The 54th Regiment, Georgia Volunteer Infantry

by William A. Bowers, Jr.

Photograph of the 54th Georgia Volunteer Infantry Flag used Courtesy of the Georgia Historical Society

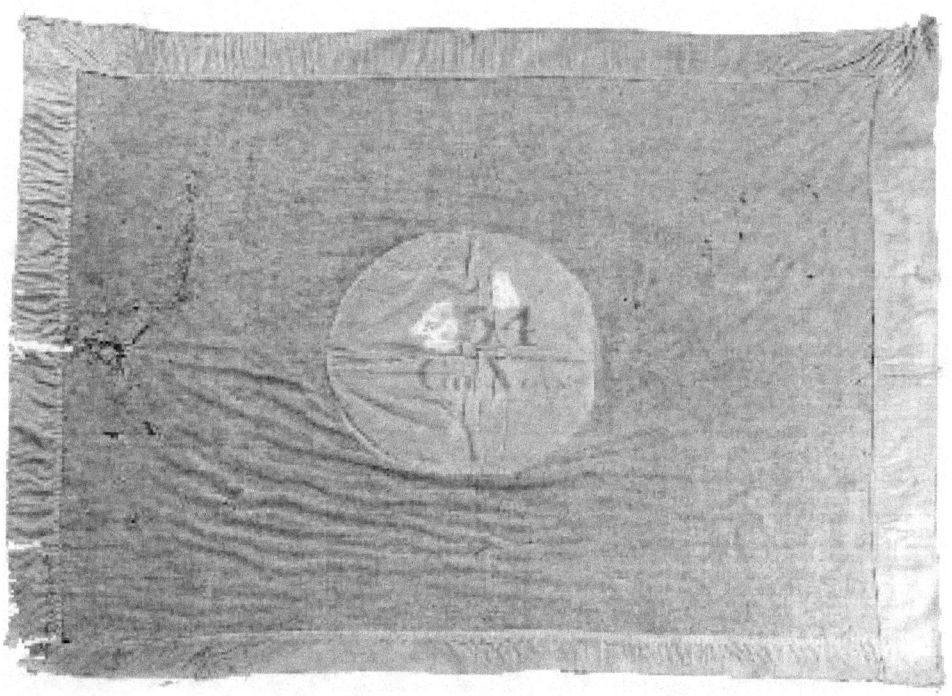

54th Georgia Volunteer Infantry Flag

Preserved at the Georgia Historical Society

501 Whitaker Street, Savannah, Georgia

2015 ©William A. Bowers, Jr.

ALL RIGHTS RESERVED

No part of this book may be produced in any form, by photocopying or by any electronic or mechanical means, including information storage or retrieval systems, without permission in writing from both the copyright owner and the publisher of this book, except for the minimum words needed for review.

ISBN: 978-0-9861109-0-0
Library of Congress Control Number: 2015936497
Published by

Swampfox Publishing Company

Edited by Deloris W. Bowers and Barbara Sachs Sloan
Interior Design by KathleenWalls
Cover Design by William A. Bowers, III

Printed in USA for Swampfox Publishing Company

HISTORY

of the

54th REGIMENT
GEORGIA VOLUNTEER
INFANTRY

CONFEDERATE STATES ARMY

Compiled by:

WILLIAM A. BOWERS, JR.

ACKNOWLEDGMENT AND THANKS:

The Compilation of a Regimental History is a long and arduous task. The nearly 21 years taken to bring this work to this point is worth all the toil to make this information available to those interested in this "Storied Regiment." There are so many people who have aided my research and given encouragement to me in this quest. There are too many to name them all.

Almost 22 years ago I met then Captain James W. Bowen, who was at the time living in Wayne County, Georgia. We struck up a friendship, and I discovered that he had been compiling a history of the 54th Georgia Volunteer Infantry Regiment. He gave me a copy of his work, and I began to study the movements of the 54th. He was the inspiration to begin my work on the 47th and then later the 27th Georgia Regiments. I even set up part of my histories very similar to the timeline he had utilized for the 54th Georgia. I remember when he came to speak at our Sons of Confederate Veterans meeting and enlightened all of us about the 54th Georgia. In January 2014 I tracked him down in Tattnall County, Georgia, and renewed our acquaintance. I inquired as to how close he was to publishing his history of the 54th Georgia since my second one, the 27th Georgia, was just off the presses. He informed me that he was not in the position to do any more with the history but if I would like to take what he had and finish it and publish it I would be welcome to do that. I went and had a visit with him where he handed over his research and work on the 54th Georgia. He also shared many research books with me for my use in this quest. As my goal was to ensure that the histories of all four companies of regular infantry from Appling County, Georgia, were put into a form where those who were interested in them or who were descended from those valiant soldiers could easily obtain all the available information about them. That has been my goal with the first two books in this work and with the final book of the "Appling County Trilogy" which has consumed more than 21 years of my life but was worth every minute of it. I again want to thank the Reverend James W. Bowen, for without his work this book could not have been possible.

Having said that, I need to thank my wife, Deloris, for standing by me in thick and thin. She was always there when I would bog down in research. I also want to thank her for all her proofreading assistance on this work. She and my son, Billy, have been in so many libraries and cemeteries and on so many battlefields with me as I attempted to understand facts surrounding the events and locate where my ancestors had been and their part in the battles. As I was bringing this book to a conclusion I suffered many health setbacks. This forced Deloris and Billy into the important role of getting the book prepared for printing. Without their work during this critical point in time, this project may not have come to fruition.

I also want to thank my son, Billy, for keeping me up to date with my computer and designing the covers, bookmarks and posters for all three books.

Thanks to my sister, Elizabeth Bowers Hall, for all her proofreading assistance on this and other works.

I would like to also thank my cousin Robert Shane Forrester. His "From the White Sand to the Red Clay" was a most informative read. His research on his ancestors who were in Company B and his compilations on the company including his ancestor, Captain George W. Moody, who was the commander of Company B, were very beneficial. His hard work and resources were most valuable to me in my compilation.

I wish to thank my fellow members in the Appling Grays Camp # 918 Sons of Confederate Veterans for helping me get started and encouraging me along the way. Also I would like to thank the members of the Sons of Confederate Veteran Camps around Georgia for their help and encouragement and for sharing information with me.

Special thanks to my Aunt Mary Ketus Holland and my Uncle Zachry Grantham Holland who researched the family genealogies and sparked my interest in the period which concluded in my becoming a part of the Sons of Confederate Veterans.

My debt is great to these and all the others who have assisted at the State Parks and National Parks that I have visited and all the patient librarians and government officials who have put up with my inquiries.

Special thanks to my eighth grade Georgia history teacher, Mrs. Carolyn McCall, for piquing my interest in the "War For Southern Independence" and for taking our class to Atlanta to expose us to more.

Thanks to my cousin, friend and author, E. Randall Floyd, who shared my beginnings of interest in the 2nd grade as we would draw Confederate Soldiers in battle on scraps of paper "way back then."

Last but not least the descendants of the 54th soldiers who have shared information, photos and data with me.

Table of Contents

Title Page with Picture of Original Flag	A
Copyright page	B
Second Title Page	C
Acknowledgment and Thanks	D
Table of Contents	F
Photographs Index	F
Introduction	G
Brief History 54th Regiment	1
Main History 54th Regiment	5
Biography Charlton Way	170
Biography Morgan Rawls	172
Biography of Hugh D. Mercer	173
Confederate Veteran May 1903	175
Confederate Veteran April 1989	176
Biography of General Taliaferro	185
Biography of General James Argyle Smith	187
Biography of General William H. T. Walker	188
Biography of General Patrick Cleburne	190
Biography of General Nathan Bedford Forrest	192
54th Georgia Field, Staff and Band	219
54th Georgia Company Commanders	221
54th Georgia Company Rosters	241
54th Georgia Alphabetical Rosters	222
54th Georgia References	I

Photographs

54th Georgia Battle Flag	cover
54th Georgia Battle Flag (Original)	A
Lieutenant Colonel Morgan Rawls	172
General Hugh Weedon Mercer	173
General William Booth Taliaferrro	185
General James Argyle Smith	187
General William H. T. Walker	188
General Patrick Cleburne	190
General Nathan Bedford Forest	192
Pictures of the Men of the 54th Georgia	198

INTRODUCTION

The brave and heroic men who fought, bled and died for the cause of the Confederate States of America were unequaled in the performance of their duty. For four years they held at bay the most powerful and well-equipped army in the world. This under-fed, under-equipped, sometimes rag-tag army fought on. They would have followed their leaders still despite privation and starvation and being outnumbered two to one on most occasions. There has been altogether too little of their history preserved for posterity.

When I became interested in retracing the footsteps of my Confederate ancestors, this fact became painfully obvious. As I searched for information on units such as the Fifty-fourth Regiment, Georgia Volunteer Infantry, only small bits and pieces emerged. A paragraph here and a page there was the extent of their traces that were available. The more research that was performed the more the story of the regiment began to unfold. I realized what I needed to do was to compile all the small fragments that I had been able to uncover into a comprehensive history so that those who were to follow in the search would have the history of this valiant and much campaigned regiment readily available. It seemed that wherever the thick of the battle was, you would find the Fifty-fourth Georgia. This regiment was called upon to perform some very difficult missions, and their valor was quite evident. Their leaders were courageous and without fear, leading their troops in an exemplary fashion.

To my great-great-grandfather, George Willis Herndon, of Company B, and my uncles, Privates David S. Carter, Isaac Herndon, Middleton Miles and Abraham Molton Eason, of Company B, and all my cousins who were in the regiment, I dedicate this work. It is to honor their sacrifice and dedication that this history is submitted.

WILLIAM A. BOWERS, JR.

H

The Fifty-Fourth Regiment Georgia Volunteer Infantry

A Brief History of a Most Gallant Regiment

In April and May 1862, 10 companies of men converged on camp Davis at Guyton, Georgia, a camp of instruction. Those companies were from Appling County, Berrien County, Bibb County, Effingham County, Emanuel County, Screven County and Muscogee County. Many of the men were from units of Georgia State Troops whose one-year enlistment was up. They elected officers and drilled and trained into cohesive units. Colonel Charlton Way was elected to lead them, and Lieutenant Colonel Morgan Rawls was elected the second in command with Major William H. Mann elected as the third in command.

They were transferred to Beaulieu Battery near Savannah to become a defense force for the battery. They also spent time at Rose Dew and Coffee Bluff, both near Savannah, in protection of batteries that were located there. In July 1863 they were transferred via rail to Charleston, South Carolina, and were encamped on James Island near Charleston. They were involved in the skirmish to block federal forces which had landed on James Island and were threatening Charleston.

On 10 July 1863 federal troops began to threaten Battery Wagner located on Morris Island. Confederate troops were rushed to the scene. At that point there were roughly 3,700 federals on Morris Island facing 1,200 Confederates within and around Battery Wagner. After an unsuccessful attempt to take the fort, federal forces laid siege to the outpost. The 54th Georgia moved in and out on rotation to the fort and was involved in the actions there. At one point Lieutenant Colonel Rawls was in command of the fort. On August 1 when the 54th was scheduled to leave Morris Island, enemy fire caused them to take up a position between batteries Wagner and Gregg. The next day they were able to move out in the rotation. Brigadier General Thomas L. Clingman noted the service of the 54th Georgia, commanded by Lieutenant Colonel Morgan Rawls, during exposure to extraordinary fire from the federal fleet while stationed between Battery Wagner and Battery Gregg (out on an open beach). Several ironsides, monitors and some wooden vessels kept up rapid and dangerous fire for many hours at close range on these men.

On August 31 companies A, F, H and I were detached on the command of Lieutenant Colonel Morgan Rawls, while the remaining companies stayed under the command of Colonel Charlton Way.

Between August 23 and September 6 they suffered nine killed, including Captain Augustus S. Roberts of Company D, and 14 wounded. The 400 Confederates who were left at Battery Wagner and on Morris Island were facing more than 11,000 federals. Finally on September 6 the cannons were removed and they evacuated Battery Wagner. Some of the wounded died as late as November in Charleston hospitals.

On October 28 all of the detached companies returned and the Regiment was at full strength on James Island.

On December 24 they were ordered to Pocotaligo, South Carolina. In early 1864 they returned to the Savannah area where they were once again placed in support of the batteries at Rose Dew, Coffee Bluff and Beaulieu.

On April 22 General Mercer received orders to proceed to Dalton, Georgia, to join with the Army of Tennessee. By April 30, 1864, the 54th Georgia was placed in Brigadier General Mercer's brigade. They were joined with the 57th and the 63rd Georgia. They were later joined by the 1st Georgia Volunteers to make up the largest brigade in the Army of Tennessee. They became nicknamed the "Silver Forks" or the "New Issue" due to the fact that they had just been issued new uniforms prior to being sent to Dalton. These uniforms were complete even with regulation markings for the officers and non-commissioned officers.

General Sherman began his campaign down into Georgia, and Mercer's Brigade was thrown in their front near Dalton, Georgia. On May 6, 1864, they were in the battle of Rocky Face Ridge. On May 8 they were involved in the battle at Dug Gap. May 13 they were heavily involved in the battle at Resaca. Although the Confederates numbered only 60,000, they faced over 100,000 federals. General Johnston, "Old Joe" as they affectionately called him, would anticipate General Sherman's movement and be in a fortified position awaiting his attack. During this campaign General Johnston would make the federals pay dearly each time they attacked his works. On May 17 they were again in action at Adairsville. That battle lasted about three days, and then on May 25 they were involved in the battle at New Hope Church. They began operations around Marietta on June 4 which included fights at Big Shanty and Golgotha Church. The regiment was under constant harassment from federal sharpshooters at this time. They continued fighting around Marietta, ending up on June 22 in the battle of Kolb's farm, which concluded on June 24. They were then moved to a location on Pigeon Hill located on Burnt Hickory Road, in the line at Kennesaw Mountain. On June 27 when Sherman's troops attacked, Mercer's Brigade was located right by Burnt Hickory Road. They caught the full impact of the attack. The 54th had eight men killed and 10 wounded with two captured, but Sherman was unable to move the Confederates from their strong position, so his men retreated. During the same day on Cheatham's Hill the federals paid dearly for their assault there. On July 2 and 3 they were in action again and lost more men.

President Jefferson Davis replaced General Joseph E. Johnston with General John Bell Hood. On July 9, 1864, the 54th Georgia and Mercer's Brigade took up a position along Peachtree Creek. On July 20 the attack was initiated by Walker's Division of General Hardee's Corps. In the battle of Peachtree Creek the 54th suffered heavy losses. Again on July 22 General Hood ordered the attack on the federal forces, and the battle of Atlanta began. Major General Walker was killed by federal sharpshooters, and General Mercer took command of the division. The 54th suffered 14 killed, including Major William Henry Mann. They also suffered 30 wounded, including Lieutenant Colonel Rawls and Captain Thomas Grigsby of Company G. July 23, 1864, General Mercer ordered the brigade to withdraw. The brigade and the 54th were then ordered south of Atlanta to protect the railroad from Macon and on August 31 were near the angle at the battle of Jonesboro. Again they suffered many casualties. They were again engaged on September 4, 1864, near Lovejoy Station. They continued fighting around Atlanta, and in November, General Hood decided to move into Tennessee on what has become known as the "Tennessee Campaign." On November 19, 1864, Mercer's (Smith's) Brigade was detached and sent to Cheatham's Ferry to aid a supply wagon train in his attempt to cross the Tennessee River on the ferry. The reason was stated as they were a coastal brigade and should have some knowledge of boats and water.

On November 28 the brigade left Cheatham's Ferry in order to catch up with the main Army which was engaged on November 30 in the battle of Franklin, Tennessee. They were two days late to be in the Battle of Franklin where their division commander Major General Patrick R. Cleburne was killed, just behind the Carter house. One of the soldiers in the brigade said that being detached in order to get the supply of salt across the river turned out that "the salt had saved their bacon," for they would have been in the heart of the battle at Franklin, where the heaviest casualty rate occurred.

The brigade, including the 54th Georgia, rejoined their division in front of Nashville on December 6 and were in Smith's brigade because General Mercer had returned to Savannah due to bad health. December 7 the brigade reported to Major General Nathan Bedford Forrest who was operating near Murphysboro, Tennessee, and were assigned to his command. The brigade then destroyed the railroad between Murphysboro and Nashville to impede the federal supplies bound there. December 15 under Major General Bedford Forrest's orders, the brigade crossed the Stones River and marched east to capture a federal forage train, as the battle of Nashville was begun. They were in action under General Forrest at Murphysboro, Tennessee. General Forrest personally chose Mercer's Brigade to be a part of his rear guard command. They then were engaged in action as the rear guard as General Hood withdrew back across the Tennessee River. The winter in Tennessee was the most severe that anyone could remember. General Forrest, noticing that most of the men in Mercer's Brigade had no shoes, ordered them transported in wagons (several references have been made to bloody footprints in the snow). The snow was so bad, and due to the fact that their shoes were entirely worn out, several men suffered from frostbite on their feet. Upon seeing this General Nathan Bedford Forrest ordered some supply wagons emptied, and the 54th and the rest of Mercer's Brigade would ride in these wagons, stopping to form up in battle line and engage the pursuing enemy. They were in action again at Triune and Columbia, Tennessee. By December 21, 1864, the effective total of the 54th Georgia was 168 men. On December 22, 23 and 24 they were still in action as an element of the rear guard and they were in action again at Pulaski, Tennessee. On December 28 after all of General Hood's forces had recrossed the Tennessee River, the brigade withdrew into northern Alabama.

They then went into Mississippi where many were hospitalized. After spending a period of time, the brigade was ordered to North Carolina to join with their old commander, General Joseph E. Johnston. They made their way back across Alabama and then from Columbus to Macon to Milledgeville and Augusta. The 54th Regiment entered into North Carolina, arriving near Bentonville on March 18, 1865. They were assigned to Bate's Corps. By this time the 54th had been combined with the Fourth Georgia Sharpshooters in a consolidated Regiment, due the lack of soldiers in both regiments. On March 19, 1865, they were on the extreme right of the attack in the fight at Bentonville, North Carolina, and drove two lines of the enemy in from their breastworks before being compelled to withdraw. The Confederates at Bentonville fought an army four to five times their size to a standstill. They were engaged some at Salisbury, North Carolina, on April 12, and on April 26, 1865, what remained of the 54th Georgia and Mercer's Brigade in North Carolina surrendered with General Joseph E. Johnson at Greensboro, North Carolina. Some soldiers who were hospitalized in Floyd House in Ocmulgee Hospital in Macon, Georgia, were captured on April 20 through April 22. Some detached elements, mostly Company B and Company K, surrendered May 10 in Tallahassee, Florida, with General Sam Jones. From May 18 to 30 the last of the Regiment who had been cut off from their command surrendered at Augusta, Georgia.

The 54th Regiment - Georgia Volunteer Infantry Confederate States Army

The following is a historical sketch depicting the events that took place, during the time of the War Between the States, between the years of 1861 and 1865. It will hopefully shed light on all that was encountered by the brave officers and men that gave so much for a cause, so dear to them. This will record their gallant deeds and track the regiment through this trying and tumultuous period of time:

"Coastal Service in Georgia and South Carolina"
1861

3 January, 1861
A local militia unit, authorized by Governor Joseph E. Brown, seized Ft. Pulaski.

16 January, 1861
Georgia secedes from the Union and in February, joined the Confederacy.

18 July, 1861
Charlton Hines Way elected Captain of Way's Independent Company Georgia Infantry. His Company was placed on Tybee Island, Georgia.

3 October, 1861
Company A, 1st Regiment, 1st Brigade of Georgia State Troops had the following changes:
William H. Mann elected Captain
Richard Bennett elected Second Lieutenant
George W. Eason appointed First Sergeant
Silas Thornton appointed Fifth Sergeant

10 October, 1861
Company K, 2nd Regiment, 1st Brigade of Georgia State Troops had the following change: George W. Moody elected First Lieutenant.

16 October, 1861
In a short notice entitled "A Regiment for the War" in the "Daily Morning News," Savannah, Georgia the birth of the 54th Regiment was announced. The new commander was named as Charlton H. Way, a graduate of the Georgia Military Institute (1855). Charlton Hines Way was born in Liberty County, Georgia on 5 October 1834. In another article is an advertisement by Charlton H. Way (then captain commanding the Forest City Rangers, known popularly as the "Jackass

Artillery" on Tybee) for volunteers for his new regiment.

29 October, 1861
Col. Hugh W. Mercer appointed Brigadier General.

1 November, 1861
Federal troops occupy Hilton Head, Port Royal, and Beaufort, South Carolina.

25 November, 1861
Shortly after a Confederate garrison had been withdrawn from Tybee Island, a Federal force moved onto the Island unopposed. This is believed to be the first U.S. flag raised over the State of Georgia during the War Between the States.

26 December, 1861
Maj. Charles H. Olmstead elected Colonel.

1862

6 February, 1862
54th Regiment, Georgia Infantry Staff had the following change:
Abner B. Campbell appointed Chaplain.

11 April, 1862
Col. Charles H. Olmstead, in command at Fort Pulaski, Georgia, surrendered to Federal troops.

16 April, 1862
Private Thomas Allen of Company C died at Beaulieu, near Savannah, Georgia.

18 April, 1862
Company A and K of the 54th Regiment Georgia Infantry were formed at Camp Davis in Guyton, Georgia.

Company A, 54th Regiment, Georgia Infantry had the following changes:
Thomas W. Brantley elected Captain
John A. McManus elected 1st Lieutenant
John H, Dunlap elected 2nd Lieutenant
W. E. Jenkins elected Jr. 2nd Lieutenant
Robert William Smith elected 1st Sergeant
James N. Harris elected 2nd Sergeant
A. J. Brantley elected 3rd Sergeant
J. W. Thurman elected 4th Sergeant
George D. Knight elected 5th Sergeant

Company K, 54th Regiment, Georgia Infantry had the following change:
George W. Eason elected Captain
Joseph H. Hannon elected 1st Lieutenant
Richard Bennett elected 2nd Lieutenant

Green Berry Ritch elected Jr. 2nd Lieutenant
Henry A. Bennett elected 1st Sergeant
John M. Bennett elected 2nd Sergeant
G. M. T. Overstreet elected 3rd Sergeant
G. E. Williams elected 4th Sergeant
Perry McCullar elected 5th Sergeant

21 April, 1862
Company B of the 54th Regiment Georgia Infantry was formed at Camp Davis in Guyton, Georgia.

Company B, 54th Regiment, Georgia Infantry had the following changes:
George W. Moody elected Captain.
Lafayette Phillips elected 1st Lieutenant
James l. Moody elected 2nd Lieutenant
John Jackson Roberson elected Jr. 2nd Lieutenant
Jacob H. Moody elected 1st Sergeant
George McCall, Jr. elected 2nd Sergeant
William R. Carter, Sr. elected 3rd Sergeant
John W. Dukes elected 4th Sergeant
S. M. Crosby elected 5th Sergeant

22 April, 1862
Company C of the 54th Regiment Georgia Infantry was formed at Camp Davis in Guyton, Georgia.

Company C, 54th Regiment, Georgia Infantry had the following changes:
Daniel A. Green elected Captain
R. B. Knight elected 1st Lieutenant
Isaac D. G. Lamb elected 2nd Lieutenant
Benjamin B. Sammons elected 1st Sergeant
Thomas W. Goodwin elected 2nd Sergeant
William H. Turner elected 3rd Sergeant
John M. McClendon elected 4th Sergeant

30 April, 1862
Company D of the 54th Regiment Georgia Infantry was formed at Camp Davis in Guyton, Georgia.

Company D, 54th Regiment, Georgia Infantry had the following changes:
Augustus S. Roberts elected Captain

Joseph Miller elected 1st Lieutenant
Michael Jenkins elected 2nd Lieutenant
Henry Sasser elected Jr. 2nd Lieutenant
David L. Bragg elected 1st Sergeant
Jackson Lariscy elected 2nd Sergeant
William M. Lariscy elected 3rd Sergeant
Jasper Bragg elected 4th Sergeant
Robert W. Shealy elected 5th Sergeant

6 May, 1862
Company E and I of the 54th Regiment Georgia Infantry were formed at Camp Davis in Guyton, Georgia.

Company E, 54th Regiment, Georgia Infantry had the following changes:
J. D. Evans, Captain
H. M. Talley elected 1st Lieutenant
James H. Griffin elected 2nd Lieutenant
Joel W. Swain elected Jr. 2nd Lieutenant
Littleton l. Albritton elected 1st Sergeant
R. G. Turner elected 2nd Sergeant
William J. Lamb elected 3rd Sergeant
Jehu Patten elected 4th Sergeant
Stephen W. Avera elected 5th Sergeant

Company I, 54th Regiment, Georgia Infantry had the following change:
Morgan Rawls, Captain
Leander L. Elkins, elected 1st Lieutenant
James F. Rawls 2nd Lieutenant
Frank E. Bourquin elected Jr 2nd Lieutenant
Harrison C. Elkins elected 1st Sergeant
Thomas E. Nease elected 2nd sergeant
Joseph h. Ganann elected 3rd Sergeant
Edward E. Foy elected 4th Sergeant

Private James Walters of Company C died at Beaulieu, near Savannah, Georgia.

10 May, 1862
54th Regiment, Georgia Infantry Staff had the following change:
James Erwin Godfrey Jr. transferred to this regiment as Surgeon.

12 May, 1862
Company G and H of the 54th Regiment Georgia Infantry were formed at Camp Davis in Guyton, Georgia.
Company G, 54th Regiment, Georgia Infantry had the following

changes:
George Walton Knight elected Captain
N. B. Roberts elected 1st Lieutenant
Grigsby E. Thomas, Sr. elected 2nd Lieutenant
Samuel B. McClary elected Jr. 2nd Lieutenant
Samuel B. Harned elected 2nd Sergeant
Thomas J. Ritch elected 3rd Sergeant
Benjamin F. Odom elected 4th Sergeant

Company H, 54th Regiment, Georgia Infantry had the following change:
Charles R. Russell elected Captain
T. F. Brewster elected 1st Lieutenant
John K. Bedell elected 2nd Lieutenant
Aaron Land elected 1st Sergeant
Alexander Teal elected 2nd Sergeant
M. L. Brawner 3rd Sergeant
William J. Hart elected 4th Sergeant
Clay M. McCoy elected 5th Sergeant

13 May, 1862
Company F of the 54th Regiment Georgia Infantry was formed at Camp Davis in Guyton, Georgia.

Company F, 54th Regiment, Georgia Infantry had the following changes:
Walter S. Chisholm elected Captain
John W. Anderson, Jr. elected 1st Lieutenant
Hamilton McDevit Branch elected 2nd Lieutenant
Charles C. Hunter elected Jr. 2nd Lieutenant
Phillip R. Falligant elected 1st Sergeant
Robert M. Butler elected 2nd Sergeant
William A. Shaw elected 3rd Sergeant
Charles F. Bailey elected 4th Sergeant
Thomas B. Mell elected 5th Sergeant

15 May, 1862
First reported desertion from the 54th occurred at Savannah, Georgia.
16 May, 1862
54th Regiment, Georgia Infantry Staff had the following changes:
Capt. Charlton H. Way elected Colonel
Capt. Morgan Rawls elected Lieutenant Colonel
Capt. William H. Mann elected Major

Company I, 54th Regiment, Georgia Infantry had the following change:
Leander L. Elkins, elected Captain
Joseph W. Brewer elected 1st Lieutenant

2 June, 1862
Federal troops moved onto James Island, South Carolina.
6 June, 1862
Brigadier General Hugh W. Mercer appointed Commander of the Military District of Georgia.
30 June, 1862

(Command Structure)
Department of S.C. and GA. Commander
(Maj. General. John C. Pemberton)
Military District of Georgia Commander
(Brigadier General. Hugh W. Mercer)
54th Georgia Regiment Commander
(Col. Charlton H. Way)

2 July, 1862
Private Boyed of Company G died of fever at Savannah, Georgia.
12 July, 1862
Sergeant Ricks of Company A died of fever at Savannah, Georgia.
15 July, 1862
Lieutenant Lafayette N. Phillips of Company B died.
16 June 1862
Federal troops complete withdrawal from James Island, South Carolina.
Private S. Moon of Company A died.
Lieutenant James L. Moody of Company B died.
17 July, 1862
Sergeant Jesse L. Peoples of Company E died at Savannah, Georgia.
20 July, 1862
Company F detached by order of General Mercer to report to Lieutenant Colonel William S. Rockwell, Provost Marshall, at the Chatham County jail to guard Federal Prisoners there and to stand picket duty at the railroad depot.
21, July, 1862
Private Causey of Company A died of fever at Savannah, Georgia.
22 July, 1862
Company B, 54th Regiment, Georgia Infantry had the following changes:
Michael Branch elected 2nd Lieutenant
24 July, 1862

Private Hurst of Company D died at Savannah, Georgia.
26, July, 1862
Private Emanuel Wright of Company G died at Savannah, Georgia.
27 July, 1862
Company K, 54th Regiment, Georgia Infantry had the following changes:
Richard Bennett elected 1st Lieutenant
Green B. Ritch elected 2nd Lieutenant
Private S. F. Boyd of Company G died at Savannah, Georgia.
29 July, 1862
Private John R. Burgstiner of Company I died of disease at Savannah, Georgia.
8 August, 1862
Private J. J. Bedenfield of Company C died of disease at Savannah, Georgia.
10 August, 1862
Sergeant Claudius F. Rahn of Company I died of disease at Savannah, Georgia.
17 August, 1862
Private W. Loukie of Company D died of disease at Savannah, Georgia.
18 August, 1862
Private J. Jordan of Company A died at home of disease.
25 August, 1862
Private T. J. Lanier of Company G died of disease at Savannah, Georgia.
Private Matthew E. Crosby of Company I died of disease at Savannah, Georgia.
1 September 1862
The Regiment was sent to Camp Anderson at Beaulieu Plantation, close to the Vernon River, in support of an artillery battery that was placed there.

Special Order No. 6 transferred the best marksmen from the 54th Georgia to the 1st Georgia Sharpshooters. This caused dissention among the companies since the companies were formed in communities where all the members were neighbors. Several of the officers disagreed with the practice and Captain George Eason of Company K and 2nd Lieutenant John Jackson of Company B were both arrested, court martialed and cashiered for refusing to obey Special Order No. 6 (They would not parade their troops for selection).

Private William Walters of Company E died at Beaulieu near Savannah, Georgia.
15, September, 1862

Private Walter Allen of Company C died at Beaulieu near Savannah, Georgia.
Private Walter Avera of Company E died at Beaulieu near Savannah, Georgia.
Private Joseph Aiken of Company E died at Beaulieu near Savannah, Georgia.

16 September, 1862
Thomas Allen Company E died at Beaulieu near Savannah, Georgia.
James Walters of Company C died at Beaulieu near Savannah, Georgia.

17 September, 1862
Private C. A. J. Parrish of company A died at Beaulieu near Savannah, Georgia.

20 September, 1862
Private H. B. Lynn of Company K died at Beaulieu near Savannah, Georgia.
Private Stephen W. Carter of Company B died at Beaulieu near Savannah, Georgia.

25 September, 1862
54th Regiment, Georgia Infantry stationed near Beaulieu near Savannah, Georgia.

(Command Structure)
Department of S.C. and Ga. Commander
(Maj. General Pierre G. T. Beauregard)
Military District of Georgia Commander
(Brigadier General Hugh W. Mercer)
54th Georgia Regiment Commander
(Col. Charlton H. Way)

Company A, 54th Regiment, Georgia Infantry had the following changes:
John H. Dunlap 2nd Lieutenant resigned his commission
W. E. Jenkins elected 2nd Lieutenant
Rodden Smith Jr. elected Jr. 2nd Lieutenant

Private Richard Roe of Company C died at Beaulieu near Savannah, Georgia.

6 October 1862
Private William Henry Eason of Company B died at Beaulieu near Savannah, Georgia (from an accidental injury).

12 October 1862
Private Henry L. Parker of Company G died at Beaulieu near Savannah, Georgia.

16 October, 1862

Private S. Lewis of Company D died at Beaulieu near Savannah, Georgia.

22 October, 1862 The Battle at Pocotaligo, South Carolina
A small skirmish occurred at Pocotaligo, South Carolina.

31 October, 1862
Private Henry Parker of Company G died at Beaulieu near Savannah, Georgia.

November, 1862
Capt. George W. Eason dismissed from Company K.

2 November, 1862
Private Malachi Easters of Company E died at Beaulieu near Savannah, Georgia.

10 November, 1862
Col. Charles H. Olmstead exchanged at Aiken's Landing, Virginia.

15 November 1862
Private Archibald Vann of Company A died in Macon, Georgia.

21 November 1862
Private John T. Faircloth of Company C died in Atlanta, Georgia.

20 December, 1862
Company K, 54th Regiment, Georgia Infantry had the following changes:
Captain George W. Eason was Court Martialed and dismissed for refusal to follow orders by General Order No. 82.
Richard Bennett elected Captain
Green B. Ritch elected 1st Lieutenant
Silas Thornton elected Junior 2nd Lieutenant
Private Milton Stripling of Company H died of disease at Savannah, Georgia.

22 December, 1862
Private Henry Bennett, Sr. of Company K died at Beaulieu near Savannah, Georgia.
Private M. V. Brantley of Company A died in Macon Georgia in 1862.

1863

January, 1863
Private G. W. Herndon of Company I died in Institute Hospital.

12 January, 1863
Private Coleman of Co. F was arrested and sent to Savannah barracks for investigation.

13 January, 1863
54th Regiment, Georgia Infantry - companies F and I commanded by Captain J. W. Anderson and Captain Elkins are reported manning Savannah River Batteries at Rose Dew and two other companies C and

H on defenses at Savannah under Captains Brantley and Russell.

31 January, 1863
Company B, D, H, I and K are located at Beaulieu near Savannah, Georgia.
Company E and G is located at Coffee Bluff 12 miles from Savannah, Georgia.
Company F is located at Oglethorpe Barracks in Savannah, Georgia.

27 February, 1863
1st Lieutenant Joseph W. Brewer of Company I died.

13 March, 1863
54th Regiment, Georgia Infantry reported manning Savannah River Batteries and other defenses.

14 March, 1863
Private Owen Cummings of Company A died of illness at Savannah.

17 March, 1863
Private T. Smith of Company F died at General Hospital No. 1 at Savannah, Georgia

25 March, 1863
Private J. M. Willy of Company F died in General Hospital No. 1 at Savannah, Georgia.

April, 1863
Nine Federal Ironclads attack Fort Sumter, but are forced to withdraw.

6 April, 1863
Private Benjamin F. Kimbrough of Company F died at Savannah, Georgia.

10 April, 1863
Private J. F. Slade of Company F died in General Hospital No. 1 at Savannah, Georgia.

25 April, 1863
Special Orders No. 101, Adjutant and Inspector-General's Office, Richmond, Article #XV reads as follows: "The following named officers will have their names dropped from the rolls for having disgracefully deserted their companies in the presence of the enemy, and will from this day cease to be officers of the C.S. Army: Captain D.A. Green, Company C, and Lieutenant G. B. Ritch, Company K, Fifty-fourth Georgia Volunteers.
Company C, 54th Regiment, Georgia Infantry had the following change:
R. B. Knight elected Captain

2nd Lieutenant Silas Thornton of Company K shown on roster as located at Legare's Plantation, James Island, South Carolina.

May, 1863
Private W. Charlton Westberry of Company K killed near Charleston, South Carolina.

8 May, 1863

(Command Structure)
Department of S.C. and GA. Commander
(Maj. General Pierre G. T. Beauregard)
Military District of Georgia Commander
(Brigadier General Hugh W. Mercer)
Brigade Commander
(Brigadier General. William B. Taliaferro)
54th Georgia Regiment Commander
(Col. Charlton H. Way)

1 June, 1863
Private William O. Moore of Company A died.
2 June, 1863
Private J. H. Morris of Company F died at Rose Dew, Georgia.
30 June, 1863
Company A is part of the Siege Train near Isle of Hope, Georgia.
2 July, 1863

(Command Structure)
Department of S.C. and GA. Commander
(General Pierre G. T. Beauregard)
Military District of Georgia Commander
(Brigadier General Hugh W. Mercer)
Brigade Commander
(Brigadier General. William B. Taliaferro)
54th Georgia Regiment Commander
(Col. Charlton H. Way)
Company A detached to S.C. Siege Train Commander
(Maj. George L. Buist)

Private J. H. Morris of Company E died at Rose Dew near Savannah, Georgia.
8 July, 1863
Three Federal brigades (about 3000 men) concentrate on Battery Island, in preparation for moving onto James Island, South Carolina.
9 July, 1863
On a day of heavy storms, Federal troops move onto James Island, South Carolina and skirmish with Confederate troops. Urgent request goes out for Confederate reinforcements from Wilmington, North Carolina and Savannah, Georgia.
10 July,1863 Siege of Battery Wagner (Morris Island, South Carolina)
Federal Infantry make a dawn attack from southern end of Morris Island supported by Federal Ironclads and Artillery from Folly Island. The Federals push to within 600 yards of Battery Wagner by evening. Col. Olmstead arrived from Savannah and is immediately sent to

Battery Wagner where he places his Georgia troops on the wall around midnight. At this time, there were approximately 3,700 Federals facing 1,200 Confederates.

11 July, 1863
Three Federal Regiments attacked Battery Wagner but were driven back. After the unsuccessful daylight assault, Federals placed siege artillery on the Island.

13 July, 1863
Brigadier General Taliaferro took command of the defenses on Morris Island, after taking a leave of absence from his command in Georgia and coming straight to Charleston, South Carolina. Federals strengthened the number of troops on Morris Island to 6,000 men facing 1,300 Confederates.

15 July, 1863
54th Regiment, Georgia Infantry ordered to Secessionville, James Island, S.C.

16 July, 1863
Over six thousand Federals launch a pre-dawn attack against a 500 man Confederate garrison on James Island, South Carolina. The Federals retreated after heavy losses. A subsequent Federal Commander wrote that he would need 40,000 men with a suitable complement of heavy and light artillery to prosecute an attack on Charleston from James Island. 800 men of the 54th Georgia were assigned to assist Colquitt's Brigade.

54th Regiment assaulted and drove Federal forces from James Island, S.C. and captured 14 union soldiers at the house on Legare's Plantation belonging to the 54th Massachusetts Regiment. This action caused the union forces to withdraw form Battery Island on the Stono River.
Company C, 54th Regiment, Georgia Infantry had the following changes:
Captain R. B. Knight resigned
Thomas M. Brantley elected Captain

17 July, 1863
JAMES ISLAND, July 17, 1863.

CAPTAIN: I have the honor to submit to the general commanding the following report of the part taken by my command in the reconnaissance made on the morning of the 16th instant:

At 10.45 p. m. on the 15th instant, I received an order from the general, commanding the forces on James Island to report at Secessionville, at 12
o'clock that night, with the Fifty-fourth Georgia Regiment, a section of two 12-pounder howitzers from the Chatham Artillery, and Captain [J. C.] Edwards' company of cavalry. The troops were rapidly put in motion

and arrived at the point indicated at the hour designated in the order.

My instructions having been to allow General Colquitt's brigade to cross the marsh in front of Secessionville by Rivers' causeway, and move down upon it left (my command moving, en echelon, upon the right and in rear of his) as soon as I found his left had moved, I put the column in motion, consisting of the Fifty-fourth Georgia and Thirty-first North Carolina Regiments, moving by a flank and making a detour to the right to avoid the dense and almost impassable abatis immediately in front. The artillery, however, were obliged to move up the road leading from the front of the work at Secessionville toward the extreme left point of the woods known as Grimball's, while the cavalry remained near Rivers' causeway to aid in any rapid movement necessary to cut off the retreating picket stationed upon the right of the marsh. This charge in the disposition of these portions of my command were rendered necessary by the condition of the ground over which the artillery had to be moved, and the evident precipitancy with which the enemy upon the right of the marsh were retreating.

Arriving about 600 yards from the line of pickets thrown out by the enemy, I deployed as skirmishers 200 men of the Fifty-fourth Georgia Regiment in front of the column and moved rapidly forward; but crossing the abatis in front of their line I found that, alarmed by the fire from general Colquitt's commandant, the force moving down upon their front, they had (together with all that portion of their force stationed upon the right of the marsh) retreated, leaving their camp strewn with muskets, accouterments, blankets, over coast, provisions, &c.

After crossing the abatis through which my skirmishers had passed, I brought my command in line of battle and (agreeable to the instructions received) awaited the appearance of General Colquitt's command, which it was intended should cross over from the left to the right of the marsh by the lower causeways. At this point, my command was perceived by the enemy's light batteries, which had been stationed upon a hill and apparently (in the gray of the morning) within an earthwork. A terrible fire was opened upon us from these batteries in front, but, as usual, proved to be almost entirely harmless.

After remaining in this position some twenty minutes, General Colquitt's command made its appearance. My guides were under the impression that it was a column of the enemy endeavoring to it was impossible to distinguish their standards. Another reason induced me to believeth statements of my guides, viz, the total cession of musketry from the other side of the marsh, where General Colquitt's command had moved, and the continued fire from the enemy's batteries upon me.

But reasoning if it were a column of the enemy that they could turn my right and cut me off from the route marked out in my instructions, or if it was General Colquitt's command that the time had arrived for me to move up in conjunction with him, I recrossed the hedge and ordered the command to move up to Grimball's woods, having carried out entirely the portion of the work assigned me.

I cannot close this report without expressing the among of obligations which I owe to Lieutenant G. H. Moffett, who acted as my guide throughout the entire movement.

The casualties in my command were 2 killed, in the Thirty-first North Carolina Regiment, by explosion of a shell, and some slight contusions from the same cause in the Fifty-fourth Georgia.

I have the honor to be, captain, very respectfully, your obedient servant,

CHARLTON H. WAY,
Colonel Fifty-fourth Georgia, Commanding.

18 July, 1863

Federal forces assaulted Battery Wagner, which was located on Morris Island, and sustained heavy losses. (This is the final battle scene depicted in the movie "GLORY".) Brigadier General William B. Taliaferro was Battery Wagner Commander during that battle.

CHARLESTON, S. C.,

July 18, 1863.

CAPTAIN: In obedience to instructions received on evening of 15th instant, I moved to Secessionville with portions of Companies A, Captain [J. C.] Edwards; C. Captain [W. G.] Smith, and G, Captain [B. W.] McTuireous, of the Fifth South arolina Cavalry stationed on James Island-in all about 120 men, the remainder being on various duties-and reported to Colonel Way, Fifty-fourth Georgia Volunteers, at 12 p. m. precisely. The cavalry was formed in rear of Colonel Way's column, and in this position moved forward until the column reached causeway leading to Legare's Point, when Colonel Way moved his infantry in line to right. A portion of the cavalry, under Captain Edwards, was ordered across causeway to cover the ground on left of road leading to Legare's house, the remainder halting at causeway. A few moments later another detachment of cavalry was ordered forward. I moved promptly and reported to General Hagood at Legare's house, when I received instructions to sweep the rear of Legare's house which was promptly and, I think, thoroughly done, driving some 30 or 40 negroes and 2 white men into the marsh and intercepting some 10 negroes, who were returned to the rear under infantry guard. Those that took to the marsh the cavalry could not reach, but some 40 infantry were soon firing upon them, and (I am impressed) at least 20 men were killed and wounded at this point, among them 2 white men. Many took to the river beyond, and some may have been drowned. Some 4 negroes were killed and 1 or 2 taken on left of road leading to Legare's house.

The officers and men behaved well, under a heavy fire from the enemy's gunboats and a field battery.

I have no casualties to report.

I have the honor to be, respectfully, your most obedient servant,

R. J. JEFFORDS,
Lieutenant-Colonel, Commanding

22 July, 1863
Abraham Eason of Company B died of disease.

29 July, 1863
54th Regiment, Georgia Infantry was on duty at Battery Wagner, South Carolina under the command of Lieutenant Colonel Morgan Rawls.
Wounded: Private Isaac Lamb – Co. C
          Private Benjamin Sirmans - Co. E. (both legs shot off - mortal)
          Both were admitted to the Trapman Street Hospital in Charleston, South Carolina.

30 July, 1863
54th Regiment, Georgia Infantry was on duty at Battery Wagner.

(Command Structure)
Dept. of S.C., Ga., and Fla. Commander
(General Pierre G. T. Beauregard)
1st Military District of S.C. Commander
(Brigadier General Roswell S. Ripley)
1st Sub-Division Commander
(Brigadier General Johnson Hagood)
54th Georgia Battalion Commander
(Col. Charlton H. Way)
(Companies B, C, D, E, G, and K)
Military District of Georgia Commander
(Brigadier General Hugh W. Mercer)

William A. Bowers, Jr.

Brigade Commander – (Col. George A. Gordon)
Detached 54th Battalion Commander –
(Lt. Col. Morgan Rawls)
(Companies F, H, and I)
Company A detached to S.C. Siege Train Commander –
(Maj. George L. Buist)

31 July, 1863
HDQRS. 1ST MIL. DIST., DEPT. OF S. C., GA., AND FLA.,

Charleston, July 31, 1863.

GENERAL: I have the honor to report that on last night the Twentieth South Carolina Regiment was sent to Battery Wagner, and the Sixth Georgia Regiment brought away with the Eighth North Carolina Regiment, which last was relieved the night before by the Fifty-first North Carolina Regiment, but was not removed from Morris Island on account of the late hour of the arrival of the steamer at Cumming's Point. Major F. F. Warley relieved Captain Chichester as chief artillery officer of the post.

The garrison at present consists of the Twentieth South Carolina Regiment; Fifty-first North Carolina Regiment; Company C, Lucas' battalion artillery; Fifty-fourth Georgia Regiment; Sixty-first North Carolina Regiment; Company G, [First] South Carolina Artillery; 30 light artillerists from [John F.] Wheaton's battery; detachment of [Thomas E.] Gregg's company, siege train for two siege howitzers, and 10 couriers.

1 August, 1863
54th Regiment, Georgia Infantry awaited transfer from Battery Wagner. On that evening the wounded and sick were transported, however due to enemy fire, the main force of the 54th was unable to leave Morris Island and moved to a position in the sand dunes between Batteries Wagner and Gregg.

HEADQUARTERS BATTERY WAGNER,

August 1, 1863 - 6 p.m.

CAPTAIN: I have the honor to report that on my arrival this morning, I found the following garrison at this battery:
Infantry:
54th Georgia, Lieutenant-Colonel Rawls, present, about... 388

51st North Carolina, Colonel [Hector] McKethan, present, about.. 474
20th South Carolina, Lieutenant-Colonel Dantzler, present, about.. 460
19th Georgia, Colonel [A.J.] Hutchins, present, about.... 260
Artillery:
Company A, Second South Carolina, Captain W.M. Hunter...... 70
Company E, Charleston Battalion, Captain [F.T.] Miles.... 46
Detachment Chatham Artillery, Lieutenant T.A. Askew.......... 29
Detachment Company C, Siege Train, Captain Thomas E. Gregg. 26

Total... 1,753

These numbers are approximative, and about 150 are more or less sick. The Fifty-fourth Georgia was stationed to-day in the sand-hills, in reserve, and is in readiness to leave on the arrival of the Charleston Battalion, which will furnish labor at Cumming's Point and guard the beach to-night. The Nineteenth Georgia furnishes the picket and reserve in the fort to-night, and the Fifty-first North Carolina and Twentieth South Carolina man the lines and furnish engineer and ordnance fatigues. (Two companies of Nineteenth Georgia are on James Island.)

Shelling began about 8.30 a.m., and lasted, say, half an hour, doing no harm save a slight injury to the front transom of the 8-inch shell gun, which can still be used.

At 10.45 a.m. Private [Malcolm] Galbraith, Company D, Fifty-first North Carolina, was slightly wounded in side and knee by sharpshooters of the enemy. Private [William F.] Rowe, Company A, Fifty-first North Carolina, was slightly wounded by mortar shell, early this morning, before my arrival.

At a quarter before 1 p.m. the enemy opened fire with large Parrott gun from a small wooden gunboat 1 to 1 1/4 miles off, and kept it up slowly till about 4.30 p.m., without injury. All is now quiet.

The men were sent to the bomb-proofs about 8.30 a.m. a portion being allotted to each regiment. It is, however, very difficult to protect them. Most of the Twentieth South Carolina had to be sent to the sand-hills, with the Fifty-fourth Georgia, and scattered about the fort.

Please send down some writing paper, and at least six lanterns for the bomb-proofs.

The columbiad carriages are reported as altered, and likely to fit. Every effort will be made to get the guns up to-night.

The enemy are strengthening heavily their works in our front.

LAWRENCE M. KEITT,
Colonel, Commanding.

2 August, 1863
54th Regiment, Georgia Infantry successfully transferred from Morris Island.

CHARLESTON, S. C.,

August 2, 1863.

GENERAL:I have the honor to report that last night the steamer Chesterfield proceeded to Cumming's Point, having on board the Charleston Battalion, which was proceeding to the relief of the Fifty-fourth Georgia Regiment, and a quantity of ammunition, and a lot of sand-bags. She arrived, landed the Charleston Battalion, took on board the sick and wounded of the Fifty-fourth Georgia, and was proceeding to land her stores and take the regiment on board, then on its way from Fort Wagner, when a wooden gunboat from the enemy came within range and opened a heavy fire, driving the steamer from Cumming's Point to Fort Sumter. The captain and mate being ashore, of course the enemy having the range, it being a bright moonlight night, and the transport steamer being of the weakest kind, it was imprudent to expose her again that night. A portion of the cargo, which was not landed, was sent down in small boats, and the attempt will be made to receive the regiment to-night before the moon rises; but I beg respectfully to represent that unless some measures can be taken to prevent such impertinence on the part of the enemy, our transportation, which is already of the weakest kind, will soon be cut up, and when that is gone our first requisite for carrying out the defense of Charleston is taken from us. My means for effecting the object are in the guns of Sumter, Moultrie, Batteries Gregg and Wagner. Battery Wagner is of course crippled, Battery Gregg is weak in number and range of its guns compared with the enemy's Parrotts, and Sumter and Moultrie are 1,200 yards farther distant from the enemy than the landing at Cumming's Point. Moreover, from the scarcity of our naval force and its inactivity, the enemy infest the creeks and give signals of our operations. The necessity of some movable offensive means for the prevention of this annoyance is absolute, in my opinion.

One gun was put in position in Battery Wagner last night, and the other is in such a state that it will be in position, and in readiness for service in an hour or so after dark to-night, in all probability.

Very respectfully, your obedient servant,

R. S. RIPLEY,
Brigadier-General.

16 August, 1863
Elijah Dickson of Company K died.
21 August, 1863
Charleston, August 21, 1863.

GENERAL: I have the honor to report the various operations for the defense of Charleston against the present attack, from August 1, on which day Colonel L. M. Keitt, Twentieth South Carolina Volunteers, relieved Brigadier-General Clingman in command of Battery Wagner:

The work of repairing and strengthening Battery Wagner had been progressed with until the battery had become quite as strong as it originally was. The commanding general having determined to keep up and increase the armament, spare carriages and chassis and one 10-inch gun were transported on the night of July 30 to Battery Wagner, and arrangements made for getting them in position. This delicate and important work was accomplished, under the direction of Lieutenant-Colonel [J. A.] Yates, by Captain [Francis H.] Harleston, First South Carolina Artillery, and Mr. A. D. Lacoste, with Captain Harleston's company [D], First South Carolina Artillery, assisted by heavy details from the garrison of Battery Wagner. The enemy during the day was principally employed on his works of attack, but kept up an occasional fire upon the battery, doing no damage. In the evening, he opened on the light-draught steamer Chesterfield, at Cumming's Point, driving her off, and for the first time attempting to interrupt our communication with Morris Island.

The Fifty-fourth Georgia Regiment was relieved from Morris Island by the Charleston Battalion. The guns of Battery Wagner were generally silent during the day. Fort Sumter and Battery Gregg opened upon the enemy whenever they were observed at work within range. Battery Simkins, at Shell Point, kept up a steady fire. Our works in process of erection on James Island progressed steadily, and the troops in that locality were held in readiness for such movements as might become necessary, under Brigadier-General Taliaferro.

During the morning of the 2nd, Battery Simkins kept up its fire on the enemy's works, which did not reply until about 2 o'clock in the afternoon, when they opened sharply from the land works and one gunboat, keeping up a fire during most of the afternoon, which was replied to by Batteries Wagner, Gregg, Simkins, and Fort Sumter. At night the enemy again opened, with mortars and Parrott guns, toward Cumming's Point, to cut off the communication. No material damage occurred, and in other portions of this command all was quiet.

The fire from the enemy's batteries was kept up on Battery Wagner quite steadily during the morning of the 3rd, having the effect of killing 1 man and wounding 2 officers and 12 privates, most of them slightly. Battery Wagner replied but little to the enemy's fire, the garrison being at work. The carriages for the two 10-inch guns proved to be so badly fitted as to cause delay in getting them ready for service. Fort Sumter and the exterior batteries kept up a fire on the enemy's advanced works. At night the Twentieth South Carolina Volunteers and detachments of the Fifty-first North Carolina Regiment were relieved by the Twenty-first South Carolina Volunteers. As the communication by means of steamers was quite dangerous, the exchange was effected by means of small boats, manned by crews from the navy. These performed their duty well, and my thanks are due to Flag-Officer J. R. Tucker, C. S. Navy, and the officers and men of his command for the valuable assistance rendered.

August 25, the enemy had commenced building another battery in the marsh south of that from which he opened fire upon the city. Fire was opened upon it from Simkins and Cheves, but soon discontinued, circumstances showing it to be a sham. The practice against Fort Sumter commenced about 9.30 o'clock, and continued throughout the 25th. One hundred and seventy-five shot and shell were thrown, of which 62 struck outside and 36 inside. The damage was only to increase the debris and explode an ammunition chest. There were no casualties.

At Battery Wagner, the enemy was unusually quiet, firing but few of his land batteries, until about 3 o'clock in the afternoon, when he opened an incessant fire from his mortars upon the fort and the space between it and the rifle-pits. Toward evening, he was observed from the observatories in the city to be accumulating forces in his works of attack, and orders were sent to Batteries Cheves and Simkins and Fort Moultrie to open upon them. Soon after dark, he advanced upon the rifle-pits in front of Wagner, but General Hagood's forces were, fortunately, prepared to receive him. His mortar practice ceased and his infantry assaulted fiercely, but the position was held with courage and spirit, and success crowned the efforts of the brave men of the Sixty-first North Carolina and Fifty-fourth Georgia Regiments, who constituted the advanced pickets and reserve. The latter regiment had been on duty during the day and had just been re-enforced by the Sixty-first going to its relief under Colonel [W. S.] Devane.

Captain [A. S.] Roberts, of the Fifty-fourth, a gallant soldier, was mortally wounded. The casualties were 5 killed and 19 wounded.

24 August, 1863
54th Regiment, Georgia Infantry was on duty at Battery Wagner.
BATTERY WAGNER, August 24, 1863

CAPTAIN: The fire opened on the enemy's advanced lines, commenced on yesterday from one of the 8-inch shell guns and the remaining serviceable 8-inch siege howitzer, was continued throughout the night from the latter, the former having been greatly disabled by the recoil.

At daylight it was apparent that the enemy, had worked diligently under our fire. He had not only repaired damages, but had greatly strengthened his work of the night before. This morning the fire from the 8-inch howitzer was continued under heavy fire from three 30-pounder Parrott guns, about 800 yards distant, and a 200-pounder battery, until the howitzer was dismounted and ruined by a 200-pounder bolt striking it full on the face.

I beg leave here to make honorable mention of Lieutenant [F.C.] Lucas and a detachment from Captain [T.B.] Hayne's company, Lucas' battalion, for the gallant manner in which, under a fire of great rapidity and almost unprecedent precision, they repaired to this piece and fought it for the encouragement of some of those to whose charge it had been committed.

Many of Captain [W.H.] Kennady's company of Second Regiment Artillery could not be induced to man the piece. Those who did their duty were wearied by the labors of the night before. Under these circumstances, the officers and men mentioned repaired to the gun and fought most gallantly until the piece was dismounted. I regret to say that 3 of this detachment were wounded; their names will be reported.

After the loss of the 8-inch howitzer, I ordered efforts to be made to work the mortar in the right bastion of the battery, which has long been silent on account of its unserviceable condition. I also ordered the 42-pounder carronade in the salient to be moved to the position formerly occupied by the 8-inch howitzer, disabled some days ago. Fire was opened from the mortar with great effect. The working parties and many of the enemy's riflemen were driven from their position. This fire, which has been constantly kept up during the day, will be continued.

The 42-pounder carronade has not been fired, owing to prudential motives, but will unite in the fire to-night. Lieutenant [W.E.] Erwin, with a detachment of Company K, First Regiment Artillery, who were in charge of the 10-inch columbiad, volunteered for service of the mortar, and deserve praise for their gallant services.

They also exhibited much coolness on yesterday while engaging the Ironsides.

The enemy's battery above referred to has replied constantly to the mortar, but has accomplished nothing.

I deem it my duty to say that the efficiency of the battery is much decreased by the habitual disregard or inability to fill the requisitions of the chief of artillery, and ordnance officer.

The 32-pounder guns and howitzers are worthless at this time, owing to the want of shell and shot. It would be wiser to remove them, under the circumstances, and give us smaller and less valuable ordnance, with a full supply of ordnance stores, for protection against assault. The 8-inch shell guns will stand but little service in their present condition, and are saved for emergencies.

Exposed as we are to almost continual firing from the enemy's heaviest guns, a mechanic should be frequently sent to inspect and repair the gun carriages; in no other way can the efficiency of the ordnance be maintained.

The necessary repairs to-night can with difficulty be made in consequence of the want of sand-bags, which have been repeatedly required for in the last two days. Colonel Harris, chief engineer, visited the post last night and approved the plan adopted for meeting the enemy's attempt at flanking, by sap, our rifle-pits. That work (extremely important, in my opinion) cannot go on efficiently to-night on account of the absence of sand-bags. In connection with this work, my thanks are due to Captain [Edward] Mallett, Sixty-first North Carolina, for valuable suggestions and superintendence.

Yesterday Sergeant Ehbrenstein, of the same regiment, volunteered and succeeded in remounting a gun for which it was thought we would be compelled to use a gin, and consequently have to wait for night. He is a valuable man, and has been ordered to report temporarily to the engineer for duty with him.

Casualties to-day, 5 wounded; 1 killed is included in to-day's report. He was reported wounded yesterday in the pits by a shell from Simkins, but was, in fact, killed.

The same battery threw fragments from two of its shell into this fort again o-day. I respectfully request that steps be taken to stop this thing.

Effective strength, 935.

Respectfully submitted.

JOHNSON HAGOOD,
Brigadier General, Commanding

(A second report)

BATTERY WAGNER,

August 24, 1863

CAPTAIN:Owing to the want of sand-bags, of which we are much in need, the repairs on the parapets have been much retarded. The line of rifle-pits has been extended in a northwestward direction; but this work could not be expedited as we wish in consequence of absence of sand-bags. The direction of the line of the rifle-pits of the enemy has been changed, making the distance between the two opposing lines greater. A strong line for our rifle-pits is now being worked upon across a marsh, which renders our position much stronger; but owing to absence of sand-bags to form bases as initial points, the work is attended with danger, and we make slow progress.

The southwest flank of Battery Wagner has been repaired along the whole line, but not perfectly; the plank revetments have been braced and steps for infantry more strongly secured. A new platform has been made for a 6-pounder howitzer, brass, and the gun mounted on the land face. Coverings of loose sand have been placed over the bomb-proof near headquarters, which had been weakened by shell from the enemy; but not effectually owing to the great want of sand-bags and material for transporting earth; hand barrows have been made, but for want of proper lumber not as many as are required. There exists great need of timber for the purpose of erecting platforms or repairing injuries.

The engineer department is very much cramped by the want of

carpenter's tools and an engineer's level.

A ditch has been begun between the line of the enemy's pickets and ours.

Covering is needed upon the tops of all the bomb-proofs, owing to the action of the wind and shot, and unless sand-bags are immediately sent the delay with result injuriously. The fire of the 10-inch mortar, to which allusion was made by me on yesterday, was continued during the night; fire was opened from the 42-pounder carronade on salient, and was kept up till morning, when the embrasure was closed to mask the gun from the enemy. The mortar firing was continued during the day. In the afternoon, fire was opened from the carronade upon the advanced working parties of the enemy. This fire we had quickly to discontinue to save the piece from being dismounted by the enemy's fire, which is surprisingly accurate.

Up to 3 p.m. the enemy were unusually quiet to-day; but few of his land batteries had been used. Pretty constant fire had been kept up upon the position of our mortar, but without effect. The use of the mortar has tended greatly to annoy and retard the enemy. I hope a full supply of 10-inch shell will be kept here; we have now but few left.

The sharpshooters have been busily engaged on both sides during the day.

Shortly after 7 p.m., the picket for relief having been but a short time out, a rapid fire of small-arms began. The enemy's fire from mortars, which had been incessant for several hours, the shells generally falling in front of or behind the battery, ceased in a great measure, and, as the fire of small-arms increased in rapidity, abated almost entirely. The fight continued until 8.30 p.m. Our position was held with indomitable courage, and success crowned the efforts of the gallant troops engaged-the Sixty-first North Carolina and the Fifty-fourth Georgia Regiments. The latter constituted the day picket and had just been re-enforced by the former, under the command of Colonel W.S. Devane,

Captain Mallett acting as major.

I regret to have to announce that Captain Roberts, of the Fifty-fourth Georgia Regiment, is reported mortally wounded while nobly discharging his duties. His loss is severe, alike to his command and country. Casualties, 5 killed, 19 wounded. Four of these were wounded by a shell from Mitchel's battery. It is proper to state, however, that the fire from this battery last night was generally accurate and very serviceable. Some of the shells were thrown exceedingly wild. One that did not explode I saw fall in the parade of Battery Wagner.

I feel it a duty that I owe to the service to call the attention of the brigadier-general commanding to the perilous delay in supplying Battery Wagner with ordnance stores and with engineer materials, as well as to the miserably inefficient transportation system in operation. If Battery Wagner falls, it will be largely due to these causes.

In concluding my report of five days and six nights of almost incessant battle at this post. I must be permitted to express my grateful thanks to my adjutant, Captain Molony; to my aides, Captain Tracy and Lieutenant [B.] Martin; to my chief of artillery, Major Warley; to Major Champneys (the engineer at the post for the last three days), and to Captain Hill, ordnance officer, for their efficient services in their several departments. I was relieved at 10 p.m., 25th, by Colonel Harriso n.

Respectfully submitted.

JOHNSON HAGOOD,
Brigadier-General, Commanding.
BATTERY WAGNER,

Thomas M. Lewis of Company D killed.
25 August, 1863
54th Regiment, Georgia Infantry performed advance picket duty. Attack on Battery Wagner began around 7 p.m. 54th Georgia and 61st North Carolina held their positions. Reports show the 54th Regiment, Georgia Infantry was reduced by 75 men during this skirmish.
Company D, 54th Regiment, Georgia Infantry had the following change:
Captain Augustus S. Roberts was severely wounded and Joseph Miller appointed Captain
Wounded: Private Wiley Carter – Co. B (both eyes shot out)
Private James Tillman Eason – Co. B (between the eyes)
Private J. S. Moore – Co. C (left leg crushed by shell \amputated above knee)
Private J. B. Lamb – Co. C (right thigh broken by a mini ball)
Private William M. Oglesby – Co. C (wound n shoulder and concussion)
The above were admitted to the 1st Georgia Hospital at Charleston, South Carolina.
Private J. G. Ellis – Co. C (wounded in the right

hand with several fingers blown off – admitted to Citadel Hospital at Charleston, South Carolina.)

26 August, 1863
54th Regiment, Georgia Infantry was on duty at Battery Wagner.

27 August, 1863
Captain Augustus S. Roberts died early and his remains were forwarded to Screven County.

29 August, 1863
54th Regiment, Georgia Infantry relieved from Battery Wagner and sent to Fort Johnson via Fort Gregg. Twenty-four men from the 54th were killed or wounded from the 23rd until the 30th of August.

Killed:
- Sergeant Samuel M. Crosby – Co. B
- Private Isham Crosby – Co. B (died of wounds)
- Private Isaac Herndon – Co. B (died of wounds)
- Private Seaborn Oglesby, Jr. – Co. C
- Captain Augustus S. Roberts – Co. D
- Private William R. Forehand – Co. D
- Private Thomas M. Lewis – Co. D
- Sergeant R. G. Turner – Co. E

Wounded:
- Private Leonidas Alexander Ford – Co. A
- Private W. Carter – Co. B
- Private Isham Crosby – Co. B
- John Tillman Eason – Co. B
- Private Isaac Herndon – Co. B
- Private A. D. Crooms – Co. C
- Private J. G. Ellis – Co. C
- Private J. B. Lamb – Co. C
- Private J. S. Moore – Co. C
- Private William M. Oglesby – Co. C
- Private John A. Baughman – Co. D
- Private Archibald Oglesby – Co. D
- Private William Gaskins – Co. E
- Private Benjamin Jonathan Sirmons – Co. E
- Private Andrew J. Ellis – Co. G
- Private G. W. Touchtone – Co. K

31 August, 1863

(Command Structure)
Dept. of S.C., Ga., and Fla. Commander
(General Pierre G. T. Beauregard)
1st Military District of S.C. Commander
(Brigadier General Roswell S. Ripley)
1st Sub-Division Commander
(Brigadier General William B. Taliaferro)
54th Georgia Battalion Commander

(Col. Charlton H. Way
(Companies B, C, D, E, G, and K)

Military District of Georgia Commander
(Brigadier General Hugh W. Mercer)
Detached 54th Georgia Battalion Commander
(Lt. Col. Morgan Rawls)
(Companies A, F, H, and I)

1 September, 1863
54th Regiment, Georgia Infantry transferred to Morris Island.
6 September, 1863
Reports show that only 400 Confederates were left on Morris Island facing 11,000 Federals. The Confederate Commander at Battery Wagner sent a message asking that if his men could not be evacuated, he preferred to make a sortie against the enemy. Morris Island was evacuated. After almost two months under incredible conditions, subjected to possibly the heaviest artillery fire ever experienced in such a small area, Battery Wagner had stood defiant. Small groups of Confederate soldiers, like those of the 54th Georgia, held off a well-equipped force of 11,000 Yankees armed with some of the heaviest artillery then known. The Federals were also aided by a fleet of heavily gunned and armored vessels. It has been determined that it cost two Federal casualties for every yard of the 1,300 yards they "won" during those two months. The Rebels had the will to fight, and fight they did. One of the last Rebels to evacuate Battery Wagner was a soldier from Georgia, who, arriving safely in Charleston, said he wasn't "afeared of hell no more, it can't touch Wagner." There were some Georgia troops present who had been in all the big battles in Virginia; they all said "that nothing they ever experienced could approximate conditions" at Wagner. The heroic Rebel defense of Battery Wagner had come to an end.
Killed: Sergeant Samuel M. Crosby – Co. B
Wounded: Private A. D. Crooms – Co. C
                 Private J. S. Moore – Co. C
                 Private John A. Baughman – Co. D
10 September 1863
Private Daniel Bragg of Co. D died in Charleston, South Carolina.
14 September 1863
Private Reubin Register of Company E died of Typhoid Fever at Charleston, South Carolina.
20 September, 1863
Private J. S. Moore of Company C died at home of wounds.
Private Reuben Register of Company E died of illness at Charleston, South Carolina.

22 September, 1863
Company F, 54th Regiment, Georgia Infantry had the following change:
John W. Anderson Jr. elected Captain
Private Stephen W. Carter of Company B died of fever in Savannah.
Private Eatonton W. Lamb of Company G died in Confederate General Hospital No. 1 at Columbia, South Carolina.

25 September, 1863
Brigadier General Thomas L. Clingman noted the service of the 54th Georgia commanded by Lieutenant Colonel Morgan Rawls during exposure to extraordinary fire from the Federal fleet while stationed between Battery Wagner and Battery Gregg (out on an open beach). Several Ironsides, monitors, and some wooden vessels kept up a rapid and dangerous fire for many hours at close range on these men.

28 October, 1863
Major General J. F. Gilmer requested the 54th Georgia be recombined at James Island. This meant bringing companies A, F, H, and I from Georgia to join the six companies already in South Carolina. (Companies F, H, and I were stationed two at Rose Dew and one was stationed on heavy Artillery duty at Beaulieu)

29 October, 1863
Company E, 54th Regiment, Georgia Infantry had the following changes:
H. M. Talley elected Captain
James H. Griffin elected First Lieutenant

30 October, 1863
Sergeant Benjamin B. Sammons of Company C died.

1 November, 1863

(Command Structure)
Dept. of S.C., Ga., and Fla. Commander
(General Pierre G. T. Beauregard)
7th Military District of S.C. Commander
(Brigadier General William B. Taliaferro)
Eastern Division Commander
(Brigadier General Johnson Hagood)
54th Georgia Battalion Commander
(Col. Charlton H. Way)
(Companies B, C, D, E, G, and K)

Military District of Georgia Commander
(Brigadier General Hugh W. Mercer)
Detached 54th Georgia Battalion Commander
(Lt. Col. Morgan Rawls)
(Companies A, F, H, and I)

13 November 1863
Private Isaac Herndon of Company B died in Charleston, South Carolina of wounds.

25 November, 1863
Private Isham Crosby of Company B died in the Wayside Hospital at Charleston, South Carolina.

December, 1863
Private Henry Bennett, Sr. of Company K died of Typhoid Fever in Savannah, Georgia.

24 December, 1863
Major General J. F. Gilmer took temporary command of the District of Georgia and 3rd Military District of South Carolina. The six companies of the 54th which had been supporting Charleston were ordered to Pocotaligo, South Carolina.

CHARLESTON, S. C., December 24, 1863.

Brigadier General JOHNSON HAGGOD,

Royal's, James Island:

The battalion of the Fifty-fourth Georgia Volunteers, the Twelfth Battalion Georgia Volunteers, excluding the company in the siege train, and the Thirty-second Georgia Infantry have been ordered to Pocotaligo, to report for temporary service in the Third Military District. They must carry five days' rations. Have the troops at the Savannah Railroad depot, with rations, as soon
as possible.

By command of General Beauregard:

JNO. M. OTEY,
Assistant Adjutant-General

31 December, 1863

(Command Structure)
Dept. of S.C., Ga., and Fla. Commander
(General Pierre G. T. Beauregard)
3rd Military District of S.C. Commander
(Brigadier General William S. Walker)
Pocotaligo Sub-District
54th Georgia Battalion Commander

William A. Bowers, Jr.

(Maj. William H. Mann)
(Companies B, C, D, E, G, and K)

Military District of Georgia Commander
(Brigadier General Hugh W. Mercer)
Detached 54th Georgia Battalion Commander
(Maj. George L. Buist)
(Companies A, F, H, and I)

Company A is located at Harrack's Place
Company F and I are located at Rose Dew Island Battery near Savannah
Company H is located at Beaulieu near Savannah

In 1863
Private W. H. Martin of Company C died of disease.
Corporal Benjamin Spell of Company D died in Charleston, South Carolina.
Private Jasper Patterson of Company K died at James Island near Charleston, South Carolina.

1864

12 January, 1864
A plot by Company F of the 54th Regiment, Georgia Infantry (stationed at Rose Dew, Savannah River battery) to desert their post was uncovered. Private Coleman, Company F, 54th Georgia was arrested and sent to barracks in Savannah as a result of an investigation.

14 January, 1864
A mutiny was suspected in the Fifty-fourth and Fifty-seventh Regiments. The following is the correspondence:

HEADQUARTERS,

Savannah, Ga., January 14, 1864.

Brigadier General THOMAS JORDAN,
Chief of Staff, Charleston, S. C.:

GENERAL: The past two or three days have brought to light a bad state of affairs here. Among the troops stationed at the batteries on Rose Dew Island, mouth of the Little Ogeechee River, there are at least a few men of bad spirit who have been attempting to excite the troops there and at other points around Savannah to acts of insubordination and desertion. It is to be feared even that a spirit of discontent has spread throughout the whole command at Rose Dew, extending possibly to other companies.

As reported by a corporal stationed at Beauleiu, the conspirators proposed to march away from their post on the island yesterday evening, going in a body with their arms to the interior of this State. They expressed themselves tired of the war and said they thought such a step on their part would end it. A secret oath had been exacted of all admitted to their confidence not to divulge their intentions.

Believing these reports might be well founded, I advised Brigadier-General Mercer, commanding the District of Georgia, to send Colonel Olmstead's regiment and a part of Colonel Gordon's command last evening to take position near the Little Ogeechee to observe the enemy in his threatened advance from that quarter, with private instructions to watch the garrison at Rose Dew Island.

These dispositions were made and the suspected troops watched. No movement was attempted by them during the night.

By order of General Mercer a board of officers is now engaged in a rigid investigation of the whole matter, and as soon as the facts are known the guilty men will be arrested and placed in close confinement for trial and punishment. This spirit of discontent has ripened into an intent to desert under the influence of idleness, a want of active service for officers and men, and I am satisfied it will be best to exchange some of the troops here for others, sending the disaffected to Charleston or some other point where they will be in the presence of the enemy.

The companies at Rose Dew are Company F (Captain J. W. Anderson), Company I (Captain Elkins), Fifty-fourth Georgia Regiment, and Jackson Guards (Captain Tanner), who claims to belong to the Fourth Florida Battalion, but is considered here as commanding an independent company. There are two other companies of the Fifty-fourth Georgia Regiment here, commanded by Captains Russell and Brantley; the latter is with the siege train.

As a change of duty may be the means of improving the tone of these disaffected troops, I propose to order the four companies of Colonel Way's regiment, Fifty-fourth Georgia, and the Jackson Guards, Captain Tanner, to the Third Military District of South Carolina, and replace them here by the Twelfth Georgia Battalion, Major Hanvey.

The Fifty-seventh Georgia Regiment should be sent on duty in presence of the enemy, say at Charleston or some other point, and another regiment sent here to replace it. The men of this regiment complain, as stated by Brigadier-General Colston, that they were not properly exchanged after their capture at Vicksburg. Will the commanding general take these troops to Charleston and send a good regiment to replace them here? If this cannot be done, perhaps an exchange might be arranged so as to bring a regiment from the Army of Tennessee or from Virginia.

The inclosed report from Brigadier-General Colston gives a clear statement of what has transpired up to this hour, and I concur fully in the recommendations therein made. Prompt action will probably be the means of avoiding future trouble, and add to the general efficiency of our available strength.

The individuals found guilty of exciting their companions in arms to discontent and desertion should be promptly punished.

I am, general, very respectfully, your obedient servant,

J. F. GILMER,
Major-General and Second in Command
HEADQUARTERS COLSTON'S BRIGADE,

January 14, 1864.

Captain G. A. MERCER,
Assistant Adjutant-General:

SIR: On Tuesday, 12th instant, a communication was received from Captain Hanleiter, commanding Beaulieu Battery, to the effect that a non-commissioned officer had informed him of the existence of a plot among the garrison at Rose Dew, the purpose of which was to abandon the post at Rose Dew with arms, ammunition, &c., to win over the troops at Beaulieu if possible, to advance toward Savannah, taking with them the Terrell Artillery at White Bluff, whose adhesion was considered certain, also some State troops camped on the Skidaway road, and to come to the camp of the Fifty-seventh Georgia, upon whom they seemed to rely as ready to join them, the whole to make their way to the interior of the country, their avowed purpose being to induce by their example as many of the troops as possible to imitate them and by refusing to bear arms any longer "to put an end to the war." The plot was to be executed on last night. I immediately send Captain W. T. Taliaferro, my assistant adjutant-general, to Beaulieu and Rose Dew to investigate the matter. In the mean time an order was sent from district headquarters for the arrest of Private Coleman, Company F, Fifty-fourth Georgia, and he was sent on to the barracks at Savannah. From the result of investigations made by Major Hartridge, commanding at Rose Dew, and Captain Taliaferro it became evident that the plot, which at first appeared so improbable, did really exist.

On yesterday I ordered about 300 men from the First Georgia Regiment and the First Florida Battalion, under the command of Colonel Olmstead, First Georgia, to repair to the causeway connecting Rose Dew Island with the mainland and cut off the communication between the two. Captain Guerard's battery of artillery was ordered to support him. One hundred and fifty men from the Sixty-third

Georgia Regiment, under Major Allen, were ordered to report to Colonel Olmstead. These movements of troops were made ostensibly for the purpose of meeting some demonstrations of the enemy by way of the Ogeechee.

No attempt of any kind was made on last night by the garrison at Rose Dew. The arrest of Coleman and the concentration of troops has evidently frustrated the design, but from the report of Sergeant Hinson to Captain Tanner (Jackson Guards, at Rose Dew), the attempt was not given up until late yesterday evening. Another non-commissioned officer confessed last night to Captain Tanner that nearly the whole company had agreed to go off that night. All the parties concerned were pledged to secrecy by an oath.

A board has been ordered by district headquarters to investigate further into the matter. The troops sent to Rose Dew to check any attempt will remain there until further orders. I would respectfully offer the following suggestions:

First. That a court-martial be convened forthwith for the immediate trial of the parties implicated; that the proceedings of this court be revised at once by the proper authority and the sentences be immediately carried into effect. A terrible and very prompt punishment is indispensable in such an extreme case.

Second. That the troops at Rose Dew be removed from that post and their place upplied by others upon whom reliance can be placed.

Third. That the Fifty-seventh Georgia Regiment be transferred either to the Army of Tennessee or of Virginia. The spirit of this regiment (the Fifty-seventh Georgia) is bad. The troops say that they have never been properly exchanged, and the impression prevails, probably with good reason, that they will not fight if brought before the enemy. They are demoralized by the influence of home, to which they are too near, their friends and relatives persuading them that they have not been properly exchanged and ought to be at home. Their presence here may have a bad effect upon the other troops and their spirit and tone may be improved by removal to more distant points.

It will be necessary, of course, to send other troops in the place of those removed.

I am, sir, very respectfully, your obedient servant,

R. E. COLSTON,
Brigadier-General, Commanding

Brigadier General Hugh W. Mercer convened a board of officers to investigate the plot previously mentioned. Maj. General. J. F. Gilmer recommended "the four companies of the 54th Regiment, Georgia Infantry be sent to Charleston or some other point where they will be in the presence of the enemy".

31 January, 1864

(Command Structure)
Dept. of S.C., Ga., and Fla. Commander
(General Pierre G. T. Beauregard)
3rd Military District of S.C. Commander
(Brigadier General William S. Walker)
54th Georgia Battalion Commander
(Col. Charlton H. Way)
(Companies B, C, D, E, G, and K)

Military District of Georgia Commander
(Brigadier General Hugh W. Mercer)
Detached 54th Georgia Battalion Commander
(Maj. Alfred L. Hartridge)
(Companies F, H, and I)
Detached 54th Georgia Regiment, Company A

7 February, 1864
The Regiment was in the Savannah Area and were close to Red Bluff, South Carolina protecting the batteries on the river.

23 February, 1864
Private Abraham Eason of Company B died of Chronic Dysentery.

24 February, 1864
Company B is ordered from Hardeeville to Pocatalligo and then to Dalton's Bluff, South Carolina.

27 February, 1864
   2nd Lieutenant Silas Thornton shown in command of Company K.
28 February, 1864
   Company A is located at Harrack's Place.
   Company C is located at Dalton's Bluff, South Carolina (orders to proceed from Hardeeville, South Carolina to Pocataligo, South Carolina then to Dalton's Bluff, south Carolina).
   Company H is located at Battery Stephen Elliott.
27 March, 1864
   Private Burns Stewart of Company E died in service.
31 March, 1864

   HEADQUARTERS HARDEEVILLE SUB-DISTRICT,

   March 31, 1864.

   CAPTAIN: I have the honor to report, for the information of the general commanding, that at 11 o'clock to-day one gun-boat and a tug proceeded up the Colleton River as far as the upper end of Spring Island. Stopping first at Seabrook's settlement, they landed a small party, apparently for the purpose of reconnoitering. The 2 pickets stationed there fired upon them, with what effect is not known. The party returned to the boat after having stolen a gun, a saddle, and some clothing, belonging to Mr. Crowell. I ordered Colonel Johnson's cavalry down immediately, but before they could reach the spot the boats had returned.

   The enemy have been reconnoitering Foot Point and its vicinity for the last two or three days, usually in small boats, and may possibly intend landing there in force. The general commanding is fully aware of the utter impracticability of holding Foot Point should the enemy design occupying it in force. If anything serious is meant by these movements, their intention must be simply to land and hold the position as a base upon the mainland. The general commanding may rely upon my using all the means at my disposal to prevent and thwart their designs, and upon my giving him prompt information in regard to anything which may occur.

   Very respectfully, your obedient servant,

   CHARLTON H. WAY,
   Colonel, Commanding Sub-District

5 April, 1864
   The 54th was sent to Pocotaligo, South Carolina via the Charleston and Savannah Railroad. They were encamped at the Frazier Farm near

Beaufort.
16 April, 1864
Special Orders No. 89
Adjt. And Insp General's Office
Richmond, April 16, 1864

XL. The First, Fifty-fourth, and Fifty-seventh Regiments Georgia Volunteers will proceed by railroad, under the command of Brig. Gen. H. W. Mercer, to Dalton, Georgia, and report to General Joseph E Johnston, commanding, &c., To relieve the Fifth, Forty-seventh, and Fifty-fifth Regiments Georgia Volunteers.

The last-named to regiments under the command of Brig. Gen. J. K. Jackson, will proceed by railroad to Savannah, Georgia, as they are successively relieved.

By command of the Secretary of War:
JNO. Withers,
Adjutant-General Assistant

22 April, 1864

HDQRS. DEPT. OF S. CAROLINA, GEORGIA, AND FLORIDA,
Charleston, S. C., April 22, 1864.
General S. COOPER,
Adjutant and Inspector General, Richmond, Va.:

GENERAL: I have had the honor to receive extracts from Special Orders, Numbers 89, War Department, S. C., ordering the First and Fifty-fourth and Fifty-seventh Regiments Georgia Volunteers to proceed to Dalton, Ga., to relieve the Fifth, Forty-seventh, and Fifty-fifth* Georgia Regiments; also the Sixty-third Georgia Volunteers to proceed to the headquarters of the Department of Northern Virginia.

I would respectfully beg leave to substitute the Sixty-fourth Georgia Regiment, now returning from Florida, for the First Georgia Regiment, for the following reasons: This latter regiment is serving as artillerists at the principal batteries on which we rely for the defense of Savannah, namely, the Savannah River batteries, Fort Bartow, lines and batteries on Whitemarsh Island, and at Fort McAllister. Their military training has been as heavy artillerists, and I have none to replace them. It has been necessary also to assign the colonel (C. H. Olmstead) to the command of the Third Military District of South Carolina. I therefore earnestly suggest that the substitution of the Sixty-fourth Georgia Regiment for the First Georgia Regiment be authorized. The Sixty-third Georgia Regiment has been serving also as heavy artillerists, but I can supply their places in part by the Twelfth Georgia Battalion, which was originally organized for an artillery battalion. The Fifty-seventh Georgia Regiment has been sent, as ordered, to relieve the Fifth Georgia Regiment, in guarding prisoners at Andersonville. The Fifty-fourth Georgia Regiment will move as ordered at the earliest practicable moment; also the Sixty-third Georgia Regiment.

I am, general, very respectfully, your obedient servant,

SAM. JONES,
Major-General, Commanding

23 April, 1864
Brigadier-General Mercer received orders from the Confederate High Command to take three Regiments (one being the 54th) and proceed to Dalton, Georgia in order to join the Army of Tennessee.

24 April, 1864
Private Bartlett Wiley Green of Company G died in General Hospital No. 1 at Savannah, Georgia of Pneumonia.

"Joining the Army of Tennessee"

26 April, 1864
Brigadier General Hugh W. Mercer relieved of command of the Military District of Georgia and begins trip to join General Joseph E. Johnston commanding the Army of Tennessee C.S.A. at Dalton.

30 April, 1864
54th Regiment, Georgia Infantry reaches Dalton, Georgia.

3 May, 1864
Mercer's Brigade was formed and sent to Report to General Johnston at Dalton, Georgia. The four regiments in Mercer's Brigade were the 1st Georgia, the 54th Georgia, the 57th Georgia and the 63rd Georgia Regiments. Due to their inexperienced look and brand new uniforms with regulation chevrons (which they no longer had) the veteran soldiers called them; "Band Box Soldiers" or "Silver Forks" or "New Issue".

One incredulous Tennessee sergeant wrote home;
"This morning I saw a regiment 1400 strong, just from Savannah. It has been in service for nearly three years but has never been a fight. We expect to show it the "elephant" in a few days".
The Tennessean did not know that elements of the brigade had seen action at Battery Wagner and James Island in the Charleston Area and were in the battle at Champion Hill near Vicksburg and were in the Siege of Vicksburg.

Lieutenant Hamilton Branch of Company F wrote to his mother Charlotte Branch:

"…………..Dalton Ga

……..I arrived here this forenoon after a series of adventures safe and sound. The train I came on collided with a freight train and bruised one man pretty badly and smashed the cars pretty badly. We are in Genl Walkers Division and Genl Hardees Corps……………..

………… we are in camp to about 3 miles from here in the direction of Cleveland (Cleveland, Tennessee)……………"

4 May, 1864

(Command Structure)
Army of Tennessee
(General Joseph E. Johnston)
Corps Commander
(Lt. General William J. Hardee)
Division Commander
(Maj. General William H. T. Walker)
Brigade Commander
(Brigadier General Hugh W. Mercer)
54th Georgia Battalion Commander
(Colonel Charlton H. Way)

Brigadier General Mercer's Brigade consisting of the 54th, 57th, and 63rd was assigned to the Corps of Lieutenant General William J. Hardee and under the Division of Major General William H. T. Walker then located 3 miles east of Dalton.

Lieutenant Hamilton Branch of Company F wrote to his mother Charlotte Branch:

."……. Bivouac Mercer's Brigade Dalton

We are about 3 miles from Dalton in the direction of Cleaveland, we are in Walker W H T Division and in General Hardees Corps, there was a dispute in reference to which Division we belong to, Walkers or Pat Cleburnes, but it has been decided in favor of Walker I believe. The country here is more hilly than the portion of Virginia through which I passed, it is very cold up here at nights, we had a very heavy frost night before last. The train on which I came from Marietta backed into a freight train near Frankfurt in a general smash up was the consequence, one man about the middle of the train was pretty badly hurt but that was all, the cars though were broken pretty badly. I was in the back car and strange to say it was the least hurt of them all………"

"…………The army up here are in fine spirits and confident of victory in the coming fight and if the people at home will only do there duty and keep the disasters away from home there is no doubt but we will whip them…………."

5 May, 1864
General William T. Sherman began his campaign into north Georgia. Federal skirmishers drove in Confederate pickets near Tunnel Hill and advanced against Rocky Face Ridge.

6 May, 1864   the Battle at Rocky Face Ridge, Georgia
The Army of Tennessee C.S.A. was entrenched between Dalton and Rocky Face, Georgia. The Brigade was called "Mercer's", "New Issue", or "Silver Spoons" after the commander and the fact that this brigade was issued new uniforms and paid just prior to departure from Savannah. The latter two nicknames quickly faded, however "Mercer's", remained until near the end of the War. Walker's was a reserve division, meaning it had no fixed place in the line of battle, but was moved from point to point as required.

8 May, 1864   Dug Gap, Georgia (Near Dalton, Georgia)

Lieutenant Hamilton Branch of Company F wrote to his mother Charlotte Branch:
"……….. Bivouac Mercer's Brigade

……….we have been marching and counter marching all the time, the enemy are advancing and we expect the big fight tomorrow and we intend to give them a good whipping and tried and end the war, they have been skirmish in all day, we have just returned from a tramp to help Genl Hood but after marching about two miles he sent us back. But I must stop as the enemy have begun the attack and our long roll is beating again………."

Wounded: Private Joseph Hamilton Stephens – Co. E

9 May, 1864   Rocky Face Ridge
The battle of Rocky Face Ridge occurred. Mercer's Brigade took an advanced position on Rocky Face Ridge where its pickets were driven in and the trenches shelled resulting in a few casualties. The Brigade marched back and forth between Dalton and Resaca and saw little action.

Wounded: Private Needham A. Barfield – Co. G

10 May, 1864
Lieutenant Hamilton Branch of Company F wrote to his mother

Charlotte Branch:

"..........Bivouac Mercer's Brigade 3 miles from Resaca Geo

I wrote to you on the evening of the eighth just as the long roll was beating. After falling into line we marched about three miles from our position and about five miles from Dalton. Here on the top of a high hill we were put into the trenches and made to stay there all night. Our trenches were on the two sides of a battery of eight guns which commanded the Valley below us. Col. (George W.) Gordon was in the trenches in the left and Col. (Charlton H.) Way in those on the right. above the center of Col. Way's line the pioneer corps then built us a small battery for two guns and the next day Capt. (R. T.) Beauregard was sent there with two 10 lb. Parrot guns. We stayed in the trenches all of the 9th and about 3 oclock a. m. our large battery were attacked by a few of the enemy and were repulsed. Before this attack there was skirmishing from early dawn and about 2 p. m. oclock Lt. (William E.) Reddick, a very nice young man and gallant officer, was killed whilst standing on the parapet. He was killed by a sharpshooter from a great distance. the enemy threw quite a number of shell over us and a few minnie balls.

Our boys all behaved very well. We were under fire about two hours. Capt. (George Anderson) Mercer and the Capt. (Edward W) Drummond both had narrow escapes. We were kept in the trenches untill about 1 oclock a. m. of the tenth when we were taken out and marched to this place which is 11 miles from Dalton. We arrived here about 10 oclock but as there is no chance of a fight here now, the enemy having fallen back, I suppose we will go back to Dalton tomorrow. We had an awful time marching to this place. We had to come down a very steep side of the mountain in the dark. I do not know when the big fight will come off but suspect before long. we had four or five men wounded in our Regiment nine in our co.........."

13 May, 1864 the Battle of Resaca, Georgia

The battle of Resaca occurred. Reports of two Federal Union Divisions attempting to cross the Oostanaula River near Lay's Ferry prompted General Johnston to send Walker's Division to drive the Federals back in that area. The Federals crossed the River on the 15th and repulsed an attack by parts of Walker's Division, Mercer's Brigade being the only part of the attack to drive the Federals back. Orders were then given to retreat, and the army marched to Calhoun, Georgia. During this march the Brigade patrolled the Western and Atlantic Railroad along with Brigades of Jackson, Stevens, and Gist. Leonidas Polk's Army of Mississippi arrives to join the Army of Tennessee. There were at this

point 100,000 Federals facing 60,000 Confederates.
Wounded: Private Joseph H. Grooms – Co. I

Lieutenant Hamilton Branch of Company F wrote to his mother Charlotte Branch:

"………Bivouac Walker's Division near Calhoun, Geo.

…………I wrote to you on the 10th and immediately after writting we were marched out and formed into line of battle, we've then stacked our arms and went to sleep. About 10 oclock it commenced raining and I have never seen it rain harder than it did. I was awakened by slipping down the hillside on which I was sleeping it was a very steep one and the water running under me cause me to slide. I was sleeping on and covering with one blanket viz Sam Douses who was sleeping with me or rather I with him as I have not seen my blanket since we started to march as I put it in Genl Mercers waggon and that has not been seen since. the rest of my baggage was put in the officers waggon also and that has not been seen since, so that I now only carry my sword, sash, haversack and canteen. My cloths are very dirty as we have been marching for the last week on very dusty roads and I have not been able to change my cloths.

I arose the morning after the rain and dried my cloths, after which we fell in and were marched to Resaka which was about 3 miles. But we were too late, for the enemy had gone back. After staying their about two hours we were marched back and bivouacked at the old place. The next day the 12th, about 4 oclock p. m. we fell in and were marched through Resacka and across the Ostanula to this place where we arrived about 9 oclock p. m. Here we have been ever since, and do not know when we will move but have been expecting to go every minute.

Genl Walker has just gone out and is shelling a party of the enemy who are putting a battery up on the river in front of us. Genls Johns(t)on and Sherman are playing a large game of Chess but Johns(t)ons boys are sure to carry him through. We do not know why we have been moved away down here but we know that it is all right………….."

Wounded: Private Needham Barfield – Co. G (left arm)
Private Joseph C. Grooms – Co. I

15 May, 1864   near Gilgal (Golgotha) Church
Mercer's Brigade was assigned to duty as a part of the advance line for Hardee's Corps. Around noon the union artillery fire changed from sporadic to intense. Hardee's advance troops were then attacked by General Hooker's federal core. Shortly after 1:30 pm Mercer's Brigade,

which was heavily engaged, received orders to fall back. While doing so they were under heavy enemy fire and lost 20 men killed or wounded. The 54th Georgia had five casualties.

Wounded:
        Private B. R. Graham – Co. C
        Private McKibber Jenkins – Co. C
        Lieutenant James H. Griffin – Co. E
        Corporal John W. Slaughter – Co. G
        Private John B. Harrell – Co. G

Lieutenant Hamilton Branch of Company F wrote to his mother Charlotte Branch:

"……………In line of battle below Calhoun Ga near the lines.

The long roll was beaten to send us on picket. we went on picket on the river about ¼ mile from Calhoun. we remained on picket all night and the next morning we were ordered to rejoin our regiment which has been ordered to reinforce the forces at Resaca.

We marched about two miles and met our regiment. we then marched down and crossed the Oustanula at Resaca on a pontoon bridge just above the Rail Road bridges. In doing this we were subjected to the fire of a yankey battery about ½ mile off but we crossed with only the loss of two men killed and four wounded, all of the 63rd Ga. We then marched through Resacka and about two miles above the rail road where we formed a line of battle and stayed about 1 hour and a half during which time we were occasionally favored with a S(hrapnel) shell, round shot or minnie ball. but fortunately no one was hurt. We then marched on about a mile and were put into the trenches where we stayed untill about 10 oclock when we were ordered to this place, which is about 12 miles from Resaca by the road. In re-crossing the river last night we crossed on the rail road bridge and were not troubled at all. in going into the trenches we were subjected to a fire of many rifles and had three or four wounded, viz. 1st Lt. (James H.) Griffin shot through the left lung and 1stLt. (Grigsby E.) Thomas (Sr.) shot in the face and one or two men.

We are now in line of battle away down on the flank, for what purpose we know not. You must excuse bad writting as I am lying down and Johnnie is asleep with his head resting on me, and also I have been up two nights now and have been marching all of one night and day. I must close now as I want to try and get a little sleep before going into the fight……"

16 May, 1864

After being engaged all day in different parts of the line, Mercer's brigade withdrew after dark to a position behind the lines of General Walker's and General William B. Bates' divisions in order to regroup.

Wounded: Private Daniel Lewis – Co. C
Lieutenant Grigsby E. Thomas Sr. – Co. G
Private John B. Harrell

Captured: Private Rice W. Britt – Co. C
Private William Albert McCants – Co. H

Lieutenant Hamilton Branch of Company F wrote to his mother Charlotte Branch:

"………Calhoun Geo

………I write to let you know that we are still quite well, but dirty. Genl (John K.) Jackson attacked the enemy yesterday and drove them to there breastworks when he very foolishly charged them without having a support and was repulsed. so last night about 10 Oclock we fell back to this place. Why we fell back I know not for the enemy were not troubling us at all. it may be though that the enemy are moving his forces to Rome and if so we will go there too.

last night was the third night during which we have been on the march. but last night we rested half the night and therefore feel quite fresh this morning. We have not been into a fight yet. it is reported that after our forces fell back from Resaca that the enemy captured two of our hospitals and killed all the wounded. Also that they fired into our ambulances and killed the wounded. I do not know that this is true but is reported so. Bob Butler is well and in fact all the boys are well. Remember me to all my friends. Write to me soon and often. We have looked whipped the enemy on all sides thus far. we are falling back gradualy, that is fall back 8t or 10 miles and then stay three or four days. I do not know how far back we will go but it is all right. General Johns(t)on knows what to do, and he will come out all right………"

17 May, 1864 the Battle of Adairsville, Georgia

At Adairsville, General Johnston came up with a plan to divide Sherman's three Federal armies and attack at Cassville, Georgia. Hardee's Corp was given the assignment of protecting the army supply train, taking a longer route, and drawing the attention of the larger Federal forces. Two other Confederate corps would attack the smaller Federal forces at Cassville. Hardee's Corp fought steadily as it retreated through Kingston, Georgia into Cassville. General Johnston's plan worked well until the two Confederate corps at Cassville were approached by a Federal cavalry division and decided the plan would not work. General Johnston then decided to make a stand, but on the night of the 19th, corps commanders Lieutenant General Polk and Lieutenant General Hood met with General Johnston, without Lieutenant General Hardee being present. The two corps commanders convinced General Johnston that Cassville could not be held. Lieutenant General Hardee was outraged when he heard the division to again retreat, but the Army of Tennessee began withdrawing on the morning of the 20th.

Wounded: Private Solomon Baker – Co. A
Captured: Private F. N. Lawrence – Co. A (near Calhoun Georgia)
Private Francis M. Lawson – Co. A (near Calhoun, Georgia)

18 May, 1864   # Kingston, Georgia

Mercer's Brigade was again positioned in the front lines near Mud Creek. In this position they were again under heavy fire. When General Johnston began to withdraw his troops to form up at Kennesaw Mountain Mercer's Brigade as pickets to protect the rear of this movement.

Captured: Private James J. Keane – Co. F

Lieutenant Hamilton Branch of Company F wrote to his mother Charlotte Branch:

"............Bivouac Co. F 54th Ga, Mercers Brigade, Walkers Division Hardee's Corps, Army of Tenn

…………..on line of battle near Bartow Georgia

…….After writting to you on the 16th we, our brigade, were marched about 7 miles down towards the river for the purpose of cutting off a party of yanks, but when we arrived there we found that they had gone. we then had the pleasure of marching back over the same ground to reinforce Genl Walker who skirmishers were engaged with the enemy. we went back in a hurry as we were liable to be cut off. when we arrived back we found the Gallant Major (Arthur) Schaaf with his brave battalion engaged with the enemy near Calhoun. There were other skirmishers but they did not act as well as they ought to have done. the enemy were driven back two miles, the Sharp Shooters suffered severely. Maj Schaaf escaped unhurt, although he led two charges on the enemy. The brave Capt (Horace D.) T(w)yman, than whom no more gallant officer lives, had his right leg broken and received a flesh wound in his left. they also lost severely in men. we formed a reserve line of battle here and waited until night when we fell back to (Adairsville). Here we staid all day and the enemy appearing in the evening (General

Benjamin F.) Cheatham was sent out to drive them back, which he did. we lay in line of battle here until 1 AM when we started to fall back again and have now reached this place, which is about two miles from Bartow. we expect to fall back again tonight and do not know where the General intends to stop, but this we do know-that when he stops he is agoing to fight the battle of the war and that God helping he is agoing to give them the worst whipping they have had. My boys are all well but nearly worn out and we, Walkers Foot Cavalry, have been doing all the strategy for Genl Johnston and have marched night and day for the last 10 days with very little rest. It is now about 10 (a)m and as I want a little sleep before we start again, which I suppose will be about dark, I must close………"

19 May, 1864 the Battles of Kingston and Cassville Georgia

Captured: Private James B. Morrison – Co. A
Private John R. Hodges – Co. F
Private Martin Dunn – Co. G
Private William Scott Wade – Co. G

Lieutenant Hamilton Branch of Company F wrote to his mother Charlotte Branch:

"………..In line Battle, Mercers Brigade Bartow, Ga

After writing you yesterday, for a wonder, we did not move, but had one good nights rest, although I was awakened about one Oclock by fire, it being near my head. It was caused by some large rails being put on the fire and they burned to the ends and set the leaves on fire and they burned to my bed which was about eight feet from the fire. My bed fellow, Sam Dowse, had his hat in haversack burned. I awoke just in time to save his cartridge box, although the strap was burned I got through with a small hole burned in the side of my hat and the silk and velvet burned off one part.

This morning we were sent to the front to relieve General (Lucius E.) Polk's Brigade who were acting as rear guards. We then threw out skirmishers and fought them for awhile, then fell back drawing them after us. We fell back about a mile to where our army was in line of battle and took our place in line on the top of a hill in an open field. Here the enemy commenced shelling us and shelled us for about two hours, killing one man and wounding several. My company lost none. This line was formed for the purpose of checking the enemy, which we did. Here Colonel Way read an order from General Johns(t)on, praising our army for the soldierly qualities they had shown during the falling back. General Mercer then said to us 'Silver Forks show what metal you are made of.'…………….."

20 May, 1864
    Captured: Private Issac J. Lanier – Co. I

21 May, 1864
    Lieutenant Hamilton Branch of Company F wrote to his mother Charlotte Branch:

"………..Bivouac Co. F 54th Ga. Reg Inft Mercers Brigade Walkers Division Hardees Corps, Army of Tennessee

……We are now only 43 miles from Atlanta. we are between Etowa station and Altoona. we laid down behind our stacks after my last letter was written and slept until 1 O'clock when we were ordered to move which we did and marched through Cass Station and Cartersville. About good daylight-we arrived at Etowa Station where we staid until about 12 Oclock to allow our army and waggons to cross the river. there were four bridges across the river, viz. the railroad, dirt road and two pontoon bridges. I went to the river and had a good bath but had to put my same dirty cloths on. I then sat down and saw a greater portion of the army cross the river. I counted 105 regiments of infantry crossing and I know there were two brigades Jackson and (States Rights) Gists, behind me.

After crossing the river we marched to this place where we have slept all night. I have been in and taken another wash and feel quite well this morning although hungry. Genl Johns(t)on thinking that the enemy were about to stop following him, determined to advance from Cassville, Bartow upon them, but finding that they were intended following him, he has commenced falling back again, and no one knows where he will stop. My company are all well. God has protected us and we have not lost a man out of the company. Johnny sends his love to you. Do send me anything to eat as soon as you get a chance. there is no use sending it except by someone. Today is 21st May, just three years since we left Savannah for Virginia……….."

22 May, 1864
    Private J. C. Blue of Company B died in Columbus, Georgia.

23 May, 1864
    Hardee's Corp sent toward Dallas, Georgia.

24 May, 1864
    Lieutenant Hamilton Branch of Company F wrote to his mother Charlotte Branch:

"……..Bivouac Mercers Brigade, Near Powder Springs Ga

I have been so worn out that I just did not feel at all like doing anything but resting whilst we were in Bivouac near Altoona, from which place I wrote you on the 20th. We stayed at that bivouac nearly three days and therefore had quite a good rest. We left that bivouac on Monday the 23rd at 10 AM Oclock. The sun was shining very brightly and it was very warm indeed. we marched very slowly until 4 ½ Oclock PM when we went into bivouac having marched but 6 miles, although as it was so warm it appeared to be about 12. We stayed at this bivouac until about 4 ½ AM. when we were awakened and fell in ranks and marched until about 5 PM when we were halted and marched into our present bivouac. we have not the prospect of a pleasant night, for as the boys say there are rain seeds on all sides.

I'm still quite well although I have chafed today for the first time, as we have stopped near a creek I have just been down and taken a wash and have received from Buck (William B.) Hassett the bottle of camphor which you sent to me and have used some of it and I think it has helped me. All the boys are well. there are some of the countrymen who have been sent off sick and Jas (J.) Keane was lost from the company on the 11th and has not been heard of since. we think he has been taken prisoner.

Mother you not think that Mrs. Robinson could now and then send me a little bundle of eatables, if so please send her a small box, say about 50 or 100 pounds. We are now only 22 miles from Atlanta by the dirt road........."

25 May1864 the Battle of New Hope Church, Georgia
Hardee's Corps entrenched on high ground just east of Dallas.
Wounded: Sergeant Benjamin F. Odom – Co. G
            Private William Williams – Co. G
            Private William Simmons – Co. I

Lieutenant Hamilton Branch of Company F wrote to his mother Charlotte Branch:

"..........Bivouac I don't know where Company F 54th Ga Mercers Brigade

After writting yesterday we were presented by Buck Hassett & Co. with a goose, which I had killed and then proceeded to clean and divide, after which I fried the Capt (John W. Anderson, Jr.) & mine and having a piece of cornbread we fried that and sat down to supper. Just as we had finished eating, which occupied some time as the goose was quite tough, it commenced raining. we then layed down and went to sleep. it rained until 12 O'clock. at 1 AM we were called and found ourselves ringing wet. we got up and put on our trappings and started back over the same road on which we marched yesterday. we marched I do not know how far but I think about 3 miles, and then went into the woods about ½ mile where we stopped and stacked arms. we had just got the sleep when we were made to get up and fall in and marched about ¼ of a mile where we now are. thus you see we have marched back towards the enemy but for what purpose unless for strategy I do not know.

The stoper was knocked out of my ink bottle yesterday and all the ink emptied into my haversack. I put the bottle and my pomade divine which was covered with link down by my haversack to dry out and in leaving last night forgot them.

My boys all look badly this morning, having marched, fasted and been wet. they have had nothing to eat now in two days………."

26 May 1864 the Battle of Dallas, Georgia
Major General Walker's Division, as part of Hardee's Corps, occupied the left end of the Army of Tennessee east of Dallas and skirmished with Federals there.

Lieutenant Hamilton Branch of Company F wrote to his mother Charlotte Branch:

"……….Mercer's Brigade, on the march to the front

After writting to you on yesterday I laid down and went to sleep, and slept about two hours. I then got up and felt quite refreshed. we staid at that bivouac until about 4 PM when we fell in and were marched 1/2 mile to the right through the woods. here we formed line of battle and rested. from that place we could hear quite a heavy skirmish going on a little to our right and front. we staid in line of battle until about 7 PM when we were marched through the woods on by roads until 10 Oclock PM when we were halted allowed to go to sleep.

Just at this place quite an amusing incident occurred. we had stopped in the road sometime in some of us were resting ourselves on the ground. all were not down because it had been raining the whole time that we were on the march and they were afraid to be on the wet ground. I was at the head of my company and Judge B(rewer) and Joe Ganaan were at the front of theres, therefore we were together. I was laying down on the ground Judge was sitting on his blanket roll at my head and Joe was half lying down by Judge. I had just dosed off when someone hit me on the knee and I heard a noise as if the horses of an ambulance were running away with it down the road. so I just rolled over into the woods and jumped up, and looking around not a man was to be seen on the road which just a moment before was crowded. they had all taken to the woods, Judge says that he thought the thing was upon him and that he was going to be run over and therefore he closed his eyes to receive it. just then Joe whispered Yanks and judge says have they gone by and opened his eyes. this noise was heard by the whole division and they all jumped into the woods. As yet no one has been able to account for the noise as nothing has been seen, but it is thought that some horses in the rear must've run away but were stopped suddenly. We laid down at this place until 2 AM when we were called and marched into a big road and up to where we are now. we have stacked arms and are about 1 ½ miles from the enemy and are awaiting orders. Ed Foy was sent off to the hospital yesterday, nothing serious I think........."

27 May 1864 the Battle of Picket's Mill, Georgia

Union troops attacked General Patrick Cleburne's men who were behind breastworks in the woods on the Picket property. Cleburne's "crack soldiers" inflicted severe causalities with a withering and galling fire from their muskets.

Captured: Private John Farmer – Co. K

Private Solomon Baker of Company A in hospital at Macon, Georgia with a Gunshot Wound to the right knee.
Private John H. Nesmith of Company F died of disease at Atlanta, Georgia.

Lieutenant Hamilton Branch of Company F wrote to his mother Charlotte Branch:

"...............In line of battle, near Dallas, Georgia

"................After writting yesterday we were marched to near New Hope Church and formed into line of battle. here we were kept all day and until 1 AM this morning. heavy skirmish and was kept up during this time in our front. we were then formed in marched to this place where we now lie in line acting as a reserve to our line of battle which is about 50 yards to the front and as covered by breastworks. we have been moved once or twice to the right and left, as the skirmishing indicated the point to be attacked. My boys are all well so far. If you have not spoken to Aunt Lizzie you need not, as Bob is attending to his business better now. We all think there will be a fight here in a day or two. Genl Johns(t)on has been offering the enemy battle for two days now but he has not excepted yet. ...."

28, May, 1864
    Wounded: Private William H. Kitchens – Co. A
Private John Washington Elliott of Company F died in the hospital at Macon, Georgia.
Private John W. Bennett of Company K died of Pneumonia in the hospital at Atlanta, Georgia.

Lieutenant Hamilton Branch of Company F wrote to his mother Charlotte Branch:

"............In line of battle as reserves to Cheatham's Division near New Hope Church

After writting on yesterday we were marched a mile and a half to the right over two very high hills and up to the top of another one, when we formed line of battle and sent out skirmishers. I do not think the army had ever been on these hills as there was no signs of them. the sides of the hills where as near perpendicular as it is possible for a man to climb up. we built small stone works here and staid until 1 Oclock AM when we were ordered to this place to report to Genl Johnston. we arrived your 5 AM. Whilst at our stone works we were subjected to the fire of the sharpshooters, but lost no one out of my company. Our skirmishers charged the enemy at that place and drove them in. There was quite an engagement on our right yesterday. we drove the enemy back two miles I believe, and captured a number of prisoners. We are expecting a fight here every day now. On the march last night I was so sleepy that I was dozing off all the time. Judge Brewer is still well. Remember me to all my friends. I have been living high for the last day. our boys were so starved that they asked General Mercer to let them kill some hogs and he gave them permission so that we have been living on fresh pork.........."

30 May, 1864   **near Dallas Georgia**
    Captured: Private General M. Kersey – Co. K
31 May, 1864
    Wounded: Private V. Nix – Co. E
Private William Albert McCants of Company H died in the hospital at Military Prison at Louisville, Kentucky.

Lieutenant Hamilton Branch of Company F wrote to his mother Charlotte Branch:

"......On Skirmish line
We remained the whole of yesterday in the same position that we were

the day before until about 2 PM when we were sent out on picket where we now are. for a wonder our brigade has been allowed three nights sleep, that is the three last nights. We were allowed two but of course as we, that is my company, was on picket last site we could not sleep at all. everything has been very quiet here for the last two days. scarcely a gun has been fired. I went down this morning washed all over and put on my clean cloths and you do not know how proud I feel. I wish you could see the cloths that I took off. They are as dirty as dirty can be. All the boys are well. the Capt (Fred Hull) has had a chill and some fiver. do not tell anyone as he has not been very sick. The O L I are on picket with us. Harmon and Paul (Elkins) are well, also Judge B…………."

1 June 1864
Private William H. Kitchens of Company A admitted to Ocmulgee Hospital at Macon, Georgia with a gunshot wound.

2 June, 1864
Lieutenant Hamilton Branch of Company F wrote to his mother Charlotte Branch:

Hd Qrs Co F54th Ga, Infty Mercers Brigade Walkers Division
Hardees Corps Army of Tenn

"………..In the trenches near New Hope

After writing to you on the 31st we remained on picket until 5 PM when we were relieved by Co H 54th. I had persuaded Capt Anderson in the mean time to go to the rear and he went about 2 PM leaving me in command of the company. after being relieved from picket I brought my company back to this place where we remained all yesterday the 1st, although we were expecting to move every minute as Genl Johns(t)on was up on this hill looking at the enemy who were evacuating the left of their line, our men occupying their breastworks as soon as they left them. In Dallas they left an envelope on which they had written off for Chattanooga will be back in a few days with something to eat. they left a number of our wounded in Dallas.

On the 31st I went on the top of Edwards Mountain which is just to our left and upon which Col (George W.) Gordon is stationed. from that place I had a magnificent view of the country in our front. I could see two lines of the enemys fortifications and also their waggon trains and cavalry passing. our battery on the top of the skill fired six shots at a house in the valley from which the enemy sharp shooters were annoying our men. at this signal the skirmishers from Genl J K Jacksons Brigade advanced and set the hose on fire and burned it to the ground………."

3 June, 1864
Lieutenant Hamilton Branch of Company F wrote to his mother Charlotte Branch:

"………in line of battle 4 miles to right of New Hope
After writting yesterday it commenced raining and rained very hard for about an hour. I having nothing to protect me got quite wet but by going to a fire and taken off my cloths and holding them to the fire I got them dry. by this time it commenced raining again but not very hard. after raining while we were ordered into line and started to march at 4 PM and marched over very boggy roads until 12 Oclock midnight when we were halted in the woods and laid down on the wet ground and went to sleep and slept until this morning when we formed line of battle and are now supporting Genl (Carter L.) Stevenson but there is no telling where we will be tonight. I am not bothered with anything on a march now's as since we left Dalton the only things I carry my sword, haversack and canteen. I sleep on the ground and cover with nothing. The boys are all well. That is all of my boys that you know. a great many have been sent off to the hospitals but none but (George W.) Brownell and (William H.) Bradl(e)y from Savh. Judge, Harmon and Paul are all well. Bob is well. We do not know when we will have a fight but are expecting one every day. I received your letter of the 26th with copies of Santys. I am very glad to hear from him but am sorry that the poor fellow has suffered so much (his brother, Lieutenant Sanford Branch was one of the "Immortal 600" Confederate Officers imprisoned by the Federal Army). I hope that he will soon be exchanged and be at home with you…….."

"……..Our army is still in fine spirits and confident, God helping us, of victory. The enemy are on short rations and not in fine spirits, for they have found us not demoralized but only drawing them into a trap……….."

8 PM

"…………….In line of battle 3 miles left of Altoona

I wrote you a letter today and gave it to Dr. (I. E.) Godfrey to mail for me, but since then I have seen Mort Ferres who tells me that you are in Atlanta. Mother if you have brought anything for me from home do not send too much at once as I cannot carry it. if you send to Savh Committee at Marietta care of Mr (John) Reil(l)y, Forage Master, Mercers Brigade he says that he will bring anything for me. he goes ever second day. he will be in Marietta tomorrow afteroon, the 4th at 3 or 4 Oclock and every other day as long as we are around about this country here which I hope will not be long as I want to advance. he will be in Marietta on Monday again. something to eat will go right well. All here are well. Capt A(nderson) is at the infirmary about two miles from her. I received your letter of the 24 this afternoon but have never recd yours of the 3rd. I am very glad to hear from Hollie and Santy........."

4 June, 1864   Operations near Marietta, Georgia

After these battles, the Federal Army again began flanking movements and the Army of Tennessee retreated towards Kennesaw, Georgia.

Wounded: Private W. H. Kitchens – Co. A
                Private Edward Jefferson Ritchey – Co. A
                Private William Simmons – Co. D
                Private Benjamin F. Odom – Co. G
                Private William Williams – Co. G

William Albert McCants of Company H died at Louisville, Kentucky prison.

John W. Bennett of Company K died of illness.

Lieutenant Hamilton Branch of Company F wrote to his mother Charlotte Branch:

"..........In line of battle between Altoona and Acworth

We remain in the place from which I wrote to you yesterday until last night at eleven oclock when we started for this place, where we arrived this morning at 4 Oclock. it rained almost the whole of yesterday and therefore the roads were in an awful state. last night we were formed into line at 8 PM and kept in line until we started on the march. this morning after building breastworks we were moved from them about 300 yards to this place where we again built breastworks. I am glad to hear that you are taking of Capt T(w)yman. If you come across Capt (Lewis A.) Picquett of the 63 Ga look after him also. Charlie Davis of my company has been sick sometime and today I have sent him to the rear. If he gets to Atlanta take care of him.........."

The Confederate troops who were on the Dallas-New Hope line fell back on June 4 and marched during the darkness with incessant rain pouring on them for 10 miles. They slogged through up to knee-deep mud.

Colonel Olmstead 1st Georgia Infantry wrote of this night and of the misery encountered in the march.

"................. the roads too were particularly bad, there had been a great deal of rain and the constant passage of artillery and transportation trains had cut them up most abominably......... The memory of night marches over these roads is like a nightmare to me as I think of them; horses and men wearied and exhausted, stumbling along, through red clay, mud and darkness-prolonged waiting every few hundred yards when somewhere in front a stalled wagon or a broken down caisson would block the road............

These night tramps were generally made in moody silence. I remembered to have fallen asleep in the saddle often, waking with a start wondering where I was when the order came to move on. This is a side of war the histories do not lay much stress upon but every old soldier bears it in mind"......................"

5 June, 1864   Operations near Marietta, Georgia

Killed: John W. Miller of Company H killed
Wounded: Private Abraham E. McLeroy – Co. H
Emanuel Hurst of Company I died in hospital.

Lieutenant Hamilton Branch of Company F wrote to his mother Charlotte Branch:

"……..In line of battle somewhere around Marietta

We stayed at our old line of battle all day yesterday and until 11 PM when we were formed and marched over the worst road I've ever marched on to this place. we arrived here about 7 Oclock this morning. it rained all day yesterday and almost all night. I am covered from head to foot with mud as I fell down seven times on the march and the mud was from 6 to 18 inches deep. I do not know exactly where we are but think not more than 5 miles from Marietta. Capt Bailey of the Savh Comm was with us yesterday. Good news from Lee it is not (the repulse of the Yankees at Cold Harbor, Va). our men are very anxious to turn around upon the enemy and give them a good thrashing and with the help of the Almighty if Genl Johns(t)on will put us upon them we will annihilate them. Old Joe is all right and will give us the word……"

6 June, 1864   Operations near Marietta, Georgia

Private Francis M. Ryle of Company A admitted to Ocmulgee Hospital with a Gunshot Wound.
Private William W. Glisson of Company C In hospital at Macon, Georgia with gunshot wound.

The 54th Regiment, Georgia Volunteer Infantry

Lieutenant Hamilton Branch of Company F wrote to his mother Charlotte Branch:

"……………In line of battle near Marietta Geo

We have only moved fifty yards to the rear of our position of yesterday, and therefore have had another nights sleep, which has greatly refreshed us and today we are all ready to go it again. our front line have built breastworks but we do not know that this is to be our permanent line of battle and therefore we are expecting to be moved every moment.

Mother I will now give you a few of my wants. I want some paper and envelopes as the sutlers ask entierly too much for it. also some stamps. also a five dollar bill as I owe a man three and a quarter, and if you have an opportunity to do send me about a canteen full of molasses. could you not send home and get a little good syrup from Mrs. Brewer or Aunt Luff and send me a little now and then as long as I am near Marietta.

Mister Riley left here for Marietta again today he says that he has told the Savannah Committee to save any they get from me and that he would bring it to me. do not send too much as I did not stay long enough at one place to eat much and cannot cary much on a march as there is only Sam Dowse and myself to carry it.

My friend Captain Piquetts mother is with him in Marietta I believe. I am very sorry for him poor fellow as he has lost a leg. Remember me to Capt T(w)yman. How is he getting along. I received your letter of the 1st this morning. if you would send your letters by mail I would get them a great deal sooner as we have a mail every day. if you do not hear from me for several days now and then you must not imagine that I am hurt for I may not be able to write sometimes or that is to send the letters off, especially if we commence fighting, for Genl Joe J makes everyone go into a fight even to postmasters. if you do not promise me this I will write only once a week and now and then instead of every second or third day as I have been doing ever since we have been in danger……………"

Lieutenant Hamilton Branch of Company F wrote to his mother Charlotte Branch:

(second letter)
June 6, 1864

"…………Wonder of wonders we have had another whole night's sleep and have not moved for a whole day. I have spent the day with the Oglethorpes, 1st Ga. they are all quite well. we had quite a nice dinner, viz. fried cornbread and bacon for the first course and fried bacon and cornbread for the second course and for dessert we had bacon and cornbread fried. you know that I enjoyed the dinner in fact and could not help it. strawberries and cream, marmalade, custard, curds, clabber sweet milk, waffles and scrambled eggs are know wheres……"

"…….No signs of a fight at present. We are all ready though, the enemy are reported fortifying at the Altoona Heights………."

8 June, 1864   near Lost Mountain

Lieutenant Hamilton Branch of Company F wrote to his mother Charlotte Branch:

"In the front trenches near Lost Mountain

………After having eaten an exceedingly large dinner, I sit down on a rail with my paper and ink on another rail (the one serving as my stool, and the other as my desk. I have managed this by throwing one end of the third rail of the fence down on the ground for the seat and then using the top one which is flat for a desk. what do you think of the idea.) for the purpose of writing to you. We did not move at all yesterday and therefore had another good night sleep this morning about 7 Oclock Maj. (Nathaniel O.) Tilton our division Qr Mr called to tell me that he had seen McF(arland?) and that he had told him to tell me that you were well and that he also was to have given him a bundle for me but they had missed one another. about 10 Oclock Fred Hull called and told me that he had a basket for me and so I went over with him and received it. just after opening the and takeing the things out we were ordered to fall in and so after giving Lts H(unter) & (Phillip R) F(alligant) something, Sam (Dowse) and I put the rest into our haversacks and started off. we marched about 1 ½ miles to this place, after getting my company fixed in the trenches I started to find Sam who had been sent off on guard. I found him at a farmhouse guarding a garden, he had had the ham boiled and so we sat down under a nice oak and eat our dinner. and we are both now suffering from having eaten too much. the things came safely. the rye bread was a little mouldy, the cake was splendid, also the butter. the biscuits were a little hard and the ham will do us more good than all. I am very very much obliged to you for the treat and Sam says that he is also……."

9 June, 1864   the Battle at Big Shanty near Marietta

Killed: Private John W. Miller – Co. I
Private Emanuel Hurst of Company H died of typhoid fever in Oliver Hospital at La Grange, Georgia.

10 June, 1864   near Lost Mountain
Wounded: Private James Teel – Co. A

General Sherman resumed his advance and General Johnston ordered his troops to block the move. Mercer's Brigade had been in the trenches in front of Lost Mountain for two days. The brigade was in the trenches in line of battle in the forward position ahead of the left-center in order to stall union advances toward that sector.

Lieutenant Hamilton Branch of Company F wrote to his mother Charlotte Branch:

"……………..Skirmish Line of Troops, In front trenches, near Lost Mountain

After writing you on yesterday the enemy reported advancing and therefore we were moved to the right about 300 yards to fill up a gap on the lines. this we did, but the enemy observing us, after we had taken our position, opened on us with their cannon and did some very pretty firing, exploding some of their shells just in front of us and striking our battery four or five times. they fired fourteen shots when they found that we had a battery on our left, and they accordingly ceased firing. just before they began with their artillery, we saw their skirmishers make the charge to our left, and retire and then make another charge and take position behind a rail fence. they were about a mile and a quarter from us. after their artilery had fired on us we saw no more of them until this morning, although we were expecting them all night and we were ready for them. this morning about 10 AM we saw their skirmishers make another charge, over the same ground as in yesterday, and passed over the fence which they occupied on yesterday and go into the woods. then a body of troops advanced, and halting at the edge of the woods near a barn on the field through which their skirmishers had charged, they carried the rail fence alluded to and made a breastwork along their line. they then moved back and forward in the old field and drove some cows into their line. about this time it commenced raining and we were ordered on picket, where we are now. the enemy fired on us as we came up here, and their balls are now whizzing all around me but my men are protected by the piles of rails and rocks and are safe, unless struck by cannon balls. my head quarters are on the right of my company which is on the top of a good little hill in the middle of and old field, so that I have a good view but I have to keep my head down pretty close. their pickets are about 300 yards from me and are throwing their balls pretty near to me. All the boys here are well. Dr (I. E.) Godfrey told me this morning that Capt A(nderson) was quite sick and that he thought he had pneumonia and that he thought that he would send him to a hospital. look out for him. If he goes I think he will go to empire Hospital………"

11 June, 1864 Operations near Marietta, Georgia (Golgotha Church)
General Johnston entrenched in the "First Kennesaw" or "Lost Mountain" line. Walker's Division took position near "Gilgal" or "Golgotha" church.

Lieutenant Hamilton Branch of Company F wrote to his mother Charlotte Branch:

"On skirmish line
…………The enemys skirmishers continued to fire on us during the whole of yesterday but ceased at dark and did not commence again until this morning. one of their sharpshooters made a very pretty shot at me just now, as I was changing my position from my Hd Qrs to this picket post which is shaded, being covered with brush. he fired at me but I happen to be just passing in the rear of a rail pile and his ball hit that instead of me. I saw a sight yesterday which I do think would make the greatest coward fight, vis. just in front of my line and between me and the enemy there is a house inhabited by a man, his wife and six little children with a negro man his wife and four little children. Lt H J (was) put at this house with a squad of men to act as the videttes. the enemy fired two shell at this house yesterday which of course scared the inmates and made them take to their cave. J. and we all advised him to move to the rear as there may be a fight here any moment and so after passing the night in great suspense he sent his family off this morning. they past along our line and a ball from the enemy came very near hitting them. I did feel awfuly to see them leaving their home thus. I expect to be relieved from picket this afternoon and will return to the trenches. I forgot to state that our battery shelled the enemy yesterday doing excellent firing. My last letters from you are dated 2 & 5. Do write. send paper and envelopes as I am out. I have not seen McF yet---with much love……………..
PS no one hurt on my side yet……………."

12 June, 1864   Operations near Lost Mountain
Lieutenant Hamilton Branch of Company F wrote to his mother Charlotte Branch:

"…………In front Trenches, near Lost Mountain, Geo

We were relieved from picket yesterday about 4 Oclock and sent back into the trenches. whilst the pickets were being relieved, I was standing by tree with the Lieut who relieved me and two of the men were standing by me. I was showing the men where they were to go when a yankey took a shot at me. his furlough giver struck the tree and fell at my feet—I picked it up. it was pretty well mashed. I got my men all off safely. one of the Lieuts who relieved the company on my left was wounded in the neck just after relieving the company…………….."

13 June, 1864 Operations near Lost Mountain
2nd Lieutenant Silas Thornton of Company K wounded.
14 June, 1864 Operations near Lost Mountain
Federals attacked Pine Mountain, near the middle of the Confederate line.
  Corps Commander, Lieutenant General Leonidas Polk killed.
  Major William H. Mann, 54th Georgia captured, but escaped.

Lieutenant Hamilton Branch of Company F wrote to his mother Charlotte Branch:

"……………..In Front Trenches, near Lost Mountain, Geo

…………Still in front. I do not know why we have not been relieved from this duty yet, our men are fully well worn out. we have one or two men wounded out of the brigade every day, but have had no one killed. the balls of the enemy are continualy falling where I now sit—I suppose they fire at our pickets and fired too high and the balls come to where we are. the enemys breastworks are in full view of us and are distant about 1200 yards. we have not been expecting a general engagement around here. Sherman is not agoing to fight if he can help it, but will flank us as long as he can, and Genl Johns(t)on cannot afford to lose the men that he would if he were to attack the enemy on his works. Genls Lee and J. Johns(t)on have got to take care of their men. the army here are confident that we can whip Sherman in an open fight. we cannot afford to lose Atlanta and the people there may rest assured that this army will have to be whipped before the enemy can have Atlanta.

It has just been reported that Lt. Genl (Leonidas K.) Polk was killed today whilst riding up the lines with Genl Johns(t)on. we are all very sorry for he was a good man……..''

Union Reports were:
Near Marietta, Ga., June 14, 1864.

Major CAMPBELL,

Assistant Adjutant-General, Twenty-third Army Corps:

MAJOR: From information got from eight deserters from the First Georgia Rebel Regiment, who came into my lines yesterday and gave themselves up, I don't know but that it would be possible for me to storm and carry a portion of the enemy's line in my front if the general thinks it of sufficient importance to warrant the necessary expenditure of life and limb. Some of them say there is a division in my front, and others a brigade. General Mercer is in command of them. I am not sufficiently conversant with General Sherman's plan of operations now to judge of the propriety or impropriety of trying to make an advance at this point. In case it is thought best for to make the effort, I would suggest that General Cox be instructed to make a strong demonstration in his front to operate as a diversion in my favor. If the general should think it advisable for me to make the effort, I would like to have him ride over here if his business will permit, in order that I may consult with his more fully.

Please answer by bearer.

I am, major, yours, respectfully,

MILO S. HASCALL,
Brigadier-General of Volunteers, Commanding Division.

15 June, 1864   Operations near Lost Mountain

June 15 1864
On the 15th, as a part of the general demonstration along the line, the Second Brigade, Colonel Bond, made a movement from the extreme right, which, with the strong demonstration made on the front, compelled a retrograde movement of the enemy, and Colonel Cooper, First Brigade, and Colonel McQuiston, Second Brigade, moved forward to take possession of the vacated works. Captain Shields with his battery (Nineteenth Ohio) and Sixth Michigan, Captain Paddock, did good service in this operation. Moving on, they were found in still greater force, and in a better chosen position, with their left on the Lost Mountain. General Butterfield's division of the Twentieth Army Corps, becoming heavily engaged with the enemy, apparently near the angle of their line, the refuse part of which was evidently in our front, Colonel Cooper, with his brigade, was ordered to press forward, develop their position, and to make a diversion in his favor. The works were reached, but night came on, and the brigade was withdrawn. During this day's operations, 16 prisoners were captured and 8 deserters came into our lines. On the 16th the command moved into position nearer the main

works of the enemy, and in so doing, drove back the skirmishers of the brigade commanded by the rebel General Mercer. By dark the whole division, First and Second Brigades in line, Third [Brigade] and First [Second] Brigade (First Division), in reserve, had secured a strong position, very near the enemy's works, so near that our skirmishers were fired on from his main works. During the day 33 men from the First Georgia gave themselves up, or were captured, on the skirmish line. During the night of the 16th the enemy evacuated his works. All of which is respectfully submitted.

MILO S. HASCALL.
Brigadier-General Volunteers, Commanding Division.

Federal Army attacked near Golgotha church.
Killed: Sergeant Harrison C. Elkins – Co. I
Wounded: Private D. D. Boatright – Co. C.
Captured: Private A. O. Wheeler – Co. A
                    Private Mathias Elbert – Co. E
                    Private Henry Ettinger – Co. F
                    Private Samuel Templeton – Co. F
                    Corporal James A. Kessler – Co. I

Lieutenant Hamilton Branch of Company F wrote to his mother Charlotte Branch:

"…………Still in the advance. Private H(enry) Ettinger of my company deserted to the enemy last night. he was a jew and is no loss to the company. his father and mother went from Petersburg to the enemy about a month ago. a yankey deserter was brought in last night. he is a young Kentuckian, was formerly in our army. he says that he knows nothing. the army are confident he says of success. You say you received my note of the third. did you receive my letter of the 3rd. how is Miss Alice. give by kind regards Captain T(wyman). I do not see any chance of our being relieved from here at present. all are quite well here………."

16 June, 1864   Operations near Lost Mountain

General Johnston swung the left half of the Confederate battle line, including Walker's Division, to a new position parallel to and just east of Mud Creek. This action halted General Sherman's advance temporarily. But then General Sherman began to flank again. This calls General Johnston to pull back his forces and reform. He formed his defense and a triangle on the high ground at the three mountains Lost, Pine and Kennesaw. Pine Mountain was at the point of the triangle and was the first to go in the union assault. This created a situation where the center of the Confederate line lay vulnerable to General George Thomas's union troops. Due to this occurrence Lost Mountain and it's defenses were abandoned and General Johnston began to concentrate his strength at Kennesaw Mountain. As he laid out his defenses along the Kennesaw Mountain Line he had the Chattahoochee River to his back.

Killed: Private Harrison C. Elkins – Co. I
Wounded: Lieutenant Silas Thornton – Co. K

Lieutenant Hamilton Branch of Company F wrote to his mother Charlotte Branch:

"…………In mainline of trenches, in between Lost and Kennesaw Mountain

Just after I had finished writing you on the 15th the enemy commenced shelling our line and after shelling for about an hour when they began to advance and they were met by our skirmishers who fought them bravely, until our line fell back which we did because Genl (M. P.) Lowery who was on our right had fallen back. It appears that Genl (William B.) Bates who was on the right fell back from some cause or other which exposed Genl L to an enflading fire and caused him to fall back which he did, first sending a notice to Genl M(ercer) that he was preparing to do so, but before Genl M could order us to fall back he received an order from Genl Cleburne to fall back immediately and also a notice from Genl L that he had fallen back and was in the main line. this of course left our right exposed and the enemy took advantage of this, therefore we had to go way around by the left which we did without loss, and took our position at the foot of Lost Mt in the main trenches here.

we staid until 12 Oclock at night when we were ordered to rejoin our division which was about 1 mile on our right, but we had to go around about way which took us until morning day break. we are now in the trenches and expect to have a fight but do not know. the enemy are right in our front. We lost several men from our brigade wounded, some killed and about 20 taken prisoner. Amongst the killed was 1st Sgt (Harrison) Clay Elkins of the Georgia Rangers, and no man would be missed more than he. a shell came through the breastwork and exploded breaking his thigh and also striking him in the back. as he was struck he raised up and cried They have killed me boys but dont give it up hold your own, and he continued to tell us to do this until he was carried off. He was taken to the division hospital where he died about ½ 4 Oclock………."

17 June, 1864   Operations near Marietta, Georgia

Captured: Sergeant George D. Knight – Co. A
Private Heze Vickery of Company D was admitted to Ocmulgee Hospital at Macon, Georgia.
Private Wiley Herndon of Company K was admitted to Ocmulgee Hospital at Macon, Georgia.

Lieutenant Hamilton Branch of Company F wrote to his mother Charlotte Branch:

"………….In main line of trenches near Lost Mountain

The enemy attacked us this morning in our front lines and the brigade on our right falling back caused us to fall back, which we did in good order. We were exposed to a heavy fire of shell and minnie balls. None of my boys were hurt. Clay Elkins of Co. I was hit on the leg with a shell, the Dr. says Mortaly. he was a noble boy. he cried they have killed me boys but dont give it up, hold your own. Cpl (James A.) Kesler of the same Co. lost part of a finger and was struck in the face……….."

18 June, 1864   Operations near Marietta, Georgia
Skirmishing continued and that night, General Johnston withdrew the Army of Tennessee to the southeast where he formed the heavily entrenched "Kennesaw Mountain Line". Mercer's Brigade took and entrenched position just south of Pigeon Hill along Burnt Hickory Road. Artillery dueling and skirmishing continued until the 26th of June.
Wounded: Lieutenant Samuel B. McClary – Co. G
              Corporal James T. Hamer – Co. H
              Private J. Taylor Chalker – Co. H wounded.
Captured: Private Bryant Wood – Co. A
              Private Daniel Wood – Co. A
              Sergeant Charles F. Bailey – Co. F
              Private William T. Coleman – Co. F
              Private Ira Payne – Co. F
              Lieutenant Samuel B. McClary – Co. G
              Private Thomas Edwards Goulding – Co. G
              Private Lafayette McDonald – Co. G
              Private Walter Brannen – Co. H
              Private Hickerson Kilchrist – Co. H
              Private Thomas H. Palmer – Co. H

Several men from companies A, F, G, and H captured.

Lieutenant Samuel McClary of Company G died of wounds at receiving hospital Marietta, Georgia.

Disaster struck late that night. Colonel Olmstead 1st Georgia Infantry wrote of that moment.

"................. Major Allen of the 63rd was the officer in command of the pickett and his orders were to remain in position for a certain time after the Brigade had retired and then to withdraw quietly and follow it without attracting the attention of the enemy. When Allen joined us about daybreak he brought in the details of the 54th, the 57th, and the 63rd Regiments but not that of the 1st. On being asked about them he expressed great sorrow and chagrin and said that in some way he had lost touch with them in the black darkness of the night and had not been able to communicate the orders for withdrawal. He also said that the orders given to him to preserve quiet, had prevented any loud calling to locate the detail and that failing to find Captain Levy he had to come in without him when the time was up................ Captain Levy wrote to me sometime afterward from the Federal prison on Johnson's Island, Lake Erie to which he (and his men) had been taken after his capture.........."

19 June, 1864   Operations near Marietta, Georgia

Several men from Company A captured.

Killed:	Private P. D. Phelan – Co. F
	Private James Weldon – Co. F
Wounded:	Lieutenant Phillip Falligant – Co. C
	Private Robert Elliott – Co. C
	Private H. T. Kirkland – Co. C
	Private James N. Layfield – Co. C
	Lieutenant Samuel B. McClary – Co. G
	Private Irwin Cowart – Co. E
	Lieutenant Charles Hunter – Co. F
	Corporal Thomas Hinely – Co. F
	Private L. Bragg – Co. F
Captured:	Sergeant James N. Harris – Co. A
	Sergeant Jeremiah W. Thurmon – Co. A
	Private George W. Henderson – Co. A
	Private James W. Henderson – Co. A
	Private Riley A. Herrington – Co. A
	Private William G. Mulkey – Co. A
	Private Reuben J. Roberts – Co. A
	Private William H. Roberts – Co. A
	Private James N. Layfield – Co. C
	Corporal Charles F, Bailey – Co. F
	Private William Coleman – Co. F
	Private Ira Payne – Co. F
	Private James Samuel Spear – Co. F
	Private James F. Spear – Co. F

The 54th Regiment, Georgia Volunteer Infantry

Private Richard Taylor of Company A died at Marietta, Georgia.

Lieutenant Hamilton Branch of Company F wrote to his mother Charlotte Branch:

"…………In line of battle, 3 miles from Kennesaw Mt. and 4 from Marietta

We remained on main trenches until 10 Oclock PM when we fell back about 2 miles to this place. I do not think that our right fell back any but only Genl Hardee who was commanding the left. the enemy could have done us a great deal of damage last night, for it was a very still night and their sharpshooters were only 50 and 100 yds from our breastworks in some places. and if they had notified their General and he had opened on us with his artilery which he had it in position he could have hurt us greatly for we (were) in range of his guns for an hour after we left the breastworks.

The 1st Ga lost quite a number yesterday in a skirmish Lt Cyrus Carter was mortaly wounded. If you were in Marietta today I could get to you as there is no chance of a fight here today. I think that we will fall back to the Chattahoochee in a few days……………"

(second letter)

"………………In line of battle, foot of Kennesaw Mountain

After writing to you on the 17th we were moved about ¾ mile to the right and put into the front trenches near the Marietta road. my company was then ordered out on picket but Genl Hardee considering it dangerous for us to go out in the day ordered us to wait until night fall and so we stacked our arms and eat our dinner. the enemy then commenced shelling us and shelled us very heavyly for about 1 hour. at dark we went out in front of our breastworks, that is four of our companies with mine on the right. we were then deployed on the left file of the left company and advanced to form a new line of pickets, as the pickets from Genl Cheathams division whom we were to relieve had been driven in. my company was the only one that herd the order and advanced. we advanced about 500 yards when we met Genl C(heatham's) pickets and I relieved them and found that there was no one on my left, and I immediately went back to try and find them which I did and was bringing them up when the enemy charged my company and were driven back. I then joined my left to the right of the other companies and prepared to fortify a picket line in the rear of the pickets. we worked all night but did not finish fortifying. the enemy attempted to make another advance but faded during the night. a little before day I put by men in into the pits and made ready for the enemy, it then commenced raining and raining hard until about 9 oclock. I made my boys fire as often as they could during the rain so as to try and keep their loads drive. the pit that I was in (the second from the right) became halffull of water and I suppose the others were the same, and about a ¼ 8 I found that not a gun in my pit would fire. a Lt. and 30 men from Co. A had been put on my right and between me and Genl (William Henry) Carrolls pickets.

About a ¼ 9 it stopped raining and the enemy advanced to my right and extended down just past the left of my company. when they arrived about 40 yds from me I gave the order to rise and fire. the men then got up and told me that the men on my right had fallen back. the men tried to fire but not a gun would fire. seeing then that the men on my right had fallen away back, I gave the order to fall back which we did, the enemy advancing with two lines of skirmishers supported by lines of battle. they advanced until within sight of our batteryes when they opened on them and the men with the stars & stripes fell back. Our men, all but my company and Cos. A & C, were then ordered to advance and three Cos of the 1st Ga to assist them, they advanced and skirmished with the enemy until night. the skirmishing was very heavy.

I will now give you an account of myself. I sat in the pit until I was cramped all over and chilled. I could not stand up because the breastworks was not high enough and the enemy were fireing the whole time. when I got up I could hardly move. after getting out of the pit, I stoped to look back after my company to see if they were all right. I found that two of the men in my pit were not out. I then told them to get out which they did. I then fell back and got behind the breastworks. as soon as the enemy were driven back by our cannon I was ordered out again, and I reported that not a gun in my company would fire and he ordered me to go and have the loads drawn. I had already ordered Lt. (Charles C.) Hunter to take what men I had with me and carry them out, which he started to do but was shot before he got over the breastworks. he was shot high up in the hip, severe but not dangerous. in the mean time I was looking up at the rest of my company who were around the fires in the brigade trying to dry themselves. Lt. (Philip R.) Falligant then came up and informed me that Lt. H was wounded and I then told him to carry them, the men, around to the brigade ordinance train and I would meet him there. we went there and was informed that the loads could not be drawn and that I had better see Capt Hardin who was a mile and a half off. Then I told Lt. F to take the company back to the breastworks and that I would try and see Capt H. Lt. F did this and was shot very slightly in the calf of the leg. he is here.

I and Sam Dowse went to look after Capt. H but could not find him. I then went into a house and tried to dry myself and then went to sleep and slept until dusk. I then found that we were preparing to fall back and as I was barefooted thought I might better go ahead will which Sam and I did. we went until we arrived at Marietta where we found that the army was not coming back that far, but was agoing to stop about 1 ½ miles from Marietta. we then went to bed upstairs in the Marrietta Hotel and slept until morning. hearing here that Lt. F. was wounded I thought that I had best go back which I did but found that Lt. F. did not have to go to the rear. if I had known this I would have stayed in tried to give me a pair of shoes in Marietta. I have been barefooted two days and it is pretty hard although by the time you get this I will have received a pair. if it were not for the rocks I could get along better.

I received your note of the 17th of today. I could not have gone to see you even if I had received it before. if we do not have a big fight in a day or two I could see you if you were here. or if you were here now I might get to see you. Do you receive my letters regularly, you do not tell me. I write them about every other day.

I lost two men killed yesterday, viz P. D. Phealan (Phelan) and Jas Weldon, three wounded ,viz Lt. Hunter, Priv. L Bragg and Cpl Thos (H.) Hinely and four missing viz Sgt. (Charles F.) Bailey and Priv (James Samuel) Spear, (William T.) Coleman, and (Ira) Payne. I am afraid that some of the missing are killed. I am as well as could be expected to when I first started to retreat from picket I thought sure that they would take me as I could hardly move being cramped and chilled so. Bob Butler is well and all the boys but those I have mentioned. that is they are as well as they can be. I do not know whether they will fight here are not, the enemy followes pretty closely they are now in our front.

I received the paper and envelopes, also the syrup which was splendid. Sam and I have feasted off of it for two days. you do not know how nice it is. if John Riley goes to Atlanta you can send me a little more of the same sort. Remember me to all friends everywhere and when you write let me know how they are getting along Effingham Co.and Savannah. tell Cousin Maria that she has not answered my last letter yet. Remember me to her and Ms. H also to Capt T(w)yman. tell him that his battalion (1st Battalion Georgia Sharpshooters) has only 30 for duty today............."

20 June, 1864   Operations near Marietta, Georgia

Colonel Olmstead recalled and chuckled years later when he thought of what a young lieutenant of the 57th Georgia, James Everett, remarked in the middle of all the chaos, "boys, I'm going to get a cannon on my plantation when the war ends. There's nothing like it to make lazy people work!"

Wounded: Private Miles W. Kitchen – Co. A
            Private J. D. Britt – Co. A
            Private James Nathan Morgan – Co. H

William O. Rahn of Company I died of illness at home in Effingham County, Georgia.

21 June, 1864   Operations near Marietta, Georgia

Captain George Mercer wrote in his journal:

"…………slept in heavy rain, cold, wet and uncomfortable. Formed a line of battle at 7 AM and constructed works and set out picket. Men broken down and completely exhausted with constant work and no rest. I slept for the first time in five nights. Very heavy rain during the day……….."

Wounded: Private Abraham Molton Eason – Co. B (right arm)

J. D. Britt of Company A died of wounds.

22 June, 1864   Operations near Marietta, Georgia

The Battle of Kolb's Farm, Georgia occurred today, involving Hood's Division.

As Mercer's Brigade began building their works on Kennesaw Mountain it had undergone a great transformation. All of the men were seasoned veterans. They had seen the "elephant". In their fights against Sherman's men they had suffered 435 casualties: 29 killed, 224 wounded, and 182 missing in action. During the next few days they would be required to muster up tremendous courage and stamina to endure the hard fighting ahead.

Lieutenant Hamilton Branch of Company F wrote to his mother Charlotte Branch:

"……………In the trenches left foot of Kennesaw Mountain

……We have remained of this place ever since I last wrote you, viz. on the 19th. we have been busy building the trenches which we now occupy. their has been constant rains, both of water and many balls, for the last three days, and on the 20th there was a very heavy artillery fire from the anemy. I received your note on the 20th and started immediately to see you. Dr Elliott of the 1st Ga very kindly gave me a seat in an ambulance, but after riding 100 yds I found that the ambulance would not reach Marietta until morning with the load it had in it, viz two wounded men and myself and I therefore got out and walked to the division hospital, where I arrived about 10 PM. the roads were in very bad order in my feet were hurt quite badly by the stones, as I'll still was barefoot, and my socks were worn out. I slept with Charlie (Charles W.) Godfrey at the hospital and started next morning to find you which I did about 10 AM. I felt a great deal better. after washing and putting on my cloths I felt a great deal better, and the Capt. and I both felt a great deal better after eating the two nice meals that we did.

After leaving you we went to the Griffin Relief Association and the Capt getting his things we started for this place, where after wadeing through the mud we arrived about 7 PM. my company then went on picket and are still there. they are held in reserve about two hundred yards from the enemy and about fifty from our picket line. the enemy have been shelling our trenches, one of their shells exploded in the top of the tree against which I am leaning in the limbs and leaves fell all around me. it would make you laugh to see Bill (William Pender), the negro boy, hug the ground. every ball that goes anywheres around us makes him lie close.

We are all and ready for the fight. it is thought that the big fight will come off here as we have no good position to fall back from here. as we can be flanked behind this better than we can hear. Charlie G's shoes fit me pretty well. On the road a man told me I had better fall down and waller as my socks would have to be dirtied anyhow……….."

Private Isaiah D. Britt – Co. A died.
Private George Correell of Company C captured.

24 June, 1864 on Kennesaw Mountain

Mercer's Brigade was positioned to the left of Burnt Hickory Road with General Cockrell's Brigade to their right and General J. Jackson's Brigade to their left.

Wounded:	Private Moses L. Overstreet – Co. B
	Lieutenant Hamilton McDevit Branch – Co. E
	Private Joseph Adkin Hewell – Co. H
Captured:	Private George Correll – Co. C

Private George Taylor of Company F. died in Oliver Hospital at La Grange, Georgia.

25 June, 1864 on Kennesaw Mountain

Lieutenant Hamilton Branch of Company F wrote to his mother Charlotte Branch:

"…………..left foot Kennesaw Mt

………There's nothing you up here, everything is exceedingly quiet, even the sharpshooters have almost ceased firing. the old saying of their always being a storm after a calm may be proved true up here. some think that we are agoing to fall back whilst others think that we will have the big fight. will take place here. Our guns on Kennesaw have just opened, on what I know not, the enemy are reported moving this morning. I do not know in which direction.

We arrived here safely last night and all the boys are quite well this morning. I met Isaac Cohen (of the Savannah Relief Committee) yesterday as I was coming out. he appeared to be very glad to see me and invited me to come over and see him at the hospital. he said that he would try and give me something to eat. the enemy are shelling us in return for our compliments to them from the mountain this morning. I have not seen Capt (William H.) Ross yet, as he has been absent all day. I will see him this evening I expect…………………………….Have the Savannah Committee decided where they will locate yet. You must be ready to leave Marietta and get some of the committees to let you know when they are ordered off as I do not want you to fall into the enemys hands………………..''

26 June, 1864

Private Thomas Jefferson Horn of Company H died of fever in Cannon Hospital at La Grange, Georgia.

27 June, 1864   The Battle of Kennesaw Mountain

Frustrated by his inability to bring General Johnston to a decisive battle, General Sherman decided on a large frontal assault of Johnston's Kennesaw Mountain Line. Federal Maj. General McPherson's Army of the Tennessee was chosen to attack along Burnt Hickory Road. About 8:30 a.m., after a morning artillery duel ended, three Federal brigades moved east toward the Confederate lines. They deployed on a half-mile front across the Brunt Hickory Road in two columns of regiments facing entrenched Confederates. The Federals encountered Mercer's Brigade in two lines of rifle pits. The six companies of the 63rd Georgia were placed as skirmishers only 20 yards from the woods line. When the federal forces came they came in such force that they overwhelmed the six companies with two brigades of federals, some 10,000 men. Those who were able to return back to Mercer's main line did so with haste. The Federal troops overran the brigade capturing or disabling more than 100 men. Mercer's Brigade was entrenched and put up a terrific fight. The federal troops wrote of sheets of flame coming from the muskets in their rifle pits. The galling fire from the rifle pits took its toll on the federals who were advancing upon them. It did not take long for the federal commanders to realize that the Confederate position could not be taken. Although they tried, they failed. They were soon pinned down and retreated that night.

According to an eyewitness report (his father in law Captain George W. Moody of Company B), Private Middleton Miles of Company B was shot mortally through the lungs while attempting to assist the 63rd Georgia pickets as they were withdrawing from their position.

Killed:	Private Middleton Miles – Co. B
	Private Jacob Moody – Co. B
	Private Jacob M. Moody – Co. B
	Private Erwin Cowart – Co. E
	Private Benjamin F. Bishop – Co. G
	Private Jesse Bryan – Co. G
	Private Samuel B. McClary – Co. G
Wounded:	Private Joseph J. Churchill – Co. A
	Private James Mixon – Co. A.
	Private John R. Ogden – Co. B
	Private Moses L. Overstreet – Co. B
	Private Lundy Layfield – Co. C
	Private Michael Peavy – Co. C
	Private John S. Roberts - Co. C
	Private Boswell Goens – Co. G
	Private Simon Peter Hunter – Co. G
	Private James N. Layfield – Co. G
	Private Joseph Adkin Howell – Co. H
	Private James Nathan Morgan – Co. H
Captured:	Private Robert W. Shealy – Co. D

William A. Bowers, Jr.

Private James N. Layfield – Co. G

28, June, 1864 on Kennesaw Mountain

Lieutenant Hamilton Branch of Company F wrote to his mother Charlotte Branch:

"…………..Near Kennesaw Mt.

………..I am very well indeed as are all the boys. Capt. Anderson is not very well this morning in fact he ought not to be here in the front. do see Mr. Wynn and try and get some wheat bread from him for the captain as he is not able to eat the cornbread and bacon which they give us out here. if you can send anything out to him that he would relish you will be conferring a great favor on this gallant soldier as well as obliging……….

……………….The Capt will not go to the rear but keeps about here. Remember me to all. Pat Cleburne and Cheatham gave them fits yesterday and Genl Cottrell of Missouri just piled them on top of one another. this was on our right and left. we were not engaged. It is said here that Col. (George W.) Gordons men were surprised yesterday and that they did not act very well.

I will write you tomorrow. If you send me a morning's edition please do so. Write me also if you have time. Bill will be in town until about 1 Oclock………………"

Private Thomas Jefferson Horne of Company H died in Cannon Hospital at LaGrange, Georgia.

As the men of Mercer's Brigade hunkered in their Kennesaw trenches and waited to retreat toward Atlanta, they became preoccupied by hunger. Several years after the war Colonel Olmstead 1st Georgia Infantry described the menu of the Confederacy for his grandchildren:

"…………..The ration as prescribed by the regulations is varied and ample, but with us it consisted of cornbread, meat (generally bacon and sometimes stringy beef) and a little salt; the coffee, sugar, molasses, beans, flower etc. that are so alluring in the printed list of rations, were conspicuous by their absence.

From every Regiment men were detailed to form what was known as the "cooking brigade" who performed these ministrations in camp well to the rear. Cornbread was all they cooked, the meat being issued raw for each man in each mess to treat as taste and opportunity might permit. The bread was prepared and dutch ovens and each individual "pone" bore the sign manual of the cook who had pressed it into shape. The fingerprints were plainly to be seen, with transverse ridges between, on every one of them. I reflected sometimes upon the degree of cleanliness of these fingers, but it was just as well not to let the mind dwell upon that seem to particularly."

Food preservation from day-to-day was a limited item. It resulted in stale rations and frequent food poisoning. Colonel Olmstead 1st Georgia Infantry recalled:

"…………The rations were usually brought up in the Commissary wagons to the main line in the dusk of the evening, to avoid the fire of the enemy; then what the men did not eat at once was stored away for the next days consumption in the haversack, or "war bags" to be brought forth, when needed, encrusted with the stale crumbs, fragments of tobacco and sand, always to be found in the bottom of these receptacles.

"Pretty poor fair" you would say and I am ready to agree with you, but in that campaign there was enough of it and most of us attacked it with appetites and digestions that regarded quantity more than quality……………"

29 June, 1864 on Kennesaw Mountain

Lieutenant Hamilton Branch of Company F wrote to his mother Charlotte Branch:

"………..Near Kennesaw Mt

………..We received the things yesterday evening for which Capt and I are much obliged. the Capt is looking better this morning I think that with a little good food and the fresh air of these hills that he will soon be well again. the boys are all well today. everything was quiet around us yesterday I went on the mountain yesterday. I will write to you in a day or two. what was the date of my last letter to you. have you seen little (Albert R.) Hunt of my company. he shot himself accidentally yesterday. he is at the infirmary I think ……………… I have a pair of shoes, they are new now Miss Jessee W. wrote that she was very glad to hear the report of my capture contradicted……………"

Private William T. Johnson of Company H admitted to Ocmulgee Hospital at Macon, Georgia with a Gunshot Wound.

30 June, 1864 on **Kennesaw Mountain**
The Army of Tennessee was at Kennesaw Mountain.

(Command Structure)
Army of Tennessee
(General Joseph E. Johnston)
Corps Commander
(Lt. General William J. Hardee)
Division Commander
(Maj. General William H. T. Walker)
Brigade Commander
(Brigadier General Hugh W. Mercer)
54th Georgia Regiment Commander
(Lt. Col. Morgan Rawls)

Samuel W. Moore of Company A died of illness at Atlanta.
July 1864
Sergeant George W. Williams of Company K was wounded near Atlanta, Georgia.
1 July, 1864 on **Kennesaw Mountain**
Private R. H. Lee of Company I died at Walker Hospital at Columbus, Georgia of Pneumonia.
Private J, S Moore of Company A died at Atlanta, Georgia.
2 July, 1864 on **Kennesaw Mountain**
General Sherman began a flanking movement. General Johnston's Army of Tennessee retreated to the "Smyrna Camp Ground Line" and entrenched.
Killed: Private A. W. Reynolds – Co. D
Captured: Private John D. Duncan – Co. G

Lieutenant Hamilton Branch of Company F wrote to his mother Charlotte Branch

"…..In the trenches Kennesaw Mt.

……Since writing to you last there has nothing of interest transpired. the enemy shelled us almost every day, and on the 27 after shelling pretty heavily, then advanced on Genls Cleburne & Cheatham (who are to the left of us) in from three to seven lines of battle, and were repulsed losing about 4000 men. they also charged Genl (Samuel G.) French (who is on our right and occupys Kennesaw Mt) and were repulsed, losing about the same number. amongst the enemys killed were two generals, and one colonel that we knew of, viz Genls (Daniel) McCook and (Charles G.) Harker.

on the 28th Sgt. (William A.) Shaw and myself climbed to the top of Kennesaw, a few of the enemys shell passed over the Mt and exploded near us. a few minie balls also fell around us, but by getting under the rocks when we heard them coming, we excaped unhurt. On arriving at the top we went in to one of the batterys, and I borrowed a glass from the man on duty there but was told not to expose myself as the enemy would fire at me from their battery in front of the mt. I looked out of the embrasure and had just fixed my glass when seeing a smoke arise from the battery below, I jumped behind the parapet and the shell exploded just over us. I then went to look again and they fired at the same place, the shell exploding about the same place. the men told me that their 1st Lt. had been killed right where I was standing and so I concluded to move. I then went about 10 feet to the left and getting behind some bushes I had a fine view of the country around and of our and the enemys trenches, also of their waggons, a large number which were parked in two old fields about three miles off. I then started down and arrived at the trenches safe and sound.

I forgot to state that the enemy came on 6 companies of the 63 Ga. who were on picket, before they knew it and killed and captured quite a number of them. they left their dead and wounded on the field. the next day whilst the 54 Ga. were on picket on the line established after this surprise, a wounded man was heard in front of our line, crying for water. Capt. (James N.) Shinholter of the 57 got up, and ran out to him with a canteen of water and telling them to try and crawl into our lines, ran back to his post, the enemy fireing at him all the time. after getting back one of the men said that if anyone would go with him he would go out and bring the man in. so Capt. S goes out again and with the help this man brought the wounded man in. the skirmish lines were about 200 yds apart and the man was in the middle of them.

We went on picket on the… (Letter is torn)… anyone being hurt. the enemy commenced earlly this morning to shell us, and shelled us very heavyily for about three hours, and in fact they have been shelling us all day but have not advanced. We expect the big fight the come off in a day or two, and if it does we will give the enemy a good whipping, but Genl Johnston may fall back from here, for the purpose of drawing the enemy down to the river. if he does it will be for the best and you may be sure that it will be all right. All the boys are well…….."

Mercer's Brigade retreated from Kennesaw Mountain with General Johnston's Army. It was a gloomy night and they marched across the campus of Georgia Military Institute. Colonel Olmstead 1st Georgia Infantry recall the poignancy of the moment:

"……………The night was dark and the little country road narrow, so progress was exceedingly slow…….. I sat on my horse taking little "cat naps", indifferent to surroundings, when suddenly the sense of being in a familiar spot aroused me. We were marching up the rear of the hill on which the old Georgia Military Institute was located. It was the school in which I had been educated in which I had spent four happy years

Many had been my dreams of the future while there but never had there been forecasts of such an event as marching with an army corps at midnight food is beloved spot. Every inch of its soil every brick of its buildings was dear to me and is saddened my soul to believe that its destruction was near. It had furnished too many officers to the Confederate Army to be spared and Sherman ordered it to be burned on the following day…………….

………You may be sure that memory was busy and that my mind was full of the associations so strangely awakened. My dearest friend at the Institute had been John Patton of the Class of 1857….. He had been the best man at my wedding and I looked forward to the enjoyment of his friendship while my life lasted. And now riding there in the dark there cane, with bitter pang, they thought that for nearly two years he had slept in a soldiers grave. He was killed in the battle of South Mountain in Lee's invasion of Maryland in 1862.

There were recollections too of many of the old Cadet Corps who had laid down their lives for the South, (in almost every battle of the War some of them had perished,) and their faces haunted me as I rode through the familiar grounds……….."

3 July, 1864 at Smyrna Campground

Walker's Division and Mercer's Brigade were set up in a strong defensive position at Smyrna Camp Ground. This commanding position that was held by Walker's division was well fortified with the exception of one small hill that was in Mercer's Brigade's front. General Hardee had concerns about the hill thinking that it might be a site where union artillery could cause problems. General Hardee ordered General Walker to take the hill. General Mercer was sick and Colonel Olmstead was now in temporary command of Mercer's Brigade. Colonel Olmstead later wrote how he had strongly objected to the order from General Hardee to take the hill in their front:

"…………..During the day General Walker…….. ordered me to send a Regiment out to seize and hold the hill, saying that General Hardee feared the enemy would take it for an artillery position. Of course there was no such thing as demurring but I took the liberty of pointing out to General Walker that any troops sent out there would be isolated and, moreover that should the enemy put a battery up on the hill he could not use it since the summit was within range of the musketry fire of our main line. The General said he was aware of these facts but that the orders to him were imperative and must be obeyed…………."

"………… (I ordered them out) with full realization that the duty before (them) was perilous in the extreme and believing, in spite of Division and Corps Commanders that it was a needless risk. The Regiment had scarcely reached its post and begin to fortify when a heavy artillery fire was opened upon it and in a very few minutes a number of the men were killed and wounded.

Then there was an abundance of the enemiy skirmish lines upon either flank and to avoid being cut off and surrounded there was nothing for the Regiment to do saved to retire to the mainline. When this was done the enemy rushed a battery to the top of the hill as had been anticipated, but we opened upon the gunners at once with rifle fire and drove them rapidly away. They left the guns standing without a man near them and there they remained harmless and silent all the rest of the day and were removed under the cover of the night.

My judgment in the premises had been justified but that did not bring back the lives that were lost nor heal the grievous wounds that had been inflicted. How many instances of this kind there must have been during these long four years of war; How many lives recklessly squandered through insufficient consideration before the giving of orders…………"

Wounded:	Lieutenant Edward W. Miller – Co. D
	Corporal William A. Taylor – Co. D
	Private Monk L. Jackson – Co. F
Captured:	Private Martin L. Brantley – Co. A
	Private Talbor Combs – Co. A
	Private William Bray – Co. F
	Private John L. Lightbourne – Co. F
	Private Richard Lane Ellison – Co. G
	Private John H. Mulkey – Co. G
	Private Joseph James Platt – Co. G
	Private William C. Williford – Co. G
	Private Elijah Dickson – Co. K
	Private James Dickson – Co. K
	Private Isaac Odom – Co. K

Lieutenant Hamilton Branch of Company F wrote to his mother Charlotte Branch:

"………..In line of battle 6 miles from Marietta and 7 from the river building trenches

…………As I inferred yesterday we fell back from our position, near Kennesaw Mt. At 11 Oclock last night we got off very nicely, the enemy did not bother us at all. we passed through the (Georgia Military) Institute grounds, also through Mr. (Roswell) Kings place. he has a very nice place indeed. We arrived here about 6 Oclock this morning pretty tired as we had been resting such a long time that we were stiff. I mean by resting that we had not been marching. we staid at Kennesaw …… (letter torn)… …..for all the time and did not have anyone at all hurt by the enemy whilst at Kennesaw nor have we had anyone hurt on our march from there. the enemy are now 1 ½ miles from here. Col. (Robert H.) Anderson is bringing up the rear with his brigade of cavalry.

(John) Mc(Pherson Berrien) has just passed here, he is quite well. they (the Oglethorpe Light Infantry) have had six or seven wounded already today. I do not know how long we will stay here but expect for a few days anyhow, as long as Old Joe sees fit. Anyhow the country here is quite level and neither army will have much the advantage of the other except that we will have our breastworks and they will have to charge them and if they do that we will ruin them, as troops behind breastworks always have a great advantage over those charging them………"

4 July, 1864 at Smyrna Campground
Private Moses Tucker of Company A wounded in the left leg.
Private Barney McAdams of Company H was wounded in the ankle.
Private William W. Sapp of Company K wounded near Marietta, Georgia.

Lieutenant Hamilton Branch of Company F wrote to his mother Charlotte Branch:

"…………In the trenches of Co. F 54th Ga Smyrna Church

………….After writting by Bill we finished building our breastworks and are now pretty well fixed. we had not quite finished our battery that was being built just to our left, when the enemy having driven in the skirmishers, opened on us. they shelled pretty heavily for a while but our batteries opening on them they stopped. quite a number of our skirmishers have been killed and wounded in the last two days. Lt. Robt (Henry) Lewis of the 1st Ga was dangerously wounded yesterday and Lt. (J. T.) Mann of the 54th Ga dangerously this morning. the enemy brought their artilery up very near our picket line and as they, the pickets, only had rail breastworks they were slaughtered in one pit. 5 were killed in the rest (4) wounded, the slightest wound being a leg shot off.

I have not had any hurt thus far. We are now building a stockade and I expect we will stay here a day or two anyhow. Sherman did not eat dinner in Atlanta on this the 4th of July, nor will he there at all unless we send them there, and then he will not be able to stay very long.................."

5 July, 1864   at the Chattahoochee River
Private Monk Jackson admitted to Ocmulgee Hospital in Macon, Georgia with a gunshot wound.
Private John Parker of Company D died in Catoosa Hospital at Griffin, Georgia.

Lieutenant Hamilton Branch of Company F wrote to his mother Charlotte Branch:

"............In line of battle, 1 mile from the Chattahoochee River

.............We remained in Smyrna Church and 11 Oclock last night when we fell back to this place. we are near the Atlanta Road and are 8 miles from Atlanta. it is thought that we will not cross the River but fight here, but I do not think so. anyhow we are fortifying here. the enemy did not follow was very closely today, in fact we have not had a gun fired at us today. As soon as we stopped here I heard that there was some potatoes to be bought about a mile from here and therefore I went down and grubbed about two quarts up out of the ground they were very nice indeed. I also got a splendid mess of blackberries and some apples. Last night the enemy at a band playing in front of us and were huzzaying for about three hours as if someone was making them a speech they were evidently drunk. Lt. Mann died yesterday........................"

6 July, 1864   at the Chattahoochee River
Federal forces reached the Confederate lines and heavy skirmishing occurred.
That night, General Johnston withdrew the Army of Tennessee to a heavily fortified line on the north bank of the Chattahoochee River, overlooking Nickajack Creek. This position was known as "Johnston's River Line," and proved too strong for an assault, thus a Federal flanking

movement began.

Killed: Private William N. Habersham Jr. – Co. F
Lieutenant John T. Mann – Co. K
Wounded: Private Barney McAdams – Co. A
Private Moses Tucker – Co. A
Private William W. Sapp – Co. K
Private James Jefferson Dickson – Co. K

Private H. W. Roberson of Company K died in Fair Grounds Hospital n Atlanta, Georgia.

Lieutenant Hamilton Branch of Company F wrote to his mother Charlotte Branch:

"…:………In reserve of Walker's Division, ½ mile of Chattahoochee River

……….After writing to you on yesterday we were moved 1 mile to the left and placed in position behind a portion of the stockade erected by Genl (Francis A.) Shoup, Genl Johnston's Chief of Artillery. this was the strangest sight we have seen since we have been here. it put me in mind of the fortifications I have read of in the account of the first American settlers lives. It was made thus—on every little rise and commanding ever little valley there were built redouts and blockhouses and all between these there were rails and logs about 12 feet in length stuck up in the ground close together, the whole forming (as some of the men remark) a wall between the Cornfeds and the Wheatfeds, and I would have liked it better if the wall had been a half mile in high and had been built farther north. we remained at that place doing nothing until dark when Bill arrived and we went to work with a good will. after eating we were ordered to pull down the stockade and build a breastwork instead. this we did working all night and until 9 Oclock this morning when we were ordered to stop work and fall in. this we did and were moved back into the woods about 200 yds where we dined. immediately after dinner, or in fact before, Capt. Anderson had finished for he had to eat as he was marching. we were ordered off and marched about 1 mile to this place and were put on reserve of our division. as soon as we stopped I put for the river and took a nice bath and put on my clean cloths. I then went back and just as I had arrived and was sitting down writing to you, we were ordered off again and are now (after having marched 1/2 mile to the left) in the trenches, and ready for a fight. we do not know how long we will stay here, and would not be at all surprised if we were moved in five minutes. thus it is we work all night and march all day and rest all the other time. therefore we soldiers have plenty of rest and time to spare. We have not had a gun fired at us now for thirty-six hours. In fact there is very little fireing along the lines now. the enemy are shelling our pontoon bridges both on the right in the left and we are now putting some in the center. I do not know whether we will cross the river are not. Old Joe knows what he is at and will take care of us and do what is best..............."

"..................in the trenches two minutes later
................Capt. Anderson desires you to get him 1 lb pure coffee and also try and get him 1 lb Charleston coffee (substitute) and have the coffee parched, and then run them through the mill together and then put the rest of the $20 coffee in sugar. Please cover my canteen. have it scoured out and make a new strap out of a piece of one of those Joe Brown shirts and then beg a cork and run the piece of iron through it and send it back by Bill. also try and get my sword scabbard mended and send it back to me as soon as you can. Mother please have my cloths washed and then mend them. I received three sheets of this paper today. the young man Charlie G. Gave it to thought that (it) was his and used it all up. do try and get my knapsack from our wagons and send me my toothbrush. you can get some of the QM to get it for you are Mr. Reily will do it. Give my love to Cousin M. And tell her to write me, and also the next time that she sends me a note by Bill to put her name to it. Also give my love to Miss Alice Gordon and to Mrs. Hathaway. Write to me often and by Bill this time. I wrote you yesterday. as soon as there is a chance of no fighting I will try and get in to see you. I will have to carry this sick to the infirmary which is about 3 miles from here in a day or two. Send the letter to Lt. Jas Hunter by Express..............."

Private David Sallis of Company H died.
Private John Parker of Company D died in Catoosa Hospital at Griffin, Georgia.
Private H. P. Roberson of Company K died at Fair Grounds Hospital No. 2 at Macon (Atlanta), Georgia.

7 July, 1864   at the Chattahoochee River
Lieutenant Hamilton Branch of Company F wrote to his mother Charlotte Branch:

"...............In the trenches ½ mile from the Chattahoochee River

............As you see by this we have not moved since yesterday, nor have we had more than a half ours work to do. the enemy have given us quite a rest. they are very quiet in the front of us, and the hill's running down into a branch and then going up on there side. they cannot see us and on account of the bush being cut down in front of us and the hill's being pretty steep, they would have a hard time getting to us. therefore we are let alone. I am very glad of it for we have been exposed to their fire, and consequently under the necessity of keeping down in our holes, for such a length the time.

If Sherman would only charge Johnston. Where he now is, the Yanky Army of Tenn would only exist in name, but old Joe will have to attack him I am afraid. afraid because we will lose so many of our precious men's lives doing it. We are all quite well and are in good spirits although we do want this falling back to stop…………"

8 July, 1864
Private James Mixon of Company A admitted to Ocmulgee Hospital at Macon with a gunshot wound.

Lieutenant Hamilton Branch of Company F wrote to his mother Charlotte Branch:

"……………….On picket line

After writting on yesterday we were ordered on picket and went out about three hundred yards in front of our trenches, to relieve the 1st Ga. we arrived there safely and have had quite an easy time of it. We are in a thick woods and have a strong line of videttes about 200 hundred yards in front of us, the enemy are firing all the time and our men reply occasionaly. the balls fired at our videttes pass all around us, we have not had but one man hurt and he was shot by a stray ball a few minutes ago. his name is John Pierce. he was struck in the hand and also in the leg. We will be relieved in about an hour. There were two dispatches received by the grapevine today, viz. that we are to man the heavy guns around Atlanta and also that we are to be sent to Charleston. We are all quite well. Give my love to Cousin M. Mrs. Hathaway and Miss Alice. I have not heard from you since you left Marietta. I do not know what old Joe intends doing but it will be all right……………"

9 July, 1864
The Federal army successfully crossed the Chattahoochee on the flank of General Johnston who then retreated across the river. Mercer's Brigade was ordered to hold the Chattahoochee River Bridge for the retreating Army of Tennessee. The bridges were then burned and the Army of Tennessee took up a position on the south bank of Peachtree Creek only a few miles from Atlanta, Georgia.

Seaborn Jones Hightower of Company H wounded.
Private Joseph Adkin Hewett of Company H admitted to Ocmulgee Hospital at Macon with a Gunshot Wound.

Private Seaborn Jones Hightower of Company H admitted to Ocmulgee Hospital at Macon with a Gunshot Wound.

Lieutenant Hamilton Branch of Company F wrote to his mother Charlotte Branch:

"....................Bivouac on banks of Chattahoochee River

................We were relieved from picket about 1 hour after I wrote you on yesterday and returned to our place in the trenches, where we arrived about 8 Oclock PM. We remained there all night were called at daylight this morning and fell in. we were then marched across the river and on to within about a mile of the railroad where the Savh Comm now are. here we were stopped and I was sent to the division hospital with the sick. after turning over the sick I went about a half mile further to the committee. here Mr. Solomon gave me some bread, butter and honey. I then went back to the hospital and taking the men that were to go back to the front started for my command. I found them about two hundred yards from where I left them, and engaged in building a battery. I then eat supper and after eating the Capt and myself went down to the river took a nice bath, from which we have just returned. (I had proceeded thus far when the fire by which I was writing went out.) We found that the brigade had moved about three hundred yards to the right and were lying down in an old field awaiting orders. we staid there until about 11 Oclock, when we were moved back into the woods where we are now agoing to sleep..............."

The Army of Tennessee retreated to the south bank Chattahoochee River utilizing pontoon bridges. They were fully protected by earthworks. As Mercer's brigade filed past him Colonel Olmstead 1st Georgia Infantry struck up a conversation with an officer:

"..............I observed Capt. Wallace Howard of the 63rd Ga. watching the crossing of the troops and gazing with melancholy earnestness upon the hills on the opposite side. I made some remark to him about are nearing the point, Atlanta, where the great battle must be fought. "I don't know". He replied "I don't like giving up so much territory, it looks to me like the beginning of the end and as though we were going right straight down to the Gulf of Mexico."

Hearing his pessimistic talk gave me the first real doubts that had ever entered mind as to the ultimate success of the Southern Cause. I reflected however that his home was in the country occupied by the enemy--- a fact that would naturally explain his low spirits, and the thought cheered me but he was not very far from the truth............."

10 July, 1864

(Command Structure)
Army of Tennessee
(General Joseph E. Johnston)
Corps Commander
(Lt. General William J. Hardee)
Division Commander
(Maj. General William H. T. Walker)
Brigade Commander
(Brigadier General Hugh W. Mercer)
54th Georgia Regiment Commander
(Lt. Col. Morgan Rawls)

Lieutenant Hamilton Branch of Company F wrote to his mother Charlotte Branch:

"……………..We had quite a nice sleep last night. Our army crossed over the river during the night and we have taken up the pontoons, and burned the bridge. (About the bridge, I have only heard) we are now in bivouac about 400 yards from the river and the enemy are in plain view on the other side. some of our pickets in some of theirs were swimming together this morning, but they are now firing on each other. We have been left here as rear guard to keep them from crossing for a while. our brigade is here and Polk's and another. It has been raining for the last hour two. Much to our surprise the enemy have not planted their batteries opposite to us, nor have they fired a shell at us yet ………….."

11 July, 1864
Lieutenant Hamilton Branch of Company F wrote to his mother Charlotte Branch:

"On rear guard south bank of the Chattahoochee River

…………………..I send all my extra clothing to you by William. do not send me anymore, until you receive a request for them from me, as I cannot carry them with me, and on a push one suit will do me for a week or two. The cake from home was very nice although a little mouldy. How about the ham. Where is it? Is it boiled, we have no way of boiling it up here.. You had better send the things up for Judge (Brewer) by William. Send me something, never mind what, to eat. if you have the preserves you had better keep them two or three days as I may get to see you, and can bring them out with me.

The Capt. says that if the relief committee have more potatoes or peas or rice than they need that a little would be quite acceptable just now. If you can get a small vial with a tight fitting cork send it to me to carry my ink in. I wish you could see me now that my hair is so short, since my (hair) has been cut it has become quite fashionable to wear the hair short and it is said that on account of the scarcity of fine tooth combs in the Confederacy, Jeff (Davis) is agoing to have all the mens hair cut short.... Mister Solomon gave me some cloth for handkerchiefs which I am now using. Write to me by Bill as that is the quickest way. also send an answer to my request of the 4th………………………..
……………………..Nothing new turned up after I wrote you on the 10th. we remained at the same bivouac in line, until this morning about 12 Oclock when we fell in and were marched back about 100 yds. so as to be covered by a ridge of hills. this was done so as to protect us in case we were shelled. About 10 this morning a body of the enemy were seen sitting down under an oak tree about ½ mile off. Capt (Hiram M.) Bledsoe (commander of the Missouri Battery) immediately threw a shell which, exploding just in front of them, made them skedaddle for protection. It has been raining for the last two hours and I'm afraid that we will have a bad night of it. I and all the boys are well. I had a tooth extracted on day before yesterday. it was much decayed………………….."

12, July, 1864
Lieutenant Hamilton Branch of Company F wrote to his mother Charlotte Branch:

"On Picket on the riverbank of the Chattahoochee near the RR Bridge.

……….We were ordered on picket soon after I had written to you on yesterday and came down here to relieve the 1st Ga. We are in pits about 10 yards from the river. this morning we made an agreement with the enemy not to fire on one another, and so our boys have been amusing themselves all day talking with the enemy. the troops imediately opposed to us belong to the 20th Army Corps Genl Hooker and are detachments from 123 NY, 5th Conn & 141 NY & 46 Penn which compose Genl Knipes Brigade. the yanks are very anxious to trade for tobacco. they say that they will give Indian rubber cloths, knifes, coffee or anything for tobacco. For the first time since we have been out here are whole regiment is on picket together. All the boys are well and in good spirits. How is Sgt. (Robert) Butler getting………….."

The river was narrow at this location. Only a little over 200 feet wide therefore the soldiers of both armies were able to communicate with each other. They had been known to swim together and to trade for items that were in short supply on either side. After this fraternization with the enemy was discouraged by orders of the Confederate Command.

After Colonel Olmstead received the orders from General Johnston to see to it that the restrictions on fraternization were carried out he recorded a moment of observation:

"………..….. I was detailed as division officer of the day with instructions to see to the maintenance of this order. The duty involved a constant oversight of a long section of the river bank; a miserable, cold Northeast rain storm set in during the night and the early mornings found me soaking wet, chilled to the bone and fagged out from want to sleep, just the conditions to make a man willing to give his head for a cup of coffee, (a stimulant that we knew nothing of in our army.)

Looking across the river I saw two Yankee soldiers walking along with a pole, stretching from the shoulders of one to those of the other from which was suspended a smoking cauldron of hot coffee. They were on their way to give a little mornings refreshment to their line of pickets. I could almost smell the delightful aroma, and a green eyed envy took possession of my soul…….. It would have been a great relief to put a bullet through that cauldron, though I have often thought how mean it was to harbor such a feeling. None of us know however how mean we can be until an occasion arises for the development of the "Old Adam" in us…….…..."

13 July, 1864
    Captured: Private William Williford - Co. G
14 July, 1864
    Wounded: Private Eugene Miller – Co. D
Private Boswell Goens of Company G died at Flewellen Hospital at Barnesville, Georgia.

15 July, 1864
    Private David H. Moody of Company B on rolls of Ocmulgee Hospital at Macon with a gunshot wound.
    Private James J. Fields of Company C on rolls of Floyd House Hospital at Macon with a gunshot wound.
    Private William Henry Harrison Griffin of Company E on rolls of Ocmulgee Hospital at Macon with a gunshot wound.
17 July, 1864
    Lieutenant Hamilton Branch of Company F wrote to his mother Charlotte Branch:

"……………Bivouac in line two miles south of Chattahoochee River,

The 54th Regiment, Georgia Volunteer Infantry

............Since writing to you on the 12th our regiment has been relieved from picket and is now in the rear enjoying a rest we were relieved by a regiment from Genl Cheathams Division after being relieved which was about 9 PM we were marched 1 mile to the rear and went to sleep. we (were) called at daylight 13th and marched to our brigade which had been relieved on the morning of the 12th. after joining the brigade I was sent off with the sick to division hospital. after finding it, which I did about 8 Oclock PM, I went to Atlanta where I remained until the 16th when I returned to bivouac and found the regiment still in the woods resting. I went to see Mrs. Gordon on the 15th. Whilst in Atlanta I dressed in a borrowed biled shirt, calico jacket and blue pants.

We have no idea up here what Genl Johnston is agoing to do. a great many think that he will attempt to cut Sherman's Army in two and fight it by detail. others think that he intends to fall back from here. the army have vastly improved by their rest in our being got ready for the next move, whatever that may be......................"

After a long time of Jefferson Davis, being dissatisfied with the leadership of General Joseph Eggleston Johnson, was ready to replace him as the head of the Army of Tennessee. Although General Johnston had pleaded with President Davis to send a unit such as General Nathan Bedford Forrest in General Sherman's rear to destroy his supply lines from Chattanooga which would render him unable to continue to press the fight into Georgia, President Davis would not deploy a unit for that purpose. Realizing that the Army of Tennessee was outnumbered by odds of 2 to 1 Johnston had intended to fight a defensive war. Thus far he had been successful for every time the federal Army would attack their losses would be far greater than that of the Army of Tennessee and would have by any man's measure been considered defeats.

President Davis desired that General Johnston attack the federal forces in an attempt to destroy them. General Johnston did not agree with that tactic. President Davis had sent a telegram to General Johnston urging him to press the attack and General Johnston replied by telegraph.

"…….. Your dispatch of today received............ As enemy had double or number, we must be on the defensive. My plan of operations must, therefore, depend on that of the enemy. It is mainly to watch for an opportunity to fight to advantage................"

With that President Davis sent a telegram relieving General Joseph E. Johnston from command of the Army of Tennessee and replacing him with General John Bell H.ood

18 July, 1864
Lieutenant General John Bell Hood was appointed Commander of the Army of Tennessee. Mercer's Brigade reported 2000 men present along Peachtree Creek.

19 July, 1864

Lieutenant Hamilton Branch of Company F wrote to his mother Charlotte Branch:

".......In trenches 1 ½ miles right from RR and 4 from Atlanta

.......I received your letters of the 17th on yesterday whilst on the march from our bivouac, (where we were when I wrote to you on the 17th) to this place. we remained at our bivouac after my last letter was written until yesterday morning at 12 Oclock when we fell in and marched to this, where we arrived at dark. we have built breastworks here but it is thought that they are only to be used in an emergency and that we are to advance on the enemy.

We learned yesterday to our great surprise and sorrow that our beloved gallant commander (Joseph E Johnston) had been relieved from the command of this army. I never have seen or heard of an army so wrapped up in a commander as this army proved itself to be on yesterday. when it was announced to everyone seemed to feel as if they had lost her best friend and the general remark was, well this army is lost, and everyone seemed to be whipped. as for myself I have never felt so downhearted in my life as I did on yesterday, and if we had not have been ordered off, I know that I could not have help from crying. Genl Johnston had the love and confidence of every man in his army, and not one doubted but that he would annihilate Sherman before he finished the campaign.

Genl Hood the present commander of this army is a fighting man and no doubt a fine officer and under him we will gain the victory, but he is not Genl Johnston. On passing Genl Johnston's headqrs, yesterday every company, regiment and brigade gave three cheers as they passed. and each marched by with cullors (sic) unfurled. We expect a general engagement soon. All are well............"

When Colonel Olmstead was 75 years old, in 1912, he looked back on this pivotal moment in the life of the Army of Tennessee and summarized the dominant view of the Confederate soldier that had been under General Joseph E. Johnston's command:

"…………..The removal of Genl. Johnston at the crisis of the Campaign was one of the most lamentable events of the entire war. Its effect upon the morale of the Army was immediately disastrous; it took the heart out of the men for he was their idol and they believed in him in spite of the long retreat from Dalton to Atlanta. They knew that Sherman's Army was much larger than our own and that the falling back had been unavoidable……….. But they had seen every assault of Sherman's repulsed with bloody loss and realized that every mile of advance brought him that much farther from his base and would add to his discomfirture in the event of defeat……….. They were prepared to follow him to the death and I believe to this day that but for his removal Atlanta would not have fallen.

The causes, or rather, the cause that led to this most unhappy action was a difference between President Davis and General Johnston that might almost be considered a personal enmity; the two men were both high-spirited, quick-tempered and stubborn in holding to their own views, while neither understood the other nor gave him credit for the virtues and high qualities that he really possessed. Gen Johnston had a grievance from the beginning of the war in relation to his rank in the Confederate Army…… It so embittered him as entirely to prevent his giving to Mr. Davis the frank confidence that always existed between the latter and Genl Lee. There was probably fault on both sides and it is difficult now to say who was the most to blame though it is quite sure that had friendly good will been present between them, no distrust and suspicion in one, nor haughty reserve in the other, the battles around Atlanta would not have been fought under the leadership of General Hood. Of General Johnstons abilities as a military man there was but one opinion in the Confederacy, and time has not altered the judgment of his contemporaries. In everything save, courage, where they stood his equals, he was head and shoulders above Genl Hood upon whom his mantle was about to fall……………………."

In a letter to his wife, Mary Townsend Walker, General William H. T. Walker, Division Commander, expressed his feelings on General Johnston being relieved and General Hood being given command of the Army of Tennessee:

"………………I was handed early this morning before I got out of blanket (I won't say bed) an order of Genl. Johnston turning over the command of the army to Lt. Genl. Hood. I thought when I saw Bragg come that he had come to relieve him but I knew he had something on hand.

I have feared this all along. Now that it is all over, I tell you….. That I never have approved of our falling back but have been in favor of a fight and I have felt satisfied in my own mind that if Johnston fell back behind the Chattahoochee he would be relieved and when I saw Bragg I jumped at the conclusion that he had come to relieve him.

Johnston and I have always been friends. For over a quarter of a century we have known each other…. I admire him and am fond of him and dislike exceedingly to see him leave us.

Hood has "gone up like a rocket." It is to be hoped…. That "he will not come down like the stick" (the stick attached to a skyrocket). He is brave. Whether he has the capacity the command armies (for it requires a high order of talent) time will develop. I will express no opinion.

A fight is now obliged to come off if Johnston has been relieved for falling back (as I take it for granted he was), it is as much as to say to Hood don't you try the same game…………"

Sam Watkins of Co. H, 1st Tennessee Infantry wrote in his diary:
"…………….Such was the fact General Joseph E Johnston had been removed and General J.B. Hood appointed to take command… Old Joe Johnston had taken command of the Army of Tennessee when it was crushed and broken at a time when no other man on earth could have united it. He found it in rags and tatters hungry and heartbroken the morale of the men gone their manhood vanished to the winds their pride a thing of the past. Through his instrumentality and skillful manipulation all these had been restored... We privates loved you because you made us love ourselves… I lay down my pen I can write no more my heart is too full. Reader this is the saddest chapter I ever wrote……………."

(Command Structure)
Army of Tennessee
(General John Bell Hood)
Corps Commander
(Lt. General William J. Hardee)
Division Commander
(Maj. General William H. T. Walker)
Brigade Commander
(Brigadier General Hugh W. Mercer)
54th Georgia Regiment Commander
(Lt. Col. Morgan Rawls)

20 July, 1864   the Battle of Peachtree Creek

Walker's Division with Mercer's Brigade on the extreme right attacked through a heavily wooded area broken by steep hills and ravines. At first the division drove the Federal army before them but were soon repulsed. Hardee's Corps was withdrawn to the outer line of Atlanta's defenses.

Killed:	Private E. Peel of – Co. D
Wounded:	Lt. Colonel Morgan Rawls
	Private Miles W. Kitchens – Co. A
	Private F. M. Ryle – Co. A
	Sergeant E. H. Bryant – Co. C
	Private J. C. Johnson – Co. C
	Private H. T. Scott – Co. C
	Private John F. Simpson – Co. C
	Private J. B. Newton – Co. D
	Private John Moses Westberry – Co. K
Captured:	Private William Dunlap – Co. A
	Private Frederick Grist – Co. A
	Sergeant John Selves – Co. C
	Sergeant John Silvers – Co. C
	Private John B. Hall – Co. C
	Private John K. Hall – Co. C
	Private J. C. Johnson – Co. C
	Private Rice D. Silvers – Co. C
	Private Thomas J. Stephens – Co. C

Private Ira Payne of Company F died at Camp Morton, Indiana prison.

21 July, 1864
Hardee's Corp was ordered on a night march south along McDonough Road with the objective of reaching and attacking behind the left flank of McPherson's Federal army.

Lieutenant Hamilton Branch of Company F wrote to his mother Charlotte Branch:

"…………..In reserve of troops in trenches in front of Atlanta

……………We were sent on picket after I wrote you on the 19th and went out and built rifle pits on the picket-line. we remained on this line until about 10 Oclock on the 20th when we were ordered to move to the right along the picket line so as (to) be in front of our division. (Hardees Corps had been moved to the right about a mile preparatory to being advanced on the enemy) we marched to the right about a half mile then halted and prepared to advance as skirmishers. we were then moved still farther to the right, and prepared again to advance. but before doing so we were moved still farther to the right. we then found that a line of battle from our division, composed of (Gen C. H.) Steven's and a part of Mercers Brigade had already advanced and was charging the enemy. in this charge Genl Stevens was shot in the head, supposed to be mortaly wounded. as we were not needed now we were ordered to fall in on the right of Genl (S. R.) Gist who was held up in reserve. this we did and found that the line in front had fallen back thus leaving us in the front.

Capt Anderson was then sent out with Co. A, C & F to act as skirmishers in front of Gist Brigade. just after we were deployed I found that about 300 yds of me and just on the top of the hill a body of men were fortifying. As I did not know whether they were friends or foes I went and reported the fact to Genl G who ordered scouts sent out to find who they were but the scouts not liking to go I went myself and got within fifty yds of a sharpshooter before I knew it. but he did not fire on me and there I stood looking at him and he at me for a full minute. I then jumped behind a tree and comenced to fall back to the skirmishers. The sharpshooters then opened and we fired on one another until we were relieved which was about 8 Oclock P. M.

We then fell back with Gists brigade to the breastworks, about a mile from where our brigade was in the morning. we stopped behind the breastworks where they passed through some gentlemans place, and a beautiful place it had been, but now alas nearly ruined. we slept here all night, and at daybreak were awakened and marched about two miles to the right along the breastworks. we were then stopped and put in the trenches. we remained here about one hour and a half and were then marched about a half mile to the left, and put in reserve about 50 yards from the trenches and at the foot of the hill.

we are now lying down here and trying to rest. we do not know what the next move will be. I have not heard officialy the result of the fight on yesterday, but it was reported that Genl (George) Maney commanding Cheatham's Division forced the enemy back on the left a mile and into the Peachtree Creek, and Genl (William B.) Bates with his division did the same thing on the right. Genl (C. H.) Stevens had to charge up a hill about a quarter of a mile in length. the right of his brigade drove the enemy back to the Creek also, but owing to the formation of the ground and the strength of the enemys position the left (where Genl Stevens commanded in person and where he was wounded) was not able to dislodge the enemy and consequently the right had to fall back.

We lost quite a number but I understand the enemy suffered a great deal more. I did not have anyone hurt in my company and only one or two were wounded in the regiment I believe. We are all well. Sam Dowse has gone to the division hospital, he is quite sick..........."

22 July, 1864   the Battle of Atlanta, Georgia
12:15 p.m. – After again turning north and believing he was in the rear of McPherson's Federal army, Walker's Division with Mercer's Brigade in the center attacked a well-positioned Federal force.

Major General William H. T. Walker was killed instantly by a Federal sharpshooter.

Brigadier General Hugh W. Mercer took command of the division and ordered Col. William Barkuloo of the 57th Georgia to take command of the brigade.

The brigade was initially placed in reserve of Gist's and Stevens' Brigades, on the right of the Fair Ground Road. Federal forces were in front about three quarters of a mile. Brigadier General Mercer ordered the brigade to advance. The brigade moved down the slope of a hill into a valley overlooked by Federal forces. The valley was clear of woods and exposed the brigade to a very accurate Federal artillery fire from a hill.

A retreat was ordered and the brigade was then placed under command of Brigadier General Marchk Lowrey. Command of the brigade was then turned over to Lt. Col. Morgan Rawls of the 57th Regiment, Georgia Infantry.

5 p.m. – The brigade moved to a point near to and southwest of the Fair Ground Road, about two and a half miles from Atlanta.

The brigade again assaulted a Federal position, carrying two lines. In the assault on the second line, Lieutenant Colonel Rawls was severely wounded and carried from the field. While being moved to the rear in a blanket by two comrades, the wounded man's blanket was torn in two by a cannon ball, which miraculously did not touch Lieutenant Colonel Rawls.

Lieutenant Colonel Cincinnatus S. Guyton of the 57th Georgia took command. Federal forces still occupied a third line of defenses about 30 paces away, with both sides firing rapidly. The brigade was in a state of confusion because it was now under close fire and mixed with several other Confederate units. Lieutenant Colonel Guyton ordered an advance on the third line, but the men could not be induced to go any further.

9 p.m. – The brigade was ordered to hold the ground by Brigadier General Lowrey. Division Commander Major General William Henry Talbot Walker killed.

Killed:
    Major William Henry Mann
    Private Wesley L. Howard – Co. A
    Private C. C. Morgan – Co. C
    Private Henry Bragg – Co. D
    Private Henry S. Lewis – Co. D
    Private William Habersham – Co. F
    Lieutenant Grigsby E. Thomas Sr. – Co. H
    Private James Alford – Co. H
    Private William LaFayette Howard – Co. H
    Lieutenant Joseph H. Ganann – Co. I
    Private John L. Bennett – Co. K
    Private Joel C. Griffis – Co. K
    Private Ezekiel Stafford Knight – Co. K
    Private Isham Reddish Knight – Co. K
    Private J. R. Knight – Co. K

Wounded:
    Lieutenant Colonel Morgan Rawls
    Private James Alford – Co. A
    Private James A. Tidwell – Co. A
    Lieutenant Michael Branch – Co. B
    Private Swain Anderson – Co. B
    Private Isham Carter – Co. B
    Private Joseph Deen – Co. B
    Private Swain M. Anderson – Co. C
    Private Jesse C. Morgan – Co. C
    Private James Ross Webb - Co. C
    Private William Griner Jr. – Co. D
    Private Joseph W. Hurst – Co. D
    Private Francis Allen Oglesby – Co. D
    Private James Madison Baskin – Co. E
    Private Lewis Lodge Griffin – Co. E
    Private A. M. Wood – Co. E
    Captain Thomas Grigsby – Co. F
    Private Issac Barron – Co. F
    Private R. E. Brantley – Co. F
    Private James E. Dennard – Co. F
    Private William Kelly – Co. F
    Private Martin Hinges – Co. F
    Private A. L. Sammons – Co. F
    Private George Waters – Co. F

Private A. M. Wood – Co. F
Captain Thomas E. Grigsby, Sr. – Co. G
Corporal James Ross Webb – Co. G
Private James D. Ely – Co. H
Private Joseph G. Goodman – Co. H
Private Henry Twilley – Co. H
Sergeant Edward E. Foy – Co. I
Lewis B. Dasher – Co. I
Private David Mitchell Morton – Co. I
Private David M. Morton – Co. I
Private John R. Nease – Co. I
Private Leonard J. Nease – Co. I
Private M. A. Bennett – Co. K
Private William Reese Nicholas -Co. K
Private James McGillis Knight – Co. K
Private G. W. Williams – Co. K

Captured:
Private Thomas B. Mell – Co. F
Private James A. Clegg – Co. G
Private Joseph G. Goodman – Co. H
Private John L. Bennett – Co. K

Sergeant Edward E. Foy of Company I in the hospital at Atlanta, Georgia.
Private Daniel Wood of Company A died at Camp Morton, Indiana prison.
Private Hickerson Kilchrist died at Camp Morton, Indiana prison.

23 July, 1864
Captured: Sergeant Thomas B. Mell – Co. F
Brigadier General Hugh W. Mercer ordered the brigade to withdraw.

Lieutenant Hamilton Branch of Company F wrote to his mother Charlotte Branch:

"…………..In trenches 2 ½ miles S/E from Atlanta

……After writing on the 21st we were moved from reserve into the trenches about a mile to the left. we remained here until dark when we fell in again and were marched through Atlanta and about 6 miles beyond in the direction of the East Point. we arrived at the 6 miles about 2 Oclock A. M. We were then halted and went to sleep. We slept until daybreak when we were formed and marched on about 6 miles. this brought us in the rear of the enemy. we then formed line of battle. Cheatham on the left next Cleburne then Walker and Bates on the right. one half of each division was in the front line and the other in the rear. in this way they forwarded through the woods and charged the enemy. we did not charge but were kept under a heavy shelling. here a shell killed Charlie Davis and wounded John Breen (and) J. E (James Elkin) Dennard. After staying here about 1 hour we were ordered to charge the enemy in our front so as to relieve Genl Cleburne who had charged and taken two lines of the enemys breastworks, and Gist and Stevens having been repulsed left of him liable to be flanked and cut off. we advanced on the enemy who were formed in this shape (here he has drawn a trench at angles showing Mercer's position and the union position) and had their artilery posted all along the front line.

we advanced about 200 yds when it was found that it was madness to advance our little brigade and therefore we ordered to halt and after a while to fall back. we fell back to our old position and were then ordered to join with Cleburne on our left. this we did and were then marched to the right a little ways and formed line of battle on an old field. Genl Lowrey then came galloping up to us and told us that we now had the Yanks where we wanted them, and that now we would charge them and not leave one to tell the tale, and he says I know that you are just the boys to do it.

We then advanced about a quarter of a mile through the woods and then with Lowery's Brigade on our right we charged one line and drove them from it. we then jumped over this line and charged the second and drove them from that also. here the big mistake was made, for we were ordered to halt. The enemy were now behind another line about ten yards in front of us and pouring a galling fire into us, for the line that we had taken had three gaps in it and through these they fired on us. it was here that Lt. Col. (Morgan) Rawls was wounded and Maj. (William H.) Mann, Lt. (Joseph H.) Gnann Co. I, and (William) Neyle Habersham and A. M. Wood Co. F, besides others killed. Pvt. Geo Waters, R. E. Brantley, A. L. Sammons were wounded in the charge in M(artin) Henges was wounded by stray ball. in the morning Ike (Isaac) Barren was also slightly wounded. Tom Mell is missing. the other boys are all well. If we had not been halted in the second line we could have taken the third line and thus cut two corps of the enemy off, but as it was we had to remain behind the second line and keep firing at the enemy and they at us, both behind breastworks and only 20 yds apart.

We remained in this position until 12 Oclock when we were ordered to establish a picket line and then fall back. this we did to the lines that Cleburne had taken and we have now fortifyed ourselves and are awaiting the next move.

We have punished the enemy severely, killing a great number and

taking a quantity of prisoners and a number of guns. Our loss has been quite severe. Genl Walker is killed and Genl Gist wounded. the gallant Lt. Joe Clay Habersham is also killed. Several Colonels in our division are killed. Poor Mrs. Habersham. The Yankey General (James B.) McPherson is reported killed and Genl Blair captured whilst behind the breastworks one of Cleburnes men gave me a sword which he had captured I have sent it to the Relief Committee to be forwarded to you……………
…………(P. S.) Capt (John) Scriven Turner and Lt. O'Neal (Henry T. O'Neill) of the 1st are killed."

(second letter)

"………On the battlefield

We charged in captured the enemy works on yesterday. Habisham, Davis, and Wood are all that I know off being killed in my company. John, Charlie and myself thanks to our heavenly father are safe. Maj (William H.) Mann and Capt Scriven Turner and Lt. Habersham are killed. Col. (Morgan) Rawls and Col. Olmstead are wounded……….."

24 July, 1864

General Hood distributed the three brigades which had been under Maj. General William H. T. Walker to other divisions within the same corps. Mercer's Brigade was transferred to Maj. General Patrick R. Cleburne's Division under Brigadier-General J. Argyle Smith. Smith was at that time on furlough recovering from wounds and Colonel Olmstead was placed in charge. The brigade was in trenches southeast of Atlanta, near the Fair Ground Road.

Wounded: Lieutenant Hamilton McDevit Branch – Co. F
Private James Elkin Dennard of Company F admitted to Ocmulgee Hospital at Macon, Georgia with a gunshot wound to the lid of the right eye with severe contusion.
Private George Waters of Company F admitted to Ocmulgee Hospital at Macon, Georgia with a gunshot wound.

The morning of July 24 Company F and Company I, who were stationed as pickets in the trenches on the Confederate right, were attacked by an enemy force. They successfully countered that attack and drove the enemy back.

Report of Lieutenant Colonel Cincinnatus S. Guyton, Fifty-seventh Georgia Infantry, commanding Mercer's brigade, of operations July 22-24.

CAPTAIN: I have the honor to report through you to the major-general commanding that about 5 p. m. on the 22nd of July the brigade (Lieutenant-Colonel Rawls, Fifty-fourth Georgia commanding), under the direction of Brigadier-General Lowrey, moved by the left flank to a point near to and southwest of the Fair Ground road, and distant from Atlanta two miles and a half, opposite the works then occupied by the enemy. From this position we assaulted the enemy's works, carrying two lines. In the assault on the second line Lieutenant-Colonel Rawls was wounded and carried from the field, when the command devolved on myself. The enemy was at this time occupying a third line of works distant from the line occupied by us about thirty paces, both sides firing rapidly. The brigade was in the utmost state of confusion as regarded its organization, the regiments being intermingled with each other and the right of Maney's brigade. On assuming command, I immediately ordered an advance, but the men could be induced to go no farther, which I think was owing in part, if not altogether, to want of organization, officers being unable to form their commands under so close and deadly fire. About 9 p. m. I reported, through Captain Gordon, assistant inspector-general, of Brigadier-General Mercer's staff, the condition of affairs to Brigadier-General Lowrey and asked for instructions, and was ordered to hold the position, which was done until 3 a. m. on 23d, when orders were received from Brigadier-General Mercer to withdraw and report to him at his headquarters. This was accomplished in tolerably good order.

The casualties of the day, ending 3 a. m. 23d, were 30 killed, 129 wounded, and 20 missing.

July 23, at 5 a. m. the brigade moved in position on the line to the right of Major-General Cleburne's division and commenced to intrench. July 24, the brigade was engaged in strengthening its position and policing the ground. Colonel Berkeley, Fifty-seventh Georgia, reported and assumed command.

During my temporary command I found the assistance rendered by Captains Mercer and Gordon, of Brigadier-General Mercer's staff, of great service, and I cannot speak in terms too highly of their gallant conduct on 22d.
I am, captain, with much respect, your obedient servant,

C. S. GUYTON,
Lieutenant-Colonel, Commanding.

25 July, 1864
The brigade joined Maj. General Cleburne's Division.

Private Isham Carter of Company B admitted to Ocmulgee Hospital at Macon, Georgia with a Gunshot Wound.
Private William H. H. Griffin shown on the rolls of Ocmulgee Hospital in Macon, Georgia with Gunshot Wound to scalp.
Private William Hughes of Company B died of Fever near Atlanta, Georgia.
Private George Waters of Company F admitted to Ocmulgee Hospital at Macon, Georgia.

(Command Structure)
Army of Tennessee
(General John Bell Hood)
Corps Commander
(Maj. General Patrick R. Cleburne)
Division Commander
(Brigadier General George Manly)
Brigade Commander
(Colonel Charles Olmstead)
54th Georgia Regiment Commander
(Capt. Thomas W. Brantley)

26 July, 1864
The brigade was occupied in clearing up the ground and completing field works.
Private David Mitchell Morton of Company I admitted to Ocmulgee Hospital at Macon, Georgia with a Gunshot Wound.
Private Reuben J. Roberts of Company A died at Camp Morton, Indiana prison.
Private Bryant Wood of Company A died at Camp Morton, Indiana prison.

27 July, 1864
The brigade moved into trenches south of Atlanta near the Georgia Railroad.
Captured: Sergeant Robert W. Shealy – Co. D

Private Reuben L. Roberts of Company A died at Camp Morton, Indianapolis, Indiana.

28, July, 1864   the Battle of Ezra Church
General S. D. Lee's Corps attacked federal General Logan's XV Corps at Ezra Church.
Private Daniel Wood of Company A died at Camp Morton, Indianapolis, Indiana.

29 July, 1864
Private Jonathan W. Knight of Company F furloughed from Floyd House Hospital at Macon, Georgia (Gunshot Wound).

Private Henry Patton of Company G died at Macon, Georgia.
Private Elias D Thomas of Company K roll shows him in Floyd House Hospital at Macon, Georgia with a Gunshot Wound.
Private J. C. Johnson of Company C admitted to Ocmulgee Hospital at Macon, Georgia with a Gunshot Wound to the hand.

31 July, 1864
The Army of Tennessee was in field-works near Atlanta.

(Command Structure)
Army of Tennessee
(General John Bell Hood)
Corps Commander
(Maj. General Patrick R. Cleburne)
Division Commander
(Brigadier General George Manly)
Brigade Commander
(Colonel Charles Olmstead)
54th Georgia Regiment Commander
(Capt. Thomas W. Brantley)

Private James Railey of Company A died at Thomaston, Georgia.

1 August, 1864
Private Arthur Turner of Company B died of illness at Richmond, Virginia.
Corporal Abraham L. Kirkland of Company C died in Filmer Hospital at Forsyth, Georgia of a Gunshot Wound.
Private William A. Robinson of Company H is shown in Floyd House Hospital at Macon, Georgia with a Gunshot Wound.
T. W. Brantley promoted to major of the 54th Regiment.

2 August, 1864
Col. Charles H. Olmstead returned from the hospital and by order of Maj. General Cleburne assumed command of the brigade while Brigadier General Mercer was on a leave of absence.
Wounded: Lieutenant Michael Branch – Co. B

3 August, 1864
Sergeant Major J. M. Bennett died in Macon, Georgia.
Sergeant E. H. Bryant of Company C died of wounds.

6 August, 1864 the Battle of Utoy Creek
Cleburn's Division was in the reserve on the Confederate left as Generals Bate and Clayton attacked three Corps of Federals.
The brigade marched to Baugh house, on the Campbellton Road where it halted for the night.
Private James B. Morrison of Company A died at Rock Island, Illinois prison.

7 August, 1864
Maj. General Cleburne wrote, "If General Hardee expects Mercer's Brigade to do any good, a brigade commander is immediately necessary.

Its present commander is not efficient".

9 August, 1864 near Decatur, Georgia
Wounded: Private Berry A. Stripling – Co. H

10 August, 1864
Brigadier General Mercer assigned to duty with the reserves of Georgia.

14 August, 1864
Jonathan N. Knight of Company E died while home on sick furlough.

17 August, 1864
Private Charles Sewell Wilkins of Company I died.

18 August, 1864
Private Cuyler Vickery, Jr. of Company D in Ocmulgee Hospital at Macon, Georgia with fractured leg.

22 August, 1864 near Jonesboro, Georgia
Wounded: Private Nathan Taylor – Co. D
Private George Washington Knight – Co. E
Private William T. Johnson of Company A admitted to Ocmulgee Hospital at Macon, Georgia with a Gunshot Wound.

24 August, 1864
Private Nathan Taylor of Company D admitted to Ocmulgee Hospital at Macon, Georgia with a Gunshot Wound.
Private George Washington Knight of Company E admitted to Ocmulgee Hospital at Macon, Georgia with a Gunshot Wound.

25 August, 1864
Company K, 54th Regiment, Georgia Infantry had the following change:
Silas Thornton appointed First Lieutenant and Company Commander.

27 August, 1864

30 August, 1864
At daylight the brigade again moved a short distance. At 9 p.m., the brigade began a march to Jonesboro, Georgia reaching the village by early morning.

31 August, 1864 the Battle of Jonesboro

(Command Structure)
Army of Tennessee
(General John Bell Hood)
Corps Commander
(Lt. General William J. Hardee)
Division Commander
(Maj. General Patrick R. Cleburne)
Brigade Commander
(Colonel Charles H. Olmstead)
54th Georgia Regiment Commander
(Colonel Charlton H. Way)

Sunrise - The brigade arrived at Jonesboro.
- The division was placed on the extreme left of a battle line just west of Jonesboro facing and parallel to the Flint River.
- Col. Olmstead, commanding the brigade was placed between Lowrey's Brigade on his left and Finley's Brigade on his right.

3:30p.m.-The brigade moved forward and took two lines of entrenchment's. They attacked Kilpatrick's federal cavalry and Ransom's XVI corps of federal infantry.
- The brigade crossed the Flint River and engaged another line.
- The brigade was ordered to recross the Flint River.
- The brigade was ordered to return to their original position.

Night - The brigade was withdrawn to the right of the corp.

(Command Structure)
Army of Tennessee Commander
(General John B. Hood)
Corps Commander
(Lt. General William J. Hardee)
Division Commander
(Maj. General Patrick R. Cleburne)
Brigade Commander
(Col. Charles H. Olmstead)
54th Georgia Regiment Commander
(Col. Charlton H. Way)

Killed:	Private John Dickson – Co. K
Wounded:	Sergeant Robert William Smith – Co. A
	Private Edward Jefferson Ritchey – Co. A
	Private John Bell - Co. C
	Private Henry Bennett – Co. K
	Private Hiram Bennett – Co. K
	Private John Smith Medders – Co. K
	Private Daniel Leon Williamson – Co. K
Captured:	Private J. Carter Huckaby – Co. H
	Private Thomas l. Bettick – Co. I
	Private Thomas Luke Blitch – Co. I
	Private Thomas Luke Smith – Co. I

1 September, 1864

The Army of Tennessee was at Atlanta and Jonesboro.

(Command Structure)
Army of Tennessee Commander
(General John B. Hood)
Corps Commander
(Lt. General William J. Hardee)
Division Commander
(Maj. General Patrick R. Cleburne)
Brigade Commander
(Col. Charles H. Olmstead)
54th Georgia Regiment Commander
(Col. Charlton H. Way)

The battle of Jonesboro continued.

Sunrise - Cleburne's Division relieved General Stevenson's Division and pickets, sent from Mercer's Brigade to relieve Sevenson's pickets, were captured.

Morning - The brigade was fired upon by Federal sharpshooters.

12 p.m. - Federal forces attacked in front, but beyond opening a brisk fire upon the skirmish line, made no other demonstrations. Mercer's Brigade was near the center opposing Walcatt and Wells Jones Federal Brigades.

Killed:	Private Wesley L. Howard – Co. A
	Private William Craven Patterson – Co. A
Wounded:	Private Robert William Smith – Co. A
	Private Franklin Holloman – Co. A
	Private William B. Carter – Co. B
	Private C. T. Spinks – Co. H
	Private John S. Medders – Co. K
Captured:	Private Timothy Thornton – Co. B

Colonel Olmstead wrote in his after action report:

After passing the second line we came upon Flint River, which at that point runs through a dense swamp. Here it was intended that we should halt, but as the brigade on our left kept going forward, our men also (though our line was much broken by the passage through the swamp) pushed up on a hill and through an open field to the enemy's third position. Here we halted and reformed our line, and the order having been given by the division commander, retired across the Flint. Our loss in the charge was slight-only 10 men wounded. That night we were withdrawn to the right of the army, and relieved General Stevenson's division just before daylight on the morning of the 1st. Our new line was not a good one; it was imperfectly laid out and only partially completed, and the enemy and gotten so close onto it that in sending out our pickets to relieve General Stevenson's pickets, some 33 of our men were captured. As daylight came on we were much annoyed by sharpshooters. In the afternoon a line of battle appeared in our front, but beyond opening a brisk fire upon our skirmish line, made no other demonstration. The brigade took no other part in the fight of the 1st, though our lesson that day amounted to 61 in killed, wounded, and captured. My officers and men have all behaved with gallantry, and deserve praise due to brave men.

I am, captain, very respectfully, your obedient servant,

CHAS. H. OLMSTEAD,

Colonel, Commanding Mercer's Brigade.

2 September, 1864

Colonel Olmstead now in command of Mercer's Brigade wrote the following;

"................The order to march came about 10 o'clock and the men moved out as silently as possible. A certain amount of noise could not be avoided and that was accounted for to the enemy by sundry calls to the various Regiments to come and draw their rations.

We got away from the trenches without molestation and marching all night reached Lovejoy's Station on the Macon and Western Railroad about daylight. The memory of that night's march is like a horrible dream. I was so tired physically as scarcely to be able to sit on my horse, and the mental depression, deep enough because of our own failure, was the more profound as the red glare in the Northern sky and the soul and rumble of distant explosions told that Hood was burning his stores and abandoning Atlanta to Sherman. The long campaign had ended in defeat and disaster.........."

Captain George Mercer, after surveying the union lines, reflected on the predicament of General Hardee's Corps;

"...............Hardee's Corps in position of great danger unless the rest of the Army forms a junction. Yesterday our army was completely dislocated; stated today that Atlanta had been abandoned, and the rest of the Army near enough to form a juncture. From the level nature of the Country, our men on the main line and in rear of it, are greatly exposed to random bullets from the skirmish line; already some of been killed and wounded……. Prisoners report five Corps opposite to us. Heavy shelling all afternoon. Shrapnel, shell and grape fall around our (headquarters) in profusion………….."

Captured: Corporal Reddick J. Speir – Co. I
3 September, 1864
Captured: Private William Albert Nease – Co. I
4 September, 1864   **near Lovejoy Station, Georgia**
Wounded: Private James J. Jones – Co. G
5 September, 1864
Headquarters Mercer's Brigade
In the Field, September 5, 1864

CAPTAIN: I have the honor to submit the following report of the part taken by this brigade in the engagements of August 31 and September 1:

On the morning of the 31st, after a fatiguing night's march, I received orders to place the brigade in line of battle, Lowery's brigade being upon our left and Finley's brigade, of Brown's division, on our right. We remained in this position until between 3 and 4 o'clock in the afternoon, when the order to advance was given, and the line pressed forward, taking the direction from the left. At first the advance was slow and steady, but on coming in sight of the first position of the enemy, the men could not be restrained and rushed on at the double-quick. The resistance of the enemy was exceedingly slight, and without difficulty we carried his first position and a second line not far behind it. Neither of these lines were very formidable. They were apparently only temporary works. After passing the second line we came upon Flint River, which at that point runs through a dense swamp. Here it was intended that we should halt, but as the brigade on our left kept going forward, our men also (though our line was much broken by the passage through the swamp) pushed up on a hill and through an open field to the enemy's third position. Here we halted and reformed our line, and the order having been given by the division commander, retired across the Flint. Our loss in the charge was slight-- only 10 men wounded. That night we were withdrawn to the right of the army, and relieved General Stevenson's division just before daylight on the morning of the 1st. Our new line was not a good one; it was imperfectly laid out and only partially completed, and the enemy had gotten so close onto it that in sending out our pickets to relieve General Stevenson's pickets some 33 of our men were captured. As daylight came on we were much annoyed by sharpshooters. In the afternoon a line of battle appeared in our front, but beyond opening a brisk fire upon our skirmish line, made no other demonstration.

The brigade took no other part in the fight of the first though our loss on that day accounted to 61 in killed, wounded, and captured.

My officers and men have all behaved with gallantry, and deserve praise due to brave men.
I am, captain, very respectfully, your obedient servant,

CHAS H. OLMSTEAD,

Colonel, Commanding Mercer's Brigade
Captain Palmer, Assistant Adjutant-General

7 September, 1864
Lieutenant Robert William Smith of Company A admitted to Ocmulgee Hospital at Macon, Georgia with a Gunshot Wound.
Private Martin Hinges of Company F is shown on a roll of Floyd House Hospital at Macon, Georgia with a Gunshot Wound.
Private Thomas W. Woods of Company K severely injured in a train collision near Barnesville, Georgia.

Lieutenant Hamilton Branch of Company F wrote to his brother Lieutenant Sandford Branch:

"……………..Bivouac Cleburnes Division

As you see by this my arm has healed enough for me to return to duty. I left Mother on the third. she was very well, only anxious to hear from you. your last letter was dated the 24th July, the very day on which I was wounded. Joe (Josiah Law) Holcombe was killed on the 31st Aug. all the other boys are well……………"

9 September, 1864
Private James Nixon of Company A admitted to Ocmulgee Hospital at Macon, Georgia with a Gunshot Wound.
Private Thomas W. Woods of Company K was severely injured in a collision near Barnesville, Georgia.

10 September, 1864
Wounded: Sergeant William Joseph Lamb – Co. E

On this date Federal and Confederate generals agreed to an armistice that was to last 10 days. The Army was reorganized and since General

Walker had been killed 54th Georgia and Mercer's Brigade which would become known as Smith's Brigade, since due to ill health General Mercer would be reassigned to Savannah and the defenses thereof, were reassigned to General Patrick Cleburne's Division. General James Argyle Smith was the new brigade commander. General Hood had developed a new strategy that included taking his army into Tennessee with Nashville as the goal. Their mission was to cut all of the union supply lines thus forcing General Sherman to abandon his mission and pull back into Tennessee.

Wounded: Sergeant William J. Lamb – Co. E

HEADQUARTERS LOWREY'S BRIGADE,
Jonesborough, Ga., September 10, 1864.

SIR: Having commanded Cleburne's division in the battles of Jonesborough on the 31st ultimo and 1st instant, I respectfully submit the following report of the part taken by the division in said battles:

The division arrived at Jonesborough about sunrise on the morning of the 31st of August, having marched all the night previous. After a few hours' rest I placed the division in position on the extreme left of the line, west of Jonesborough, on the Jonesborough and Fayetteville road, in a direction parallel with and facing Flint River. The line was formed in the following order: Granbury's brigade on the left; Lowrey's, Colonel John Weir commanding, in the center; Mercer's, Colonel Charles H. Olmstead commanding, on the right, and Govan's in reserve in rear of Granbury's. Brown's division was next on my right. Each man was provided with sixty rounds of ammunition, and all were informed that General Hood expected them to go at the enemy with fixed bayonets, and drive them across the river. General Granbury's left regiment was made the battalion to the left and swing gradually to the right. Strict instructions were given to brigade commanders to keep their lines well regulated, and in halting and dressing the line to be governed by the left brigade. About 3.30 p. m. the division moved forward in good order and soon encountered the enemy in an open field, strongly posted behind the rail breast-works, with four pieces of artillery. From prisoners taken the force was ascertained to have been cavalry dismounted, under command of the Federal General Kilpatrick. Both artillery and small-arms opened vigorously on my lines, but after a short contest the enemy fled in confusion, and were pursued by my command with great impetuosity. A portion of this force made a slight stand at a second line of works, to hold us in check while the remainder crossed Flint River; but the stand was only slight, and all soon fled in great confusion, leaving in front of

Lowrey's brigade 2 pieces of artillery in a deep slough near the creek. Contrary to instructions, Granbury's brigade crossed the river for the purpose of driving a battery from the next hill, which was doing some execution in our lines. Too full of impetuosity, Lowrey's and Mercer's followed the example, and the enemy was driven from another line of works beyond the river. I immediately ordered the brigade commanders to bring their commands back and form their lines on this side of the river. Observing that we were far in advance of the troops on our right, and that the connection on the right was entirely broken, I immediately ordered Brigadier-General Govan to change the direction of his line and unite with the forces on our right, and press the enemy's flank, if a flank could be found, assuring him that I would join him with the other three brigades as soon as possible. Pending the movements and the reformation of the other brigades, I galloped to the right to make observations. I found that the enemy was in good works, the right to make observations. I found that the enemy that Cheatham's division, under command of Brigadier-General Maney, had come in and occupied the ground between my command and the enemy's infantry works. But supposing a charge would be ordered, I was making all haste to get in position to join in the assault, when I received an order from Major-General Cleburne to return to the position from which I started. On arriving at that Lieutenant-General Lee; but having proceeded in that direction about 600 yards I was ordered by Lieutenant-General Hardee to halt and await further orders. Again I was soon ordered back to the place from which I commenced the advance.

In the engagement the loss of the division was 28 killed and 147 wounded; total, 175.

Both officers and men acted with their usual gallantry, and in obedience to the order given drove across the river all the enemy that was in their front. The right of the enemy's infantry works rested on the river at a point to the right of where my right rested when the move commenced. It would have required a complete change of front to leave formed a line parallel with the enemy's infantry works, and no assault could have been made on the flank, as it rested on the river. I did not swing as much to the right as I intended to do, for the reason that the enemy was farther to my left than was expected, and to have done so would have left the enemy in works on this side of the river on my left flank and in my rear. My left brigade encountered the strongest force of the enemy and sustained the greatest loss. A few moments previous to the advance a battalion of engineer troops and the Third Mississippi Cavalry (dismounted) were sent to report to me, and were by me ordered to report to Brigadier-General Granbury. Of the conduct of these troops General Granbury makes favorable mention in his report. Captain Key advanced with the division with two batteries, which were efficiently handled and used with as much effect as the formation of the ground and the circumstances would admit.

At 1.30 a. m. the 1st instant I received an order from Major-General Cleburne to relieve Lee's corps with Cleburne's division. This threw me on the right of the line, and to relieve the whole corps I had to form on one rank. This I did with the brigades in the following order: Mercer's brigade on the left and uniting with the right of Brown's division, Lowrey's brigade left center, Granbury's right center, and Govan's brigade on the right. The general direction of the line was almost due north and south and parallel with the railroad, the right of Govan's brigade turning back into a skirt of woods nearing the railroad. Mercer's, Lowrey's, and a portion of Grandury's brigades found an inferior line of intrenchments incomplete on ground badly selected, and very near the enemy, and a portion of Granbury's and the whole of Govan's found no works at all, but a few fence rails scattered along on a line that had been marked out. The pickets of Mercer's brigade, in deploying in thick woods near the enemy, were attacked and 33 of them captured. In consequence of the nearness of the enemy and the unfavorableness of the ground, a few vedettes had to suffice for a picket-line that day. The men of all the brigades went vigorously to work, and amid shelling and sharpshooting soon had a tolerably good line of works. Early in the afternoon, information having been received that the enemy was moving to our right, I was ordered by Lieutenant-General Hardee to select a line on the right of Govan's brigade for two other brigades which had been ordered to report to me. On making a hasty examination of the ground I found it absolutely necessary to change a portion of Govan's line in order to get good ground and the proper direction for the two brigades. Having the line hastily marked out by a small detail from Govan's brigade, I ordered Brigadier-General Govan to place his right regiment on the rear line, prepare new works, and destroy the old work in his front. I urged him to have this work done at once, assuring him that there was no time to lose. Brigadier-General Lewis soon reported to me with his brigade, and Colonel McCullough, in command of Gist's brigade. I placed Lewis' brigade in position, with his left connecting with Govan's right, and his right resting on the railroad, and continued the line with Gist's brigade on the east side of the railroad, turning his right back almost parallel with the railroad. These brigades were formed in thick woods, and going vigorously to work soon had temporary works, and the bushes thinned out in their front, forming an inferior abatis. I in person superintended the deployment of a line of skirmishers in front of Gist's brigade, and the pioneers of Cleburne's division soon cut down bushes in their front, forming a good abatis. I also ordered that the skirmishers should be extended 200 or 300 yards to the right of the brigade, and that one man of every four should be advanced 400 or 500 yards, to deceive the enemy and check his advance. This done, I was informed by Lieutenant-General Hardee that another brigade had been ordered to report to me, to continue the extension of the line to the right; but by my request he sent an engineer to select the line, and placed Brigadier-General Lewis in command of his own brigade, Gist's, and the one en route for the right of the line. Before I had time to give my further attention to the point where the works were to be changed on Govan's line, the enemy was advancing on my whole front. He made a vigorous assault on Govan's line at the angle formed by the change above alluded to, but the assault was repulsed. He then advanced in three separate columns, all converging upon this point, and in the second assault he carried that part of the work. This necessitated the giving up of the whole of the ground occupied by Govan's and Lewis' brigades. Brigadier-General Govan, about 600 of his officers and men, and 8 pieces of artillery here fell into the enemy's hands. Brigadier-General Granbury then threw his line back and began to form a line perpendicular to his original one, but, by my order, he immediately reoccupied his works and held them until after the close of the engagement. Colonel P. V. Green reformed a portion of Govan's brigade, charged, and retook a portion of the works, but could not hold them. Major-General Cleburne threw Vaughan's brigade into the lurch, which, with the assistance of the remaining portions of Govan's and Lewis' brigades, completely checked the advance of the enemy. Heavy demonstrations were made upon my whole front, but no determined assault, except upon Govan's brigade.

By personal observation since the battle I find that the new work ordered for the right regiment of Govan's brigade was in a very imperfect state, and that the old work in front had not been destroyed as I had ordered. Colonel Green, now commanding Govan's brigade, is of the opinion that the heavy shelling of the enemy prevented the execution of the order above mentioned. The old work furnished cover to the enemy and gave them great advantage over the men in the incomplete new work. Our whole force being in one rank, and the enemy having this advantage, to hold the work was impossible.

The men acted most gallantly, pouring a heavy fire into the massed columns of the enemy and inflicting heavy loss, as the extensive graveyards of the enemy now show. He could not advance over the temporary works which he had taken, and in his heavy and confused masses could not seriously injure us.

Night came and closed the contest, and at 11 p. m. we quietly withdrew.

Each brigade sustained some loss during the day, but the principal loss was in Govan's brigade. (For particulars in regard to loss please see reports of brigade commanders.)

The loss of the division on that day, as taken from the reports of brigade commanders, was 55 killed, 197 wounded, and 659 missing. The whole loss of the division in the two days in killed, wounded, and missing was 1,086.

The staff officer with me in these battles were Lieutenant Jetton, of Major-General Cleburne's staff, and Captain J. P. Walker, Lieutenant W. J. Milner, and Lieutenant T. T. Riley, of my own staff, all of whom were prompt to render me all the necessary assistance and acted with great gallantry.

All of which is respectfully submitted.

M. P. LOWREY,
Brigadier-General

13 September, 1864
Private James P. Hodges of Company I died in C. S. A. Hospital at Jackson, Mississippi.

14 September, 1864
Private Jonathan G. Hodges of Company I died in hospital died in General Hospital at Shelby Springs, Alabama.
Lieutenant Henry A. Bennett of Company K is shown on report of Mercer's Brigade in camp near Jonesboro, Georgia as being wounded.

18 September, 1864
On this date the Army of Tennessee which was now rested marched along the West Point Railroad toward Newnan, Georgia.
Captain Philip R. Falligand died of disease while attempting to rejoin his command of Company F.

20 September, 1864
The Army of Tennessee was near Palmetto, Georgia.

(Command Structure)
Army of Tennessee Commander
(General John B. Hood)
Corps Commander
(Lt. General William J. Hardee)
Division Commander
(Maj. General Patrick R. Cleburne)
Brigade Commander
(Col. Charles H. Olmstead)

William A. Bowers, Jr.

54th Georgia Regiment Commander
(Col. Charlton H. Way)

Private J. E. McConnell of Company E died at Fair Grounds Hospital No. 1 at Atlanta, Georgia.

21 September, 1864
In the Field, September 21, 1864.

MAJOR: I have the honor to submit the following report:

On the 2nd of August I returned to duty from the hospital, and by order of General Cleburne assumed command of the brigade, then in position on the right of the lines about Atlanta. August 3, moved from the trenches to give place for the militia, and marched two or three miles to the left, taking position in reserve, where we remained quietly until August 6. Marched still farther to the left, halting for the night at the Baugh house, on the Campbellton road. At daylight on the following morning took position on main line and intrenched. Nothing of importance took place here except slight skirmishing on the picket-line. On the morning of the 29th discovered that the enemy had disappeared entirely from our front. At 3.30 p. m. marched to the left, near East Point. August 30, moved at daylight, still going to the left. Halted at 8 o'clock and commenced to fortify. At 9 p. m. took up line of march for Jonesborough. On the road all night, reaching the village in the early morning.

For the operations of the brigade on August 31 and September 1 I beg to refer you to inclosed report, marked A. Inclosed also is a list of casualties in brigade from July 20 to September 1, inclusive, marked B. The reports of operations from July 20 to the date on which I assumed command are being made out by the proper officer, and shall be forwarded as soon as completed.
Very respectfully, your obedient servant,

CHAS. H. OLMSTEAD,
Colonel, Commanding.

List of casualties in 54th Regiment from July 20 to September 1, 1864, inclusive.

54th Regiment	Killed	Wounded	Missing
July 20	.....	5	5
July 22:	14	42	5
July 24	1	1	.....
August 4	.....	1	.....
August 15:	.....	1	.....
August 20	.....	2	.....

August 22	......	1	......
August 23	1	......	......
August 31	.....	8	......
September 1:	2	......	......
RECAPITULATION	18	65	10

22 September, 1864

September 22, 1864.

CAPTAIN: I have the honor to report through you to the major-general commanding the following: On the morning of the 22nd of July Brigadier-General Mercer notified me of the death of Major-General Walker and ordered me to take command of the brigade. At that time we occupied a position in rear of a line supposed to be held by the brigades of Gist and Stevens (being in reserve for those brigades), on the right of the Fair Ground road. I immediately assumed command, and having learned from officers and men who, passed through the brigade before General Mercer left that Gist's line had been driven in, and in all probability that Stevens' had met with the same misfortune, I sent scouts to the right, left, and front, to report any advance of the enemy, and to ascertain if there were any Confederate forces within supporting distance. The Federal forces were in my front, about three-quarters of a mile distant, and from one point of the line in view. I soon ascertained that the brigade was unsupported on either flank. About this time General Mercer informed me that the enemy in our front were retreating and ordered me to advance. The brigade accordingly moved forward down the slope of the hill, and as we neared the valley separating our position from the hill occupied by the enemy the woods became more open and exposed us to the view of the Federals and to a heavy fire of artillery. The valley was narrow and destitute of trees and other shelter, excepting along the edge of a small stream running diagonally across it. I ordered a halt as soon as the brigade reached the fringe of bushes along the branch and proceeded to reconnoiter the position of the enemy, who I had discovered strongly posted on emerging from the woods. In this I was ably seconded by Captains Mercer and Gordon, of Brigadier-General Mercer's staff. We found the enemy, whom I had discovered strongly posted on emerging from the woods. In this I was ably seconded by Captains Mercer and Gordon, of Brigadier-General Mercer's staff. We found the enemy drawn up in three lines of battle on the crest of the hill and supported by two batteries. Between us and them the ground was open and afforded no shelter for an advance. They were distant about 500 yards, and their lines outflanked ours both to the right and left. Having ascertained these facts, I determined to withdraw the brigade at once from under the heavy fire of artillery then pouring into our ranks. Having given the command, the troops fell back in good order to about their former position, having lost about 15 killed and wounded. I reported to General Mercer the condition of affairs, and in a short time he ordered me to report to Brigadier-General Lowrey, on our left. As soon as I reached the place designated I was directed to march the brigade around to near General Hardee's quarters, from where, by direction of a staff officer, I advanced some 500 or 600 yards up the road and formed line of battle at right angles with and to the left of the road, the right of the line resting on it. While forming this line the report reached me that General Cleburne had carried the enemy's works, capturing several pieces of artillery and 2,000 prisoners, and had no use for us. Being but recently from a sick bed, and exhausted by the fatigues of the day, I here turned over the command to Lieutenant-Colonel Rawls, Fifty-fourth Georgia, and reported to the brigade hospital.

July 24, again assumed command of the brigade, then in the trenches southeast of Atlanta, near the Fair Ground road. July 25, in the morning the brigade was assigned to Major-General Cleburne's division, and Brigadier-General Mercer returned to his place. In the evening he was relieved and I again placed in command. July 26, we were occupied in clearing up the ground and completing the works. July 27, at 7.30 a. m. we moved into the trenches south of Atlanta, with the left resting upon the Georgia Railroad. All quiet along the front; the brigade employed in completing the trenches and placing obstacles in front. From this time until the 2nd of August there was no change in our position, except shortening our front by closing to the right. During this time the men were employed in strengthening the defenses, clearing off and policing the ground, until, on the morning mentioned, I received an order, of which the following is a copy, appended, whereupon I turned over the command to Colonel Olmstead.
Respectfully submitted.

WM. BERKELEY,
Colonel Fifty-seventh Georgia

Private Samuel B. Finney of Company A was admitted to Ocmulgee Hospital at Macon, Georgia with a Gunshot Wound.

24 September, 1864
    Wounded: Lieutenant Hamilton Branch – Co. F

25 September, 1864
Brigadier-General J. Argyle Smith returns to action and assumes command of Mercer's Brigade.

28 September, 1864
Lieutenant General William J. Hardee transferred to defense of

Savannah. Major General Benjamin F. Cheatham appointed as Corp Commander over Cleburne's Division.

Lieutenant Hamilton Branch of Company F wrote to his brother Lieutenant Sandford Branch:

"……….At Home

………..Yours of the 29 was received this morning and I was very glad to hear that you were well and I hope that you are made soon be with us. My wound has healed up splendidly and I am enjoying splendid health. Mort Davis was married about the first of the month. All your friends are well and are also all at home. There has been church up home every day you for the last week. All the ducks were there and I enjoyed myself very much. My dear brother if you need anything write to me and let me know and I will send it to you. When you write remember me to all the boys at Point Lookout. With much love and hoping to see you soon…………"

29 September, 1864

All officers had been ordered to remain with their commands as they were due to receive orders for an immediate troop movement. Colonel Charles Olmstead still in temporary command of Mercer's Brigade attempted to get a brief furlough so that he would be able to spend some time with his wife who was close by. Mrs. Olmstead had grown depressed over the situation but she decided to use her charms, which were plentiful, upon the Division Commanders from whence the orders had come.

Later on Colonel Olmstead wrote of this to his children:

"……………..It looked blue enough for us until your Aunt Fan and mother went to put the matter before Gen Hardee, (whom they both knew,) carrying with them for the purposees of bribery, some of the good things that have brought up with them to reinforce our commissariat. The General was complacent enough, but said, 'ladies, this matter rests with Gen'l Cleburne who is here now; let me introduce him.'

The introduction was made and then Gen. Cleburne, who was a shy man, found himself in a tight place. He started to explain how essential it was to have all officers with the Division on that day, but every word of explanation and argument was met by gifts of peaches, apples, cakes and other appetizing things that were piled up in his arms while Gen

Hardee's stood by roaring with laughter. Of course, there was only one ending to the situation, the General surrendered at discretion for the first time in his life……."

Private James C. Clark of Company I died in Walker Hospital at Columbus, Georgia of Chronic Diarrhoea.

30 September, 1864
Private Daniel J. Hancock of Company E died of Pneumonia at Macon, Georgia.
Private James Waters of Company E died in service.

13 October, 1864
Private James Culpepper of Company B was captured near Resacca, Georgia.
Private John G. Duncan of Company G died of Small Pox at Camp Chase, Ohio.

14 October, 1864
The Army of Tennessee is in the vicinity of Dalton, Georgia.
Captured: Private Mitchell J. Newton – Co. D
                  Private Henry C. Benning – Co. F
                  Private Charles C. Bonnard – Co. H

15 October, 1864
Private James A. Jordan of Company A died in Jones County, Georgia.

The following were killed or wounded in the fighting around Atlanta, Georgia:
Killed: Private Harrison C. Elkins – Co. I
Wounded: Private Needham W. Bryant – Co. C
                  Private Samuel Richardson – Co. C
                  Private G. B. Robertson – Co. C
                  Private J. B. Newton – Co. D

24 October, 1864
Private J. P. Morrow of Company C died in Fair Grounds Hospital No. 1 at Atlanta, Georgia.

26 October, 1864
The Army of Tennessee was at Tuscumbia, Alabama.

27 October, 1864
Private J. Carter Huckaby of Company H died at Macon, Georgia.

30 October, 1864
Lieutenant Hamilton Branch of Company F wrote to his mother Charlotte Branch:

"………………Battle House, and Mobile Ala

……………..We remained in Montgomery until the afternoon of the

28th when took the train on the Ala & Fla Rail Road to Pollard and then the train on the Mobile and Great Northern RailRoad to the Ala River and then took the (steamer) Senator and went 20 miles down the river to Mobile. from the Senator we had a fine view of the enemy's fleet as well as our own and land batteries. Mr. May took Willie and myself out to ride. we went to Mr. Mays 5 miles from Montgomery and then on the way back we stopped to see the Miss Shaws of Washington, N. C. I also called on Miss Beasely three times and enjoyed myself very much. Miss Bettie is a very nice young lady. she sewed bars on my collar for me. We leave here this afternoon for Corinth. Mobile is quite a city. it is very much like New York. I am of the opinion that Mobile can be taken if the enemy try very hard. Bob Grant is here and will leave with us. I do not know when you will hear from me again and praying that God will bless you I am as ever ………………………………"

7 November, 1864

Lieutenant Hamilton Branch of Company F wrote to his mother Charlotte Branch:

"………………Bivouac Cleburnes Div Tuscumbia Ala

………………..After writing to you from Corinth Miss, I got on board the train for Cherokee Ala. after going about three miles the engine stalled and we all had to get out and push her up the hill. we then got in and went about ½ mile when she stopped again. we had the same luck all day, and succeeded in getting 14 miles during the day. at night the wood gave out and we had to lie over all night. this was at Byrnesville, Miss. the next morning we ran down about a mile and had some wood hauled up to us by waggons. we then went about 4 miles, when the engine again stopped and also one of the cars ran off the track. the engine then took the first five cars and carried them about 3 miles to Iuka Miss and leaving them there went back after the ballance of the cars of the train. returning with them, she then hitched on to the whole of the train and going on her way arrived at Cherokee Ala at 3 Oclock P.M. having been 28 hours going from Corinth to Cherokee, a distance of 30 miles. I left Cherokee at 4 and marching along the railroad about 5 miles stopped all night in a church. the next morning I marched to Tuscumbia Ala, a distance of 10 miles.

After remaining in this place three or four hours I went out to camp which is about 1 ½ miles from Tuscumbia and about 300 yds from the river. here I found all the boys looking very well after their rest. (James Potter) Williamson and (William F.) May, Capt. (James J.) Lachlison, Lt. (John K.) Bedell and myself came together and I are all well. Judge and Tom (Thomas A.) Brewer are both here and are quite well. also Lt. George Brewer a cousin of Miss Joes is here and is quite well. tell Miss

Joe that I had a talk with him yesterday in regard to my being married, but as he is a fine looking young man and did not mean me but Lt. M. (Michael) Branch of Co. B, I have concluded not to kill him but to let him off.

Harmon Elkins is all so here quite well. Doctor Godfrey examined me yesterday and says that if I will let him cut that place again and put costik in it that he will warrant to cure me in two weeks but as it does not inconvenience me very much I have concluded letting go on as it wants to until it either gets better or worse.

Remember me to all the people around home and in Savannah. Tell Sarah Brigham that I shall expect a letter from her. I do not know where we will go or what we will do but I would not be surprised if we went back somewhere between here and Corinth and spent the winter. I think that it is almost too late to go into Tennessee. We do not know anything about Sherman. (Major General Nathan B.) Forrest has brought up the four transports that he captured and they are now being unloaded at Florence (Alabama) four miles from here. the two gunboats he captured are now patrolling the river………………."

8 November, 1864
Upon rejoining his command Lieutenant Hamilton Branch of Company F wrote to his mother Charlotte Branch:

…….Hd Qrs Co. F 54th Ga Reg Smith's Brigade, Cleburne's Division Cheatham's Corps, Army of Tenn near Tuscumbia Ala

"…………Since writting to you on yesterday we have not moved and there is nothing new here. I will try and give you an account of the moves of my company during my absence. After I had written view on 23 of July we were moved about 1/2 mile to the right and put in the trenches at 8 PM. I having at the request of the men been put in Command of Co. I, was sent with Co.'s I and F to relieve the pickets of (R. C.) Tylers Brigade, this I did. the next morning the enemy advanced on my line and I drove them back and was going over my line when I was wounded the arm and went home with you. my company the next day was moved back to where we were on the 20th and a day or two afterwards were moved to Peachtree St., Atlanta where they remained a day or two and were then moved further to the left near East Point where they remained about two weeks when them were moved farther to the left and down the M& W RR two miles. here they remained about a week when they were moved down the road about two miles and built rifle pits. the next day they were moved along the works to within 10 miles of Jonesboro and that night the(y) marched to

Jonesboro where they arrived on the morning of the 31 Aug. They then charged with the division and ran the Cavalry under (Brigadier General Hugh J.) Kilpatrick about 1 ½ miles when they learned that (General Stephen Dill) Lee's Corps had fallen back, and they then fell back to their breastworks. The next day the enemy made a feint in front of our boys and massed their troops in front of (Brigadier General Daniel C.) Govans Brigade. They then charged Govan three times and were repulsed each time. they then massed a solid body of men 75 feet deep and walked over Govan's Brigade, capturing Govan and a large number of his men (about 300).

That night our Corps fell back to Lovejoy where they were joined by the rest of the army. here they remained about a week when the enemy having fallen back, they were moved back to near Jonesboro here. an armistice having been granted they remained about two weeks when they were moved to Palmetto. Here they remained until the 29th Sept (whilst here they were reviewed by the President) when they went to within two miles of the Chattahoochee and the next morning cross the river and marched to within 8 miles of Powder Springs. Having crossed Dog River, where they remained 4 days when they marched in a heavy rain 9 miles and remained all night in the woods. the next morning they crossed the Coosa River and remained all night 1 mile from the river. the next morning they marched to with 8 miles of Rome. they then went to Cedartown, Cave Springs and several other little places. they then went to Dalton and destroyed the rail road from their to Tilton. the next day they marched 19 miles from Dalton. they then marched through those valleys and went to Blue Pond. they were marched to Gadsden where they remained two days and then went to the top of Sand Mt. where they remained three nights, or that is they were that time crossing it. they then marched to near Summerville. they then marched to Decatur where they remained two days. they then marched three days when they arrived at this place where they have now been 7 days. This is as near as can gather from the boys memory.........."

9 November, 1864

Lieutenant Hamilton Branch of Company F wrote to his mother Charlotte Branch:

"................We have not been moved yet although we expect to go every hour. no one knows where we will go although most people think that we will make a big raid into Tennessee and then go into winter quarters somewheres around here. we were ordered to march this morning at sunrise but the order was countermanded. The river is very high today, and may possibly keep us here a day or two longer. Was it not a pity that we could not save Forrests last capture, I mean

Johnsonville. just to think what a help it would have been to us,4 Gunboats 11 steamers, and 17 barges loaded with supplys, besides the houses and wharves filled with supplys. it was too bad that he had to burn them all. I think that 75,000 to 120,000 tons is a pretty large amount of stores for the yanks even to lose, and I think it it will tell on Sherman.

If we cross the river you must not expect to hear from me until we come back, for I will not have any way of sending a letter off. Give my love to all my friends. Tell Miss Joe that I have not seen her sweetheart yet. Have you heard from my poor dear brother lately. I have not received a letter from you yet. Harmon Elkins, Judge and Tom Brewer are here and are quite well. My leg is about the same, no better or worse. We have been having rain ever since I have been here...................."

10 November, 1864
Private Thomas V. Anderson was captured in Tennessee.
12 November, 1864
Lieutenant Hamilton Branch of Company F wrote to his mother Charlotte Branch:

Hd Qrs Co. F, Smith's Brigade Cleburns Division, Chethams Corps Army of Tenn near Tuscumbia Ala

"................Genl Hood disclosed his plans to the army today. he intends to strike at some point before the winter sets in. this point is on the Nashville and Chattanooga RailRoad, and he expects to strike it and then open communication south. then he will go into winter quarters. Forrest will have command of our calvary. Genl H (Hood) expects to be successfull and do great things. he does not intend to fight over his number, but will fight Sherman wherever he meets him. Sherman has now one corps at Huntsville, one at Stevenson, one a Chattanooga, two at Marietta and one in Atlanta. Our corps are all in the right place.

we are having fine weather now, pretty cold, as the men most of them are without blankets. the river is rising and has been for a week. we would have been on our way now but for our pontoon being too short, but it will be all right tomorrow, and then we will go. I do not know when you will hear from me again, but you must not be anxious about me, for I hope it will all be well. I hope my dear brother may soon be exchanged, and that he may remain with you. (James) Williamson is still here. Bob (Grant), Harmon (Elkins), Judge and Tom (Brewer) are well..............."

Tennessee Campaign

13 November, 1864

The Army of Tennessee under the command of General John Bell Hood crossed the Tennessee River at Florence Alabama. Cheatham's Corps was the first to cross. Colonel Olmstead, now back commanding the First Georgia Volunteers, remembered the crossing clearly:

"………The whole army massed at this point in large open fields, preparatory to crossing the river on a pontoon bridge that had been laid there. The various Brigades and Divisions were all in column of fours side by side with only a few paces separating the columns----they made a very impressive sight for it is not often that one sees an entire army in such close masses. It was a bright autumnal Sunday morning, the church bells were ringing in the little town and as the commands moved down in succession to the bridge, with colors fluttering in the sun light there was a sense of exhilaration and being part of the brilliant spectacle. The pontoons were deep in the water as we crossed and the current of the mighty river chafed and fretted against them, but all held safely to their mooring and there were no mishaps that came to my knowledge……………"

Lieutenant Hamilton Branch of Company F wrote to his mother Charlotte Branch:

"Bivouac Cleburne's Division near Florence Ala

………We left the bivouac from which I wrote you on yesterday at 8 Oclock this morning and marched to the Tennessee River opposite Florence. we then crossed the river on a pontoon bridge. (the river here is very wide and there is a great strain on the bridge). we then marched through the town which is a very pretty little place, and where there are plenty of young ladys. we then marched about a mile where we are now bivouacing. I have sent Bill to town with two pr of socks to have darned for me. I think we will leave here tomorrow morning, although we have just heard that the pontoon bridge has broken. if this is so we may stay here a day or two. We are now 45 miles from Savannah, Tenn but we will not go there as it is out of the way……,"

15 November, 1864

Lieutenant Hamilton Branch of Company F wrote to his mother Charlotte Branch:

"…………………….Contrary to expectation we did not move yesterday but remained in camp bivouac until 8 Oclock A.M. when we were formed without arms and marched to within a mile of Florence, where we were put to work fortifying. we worked all day and went back to camp about 5 Oclock P.M. It rained almost all night, and this morning we are again at work with our fortifications. we will finish them today, and then I expect if everything is ready that we will move on. we are fortifying here so that in cas(e) we fall back we can cross the river under the cover of these fortifications. We are all well and in good spirits but anxious to move forward. Williamson was at work all day yesterday. Harmon, Judge and Tom are all well. This will be my last I expect for some time. Love to all I hope Santy is with (you)…………….."

17 November, 1864
Private Benjamin T. Zipperer of Company I died in Scott Hospital at Marion, Alabama.

19 November, 1864
Mercer's Brigade was detached and sent to Cheatham's Ferry, to aid a supply wagon train in its attempt to cross the Tennessee River.

Lieutenant Hamilton Branch of Company F wrote to his mother Charlotte Branch:

"Bivouac Cleburnes Division near Florence Ala

…….After I had written to you on the 17th we were ordered to go out and strengthen our works which we did, and they are now cannon ball proof. and on yesterday that was a detail sent out to build rifle pits in front of the works, which they did, and we are now strongly fortified at this place and are only waiting for fair weather and more supplys before we advance into Tennessee. We have been having rainy weather for the last two weeks. I do not know at what point we will strike the N & C RR, but I wish that we would hurry up, for after this rain we are agoing to have very cold weather. some persons think we will go by Huntsville and take the garrison there and then go on………"

20 November, 1864
The Army of Tennessee left Florence for campaign into Tennessee.

(Command Structure)
Army of Tennessee Commander
(General John B. Hood)
Corps Commander
(Maj. General Benjamin F. Cheatham)
Division Commander
(Maj. General Patrick R. Cleburne)
Brigade Commander
(Brigadier General James A. Smith)
54th Georgia Regiment Commander

The 54th Regiment, Georgia Volunteer Infantry
(unknown)

By this time, Mercer's Brigade was commanded by Brigadier General. James A. Smith and was thereafter referred to as "Mercer's" or "Smith's" Brigade. The brigade was then detached from the Army of Tennessee and left behind for the purpose of convoying a supply train which was supposed to be ready to follow the army into Tennessee in a few days. Lieutenant Hamilton Branch of Company F wrote to his mother Charlotte Branch:

"………..The weather is a little better this morning. the clouds are breaking and it is quite cool. if this continues I think we will move forward in a day or two, and then I do not know when you will hear from me again. (William B.) Hassett has applied for a detail and if he gets it, he will leave here in a few days for Savannah. I will send some letters to you by him. please put them in my desk. Harmon, Judge & Tom are quite well. All my boys here are well.

I have with me Lt. (William A.) Shaw, Sgt. Robinson (George R. Robertson), Cpls (Hugh H.) Harrigan and (W. G.) Solomon and Privates Barren (J. J. Barron), (George W.) Brownell, (William H.) Bradley, Bryand (D. J. Bryant), (William S.) Gavan, (Albert R.) Hunt, (William B.) Hassett, (Ben J.) Helmy, (J. D.) Jarrall, Laklison (Robert or K. Lachlison), (William F.) May, (E) Nease, (William B.) Puder, (Joel P.) Rackley, (Alexander J.) Raymur, (James Potter) Williamson, and Cook Bill Pender. besides these there are up here detailed (J. O.) Andrews, (Andrew J.) Coleman, (T. A.) Miller, (John) McCormick & (A. L.) Sammons J., 28 in all. Give my love to all my friends. I shall write whatever I have an opportunity…….."

21 November, 1864

The Army of Tennessee, under the command of General John Bell Hood entered Tennessee. Smith's Brigade (formerly Mercer's Brigade) was detailed to ensure that the convoy containing all of the supplies crossed the Tennessee River at what was called "Cheatham's Ferry". They were to ensure that all of the wagon trains crossed the Tennessee River and then worked to rejoin their command north of them. The main cargo of the supply train was salt to preserve the meat and some other vital foodstuffs.

Colonel Olmstead wrote the following of the plight of Smith's (Mercer's) Brigade at the Tennessee River:

"……………..The orders finally came for the army to go forward into

Tennessee but to our great disappointment Smith's Brigade did not march with it. We were detached and sent to a place called Cheatham's Ferry some twelve miles or so from Florence to aid in getting a supply train across the River. I learned that we were chosen for this service because being men from the coast we were supposed to have some knowledge of the management of boats. We waited for two days at the Ferry before the train arrived on the other side of the river and then getting the wagons over gave pretty strenuous work for four or five days more. (Though there was no let up at night)----for the river was a mile broad, the current was strong, and two or three old flat boats were the only means of transportation. At last the job was completed and we were on the march once more, but a full week behind the rest of the army........."

Private John T. Faircloth of Company C died in Fair Grounds Hospital No. 1 at Atlanta, Georgia.
Private J. L. Webb of Company C died in Atlanta, Georgia.

Lieutenant Hamilton Branch of Company F wrote to his mother Charlotte Branch:

Hd Qrs Co F 54th Ga Reg Infty Brig Genl J. A. Smiths Brigade Maj Genl P. R. Cleburnes Division, lt. Genl F. Cheathams Corps Bt General J. B. Hoods Army of Tenn
General P. G. Beauregard;s Dept. near Florence Ala

"............The weather did not clear up as I thought it would on yesterday, but still remains cloudy and rainy. notwithstanding this we leave in a few moments for the first march of the new campaign. our destination is unknown, but we march in the direction of the Nashville and Chattanooga Rail Road. a part of our army has already gone. We have just heard of Sherman's move in the direction of Macon, and we expect the people down there to take care of his three corps whilst we take care of the remaining four under Thomas. We expect to have a hard time and to have some fighting to do, but we intend with Gods help to ruin Thomas' Army. ...."
"...............Our divisions started this morning our brigade has been left here until tomorrow when we will bring up the rear of the army. It has been snowing right lively for the last two hours. the snow melts as fast as it falls................"

22 November, 1864
The Brigade works at Cheatham's Ferry in freezing weather and occasional snowstorms to get a salt train across the Tennessee River.
A. W. Patterson of Company A captured at Gordon, Georgia.

23 November, 1864
Private Alf W. Patterson of Company A was captured at Gordon Georgia.
The Brigade still works at Cheatham's Ferry in freezing weather and occasional snowstorms to get a salt train across the Tennessee River.

27 November, 1864
The Brigade continues to work at Cheatham's Ferry in freezing weather and occasional snowstorms to get a salt train across the Tennessee River. After learning of the fate of their division at Franklin, Tennessee one of the soldiers, Sergeant Walter Clark, of the 63rd Georgia later quipped that Hoods "salt had literally saved our bacon".

28 November, 1864
The Brigade left Cheatham's Ferry to catch up with the main Army.
Lieutenant Hamilton Branch of Company F wrote to his mother Charlotte Branch:

"Bivouac Smiths Brigade near the Tennessee line

............We left bivouac at Cheathams Ferry this morning and marched to this place, which is 18 miles from the ferry. Our regiment marched in the rear of the train of 140 waggons that were to convoy to the army. the roads were very bad and the marching very hard on the men. I was compelled to ride the last 2 miles on account of my leg. We went into bivouac at 9 1/2 P.M................."

29, November, 1864
Private J. Roland, Jr. of Company K was captured in Tennessee.

30 November, 1864   **the Battle of Franklin, Tennessee**
The Army of Tennessee attacked Federal forces at Franklin, Tennessee. Thirteen Confederate officers were either killed, wounded, or captured.
Division Commander Major General Patrick R. Cleburne killed.
Mercer's Brigade arrives at Franklin well after the battle had ended. With Cleburne's death, General Smith was put in command of the Division and Colonel Olmstead was put in charge of Mercer's Brigade.
Wounded: Private Harvey M. T. Land – Co. H
                   Private William Henry Harrison Griffin– Co. E

Lieutenant Hamilton Branch of Company F wrote to his mother Charlotte Branch:

"..................We again marched in the centre and made 10 miles going in the bivouac at 5 P.M......................"

1 December, 1864
Lieutenant Hamilton Branch of Company F wrote to his mother

Charlotte Branch:

"Near Henryville Tenn

............After marching 3 miles this morning we came into the Waynesboro & Columbia Turnpike but it was not much better than the Natchez Trace road on which we have been marching. We made 15 miles today and bivouaced about 5 1/2 P.M............"

2 December, 1864
Lieutenant Hamilton Branch of Company F wrote to his mother Charlotte Branch:

"Bivouac 2 miles beyond Mt. Pleasant Tenn

...............Yesterday we marched in front of the train and today in the rear, my company being the rear guard for the brigade. after marching 9 miles the turnpike became a great deal better. We marched through Mt. Pleasant a very pretty little place and bivouaced at 7 P.M. 2 miles beyond the village. Today we heard for the first time of the Battle of Franklin and the death of Generals Cleburne and (Hiram G.) Grandbury of our division............"

3 December, 1864
Lieutenant Hamilton Branch of Company F wrote to his mother Charlotte Branch:

"Bivouac near Spring Hill Tenn

...............We marched 20 miles today passing through Columbia a very pretty place. Genl Cleburne was buried here yesterday. we also passed through Spring Hill. there are great many of the wounded from Franklin in these places. Genl Smith was born in this country. he will command our division it is thought................."

4 December, 1864
Smith's Brigade, which included the 54th Georgia, was ordered to proceed to Nashville. They stopped 6 miles from the city and took a position in trenches while awaiting further orders.

Smith's (Mercer's) Brigade which included the 54th Georgia began the move up toward the Army of Tennessee after completing their mission of getting the supplies across the Tennessee River. As they move forward and came upon the battlefield that had been Franklin, Colonel Olmstead remembering that moment wrote:

"…………We arrived at Franklin on the third day after the battle and I had opportunity to examine the ground….. Every field officer in (Cleburne's) Division was either killed or wounded while the loss of the rank-and-file was awful…. I saw several of the enemys dead still lying in the field and all along the front of the works there were little pools of congealed blood in the frozen earth where our poor Southern boys had died. In one place the horse of the Confederate General lay astride of the parapet where he and his writer had been killed. I learned that this was General Adams the commander of a Mississippi Brigade…..
…. It was impossible to avoid the thought that but for the detail that sent us to Cheathams Ferry we too would in all probability have shared the same fate………"

Lieutenant Hamilton Branch of Company F wrote to his mother Charlotte Branch:

"………..We marched through the battlefield of Franklin today, also through the town, it is a very pretty town. all of our badly wounded are here. I think the charge of our Corps at this place was the grandest charge of the war. we may 24 miles today and bivouaced 5 miles from Nashville Tenn………………"

5 December, 1864
Mercer's Brigade arrived at Nashville, Tennessee.
Corporal William W. Jeffers of Company D was captured at Brown County, Georgia.

Lieutenant Hamilton Branch of Company F wrote to his mother Charlotte Branch:

"……………..We marched to this (unidentified) place this morning and threw up rail fortifications. Here we rejoined our gallant old division, but there are few of them left……….."

6 December, 1864
Mercer's Brigade re-joined their Division in front of Nashville. Brigadier General James A. Smith was then appointed Division Commander to replace Cleburne. Col. Charles H. Olmstead was appointed Brigade Commander. The brigade was engaged in constructing a second line of works in front of Nashville, a little to the right of the Nolensville Pike.

Lieutenant Hamilton Branch of Company F wrote to his mother Charlotte Branch:

"………..On yesterday some negro troops (probably the 14th or 44th U.S. Colored Troops) advanced and drove in our division pickets. last night and today we have been fortifying our front…………….."

7 December, 1864

Mercer's Brigade was detached and ordered to report to Maj. General Nathan B. Forrest who was operating near Murfreesboro, Tennessee. Colonel Olmstead, who again was in command of the brigade, reported to his new commander after breakfast. General Nathan Bedford Forrest commanded and garrisoned more respect and mystique that any other officer. He was known as the "Wizard of the Saddle". Colonel Olmstead recounted his interview with General Forrest:

"………I left the Brigade in its comfortable camp and went to find Genl Forrest to report to him in person. A sleet storm had sprung up during the night, driven by a fierce gale and I rode right in the teeth of it, unable to see more than a few yards ahead. Poor Lady Gray's mane and tail were frozen stiff and my own hair and beard and every fold of my clothing were encrusted with ice. When the General's Head Quarters were finally reached I had to be help from the saddle, but a blazing fire of great logs, by which the General was standing quickly restored circulation, which was assisted also by a "nip" from his flask which he considerately handed me…………

The first look at him as he stood there, fully satisfied my preconceptions of the man; he appeared the born soldier that he was. Six feet and over in height, straight as an arrow, black hair, and piercing black eyes, a ruddy collection and indefinable something in his bearing that stamped him as a leader of men. That he had no education to speak of was currently reported and a little order, written by himself, that I received from them later on, gave a demonstration of the truth of this; there was scarcely a word of it that was up to the dictionary standard. But what a man he was in all that makes manhood………..".

Lieutenant Hamilton Branch of Company F wrote to his mother Charlotte Branch:

"…………….Today the negro troops advanced on our brigade pickets but were driven back. we, our brigade, held the position from which our division men were driven on yesterday………….."

8 December, 1864

The brigade arrived within 11 miles of Murfreesboro. General Forrest was at Stewart's Creek, Tennessee.

Private David Zittrauer of Company I was captured in Effingham County, Georgia.

Lieutenant Hamilton Branch of Company F wrote to his mother Charlotte Branch:

"……………………Bivouac Smith's Brigade 18 miles Nashville

…………I was sent out this morning in charge of the pickets from our regiment. as soon as we were posted we were relieved by the pickets of some other brigade and on returning to our bivouac we found the brigade just starting towards Murfreesboro. we marched 16 miles in bivouaced on the turnpike having made a very good march………………….."

9 December, 1864
The brigade was ordered to strongly fortify themselves on Stewart's Creek or at La Vergne as General Forrest might deem best. General Forrest who had his two brigades Smith's and Palmer's along with General William Bates' Division were positioned to entrap the enemy but when Bates was recalled Forrest realized his two brigades were insufficient to withstand the attack of the enemy and withdrew from the position. The brigade then engaged in destroying the railroad line between Murfreesboro and Nashville.

10 December, 1864

(Command Structure)
Army of Tennessee
(General John Bell Hood)
Corps Commander
(Maj. General Benjamin F. Cheatham)
Division Commander
(Brigadier General James A. Smith)
Brigade Commander
(Colonel Charles Olmstead)
54th Georgia Regiment Commander
(Capt. George W. Moody)

Lieutenant Hamilton Branch of Company F wrote to his mother Charlotte Branch:

"……………………On the Nashville and Chattanooga RR

……..We have been employed for the last two days destroying this Rail Road. Genl Forrest says that he intends to feed us well, and that he wants us to destroy this road totaly and then he wants us to fight well (and not do like Bates division) far he intends to capture Murfreesboro, the garrison and all their supplies if they have any clothing he intends to fit us out before he gives any to the army. It sleeted all day yesterday and it is very cold today. this is the hardest road to take up that I have ever seen………………….."

12 December, 1864

Lieutenant Hamilton Branch wrote an entry about the Battle of Franklin on this date:

"…………………..As we had nothing to eat yesterday we did not work, nor have we worked today, but have been in bivouac about ½ mile from the rail road. We have been hearing heavy fireing the last two days in the direction of Nashville. As I have just taken a good wash and put on good clean cloths and am therefore free from lice, I will tell you all I have learned about Hoods fights.

Hood sent two of his corps to make a feint against Columbia whilst Cheathams Corps was to try and (get) between Columbia and Nashville. if he had done this, Hood would have bagged the whole of Thomas' forces. Cleburnes Division arrived in their rear at Spring Hill in time and drove the enemy into the town, but he was not met by Bates division and therefore the whole of Thomas army escaped from Columbia and arrived at Franklin with the loss of only a few men. Hood then pursued him and came upon him fortifying at Franklin. he also caught a courier with a dispatch from Thomas saying that as F(ranklin) was the key to all East Tennessee that he intended to hold it. Hood immediately ordered the attack on the reception of this news and right Gallantly the attack was a made.

Cheathams Corps made the principal charge with Cleburnes Division in the centre, (John C.) Browns on the (he leaves a blank) and Bates on the L(eft). In front of Bates there was an open place of about (blank) yards. he was to charge into this and flanking the enemy sweep down their lines, whilst the others charged the breastworks. where the turnpike enters the town their is at the second line of works about 50 yds to the right a gin house or barn (at this place on the works the gallant Genl P. R. Cleburne was killed) and on the left about 75 yds there is a thorny locus thicket. the enemy had cut a part of this down for a abatte. it was to the right and left of the turnpike that Cleburne's Div charged and gallantly they charged too, although they paid dearly for it. they came against the first line of works in column of regiments by brigades and driving the enemy from them swept around by regiments into line and followed the flying foe. this they did so closely that the enemy could not fire on them until they were in 40 yds of the second line. they then opened from their works but Cleburnes men did not stop until they had reached the works and a great many going into the works were captured. the division then fought over the works but as the enemy had the advantage they could not get them out. they laid down in front of the works and the enemy would take and stick their guns over the works and shoot our men. this our men could not do as the slant was on our side our men laid there until night when the enemy left. the charge was made at three P.M. Bates division as usual failed. if they had done their part as well as Cleburne and Brown, we would have ruined the army of Thomas. our total loss in this fight was 3300. our division lost 1650, almost one half of the number they carried in. our brigade was with the salt train therefore we can say that we have been saved by salt.

Maj. Genl Cleburne and Brig Genls (Hiram) Granbury, (Ortho F.) Strahl, Gist and (John) Adams were killed and Maj Genl (John C.) Brown and Brig Genls (George W.) Gordon, (John C.) Carter and (Thomas M.) Scott were wounded. Gordon was also captured. In Brown's Div every General and Staff officer was killed or wounded. the ground over which this charge was made was as open as your hand. the distance between the first and second line was 300 yds and there was not a bush or stump even to protect them. I think it the most gallant fight of the war.

General H(ood) says that if he had had more daylight or if the enemy staid until next day that he would have had them all. he did not use any artilery on account of our women and children being in the town, but he intended to surround the town and open next morning from 108 pieces of artilery and fire 100 rounds from each piece.

After the fight at Franklin Genl Hood sent Bates over here to Murfreesboro. after waiting a day or two Hood, finding that Bates was doing nothing, sent Genl Forrest here. he immediately went to work. Bates division was ordered to advance on the town and draw the enemy out, then to keep them engaged whilst Forrest went around in the rear and captured their works. Bates went out and the enemy came to meet him and advanced a skirmish line. Bates men, seeing the skirmish line advancing, ran like a scared dog. Forrest, seeing this galloped in the midst of them and failing to rally them cursed them and knocked several of them down. in the meantime Forrest had sent his cavalry to the rear and they charged into the town and fought the enemy there but finding that Bates had failed they fell back. Genl F. says that if Bates had held his ground 30 minutes, that he would have taken the whole force of the enemy. I do not know whether he will attack them again or not but anyhow we are here waiting on him............."

13 December, 1864
Lieutenant Hamilton Branch of Company F wrote to his mother Charlotte Branch:

"............Lavergne Tenn

".........We marched from our bivouac to this place (4 miles) this morning and have been engaged tearing up the tracks. I had to destroy the tank. while doing it General Forrest came up to me and said that he wanted it destroyed totaly. Col. Olmstead told him that he had put a man there that would do it. we then had a little talk and Genl Forrest took from his pockets and gave Col. O and myself each a fine large apple..................."

Private Benjamin J. Helmey captured at Triune, Tennessee.

14 December, 1864
The brigade was destroying the railroad between Murfreesboro and Nashville.

(Command Structure)
Army of Tennessee Commander
(General John B. Hood)
Corps Commander
(Maj. General Benjamin F. Cheatham)
Division Commander
(Brigadier General James A. Smith)
Brigade Commander
(Col. Charles H. Olmstead)
54th Georgia Regiment Commander
(Capt. George W. Moody)

Lieutenant Hamilton Branch of Company F wrote to his mother Charlotte Branch:

"......................In bivouac

...........At Dr. (R. T.) Coleman's request Capt (George W.) Moody and myself accompanied him to a little sociable at Mr. Goodmans, about 2 miles from here. We had quite a nice time, there were eight ladies and eight gentlemen. we danced until 1 oclock, and also eat a very fine supper. We had and inspection today. one of the ladies of the frolic last night was a Nashville girl. The sleet which has been on the ground for the last five days thawed this morning...................."

15 December, 1864 The Battle of Nashville
Maj. General Forrest orders Mercer's Brigade to cross Stone's River and to march east from Murfreesboro to capture a Federal forage train.
Wounded: Private Edward Jefferson Ritchie – Co. A

Lieutenant Hamilton Branch of Company F wrote to his mother Charlotte Branch:

"……………..Near Lebanon Turnpike 5 miles from Murfreesboro

……...We left bivouac this morning and marched to within 8 miles of M(urfreesboro) when we turned to the left and marched to this place. Genl Forrest is in command of the party. We have been hearing the report of heavy artilery in the direction of Nashville all day. it is very quick and heavy. We had to ford a creek this morning. it was about half thigh deep. consequently the water ran all down my boot legs……………………."

16 December, 1864
The Army of Tennessee was soundly defeated at Nashville and Hood began his retreat in great disorder. He was enroute back to the Tennessee River to re-cross into Alabama. General Thomas and his army followed, but very cautiously. Major General Nathan Bedford Forrest was advised of the defeat at Nashville and was ordered to rejoin and protect the retreating army. Mercer's Brigade begins a forced march towards Columbia, Tennessee some 60 miles away.

The winter was the most severe in the history of the Nashville area. It is been said that the retreat which was a very difficult and very severe night march was reminiscent of the famous retreat of Napoleon after his defeat in Moscow. The snow and sleet, the icy wind and bitter cold was the cause of tremendous suffering of the troops, some of whom had no overcoats, cotton uniforms and whose shoes had long since worn out causing them to wrap their feet in rags for protection.
General Forrest's troopers, observing this and also observing the difficulty in those infantryman keeping pace on that frozen and harsh ground and seeing that many of them had unhealed wounds on their feet and in their legs. Those troopers of Forrest dismounted and gave their horses to the men who were barefooted and suffering from frostbite. General Forrest then began planning moves that would entrap and slow down the pursuing federal force.

Colonel Olmstead recounted in his memoirs;

"……….Then began a march that had few parallels in the war for downright hardship and suffering--- every circumstance conspired to make it such. The country was covered with sleet and snow, the weather was bitter. Many of the men of the brigade were absolutely barefooted, while all of them were clad in warm clothing that was three fourths cotton. Not one in 100 had an overcoat and added to all this was a knowledge of disaster and of the fact that the Federal army was between us and Hood. Everything combined to weigh down heart and soul with a deep sense of depression.

I cannot remember how late we marched that night but by crack of dawn on the following morning we were on the road again. And what a day that was! I saw with my own eyes, again and again, the print of bloody feet in the snow and men fell out of the columns from whom we never heard again............"

It was reported by Lieutenant Hamilton Branch of Company F that Smith's (Mercer's) Brigade lost 300 to 400 men who dropped out of the line to either die or be captured by the enemy in the 60 miles they marched in a 48 hour period of time in the bitter cold. The cost was terrific and those who survive that march would still have no rest.

Wounded:	Private J. C. Carter – Co. - B
	Private Stephen Murphey – Co. B
	Lieutenant Hamilton McDevit Branch – Co. F
Captured:	Private Anderstokes J. Best – Co. E
	Private Zaddock Best – Co. E
	Private Reuben A. Warren – Co. K

18 December, 1864   near Triune, Tennessee
The brigade reached Columbia, Tennessee late at night.

Captured:	Private Robert A. McCray – Co. E
	Private Benjamin J. Helmy – Co. F

19 December, 1864   Murfreesboro, Tennessee

Captured:	Private John J. Mulkey – Co. A
	Private Green B. Payne – Co. A
	Private Franklin Vetch – Co. H
	Private William Jasper Shearhouse – Co. I

Lieutenant Hamilton Branch of Company F wrote to his mother Charlotte Branch:

"…………….Columbia Tenn

…………..We were called at 4 A.M. on the 16th and marched all day. recrossed the creek in marched until 8 P.M., when we went into bivouac and slept until 12 when we were called in marched all night and all day and bivouaced for two hours the next night, when we again got up and put, and marched all night and day and all the next night and bivouacked two miles from this city. in the 3 days we made 60 miles and over the worst roads I have ever seen. about 200 of our brigade were barefooted. Genl Forrest made his escort take up barefoot men behind them. Our army is now on the retreat. it has been driven from its works at Nashville. I have not learned any particulars yet...................."

20 December, 1864
The Army of Tennessee was at Columbia.

(Command Structure)
Army of Tennessee Commander
(General John B. Hood)
Cavalry Commander
(Maj. General Nathan B. Forrest)
Division Commander
(Maj. General Edward C. Walthall)
Brigade Commander
(Col. Charles H. Olmstead)

Maj. General Forrest was directed to oppose the advance of the Federal cavalry and thus cover the retreat of the Army of Tennessee. Smith's (Mercer's) Brigade was ordered to report to Maj. General Edward C. Walthall as a portion of a rear guard for the army. Maj. General Walthall consolidated several brigades because they were all greatly reduced in numbers. He consolidated Mercer's old brigade with Palmer's Brigade under the command of Col. Joseph B. Palmer. This newly created division numbered about 1900 men of which 400 had no shoes. Snow covered much of the ground these men would be defending during the retreat. Along with 3,000 cavalry and officers and eight pieces of artillery this was the force expected to protect the main army from approximately 10,000 cavalry. They did! The 54th Georgia and the rest of what was Mercer's Brigade had their finest hours serving under General Forrest as the rear guard. Time after time they delivered deadly blows unto the pursuing enemy. General Forrest would lay a trap and the federal forces would oblige. As they would come into the teeth of the trap the entrenched infantry would pour withering fire into them.

Samuel B. Finney of Company A captured at Stones River, Tennessee.

Lieutenant Hamilton Branch of Company F wrote to his mother Charlotte Branch:

"................Columbia

...........On the morning of the 19th we marched through Columbia (having crossed Duck River on a pontoon Bridge) and bivouaced just on the skirts and on the Pulaski turnpike. Our army left here this morning for the Tennessee river. our brigade and 6 others together with the cavalry will hold the enemy in check and allow Hood to retreat. as soon as he gets out of the way we will follow them. Our brigade has lost 3 or 400 men. they could not keep up with us and have been captured by the enemy. my company arrived here with 2 Lts, one Cpl and 1man, but I expect 2 or 3 more of my men have crossed but are not with us. The enemy charges our corps yesterday and Old Frank drove them back and captured their battery.

From all that I can learn our men did not fight well at Nashville. a part of Bate's division and some other brigades formed a line of skirmishers. on the 15th they charged Stewarts Corps (on the left) 4 times. the first 3 times they were driven back, but the fourth time they flanked him and made him fall back a quarter and also capturing from him 16 piece of artilery and several hundred prisoners. on the 17th they charged Lee and Cheatham 6 times. the first five times they were repulsed for the six-time they broke through Bate's division. (J. J.) Finleys, and (R. C.) Tylers Brigades were running but H. R. Jackson's Georgia Brigade fought until they were captured. Genl Hood says they fought well, and Genl Smith (whose division Cleburnes was in reserve) who saw the fight says that they fought splendidly. after this army fell back. we lost several thousand prisoners but not many killed or wounded. the enemy put their negroes in front. Genl Lee was shot in the foot and Genls Ed Johnston (Edward "Allegheny" Johnson) and H. R. Jackson were taken prisoners. George and Willie Patton are missing from our brigade................."

21 December, 1864

The brigade reported 921 men present at Columbia. The 54th Regiment, Georgia Infantry reported only 168 men and 5 servants present.
Private James F. McBride of Company C was captures while home on sick furlough.

Lieutenant Hamilton Branch of Company F wrote to his mother Charlotte Branch:

"........................Our brigade in Genl Browns together with 6 others have been left here by Hood with Genl Forrest and his cavalry to hold the enemy in check until he gets out of the way with his army and men. Genl F(orrest) has taken a great fancy to our brigade in Genl Browns. he made a special request for us to be left here at the post of honor with him. the other 6 brigades volunteered to stay. this I consider the highest compliment that can be paid a brigade. Genl F. told Genl

Hood that col. Olmstead had a brigade of men. Genl H replied that he was glad for that, he had a great many children with him. I do not know when we will leave here as the enemy are not pressing us. Poor Frank (Francis Edward) Bourquin was killed last night by a tree falling on him. the tree was cut down by some of our cooks. Frank
was in bed, he is buried near the cemetery here. It has been snowing all day............"

22 December, 1864
The rearguard action begins with the brigade marching through sleet and snow to a point two and a half miles from Lynnville, Tennessee. The bitter cold continued and General Forrest aware that many of his men had no shoes unloaded supply wagons and loaded them into the wagons for them to ride in order to avoid walking in the snow. They would ride to the place of General Forrest choosing and unload from the wagons, take up a line of battle and prepare to engage the enemy. When they moved again the wagons were brought forth and they were loaded and transported to the next location of engagement. Someone had stated that for once it was an advantage to be barefooted in this bitter cold weather.

Colonel Olmstead observed his shoeless soldiers and witnessed an event that he would never forget. In his memoirs he wrote of it:

"...............Allie Shellman (was) standing on the frozen turnpike without shoes, his feet were tied up in a lot of old rags. The column filled the road and while we were waiting for the order to march at cavalry man rode by through the bushes at the side of the road. Passing, he happened to notice Shellman's condition and in an instant had one foot after another up at the saddle bow, took off his shoes and threw them at Allies feet with the remark, 'Friend you need them more than I do,' then galloped away without waiting to be thanked. One such incident as this goes a long way toward giving a firm faith in the good that is in human nature............"

Captured: Sergeant Edward F. Blair – Co. F
            Sergeant Joseph Potter Williamson – Co. F

23 December, 1864
Lieutenant Hamilton Branch of Company F wrote to his mother Charlotte Branch:

"..................14 miles from Columbia on turnpike

..........We remained here all last night and all to day until this afternoon when we moved a ½ mile towards Columbia and forward a line of battle. we remained here until dark when we went into bivouac……………………..…"

"…………..We left Columbia yesterday and marched to this place. we formed line of battle twice but the enemy did not come up to us. Genl Forrest drew them on until he got them where he wanted them. this was about 5 miles from Pulaski. he then stopped and formed line of fight. we then built rail breastworks and waited for the enemy to charge us. this they would not do. therefore Genl F. told us that when he sounded the charge that he wanted us to go forward with a vim. we had 3 brigades of infantry, (Winfield S.) Featherstones, (John C.) Browns, and (James A.) Smiths and two of Calvary. as soon as the bugle was blown we charged and drove the enemy back capturing 1 piece of artillery, about 40 horses, 50 carbines, and 15 prisoners. we had two wounded on our side Ramus (Alexander J. Ramour) of my company (who with (William S.) Gavan and Barren (J. J. Barron) had joined us at Pulaski) captured a horse and sold it for $1000………….."

In Colonel Olmstead's report he writes:

"…………Early on the morning of the 22nd, the enemy crossed the river in force above Columbia and we commenced our retreat. We retired slowly, forming line of battle occasionally, until we had gotten some six or seven miles this side of Pulaski, when the enemy pushed us so hard that it was determined to stop and fight them. Accordingly the line was formed, our position being extreme left of the infantry, with Palmers Brigade on our right. The enemy approached boldly, a heavy line of skirmishers preceded them. Upon given the signal, the whole line charged, when the enemy retreated with confusion offering but a slight resistance. We captured a number of horses and a canon. This was on Christmas day. We did not see the enemy again. On the 28th we recrossed the Tennessee, and on the 1st of January, rejoined our division at Corinth, from whence we marched to Tupelo. The conduct of men and officers in this trying retreat was admirable; they bore hardships forced upon them unflinchingly, and were ever ready to show a bold front on the approach of the enemy. I would especially call attention to the gallant conduct of Private P Murner of the first Georgia, and Private A. Vikery, of the Fifty-fourth. These men carried the colors of their respective regiments, and showed conspicuous bravery in the charge on the 25th………….."

24 December, 1864

The brigade marched to a position of defense along Richland Creek, Tennessee. Around 8 p.m., the brigade retired to the outer line of earthworks near the town of Pulaski, Tennessee.
Private J. R. Nease of Company I was captured in Savannah, Georgia.

Lieutenant Hamilton Branch of Company F wrote to his mother

Charlotte Branch:

"………………..We left our bivouac of yesterday this morning and marched to within 3 miles of this place, when we stopped and formed line of fight. We remained in line until 7 P.M. when we moved to this place and took position in the enemys old works 6 miles south of Pulaski……………….."

25 December, 1864
The brigade marched through Pulaski. A plan was made to counter attack the pressing Federal cavalry. Seven miles from Pulaski, at "Anthony's" or "King's" Hill, an ambush was prepared. When the Federal cavalry neared the troops lying in wait for them, the brigade delivered a destructive fire and then charged. The Federals retreated and the Confederate's captured a number of prisoners and horses and one piece of artillery. Private A. Vickery was specifically mentioned for his bravery in carrying the 54th Regimental colors during the charge against the Federals on Christmas Day. Around sunset, the brigade withdrew from their position and moved to Sugar Springs, Tennessee.

Captured: Private Jeremiah B. Weaver – Co. E (Pulaski, Tennessee)
Private Jethro John Wilkins Weaver – Co. E (Pulaski, Tennessee)
Private Charles Kirkman – Co. G (Pulaski, Tennessee)

The Brigade and the 54th Regiment were again on night march. Colonel Olmstead wrote of this march:

"…………..Gen. Forrest continued the retreat. That afternoon a thaw commenced and a cold rain set in; The roads were rivers of slush as the snow melted, but on we went in the black darkness, stumbling along, cold, weary to exhaustion, dead for sleep, but the march kept up until midnight when we came up with the other half of the rear guard where they had gone into bivouac.

Our men filed off into the fields to the right and left of the road but there was sorry comfort for them--- it was cultivated land and the furrows were filled with water--- they sliept as they could on the ridges between…..

After the men were placed, Matthew and I looked around forlornly for some more attractive bed than a corn hill in which to sleep….. We discovered an ambulance standing on the side of the road which no one seemed to have claimed. Into this we crept….. So ended our Christmas!……."

One soldier stated "General Forrest will set the trap and the Yankees will oblige".

Lieutenant Hamilton Branch of Company F wrote to his mother Charlotte Branch:

"…………….We marched through Pulaski this morning and leaving the turnpike turned into a very muddy road. the enemy followed us very closely, in fact they charged our men who were left to burn the bridge at Pulaski………………………."

26 December, 1864
  Captured: Private Samuel H. McDonald – Co. G

Lieutenant Hamilton Branch of Company F wrote to his mother Charlotte Branch:
"…………………….Stegar (Sugar) Creek 20 miles from Pulaski

…………We remained at our fighting ground yesterday an hour or two after the fight and then at 3 ½ Oclock P. M. we commenced to fall back again. we marched all the afternoon and until 11 at night. we crossed, that is waded, about 20 creeks and went into bivouac in a mudhole at this place. it had been raining for the last two days but as I had captured a rubber cloth on Christmas I managed to keep pretty dry. I also captured a shirt and testament off of the gun we captured. this morning we found the enemy had not been satisfied with their drubbing of yesterday, but were upon us again. Genl F. therefore made his rear consisting of two brigades of Inft and 1 of Cavalry charged them again. they drove the enemy back killing a number of horses and taking some prisoners. we then fell back during the rest of the day, and bivouaced at night near Lexington………………………."

27 December, 1864
Lieutenant Hamilton Branch of Company F wrote to his mother Charlotte Branch:

"……………..We left bivouac at daylight and fell back to Shoal Creek where we bivouaced at night………………….."

28 December, 1864
  Captured: Private John Breen - Co. F (Egypt Station, Tennessee)
The brigade recrossed the Tennessee River.

Lieutenant Hamilton Branch of Company F wrote to his mother

Charlotte Branch:

"………………Bainbridge Ala

……….We were called at 1 A.M. and marched to the pontoon (about 2 miles) when we crossed over the Tennessee and are now safe again on this side of the river, at Shoal creek. (Joel P.) Rackley and (D. J.) Bryant joined me. I left the brigade this morning and have started for the rear……………..."

29 December 1864
Lieutenant Hamilton Branch of Company F wrote to his mother Charlotte Branch:

"……………Corinth, Miss

……………..I arrived at this place this morning, dirty lousey and hungry…………………"

During the year of 1864 the following died in service:
                Private Caleb Stephens – Co. A
                Sergeant Matthew Thornton – Co. F
                Private Erasmus Hubbard – Co. H
                Private W. B. Hannah – Co. I
                Private H. P. Roberson – Co. K
                Private W. H. Roberson – Co. K

31 December 1864
John R. Nease of Company I captured.

In the year of 1864:
Private G. B. Robertson of Company C wounded.

Corporal E. D. McGar of Company C died while on sick furlough.
Private E. J. McGar of Company C died of disease in Macon, Georgia.
Private J. C. McGar of Company C died of disease in Macon, Georgia.
Private Robert D. Caesar was captured at Savannah, Georgia.

1865

January, 1865
A train wreck occurred during this time which injured several men from the brigade.
  Joseph Deen of Company B injured.
  B. R. Graham of Company C injured.

1 January, 1865
General Forrest's command rejoined the Army of Tennessee near Corinth, Mississippi. The temporary division was disbanded and Smith's Brigade rejoined Brigadier General James A. Smith's (formerly Cleburne's) Division at Corinth, Mississippi. Under General Hood's command the once mighty Army of Tennessee had been reduced in strength from General Joseph E. Johnston's 50,000 strong to a bloodied, demoralized mere 18,000 men, many of them in no shape to fight. After this General John Bell Hood resigned the command of the Army of Tennessee and General Pierre Gustave Toutant Beauregard became commander.
  Private Isham Strickland of Company B captured at Itawamba County, Mississippi.

5 January, 1865
Private Jethro John Wilkins Weaver of Company E died at Camp Chase, Ohio.

6 January, 1865
Private George W. Middleton of Company B died of pneumonia in General Hospital at Atlanta, Georgia.

10 January, 1865
Private Wiley Carter, Sr. of Company B admitted to St. Mary's Hospital at West Point, Mississippi with a Gunshot Wound.

11 January, 1865
Private Edwin A. Houston of Company H admitted to Way Hospital at Meridian, Mississippi with a Gunshot Wound.

12 January 1865
Cheatham's Corp arrived at Tupelo, Mississippi.

13-20 January, 1865
The Army of Tennessee was camped at Tupelo.
William J. Shearouse of Company I died at Camp Chase, Ohio prison.

14 January, 1865
Private George W. Ely of Company H admitted to Way Hospital at Meridian, Mississippi with Gunshot Wounds.

15 January, 1865
Lieutenant Marcus B. Ely of Company H admitted to Way Hospital at Meridian, Mississippi with a Gunshot Wound.

17 January, 1865
Private Robert F. Lachilson of Company F admitted to Way Hospital at Meridian, Mississippi with a Gunshot Wound.

18 January, 1865
Private Joseph Webb of Company C admitted to Way Hospital at Meridian, Mississippi with a Gunshot Wound.
Lieutenant James F. Rawls of Company I admitted to Way Hospital at Meridian, Mississippi with a Gunshot Wound.
Private Augustus Waters of Company I admitted to Way Hospital at Meridian, Mississippi with a Gunshot Wound.

19 January, 1865
Private Thomas L. Blitch of Company I died at Camp Douglas, Illinois prison.

20 January, 1865

HEADQUARTERS SMITH'S BRIGADE, Near Tupelo, Miss., January 20, 1865.

CAPTAIN: I have the honor to submit the following report of the operations of this brigade from December 6, 1864, to the present date:

On December 6 and 7 the command was busy constructing a second line of works infront of Nashville, a little to the right of the Nolensville pike. On the morning of the 8th we took up the line of march for Murfreesborough, having been ordered to report to General Forrest near that place. At night-fall went into camp within eleven miles of the place. From that time until December 15 the command did little else than destroy the railroad between Murfreesborough and Nashville. On the 15th marched with Palmer's brigade and a portion of the cavalry to a position considerably to the eastward of Murfreesborough. On the next day, however, we retraced our steps, and (the news of the disaster at Nashville reaching us that night) we immediately started across the country for Pulaski by forced marches. The roads were in horrible condition and the weather intensely cold, so that the sufferings of the men, who were many of them barefooted and all poorly clad, were intense. On arriving at Duck River it was found to be so much swollen by heavy rains as to be impassable. We were accordingly ordered to Columbia, which place we reached late at night on the 18th. Here we remained for three days, receiving orders to report to Major-General Walthall as a portion of the rear guard of the army.

Early on the morning of the 22nd the enemy crossed the river in force above Columbia, and [we] commenced our retreat. We retired slowly, forming line of battle occasionally, until we had gotten some six or seven miles on this side of Pulaski, when the enemy pushed us so hard that it was determined to stop and fight them. Accordingly, the line was formed, our position being upon the extreme left of the infantry, with Palmer's brigade upon our right, the cavalry upon our left. The enemy approached boldly, a heavy line of skirmishers preceding them. Upon a given signal our whole line charged, when the enemy retired in confusion after offering but a slight resistance. We captured a number of horses and one piece of artillery, a 12-pounder Napoleon. This was on Christmas day. On the following day the rear guard was again attacked, but this brigade was not engaged in the affair, nor did we again meet the enemy.

On the 28th we recrossed the Tennessee, and on the 1st of January rejoined our division at Corinth, from whence we marched to Tupelo. The conduct of men and officers in this trying retreat was admirable; they bore the hardships forced upon them unflinchingly, and were ever ready to show a bold front on the approach of the enemy.

I would especially call the attention of the general commanding to the gallant conduct of Private P. Murner, of the First Georgia, and Private A. Vikery, of the Fifty-fourth Georgia. These men carried the colors of their respective regiments, and showed conspicuous bravery in the charge on the 25th.

I am, captain, very respectfully, your obedient servant,

CHAS. H. OLMSTEAD,
Colonel, Commanding Brigade

Captain W. W. HARDY,
Acting Assistant Adjutant-General

List of casualties: 1 killed, 2 wounded, 70 missing. The missing were most of them men who broke down physically on the other side of Duck River, and are supposed to have fallen into the hands of the enemy.

CHAS. H. OLMSTEAD,
Colonel, Commanding Brigade

Private William Jasper Shearouse of Company I died at Camp Chase, Ohio.
22 January, 1865
Private Benjamin J. Helmy of Company F died of Pneumonia in Camp Chase Military Prison at Columbus, Ohio.
24 January, 1865
The following is the Report of Major General Nathan B. Forrest, C. S.

Army, commanding cavalry, of operations November 16, 1864-January 23, 1865

HEADQUARTERS FORREST'S CAVALRY CORPS,

Verona, Miss., January 24, 1865.

COLONEL: I have the honor to submit the following report of the operations of the troops under my command during the recent movements in Middle Tennessee:

While in West Tennessee I received orders from General Beauregard on the 30th of October, to report without delay to General Hood at Florence, Ala. I was then actively operating against Johnsonville, and so soon as I completed the destruction of the enemy's fleet and stores at that place I commenced moving up the Tennessee River. I halted my command at Perryville with a view of crossing the river at that point, but being without facilities, and the river already high and rising rapidly, I found it impossible to cross over. I succeeded, however, in throwing across a portion of Rucker's brigade, while I moved to Corinth with the balance of my command. My men and horses were much jaded, but I moved at once to Florence and crossed the river on the 16th and 17th of November. On my arrival at Florence I was placed in command of the entire cavalry then with the Army of Tennessee, consisting of Brigadier-General Jackson's division and a portion of Dibrell's brigade, under command of Colonel Biffle, amounting to about 2,000 men, together with three brigades of my former command at Shoal Creek until the morning of the 21st, hen, in obedience to orders from General Hood, I commenced a forward movement. My command consisted of three divisions-Chalmers', Buford's, and
Jackson were ordered to move up the military road to Lawrenceburg, and thence southeastward in the direction of Pulaski. Both these divisions had several engagements with the enemy, and were almost constantly skirmishing with him, but drove him in every encounter.

At Henryville Brigadier-General Chalmers developed the enemy's cavalry and captured forty-five prisoners. At Fouche Springs the enemy made another stand. I ordered General Chalmers to throw forward Rucker's brigade and to keep up a slight skirmish with the enemy until I could gain his rear. I ordered Lieutenant-Colonel Kelley to move by the left flank and join me in rear of the enemy. Taking my escort with me I moved rapidly to the rear. Lieutenant-Colonel Kelley being prevented from joining me as I had expected, I made the charge upon the enemy with my escort alone, producing a perfect stampede, capturing about 50 prisoners, 20 horses, and 1 ambulance. It was near night, and I placed my escort in ambush. Colonel rucker pressed upon the enemy, and as they rushed into the ambuscade my escort fired into them, producing the wildest confusion. I ordered Colonel Rucker to rest his command until 1 a. m., when the march was renewed toward Mount Pleasant, where he captured 35,000 rounds of small-arm ammunition and the guard left in charge of it. Meantime Brigadier-Generals Buford and Jackson had proceeded from Lawrenceburg toward Pulaski and encountered Hatch's division of cavalry at Campbellsville, and routed him after a short but vigorous engagement, in which he lost about 100 prisoners and several in killed and wounded. Most of my troops having reached Columbia on the evening of the 24th I invested the town from Duck River to the extreme north, which position I held until the arrival of the infantry on the morning of the 27th, when I was relieved.

Columbia having been evacuated on the night of the 28th [27th] I was ordered to ove across Duck River on the morning of the 28th. Chalmers' division was ordered to cross an Carr's Mill, seven miles above Columbia, Jackson's, at Holland's Ford, while I crossed at Owen's Ford with a portion of Colonel Biffle's regiment. Before leaving Columbia I sent my escort to Shelbyville for the purpose of ascertaining the movements of the enemy and destroying the railroad, and I regret to announce that Captain Jackson was seriously wounded on this expedition. On the night of the 28th I was joined by Chalmers' division about eight miles from Columbia on the Spring Hill and Carr's Mill road.

Jackson's division was ordered to proceed to the vicinity of Hurt's Cross Roads on the Lewisburg pike. At 11 o'clock at night I received a dispatch from General Buford informing me that the enemy had made such a stubborn resistance to his crossing that he could not join the command until the morning of the 29th. I ordered General Jackson to move along the Lewisburg pike toward Franklin until he developed the enemy.Brigadier-General Armstong notified me that he had struck the enemy, when I ordered him not to press too vigorously until I reached his flank with Chalmers' division. The enemy gradually fell back, making resistance only at favorable positions. After waiting a short time for my troops to close up, I moved rapidly toward Spring Hill with my entire command. Two miles from town the enemy's pickets were encountered and heavy skirmishing ensued. I ordered General Armstrong to form his brigade in line of battle. I also ordered a portion of the Kentucky brigade and the Fourteenth Tennessee Regiment, under Colonel White, to form, which being done I ordered a charge upon the enemy, but he was so strongly posted upon the crest of a hill that my troops were compelled to fall back. I then dismounted my entire command and moved upon the enemy. With a few men I moved to the left on a high hill, where I discovered the enemy hurriedly moving his wagon train up the Franklin pike. I ordered my command to push the enemy's right flank and Buford to send me a regiment mounted. He sent the Twenty-first Tennessee, Colonel Wilson commanding, which I ordered to charge upon the enemy. Colonel Wilson at the head of his splendid regiment made a gallant charge through an open field. He received three wounds, but refused to leave his command. About this time I received orders from General Hood to hold my position at all hazards, as the advance of his infantry column was only two miles distant and rapidly advancing. I ordered up my command, already dismounted. Colonel Bell's brigade was the first to reach me, when I immediately ordered it to the attack. Major-General Cleburne's division soon arrived, and, after some delay, was formed in line of battle and moved upon the enemy on my left. Colonel Bell reported that he had only four rounds of ammunition to the man when I ordered him to charge the enemy. This order was executed with a promptness and energy and gallantry which I have never seen excelled. The enemy was driven from his rifle-pits, and fled toward Spring Hill. I then ordered Brigadier-General Jackson to move with his division in the direction of Thompson's Station and there intercept the enemy. He struck the road at Fitzgerald's, four miles from Spring Hill, at 11 o'clock, just as the front of the enemy's column had passed. This attack was a complete surprise, producing much panic and confusion. Brigadier-General Jackson had possession of the pike and fought the enemy until near daylight, but receiving no support, he was compelled to retire, after killing a large number of horses and mules and burning several wagons.

Chalmers' and Buford's divisions being out of ammunition, I supplied them from the infantry (my ordnance being still at Columbia), when I ordered Brigadier-General Chalmers to move at daylight on the morning of the 30th to the Carter's Creek turnpike, between Columbia and Spring Hill, and there intercept a column of the enemy reported to be cut off. General Chalmers moved as ordered, but reported to me that the enemy had passed unmolested on the main pike during the night. Buford and Jackson were ordered to move forward with their divisions on the Franklin pike and to attack the enemy. They overtook his rear two miles from where General Jackson had cut his column the night previous and pushed him on to Winstead's Hill, where he was strongly posted. General Stewart's corps arriving upon the ground, I moved with Buford's and Jackson's divisions to the right, my right extending to Harpeth River, and ordered Brigadier-General Chalmers on the left. The enemy retired from Winstead's Hill toward their fortifications at Franklin. I ordered Brigadier-General Chalmers to advance on the left, which he did, charging and dislodging the enemy from every position he had taken. The enemy was posted on a strong hill on the opposite side of Harpeth River, from which position he was firing upon our troops on the Lewisburg pike. I ordered Brigadier-General Jackson to cross over and drive the enemy from this hill and to protect our right. I ordered Brigadier-General Buford to dismount his command and take position in line of battle on the right of Stewarts' corps, covering the ground from the Lewisburg pike to Harpeth River. Skirmishing at once commenced, and Buford's division rapidly advancing drove the enemy across Harpeth River, where he joined the cavalry. Brigadier-General Jackson engaged the united forces of both infantry and cavalry, and held him in check until night, when he threw forward his pickets and retired across Harpeth for the purpose of replenishing his ammunition. The enemy held strong positions commanding all the fords. I ordered Brigadier-General Buford to remount his command and hold himself in readiness for action at a moment's warning. Brigadier-General Jackson's troops being out of ammunition, and my ordnance still in the rear, Captain Vanderford furnished me with the necessary supply.

At daylight on the 1st of December I moved across Harpeth River and advanced up the Wilson pike, and stuck the enemy at Owen's Cross-Roads, in strong force. I ordered Captain Morton to open upon him with his battery. Soon afterward I ordered Brigadier-General Buford to charge, which order he executed by dislodging the enemy and capturing several prisoners. I then moved with Jackson's and Buford's divisions to Brentwood, where I was joined by Brigadier-General Chalmers. Ordering Chalmers to proceed with his division up to the Franklin and Hillsborough pike, and to cross over and intercept, if possible, the enemy retreating toward Nashville, I moved with Buford's and Jackson's divisions toward the Nashville pike, and, leading the enemy had reached Nashville, I camped for the night.

On the following morning (the 2nd) I ordered Brigadier-General Chalmers to move on the left and to guard the Hillsborough and Hardin pikes, while I proceeded to the right Buford's and Jackson's divisions and took position in sight of the capitol at Nashville. I ordered Brigadier-General Buford to move with his division across to Mill Creek and to form line of battle near the asylum on the Murfreesborough pike. Jackson's division was ordered into position so as to cover the Nashville and Mill Creek pike. My command being relieved by the infantry I commenced operating upon the railroad, block-house, and telegraph lines leading from Nashville to Murfreesborough. I ordered Buford's division on the Nashville and Chattanooga Railroad for the purpose of destroying stockades and block-houses.

On the 3rd of December stockade Number 2 surrendered, with 80 prisoners, 10 men killed, and 20 wounded in the attack by Morton's battery. On the day previous, while assaulting stockade Number 2, a train of cars came from Chattanooga loaded with negro troops. The train was captured, but most of the troops made their escape.

On the 4th I ordered Brigadier-General Buford to attack block-house Number 3, but the demand for surrender was complied with, and the garrison of thirty-two men made prisoners. An assault was also ordered on stockade Number 1, on Mill Creek, but the garrison unhesitatingly surrendered. I ordered the destruction of the block-house and two stockades, in which were captured 150 prisoners.

On the morning of the 4th I received orders to move with Buford's and Jackson's ivisions to Murfreesborough, and to leave 250 men on the right to picket from the Nashville and Murfreesborough pike to the Cumberland River. Colonel Nixon, of Bell's brigade, was left for this purpose.

On the morning of the 5th I moved, as ordered, toward Murfreesborough. At La Vergne I ordered Brigadier-General Jackson to move on the right of town and invest the fort on the hill, while I moved with Buford's division to block-house Number 4. The usual demand for surrender was sent under flag of truce and a surrender made. The garrison on the hill, consisting of 80 men, 2 pieces of artillery, several wagons, and a considerable supply of stores, also surrendered to Brigadier-General Jackson. A large number of houses, built and occupied by the enemy, were ordered to be burned.

Four miles from La Vergne I formed a junction with Major-General Bate, who had been ordered to report to me with his division for the purpose of operating against Murfreesborough. I ordered Brigadier-General Jackson to send brigade across to the Wilson [Wilkinson] pike, and moving on both pikes the enemy was driven into his works at Murfreesborough. After ordering General Buford to picket from the Nashville and Murfreesborough to the Lebanon pike on the left, and Jackson to picket on the right to the Salem pike, I encamped for the night.

The infantry arrived on the morning of the 6th, when I immediately ordered it in line of battle and to move upon the enemy's works. After skirmishing for two hours the enemy ceased firing, and showed no disposition to give battle. I ordered a regiment from Brigadier-General Armstrong's brigade, with which I made a careful reconnaissance of the enemy's position and works. On the evening of the 6th I was re-enforced by Sears' and Palmer's brigades of infantry. I ordered Colonel Palmer in position on the right upon a hill, and to fortify during the night.

On the morning of the 7th I discovered from the position occupied by Colonel Palmer the enemy moving out in strong force on the Salem pike with infantry, cavalry, and artillery. Being fully satisfied that his object was to make battle, I withdrew my forces to the Wilkinson pike, and formed a new line on a more favorable position. The enemy moved boldly forward, driving in my pickets, when the infantry, with the exception of Smith's brigade, from some cause which I cannot explain, made a shameful retreat, losing two pieces of artillery. I seized the colors of the retreating troops and endeavored to rally them, but they could not be moved by any entreaty or appeal to their patriotism. Major-General Bate did the same thing, but was equally as unsuccessful as myself. I hurriedly sent Major Strange, of my staff, to Brigadier-Generals Armstrong and Ross, of Jackson's division, with orders to say to them that everything depended on their cavalry. They proved themselves equal to the emergency by charging on the enemy, thereby checking his farther advance. I ordered the infantry to retire to Stewart's Creek, while my cavalry encamped during the night at Overall's Creek. The enemy returning to Murfreesborough, I ordered my cavalry to resume its former position.

It is proper to state here that I ordered Brigadier-General Bufored to protect my left flank, but he was so remote the order never reached him. While the fight was going on, however, he made a demonstration on Murfreesborough, and succeeded in reaching the center of town, but was soon compelled to retire.

On the 9th General Hood sent to my support Smith's brigade, commanded by Colonel Olmstead, and ordered Bate's division to report back to his headquarters. On the 11th I ordered Brigadier-General Buford to proceed to the Hermitage, and to picket the Cumberland River, so ordered the infantry to destroy the railroad from La Vergne to Murfreesborough, which was most effectually done. Brigadier-General Jackson, who had been previously ordered to operate south of Murfreesborough, captured, on the 13th, a train of seventeen cars and the Sixty-first Illinois Regiment of Infantry, commanded by Lieutenant-Colonel Grass. The train was loaded with supplies of 60,000 rations, sent form Stevenson to Murfreesborough, all of which were consumed by fire, after which the prisoners, about 200 in number, were sent to the rear.
On the 14th I moved with Colonels Olmstead's and Palmer's brigades across Stone's River and east of Murfreesborough, with a view of capturing the enemy's forage train, but on the evening of the 15th I received notice from General Hood that a general engagement was then going on at Nashville, and to hold myself in readiness to move

at any moment. Accordingly, on the 16th I moved my entire command to the Wilkinson Cross-Roads, at the terminus of the Wilkinson pike, six miles from Murfreesborough. One the night on the 16th one of General Hood's staff officers arrived, informing me of the disaster at Nashville and ordering me to fall back via Shelbyville and Pulaski. I immediately dispatched orders to Brigadier-General Buford to fall back from the Cumberland River, via La Vergne, to the Nashville pike, and to protect my rear until I could move my artillery and wagon train. From this position General Buford was ordered across to the Nashville and Columbia pike, for the purpose of protecting the rear of General Hood's retreating army. My sick, wounded, and wagon train being at Triune, I did not retreat via Shelbyville, but moved in the direction of Lillard's Mills, on Duck River. I ordered Brigadier-General Armstrong to the Nashville and Columbia pike. Most of the infantry under my command were barefooted and in a disabled condition, and being encumbered with several hundred head of hogs and cattle, my march along the almost impassable roads was unavoidably slow. On reaching Duck River at Lillard's Mills I ordered everything to be hurried across, as the stream was rapidly rising. After putting over a part of my wagon train the stream became unfordable. I was therefore compelled to change my direction to Columbia, which place I reached on the evening of the 18th.

On the morning of the 19th the enemy was reported at Rutherford's Creek in strong force. I immediately commenced disposing of my troops for the purpose of preventing his crossing. Everything being across Duck River I was ordered by General Hood to withdraw my command at 3 o'clock, which I did, and went into camp at Columbia. Chalmers' division having been sent to the right, I am unable to state anything from personal knowledge as to his operations from the 3rd to the 19th; but I learn from his official report that his line extended from the Hillsborough pike, on the right, across the Hardin and Charlotte pikes to the river, on the left; that he captured two transports laden with horses and mules; that the transports were recaptured, by leaving on his hands 56 prisoners and 197 horses and mules; that the enemy made several attempts with his monitors and gun-boats to silence his river batteries, all of which were unsuccessful; that he maintained a strict blockade of the river and his position until Ector's brigade of infantry fell back; that then prevented Hatch from gaining the rear of our army' and that he was constantly and severely engaged every day while protecting the rear of General Hood's army until he crossed Rutherford's Creek.

On the 20th General Hood, on leaving Columbia, gave me orders to hold the town as long as possible, and when compelled to retire to move in the direction of Florence, Ala., via Pulaski, protecting and guarding his rear. To aid me in this object he ordered Major-General Walthall to report to me with about 1,900 infantry, 400 of whom were unserviceable for want of shoes. The enemy appeared in front of Columbia on the evening of the 20th and commenced a furious shelling upon the town. Under a flag of truce I proceeded to the river and asked an interview with General Hatch, who I informed by verbal communication across the river that there were no Confederate troops in town, and that his shelling would only result in injury to the women and children and his own wounded, after which interview the shelling was discontinued.

The enemy succeeded in crossing Duck River on the morning of the 22nd. I at once ordered my troops to fall back in the direction of Pulaski. Brigadier-General Chalmers was ordered on the right down the Bigbyville pike toward Bigbyville. The infantry moved down the main pike from Columbia to Pulaski, the rear protected by both Buford's and Jackson's divisions of cavalry, while a few scouts were thrown out on the left flank. The enemy made his first demonstration on my rear pickets near Warfield's, three miles south of Columbia. He opened upon us with artillery, which forced us to retire farther down the road in a gap made by two high hills on each side of the road, where he was held in heck for some time. On the night of the 23rd I halted my command at and near Lynnville, in order to hold the enemy in check and to prevent any pressure upon my wagon train and the stock then being driven out.

On the morning of the 24th I ordered the infantry back toward Columbia on the main pike and my cavalry on the right and left flanks. After advancing about three miles the enemy was met, where a severe engagement occurred and the enemy was held in check for two hours. I retreated two miles, where I took position at Richland Creek. Brigadier-General Armstrong was thrown forward in front and General Ross on the right flank. Chalmers and Buford formed a junction, and were ordered on the left flank. Brigadier-General Armstrong was ordered to the support of six pieces of my artillery, which were placed in position immediately on the main pike and on a line with Buford's and Chalmer's divisions and Ross' brigade, of Jackson's division. After severe artillery firing on both sides two pieces of the enemy's artillery were dismounted. The enemy then flanked to the right and left and crossed Richland Creek on my right, with the view of gaining my rear. I immediately ordered Armstrong and Ross, of Jackson's division, to cross the bridge on the main pike and move around and engage the enemy, who were crossing the creek. Both Buford and Chalmers were heavily pressed on the left, and after an engagement of two hours I ordered them to fall back across Richland Creek. I lost 1 killed and 6 wounded in their engagement. The enemy lost heavily. Brigadier-General Buford was wounded in this engagement, and I ordered Brigadier-General Chalmers to assume command of Brigadier-General Buford's division together with his own. I reached Pulaski without further molestation.

On the morning of the 25th, after destroying all the ammunition which could not be removed from Pulaski by General Hood and two trains of cars, I ordered General Jackson to remain in town as long as possible and to destroy the bridge at Richland Creek after everything had passed over. The enemy soon pressed General Jackson, but he held him in check for some time, killing and wounding several before retiring. Seven miles from Pulaski I took position on King's Hill, and awaiting the advance of the enemy, repulsed him, with a loss of 150 killed and wounded, besides capturing many prisoners and one piece of artillery. The enemy made no further demonstrations during the day. I halted my command at Sugar Creek, where it encamped during the night.

On the morning of the 26th the enemy commenced advancing, driving back General Ross' pickets. Owing to the dense for he could not see the temporary fortifications which the infantry had thrown up and behind which they were secreted. The enemy therefore advanced to within fifty paces of these works, when a volley was opened upon him, causing the wildest confusion. Two mounted regiments of Ross' brigade and Ector's and Granbury's brigades* of infantry were ordered to charge upon the discomfited foe, which was done, producing a complete rout. The enemy was pursued for two miles, but showing no disposition to give battle my troops were ordered back. In this engagement he sustained a loss of about 150 in killed and wounded; many prisoners and horses were captured and about 400 horses killed. I held this position for two hours, but the enemy showing no disposition to renew the attack, and fearing he might attempt a flank movement in the dense fog, I resumed the march, after leaving a picket with orders to remain until 4 o'clock. The enemy made no further attack between Sugar Creek and Tennessee River, which stream I crossed on the evening of the 27th of December. The infantry were ordered to report back to their respective corps, and I moved with my cavalry to Corinth.

The campaign was full of trial and suffering, but the troops under my command, both cavalry and infantry, submitted to every hardship with an uncomplaining patriotism; with a single exception, they behaved with commendable gallantry.

From the day I left Florence, on the 21st of November, to the 27th of December y cavalry were engaged every day with the enemy. My loss in killed and wounded has been heavy. I brought out of the campaign three pieces of artillery more than I started with.

My command captured and destroyed 16 block-houses and stockades, 20 brigades, several hundred horses and mules, 20 yoke of oxen, 4 locomotives, and 100 cars and 10 miles of railroad, while I have turned over to the provost-marshal-general about 1,600 prisoners.

To my division commanders-Brigadier-Generals Chalmers, Buford, and Jackson-I take pleasure in acknowledging the promptitude with which they obeyed and executed all orders. If I have failed to do justice in this report it is because they have not furnished me with a detailed report of the operations of their respective commands.

I am also indebted to Major-General Walthall for much valuable service rendered during the retreat from Columbia. He exhibited the highest soldierly qualities. Many of his men were without shoes, but they bore their sufferings without murmur and were every ready to meet the enemy.

I am again under obligations to my staff for their efficient aid during the campaign.

All of which is respectfully submitted.

N. B. FORREST,
Major-General

Private Benjamin J. Helmey of Co. F died of pneumonia at Camp Chase Military Prison at Columbus, Ohio.

25 January, 1865
Private Thomas Razor Carter of Company B admitted to Way Hospital at Meridian, Mississippi with a Gunshot Wound.
Private William Thomas Reddish of Company B admitted to Way Hospital at Meridian, Mississippi with a Gunshot Wound.
30 January, 1865
Private Cader Hancock of Company E was admitted to Way Hospital at Meridian, Mississippi with a Gunshot Wound.
31 January, 1865
Smith's Brigade receives orders for transfer to Smithfield, North Carolina.
Benjamin J. Helmy of Company F died at Camp Chase, Ohio prison.
1 February, 1865
Smith's Brigade moves by train from Mobile and arrive at Montgomery, Alabama.
2 February, 1865

Private J. d. Bennett of Company K admitted to Way Hospital at Meridian, Mississippi with a Gunshot Wound.

3 February 1865
Private William J. Butler admitted to Way Hospital at Meridian, Mississippi with a Gunshot Wound.

6 February, 1865
Smith's Brigade having moved from Montgomery, Alabama to Columbus, Georgia arrive in Macon, Georgia. As the brigade passes through Georgia, many of the men "left the ranks to look after their families and assess Sherman's damage". This trip left the brigade with 300 men.

8 February, 1865
Private D. W. Holloway of Company H admitted to Way Hospital at Meridian, Mississippi with a Gunshot Wound.

13 February, 1865
Private James Smith of Company E died in Columbia, South Carolina at the Hospitals of the Army of Tennessee.

14 February, 1865
Private Isham Strickland of Company B died at Camp Chase, Ohio prison.

16 February, 1865
Private Samuel B. Finney of Company A died of pneumonia in the Hospital at Camp Chase, Ohio.

20 February, 1865
Private Franklin Holloman of Company A admitted to Way Hospital at Meridian, Mississippi with a Gunshot Wound.
Private Walter Brannen of Company H died at Martinsburg, Virginia.

23 February 1865
Abraham Eason of Company B died at Dalton, Georgia.

26 February 1865
Private Walter Brannen of Co H died at Martinsville, Virginia.

28 February 1865
Private William Kelly of Company F admitted to Ocmulgee Hospital at Macon, Georgia with a Gunshot Wound.

12 March, 1865
Corporal William A. Taylor of Company D died of disease while at home sick (on furlough).

18 March, 1865
As Mercer's Brigade neared the North Carolina border, General Cheatham became aware of how many of Olmsted's Georgians had taken "French leave" to see their families who were near the path they had taken. The brigade now most likely was comprised of less than 300 men total effective. General Cheatham requested an interview with Colonel Olmstead and inquired about the problems.
Colonel Olmstead recorded this after that meeting:

"............It distressed me to see how many of our men had slipped away from the ranks during the passage through Georgia, though I quite well understood and symphatized with them for going. When we were nearly up to the North Carolina line, Gen. Cheatham who then commanded the corps, sent for me to ask an explanation of this falling off in the Brigade numbers.
I told him that the men had no intention of deserting the colors, but that as husbands and fathers they had felt obliged to go to look after their families most of whom had lived in the line of Sherman's March and were now homeless and destitute. I further said that if he would send me back to Georgia I felt confident of being able to return to the army with most of the missing ones. The proposition met with his approval and he had once instructed his Adjutant General to prepare an order detailing me for this service. The paper was handed me and I started off the same day.
This was the first time I had ever been brought in contact with Genl Cheatham and it can not be said that he made a very favorable impression upon me. He was known as a man of great personal bravery, and an indomitable fighter and with a fine record upon many bloody fields. But he was also reported to be a hard drinker..... It is certainly true that during my interview with him there was decided evidence of his being under the influence of liquor. As he handed me the order he said with a gravity that was ludicrous, 'Colonel you go and bring those men back and if you want anybody shot just wink your eye.'.................."

Of course the Colonel did not want to have anyone shot. He quickly returned to Georgia and advertised in the newspapers in Augusta, Columbus and Macon for members of his Brigade, Mercer's, to return to duty. In two weeks he returned with more than 500 men.
Unfortunately by the time he returned the Battle of Bentonville had been fought. The Army of Tennessee had fired its final shot in the long war. The last major battle of the Army of the West was over. Only those members of Mercer's Brigade who went directly to Bentonville and were there in time to participate in that fateful battle. They were on the right in the line of battle.

After train rides and marches through Augusta, Georgia, Salisbury and Smithfield, North Carolina, the 54th and men of Smith's brigade were walking to Bentonville, North Carolina. Here they were assigned to Bate's Corps. Company G, 54th Regiment, Georgia Infantry had the following change:
Grigsby E. Thomas Sr. elected Captain for gallantry displayed at Bentonville, North Carolina.
W. R. Durden of Company C captured.

19 March, 1865 the Battle of Bentonville

Colonel Olmstead was sent to collect the men who had left the ranks on the trip through Georgia. The Confederate army was near Bentonville. Smith's Brigade was in line of battle. Brigadier General Smith, who commanded Cleburne's old division at the Battle of Bentonville, reports "only two of the brigades of the division (Gordon's and Smith's) were engaged. Mercer's old Brigade (now Smith's Brigade), which included the remnant of the 54th Georgia, was on the extreme right of the attack. The brigade drove a portion of the Federal Army back some distant and halted to reform. At Bentonville, Mercer's old brigade had helped the Army of Tennessee to redeem themselves in history. They had fought an army four to five times their size to a standstill.

Wounded: Private Andrew Jackson – Co. G
Private William W. Cook – Co. H

Private William T. Coleman of Company H died at Point Lookout, Maryland.

20 March 1865

Private Gilbert Watson of Company G died in Way Hospital No. 3 at Salisbury, North Carolina.

22 March, 1865

The Army of Tennessee retreats to Smithfield, North Carolina.
Private William Coleman of Co. F died at Point Lookout, Maryland.

31 March, 1865

(Command Structure)
Confederate Army Commander
(General Joseph E. Johnston)
Army of Tennessee Commander
(Lt. General Alexander P. Stewart)
Corps Commander
(Maj. General Benjamin F. Cheatham)
Division Commander
(Brigadier General James A. Smith)
Brigade Commander
(Capt. J. R. Bonner)
54th Georgia Regiment Commander
(Capt. Grigsby E. Thomas Sr.)

10 April, 1865

The Army of Tennessee undergoes a major reorganization. The 54th was reorganized by consolidating the 37th and 54th Georgia with the 4th Battalion Georgia Sharpshooters under the command of Col. Theodore D. Caswell who previously commanded the 4th.

William A. Bowers, Jr.

(Command Structure)
Confederate Army Commander
(General Joseph E. Johnston)
Corps Commander
(Lt. General William J. Hardee)
Division Commander
(Maj. General John C. Brown)
Brigade Commander
(Capt. J. R. Bonner)
54th Georgia Regiment Commander
(Col. Theodore D. Caswell)

12 April, 1865 Salisbury, North Carolina

Several men of the 54th Georgia were captured at Salisbury, North Carolina.

Captured: Private John R. Tripp- Co. C
Private Andrew Coleman - Co. F
Private Robert Lacilson, Jr. -Co. F
Private Valerius A. McGinty - Co. H

16 April, 1865

After marches from Smithfield to Raleigh and Chapel Hill, North Carolina, the 54th was now in the vicinity of Greensboro, North Carolina. Several men of Companies C and F were captured at Salisbury, North Carolina.

Lieutenant William A. Shaw of Company F captured at Ft. Tyler, West Point, Georgia.

19 April, 1865

Private Allen Williams of Company G was paroled at Newton, North Carolina.

20, 21 -22 April, 1865

Several men were captured at Macon, Georgia.
Field and Staff:
Captain Thomas W. Brantley (Adjutant)
Sergeant Major Lawrence E. Burgstiner
Company A:
Corporal J. W. Ross

Privates:
Peter Allen	William Avera	Samuel T. Campbell
William Flowers	Charles Follendore	William James
James L. Joiner	F. M. Lawrence	Joseph Mandetle
John Roberts	John J. Roberts	Henry James Sharpe

The 54th Regiment, Georgia Volunteer Infantry

John T. Stewart   J. D. Tidwell   Moses Tucker

Company B:
Private George W. Hooker

Company C:
Privates:
Simeon Lamb   Simeon Roberts

Company F:
Privates:
Isham Beck   W. J. Doggett   Albert R. Hunt
William F. May Alexander J. Raymur

Company G:
Private Henry Stewart

26 April, 1865
General Joseph E. Johnston surrenders to General Sherman at Greensboro, North Carolina and for the 54th Georgia, the war was over.
Listed are the men who surrendered at Greensboro, North Carolina:

Company A:
Corporals:
A. S. Sallas   G. Clark Smith
Privates:
James D. Dougherty James M. Fountain   J. H. Graddy
Joseph J. Harris   D. B. Hudson   John W. Hudson
James J. Jessup   S. W. Noland   William F. Sloc

Company B:
Lieutenant C. H. White
Privates:
Josiah Boatright   W. H Camel   George Willis Herndo
T. H. Kilgore   G. W. McAbee   S. T. Smith

Company C:
Lieutenant Christian Kuhlman
Sergeants:
W. R. Durden   Thomas W. Goodwin
Privates:
Corsea Antonia   Augustus H. K. Dunn L. B. Dye
W. R. Ennis   D. M. Farmer   William Thomas Griffin
Rufus T. Knight   Thomas S. Moore   Seaborn Oglesby, Sr.
Peter Parish   Thomas H. Walden   Jesse A. Wiggins

163

William A. Bowers, Jr.

Henry T. Downs

Company D:
Captain H. M. Talley

Sergeants:
John R. Barefield	David L. Bragg	George R. Robertson

Corporals:
John W. Smith	W. G. Solomon

Privates:
Eldridge G. Allmond	Elzie Allmond	J. O. Andrews
J. J. Barron	John A. Baughman	H. N. Britt
James J. Britt	John J. Britt	L. H. Britt
T. C. Clifton	Enos B. Dickey	Samuel Dowse
G. W. Dyal	P. H. Ferrell	William S. Gavin
William B. Joyner	Henry D. Lewis	John McCormick
John Isaac Peeler	B. F. Powell	Anderson L. Sammons
L. D. Sheppard	Henry E. Simmons	A. C. Simpson
A. E. Simpson	A. S. Simpson	James T. Simpson
John F. Simpson	William Henry Simpson	C. A. Sorea
J. D. Underwood	William J. Waters	Thomas C. Whitehurst

Company E:
Privates:
T. P. Bramblett	John Culpepper	J. M. Davis
William B. Easters	Samuel Guthrie	William H. Holstead
C. P. Stanley	James H. Stephens	

Company F:
Captains:
John W. Anderson	Thomas E. Grigsby, Sr.

Lieutenants:
Robert M. Butler	Charles C. Hunter

Sergeants:
John J. Jones	William H. McDonald

Corporals:
George W. Langford	Thomas J. Stripling

Privates:
Elias Alverson	J. O. Andrews	A Needham Barefield
John W. Blasingame	Thomas A. Brewer	Williamson T. Brewer
James P. Brooks	Alex J. Brown	Jesse Carr
Francis M. Crosby	John E. Davidson	A. J. Dawkins
Thomas J. Dawkins	Tomas J. Downs	George L. Grandberry
H. Hagin	James B. Hammock	James Andrew Hinley
William A. Lawes	William A. Laws	La Fayette Martin

The 54th Regiment, Georgia Volunteer Infantry

John McHugh   Angus P. Moore   E. C. Nunn
James B. Ogletree Samuel J. Smith   George J. Tarvin
La Fayette Thomas

Company G:
Captain John J. Lynn
Sergeant R. P. Hammond
Corporal James Ross Webb
Privates:
Andrew Harper   Edward S. Holloway   Francis L. Hudgens
Andrew Jackson   George W. Langford   James M. McElroy
Jno M. McElroy   Erasmus M. Murphey   Abner Slaughter
Warren A. Ware   George S. Watson

Company H:
Captain Charles R. Russell
Lieutenants:
Luther M. Dowdell Aaron Land
Sergeants:
M. L. Brawner   A. Judson Ely   William J. Hart
Corporals:
William Hancock A. J. Hubbard   Henry A. J. Kennon
William Matthew Rodgers   Ephraim S. Sallas
John J. Walker
Privates:
William Allgood   James P. Arant   Henry H. Blackman
Cornelius J. Boles James E. Bonhart   Samuel S. Cook
Thomas Dunaway William Dunaway   George W. Ely
Raymond R. Hutchison   Daniel Isom
D. G. Kilcrease
John Land   W. Pierce Langford   M. A. Marshall
William B. Moore A. J. Morgan   James Marcus Norris
Joseph Marshall Norris   William P. Phillips
C. L. Raiford
Adam C. Rodgers Samuel C. Rodgers   George M. Stripling
William M. Tarvin William Thomas   William H. H. Thomas

Company I:
Sergeant Theodore Jasper Wilkins
Corporal David Benjamin Arnsdorff
Privates:
J. C. Arnsdorff   George Washington Fetzer   John H. Grady
Robert Habersham Guyton   James Jeremiah Heidt
S. M. Scarborough Lacy W. Simmons   David Speir

William S. Speir   George W. Zeigler

Company K:
Privates:
R. C. Anderson   Demetrius Arnett   Nathaniel J..Green
John Landers   James Moss   John Wheatley
William Wilson

30 April 1865
John Allen of Company A captured at Macon Georgia.
Peter Allen of Company A captured at Macon Georgia.

2 May, 1865
The Confederate army dispersed at Greensboro.

(Command Structure)
Confederate Army Commander
(General Joseph E. Johnston)
Corp Commander
(Lt. General William J. Hardee)
Division Commander
(Maj. General John C. Brown)
Brigade Commander
(Capt. J. R. Bonner)
54th Georgia Regiment Commander
(Col. Theodore D. Caswell)

4 May, 1865
Several men of Company E surrendered at Augusta.

7 May, 1865
William C. Lindsay of Company E died of illness.

10 May, 1865
The following surrendered under Major General Sam Jones Commanding the Army of Florida to Brigadier General E. M. McCook commanding United States Forces at Tallahassee, Florida:

Company A:
Private R. L. Taylor
Company B:
Sergeant William R. Carter, Sr.
Corporals:
Phillip Marion Carter   Stephen Floyd
Privates:
James H. Anderson   John H. Anderson   George M. Carter
William R. Carter, Jr.   Joseph Deen   George Moody
Isaac I. Moody   Jacob H. Moody   George W. Nunez

The 54th Regiment, Georgia Volunteer Infantry

Silas O'Quinn, Sr. Isham Ogden John R. Ogden
Moses L. Overstreet Thomas Simmons Seaborn Smith
William Thornton Joseph C. Tillman

Company D:
Private H. S. Burke

Company E:
Sergeant Stephen Willis Avera
Corporals:
Baton May Jeremiah May L. G. Young
Privates:
Thomas A. Baker Zachariah Baker James Braden
John Crosby Marshall Green Jonathan N. Knig
Thomas L. Lamb John G. Lewis John G. Luke
William H. Luke Daniel J. McCranie William E. Morris, Jr.
David S. Robinson Samuel G. Sanders John C. Sirmon
Ira J. Sutton Jeptha N. Young
Company F:
Privates:
Allen Sapp Isham Tyre Moses/Joshua Westberry

Company G:
Sergeant John M. Rhodes
Private M. F. Harrell

Company H;
Private George Washington Williams

Company I:
Private David M. McCray

Company K:
Lieutenant Silas Thornton
Sergeants:
Perry McCullar G. M. T. Overstreet
Corporals:
David Griffis J. G. Griffis D. R. Johnson
Hampton Knight Nathaniel Stafford Knight
Timothy Williams
Privates:
Jesse Columbus Altman Hiram Bennett sham A. Bennett
Richard Bennett, Jr. Salathiel E. Bennett Clement C. Byrd
Elijah Griffis S. H. Groves James Hampton Johnson
James Knight Berry A. Leggett Alfred Lightsey

William A. Bowers, Jr.

John S. Massey	M. Calvin McCullar	Abraham E. Patterson
Solomon R. Patterson	Henry Prescott	John Henry Sapp
William W. Sapp	James M. Smith	Lewis Thomas
G. W. Touchtone	Robert Williams	

Soldiers with no specific Company listed:
Privates:

A. M. Culler	W. C. Duller	I. T. Henderson
R. M. Hensel	A. Jackson	James B. Kinert
I. Milton	S. R. Sattean	J. B. Thomas
S. Thompson	S. Tyson	W. R. Woods

12 May, 1865
Jeremiah B. Weaver of Company E died at Camp Chase, Ohio prison.

15 May, 1865
Soldiers of the 54th Regiment, Georgia Infantry who surrendered at Augusta, Georgia:
Private Samuel C. M. M. Dickey of Company D

18 May, 1865
Soldiers of the 54th Regiment, Georgia Infantry who surrendered at Augusta, Georgia:
Private J. E. Simmons of Company I
Private George W. Brownell of Company F

19 May, 1865
Soldiers of the 54th Regiment, Georgia Infantry who surrendered at Augusta, Georgia:
Captain Hartford Henry Way (Adjutant)
Private R. M. Hall Company D

24 May, 1865
Soldiers of the 54th Regiment, Georgia Infantry who surrendered at Augusta, Georgia:
Company C:
Privates:

E. P. Bedenfield	William R. Johnson	B. S. Oglesby
John K. Wiggins		

Company D:
Private Charles Thomas Jefferson Claxton
Company K:
Private Zachariah D. Bowen

26 May, 1865
Soldiers of the 54th Regiment, Georgia Infantry who surrendered at Augusta, Georgia:
Company C:
Privates:

John Boatright	Benjamin W. Johnson	James S Stephens

Company D:
Captain Joseph Miller
Lieutenant John Milo Miller, Jr.

27 May, 1865
Soldiers of the 54th Regiment, Georgia Infantry who surrendered at Augusta, Georgia:
Company C:
Corporal Houston Henry Hall
Privates:
Andrew Jackson Rich   Stephen E. Rich

30 May, 1865
Soldiers of the 54th Regiment, Georgia Infantry who surrendered at Augusta, Georgia:
Company C:
Privates:
E. R. Lamb   J. W. Oglesby

Company D:
Private William Claxton

William A. Bowers, Jr.

Charlton Hines Way

Charlton H. Way was born October 5, 1834, in Fairborn, Liberty County, Georgia. He was the son of William James Way and Mary Elizabeth Hanford. In 1841 his parents moved to Savannah, Georgia. He attended Georgia Military Institute in Marietta, Georgia, graduating with first honors in 1855. He read the law and was a student in the office of the Hon. John E. Ward, who was formerly Minister to China. He later became a commission merchant in Savannah, Georgia. He was married first to Laura Seaton, and in 1859, his second marriage was in Milledgeville, Georgia, to Francis M. Williams who was considered one of the reigning belles of Georgia.

When the War for Southern Independence broke out he volunteered for service. July 18, 1861, he was elected captain of Way's Independent Company, Georgia Infantry (Forest City Rangers). He became assistant adjutant for the Georgia State Troops. On November 1, 1861, he mustered out. May 13, 1862, he was elected colonel of the newly formed 54th Regiment, Georgia Volunteer Infantry at Guyton, Georgia. He served throughout the war in the service of the Confederate States Army and surrendered with the Army of Tennessee on April 26, 1865, in Greensboro, North Carolina.

After the war, having lost his fortune, he became a Cotton Broker and a Real Estate Developer in Savannah, Georgia. He was elected as Commissioner to the International Exposition at Paris, France, in 1867 and in 1878. Later he served his country as United States Counsel General to St. Petersburg, Russia, under President Cleveland in 1887.

His business interests made it necessary for him to spend the greater part of his last twenty years in Europe. There he amassed a large circle of friends in public and private life in England and on the European Continent. Those friends were delighted by the news of his appointment. He was conservative in politics. He had accepted the results of the war and the new conditions in the South.

Way was a strong supporter of Thomas F. Bayard, who had been a strong supporter of the South during reconstruction, for the presidency, but when Way saw the futility in securing Bayard's nomination he gave his support to and devoted all his energies for the election of Grover Cleveland, who won the nomination and presidency.

Way was considered a gentleman of an excellent education. He was brilliant and witty and possessed superb conversational powers.

Way and his family lived in a fine mansion on the Vernon River, just below Savannah, Georgia, where he and his wife entertained their friends with true Southern hospitality.

He died of stomach problems in Savannah, Chatham County, Georgia, July 1, 1901, at the age of 66 years. He is buried in Lot # 753 in North Laurel Grove Cemetery at Savannah, Chatham County, Georgia. His wife died in 1902 and is buried beside her husband.

William A. Bowers, Jr.

Morgan Rawls

Morgan Rawls was born in Rufus, Bulloch County, Georgia, June 29, 1829. He moved to Guyton, Effingham County, Georgia, at an early age. He was educated in the local schools and was training to become a farmer. He married Salina V. Elkins on October 22, 1851, in Effingham County, Georgia. He and his new family moved to Guyton, Georgia, in 1856. He ran as a candidate to the 1860 convention on the Union Party Platform and lost.

With the outbreak of the War for Southern Independence he joined the Confederate States Army and was elected captain of Company C of the 1st Brigade, Georgia State Troops, the Georgia Rangers, on September 18, 1861. The company was sent from Guyton, Georgia, to #7 on the Gould Railroad where they were formed and drilled. March 18, 1862, he was mustered out when his tour of enlistment was up. He was elected captain of Company I, 54th Regiment, Georgia Volunteer Infantry, at Guyton, Georgia.

On May 16, 1862, he was elected lieutenant colonel of the 54th Regiment, Georgia Volunteer Infantry when it was formed at Guyton, Georgia. He was wounded in the Battle of Atlanta on July 22, 1864, and while being carried to the field hospital a cannonball passed through the blanket he was being transported in without even causing him a scratch. He returned to his unit and was eventually promoted to colonel in the 54th Regiment of the Georgia Volunteer Infantry.

After the war, Rawls was a delegate to the State Reconstruction Convention in 1865. He also served multiple terms in the Georgia House of Representatives (1863–1865, 1868–1872, 1886–1889 and 1896–1904). In 1872, Rawls was elected as a Democrat to represent Georgia's 1st Congressional District in the U.S. House of Representatives during the 43rd Congress; however, he only served from March 4, 1873, until March 24, 1874. Republican Andrew Sloan was successful in contesting Rawls's election and served the remainder of the term in the 43rd Congress.

Rawls served in the office of the Clerk of the United States House of Representatives from 1874 to 1882 and 1891 to 1895. His wife, Salina, died in 1891. He died in Guyton, Georgia, on October 18, 1906, and was buried beside his wife in Guyton Cemetery located at Guyton, Effingham County, Georgia.

General Hugh Weedon Mercer

Hugh Weedon Mercer was born in Fredericksburg, Virginia, on November 27, 1808. His grandfather and namesake, Hugh Mercer, of Pennsylvania had been a general under George Washington during the American Revolution. He graduated 3rd of 33 from the United States Military Academy at West Point in 1828. He served as a 2nd lieutenant in the US Artillery, spending much of his service time in Georgia. He was given an assignment as an aide to Lieutenant General Winfield Scott in 1862, as which he served until 1834. He left the army and married Mary S. Anderson, a lady from Savannah, Georgia. He resigned his commission in 1835 and settled in Savannah. He was also an artillery officer in the local militia.

From 1841 to 1861 he was a cashier at Planters Bank in Savannah, Georgia. He started building the Italianate-style Mercer House. However, construction was interrupted by the War for Southern Independence. As a side note, no Mercer ever lived there.

In 1861, he enlisted in the Confederate Army and was commissioned as colonel of the 1st Georgia Infantry. He was promoted to brigadier general by the end of October. In August of 1862, he played a major role in impressing the first group of slaves and free blacks into service for the Confederacy. By November, however, he lost his authority to impress workers and depended on Governor Joseph E. Brown and local sheriffs to provide slaves to join the Confederate effort. He served in several capacities in the Army of South Carolina, Georgia and Florida while stationed at Savannah and Charleston.

At the beginning of the Atlanta Campaign, he left Savannah and was placed in command of a brigade consisting of the 54th Regiment Georgia Infantry, the 57th Regiment Georgia Infantry and the 63rd Regiment Georgia Infantry, which became known as Mercer's Brigade. The brigade was joined by the 1st Georgia Regiment Infantry and was engaged as the largest brigade in the then Army of Tennessee under General Joseph E. Johnston. They were in battles at Rocky Face, Dug Gap, Dalton, Resaca, Marietta, Golgotha, Big Shanty, New Hope Church and Kennesaw Mountain (where his son was wounded). His brigade then fought under General John Bell Hood at

Peachtree Creek, Atlanta, Jonesboro and Lovejoy Station. When General William H. T. Walker was killed by a mini ball in the Battle of Atlanta on July 22, 1864, command of his division devolved to General Mercer. During the Battle of Atlanta and Jonesboro he became ill and at the beginning of the campaign in Tennessee, Mercer was relieved of command and sent to Savannah, serving under Lieutenant General William J. Hardee. He commanded the 10th Battalion, Georgia Infantry, which was charged with the defense of the Savannah area. When General Hardee retreated in December of 1864, Mercer left the city, returning after the fighting ended.

The 54th Regiment, Georgia Volunteer Infantry

Confederate Veteran May 1903

INQUIRIES.
W. A. O'Neal, Commerce, Tex.

I want to correspond with my comrades who fought and suffered with me in the sixties, while contending for the principles that we then knew were right. We who still live continue to know that those principles are immortal. Though they went down in defeat, they still live and manifest themselves in many ways. I want to meet surviving members of my old company at New Orleans. Our regiment, the Fifty Fourth Georgia Infantry, fought with that grand and knightly soldier, Joseph E. Johnston, and the gallant and daring John B. Hood, from Chattanooga, Tenn., up to the last day at Greensboro, N. C., where the bitter cup was passed and the fight was ended and our faces were again turned homeward. Our Capt. N. B. Roberts and Lieut. G. E. Thomas were from Columbus, Ga., and better soldiers or braver men never lived. Lieut. Tom Granbery was idolized by the entire company. The noble and brave Lieut. Sam McLeary fell at my side on July 18, 1864, at Kennesaw Mountain, with a bullet through his brain. I sent his body to his wife in Harris County, Ga. I would be glad to see her if she still lives, and also the faithful Negro servant, Lairy, who accompanied the body home. Also First Sergts. R. P. ("Pack") Hammond and J. J. Jones, who were wounded by my side at Lovejoy Station, Ga.; Sergt. S. B. Harned, who was a native of the North, but as true to the South as any of us, and Corporals Stribling, Slaughter, Webb, and the many brave, daring private soldiers who stood shoulder to shoulder with me in all those trying scenes. Such men as A. D. Aron, Jesse Bryan, J. A. Clegg, the Dawkins boys, Jim Ellison, Jim Hammock, W. A. Laws, John Mulkey, the Granbery and McDonald boys. My tent and blanket mates were J. B. Ogletree and W. S. Wade. God bless them if they still live, for their reward is great! I also recall Corp. Parker, George Tarvin, George Taylor, John Thornton, the Williams boys, whose memory is as fresh to me as if it were yesterday. Let those who still live whose names I have written meet me at New Orleans at Georgia headquarters, and let every one wear the letter of his company and number of his regiment on his hat or breast, so we may know each other and have a hallowed reunion. I would be very glad to see Col. Charlton H. Way or Lieut. Col. Morgan Rauls. Our adjutant, T. M. Brantley, was a handsome officer, and so was Capt. George W. Moody, who commanded Company B, and who greatly resembled the sainted Bishop and General Leonidas Polk. Let us meet and greet each other once more (Veteran 1903).

W. A. O'Neal

Confederate Veteran March-April 1989
BLOODY FOOTPRINTS IN THE SNOW
MERCER'S BRIGADE
April 28, 1864- April 26, 1865
By Robert L. Brawner

On April 23, 1864 the life of coastal watch duty was suddenly broken when Brigadier General Hugh W. Mercer received orders from the Confederate high command to take three regiments of infantry from Savannah, Georgia and join the Army of Tennessee. These same orders called for the transfer of a fourth Regiment, the 63rd Georgia from Savannah to General A. R. Wright's Brigade then seeing action in the Army of Northern Virginia. At the last moment, at the request of General Mercer, the orders for the 63rd were changed and four regiments made the long trip by rail to Dalton, Georgia on April 28. Mercer's Brigade had been formed.

The infantry regiments comprising the brigade were the 1st Volunteer, 54th, 57th and 63rd Georgia Volunteer Infantry Regiments. The 1st Georgia was composed of men from Chatham County and was commanded by Colonel Charles H. Olmstead. The 54th Georgia was made up of soldiers from Chatham, Appling, Bibb, Emmanuel, Screven, Berrien, Muskogee and Effingham Counties and was under the command of Colonel Charlton H. Way. The 57th Georgia, under Colonel William Barkuloo, was comprised of warriors from Thomas, Laurens, Wilkerson, Houston, Crawford, Washington and Baldwin Counties. The 63rd Georgia was composed of men from Richmond, Chatham, Laurens, Spalding, Jefferson, Bartow and miscellaneous Georgia counties and was led by Colonel George Gordon. Company names like "City Light Guards", "Coast Rifles," "German Volunteers," "Savannah Cadets," "Russell Guards," "Smith Guards," "Bragg Rifles," "Phoenix Rifleman," "Oconee Grays" and "Oglethorpe Light Infantry" gave a sporting character to this collection of farmers, merchants and professional men.

All of the four regiments had seen combat. The 1st and 54th Georgia had seen action at Battery Wagner on Morris Island, South Carolina. The 57th Georgia had fought and surrendered at Vicksburg and was paroled and parts of the 63rd Georgia had fought in Virginia early in the war. All of the regiments had been on coastal guard duty and had fought mosquitoes, sand gnats and an occasional Yankee patrol from nearby Fort Pulaski. The life of coastal duty was usually easy but the drilling was long and General Mercer had the men of his command, about 1,400 effectives, ready for action.

Brigadier General Hugh Weeden Mercer was born at Fredericksburg, Virginia on November 27, 1808, the grandson of Revolutionary War General

Hugh Mercer. He attended West Point and graduated in 1828, 3rd in his class. Mercer was stationed in Savannah for two years during his tours of duty and here he met and married a local girl. He resigned his commission in 1841 and worked as a cashier for the Planter's Bank in Savannah until the start of the war. Mercer entered service in the Confederate forces as colonel of the 1st Georgia Volunteer Infantry Regiment, but in October 1861 he was promoted to brigadier general and was placed in command of the First Military District of South Carolina. By June of 1862 Mercer was placed in command of the defenses of Savannah and the District of Georgia. In April 1864, he was put in command of the brigade and served until the end of the Atlanta campaign when, on July 27, General Braxton Bragg wrote President Jefferson Davis that "Brigadier General Mercer is too old and infirm for the active duties of the campaign; all his commanders considered him in the way. At the same time they agree with me in an indisposition to mortify the valiant and worthy old soldier by bringing him before a board. I accordingly relieved him and sent him home..." Mercer returned to Savannah with General Hardee. He remained in service and was captured on April 20, 1865 and paroled in Macon, Georgia on May 13, 1865. After the war, his health broken, Mercer lived in Savannah and Baltimore, Maryland, moved to Baden-Baden, Germany for health reasons and died there on June 9, 1877.

The brigade reached Dalton on April 30 and by May 4 was attached to General William H. T. Walker's Division of Hardee's Corps located 3 miles east of Dalton. It was the largest brigade in the Army. At Dalton the brigade was given the nickname "New Issue" because its arrival coincided with a new issue of Confederate money that was almost worthless. The men fought so well in their first engagement that this name was soon dropped. They were also called "Silver Fork Brigade" but this was also soon dropped. Walker's was a reserve division, it had no fixed place in the line of battle but was moved from point to point as required. The brigade took an advanced position on Rocky Face Ridge and first sighted the enemy on May 9 when its pickets were driven in and the trenches were shelled resulting in a few casualties. May 10 to 13 was spent marching and back and forth from Dalton to Resaca. The Battle of Resaca erupted on May 14 and reports of two Union divisions attempted crossing the Oostanaula River near Lay's Ferry prompted General Johnston to send Walker's Division to drive the enemy back. The Yankees under Brigadier General Thomas Sweeney had, to the relief of all concerned, pulled back but soon Federal artillery began shelling the brigade's position. On May 15, Yankee troops again crossed the river. They repulsed an attack by parts of Walker's Division, Mercer's Brigade being the only part of the attack to drive back the enemy. The evening of May 15 saw orders to retreat and the army marched to Calhoun, Georgia. During the march the brigade was employed in patrolling the Western and Atlantic Railroad along with the brigades of Jackson, Stevens and Gist.

From May 16 til June 26 the brigade's duty consisted of skirmishing, falling back with the army, building breastworks and picket duty. On May 19 at Cassville, Georgia the brigade was positioned in front of the division and the 63rd Georgia was placed in advance of the brigade in support of the skirmish line. These skirmishers were under the command of Major J. V. H. Allen. In the heat of the battle, the 63rd was nearly surrounded by the enemy but retreated in time to rejoin the main force. There was skirmishing near Dallas, Georgia on May 28 and at Gilgal Church on June 15 and 16 the brigade skirmished with General Butterfield's Division of the 20th Corps. The brigade near Gilgal Church, through an oversight, was almost cut off from the division and captured. While making their escape, the 1st Volunteers suffered many casualties. On the 18th of June there was heavy skirmishing and six companies of the 63rd Georgia retook a number of rifle pits and held them all day against artillery and infantry fire while suffering considerable loss. The Battle of Kennesaw Mountain began on June 27.

On June 28, Walker's troops were on the top of Little Kennesaw Mountain and were attacked by units of McPherson's troops under Colonel Dan McCook. All of the rifle-pits in the front of the brigade, then held by soldiers from the 63rd Georgia, were taken by the rapid advance of the Yankee line of battle and some of the men were bayoneted. This lost ground was "regained by a gallant counterattack" and the battle moved away. The 63rd Georgia and the brigade were complemented by General Walker on the following day for their parts in the battle.

From June 28 to July 4, all was quite around the brigade and on July 5 the order for retreat was again received. The men marched to a position near Smyrna Church a few miles north of the Chattahoochee River. General Mercer became ill during this encampment and Colonel Olmstead assumed command of the brigade. While at Smyrna Church, the brigade was sent to fortify a hill near camp but was pushed back with casualties by artillery and skirmishing. The army crossed the Chattahoochee River on July 10 and Mercer's Brigade was left guarding points near the river by General Walker. Both armies rested across from each other on the banks of this river. Colonel Olmstead tells of soldiers meeting nightly in the middle of the water to exchange tobacco and sugar. He also relates of smelling the aroma of fresh coffee from the enemy side and how his men wished they could cross the river and raid the enemy camp. Then came the terrible and bloody battles for Atlanta.

On July 17, General John B. Hood replaced General Johnston as commander of the Army of Tennessee and Southern forces that had been on the defensive since the first part of May now took the offense. Mercer's Brigade was in the thick of this fighting. On July 20 during the Battle of Peachtree

Creek, Walker's Division attacked the II Army Corps under Brigadier General John Newton on the left front. The brigade never really got into the main action of this assault because they had to march over bad ground and through impenetrable thickets of briars. They spent most of their time skirmishing with the enemy and during one hot session relieved Lowery's Brigade. The morning of July 22 dawned hot and bright and Walker's Division was up early marching toward the enemy. Bad terrain again made travel almost impossible but progress was being made when the division came upon Leggett's Hill. Here, General Walker was killed by a Union picket before any action was taken. "A Federal division was hotfooting it along and reached a site at exactly the same time as Confederate General Bate and Major General Hugh Mercer (who immediately had succeeded the dead General Walker) dashed forward to lay into Blair's Federals on Leggett's Hill. It set off the first clash of the actual Battle of Atlanta; and for more than two hours a Federal battery poured shells and solid shot into Bates' and Mercer's weary troops." When Mercer took over the division, Lt. Colonel Rawls of the 54th Georgia assumed command of the brigade. Rawls was wounded and Colonel Guyton of the 57th Georgia took command until the battle was over.

There were three lines of battle of Federal infantry on Leggett's Hill supported by two batteries. Mercer's Brigade begins the battle on the right of Fair Ground Road in the rear of the brigades of Gist and Stevens. The men were ordered to advance across a small valley and attack the enemy on the crest of the hill. They did this and carried two of the enemy lines but were stopped by the third line. The two battle lines were a mere 30 yards apart and stood firing at each other. Another advance was ordered by Colonel Guyton but, owing to heavy fire from the enemy, exhaustion and disorganization of the troops and officers, an advance was not made. The brigade held its position until 3 a.m. on the 23rd, then was withdrawn. On July 23, at 5 a.m., the brigade moved to the right of Major General Patrick Cleburne's division and entrenched. It was a bloody two days as 30 were killed, 129 wounded and 20 were missing.

July 24 was a busy day for the division and the brigade. Walker's division was broken up and scattered throughout the corps. General Mercer was relieved of command and returned to the coast. The unit was transferred to Cleburne's Division and placed under the command of Brigadier General J. Argyle Smith. Smith was at the time on furlough recovering from wounds and Colonel Olmstead was placed in charge. While all of these moves were happening the brigade spent its time strengthening their position and walking picket duty. Little was done from July 24 until the end of August. The brigade spent its days on the left of the army guarding the railroad between Atlanta and Macon and was in some hot picket duty in the trenches around Atlanta.

On August 29, the brigade woke to find that "the enemy had disappeared entirely from our front". August 30 and 31 were spent marching past East Point, Georgia and toward Jonesborough, 20 miles south of Atlanta. The village was reached in the early morning hours of the 31st. The brigade was placed in line of battle with Lowery's Brigade on the left and Finley's Brigade of Brown's Division on the right. The Federal position on the Flint River was immediately attacked. "Between 3 and 4 o'clock on the afternoon of the 31st, the order to advance was given and the line pressed forward taking the direction from the left. At first the advance was slow and steady, but on coming insight of the first position of the enemy, the men could not be restrained and rushed on at the double quick. Two lines were carried and the enemy retreated across the Flint."

On the morning of September 1, the brigade relieved part of General Stevenson's Division and a new line of battle was formed. Sharpshooters were an annoyance during the morning and in the afternoon a brisk skirmish started up but no other action was taken. The Battle of Jonesborough was over. The fighting was in vain, however, because on this day Hood evacuated Atlanta. It had been a bloody struggle as the brigade reported casualties from July 20 to September 1 of 46 killed, 200 wounded and 59 missing.

The armies spent the first part of September catching their breaths and renewing much needed supplies. There had been continuous fighting since May 9 and the victorious Federals and demoralized Confederates needed a break from the action. The brigade marched from the battle at the Flint River to Lovejoy Station south of Jonesborough to guard the Macon and Western Railroad. On September 8, the Yankees abandoned their front at this town and the brigade moved to a site one mile above Jonesborough where they remained for 10 days. The army left Jonesborough and marched through Fairburn and by September 19 camped at Palmetto, Georgia for 10 days. On September 25 General Smith assumed command of the brigade and on the 26th the army was reviewed by President Davis. After the ceremonies, members of the brigade were told by General Cleburne to "go to the river and wash themselves." September 29 saw the beginning of the march toward the north and by October 13 the Army of Tennessee and Smith's (formerly Mercer's) Brigade were in the vicinity of Dalton again. Their time in this area was spent tearing up tracks of the Western and Atlantic Railroad in an attempt to disrupt Federal supply lines. By October 26 the army had marched through Decatur and Gadson, Alabama and camped at Tuscambia. Hood's strike into Tennessee was poised to begin and the army was in for terrible times. Mercer's Brigade would be no exception.

On November 12, General Hood and the "hard luck Army of Tennessee" crossed the Tennessee River on their way north. This was the start of a disastrous and bloody campaign that would break the spirit of the army at the horrible "victory" at Franklin and then break its back at Nashville. After this action which began with "one fourth of the effective infantry without shoes and most without proper winter clothes," the army would only be a shadow of itself and would cease to be an effective force.

When the army crossed the river Mercer's (or Smith's) Brigade was detached on November 19 was sent to Cheatham's Ferry, 12 miles away, to aid a supply wagon train in its attempt across the river. From November 21 to the 27 the brigade worked in freezing weather and occasional snowstorms at the ferry. The train was carrying salt and as Sergeant Walter Clark of the 63rd Georgia said "salt saved our bacon." The brigade left the train on November 28 and did not reach the Franklin battlefield until November 30, well after the battle had ended. In this battle General Cleburne was killed and his division was decimated, a fate which would have surely befallen the brigade. With Cleburne's death, General Smith was put in charge of the division and Colonel Olmstead again commanded the brigade. On December 5, after six days of marching, the brigade arrived at Nashville, Tennessee and rejoined the division. December 6 and 7 were spent on picket and breastwork duty and the men were in line of battle on the right flank of the army. Then luck intervened again.

Colonel J. B. Palmer, who replaced the ailing General Smith at Nashville, writes "On the 7th (December) my brigade, commanded by Colonel Olmstead, of the 1st Georgia Regiment, was again detached and ordered to report to Major-General Forrest, who was operating near Murfreesboro." Forrest writes "On the 9th General Hood sent to my support Smith's brigade, commanded by Colonel Olmstead." The brigade reached Forrest on December 9 and were ordered to "strongly fortify themselves on Stewart's Creek, or at La Vergne, as General Forrest might deem it best, to constitute a force in observation of the enemy." From December 9 to the 15th the brigade spent their time in the sleet and snow destroying miles of railroad track between Nashville and Murfreesboro. The 15th saw orders from Forrest for the brigades under Olmstead and Palmer to cross Stone's River and march east from Murfreesboro to capture a Federal forage train. The Battle of Nashville began this day and on the 16th General Forrest received word from Hood concerning the defeat of the army and was ordered to rejoin the main force. Forrest and his command immediately turned and headed for Columbia, Tennessee 60 miles away.

It was a brutal march. The men had nothing to eat save a few ears of corn each. Their clothing was in rags and many had no shoes. The weather was extremely cold, the rain mixed with sleet turned the roads into frozen mud pits. Despite these adverse conditions the brigade made 35 miles in a 21 hour march, rested for five hours and marched the remaining 25 miles to Colombia arriving late on the 18th December.

At Columbia, the brigade was ordered to report to Major-General E. C. Walthall who, along with Forrest, was assigned to form a rear guard to protect the retreating army. While this guard was being formed the brigade spent its time manning snow filled trenches and keeping the enemy in check. General Walthall in his report of January 14, 1865 writes "he (the commanding general) directed me with a special command to be organized for the purpose, to report to Major-General Forrest to aid in covering the retreat of the army, then in motion toward Pulaski (Tenn.) his purpose being to cross the Tennessee River near Bainbridge, if practicable. This organization was made up of the following brigades viz: Brig. Gen. W. S. Featherston's; Col. J. B. Palmer's; Strahl's brigade commanded by Col. C. W. Heiskell; Smith's brigade, commanded by Col. Olmstead of Georgia; Maney's commanded by Col. H. R. Field; with three of my own command, namely Brig. Gen. D. H. Reynolds'; Ector's, commanded by Col. D. Coleman; and Quarles, commanded by Brig. Gen. George D. Johnston." Walthall also writes in his report of January 3, 1865 "These brigades were all greatly reduced in numbers, and deeming it expedient to consolidate them, that the command might be more wieldy and compact, I organized them as thus: Palmer's and Smith's brigades, under Col. Palmer; Maney's and Strahl's under Col. Field; Reynolds' and Ector's under Brigadier-General Reynolds; and Featherston's and Quarles', under Brigadier-General Featherston. In all, Forrest and Walthall commanded 1,900 infantry, 3,000 cavalry and officers and eight pieces of artillery. Smith's Brigade totaled 319 effectives of a total of 463 present. With this small band of poorly fed and badly clad warriors the commanders were expected to protect the main Army from approximately 10,000 cavalry under General Wilson. This they did!

On December 22, the rear guard began a slow retreat toward Pulaski skirmishing continually with the enemy. The country was covered with sleet and snow and the temperature was bitter. Many men were barefooted, clad in clothing that was mostly cotton and "not one in a hundred had an overcoat." Colonel Olmstead writes of seeing "prints of bloody feet in the snow" and relates the story of a cavalryman stopping to give a foot soldier his boots with the remark "you need these more than I do." Conditions worsened to the point that Forrest ordered some of the wagons to be emptied. The men would then ride in them until the enemy appeared, then they would jump out, form a line of battle, skirmish and when the enemy pulled back they would jump back in the wagons and continue the retreat.

On December 24, the guards arrived at Richland Creek, seven miles from Pulaski and were then ordered to man earthworks near the town. Christmas morning found the brigade passing through Pulaski and on the road to Bainbridge. The Federals began to press the unit and Forrest stopped the guard and prepared for battle. Walthall writes "it was determined to turn upon him (Federals) and a line was selected on Anthony's Hill, about seven miles from Pulaski. Here Featherston's and Palmer's commands, with a brigade of cavalry on either flank, were put in ambush to await the enemy's approach. When the attacking force neared the troops laying in wait, the latter delivered a destructive fire, and a section of artillery belonging to the cavalry, concealed nearby, opened upon it with considerable effect. The enemy retreated in disorder and my command, by prompt pursuit, captured a number of prisoners and horses and one piece of artillery." On the following day, the 26th, the rear guard was attacked again and repulsed the enemy but the brigade saw no action and did not meet the enemy again as the unit retired to Sugar Creek.

By the end of the December 27, the rear guard had marched to the Tennessee River and was arranged in a line of breast works, but no contact had yet been made with the Federals. On December 28, the Army of Tennessee having already crossed the river to safety, the now immortal rear guard crossed, Smith's brigade being the next to last command to do so. The brigade then marched to Corinth and then Tupelo, Mississippi where it went into winter camp on January 13. Hood's Tennessee campaign had ended in disaster, but the brigade had done its part in saving the army. During this short campaign the brigade had casualties of one kill, two wounded and 70 missing.

The weary soldiers would only be able to rest for two weeks as orders came transferring the entire army to Smithfield, North Carolina to join the units of Johnston and Hardee in an attempt to halt Sherman's army in its march to join the Army of the Potomac. The brigade traveled by train from Mobile to Montgomery, Alabama on February 1 and then to Columbus, Georgia and by the 6th had reached Macon, Georgia. As the brigade passes through Georgia, many of the men "left the ranks to look after their families and who could blame them for doing so". This trip left the brigade with 300 men.

On March 18, after train rides and marches through Augusta, Georgia, Salisbury and Smithfield, North Carolina, the men were found walking to Bentonville, North Carolina. Here they were assigned to Bate's Corps as Cheatham and the division had not arrived.

At 10 a.m. on March 19, the brigade was in line of battle. Brigadier-General Argyle Smith who commanded Cleburne's old division at the Battle of Bentonville reports "only two of the brigades of the division (Gordon's and my own) were engaged, the other two (Lowery's and Granbury's) being still in the rear. I was placed in position on the right of Clayton's division, Govan's brigade on the left and Smith's on the right. The enemy suddenly appeared on our front pushing his lines up within 30 or 40 paces of my left. He was, however, soon forced to retrace his steps in confusion, leaving a number of his dead and wounded in my possession. My breastwork was soon completed."

"I soon received an order to be in readiness to advance at 12:45 p.m. After advancing about 200 yards, the enemy opened a heavy fire on us from his works about 400 yards in our front. This fire only staggered us for the moment; another moment he was driven in great disorder from his strongly entrenched position. The pursuit was kept up until we had reached a road running parallel with our works and about a mile from them. Here the line was halted to reform." This fighting occurred against units of the Federal 14th and 20th Corps. March 20 and 21 brought heavy skirmishing between the two armies and on March 22 the brigade retreated to Smithfield. At Bentonville, the brigade had helped the Army of Tennessee to redeem themselves in history. They had fought an army four to five times their size to a standstill.

The army was reorganized on April 10 and the much depleted brigade was placed in the division of Major-General John C. Brown. It was consolidated into three regiments: the 1st Florida (consolidated 1st, 3rd, 4th, 6th and 7th infantry and 1st Cavalry) under Lt. Colonel Elisha Mashburn, the 1st Georgia (consolidated 1st, 57th and 63rd Georgia Infantry) commanded by Colonel Charles Olmstead and the 54th Georgia (consolidated 37th and 54th Georgia and 4th Battalion Georgia Sharpshooters) under Colonel Theodore D. Caswell. Before the battle of Bentonville, Colonel Olmstead was sent to collect the men who had left the ranks on the trip through Georgia and the 500 soldiers he returned with brought the brigade's effectives to approximately 800. A march southward through Raleigh and Chapel Hill, North Carolina brought the brigade to the vicinity of Greensboro on April 16. Ten days later on April 26, General Joseph Johnston surrendered his command to General Sherman and for the brigade the war was over. Defeated but standing straight and tall, bloody but still full of fight, they had done their duty. It was time to start the long walk home.

This article is dedicated to the memory of Sergeant M. L. Brawner of Company "H" of the 54th Georgia Infantry Regiment.

General William Booth Taliaferro

William Booth Taliaferro was born in Gloucester County, Virginia, to a prominent family of English-Italian origin who settled in Virginia in the 1600s. He was the nephew of James A. Seddon, who would become Secretary of War for the Confederate States of America under Jefferson Davis. Taliaferro attended Harvard University and William and Mary College, graduating from the latter in 1841.

William Taliaferro joined the United States Army during the Mexican-American War, fighting as a captain in the 11th and later as a major in the 9th United States Infantry regiments.

After the war, Taliaferro's interest in state politics led him to seek office and be elected. He served as a member of the Virginia House of Delegates and was a prominent backer of James Buchanan's presidential campaign in 1856. He also continued his military service as commander of a division of the Virginia State Militia. He was placed in command at Harpers Ferry after John Brown's raid and capture of that town's arsenal.

After the state of Virginia seceded in 1861, Taliaferro became commander of Virginia's State Militia with the rank of major general. Later he took command of the 23rd Virginia Infantry as colonel. He fought several engagements in 1861 and by the end of the year had ascended to brigade command, where he led Confederate forces at the Battle of Greenbrier River in what is now West Virginia.

General Taliaferro's Brigade was under Major General Thomas J. "Stonewall" Jackson's command at the end of 1861. He remained with General Jackson for several months, eventually rising to division command in 1862. Taliaferro was seriously injured at the Battle of Second Manassas (Second Bull Run) but returned to the field in time for the Battle of Fredericksburg, his last battle under General Jackson.

General Taliaferro's reputation was that of a strict and aloof commander who alienated many of his troops. There is at least one known circumstance when one of his troops actually assaulted him, though Taliaferro was unscathed. Taliaferro chafed under the command of General Jackson, complaining to his political colleagues in Virginia about Jackson's tactics and treatment of the men. General Jackson later protested Taliaferro's promotion to brigadier general while Taliaferro was still under General Jackson's command; however, Jackson respected Taliaferro's leadership and military ability and did not continue to stand in his way. Jackson later would select Taliaferro for temporary divisional command in specific engagements.

After the Battle of Fredericksburg, General Taliaferro was given command of the District of Savannah. In this capacity he led troops on James Island then at the Battle of Battery Wagner on Morris Island. General Taliaferro was commended for his service in that battle.

In 1864, Taliaferro was given command of all forces in the Eastern district of Florida, which made him the overall commander when the Battle of Olustee (Battle of Ocean Pond) occurred on February 20. On March 5, 1864, he returned to James Island, South Carolina, where he was made commander of all the forces in that state. Taliaferro was still in command when General Sherman and his federal forces entered the state from Savannah. General Taliaferro returned to Virginia when the Army of South Carolina, Georgia and Florida surrendered later that year.

After the war, William Taliaferro lived in Gloucester County, Virginia. He served again in the state legislature and as a judge and sat on the board of the College of William and Mary and the Virginia Military Institute. He died at his home, "Dunham Massie," on February 27, 1898, at the age of 75. He is buried in Ware Church Cemetery, Gloucester County, Virginia. His collection of papers is located at the Special Collections Research Center at the College of William and Mary.

General James Argyle Smith

James Smith was born July 1, 1831, in Maury County, Tennessee. He was raised in the state of Tennessee. He went to the Military Academy at West Point on July 1, 1848, graduated in 1853, and became a 2nd lieutenant in the infantry. Smith served in various posts in the west including the Jefferson Barracks Military Post. Smith fought at the Battle of Ash Hollow against the Sioux in 1855. Then from 1857 to 1858, Smith fought in the Utah War against the Mormons. One year after returning from the Utah War, Smith was promoted to a first lieutenant. In May 1861 he resigned his commission to join the Confederate Army.

Smith joined the Confederate Army in 1861 with the rank of lieutenant. In March 1862 he became a major and the adjutant-general to General Leonidas Polk. At the Battle of Shiloh, Smith became the lieutenant colonel of the Second Tennessee Infantry Regiment. General Bushrod Johnson commended Smith on his bravery at the Battle of Perryville. He was put in command of the 5th Confederate Infantry. His bravery was also noticed at the Battle of Murfreesboro, Tennessee, by both General Cleburne and General Leonidas Polk. After his performance in the Battle of Chickamauga and the praise he received from General Polk, Smith was promoted to brigadier general. At the Battle of Missionary Ridge, Smith attacked Sherman's flank preventing the Union Army from blocking off General Bragg's retreat. During the Battle of Missionary Ridge Smith was shot through both thighs while leading his men. After recovering from his wounds, Smith fought at the Battle of Atlanta where his brigade captured 15 artillery pieces. During this battle he was wounded again. After the Battle of Atlanta he took command of Mercer's Brigade when General Mercer was reassigned to Savannah due to bad health. Smith was in the division under the command of General Patrick Cleburne when the Battle of Franklin, Tennessee, occurred and after General Cleburne's death, Smith took over command of his division at Nashville. Smith and General William Bate led Cheatham's corps at the Battle of Bentonville.

After starting a farm in Mississippi, Smith was elected the Mississippi State Superintendent of Public Education from 1878 to 1886. He then became an agent of the Bureau of Indian Affairs from 1893 to 1897. He later became the Marshal of the Supreme Court of Mississippi. James Argyle Smith died on December 6, 1901, in Jackson, Mississippi, and was buried at the Greenwood Cemetery.

General William Henry Talbot Walker

General William H. T. Walker, otherwise known as "Fightn' Billy," was born November 26, 1816, in Augusta, Georgia, the son of Freeman Walker (US Senator from Georgia and mayor of Augusta, Georgia) and Mary Garlington Creswell. His father died when he was only 11 years old. He received his early education at Augusta's Richmond Academy. He entered the United States Military Academy at West Point in 1832, graduating in 1836, 46th out of 59 cadets.

July 1, 1837, Walker was appointed brevet second lieutenant and assigned to the 6th United States Infantry where he served in the Seminole Wars. He was wounded three times in the battle at Okeechobee and kept pressing forward until the third wound. Colonel Zachry Taylor cited him for his gallantry and bravery. By 1845 he had been promoted to the rank of captain. During the Mexican War he was wounded in his performance in the battles. His performance and bravery in leadership won him promotion to the rank of major. In the next battle he was wounded in the back, and his gallantry caused him to be promoted to lieutenant colonel. He also earned the nickname "Shot Pouch" for his multiple wounds in those battles.

On May 9, 1846, he married Mary Townsend in Albany, New York. They had four children: two sons and two daughters.

After the Mexican War he was assigned to recruiting duty for the United States Army until 1852. He also served as Commandant of the Cadets at West Point from 1854 to 1856. The head of his staff was Captain Robert E. Lee.

At the outbreak of the War for Southern Independence he chose to fight for his home state, Georgia, and also for the Confederate cause. He resigned his commission December 20, 1860, and was then appointed colonel in the Georgia State Militia on February 1, 1861. He was transferred to the regular Confederate Army Infantry as a colonel on April 25, 1861. He was promoted to brigadier general May 25th. He was then assigned to the 1st Brigade, 4th Division, Potomac District of the Department of Northern Virginia on October 22nd. Seven days later he resigned his commission and then rejoined the Georgia Militia and was made a brigadier general, serving there from November 1861 to January 1863. He resigned his commission in the militia to rejoin and reenter the Confederate States Army where he resumed with the rank of brigadier general on February 9, 1863. In May of 1863 he was assigned command of a brigade in the Confederate Department of the West. On May 21, 1863, he was promoted to division commander. On May 23, 1863, he was promoted to major general. This promotion was strongly endorsed by the commander of the department, General Joseph Eggleston Johnston. General Johnston believed in Walker's ability to lead a division and chose him over the other candidates.

Walker was in the Vicksburg campaign that summer under General Johnston. Walker and his division were then transferred to the Department of Mississippi and Eastern Louisiana in July 1863 and served there until August 23, 1863, when the command was added to the Reserve Corps of the Army of Tennessee. He fought in the battle of Chickamauga, Georgia, in September as the commander of the reserve corps of the Army of Tennessee.

December 1863 Walker and his division were made a part of Lieutenant General William J. Hardee's First Corps of the Army of Tennessee. He was highly respected by his men and would command the division with valor and gallantry up until his death in combat July 22, 1864, in the battle of Atlanta, when he was shot from his horse by a Federal picket, instantly killing him. The Confederacy lost one of its brightest stars and most able generals that day. Brigadier General Hugh W. Mercer took over command of the division.

General William Henry Talbot Walker is buried in the Walker Cemetery located at Georgia Regents University in Augusta, Richmond County, Georgia.

An upturned cannon marks the place where Walker was killed in Glenwood Triangle on Glenwood Avenue in Atlanta, Georgia.

General Patrick Ronayne Cleburne

Patrick Cleburne was born March 1828 in Ovens, County Cork, Ireland, the second son of Dr. Joseph Cleburne, a middle-class physician of Anglo-Irish ancestry. Patrick's mother died when he was 18 months old, and he was an orphan at 15. He followed his father into the study of medicine but failed his entrance exam to Trinity College of Medicine in 1846. In response to this failure, he enlisted in the 41st Regiment of Foot of the British Army, subsequently rising to the rank of corporal.

Three years later, Cleburne bought his discharge and then immigrated to the United States. After spending a short time in Ohio, he settled in Helena, Arkansas, where he became a pharmacist.

When the war broke out in 1861, Cleburne joined the local militia company (the Yell Rifles) as a private. He was soon elected captain. He led the company in the seizure of the U.S. Arsenal in Little Rock in January 1861. When Arkansas left the Union, the Yell Rifles became part of the 1st Arkansas Infantry, later designated the 15th Arkansas, of which he was elected colonel. He was promoted to brigadier general on March 4, 1862.

Cleburne served at the Battle of Shiloh, the Battle of Richmond (Kentucky), where he was wounded in the face, and the Battle of Perryville. Cleburne was promoted to division command and served at the Battle of Stones River, where his division drove the federal troops there back to the Nashville Pike. He was promoted to major general on December 13, 1862.

During the campaigns of 1863 in Tennessee, Cleburne and his soldiers fought at the Battle of Chickamauga. At the Battle of Wauhatchie near Chattanooga they conducted a rare night assault. They successfully resisted a much larger Union force under Major General William T. Sherman on the northern end of Missionary Ridge during the Battle of Missionary Ridge. In May and June of 1864 in the Atlanta Campaign, which included the Battle of Ringgold Gap in northern Georgia, and at the Battle of Pickett's Mill his "crack troops" repulsed a larger Federal force inflicting a great number of casualities on General Sherman's army. Cleburne and his troops received an official "Thanks" from the Confederate Congress for their actions during this campaign.

Cleburne's strategic use of terrain, his ability to hold ground where others failed, and his talent in foiling the movements of the enemy earned him fame and gained him the nickname "Stonewall of the West." Federal troops were quoted as dreading to see the blue flag of Cleburne's Division across the battlefield. General Robert E. Lee referred to him as "a meteor shining from a clouded sky."

It had become obvious to Cleburne that the Confederacy was losing the war because of the growing limitations of its manpower and resources. In 1864, he dramatically called together the leadership of the Army of Tennessee and put forth the proposal to emancipate slaves and enlist them in the Confederate Army to secure Southern independence. This proposal was met with polite silence at the meeting, and while word of it leaked out, it went unremarked on, much less officially recognized.

Prior to the campaigning season of 1864, Cleburne fell in love and became engaged to Susan Tarleton of Mobile, Alabama. Their marriage was never to be, as Cleburne was killed in the Battle of Franklin, just south of Nashville, Tennessee, on November 30, 1864. He was last seen advancing on foot toward the Union line with his sword raised, after his horse was shot out from under him. Accounts later said that he was found just inside the federal line and his body carried back to an aid station along the Columbia Turnpike. Confederate war records indicate he died of a shot to the abdomen or possibly a bullet that went through his heart. When the soldiers found his body, his boots were gone, as were his sword, watch, and anything else of value.

According to a letter written to General Cheatham from Judge Mangum post-war, Cleburne's remains were first laid to rest at Rose Hill Cemetery in Columbia, Tennessee. At the urging of Army Chaplain Bishop Quintard, Judge Mangum, staff officer to Cleburne and his law partner in Helena, had Cleburne's remains moved to St. John's Episcopal Church near Mount Pleasant, Tennessee, where they remained for six years. He had first observed St. John's during the Army of Tennessee's march into Tennessee during the campaign that led to the Battle of Franklin and commented that it was the place where he would like to be buried because of its great beauty and resemblance to his Irish homeland. In 1870, he was disinterred and returned to his adopted hometown of Helena, Arkansas, with much fanfare, and buried in Maple Hill Cemetery, overlooking the Mississippi River.

William A. Bowers, Jr.

General Nathan Bedford Forrest

Nathan Bedford Forrest was born July 13, 1824, in Bedford County, Tennessee, to a poor family. His father, William Forrest, a blacksmith, died when he was six years old, leaving him with 11 siblings. At 17 years of age he became the head of his family. He went into business with his uncle in Hernandez, Mississippi. When his uncle was shot and killed in an argument with the Matlock brothers, in a confrontation with them Forrest shot and killed two of them with a two-shot pistol and wounded two other brothers with a knife which had been thrown to him (one of them served under Forrest during the War for Southern Independence). He became a successful businessman and planter, owning several cotton plantations in the delta region of west Tennessee. He was a slave owner and trader in that area. In 1858 he was elected a Memphis City Alderman as a Democrat. He supported his mother and put his younger brothers through college. By 1861 he had become a millionaire and was one of the richest men in the South.

He was known as a Mississippi Gambler and a Memphis speculator and at one point was the captain of a riverboat which plied the river between Memphis and Vicksburg. The following is a quote about him. "He was known to his acquaintances as a man of obscure origin and low associations, a shrewd speculator, negro trader and duelist, but a man of great energy and brute courage."

In 1845 he married Mary Ann Montgomery and started a family.

When the war broke out he joined the Tennessee Mounted Rifles as a private on July 14, 1861. He had no prior military training or military experience but excelled as a commander and demonstrated leadership potential and an uncanny gift for military tactics which he would use to almost perfection in the next four years. After Tennessee was split in loyalties, Forrest posted ads to join his regiment for "men with good horse and good gun" adding "if you wanna have some fun and to kill some Yankees."

He was six feet two inches tall and 210 pounds. Forrest was physically imposing and intimidating, especially compared to the average height of men at the time. He used his skills as a hard rider and fierce swordsman to great effect. (He was known to sharpen both the top and bottom edges of his heavy saber.) He became known as the "Wizard of the Saddle" for his ability to read the battlefield and know the correct decision to make. According to an evaluation of the contemporary records it has been determined that Forrest may have killed more than thirty enemy soldiers with saber, pistol and shotgun. He was in an altercation with an artillery officer who shot him in the hip but received a mortal stab wound from Forrest.

Forrest's command included his Escort Company (these were his "Special Forces"), for which he selected the best soldiers available. This unit, which varied in size from 40 to 90 men, was the elite of the cavalry.

Forrest received praise for his skill and courage during an early victory in the Battle of Sacramento in Kentucky, where he routed a Union force by personally leading a cavalry charge that was later commended by his commander, Brigadier General Charles Clark. Forrest then distinguished himself further at the Battle of Fort Donelson in February 1862. His cavalry captured a Union artillery battery, and then he broke out of a Union Army siege headed by then Major General Ulysses S. Grant. Forrest rallied nearly 4,000 troops and led them across the river.

A few days after Fort Donelson, with the fall of Nashville imminent, Forrest took command of the city. Local industries had several million dollars' worth of heavy ordnance machinery. Forrest arranged for transport of the machinery and several important government officials to safe locations.

April 6 to April 7, 1862, a month later at the Battle of Shiloh, Forrest commanded a Confederate rear guard after the Union victory. In the Battle of Timbers, Forrest drove through the Union skirmish line. He was unaware that the rest of his men had halted their charge when reaching the full Union brigade, Forrest charged the brigade single-handedly and soon found himself surrounded. He emptied his Colt Army revolvers into the swirling mass of Union soldiers and pulled out his saber, hacking and slashing. A Union infantryman fired a musket ball into Forrest's spine with a point-blank musket shot, nearly knocking him out of the saddle. Forrest grabbed an unsuspecting Union soldier, hauled him onto his horse to use as a shield, dumped the man once he had broken clear and was out of range, then galloped back to his awe-struck cavalrymen. A surgeon removed the musket ball a week later, without anesthesia, which was unavailable. Forrest would likely have been given a generous dose of alcohol to muffle the pain of the surgery.

By early summer, Forrest commanded a new brigade of "green" cavalry regiments. In July he led them into middle Tennessee under orders to launch a cavalry raid. On July 13, 1862, he led them into the First Battle of Murfreesboro, which Forrest is said to have won.

According to a report by a Union commander: "The forces attacking my camp were the First Regiment Texas Rangers (8th Texas Cavalry, Terry's

Texas Rangers, ed.), Colonel Wharton, and a battalion of the First Georgia Rangers, Colonel Morrison, and a large number of citizens of Rutherford County, many of whom had recently taken the oath of allegiance to the United States Government. There were also quite a number of negroes attached to the Texas and Georgia troops, who were armed and equipped, and took part in the several engagements with my forces during the day."

He was promoted in July 1862 to brigadier general and was given command of a Confederate cavalry brigade. In December 1862 Forrest's veteran troopers were reassigned by General Braxton Bragg to another officer, which Forrest protested vehemently. Forrest had to recruit a completely new brigade, composed of about 2,000 inexperienced recruits, most of whom lacked weapons. Again, Bragg ordered a raid, this one into west Tennessee to disrupt the communications of the Union forces under Grant, threatening the city of Vicksburg, Mississippi. Forrest again protested that to send such untrained men behind enemy lines was suicidal, but Bragg insisted, and Forrest obeyed his orders. On the ensuing raid, he showed his brilliance, leading thousands of Union soldiers in west Tennessee on a "wild goose chase" to try to locate his fast-moving forces. Never staying in one place long enough to be attacked, Forrest led his troops in raids as far north as the banks of the Ohio River in southwest Kentucky. He returned to his base in Mississippi with more men than he had started with. By then all were fully armed with captured Union weapons. As a result, Union General Ulysses S. Grant was forced to revise and delay the strategy of his Vicksburg Campaign.

"He was the only Confederate cavalryman of whom Grant stood in much dread," a friend of Grant's was quoted as saying. General Sherman also noted in his memoirs that he feared General Forrest cutting his supply lines into Georgia during the Atlanta Campaign (General Joseph E. Johnston had urged Present Davis to do that very thing.).

Forrest continued to lead his men in small-scale operations until April 1863. The Confederate Army dispatched him into the back country of northern Alabama and west Georgia to defend against an attack of 3,000 Union cavalrymen commanded by Colonel Abel Streight, with a force far smaller in number. Streight had orders to cut the Confederate railroad south of Chattanooga, Tennessee, to cut off Bragg's supply line and force him to retreat into Georgia. Forrest chased Streight's men for 16 days, harassing them all the way. Streight's goal changed to escape the pursuit. On May 3, Forrest caught up with Streight's unit east of Cedar Bluff, Alabama. Forrest had fewer men than the Union side, but he repeatedly paraded some of them around a hilltop to appear a larger force and convinced Streight to surrender his 1,500 exhausted troops.

Forrest served with the main army at the Battle of Chickamauga (September

18 to September 20, 1863). He pursued the retreating Union army and took hundreds of prisoners. Like several others under Bragg's command, he urged an immediate follow-up attack to recapture Chattanooga, which had fallen a few weeks before. Bragg failed to do so, upon which Forrest was quoted as saying, "What does he fight battles for?" After Forrest made death threats against Bragg during a confrontation, Bragg reassigned him to an independent command in Mississippi. On December 4, 1863, Forrest was promoted to the rank of major general.

On March 25, 1864, Forrest was at Paducah, Kentucky, where he unsuccessfully demanded surrender of U.S. Col. Stephen G. Hicks: "... if I have to storm your works, you may expect no quarter."

On April 12, 1864, General Forrest led his forces in the attack and capture of Fort Pillow on the Mississippi River in Henning, Tennessee.

Forrest's greatest victory came on June 10, 1864, at the Battle of Brice's Crossroads. Forrest led other raids that summer and fall, including a famous one into Union-held downtown Memphis in August 1864 and another on a Union supply depot at Johnsonville, Tennessee, on October 3, 1864, called the Battle of Johnsonville.

In December, in the Franklin-Nashville Campaign, he fought alongside General John Bell Hood, the commander of the Confederate Army of Tennessee in the disastrous Battle of Franklin.

After his defeat at Franklin, Hood continued to Nashville. Hood ordered Forrest to conduct an independent raid against the Murfreesboro garrison. After success in achieving the objectives specified by General Hood, Forrest engaged Union forces near Murfreesboro on December 5, 1864. In what would be known as the Third Battle of Murfreesboro, a portion of Forrest's command (General Bate's men) broke and ran. After Hood's Army of Tennessee was all but destroyed at the Battle of Nashville, Forrest distinguished himself by commanding the Confederate rear guard in a series of actions that allowed what was left of the army to escape. For this, he earned promotion to the rank of lieutenant general. He was successful at places such as Columbia and Pulaski, Tennessee. In this a statement that was made by one of his men, "General Forrest would set the trap, and the Yankees would oblige."

In the rear guard action Forrest's compassion was demonstrated when he discovered his Georgia rear guard troops were in possession of only worn-out brogans which were causing injury to their feet due to the Tennessee snow. Upon discovering their plight he ordered wagons to be unloaded and created the first use of "personnel carriers" as he used them to transport his troops from location to location where they would unload and form line of battle to meet the enemy. After each fight they were again loaded in the wagons and transported to the next potential battle site.

In 1865, Forrest was tasked to defend the state of Alabama against Federal troops. When he received news of Lee's surrender, Forrest also chose to surrender. On May 9, 1865, at Gainesville, Forrest read his farewell address.

Forrest was one of the first men to grasp the doctrines of "mobile warfare" that became prevalent in the 20th century. Paramount in his strategy was fast movement, even if it meant pushing his horses at a killing pace, which he did more than once. Noted Civil War scholar Bruce Catton wrote: "Forrest ... used his horsemen as a modern general would use motorized infantry. He liked horses because he liked fast movement, and his mounted men could get from here to there much faster than any infantry could; but when they reached the field they usually tied their horses to trees and fought on foot, and they were as good as the very best infantry."

Forrest became well known for his early use of "maneuver" tactics as applied to a mobile horse cavalry deployment. He sought to constantly harass the enemy in fast-moving raids and to disrupt supply trains and enemy communications by destroying railroad track and cutting telegraph lines, as he wheeled around the Union Army's flank.

After the war, with slavery abolished, Forrest suffered a major financial setback. He became interested in the area around Crowley's Ridge during the war and settled in Memphis, Tennessee. In 1866 Forrest and C. C. McCreanor contracted to finish the Memphis & Little Rock Railroad. He built a commissary in a town forming along the rail route which most residents were calling "Forrest's Town," incorporated as Forrest City, Arkansas, in 1870.

He later was employed at the Selma-based Marion & Memphis Railroad and eventually became the company president. He was not as successful in railroad promoting as in war, and under his direction, the company went bankrupt.

Nearly ruined as the result of the failure of the Selma, Marion and Memphis Railroad in the early 1870s, Forrest spent his final days running a prison work farm on President's Island on the Mississippi River. There were financial failures across the country in the Panic of 1873. Forrest's health was in steady decline. He and his wife lived in a log cabin they had salvaged from his plantation.

During the Virginius Affair of 1873 Forrest, who had known some of the Southern filibusters on the vessel as friends, wrote a letter to the then General-in-Chief of the United States Army William Tecumseh Sherman and offered his services in case of war with Spain. Sherman, who in the War Between the States had recognized what a deadly foe Forrest was, replied after the crisis settled down by thanking Forrest for the offer and stating that had war broken out he would have considered it an honor to have served side-by-side with him.

Forrest died in Memphis in October 1877, at the home of his brother Jesse, reportedly from acute complications of diabetes. He was buried at Elmwood Cemetery. In 1904 the remains of Forrest and his wife, Mary, were disinterred from Elmwood and moved to a Memphis city park originally named Forrest Park in his honor.

William A. Bowers, Jr.

Confederate Veterans – Appling County, Georgia

CONFEDERATE VETERANS IDENTIFIED—All of the above Confederate veterans were identified by R. S. Wolfe and H. G. (Cap) Branch. The picture was taken at the site of the old Spring Branch Baptist Church in 1908. Several readers recognized some of them. They are, front row, left to right, Ben B. Milikin, Henry W. Beecher. John Gardner. Mathew (Luck) Johnson, Absalon Stone, Duncan Campbell, Tom Knight, Daniel W. Long, Jacob White and Lovett Baxley; back row, Jim Hall, Berry White, W Lumpkin Beecher, Joe Baxley, W. Alfred Beecher, Nat A. Thomas, Clem Byrd, Noah Altman W. D. Simmons, Mitchell Stone, E. T. Kennedy and Thomas H. Willoughby.

The 54th Regiment, Georgia Volunteer Infantry

Company A – Lamar Infantry – Bibb County

Private Samuel T. Campbell

Private Urias K. Kitchens, Jr.

William A. Bowers, Jr.

Company B – Appling Volunteers – Appling County

Lieutenant Michael Branch

Corporal Phillip Marion Carter

Private Jesse Crummey

The 54th Regiment, Georgia Volunteer Infantry

Private Isham Crosby

Private Jesse Carter

William A. Bowers, Jr.

Private George Willis Herndon

Private George "Tobe" Moody

Silas O'Quinn Sr.

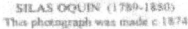

Isham, Francis M., and S. Aleck O'Quinn

Private Silas A. O'Quinn

Company C – Bartow Infantry – Emanuel County

Captain Daniel A. Green

Private Henry H. Hall

Lieutenant Phillip Falligant

The 54th Regiment, Georgia Volunteer Infantry

Company D – Screven County

Private Jasper Bragg

Private Henry Overstreet

Andrew Jackson Becton

Private Madison M. Dickley

William A. Bowers, Jr.

Among those pictured is William Joseph Lamb, who long resided in Georgia Militia District 1144, the Ray's Mill (nka Ray City) District, Berrien County, GA.

Picture courtesy of O. H. P. Johon, Sr. of Berlin, Georgia

CONFEDERATE VETERANS
HAHIRA, GA., JANUARY 1st, 1908

(1) W. A. Ram, Dec 31, 1845 (2) J. W. Rouse, Aug 12, 1843 (3) H. C. Lang, July 13, 1839 (4) E. J. Williams, Oct 21, 1842 (5) J. A. Mobley, June 23, 1839 (6) M. M. Howard, Dec 19, 1848 (7) J. H. Tillman, 1842 (8) Hardy Christian, Aug 31, 1838 (9) Jno L. Right, Dec 20, 1844 (10) J. P. Powers, 1840 (11) M. C. Futch, Aug 20, 1836 (12) C. H. Shaw, June 8, 1842 (13) S. B. Dampier, Nov 18, 1835 (14) T. A. Judge, Nov 22, 1843 (15) J. W. Taylor, Oct 25, 1833 (16) B. J. Sirmans, Feb 24, 1847 (17) S. W. Register, Aug 5, 1839 (18) A. Cowart, Dec 29, 1843 (19) J. T. Courson, Mar 22, 1848 (20) J. M. Patterson, May 27, 1840 (21) Elbert Mathis, Oct 4, 1836 (22) M. A. Tolar, Dec 8, 1832 (23) J. H. King, Nov 3, 1839 (24) G. W. Robinson, May 1, 1833 (25) W. M. Watson, 1840 (26) Jessie Moore, June 12, 1839 (27) N. J. Money, Mar 28, 1845 (28) A. Dixon, May 10, 1847 (29) W. J. Lamb, Apr 20, 1837 (30) Troy Thomas, Jan 13, 1833 (31) W. W. Joyce, May 3, 1832 (32) W. H. Green, Apr 13, 1834 (33) W. H. Dent, Oct 12, 1844 (34) Jas. W. Parish, Mar 2, 1847 (35) Unknown (36) Unknown (37) Unknown (38) Blu Sirmans, Nov 15, 1839 (39) J. A. Lawson, July 10, 1836 (40) J. J. Parrish, Sept 11, 1834 (41) R. W. Roan, June 18, 1846 (42) A. T. Tadlock, March 27, 1835 (43) W. R. Starling, May 3, 1831 (44) W. M. Lawson, Sept 7, 1834 (45) W. E. Stephens, Dec 15, 1849 (46) G. W. Powell, March 3, 1847 (47) J. F. Barfield, July 7, 1833 (48) W. W. Rutherford, Oct 18, 1825 (49) J. J. Hutchinson, Oct 1, 1843 (50) G. C. Hodges, Oct 13, 1846 (51) T. E. Swilley, Sept 22, 1843 (52) J. I. Martin, Spt 21, 1844 (53) E. J. Shanks, March 3, 1840 (54) H. L. Smith, Dec 28, 1841 (55) G. W. Stephens, Jan 8, 1833 (56) T. A. Roberts, July 6, 1844 (57) T. L. Wiseman, June 4, 1838 (58) W. W. Wilkderson, June 10, 1830 (59) H. B. Lawson, Aug 28, 1844 (60)

The 54th Regiment, Georgia Volunteer Infantry

Company E – Berrien County

Private S. W. Avera Private Lewis Lodge Griffin

Private Thomas D. Futch

William A. Bowers, Jr.

Private William J. Lamb   Corporal George Washington Knight

Private Jehu Patten

The 54th Regiment, Georgia Volunteer Infantry

Private David S. Robinson

Private James Patton

Private Reuben Register

Company F – Savannah Cadets – Chatham County

Lieutenant
Hamilton Branch

Private Isham Tyre

The 54th Regiment, Georgia Volunteer Infantry

Company G - Muscogee County

Private Benjamin Bishop

Company H – Russell Guards – Muscogee County

Lieutenant T. F. Brewster

Lieutenant Aaron Land

Private Harvey M. T. Land

The 54th Regiment, Georgia Volunteer Infantry

Private James McCurdy Rodgers

Corporal John D. Skelton

Company I – Effingham County

Private Edwin Hinley

Private James Jeremiah Heidt

Private Lewis A. Mingledorf

Private Lewis W. Rahn

William A. Bowers, Jr.

Company K – Satilla Rifles – Appling County

Private General Kersey (left)

Private James Christopher Columbus Davis (right)

Lieutenant James Edwin Hannon

JAMES EDWIN HANNON
1826 – 1907

The 54th Regiment, Georgia Volunteer Infantry

Private James A. Thornton

Private G. W. O'Quinn

Sergeant George M. T. Overstreet

Private Moses J. Westberry

Private John Westberry

Private Isham Tyre

The 54th Regiment, Georgia Volunteer Infantry

Roster of the Field, Staff, and Band
54th Regiment, Georgia Volunteer Infantry
Army of Tennessee C.S.A.

Name	Highest Rank Attained	Remarks
Charlton Hines Way	Colonel	
T. D. Caswell	Colonel	
Morgan Rawls	Lieutenant Colonel	See Company I
William Henry Mann	Major	
Thomas M. Brantley	Adjutant	See Company A & C
J. T. Hunt	Adjutant	
Hartford Henry Way	Adjutant	Company G
Abner B. Campbell	Chaplain	
James Erwin Godfrey Sr.	Chaplain	
Dixon G. Russell	Ensign	
Hartford Henry Way	Sergeant Major	See Company G
J. H. Bennett	Sergeant Major	See Company K
Lawrence E. Burgstiner	Sergeant Major	See Company I
Thomas A. Burke	Quartermaster	
William H. Mansfield	Quartermaster	
John G. Clarke	Assistant Quartermaster	
James Erwin Godfrey Jr.	Surgeon	
J. J. Callaway	Assistant Surgeon	
Camillus T. Coleman	Assistant Surgeon	
W. B. Richardson	Assistant Surgeon	
H. M. Talley	Assistant Surgeon	See Company E
T. F. Brewster	Hospital Steward	See Company H
Joseph S. Stevenson	Hospital Steward	See Company H
J. G. Eberhart	Hospital Steward	
P. H. Ferrell	Commissary	See Company C

William A. Bowers, Jr.

Lemuel Rhodes Forbes	Commissary Sergeant	See Company B
Daniel L. Moses	Ordinance Sergeant	See Company F
Martin F. Miller	Ordinance Sergeant	See Company E
W. B. Strawbridge	Ordinance Sergeant	See Company H
J. W. Turner	Ordinance Sergeant	
Joseph Potter Williamson	Asst. Ordinance Sergeant	See Company F
Nickerson Godfrey	Cook	
Joseph Clayton	Chief Musician	See Company A
William Quinn	Drum Major	
T. Bennett	Musician	See Company F
Mathew Branham	Musician	See Company D
John Brooker	Musician	See Company G
Henry Freeman	Musician	See Company H
Charles Gorman	Musician	See Company H
Lucius Griffin	Musician	See Company G
Samuel Huson	Musician	See Company K
Jim (negro)	Musician	
Jim Jones	Musician	
George Jones	Musician	
R. Massette	Musician	See Company A
— Mims	Musician	
John Nordette	Musician	See Company A
Mims —	Musician	
George Rees	Musician	
G. T. Sanders	Musician	See Company K
John M. Thurmond	Musician	See Company K
William S. Williams	Musician	
Andrew Wood	Musician	

The 54th Regiment, Georgia Volunteer Infantry

COMPANY COMMANDERS

Company A "Lamar Infantry"	Capt. Thomas W. Brantley	Bibb County
Company B "Appling Volunteers"	Capt. George W. Moody	Appling County
Company C "Bartow Infantry"	Capt. Daniel A. Green Capt. R. B. Knight Capt. Thomas Brantley	Emanuel County
Company D "Yancy Guards"	Capt. Augustus Roberts Capt. Joseph Miller	Screven County
Company E "Berrien County Guards"	Capt. J. D. Evans Capt. H. M. Talley	Berrien County
Company F "Savannah Cadets"	Capt. Walter S. Chisholm Capt. John W. Anderson	Chatham County
Company G "Georgia Invincibles"	Capt. George W. Knight Capt. N. B Roberts Capt. Thomas E. Grigsby, Sr. Capt. John J. Lynn	Muscogee County
Company H "Russell Guards"	Capt. Charles Russell	Muscogee County
Company I "Georgia Rangers"	Capt. Morgan Rawls Capt. Leander L. Elkins	Effingham County
Company K " Satilla Rifles"	Capt. George Eason Capt. Richard Bennett 1st Lt. Green B. Ritch 1st Lt. Silas Thornton	Appling County

William A. Bowers, Jr.

The following lists the members of companies which formed the 54th Regiment, Georgia Volunteer Infantry. Those names in bold were wounded and those in bold/underline died during the war.

Company A - Bibb County, Georgia
"Lamar Infantry"

James Alford
David Allen
J. Allen
John Allen
Peter Allen
John Armor
J. W. Armor
W. H. Ashley
John F. Avera
William Avera
James B. Bailey
Solomon Baker
Charles Banks
J. C. Barfield
John R. Barfield
E. F. Bass
Matthew W. Bass
John T. Bates
H. Bates
E. H. Beasley
J. F. Beasley
P. R. Bird
Charles Blaker
James E. Bonhart
Benjamin Bowers
James A. Bowers
A. J. Brantley
Horatio S. Brantley
H. A. Brantley
H. T. Brantley
Martin L. Brantley
M. V. Brantley
T. W. Brantley
Thomas W. Brantley
W. J. W. Brantley
William Brice
H. N. Britt

<u>Isaiah D. Britt</u>
<u>J. D. Britt</u>
James J. Britt
John J. Britt
L. H. Britt
O. D. Britt
L. R. M. Bronson
James P. Brooks
W. F. Brown
Robert Burkett
<u>J. Causey</u>
Samuel T. Campbell
J. H. Cherry
Joseph J. Churchill
Joseph Clayton
J. W. Cobb
G. W. Cook
Talbot Coombs
J. F. Courson
James M. Crawford
<u>Owen Cummings</u>
J Cunningham
William Cunningham
Joseph Davidson
H. C. Davis
J. M. Davis
A. C. Dennis
James D. Dougherty
Benjamin Downs
Jefferson Dumas
John H. Dunlap
William Dunlap
J. Dyer
Z. Dyes
S. Elliott
J. B. M. Ellsion
Elbert Fagan

C. Falvey
Henry Faulk
Robert James Faulk
Robert L. Felts
G. T. Fennell
Samuel B. Finney
Thomas Flinn
William R. Flowers
Charles E. Follendore
Joseph F. Follendore, Sr.
Leonidas Alexander Ford
James M. Fountain
William T. Fountain
Thomas Freeny
J. D. Fuller
John Gaffney
J. N. Garland
James W. Garland
D. J. Giles
J. J. Gill
J. H. Graddy
Frederick Grist
Burrell B. Grooms
G. W. Guthrie
Charles Hamby
R. P. Hammond
Charles Hansley
J. C. Hardee
Thomas C. Hardy
D. C. Hargrove
J. A. Harrington
F. Harris
J. J. Harris
James N. Harris
Joseph J. Harris
E. W. Harvey

The 54th Regiment, Georgia Volunteer Infantry

W. M. Heath
W. R. Heath
George W. Henderson
James W. Henderson
L. O. Hengraw
John Herrington
Riley A. Herrington
Alford Hicks
H. Hicks
John R. Hodge
Franklin Holloman
J. W. Horton
A. Hotaling
Daniel S. House
W. House
Wesley L. Howard
William Hoyt
David Bishop Hudson
John Wesley Hudson
William James Hudson
William Hysler
P. W. Jackson
William James
William E. Jenkins
James J. Jessup
D. J. Jiles
F. W. Johnson
S. A. Johnson
William T. Johnson
James L. Joiner
John J. Jones
N. S. Jones
W. S. Jones
J. Jordan
Jacob J. Jordan
James J. Jordan
Richard Jordan
Christopher C. Ketchem
Benjamin Kimbrew
E. S. Kimbrew
Thomas M. Kimbrew
Thomas Duaugn King
John Kirby
C. M. Kitchens
Miles W. Kitchens

Oran W. Kitchens
Uriah K. Kitchens
William H. Kitchens
George D. Knight
William J. Land
W. J. Langston
F. M. Lawrence
F. N. Lawrence
Francis M. Lawson
F. C. Lester
Robert Henry Lewis
W. S. Lones
John C. Lyles
J. C. Lyster
W. L. Lyster
Joseph Mandetle
John Mann
J. F. Marshall
D. Mason
Daniel M. Mason
John B. Mason
John Martin Mason
S. O. Mason
Robert Massette
S. D. May
Barney McAdams
J. A. McManus
H. McTague
J. R. Mitchell
Robert J. Mitchell
James Mixon
J. S. Moore
Samuel W. Moore
Seborn O. Moore
William W. Moore
James Morrison
James B. Morrison
John J. Mulkey
William G. Mulkey
C. M. Newsome
H. Newson
James Nixon
George W. Noland
S. W. Noland
W. A. Noland

John Nordette
C. A. J. Parrish
C. C. Parrish
E. C. Parrish
Alf W. Patterson
Samuel L. Patterson
William Patterson
Green B. Payne
T. Powers
W. Rabun
William Rabun
W. J. Ragg
James Railey
T. J. Raine
N. L. Richardson
W. L. Richardson
_____ **Ricks**
Thomas J. Ritch
Edward Jefferson Ritchey
M. G. Rittenberry
John J. Roberts
J. L. Roberts
John Roberts
R. Roberts
Reuben J. Roberts
Solomon Roberts
William H. Roberts
J. T. Rockmore
J. W. Ross
A. J. Rutledge
William G. Rye
Francis M. Ryle
A. S. Sallas
A. T. Sanders
William Sawyer
William B. Scott
Henry James Sharpe
A. P. Simmons
R. Simmons
William Simmons
George Sizemore
J. J. Skinner
F. B. Slocumb
William F. Slocumb
C. Smith

William A. Bowers, Jr.

Cicero C. Smith
G. Clark Smith
Henry Luke Smith
John j. Smith
John W. Smith
Robert William Smith
Rodden Smith Jr.
W. D. Smith
Charles Sonneborn
Caleb Stephens
Joe Stevens
Joseph Stevens
John T. Stewart
Silas Stewart
Henry W. Stringer
Jerry Taylor
R. L. Taylor
Richard Taylor
James Teel
Jeremiah W. Thurman
George W. Tidwell
James A. Tidwell
Moses Tucker
Stephen Tucker
Archibald Vann
Wiley Vann
B. Vincent
William H. Visage
James Wells
William Wells
Allen O. Wheeler
J. M. Wheeler
J. D. White
W. W. Wiggins
John H. Wilder
James Wilkinson
U. L. Williams
A. J. Wood
Bryant Wood
Daniel Wood
H. Wood
J. C. Wood
W. H. T. Wood
James William Franklin Woodall
J. Woodson

William W. Wrye
Samuel Wynn
David Zittman

The 54th Regiment, Georgia Volunteer Infantry

Company B - Appling County, Georgia
"Appling Volunteers"

W. P. Adair
James H. Anderson
James J. Anderson
John H. Anderson
Swain M. Anderson
Thomas V. Anderson
W. Atkinson
Charles Banks
S. J. Bankston
Michael Baxley
Mitchell Baxley
J. E. Beck
J. M. Bloodworth
W. M. Bloodworth
J. C. Blue
Josiah Boatright
Michael Branch
T. J. Buckalew
Elias Bullard
Irving Bullard
T. W. Burt
H. W. Burt
W. H. Camel
David Carter Jr.
David Carter Sr.
David S. Carter
George M. Carter
Isaac Carter Jr.
Isaac Carter Sr.
Isaac D. Carter
Isham Carter
J. C. Carter
J. W. Carter
J. W. Carter
Jackson Carter
James H. Carter
Jefferson Carter
Jesse Carter
Paul Carter
Paul A. Carter

Phillip Marion Carter
Stephen W. Carter
Thomas H. Carter
Thomas Razor Carter, Sr.
W. Carter
Wiley Carter Jr.
Wiley Carter Sr.
William B. Carter
William J. Carter
William R. Carter Sr.
Wilson Carter
R. M. Causey
Pickens Clark
William Cook
Joshua S. Cowart
J. M. Crawford
Abraham Taylor Crosby
Berry W. Crosby
David Crosby
Isham Crosby
James Crosby Sr.
Samuel M. Crosby
Samuel Crosby
Elias Crummey
James Culpepper
Joseph Deen
T. W. Deen
T. W. Dent
John W. Dukes
J. H. Dukes
T. D. Dukes
G. W. Dyal
Abraham Eason
Abraham Molton Eason
Felix K. Eason
George Eason
James Tillman Eason
Moses Leonard Peek Eason
William Henry Eason
Stephen Floyd

Lemuel Rhodes Ford
J. H. Gannon
J. M. Goggins
J. F. Gordon
J. A. Gunn
W. C. Gunn
A. F. Hamil
J. Hand
Stephen Harden
H. C. Harris
Isaac T. Henderson
E. Herndon
G. W. Herndon
George Willis Herndon
Isaac Herndon
James Herrington
John Herrington
J. G. Hightower
W. C. Hood
George W. Hooker
J. W. Howard
Isham Hughes
M. H. Hughes
William Hughes
John Hughey
John W. Hughey
J. L. Hunt
W. A. Jackson
James Joiner
Russell B. Jones
Kindred L. Keene
T. H. Kilgore
Alfred Lane
Bryant Leggett
J. B. Lesnur
R. F. Lester
R. Long
Robert A. Long
Thomas Long

225

J. A. Lowrey
W. C. Maddox
P. F. Matthews
George W. McAbee
George J. McCall Jr.
David McGauley
George W. Middleton
Middleton Miles
David H. Moody
George Moody
George W. Moody
I. I. Moody
Isham Moody
Jacob Moody
Jacob H. Moody
James L. Moody
James M. Moody
Stephen Murphey
William M. Murphey
George W. Nunez
Isaac Ogden
Isham C. Ogden
James Ogden
John R. Ogden
D. M. Oliver
J. R. Oliver
Francis O'Quinn
Silas A. O'Quinn Sr.
Moses L. Overstreet
William Overstreet
S. A. Patton
Lafayette N. Phillips
John F. Pickles
T. W. Powell
William Thomas Reddish
Thomas J. Reed
Edward Jefferson Ritchie
John Jackson Roberson
Joseph D. Roberson
T. Roberson
G. W. Ross
David R. Rowell
J. W. Rumsey
J. P. Seagraves

John A. Sharpe
John T. Sharpe
J. R. Sikes
David Simmons
Thomas Simmons
W. B. Simonton
S. T. Smith
Seaborn Smith
T. A. Smith
Thomas Smith
Warren Smith
Eli Stafford
Zachariah Steedley
H. J. Stephens
John Stewart
J. W. Stocks
T. M. Stocks
Isham Strickland
Jacob Strons
D. W. Summerall
P. H. Taylor
M. T. Thigpen
W. R. Thompson
Timothy Thornton
William Thornton
Joseph C. Tillman
M. W. Thompkins
Benjamin A. Trice
Arthur Turner
Archibald J. Williams
Henry A. Williams
J. A. Williams
James A. Williams
Joseph Williams

Company C - Emanuel County, Georgia
"Bartow Infantry"

Thomas Allen
Walter Allen
D. W. Anderson
Swain M. Anderson
Corsea Antionio
E. P. Bailey
J. M. Bailey
J. R. Bailey
L .L. Bailey
N. L. Bailey
Benjamin Barbee
John M. Beck
E. P. Bedenfield
J.J.Bedenfield
John Bell
John Bishop
B. Boatright
Daniel D. Boatright
John Boatright
William Boatright
Thomas M. Brantley
Rice W. Britt
J. S. Brown
E. H. Bryant
Needham W. Bryant
Daniel B. Cannady
Jesse D. Carr
H. Cawell
F. Cheek
B. P. Coker
Andrew J. Coleman
William T. Coleman
J. D. Conwell
A. D. Crooms
W. Davis
D. Devereaux
L. Devereaux
Henry T. Downs
Newton Drew

Augustus H. K. Dunn
J. Durden
L. H. Durden
W. R. Durden
L. B. Dye
George Eberhart
Robert Elliott
J. G. Ellis
W. R. Ennis
J. Faircloth
John T. Faircloth
Phillip R. Falligant
D. M. Farmer
Issac V. Farmer
J. M. Farmer
J. V. Farmer
P. H. Ferrell
James J. Fields
W. D. Flemming
William J. Folks
T. M. Gaines
W. M. Gaines
W. H. German
William W. Glisson
Thomas W. Goodwin
B. R. Graham
Thomas J. Gracen
J. A. Gray
Daniel A. Green
G. W. Greenway
William Thomas Griffin
D. J. Grubbs
Houston Henry Hall
J. R. Hall
James J. Hall
John B. Hall
John K. Hall
William Hardy
John Jacobs

Elias Jenkins
K. Jenkins
Levi Jenkins
McKibber Jenkins
Benjamin L. Johnson
Benjamin W. Johnson
John Johnson
John D. Johnson
Josiah C. Johnson
William R. Johnson
Joseph P. Jones
Thomas Jones
James C. Keen
John Kelly
John S. Kemp
William Kennedy
Abraham Kirkland
Edward L. Kirkland
Henry C. C. Kirkland
Henry T. Kirkland
N. G. Kirkland
R. B. Knight
Rufus T. Knight
Christian Kuhlman
Edwin J. Lamb
E. R. Lamb
F. M. Lamb
H. B. Lamb
Isaac B. Lamb
Isaac D. G. Lamb
Isaac M. Lamb
J. B. Lamb
J. M. Lamb
Simeon Lamb
Thomas G. Lamb
A. Lane
T. J. Lanier
W. D. Lawrence
James N. Layfield

Lundy Layfield
David J. Lee
Henry G. Lee
Daniel Lewis
E. G. Lewis
W. H. Martin
James F. McBride
J. McCoy
E. D. McGar
E. J. McGar
J. C. McGar
Dennis McLendon
John M. McLendon
S. T. Minton
M. D. Mobley
A. M. Moore
J. S. Moore
John T. Moore
Thomas S. Moore
C. C. Morgan
Jesse C. Morgan
J. P. Morrow
A. R. Oglesby
B. S. Oglesby
K. T. Oglesby
Seaborn Oglesby Jr.
Seaborn Allen Oglesby Sr.
William M. Oglesby
Peter Parish
Michael Peavy
Isaac John Peeler
E. Pettingaale
Andrew Jackson Rich
Stephen E. Rich
_____ Richardson
S. Richardson
S. W. Richardson
Samuel Richardson
John S. Roberts
Simeon Roberts
T. Roberts
Thomas Roberts
G. B. Robertson
Richard Roe

Anderson L. Sammons
Benjamin B. Sammons
John Sammons
Wiley G. Sammons
H. T. Scott
John Selves
William G. Sherrod
John Silvers
Rice D. Silvers
Henry E. Simmons
J. F. Simmons
R. G. Simmons
A. C. Simpsom
A. E. Simpson
Asa S. Simpson
James T. Simpson
John F. Simpson
William Henry Simpson
T. Smith
J. D. Spence
James H. Stephens
James S. Stephens
Thomas J. Stephens
Jethro Sumner
A. Thigpen
John R. Tripp
Arthue Thomas Tuliford
J. W. Turner
William H. Turner
J. D. Underwood
A. J. Veal
Amos Walden
Thomas H. Walden
James Walters
Miles B. Watkins
Abner Webb
Joseph Webb
J. L. Webb
Jesse A. Wiggins
Joseph Wiggins
John K. Wiggins

The 54th Regiment, Georgia Volunteer Infantry

Company D - Screven County, Georgia
"Yancey Guards"

Eldirdge G. Allmond	J. C. W. Collins	Moses L. Lariscy Jr.
Eliza Allmond	William Cosgrove	Moses Lariscy Sr.
J. Anderson	William Deason	William M. Lariscy
J. W. Anderson, Jr.	Enos B. Dickey	W. S. Lawrence
James J. Anderson	Madison Dickey	F. C. Lester
J. O. Andrews	J. L. Dickey	D. Henry Lewis
Corsea Antonio	Samuel C. M M. Dickey	**Henry S. Lewis**
R. Arnett	Samuel Dowse	**S. Lewis**
J. C. Barfield	G. W. Dyle	S. Lewis
John R. Barfield	H. G. Edenfield	**Thomas M. Lewis**
John A. Baughman	John A. Forehand	Thomas J. Lightfoot
Perry Bazemore	**W. R. Forehand**	**W. Loukie**
Andrew Jackson Becton	John Wesley Freeman	Johm McCormick
John Wesley Bolton Sr.	William Randolph Freeman	A. J. McCoy
Reuben Bolton	Patrick Gately	Samuel McCoy
Richard Bolton	William S. Gavin	Seaborn McCoy
M. Bonham	Thomas J. Grayson	E. W. Miller
Daniel Bragg	**William Griner Jr.**	**Edward W. Miller**
David Bragg	R. M. Hall	**Eugene Miller**
David L. Bragg	**H. E. Hartley**	John Milo Miller Jr.
Henry Bragg	J. W. Hartley	Joseph Miller
Howell Bragg	E. W. Harvey	A. S. Mincey
Jasper Bragg	Wensley H. Hobby	Hilliard Mincey
L. Bragg	**_____ Hurst**	**James B. Newton**
William B. Bragg	James Hurst	M. J. Newton
Mathew Branham	**Joseph W. Hurst**	Mitchell J. Newton
David M. Brinson	J. M. Jeffers	**Archibald Oglesby**
H. N. Britt	William W. Jeffers	**Francis Allen Oglesby**
James J. Britt	Charles J. Jenkins	Henry Overstreet
John J. Britt	Daniel T. Jenkins Sr.	Israel Parker
L. H. Britt	J. T. Jenkins	John Parker
H. S. Burke	Michael Jenkins	**John Parker**
J. D. Burke	Paul Jenkins	S. L. Patterson
W. D. S. Burke	Peyton H. Jenkins	**E. Peel**
Charles Thomas Jefferson	John Joyner	Henry W. Peel
Claxton	William B. Joyner	Isaac Peeler
W. Claxton	W. W. Kemp	E. Pierce
William Claxton	Allen Lariscy	E. N. Pierce
Thomas C. Clifton	Jackson Lariscy	John R. Pierce

229

B. F. Powell
A. W. Reynolds
W. M. Reynolds
N. H. Rhodes
W. H. Rhodes
Augustus S. Roberts
John M. Roberts
Anderson L. Sammons
D. S. Sanders
R. B. Sanders
Allen Sasser Sr.
Henry Sasser
Howell Sasser
Littleton Sasser
Robert W. Shealy
L. D. Sheppard
William Simmons
A. C. Simpsom
Asa E. Simpson
A. S. Simpson
James T. Simpson
John F. Simpson
William Henry Simpson
A. R. Smith
C. A. Sorea
William Sowell
Benjamin Spell
H. M. Talley
Jerry Taylor
Nathan Taylor
W. Taylor
William Taylor
William A. Taylor
Stephen H. Thompson
Cuyler Vickery, Sr.
Cuyler Vickery, Jr.
Hezekiah Vickery
J. H. Vickery
William Vickery
George Milton Wallace
Augustus Waters
James Waters
James Waters
John Waters
Michael Waters

William J. Waters
James A. Wells
Samuel F. Wilson

The 54th Regiment, Georgia Volunteer Infantry

Company E - Berrien County, Georgia
"Berrien County Guards"

Joseph Aiken
Littleton L. Albritton
Matthew Hodges Albritton
G. H. Avera
Stephen Willis Avera
Walter Avera
William M. Avera
E. Baker
Thomas A. Baker
Zachariah Baker
William Baldree
James Madison Baskin
Robert M. Bean
David Beckton
Anderstokes J. Best
Zaddock W. Best
James Braden
Richard Bradford
T. P. Bramlette
James Brogdon
William Brogden
Stewart Burns
D. J. Carlton
D. B. Carroll
Henry Collier
Erwin Cowart
William Crawford
John Crosby
John Culpepper
William A. Davis
Howell B. Dobson
Micajah (Malachi) Easters
William B. Easters
William Edwards
J. D. Evans
James Lucius Faulkner
William B. Faulkner
J. M. Fulson

E. A. Futch
Malcolm C. Futch
Thomas Dugger Futch
William Gaskins
James Green
Marshall Green
William Hiram Green
James H. Griffin
Lewis Lodge Griffin
Lewis Moses Griffin
Solomon Griffin
William Henry Harrison Griffin
Samuel Guthrie
Cader Hancock
Daniel H. Hancock
John Mark Hancock
J. E. Harrison
John Helton
John J. Hoffman
William H. Holstead
T. Johnson
E. J. Kinard
George Washington Knight
J. W. Knight
Jonathan N. Knight
Jonathan W. Knight
Edwin J. Lamb
Thomas L. Lamb
William J. Lamb
Joseph E. Lambert
D. P. Lane
Guilford J. Lee
James L. Lee
Jesse Lee
John Lee
John G. Lewis
William C. Lindsay

James J. Luke
John G. Luke
J. P. Luke
William H. Luke
B. F. Mainor
Elbert Mathis
John J. Mathis
Bateman May
Jeremiah M. May
Francis McArdie
James George McCall
John E. McConnell
Daniel J. McCranie
Robert A. McCrary
John McDermid
George C. McGee
W. A. McGee
George M. McKinney
Martin F. Miller
Edmund Darling Morris
J. H. Morris
William E. Morris
George W. Nash
J. H. Nash
Frenkiln Nelson
V. Nix
I. T. Noland
Joseph Oldham
William H. Outlaw
William M. Parr
James M. Patten
Jehu Patten
Elbert Wells Peabody
Jesse L. Peoples
George W. Pope
H. P. Rainey
John Ray
Rufus Ray
Reubin Register

231

David S. Robinson
Noah Roe
Zachariah Rooks
Samuel Greenberry Sanders
Benjamin Jonathan Sirmans
John C. Sirmans
J. C. Smith
James Smith
W. F. Smith
E. G. Stanford
C. P. Stanley
James H. Stephens
Joseph Hamilton Stephens
Richard Street
Ira J. Sutton
J. J. Sutton
S. J. Sutton
Joel Wooten Swain
H. M. Talley
Lewis R. Taylor
R. L. Taylor
M. L. Thomas
Thompson T. Thompson
Hiriam Tucker
John Tucker
Moses J. Tucker
R. G. Turner
L. H. Vance
S. Walters
William WaLters
James Waters
Gilbert Watson
Joseph Watson
Jeremiah B. Weaver
Jethro John Wilkins Weaver
John B. Weaver
John Webb
Jordan Webb
B. W. Williams
James E. Williams
Robert D. Woodward
Jeptha N. Young
Joel Green Young
L. G. Young

The 54th Regiment, Georgia Volunteer Infantry

Company F - Chatham County, Georgia
"Savannah Cadets"

J. Aaron
James Aaron
Wesley Aaron
John W. Anderson Jr.
J. O. Andrews
Charles F. Bailey
J. J. Barron
C. John Barry
James Beale
Islam M. Beck
J. M. Beck
John M. Beck
Anthony Bennett
T. Bennett
Henry C. Benning
Edward F. Blair
R. J. G. Blake
James F. H. Blois
George Blount
Richard Bradford
William H. Bradley
B. Bragg
L. Bragg
Hamilton McDevit Branch
R. E. Brantley
Robert M. Brantley
William Bray
J. Breen
John Breen
Thoms A. Brewer
William T. Brewer
Alex J. Brown
Edmund Wade Brown
James Brown
George W. Brownell
Benjamin Bryant
Benjamin F. Bryant
D. J. Bryant
Henry W. Butler

Robert M. Butler
Henry J. Byrd
D. Robert Caesar
John Calder
T. Calder
Charles P. Carey
B. Carr
S. Carr
James P. Chaplain
Walter S. Chisholm
George Clark
George J. Clarke
William S. Clarke
Thomas A. Cobb
James A. Cochran
T. Colder
Andrew J. Coleman
William T. Coleman
William Conner
William H. Connerat
T. Cook
C. F. Cooper
Edward Cooper
John Cooper
D. Cranson
George Crawford
Francis M. Crosby
E. B. Crozier
Charles Davis
J. Benjamin Davis
A. J. Dawkins
James Elkin Dennard
W. J. Doggett
J. M. Doty
William W. Doty
Thomas J. Downs
Samuel Dowse
E. J. Doyle
Henry S. Dreese

T. Dreese
Z. Dyes
J. M. Elliott
John M. Elloitt
John Washington Elliott
Thomas Estell
S. C. Ethridge
Henry Ettinger
Francis S. Ferrell
R. W. Flake
Leonidas Alexander Ford
Frank J. Fox Jr.
A. Freeborn
James Freeborn
Phillip R. Galligant
William S. Gavin
David F. Goins
George L. Granberry
Thomas J. Granberry
James Griffin
William W. Habersham
William N. Habersham Jr.
A. M. Hall
Charles Hamby
James B. Hammock
William T. Hannan
Charles Hansley
William Harden
Abraham Wilson Harmon
Hugh H. Harrigan
William Harris
William B. Hassett
Gustavus George Hedrick
J. J. Hedrick
Benjamin J. Helmy
Edwin Randolph Hernandez
Riley A. Herrington
Thomas H. Hinely
Martin Hinges

233

John R. Hodge
A. Hunt
Albert R. Hunt
Charles C. Hunter
Monk L. Jackson
J. D. Jarrell
John E. Jarrell
James Hampton Johnson
Thomas Joiner
John J. Jones
James J. Keane
A. N. Keifer
Lawrence Kelley
William Kelley
Benjamin F. Kimbrough
Alexander D. Krenson
K. Lachilson
Robert Lachilson Jr
George W. Langford
W. S. Law
William A. Lawes
John L. Lightbourne
James Looker
Edward T. Lovett
Thomas Lyster
John Mann
D. Mason
John Martin Mason
J. Maxwell
James A. Maxwell
William F. May
L. E. McCarthy
John McCormick
Clay McCoy
Peter McGuire
Antony McHale
John McHugh
Hector McMillan
George F. Mell
Thomas B. Mell
Henry A. Miller
Thomas A. Miller
Allen Moody
Angus P. Moore
Charles Moore
George W. Moore
J. H. Morris
Charles Mortimer
Daniel L. Moses
P. J. Mularkey
James C. Murphy
Timothy Murphy
Patrick Nagle
E. J. Nease
E. L. Neese
John H. Nesmith
E. C. Nunn
James B. Ogletree
Alexander Pacetty
Abraham E. Patterson
Ira Payne
Thomas Peel
E. Pettigrew
P. D. Phelan
John Pierce
William B. Puder
J. A. Quinn
Patrick Quinn
Joel P. Rackley
Alexander J. Raymur
G. G. Redrich
John J. Roberts
John M. Roberts
William Roberts
George R. Robertson
George A. Rose
A. J. Sammons
Anderson L. Sammons
John Sammons
D. S. Sanders
R. B. Sanders
Allen Sapp
R. D. Sasser
S. Shaffer
William L. Shaffer
James Shaw
William A. Shaw
J. F. Slade
George R. Smith
Mee Smith
Samuel J. Smith
T. Smith
William C. Smith
H. Snider
W. G. Solomon
Charles Sonneborn
James F. Spear
James Samuel Spear
William C. Staley
Robert Stripling
Thomas J. Stripling
George J. Tarvin
George Taylor
Wesley Taylor
Samuel Templeton
Grigsby E. Thomas Sr.
Lafayette Thomas
John B. Thornton
Matthew Thornton
S. T. Thornton
Phillip Tippins
Jason Tyer
Isham Tyre
Hugh Wadell
V. Walsh
George Waters
James T. Weldon
John Wiley
Charles L. Whitehurst
T. C. Whitehurst
H. Williamson
James Potter Williamson
Frank M. Willis
A. M. Wood
J. M. Wylly
John Wylly
James Yokum
Henry Young
David Zittro

The 54th Regiment, Georgia Volunteer Infantry

Company G - Muscogee County, Georgia
"Georgia Invincibles"

Andrew D. Aaron
J. T. Alexander
James Alford
Calvin R. Almond
Robert P. Anderson
John Avertt
Needham A. Barfield
Thomas J. Barrow
Benjamin F. Bishop
John Bishop
Henry Blackstock
Daniel D. Boatright
………..**Boyed**
Samuel F. Boyd
W. A. Boyd
H. M. Brakefield
John Brooker
Alex Brown
William Brown
Joel L. Bruce
William Bruce
Jesse Bryan
Jasper S. Bullard
A. Burger
Henry Burger
D. B. Cannady
J. B. Cartin
Joseph Cartledge
James A. Clegg
Vines H. Collier
J. D. Conwell
William Cooper
George Correll
E. P. Crumb
Phillip Cunningham
William Dalton
John E. Davison
A. J. Dawkins
Rufus Dawkins
Thomas J. Dawkins

Henry DeLaney
Samuel Deloach
J. Donalson
David Dortch
Thomas J. Downs
John D. Duncan
J. G. Dunn
Martin Dunn
L. B. Dye
Andrew J. Ellis
Jim Ellison
Richard Lane Ellison
James Eyles
James D. G. Ford
James W. Gatlin
W. Georges
A. W. Gibson
William D. Globle
Boswell Goens
Thomas Edwards Goulding
B. R. Graham
George L. Granberry
Thomas J. Granberry
Bartlett Wiley Green
Lucius Griffin
Jackson Grimes
W. Grimes
J. B. Hammack
James B. Hammock
R. P. Hammond
Samuel B. Harned
Andrew Harper
J. G. Harper
John B. Harrell
Moses Harrell Jr.
Moses Harrell Sr.
Edward S. Holloway
Joseph B. Holloway
Abner Howard
Francis L. Hudgeons

G. F. Hunter
George S. Hunter
Simon Peter Hunter
Andrew Jackson
Robert T. Jackson
William W. Jackson
William J. Jennings
Benjamin L. Johnson
James J. Jones
James R. Jordan
Nathaniel O. Kendrick
H. T. Kirkland
N. G. Kirkland
Charles Kirkman
George Walton Knight
Eatonton W. Lamb
George W. Langford
T. J. Lanier
William A. Laws
James N. Layfield
David J. Lee
Andrew J. Lowe
Thomas B. Lynn
J. B. Martin
Lafayette Martin
Samuel B. McClary
James McDonald
La Fayette McDonald
Samuel H. McDonald
William H. McDonald
Benjamin F. McDuffie
William McHarque
John McHugh
Joshua McKinney
Piesant McKinney
William McKinney
Jno. M. McLeroy
Asa Meadows
William Merritt
James M. Moore

Richard J. Moore
G. Morrow
John H. Mulkey
Erasmus M. Murphey
William H. Nance
Leonard J. Nease
E. C. Nunn
Benjamin F. Odom
James B. Ogletree
William A. O'Neal
Joseph O. Oswalt
Andrew J. Ousley
Henry L. Parker
L. H. Parker
Preston Parker
Sampson D. Parker
William Parkman
Jordon P. Pate
Henry Patten
Monroe Penn, Jr.
William Pepper
Thomas J. Peppers
Elijah Perdue
Charles Hardy Peurifoy
George W. Phelps
James Joseph Platt
Mark Platt
John M. Rhodes
S. E. Rich
Thomas J. Ritch
Francis Roberts
Nap B. Roberts
L. B. Rovy
----- Rucker
A. M. Slaton
Abner Slaughter
John W. Slaughter
Richard J. Slaughter
T. J. Sloman
A. A. Smith
Thomas W. Spillers
Russell Starnes
Henry Stewart
Robert Stripling
Thomas J. Stripling

George J. Tarvin
Grigsby E. Thomas Sr.
John S. Thornton
John T. Thornton
W. J. Tilley
Andrew Jackson Tucker
James Madison Hill Tucker
A. Jackson Tyler
William Scott Wade
William Wardlaw
Warren A. Ware
George S. Watson
Gilbert Watson
Hartford H. Way
James Ross Webb
E. H. West
Allen Williams
Samuel Williams
William Williams
William C. Williford
Emanuel Wright
John Wright

The 54th Regiment, Georgia Volunteer Infantry

Company H - Muscogee County, Georgia
"Russell Guards"

J. P. Aaron
J. C. Aikens
William Allgood
Elias Alverson
William Ansley
JamesP. Arant
John P. Arrow
Joseph D. Ashfield
John T. Attaway
James P. Avant
Joseph Babb
S. A. Baldwin
E. Ballard
Walter Bannon
C. J. Bates
I. Bazemore
R. F. Beal
John K. Bedell
Berry Bigby
Henry H. Blackman
J. H. Blackwell
Levi S. Blake
R. G. Blake
Samuel L. Blake
Thomas Bolan
Cornelius J. Boles
E. F. Bone
M. Bonham
James E. Bonhart
Charles C. Bonnard
Neely Bowles
V. Bowles
Walter Brannen
James Henry Branner
James Lemuel Brawner
M. L. Brawner
S. Braynard
J. L. Brewer
Thomas F. Brewster

Issac Brigman
Thomas Brigman
J. Broadaway
John M. Brown
John R. Brown
R. D. Brown
Charles Bruce
Benjamin F. Bryant
Columbus C. Buce
E. Bullard
C. C. Callings
D. L. Cape
Henry Cash
J. Tayler Chalker
J. E. Chambers
R. G. Chambers
James C. Claxton
James A. Cochran
C. Columbus Collins
James Cook
Samuel S. Cook
William W. Cook
Noah Corbitt
M. M. Crow
T. J. Crow
J. Crutchfield
Thomas Crutchfield
A. M. Culler
Owen Cummings
Thomas J. Doggett
Joseph T. Dorough
James D. Dougherty
Luther M. Dowdell
J. L. Dudley
George W. Dunaway
Lew Curtis Dunaway
Thomas Dunaway
William Dunaway
J. D. Dyal

A. Judson Ely
George W. Ely
George W. Ely
James D. Ely
Marcus B. Ely
Mary Ely (cook - slave)
W. H. Eskew
Anderson Everidge
W. B. Fain
----- Felzer
Henry Freeman
W. T. German
Jasper Goodman
Joseph G. Goodman
Charles Gorman
G. A. Green
Robert Habersham Guyton
James T. Hamer
William Hancock
J. A. Harrington
Eli Harris
William J. Hart
E. W. Harvey
William H. Harvey
John Haynes
_____ Hays
James W. Henderson
Joseph Adkin Hewett
H. Hicks
Seaborn Johnson Hightower
William J. Hightower
D. W. Holloway
L. J. Horne
Thomas Jefferson Horne
Thomas Jefferson Horne
J. W. Horton
Edwin A. Houston
William LaFayette Howard
Joseph Aikem Howard

Joseph C. Howell
A. J. Hubbard
Erasums Hubbard
Richard J. Hubbard
J. Cater Huckaby
Oliver B. Huckaby
Raymond R. Hutchinson
A. D. Isabell
J. J. Isabell
R. M. Isabell
Daniel Isom
William T. Johnson
Seaborn L. Jones
C. B. Kendrick
William Kendrick
Henry A. J. Kennon
Hickerson Kilcrease
D. G. Kilcrease
James A. Kilcrease
William Kilcrease
Aaron Land
Harvey M. T. Land
John Land
W. Pierce Langford
Moses Lariscy
R. H. Lee
M. A. Marshall
John J. Massey
Barney McAdams
William Albert McCants
Clay M. McCoy
B. B. McCraw
William H. McGee
Valerius A. McGinty
Abraham E. McLeroy
Nathan McLeroy
John W. Miller
T. S. Mitchell
Allen Moody
W. Moore
William B. Moore
A. J. Morgan
James Nathan Morgan
R. H. Morgan
Robert J. Morgan

H. J. Millinnix
Jackson A. Mullins
Henry L. Narramore
James L. Neal
_____ Neal
Amos P. Norris
James Marcus Norris
Joseph Marshall Norris
Littlebury B. Nunnally
Franklin G. O'Conner
Thomas H. Palmer
W. J. Palmer
James M. Perdue
William P. Phillips
George Tillman Pigg
W. Raburn
C. L. Raiford
J. H. Railey
Jefferson Railey
John F. Raley
John T. Railey
John Ramsey
Elias Roach
William A. Robinson
J. T. Rockmore
Adam C. Rodgers
James McCurdy Rodgers
Robert Rodgers
Samuel C. Rodgers
T. J. Rodgers
William Matthew Rodgers
R. A. Rogers
S. W. Royiston
S. Ruford
Charles R. Russell
Dickerson G. Russell
Joseph Russell
Roland A. Russell
R. H. Russell
David Sallis
Ephraim Sallis
Alberry Sanders
R. D. Sasser

W. W. Shanks
A. Silas
John D. Skelton
W. J. Skelton
G. W. Spear
James Samuel Spear
C. T. Spinks
W. W. Spinks
Joseph S. Stevenson
Abdiel Stott
W. B. Strawbridge
Benjamin A. Stripling
Berry A. Stripling
George M. Stripling
John A. Stripling
Milton Stripling
Solomon T. Tarvin
William Tarvin
Alexander Teel
Lafayette Thomas
William Thomas
William H. H. Thomas
Henry Twilley
G. A. Underwood
James P. Upton
Wiley Vann
Franklin Veatch
Nathaniel Wade
John J. Walker
William F. Whitehead
George Washington Williams

The 54th Regiment, Georgia Volunteer Infantry

Company I, Effingham County, Georgia
"Georgia Rangers"

James S. Aaron
William Aaron
James O. Abbott
T. C. Abbott
David B. Arnsdorff
Jonathan C. Arnsdorff
J. L. Arnsdorff
John Lewis Arnsdorff
Thomas L. Bettick
James S. Blassingame
John S. Blasingame
John W. Blasingame
Benjamin Blitch
Thomas L. Blitch
Willie S. Blitch
J. I. Borgsteiner
Frank E. Bourquin
George W. Bray
Joseph W. Brewer
Thomas A. Brewer
Williamson T. Brewer
W. A. J. Brown
John R. Burgstiner
Lawrence E. Burgstiner
William J. Butler
B. T. Carithers
William Chittle
James C. Clark
Charles Christopher Conaway
Francis M. Crosby
Matthew E. Crosby
Y. A. Daniel
Lewis B. Dasher
Richard A. Dasher
W. G. David
James Benjamin Davis
L. Dudley
Thomas A. Dutton
William H. Dutton
Z. E. Dutton

Levi D. Edwards
Harrison C. Elkins
Leander Lucius Elkins
Horace W. Everett
J. J. Everett
George W. Fetzer
E. C. Foy
Edward E. Foy
Abraham J. Futrelle
Micajah Benjamin Futrell
George M. Ganann
Joseph Hanin Ganann
P. D. George
J. A. Gloer
John H. Grady
J. W. Griffith
O. P. Griffith
Joseph C. Grooms
Robert Habersham Guyton
D. Hagin
H. Hagin
W. B. Hannah
Isaiah Heidt
J. J. Heidt
G. W. Herndon
Edwin J. Hinely
James A. Hinely
John M. Hinely
J. W. Hinely
James P. Hodges
Jonathan G. Hodges
R. E. Hodges
Emanuel Hurst
Felix M. Hurst
J. L. Hurst
J. S. Hurst
C. J. Jenkins
Phillip Jones
J. F. Kearney

James Kearney
James A. Kesler
W. V. Kessler
William L. Kirby
Issac J. Lanier
R. H. Lee
Charles LeRoy
E. D. Lloyd
David M. McCray
J. D. Merritt
William Merrit
George D. Mingledorff
Lewis Asbury Mingledorff
T. C. Mitchel
William B. Moody
I. V. Moore
David M. Morton
Henry O. Morton
Silas Morton
Edward Leonard Nease
James Jeremiah Nease
John Robert Nease
John Robert Nease, Jr.
John N. Nease
Leonard J. Nease
Thomas E. Nease
William Albert Nease
James Olliff
W. F. O'Kelley
George I. Patten
H, D, Patten
William C. Patten
K. W. Potterfield
R. L. T. Potterfield
S. B. Power
T. B. Power
J. M. Pullin
P. Quesenberry

Claudius F. Rahn
Lewis W. Rahn
William O. Rahn
James F. Rawls
Morgan Rawls
Zaccheus A. Rawls
John Russell
W. J. Russel
A. J. Sailors
S. M. Scarborough
Valentine M. Seckinger
G. W. Seuze
William J. Shearhouse
Andrew J. Simmons
D. T. Simmons
J. D. Simmons
John M. Simmons
Lacy W. Simmons
J. J. Smith
David Speir
Reddick J. Speir
William S. Speir
W. Spin
C. M. Stephens
Lafayette Thomas
W. A. Tolbert
C. Trice
J. C. Trice
P. A. Tullis
George H. Walthour
Augustus Waters
Charles S. Wilkins
Theodore J. Wilkins
B. A. Williams
M. Williams
J. F. Wirtman
R. T. Wolfe
George W. Zeigler
John A. Zeigler
Benjamin T. Zipperer
J. T. Zipperer
Emmett D. Zittrouer

The 54th Regiment, Georgia Volunteer Infantry

Company K - Appling County, Georgia
"Satilla Rifles"

Abel G. Acridge
Elias Altman
I. C. Altman
Jesse Columbus Altman
R. C. Anderson
Z .W. Anderson
Demetrius Arnett
Henry A. Bennett
Henry Bennett Jr.
Henry Bennett Sr.
Hiram Bennett
Isham A. Bennett
Isham D. Bennett
J. D. Bennett
J. M. (H.) Bennett
John L. Bennett
John Millender Bennett
John W. Bennett
M. A. Bennett
M. H. Bennett
Noah H. Bennett
Richard Bennett
Richard Bennett Jr.
S. C. Bennett
Salathiel A. Bennett
T. J. Booker
Hezekiah Bowen Jr.
Malachi Bowen
Zachariah D. Bowen
G. T. Brantley
Clement C. Byrd
William Cowart
F. A. Cox
John Cox
Isaiah Crook
Jesse Crummey
James C. C. Davis
James M. Davis
Joseph J. Davis

Joseph W. Davis
Elijah Dixon
Elisha Dixon
James Jefferson Dixon
James K. Dixon
John Dixon
William J. Dixon
Edward Dillon
James S. Doyle
A. J. Dunaway
D. D. Dyal
J. D. Dyal
George W. Eason
Silas O. Eason
John Farmer
George W. Farrow
W. J. Gill
A. N. Glaze
R. N. Graves
Nathaniel J. Green
J. T. Gresham
David Griffis
Elijah Griffis
Joel C. Griffis
J. G. Griffis
S. H. Groves
James H. Hannon
Samuel Hargroves
Hyde A. Harmon
J. T. Harnesburger
Stogner Riley Harris
Wiley L. Herndon
James Hogan
W. W. Hugley
Samuel Huson
D. R. Johnson
James Hampton Johnson
James F. Keane

G. H. Kersey
General M. Kersey
Richard Kirkland
E. J. Knight
Ezekial Stafford Knight
Hampton Knight
Isham Reddish Knight
J. R. Knight
James Knight
James McGillis Knight
Jonathan Knight
Nathaniel Stafford Knight
John Landers
Berry A. Leggett
Alfred Lightsey
Daniel Lynn
George W. Lynn
H. B. Lynn
John T. Mann
William H. Mann
John S. Massey
W. J. McClure
Alfred M. McCullar
M. Calvin McCullar
Perry McCullar
James Riley Medders
John Smith Medders
W. W. Medders
Edward Miles
Allen Moody
William Moody
James Moss
James Hamilton Nicholas
Josiah L. Nicholas
William Reese Nicholas
W. B. Norman
Issac M. Odum
George W. O'Quinn
G. M. T. Overstreet

J. H. Overstreet
Abraham E. Patterson
Isham Patterson
Jasper Patterson
Johnson Patterson
Solomon R. Patterson
H. T. Poss, Jr.
H. T. Poss, Sr.
Henry Prescott
N. Prescott
Stephen Purvis
Tillmon Rathbone
Green Berry Ritch
John G. Rich
H. P. Roberson
H. W. Roberson
W. H. Roberson
W. A. Rorie
J. Rowland, Jr.
R. B. Saffold
G. T. Sanders
Allen Sapp
John Henry Sapp
William W. Sapp
James Smaley
James M. Smith
J. J. Spires
J. N. Spires
Banner Thomas
Elias D. Thomas
Lewis Thomas
John B. Thompson
James A. Thornton
John B. Thornton
Jonathan Thornton
Silas Thornton
Timothy Thornton
Phillip Tippens
G. W. Touchtone
M. H. Turner
Reuben A. Warren
Jacob H. Wells
Charles M. Westberry
John Moses Westberry
M. Westberry

M. G. Westberry
Moses Josiah Westberry
W. Charlton Westberry
John Wheaty
G. W. Williams
Robert Williams
Timothy Williams
Daniel Leon Williamson Sr.
Thomas W. Woods

The 54th Regiment, Georgia Volunteer Infantry

The following is an alphabetical listing of the soldiers of the 54th Georgia Volunteer Infantry Regiment extracted from the data contained in the National Archives.

AARON, ANDREW D.: Company G, private. May 12, 1862 enlisted as a private in Co. G, 54th Regiment, Georgia Infantry at Columbus, Georgia. December 31, 1862 received pay including $50.00 bounty pay. January – February 1863 roll shows him present. January and May 8, 1864 issued clothing.

AARON (ARON), J.: Company F, private. September 6, 1862 discharged at Beaulieu near Savannah, Georgia.

AARON, J. P.: Company H, private. November 8, 1862 enlisted in Co. H, 54th Regiment, Georgia Infantry at Columbus, Georgia. November 1862 roll shows him present.

AARON, JAMES: Company F, private. May 17, 1862 enlisted in Co. F, 54th Regiment, Georgia Infantry at Savannah, Georgia and paid $50 enlistment bounty. September 6, 1862 discharged at Beaulieu near Savannah, Georgia. October 16, 1863 enlisted as a private Co. I, 54th Regiment, Georgia Infantry at Rose Dew, Georgia. October 31, 1863 received pay. November-December 1863 roll shows him present. January 1864 issued clothing.

AARON, JAMES S.: Company I, private. October 16, 1863 enlisted as a private Co. I, 54th Regiment, Georgia Infantry at Rose Dew, Georgia. October 31, 1863 received pay. November-December 1863 roll shows him present. July 20, 1864 admitted to Ocmulgee Hospital, Macon, Georgia with Remitting Febris. July 23, 1864 transferred to Emmanuel County, Georgia. He was born July 10, 1844 and died May 14, 1914. He is buried in Elam Church Cemetery at Four points, Jenkins County, Georgia. (find a grave # 51194843)

AARON (ARON), WESLEY: Company F, private. May 12, 1862 enlisted in Co. F, 54th Regiment, Georgia infantry and paid bounty $50.00. September 6, 1862 discharged at Beaulieu, near Savannah, Georgia.

AARON, WILLIAM: Company I, private. May 6, 1862 enlisted in Co. I, 54th Regiment, Georgia Infantry at Guyton, Georgia. December 31, 1862 received pay including $50 enlistment bounty. January-February 1863 roll shows him present. August 31, 1863 received pay. November-December, 1863 roll shows him present. January and June 2, 1864 issued clothing.

ABBOTT, JAMES O.: Company I, private. May 6, 1862 enlisted in Co. I, 54th Regiment, Georgia Infantry at Guyton, Georgia. December 31, 1862 received pay which included $50 enlistment bounty. January-February 1863 roll shows him present. October 31, 1863 received pay. November-December 1863 roll shows him present. January and June 2, 1864 issued clothing. Pension records show; he was absent sick at the close of the war. He was born in Effingham County, Georgia August 11, 1832 and died there May 7, 1914. He is buried in Guyton Christian Church Cemetery at Guyton, Effingham County, Georgia. (find a grave # 34458488)

ABBOTT, T. C.: Company I, private. May 6, 1862 enlisted in Co. I, 54th Regiment, Georgia Infantry at Guyton, Georgia. December 31, 1862 received pay including $50 enlistment bounty. January-February, 1863 roll shows him present. October 31, 1863 received pay. November-December 1863 roll shows him present. January and June 2, 1864 issued clothing.

ACRIDGE, ABEL G.: Company K, private. He enlisted in Co. K, 54th Regiment, Georgia Infantry. November 24, 1862 received pay ($43.26).

ADAIR, W. P.: Company B, private. He enlisted in Co. B, 54th Regiment, Georgia Infantry.

AIKEN, JOSEPH: Company E, private. He enlisted in Co. E, 54th Regiment, Georgia Infantry. September 15, 1862 died in Beaulieu, near Savannah, Georgia.

AIKENS, J. C.: Company H, sergeant. He enlisted in Co. H, 54th Regiment, Georgia Infantry.

ALBERSON, E.: Company F, private. May 12, 1862 enlisted in Co. H, 54th Regiment, Georgia Infantry at Savannah, Georgia. December 31, 1862 received pay. January 1, 1863 transferred from Co. H to Co. F. January-February, 1863 roll shows him present. November 1, 1863 received pay. November-December, 1863 roll shows him present. January 1864 issued clothing.

ALBRITTON, MATTHEW HODGES: Company E, private. October 22, 1862 enlisted as a private in Co. E, 54th Regiment, Georgia Infantry at Coffee Bluff near Savannah, Georgia. December 31, 1862 received pay. January-February 1863 roll shows him present. January and May 8, 1864 issued clothing. Pension records show he was wounded in the throat and abdomen (date and place not specified). He was born in Houston, County, Georgia March 30, 1840 and died in Berrien County, Georgia September 20, 1915. He is buried in Pleasant Cemetery in Berrien County, Georgia. (find a grave # 16662156)

ALBRITTON, W. LITTLETON: Company E, sergeant. May 6, 1862 enlisted in Company E, 54th Regiment, Georgia Infantry at Savannah, Georgia. December 31, 1862 received pay which included $50 enlistment bounty. January-February, 1863 roll shows him present. October 30, 1863 appointed 2nd lieutenant Co. E, 54th Regiment, Georgia Infantry. January 1864 issued clothing. January 24, 1865 granted a leave of absence for 18 days from the Army of Tennessee Headquarters. Pension records show; May 1, 1865 he surrendered at Thomasville, Georgia. He was born November 25, 1833 and died in Nashville, Georgia August 8, 1898. He is buried in Old City Cemetery at Nashville, Berrien County, Georgia. (find a grave # 14770528)

ALEXANDER, J. T.: Company G, private. He enlisted as a private in Co. G, 54th Regiment, Georgia Infantry. May 17, 1865 captured at Hartwell, Georgia and paroled at Hartwell Georgia.

ALFORD, JAMES: Company A, private. August 29, 1862 enlisted In

Co. A, 54th Regiment, Georgia Infantry at Savannah, Georgia. April 30, 1863 received pay. June 1863 roll shows him "Absent Without Leave". January 1864 issued clothing. Pension records show; he enlisted as a private (date and place not shown). July 22, 1864 he was wounded at Atlanta, Georgia. April 1, 1865 he was at home sick with the Measles. He was born in Harris County, Georgia February 11, 1842.

ALFORD, JAMES: Company G, private. He enlisted as a private in Co. G, 54th Regiment, Georgia Infantry.

ALLEN, DAVID: Company A, private. June 13, 1863 enlisted in Co. A, 54th Regiment, Georgia Infantry at Savannah, Georgia. June 30, 1863 roll shows him present. October 31, 1863 received pay. December 1863 roll shows him present. January – February 1864 roll shows him present. January 1, 1864 received pay. March 31, 1864 issued clothing. He was born in Kingsbury, Washington County, New York December 10, 1809. He died in Bibb County, Georgia August 2, 1864. He is buried in the Allen Family Cemetery at Macon, Bibb County, Georgia. (find a grave # 103203141)

ALLEN, JOHN: Company A, private. April 25, 1862 enlisted in Co. A, 54th Regiment, Georgia Infantry at Macon, Georgia. April 30, 1863 received pay. June 30, 1863 roll shows him present. August 31, 1863 received pay. November – December 1863 roll shows him "Absent Without Leave" since December 30, 1863. November 1863 received "Commutation of Rations" from October 30, 1863 to November 5, 1863. January 1, 1864 received pay. January – February 1864 roll shows him present. March 1, 1864 received pay. April 29, 1864 and November 1, 1864 issued clothing. November – December 1864 roll shows him absent of provost duty at Macon, Georgia (in Co. D, 1st Regiment Troops and Defences, Macon, Georgia). April 30, 1865 shown on roll as captured by 1st Brigade, 2nd U. S. Cavalry Division at Macon, Georgia.

ALLEN, PETER: Company A, private. April 22, 1862 enlisted in Co. A, 54th Regiment, Georgia Infantry at Macon, Georgia. April 30, 1863 received pay. June 30, 1863 roll shows him present. October 15, 1863 to October 21, 1863 received "Commutation of Rations". January 1, 1864 received p ay. January – February 1864 roll shows him present. April 28 and November 1, 1864 issued clothing. December 31, 1864 roll shows him absent of provost duty at Macon, Georgia (in Co. D, 1st Regiment Troops and Defences, Macon, Georgia at Camp Wright). April 21-22, 1865 shown on roll as captured by 1st Brigade, 2nd U. S. Cavalry Division at Macon, Georgia.

ALLEN, THOMAS: Company C, private. April 22, 1862 enlisted in Co. C, 54th Regiment, Georgia Infantry. September 16, 1862 died at Beaulieu near Savannah, Georgia.

ALLEN, WALTER: Company C, private. He enlisted in Co. C, 54th Regiment, Georgia Infantry. September 15, 1862 died at Beaulieu near Savannah, Georgia.

ALLGOOD, WILLIAM: Company H, private. February 28, 1865

enlisted in Co. H, 54th Regiment, Georgia Infantry at Hamburg, South Carolina. (Consolidated with Co. F, 37th Regiment, Georgia Infantry.) April 26, 1865 surrendered at Greensboro, North Carolina. May 1, 1865 paroled at Greensboro, North Carolina.

ALLMOND (ALLMON), CALVIN R.: Company G, private. May 12, 1862 enlisted in Co. D, 54th Regiment, Georgia Infantry. He was born March 12, 1830 and died March 28, 1894. He is buried in Rosemere Cemetery in Opelika, Lee County, Alabama. (find a grave # 86308765)

ALLMOND (ALLMON), ELDRIDGE GERALD: Company D, private. 1863 he enlisted in Co. D, 54th Regiment, Georgia Infantry. April 26, 1865 surrendered at Greensboro, North Carolina. May 1, 1865 paroled at Greensboro, North Carolina. He was born in Georgia August 30, 1845 and died in Vidalia, Toombs County, Georgia September 1, 1921. He is buried in Ferguson Cemetery, at Higgston, Montgomery County, Georgia. (find a grave # 59428049)

ALMAND , ELZIE (ELSEY): Company D, private. (June 26) July 21, 1962 enlisted in Co. D, 54th Regiment, Georgia Infantry at Savannah, Georgia and paid bounty $50.00. August 1862 roll shows him present. December 31, 1862 received bounty pay $50.00. January – February 1863 roll shows him present. January 1864 and April 25, 1864 issued clothing. Pension records show: April 26, 1865 surrendered at Greensboro, North Carolina. May 1, 1865 paroled at Greensboro, North Carolina. He was born in Burke County, Georgia September 2, 1843 and died in Emanuel County, Georgia March 24, 1914. He is buried in Bethel United Methodist Church Cemetery at Swainsboro, Emanuel County, Georgia. (find a grave # 66709647)

ALTMAN, ELIAS: Company K, private. October 3, 1861 enlisted as a private in Co. K, 1st Regiment, Georgia State Troops. April 1862 mustered out. April 19, 1862 enlisted in Co. K, 54th Regiment, Georgia Infantry at Savannah and paid $50.00 bounty. May 15, 1862 deserted at Savannah, Georgia. August 1862 roll shows he deserted. May 22, 1865 surrendered in Augusta, Georgia and paroled there. He was born January 20, 1844 and died October 20, 1918. He is buried in Springfield Cemetery in Bacon County, Georgia. (find a grave # 130553879)

ALTMAN, I. C.: Company K, private. He enlisted as a private in Co. K, 54th Regiment, Georgia Infantry.

ALTMAN, JESSE, COLUMBUS: Company K, private. October 3, 1861 enlisted as a private in Co. K, 1st Regiment, Georgia State Troops. April 1862 mustered out. April 18, 1862 enlisted in Co. K, 54th Regiment, Georgia Infantry at Savannah, Georgia and paid bounty $50.00. January 1, 1863 received pay. January – February 1863 roll shows him present. October 2, 1863 received pay $44.00 at Charleston, South Carolina. December 21, 1863 received pay $22.00 at Savannah, Georgia. March 18 and April 18, 1864 issued clothing. May 10, 1865 surrendered at Tallahassee, Florida. May 19, 1865 paroled at Thomasville, Georgia. Parole shows him as 5 feet 7 inches high, light hair, blue eyes and light complexion. He was born November 20, 1842 and died in Pierce County, Georgia January 11, 1899. He is buried in Patterson Cemetery at Patterson, Pierce County, Georgia. (find a grave # 16215727)

ALVERSON, ELIAS: Company F, private. November 8, 1862 enlisted in Co. H, 54th Regiment, Georgia Infantry at Columbus, Georgia. January 17, 1863 he was transferred from Co. H, 54th Regiment, Georgia Infantry to Co. F, 54th Regiment, Georgia Infantry by order of Colonel Way. January-February 1863 roll shows his transfer. November 18, 1863 he is shown on report as dieting. Pension records show: April 26, 1865 surrendered at Greensboro, North Carolina. May 1, 1865 paroled at Greensboro, North Carolina. He was born in Harris County, Georgia July 1839 and died June 10, 1908. He is buried in Barnes Cemetery in Meriwether County, Georgia. (find a grave # 90643983)

ANDERSON, D. W.: Company C, private. He enlisted in Co. C, 54th Regiment, Georgia Infantry.

ANDERSON, J.: Company D, private. December 12, 1862 enlisted in Co. D, 54th Regiment, Georgia Infantry at Beaulieu, near Savannah, Georgia. December 31, 1862 received pay (bounty $50.00). January – February 1863 roll shows him present.

ANDERSON, J. W., JR.: Company D, private. He enlisted in Co. D, 54th Regiment, Georgia Infantry.

ANDERSON, JAMES H.: Company B, private. October 10, 1861 enlisted as a private in Co. K, 2nd Regiment, 1st Brigade, Georgia State Troops. April 1862 mustered out. April 21, 1862 enlisted in Co. B, 54th Regiment, Georgia Infantry at Savannah, Georgia. Pension records show he was at home on sick furlough for 30 days beginning March 8, 1865. May 10, 1865 surrendered at Tallahassee, Florida. May 19, 1865 paroled at Thomasville, Georgia. He was born in Wayne County, Georgia June 21, 1834.

ANDERSON, JAMES J.: Company D, private, September 14, 1863 received pay $44.00 at Charleston, South Carolina. January, April and October 17, 1864 issued clothing.

ANDERSON, JAMES J.: Company B, private. September 7, 1864 admitted to Ocmulgee Hospital at Macon, Georgia with Debilitas Paralysis. August 28, 1864 admitted to Ocmulgee with Paralysis. October 4, 1864 furloughed to Pierce County, Georgia.

ANDERSON, JOHN H.: Company B, private. April 21, 1862 enlisted in Co. B, 54th Regiment, Georgia Infantry at Savannah, Georgia. December 31, 1862 received pay ($50.00 bounty). January – February 1863 roll shows him "prisoner in arrest" absent without leave 6 days. January 1864, May 18, 1864 and April 25, 1864 issued clothing. May 10, 1865 surrendered at Tallahassee, Florida. May 20, 1865 paroled at Thomasville, Georgia.

ANDERSON, JOHN W.: Company F, captain. May 17, 1861 enlisted and elected 2nd lieutenant in Chisholm's Company, Georgia State Troops. May 1862 mustered out. May 13, 1864 appointed 1st lieutenant of Co. B, 54th Regiment, Georgia Infantry. July 1862 roll shows him present at Savannah, Georgia. November 24, 1862 roll shows him present at headquarters District of Georgia. August 1862 roll shows him absent on sick leave since August 22, 1862 (the Regiment is at Beaulieu, Georgia). September, October and November 1862 rolls show him present at Beaulieu, Georgia. December 1862 roll shows him absent detailed as enrolling officer on December 30, 1862. January 2, 1863 absent on special duty. January – February 1863 roll shows him present. March 9, 1863 received pay $90.00. May 30, 1863 roll shows him absent due to court martial at Savannah, Georgia from May 4, 1863. September 26, 1863 roll shows him absent since September 20, 1863 on Quarter Master Duty. November 1863 promoted to Captain, Co. F, 54th Regiment, Georgia Infantry. November 11, 1863 received pay $11.35 for travel expense to court martial. November 27, 1863 roll show him detailed as Quarter Master Duty (to return as soon as possible). November 28, 1863 issued clothing. December 1, 1863 received pay $130.00. November – December 1863 roll shows him absent sick in General Hospital No. 1 at Savannah, Georgia. December 31, 1863 received pay $130.00. January 23, 1864 roll shows him absent due to being a witness in court martial from January 17, 1864. February 11 and 18, 1864 issued clothing. March 10, 1864 granted 10 days leave. March 14, 1864 issued clothing. July 2, 1864 received pay $130.00. April 26, 1865 surrendered in North Carolina. May 3, 1865 paroled in Hillsboro, North Carolina. He was born in Savannah, Chatham County, Georgia September 20, 1843 and died February 16, 1901. He is buried in Bonaventure Cemetery at Savannah, Chatham County, Georgia. (find a grave # 99213645).

ANDERSON, R. C.: Company K, private, November 27, 1862 enlisted in Co. K, 54th Regiment, Georgia Infantry at Beaulieu, near Savannah, Georgia. November 1862 roll shows him present and he joined November 27, 1862. January 1, 1863 received pay. January – February 1864 roll shows him present on extra duty as a courier. March 18, 1864 issued clothing. April 26, 1865 surrendered at Greensboro, North Carolina. May 1, 1865 paroled at Greensboro, North Carolina.

ANDERSON, ROBERT P.: Company G, private. January 15, 1863 enlisted in Co. G, 54th Regiment, Georgia Infantry at Savannah, Georgia. January 19, 1863 deserted at Savannah, Georgia. January – February 1863 roll shows he deserted. He was born in 1835 and died September 30, 1905. He is buried in Porterdale Cemetery at Columbus, Muscogee County, Georgia. (find a grave # 70547592)

ANDERSON, SWAINE MARSH: Company C, private. February 1863 enlisted in Co. B, 54th Regiment, Georgia Infantry. July 23, 1864 wounded in the hand, permanently disabled. Sent to hospital at Macon, Georgia and remained there for two months. He was furloughed for 60 days. He was unable to reach his command at the close of the war. He was born in Georgia October 24, 1846 and died March 17, 1923. He is buried in Hebron Primitive Baptist Church Cemetery at Garfield, Emanuel County, Georgia. (find a grave # 66648087)

ANDERSON, THOMAS V.: Company B, private. October 10, 1861 enlisted as a private in Co. K, 2nd Regiment, 1st Brigade, Georgia State Troops. April 1862 mustered out. April 21, 1862 enlisted in Co. B, 54th Regiment, Georgia Infantry at Savannah, Georgia. December 31, 1862 received bounty pay $50.00. January – February 1863 roll shows him present. January and April 25, 1864 issued clothing. November 10, 1864 captured at Nashville, Tennessee and took the Oath of Allegiance. Prisoner of War record shows him as being a resident of Pierce County, Georgia. Fair complexion, light hair, gray eyes and 5 foot 9 ½ inches high. He was born in Appling County, Georgia June 4, 1841 and died November 25, 1921. He is buried in Conner Cemetery, Raiford, Bradford County, Florida. (find a grave # 25660602)

ANDERSON, Z. W.: Company K, musician, He enlisted as a musician in the 54th Regiment, Georgia Infantry.

ANDREWS, J. O.: Company D, private. May 13, 1862 enlisted as a private in Co. D, 54th Regiment, Georgia Infantry at Savannah, Georgia. December 31, 1862 received bounty pay $50.00. January – February 1863 roll shows him present. March 1, 1863 received pay $22.00. March 10, 1863 issued clothing. May 31, 1863 received pay $16.80. July 1, 1863 through September 30, 1863 detailed as orderly and mail carrier at Savannah, Georgia at $3.00 extra per day. September 2, 1863 and October 31, 1863 received pay $22.00. October 14 and December 30, 1863 issued clothing. November 30, 1863 through December 31, 1863 detailed as orderly and mail carrier at Savannah, Georgia. November –December 1863 roll shows him absent detailed in General Mercer's office since April 10, 1863. December 1863 received pay. January 1864 issued clothing. January 1, 1864 and February 29, 1864 received pay $22.00. January 1, 1864 through April 30, 1864 received $3.00 per day extra pay for extra duty as clerk and orderly and mail carrier at Savannah, Georgia. April 27, 1864 issued clothing. April 26, 1865 surrendered at Greensboro, North Carolina. May 1, 1865 paroled at Greensboro, North Carolina.

ANDREWS, J. O.: Company F, private. May 17, 1861 enlisted as a private in Chisholm's Company, Georgia State Troops. May 1862 mustered out. May 18, 1862 enlisted as a private in Co. F, 54th Regiment, Georgia Infantry. April 26, 1865 surrendered at Greensboro, North Carolina. May 1, 1865 paroled at Greensboro, North Carolina.

ANSLEY, WILLIAM: Company H, private. May 20, 1862 enlisted in Co. H, 54th Regiment, Georgia Infantry at Savannah, Georgia and received bounty $50.00. December 31, 1862 received pay. January – February 1863 roll shows him present. October 31, 1863 received pay. November – December 1863 roll shows him present. December 31, 1863 received pay. January – February 1864 roll shows him present. January and June 2, 1864 issued clothing. Pension records show; he was "on the road returning from Nashville, Tennessee" and was discharged in Alabama in 1865. He was born in Warren County, Georgia January 1, 1842.

ANTONIO, CORSEA (CORSEY): Company C, private. April 30,

1862 enlisted in Co. C, 54th Regiment, Georgia Infantry. April 26, 1865 surrendered at Greensboro, North Carolina. May 1, 1865 paroled at Greensboro, North Carolina. He was born in Spain and was a resident of Georgia since 1858.

ARANT, JAMES P.: Company H, private. November 10, 1862 enlisted in Co. H, 54th Regiment, Georgia Infantry at Columbus, Georgia. December 31, 1862 received pay. January – February 1863 roll shows him present. September 1863 through December 1863 detailed as driving a team at Beaulieu, near Savannah, Georgia at a rate of $.25 per day. October 31, 1863 received pay. November – December 1863 roll shows him present detailed as a teamster. December 31, 1863 received pay. January 1864 issued clothing. January – February 1864 roll shows him present detailed as teamster in the Quartermasters Department since February 24, 1864. February 24, 1864 through April 1864 detailed as a teamster. April 26, 1865 surrendered at Greensboro, North Carolina. May 1, 1865 paroled at Greensboro, North Carolina.

ARMOR, J. W.: Company A, private. August 1862 roll shows he transferred to the Sharpshooters in Savannah, Georgia by Special Order No. 259.

ARNETT, DEMETRIUS: Company K, private. April 27, 1864 enlisted in Co. K, 54th Regiment, Georgia Infantry at Washington, Georgia. April 26, 1865 surrendered at Greensboro, North Carolina. May 1, 1862 paroled at Greensboro, North Carolina.

ARNETT, R.: Company D, private. October 16, 1862 transferred to Co. D, 54th Regiment, Georgia Infantry at Beaulieu, near Savannah, Georgia.

ARNSDORFF, DAVID BENJAMIN: Company I, corporal. May 6, 1862 enlisted in Co. I, 54th Regiment, Georgia Infantry at Camp Davis near Guyton, Georgia. December 31, 1862 received pay bounty $50.00. January – February 1863 roll shows he was present sick in Regimental Hospital. October 31, 1863 received pay. November – December 1863 roll shows he was present detailed as the captain's clerk. January 1864 issued clothing. April 26, 1865 surrendered at Greensboro, North Carolina. May 1, 1862 paroled at Greensboro, North Carolina. He was born December 24, 1836 and died in Effingham County, Georgia November 15, 1909. He is buried in Bethel Lutheran Church Cemetery at Springfield, Effingham County, Georgia. (find a grave # 67904172)

ARNSDORFF, JOHN LEWIS: Company I, private. May 6, 1862 enlisted in Co. I, 54th Regiment, Georgia Infantry at Camp Davis near Guyton, Georgia received bounty $50.00. December 31, 1862 received pay. January – February 1863 roll shows him present. October 31, 1863 received pay. November – December 1863 roll shows him present detailed to build houses for the company. January 1864 issued clothing. He was born in 1828 and died January 25, 1865. He is buried in Veterans Park of Effingham County at Springfield, Effingham County, Georgia. (find a grave #42380132)

ARNSDORFF, JONATHAN C.: Company I, private. November 20,

1862 enlisted in Co. I, 54th Regiment, Georgia Infantry at Beaulieu, near Savannah, Georgia. November 1862 roll shows him present. (joined November 20 at Beaulieu). December 31, 1862 received $50.00 bounty pay. January – February 1863 roll shows him present. October 31, 1863 received pay. November – December 1863 roll shows him present. January 1864 issued clothing. April 26, 1865 surrendered at Greensboro, North Carolina. May 1, 1862 paroled at Greensboro, North Carolina. He was born in Effingham County, Georgia December 5, 1835 and died June 24, 1905. He is buried in Bethel Lutheran Church Cemetery at Springfield, Effingham County, Georgia (find a grave # 67965694)

ARROW, JOHN P.: Company H, private. November 8, 1862 enlisted in Co. H, 54th Regiment, Georgia Infantry at Columbus, Georgia. November 1862 roll shows him present.

ASHFIELD, JOSEPH D.: Company H, private. May 12, 1862 enlisted in Co. F, 54th Regiment, Georgia infantry. January – February 1863 roll shows him present and due two months' pay for September and October. October 31, 1863 received pay. November – December 1863 roll shows him present. December 31, 1863 received pay. January 1864 issued clothing. January – February 1864 roll shows him present. Pension records show; He was in the hospital with Frostbitten Feet at the close of the war. He was born in Putnam County, Georgia August 5, 1832 and died in Talbot County, Georgia June 10, 1902. He is buried in Culpepper Cemetery in Talbot County, Georgia. (find a grave # 122100181)

ATKINSON (ATKISON), W.: Company B, private. He enlisted as a private in Co. B, 54th Regiment, Georgia Infantry.

ATTAWAY, JOHN T.: Company H, private. May 12, 1862 enlisted as a private in Co. F, 54th Regiment, Georgia infantry. November 1, 1863 transferred to Co. C, 27th Battalion, Georgia Infantry (non-conscript). March – April 1864 roll shows he was discharged by writ of habeas corpus in March 1864. He was born November 23, 1846 and died July 11, 1922. He is buried in Pleasant Ridge Cemetery at Arguta, Dale County, Alabama. (find a grave # 22023470)

AVANT, JAMES P.: Company H, private. November 10, 1862 enlisted as a private in Co. F, 54th Regiment, Georgia infantry. February 1864 detailed as a teamster for the Quartermaster's Department.

AVERA, G. H.: Company E, musician. He enlisted as a musician in Co. E, 54th Regiment, Georgia Infantry.

AVERA, JOHN F.: Company A, private. April 28, 1862 enlisted in Co. A, 54th Regiment, Georgia Infantry at Macon, Georgia. October 31, 1862 received pay. November – December 1862 roll shows him present. April 30, 1863 received pay. June 30, 1863 roll shows him present. January 1, 1864 received pay. January – February 1864 roll shows him present. March 31 and April 28, 1864 issued clothing.

AVERA, STEPHEN WILLIS: Company E, sergeant. May 6, 1862 enlisted as a private and was appointed 5th sergeant in Co. E. 54th Regiment, Georgia Infantry at Savannah, Georgia and paid bounty $50.00. December

31, 1862 received pay. January – February 1863 roll shows him as present sick. October 31, 1863 received pay. December 31, 1863 hospital roll for First Georgia Hospital at Charleston, South Carolina shows him present. January 1864 issued clothing. May 10, 1865 surrendered at Tallahassee, Florida. May 24, 1865 paroled at Thomasville, Georgia. He was born in Wilkinson County, Georgia January 5, 1836 and died in Berrien County, Georgia October 30, 1924. He is buried in Pleasant Grove Primitive Baptist Church Cemetery at Moultrie, Colquitt County, Georgia. (find a grave #52040194)

AVERA, WALTER: Company E, private. May 6, 1862 enlisted as a private in Co. E. 54th Regiment, Georgia Infantry at Savannah, Georgia and paid bounty $50.00. September 15, 1862 died at Beaulieu near Savannah, Georgia.

AVERA (AVREA), WILLIAM: Company A, private. May 4, 1863 enlisted in Co. A, 54th Regiment, Georgia Infantry at Savannah, Georgia. November 27, 1862 received bounty pay $50.00. December 31, 1862 received pay. January – February 1863 roll shows him present. April 30, 1863 received pay. June 30, 1863 roll shows him present. August 21, 1863 received pay $33.00 at Charleston, South Carolina. October 31, 1863 received pay. November 1863 received commutation of rations for time on sick leave. November – December 1863 roll shows him present sick in company hospital. January 1, 1864 received pay. January 1864 issued clothing. January – February 1864 roll shows him present. April 29, 1864 issued clothing. April 20 and 21 1865 he is shown as captured at Macon, Georgia.

AVERA (AVREA), WILLIAM M.: Company E, private. He enlisted as a private in Co. E. 54th Regiment, Georgia Infantry. He was born in Wilkinson County, Georgia July 3, 1834 and died in Berrien County, Georgia March 2, 1896. He is buried in the Griffin Cemetery, in Berrien County, Georgia. (find a grave # 16023640)

AVERTT (AVRETT), JOHN: Company G, private. January 22, 1863 enlisted in Co. G, 54th Regiment, Georgia Infantry at Columbus, Georgia and received $50.00 bounty pay. January – February 1863 roll shows him present.

BABB, JOSEPH: Company H, private. He enlisted in Co. H, 54th Regiment, Georgia Infantry.

BAILEY, CHARLES F.: Company F, sergeant. May 17, 1861 enlisted and appointed 2nd corporal in Chisholm's Company, Georgia State Troops. May 1862 mustered out. May 13, 1862 enlisted as 4th sergeant in Co. F, 54th Regiment, Georgia Infantry at Savannah, Georgia and paid bounty $50.00. December 31, 1862 received pay. January – February 1863 roll shows him present as 4th sergeant. September 22, 1863 appointed 3rd sergeant. November 1, 1863 received pay. November – December 1863 roll shows him present as 3rd sergeant. January 1864 issued clothing. June 18, 1864 he was captured near Marietta, Georgia. June 26, 1864 received at Military Prison, Louisville, Kentucky from Nashville, Tennessee. June

27, 1864 sent to Camp Morton, Indiana. June 28, 1864 arrived at Camp Morton, Indiana. May 18, 1865 took oath of allegiance at Camp Morton, Indiana. Described: residence – New York City, complexion –florid, hair – dark, eyes – grey, height – 5ft 4 ¾ inches. He was born November 2, 1843 and died December 11, 1933. He is buried in Evergreen Cemetery at Saint Augustine, St. Johns County, Florida. (find a grave # 9325162)

BAILEY, E. P.: Company C, sergeant. He enlisted as a sergeant in Co. C, 54th Regiment, Georgia Infantry.

BAILEY, J. M.: Company C, private. He enlisted as a private in Co. C, 54th Regiment, Georgia Infantry.

BAILEY, J. R.: Company C, private. He enlisted as a private in Co. C, 54th Regiment, Georgia Infantry.

BAILEY, JAMES BLACKSTONE: Company A, private. April 26, 1862 enlisted in Co. A, 54th Regiment, Georgia Infantry at Macon, Georgia. December 31, 1862 received pay. June 30, 1863 roll shows him present. He was born January 19, 1830 and died April 16, 1880. He is buried in Bailey – Collins Cemetery in Bibb County, Georgia. (find a grave # 25666910)

BAILEY, L. L.: Company C, private. He enlisted as a private in Co. C, 54th Regiment, Georgia Infantry.

BAILEY, N. L.: Company C, sergeant. He enlisted as a sergeant in Co. C, 54th Regiment, Georgia Infantry.

BAKER, E.: Company E, private. He enlisted as a private in Co. E, 54th Regiment, Georgia Infantry.

BAKER, SOLOMON: Company A, private. September 1, 1862 enlisted in Co. A, 54th Regiment, Georgia Infantry at Macon, Georgia. October 31, 1863 received pay. November – December 1863 roll shows him present. January 1, 1864 received pay. January – February 1864 roll shows him present. March 31, 1864 and April 29, 1864 issued clothing. May 27, 1864 shows on register of Floyd House and Ocmulgee Hospitals at Macon, Georgia with a Gunshot Wound to the right knee. (Disease continued. Ball striking the top of the patella and passing around and out at lower third of thigh.) Pension records show he was furloughed for 60 days and was at home wounded at the close of the war. He is shown as a resident of Twiggs County, Georgia. He was born in Georgia October 3, 1839 and died in Twiggs County, Georgia February 1913. He is buried in Baker Family Cemetery at Jeffersonville, Twiggs County, Georgia. (find a grave # 43929363)

BAKER, THOMAS ASA: Company E, private. May 6, 1862 enlisted in Co. E, 54th Regiment, Georgia Infantry at Savannah, Georgia and paid bounty of $50.00. December 31, 1862 received pay. January – February 1863 roll shows him present. August 31, 1863 received pay for 62 days ($24.80). September 1863 through October 1863 detailed on extra duty as a mechanic at Savannah, Georgia. October 31, 1863 received pay. January 1864 issued clothing. May 1, 1864 received pay $104.63. May 8, 1864 issued clothing. November 1863 through March 1864 detailed on extra duty as a mechanic at Savannah, Georgia. November 20, 1864 issued clothing at Convalescent Camp Wright. November – December 1864 shown in Co. C, 1st Regiment Troops and Defences, Macon, Georgia stationed at Camp Knight, Macon, Georgia as absent as Provost Guard at Albany, Georgia. May 10, 1865 surrendered at Tallahassee, Florida. May 26, 1865 paroled at Albany, Georgia. He was born in Irwin County, Georgia March 3, 1829 and died in Berrien County, Georgia May 1, 1892. He is buried in Baker Cemetery in Cook County, Georgia. (find a grave # 36793551)

BAKER, ZACHARIAH: Company E, private. May 6, 1862 enlisted in Co. E, 54th Regiment, Georgia Infantry at Savannah, Georgia and was paid $50.00 bounty. October 31, 1862 received pay. January – February 1863 roll shows him absent without leave since January 27, 1863. January 1864 and April 25, 1864 issued clothing. Pension records show he was at home on sick furlough at the close of the war.
May 10, 1865 surrendered at Tallahassee, Florida. May 26, 1865 paroled at Albany, Georgia. He was born in Lowndes County, Georgia in 1834 and died in Berrien County, Georgia in 1911.

BALDREE, WILLIAM A., SR.: Company E, private. May 6, 1862 enlisted in Co. E, 54th Regiment, Georgia Infantry at Savannah, Georgia and was paid $50.00 bounty. December 31, 1862 received pay. January – February 1863 roll shows him present. January 1864 issued clothing. May 24, 1865 surrendered and pardoned at Thomasville, Georgia. He was born in Tattnall County, Georgia May 4, 1834 and died in Berrien County, Georgia February 14, 1914. He is buried in Empire Primitive Baptist Church Cemetery at Lakeland, Lanier County, Georgia. (find a grave # 14633727)

BALDWIN, S. A.: Company H, private. He enlisted as a private in Co. H, 54th Regiment, Georgia Infantry.

BALLARD, E.: Company H (A), private. August 1862 roll shows he deserted at Savannah, Georgia on May 20, 1862. September 1, 1862 transferred to Company A on September 1, 1862 at Beaulieu, Georgia (Special Order No. 6). September 1862 roll shows his transfer.

BANKS, CHARLES: Company B, private. He enlisted in Co. B, 54th Regiment, Georgia Infantry. He was born in Wilmington, New Hanover County, North Carolina January 1, 1840 and died in Appling County, Georgia in 1909. He is buried in Midway Church Cemetery in Appling County, Georgia. (find a grave # 22578570)

BANKSTON, S. J.: Company B, private. He enlisted in Co. B, 54th Regiment, Georgia Infantry.

BANNON (BRANNON), WALTER: Company H, private. He enlisted as a private in Co. H, 54th Regiment, Georgia Infantry.

BARBEE, BENJAMIN: Company C, private. March 20, 1863 enlisted in Co. C, 54th Regiment, Georgia Infantry at Savannah, Georgia. October 31, 1863 received pay. December 1863 roll of General Hospital No. 1 at Savannah, Georgia shows him present and due 2 months' pay. February

1864 roll of General Hospital No. 1 at Savannah, Georgia shows him present and due 4 months' pay. January – February 1864 roll shows him absent sick in the hospital at Savannah, Georgia since July 10, 1863 (Dls. list furnished).

BARFIELD (BAREFIELD), A. NEEDHAM: Company G (F), private. May 12, 1862 enlisted in Co. G, 54th Regiment, Georgia Infantry at Columbus, Georgia and received bounty pay $50.00. December 31, 1862 received pay. January – February 1863 roll shows him present (previously shown on the rolls as A. Barfield through mistake). January 1864 and April 25, 1864 issued clothing. May 12 (13), 1864 wounded and left arm permanently disabled at Resaca, Georgia. April 26, 1865 surrendered at Greensboro, North Carolina. May 1, 1865 paroled at Greensboro, North Carolina (shown in consolidated Company F and absent without leave).

BARFIELD, J. C.: Company A (D), sergeant. He enlisted as a sergeant in Co. A, 54th Regiment, Georgia Infantry.

BARFIELD, JOHN R.: Company A (D), sergeant. May 3, 1862 enlisted in Co. A, 54th Regiment, Georgia Infantry at Macon, Georgia and was elected 1st corporal. April 30, 1863 received pay.
June 30, 1863 roll shows him present. He was elected 4th sergeant of Co. A, 54th Regiment, Georgia Infantry and was Quartermaster Sergeant. May 1863 through August 31, 1863 detailed as Quartermaster Sergeant (Siege Train). August 31, 1863 received pay at Savannah, Georgia. October 1, 1863 through October 31, 1863 detailed as Quartermaster Sergeant at Isle of Hope, Savannah, Georgia. October 31, 1863 received pay. November – December 1863 roll shows him present. January 1, 1864 received pay. January – February 1864 roll shows him present and due pay from September and October. March 31, 1864 issued clothing. April 29, 1864 issued clothing. April 26, 1865 surrendered in Co. D, 54th Regiment, Consolidated Georgia Infantry at Greensboro, North Carolina. May 1, 1865 paroled at Greensboro, North Carolina. He was born in Georgia in 1834 and died in Morris County, Texas June 27, 1890. He is buried in Barfield Cemetery at Dangerfield, Morris County, Texas. (find a grave # 55681343)

BARRON, ISSAC: Company F, private. He enlisted as a private in Co. F, 54th Regiment, Georgia Infantry. July 22, 1864 wounded in Atlanta, Georgia.

BARRON, J. J.: Company F (D), private. March 10, 1863 enlisted in Co. F, 54th Regiment, Georgia Infantry at Savannah, Georgia. November 1, 1863 received pay. November – December 1863 roll shows him present. January 1864 and April 25, 1864 issued clothing. April 26, 1865 surrendered in Co. D, 54th Regiment, Consolidated Georgia Infantry at Greensboro, North Carolina. May 1, 1865 paroled at Greensboro, North Carolina. (He was shown as being in Company D of the consolidated 54th Georgia.)

BARROW, THOMAS, J.: Company G, private. He enlisted in Co. G, 54th Regiment, Georgia Infantry. He was born in Macon, Bibb County,

Georgia February 25, 1842 and died in Andalusia, Covington County, Alabama August 31, 1910. He is buried in Camerons Chapel Cemetery in Brantley, Crenshaw County, Alabama. (find a grave # 16274352)

BARRY (BARREY), C. JOHN: Company F, private. May 17, 1861 enlisted as a private in Chisholm's Company, Georgia State Troops. May 1862 mustered out. May 13, 1862 enlisted in Co. F. 54th Regiment, Georgia Infantry. September 5, 1862 discharged at Beaulieu, near Savannah, Georgia. September 1862 roll shows his discharge.

BASEMORE (BAZEMORE)(BAZIMORE), PERRY: Company D, private. February 22, 1862 enlisted in Co. D. 54th Regiment, Georgia Infantry and paid bounty $50.00. December 31, 1862 received pay. January – February 1863 roll shows him present on picket duty.

BASKIN, JAMES MADISON: Company E, private. May 10, 1862 enlisted as a private in Co. E, 54th Regiment, Georgia Infantry at Savannah, Georgia and paid bounty $50.00. November and December 1862 roll shows him detailed as a boatman. December 31, 1862 received pay. January – February 1863 roll shows him present. August 31, 1863 received pay $24.80. July 1, 1863 through April 27, 1864 detailed on extra duty at Savannah, Georgia as a mechanic at an additional $.40 per day. May 1, 1864 received pay $109.13. January 1864 and May 8, 1864 issued clothing. July 22, 1864 wounded at Atlanta, Georgia. August 29, 1864 issued clothing. April 1865 he was furloughed home from La Grange, Georgia hospital. He was born in Houston County, Georgia April 6, 1829 and died in Berrien County, Georgia July 7, 1913. He is buried at Beaver Dam Cemetery at Ray City, Berrien County, Georgia. (find a grave # 110565335)

BASS, E. F.: Company A, private. April 29, 1862 enlisted as a private in Co. A, 54th Regiment, Georgia Infantry at Macon, Georgia. April 30, 1863 received pay. June 30, 1863 roll shows him present. October 31, 1863 received pay. November – December 1863 roll shows him present. January 1, 1864 received pay. January – February 1864 roll shows him present. March 31, 1864 issued clothing.

BASS, MATTHEW W.: Company A, private. September 1, 1863 enlisted in Co. A, 54th Regiment, Georgia Infantry at Macon, Georgia. October 31, 1863 received pay. November – December 1863 roll shows him present. January 1, 1864 received pay. January – February 1864 roll shows him present. March 31, 1864 issued clothing. Pension record shows he was discharged in 1864. He was born in Jones County, Georgia in 1823 and died there in 1897.

BATES, C. J.: Company H, private. November 5, 1862 enlisted as a private in Co. F, 54th Regiment, Georgia Infantry. January 1, 1863 detailed to Pioneer Corps.

BATES, H.: Company A, private. September 1, 1862 transferred from Co. H, 54th Regiment, Georgia Infantry to Co. A, 54th Regiment, Georgia Infantry (Special order No. 6) at Beaulieu, near Savannah, Georgia.

BATES, JOHN T.: Company A, private. April 21, 1862 enlisted in Co.

A, 54th Regiment, Georgia Infantry at Macon, Georgia. April 30, 1863 received pay. June 30, 1863 roll shows him present. October 31, 1863 received pay. November – December 1863 roll shows him present. January 1, 1864 received pay. January – February 1864 roll shows him absent on furlough. April 29, 1864 issued clothing. March 1, 1865 admitted to Ocmulgee Hospital at Macon, Georgia with Ulcus. March 27, 1865 returned to duty. He was a resident of Bibb County, Georgia.

BAUGHMAN, JOHN A.: Company D, private. April 30, 1862 enlisted in Co. A, 54th Regiment, Georgia Infantry at Savannah, Georgia and received bounty $50.00. December 31, 1862 received pay. January – February 1863 roll shows him present (note Camp Ward). August 29, 1863 wounded at Battery Wagner on Morris Island near Charleston, South Carolina. January 1864, April 25, 1864 and May 1964 issued clothing. February 10, 1864 through April 30, 1864 on detail special duty as a mechanic at Savannah, Georgia and Hardeeville, South Carolina. April 26, 1865 surrendered at Greensboro, North Carolina. May 1, 1865 paroled at Greensboro, North Carolina. He was born in Barnwell County, South Carolina February 24, 1832 and died in Screven County, Georgia March 14, 1904. He is buried in Sardis Cemetery at Sardis, Burke County, Georgia. (find a grave # 29411429)

BAXLEY, MICHAEL: Company B, corporal. April 28, 1862 enlisted in Co. B, 54th Regiment, Georgia Infantry at Savannah, Georgia.

BAXLEY, MITCHELL: Company B, corporal. April 28, 1862 enlisted in Co. B, 54th Regiment, Georgia Infantry at Savannah, Georgia and received bounty $50.00. December 31, 1862 received pay. January – February 1863 roll shows him absent since February 4, 1863 enrolling conscripts. December 16, 1863 received pay $104.00 at Savannah, Georgia. March 1864 discharged due to being elected to Civil Office (after being elected Sheriff of Appling County). He was a resident of Appling County, Georgia. He was born January 14, 1863 in Appling County, Georgia and died January 30, 1917 in Appling County, Georgia. He is buried in the Baxley Graveyard (Cemetery) in Appling County, Georgia. (find a grave # 62785745)

BAZEMORE, I.: Company H, private. November 10, 1862 enlisted in Co. H, 54th Regiment, Georgia Infantry.

BAZEMORE, PERRY: Company D, private. He enlisted in Co. D, 54th Regiment, Georgia Infantry. He was born November 20, 1824 and died in Sylvania, Screven County, Georgia May 2, 1888. He is buried in the Bazemore Cemetery in Screven County, Georgia. (find a grave # 23499263)

BEAL, R. F.: Company H, private. May 12, 1862 enlisted in Co. H, 54th Regiment, Georgia Infantry at Beaulieu, near Savannah, Georgia. October 31, 1862 received pay. January 16, 1863 discharged for substitute George F. Pigg. January – February 1863 roll shows him discharged for substitute George T. Pigg. He was born in 1843 and died in 1879. He is buried in Hamilton Cemetery at Hamilton, Harris County, Georgia. (find a grave #

125415873)

BEALE (BEALL), JAMES: Company F, musician. May 17, 1861 enlisted as a private in Chisholm's Company, Georgia State Troops. May 1862 mustered out. January 19, 1863 enlisted as a musician in Co. F, 54th Regiment, Georgia Infantry at Savannah, Georgia and received bounty $50.00. January – February 1863 roll shows him present. August 1, 1863 transferred to Co F, 63rd Regiment, Georgia Infantry. 1863 transferred to Co D, 63rd Regiment, Georgia Infantry.

BEAN, ROBERT M.: Company E, corporal. He enlisted in Co. E, 54th Regiment, Georgia Infantry.

BEASLEY, E. H.: Company A, private. He enlisted as a private in Co. A, 54th Regiment, Georgia Infantry.

BEASLEY, J. E.: Company A, private. He enlisted in as a private in Co. A, 54th Regiment, Georgia Infantry.

BECK, ISHAM M.: Company F, private. October 1862 enlisted in Co. F, 54th Regiment, Georgia Infantry at Savannah, Georgia and received bounty $50.00. May 1865 paroled at Macon, Georgia. He was born in Anderson, South Carolina September 29, 1826.

BECK, J. E.: Company B, private. He enlisted in Co. B, 54th Regiment, Georgia Infantry.

BECK, J. M.: Company F, private. February 12, 1863 enlisted in Co. F, 54th Regiment, Georgia Infantry at Savannah, Georgia and received bounty $50.00.

BECK, JOHN M.: Company F, private. January 19, 1863 enlisted in Co. F, 54th Regiment, Georgia Infantry at Savannah, Georgia and received bounty $50.00. November 1, 1863 received pay. November – December 1863 roll shows him present. January – February 1863 roll shows him present. January 1864 issued clothing.

BECK, JOHN M.: Company C, private. He enlisted in Co. C, 54th Regiment, Georgia Infantry.

BECKTON, DAVID: Company E, private. October 6, 1861 enlisted as a private in Co. K, 5th Regiment, Georgia State Troops. April 1862 mustered out. May 6, 1862 enlisted in Co. E, 54th Regiment, Georgia Infantry at Savannah, Georgia and received bounty $50.00. December 31, 1862 received pay. January – February 1863 roll shows him present. January 1864 issued clothing.

BECTON, ANDREW JACKSON: Company D, private. April 30, 1862 enlisted in Co. D, 54th Regiment, Georgia Infantry at Savannah, Georgia and received bounty $50.00. December 31, 1862 received pay. January – February 1863 roll shows him present. January 1864, April 25, 1864 and May 8, 1864 issued clothing. Pension records show: April 26, 1865 surrendered at Greensboro, North Carolina. May 1, 1865 paroled at Greensboro, North Carolina. He was born in Screven County, Georgia July 5, 1835 and died August 30, 1913. He is buried in Big Horse Creek Cemetery in Jenkins County, Georgia. (find a grave # 10965437)

BEDELL (BIDDELL) (BURDELL), JOHN K.: Company H, lieutenant.

May 12, 1862 enlisted in Co. H, 54th Regiment, Georgia Infantry at Columbus, Georgia. May 14, 1862 appointed 2nd lieutenant Co. H, 54th Regiment, Georgia Infantry at Savannah, Georgia. July 1862 roll shows him present at Savannah, Georgia. August 1862 and September1862 rolls show him present at Beaulieu, near Savannah, Georgia. October 1862 roll shows him present (sick) at Beaulieu, near Savannah, Georgia. November 24, 1862 shown on roll of officers listed Headquarters, District of Georgia at Savannah, Georgia. November 1862 roll shows him absent with leave (for 10 days) since November 29, 1862 from Beaulieu, near Savannah, Georgia. December 1862 roll shows him present at Beaulieu, near Savannah, Georgia. January 2, 1863 he is shown on report as sick. January – February 1863 roll shows him present. May 22, 1863 to June 1, 1863 and August 25, 1863 to August 26, 1863 he is shown as being on leave by order of General Mercer. December 5, 1863 received pay $80.00. December 15, 1863 promoted to 1st lieutenant of Co. H, 54th Regiment, Georgia Infantry. November – December 1863 roll shows him. January 13, 1864 received pay $80.00. February 24, 1864 issued clothing. February 29, 1864 15 days leave granted by General Mercer. January – February 1864 roll shows him present. June 2, 1864 received pay $180.00. July 2, 1864 received pay $ 90.00. August 25, 1864 he is shown on Inspection Report of Mercer's Brigade (Cleburne's Division) in the field near Atlanta, Georgia as sick in the hospital at Macon, Georgia. September 14, 1864 he is shown on Inspection Report of Mercer's Brigade (Cleburne's Division) in camp near Jonesboro, Georgia as sick in the Medical Board Division Hospital.

BEDENFIELD (BEDINFIELD), E. P.: Company C, private. May 6, 1862 enlisted in Co. C, 54th Regiment, Georgia Infantry at Savannah, Georgia and received bounty $50.00. December 31, 1862 received pay. January – February 1863 roll shows him present. December 1, 1863 issued clothing. January 1, 1864 received pay. January – February 1864 roll shows him absent (detached as ambulance driver by order of Major Mann on February 20, 1864). April 25, 1864 and April 28, 1864 issued clothing. May 24, 1865 surrendered and paroled at Augusta, Georgia.

BEDENFIELD (BEDDINGFIELD), J. J.: Company C, private. May 5, 1862 enlisted in Co. C, 54th Regiment, Georgia Infantry at Savannah, Georgia and received bounty $50.00. August 8, 1862 died of disease at Savannah, Georgia. August 1862 roll shows his death.

BELL, JOHN: Company C, private. October 9, 1862 enlisted in Co. C, 54th Regiment, Georgia Infantry at Savannah, Georgia and received bounty $50.00. December 31, 1862 received pay. January – February 1863 roll shows him present in hospital at Bethesda. January 1, 1864 received pay. January – February 1864 roll shows him present. April 28, 1864 issued clothing. August 31, 1864 wounded in the left leg and permanently disabled. He was born in Jefferson County, Georgia April 1, 1844 died in Swainsboro, Emanuel County, Georgia September 24, 1906. He is buried in the Swainsboro Early Settlers Cemetery at Swainsboro,

Emanuel County, Georgia. (find a grave # 38792987)

BENNETT, ANTHONY: Company F, private. He enlisted in Co. F, 54th Regiment, Georgia Infantry.

BENNETT, HENRY A.: Company K, lieutenant. October 3, 1861 enlisted as a private and appointed 4th sergeant in Co. A, 1st Regiment, 1st Brigade, Georgia State Troops. April 1862 mustered out. April 18, 1862 enlisted as 1st sergeant in Co. K, 54th Regiment, Georgia Infantry at Savannah, Georgia and received bounty $50.00. January – February 1863 roll shows him present. September 4, 1863 received pay $80.00. January 1, 1864 received pay. January – February 1864 roll shows him present. March 16, 1864 issued clothing. He was promoted to 2nd lieutenant. September 14, 1864 he is shown on report of Mercers Brigade in camp near Jonesboro, Georgia as being wounded in Medical Board Division Hospital. He was born November 7, 1838 and died in Baxley, Appling County, Georgia December 31, 1917. He is buried in Omega Cemetery in Appling County, Georgia. (find a grave # 120048341)

BENNETT, HENRY, Sr.: Company K, private. April 18, 1862 enlisted as a private in Co. K, 54th Regiment, Georgia Infantry at Savannah, Georgia and received bounty $50.00. August 1862 roll shows he was transferred to 1st Georgia Sharpshooters in Savannah, Georgia by Special Order 259. December 22, 1862 died. November 4, 1862 death benefit claim was filed by Nancy L. Bennett, his wife.

BENNETT, HENRY, Jr.: Company K, private. April 19, 1862 enlisted as a private in Co. K, 54th Regiment, Georgia Infantry at Savannah, Georgia and received bounty $50.00. June 10, 1862 he deserted. August 1862 roll shows he deserted. January 1, 1864 received pay. January – February 1864 roll shows him present. December 1863 died of Typhoid Fever in Savannah, Georgia.

BENNETT, HIRAM: Company K, private. October 3, 1861 enlisted as a private in Co. A, 1st Regiment, 1st Brigade, Georgia State Troops. April 1862 mustered out. April 18, 1862 enlisted as a private in Co. K, 54th Regiment, Georgia Infantry at Savannah, Georgia and received bounty $50.00. July 30, 1862 transferred to 1st Georgia Sharpshooters by Special Order No. 259. August 31, 1864 he was wounded in the right leg necessitating amputation at Jonesboro, Georgia. May 10, 1865 surrendered at Tallahassee, Florida. May 22, 1865 paroled at Thomasville, Georgia.

BENNETT, ISHAM A.: Company K, private. April 19, 1862 enlisted as a private in Co. K, 54th Regiment, Georgia Infantry at Savannah, Georgia and received bounty $50.00. March 18, 1864, April 25, 1864 and June 2, 1864 issued clothing. May 10, 1865 surrendered at Tallahassee, Florida. May 15, 1865 paroled at Tallahassee, Florida. He is described as: 5 feet 5 inches high, light hair, grey eyes and fair complexion.

BENNETT, ISHAM D.: Company K, private. October 3, 1861 enlisted as a private in Co. A, 1st Regiment, 1st Brigade, Georgia State Troops. April 1862 mustered out. April 18, 1862 enlisted as a private in Co. K, 54th Regiment, Georgia Infantry at Savannah, Georgia and received bounty $50.00. January 1, 1863 received pay. January – February 1863 roll shows him present. January 22, 1862 admitted to Way Hospital at Meridian, Mississippi with Diarrhoea and was transferred to Quintard Hospital. Pension records show; he was at home on sick furlough at the close of the war. He was born in Appling County, Georgia July 29, 1837 and died in Wayne County, Georgia April 27, 1920. He is buried in Stogner R. Harris Family Cemetery in Ritch, Wayne County, Georgia. (find a grave # 102035550)

BENNETT, J. D.: Company K, private. April 19, 1862 enlisted as a private in Co. K, 54th Regiment, Georgia Infantry at Savannah, Georgia and received bounty $50.00. January 5, 1864 received pay $22.00, shown as being detailed as a guard on the Atlantic and Gulf Railroad. March 18, 1864, April 18, 1864 and April 25, 1864 issued clothing. February 2, 1865 admitted to Way Hospital at Meridian, Mississippi with a gunshot wound. February 7, 1865 roll of Way Hospital at Meridian, Mississippi shows he was transferred to Quintard Hospital and furloughed for 60 days to Grady, Georgia.

BENNETT, J. M.: Field and Staff, sergeant major (Company K, private). April 19, 1862 enlisted as a private in Co. K, 54th Regiment, Georgia Infantry at Savannah, Georgia and received bounty $50.00. He was appointed Sergeant Major of the 54th Regiment, Georgia Infantry. He died August 2, 1864 in Macon, Georgia and is buried in Rose Hill Cemetery at Macon, Bibb County, Georgia. (find a grave # 100402510)

BENNETT, JOHN L.: Company (F) K, private. May 5, 1861 enlisted as a private in Co. F, 54th Regiment, Georgia Infantry at Savannah, Georgia and received bounty $50.00. September 1, 1862 transferred to Co. K, 54th Regiment, Georgia Infantry at Savannah, Georgia (Special Order No. 6). September 9, 1862 joined Co. K at Beaulieu, near Savannah, Georgia. September 1862 roll shows his transfer. January 1, 1863 received pay. January – February 1863 roll shows him present. March 18, 1864, April 18, 1864 and April 25, 1864 issued clothing. July 22, 1864 killed at Atlanta, Georgia. Death benefit claim was filed December 8, 1864 by Polly Bennett, his widow.

BENNETT, JOHN MILLENDER: Company K, sergeant major. October 3, 1861 enlisted as a private in Co. A, 1st Regiment, 1st Brigade, Georgia State Troops. April 1862 mustered out. April 18, 1862 enlisted as a private and appointed 2nd sergeant in Co. K, 54th Regiment, Georgia Infantry at Savannah, Georgia and received bounty $50.00. January 1, 1863 received pay. January – February 1863 roll shows him present. March 18, 1864 issued clothing.

BENNETT, JOHN W.: Company K, private. October 3, 1861 enlisted as a private in Co. A, 1st Regiment, 1st Brigade, Georgia State Troops. April 1862 mustered out. April 19, 1862 enlisted as a private in Co. K, 54th Regiment, Georgia Infantry at Savannah, Georgia and received bounty $50.00. January 1, 1863 received pay. January – February 1863 roll shows him present. January 22, 1864 received pay $22.00. March

16, 1864, April 18, 1864 and April 25, 1864 issued clothing. May 28, 1864 he died of Pneumonia in the hospital at Atlanta, Georgia.

BENNETT, M. A.: Company (F) K, private. October 3, 1861 enlisted as a private in Co. A, 1st Regiment, 1st Brigade, Georgia State Troops. April 1862 mustered out. April 18, 1862 enlisted as a private in Co. F, 54th Regiment, Georgia Infantry at Savannah, Georgia and received bounty $50.00. September 1, 1862 transferred to Co. K, 54th Regiment, Georgia Infantry at Beaulieu, near Savannah, Georgia (Special Order No. 6). September 1862 roll shows his transfer. September 11, 1862 joined his new company Co. K, 54th Regiment, Georgia Infantry at Beaulieu, near Savannah, Georgia. January 1, 1863 received pay. January – February 1863 roll shows him present. February 1, 1864 he is described on pay document as; 23 years of age, blue eyes, black hair, dark complexion, 5 feet 8 inches high, a resident of Appling County, Georgia and was a farmer by occupation. February 15, 1864 received pay $22.00. March 18, 1864 issued clothing. July 22, 1864 wounded in the leg at Atlanta, Georgia. Pension records show he was at home wounded at the close of the war. May 22, 1865 surrendered and pardoned at Thomasville, Georgia. He was born in Appling County, Georgia May 31, 1841.

BENNETT, M. H.: Company (F) K, private. October 3, 1861 enlisted as a private in Co. A, 1st Regiment, 1st Brigade, Georgia State Troops. April 1862 mustered out. April 18, 1862 enlisted as a private in Co. F, 54th Regiment, Georgia Infantry at Savannah, Georgia and received bounty $50.00. September 1, 1862 transferred to Co. K, 54th Regiment, Georgia Infantry at Beaulieu, Georgia near Savannah, Georgia (Special Order No. 6). September 1862 roll shows his transfer.

BENNETT, NOAH H.: Company F (K), private. May 5, 1862 enlisted as a private in Co. F, 54th Regiment, Georgia Infantry at Savannah, Georgia and received bounty $50.00. September 1, 1862 transferred from Co. F, 54th Regiment, Georgia Infantry to Co. K, 54th Regiment, Georgia Infantry by Special Order No. 6 at Beaulieu, near Savannah, Georgia. January 1, 1863 received pay. January – February 1863 roll shows him present. March 18, 1864 issued clothing. Pension records show; he was at home on sick furlough at the close of the war. May 10, 1865 surrendered at Tallahassee, Florida. May 19, 1865 paroled at Thomasville, Georgia. He is described on parole record as: 5 feet 8 inches high, light hair, grey eyes and light complexion. He was born in Georgia January 18, 1844 and died in Wayne County, Georgia May 5, 1916. He is buried in Foster Cemetery in Pierce County, Georgia. (find a grave # 38828065)

BENNETT, RICHARD: Company K, captain. October 8, 1861 enlisted as a private and elected 2nd lieutenant in Co. A, 1st Regiment, 1st Brigade, Georgia State Troops. April 1862 mustered out. April 18, 1862 appointed 2nd lieutenant of Co. K, 54th Regiment, Georgia Infantry. July 18 (27), 1862 appointed 1st lieutenant of Co. K, 54th Regiment, Georgia Infantry. July 1862 roll shows him absent from the regiment at Savannah, Georgia. August 1862 roll shows him present in arrest at Beaulieu, near Savannah,

Georgia. September 1862 roll shows him present at Beaulieu, Georgia. October 1862 roll shows him present in arrest at Beaulieu, Georgia. November 1862 roll shows him present at Beaulieu, Georgia. December 20, 1862 appointed captain of Co. K, 54th Regiment, Georgia Infantry. December 1862 roll shows him present and promoted to captain after Captain Eason was dismissed after General Court Marshal on December 20, 1862. January 1, 1863 received pay. January – February 1863 roll shows him present. March 4, 1863 received pay $130.00. April 2, 1863 received pay $130.00. May 21, 1863 tendered his resignation as captain of Co. K, 54th Regiment, Georgia Infantry. May 22, 1863 through June 2, 1863 he was on leave of absence approved by General Mercer. October 21, 1863 he is shown on roll at Legare's Point, South Carolina. October 22, 1863 letter approving sick leave due to Intermittent Fever and the fact he is in Wayside Hospital. October 23, 1863 leave granted. January 1864, April 25, 1864 and June 2, 1864 issued clothing. June 7, 1864 received pay $260.00. July 2, 1864 received pay $130.00. September 14, 1864 roll of Mercer's Brigade near Jonesboro, Georgia shows him sick in Medical Board Division Hospital since September 2, 1864. January 22, 1865 granted leave of absence for 25 days by Special order #17 at Tupelo, Mississippi. Pension records show; he was at home sick at the close of the war. He was born in Georgia February 2, 1829 and died February 16, 1891. He is buried in Hephzibah Baptist Church Cemetery at Dixie Union, Ware County, Georgia. (find a grave # 17276619)

BENNETT, RICHARD, JR.: Company K, private. October 3, 1861 enlisted as a private in Co. A, 1st Regiment, 1st Brigade, Georgia State Troops. April 1862 mustered out. April 18, 1862 enlisted as a private in Co. F, 54th Regiment, Georgia Infantry at Savannah, Georgia and received bounty $50.00. January 1, 1863 received pay. January – February 1863 roll shows him present. He was promoted to sergeant of Co. F, 54th Regiment, Georgia Infantry. May 10, 1865 surrendered at Tallahassee, Florida. May 21, 1865 paroled at Thomasville, Georgia. He was born in Georgia. The Southern Cross of Honor was bestowed on him by the Jesup Chapter United Daughters of the Confederacy in 1903.

BENNETT, S. C.: Company K, private. He enlisted as a private in Co. K, 54th Regiment, Georgia Infantry.

BENNETT, SALATHIEL E.: Company (F) K, private. April 18, 1862 enlisted as a private in Co. F, 54th Regiment, Georgia Infantry at Savannah, Georgia and received bounty $50.00. September 1, 1862 transferred to Co. K, 54th Regiment, Georgia Infantry at Beaulieu, near Savannah, Georgia (Special Order No. 6). September 1862 roll shows his transfer. September 24, 1862 joined his new company Co. K, 54th Regiment, Georgia Infantry at Beaulieu, Georgia near Savannah, Georgia. January 1, 1863 received pay. January – February 1863 roll shows him present. March 18, 1864 and April 25, 1864 issued clothing. May 10, 1865 surrendered at Tallahassee, Florida. May 23, 1865 paroled at Thomasville, Georgia. He was born in Appling County, Georgia October 2, 1843 and died in Pierce County,

Georgia May 6, 1905. He is buried in the Jesup City cemetery in Jesup, Wayne County, Georgia. (find a grave # 93859626). The Southern Cross of Honor was bestowed on him by the Jesup Chapter United Daughters of the Confederacy in 1903.

BENNETT, T.: Company F, musician. January 19, 1862 enlisted as a musician in Co. F, 54th Regiment, Georgia Infantry at Savannah, Georgia and received bounty $50.00. January – February 1863 roll shows him present.

BENNING (BANNING)(BENNINGS), HENRY C.: Company F, private. May 17, 1861 enlisted as a private in Chisholm's Company, Georgia State Troops. May 1862 mustered out. May 13, 1862 enlisted as a private in Co. F, 54th Regiment, Georgia Infantry at Savannah, Georgia and received bounty $50.00. October 31, 1862 received pay. January 5, 1863 received pay $22.00. January – February 1863 roll shows him present. November 1, 1863 received pay. November – December 1863 roll shows him absent on picket duty at Little Ogeechee Bridge. January 1864 and April 25, 1864 issued clothing. October 14, 1864 captured at Dalton, Georgia and sent to Nashville, Tennessee. October 23, 1864 he is shown on roll of Nashville Tennessee Provost Marshal as being sent to Louisville, Kentucky. October 24, 1864 arrived at Louisville, Kentucky, Military Prison. October 27, 1864 sent to Camp Douglas, Illinois. October 29, 1864 he is shown on roll of Camp Douglas, Illinois. May 12, 1865 discharged from Camp Douglas, Illinois. He took the Oath of Allegiance and is described as: a resident of Chatham County, Georgia, fair complexion, red hair, blue eyes and released to go to New York City.

BEST, ANDERSTOKES J.: Company E, private. May 6, 1862 he enlisted in Co. E, 54th Regiment, Georgia Infantry at Savannah, Georgia and received bounty $50.00. August 1, 1862 transferred to the 1st Georgia Sharpshooters by Special Order No. 259. August 1862 roll shows the transfer. December 16, 1864 captured at Nashville, Tennessee. May 16, 1865 released at Camp Chase, Ohio.

BEST, ZADDOCK W.: Company E, private. October 6, 1861 enlisted as a private in Co. K, 5th Regiment, Georgia State Troops. April 1862 mustered out. May 6, 1862 he enlisted in Co. E, 54th Regiment, Georgia Infantry at Savannah, Georgia and received bounty $50.00. August 1, 1862 transferred to the 1st Georgia Sharpshooters by Special Order No. 259. August 1862 roll shows the transfer. December 16, 1864 captured at Nashville, Tennessee. April 22, 1865 took Oath of Allegiance at Camp Chase, Ohio and joined the U. S. Army. August 17, 1865 deserted from the U. S. Army. He was born in 1844 and died in 1907. He is buried in Hopewell Cemetery at Moultrie, Colquitt County, Georgia. (find a grave # 82972152)

BETTICK, THOMAS L.: Company I, private. He enlisted as a private in Co. I, 54th Regiment, Georgia Infantry. August 31, 1864 captured at Jonesboro, Georgia. November 1, 1864 received at Camp Douglas, Illinois.

BIGBY, BERRY: Company H, private. He enlisted as a private in Co. H, 54th Regiment, Georgia Infantry.

BIRD, P. R.: Company A, private. He enlisted as a private in Co. A, 54th Regiment, Georgia Infantry.

BISHOP, BENJAMIN F.: Company G, private. He enlisted as a private in Co. G, 54th Regiment, Georgia Infantry at Savannah, Georgia. June 27, 1864 killed on Pigeon Hill at Kennesaw Mountain, Georgia. November 17, 1864 death benefit claim filed for and paid to Luck Bishop, his widow.

BISHOP, JOHN: Company G (C), private. May 12, 1862 enlisted as a private in Co. G, 54th Regiment, Georgia Infantry at Columbus, Georgia and received bounty $50.00. August 18, 1864 discharged at Savannah, Georgia. August 1862 roll shows his discharge. September 1, 1862 transferred to Co. C, 54th Regiment, Georgia Infantry at Beaulieu, near Savannah, Georgia (Special Order No. 6). September 1862 roll shows his transfer. May 20, 1865 surrendered and paroled at Augusta, Georgia. He was born May 22, 1837 and died January 1, 1898. He is buried in Bishop's Chapel Cemetery at Summertown, Emanuel County, Georgia. (find a grave # 52390077)

BLACKSTOCK, HENRY: Company G, private. He enlisted as a private in Co. G, 54th Regiment, Georgia Infantry at Columbus, Georgia and received bounty $50.00.

BLACKMAN, HENRY HARRISON: Company H, private. May 12, 1862 enlisted as a private in Co. H, 54th Regiment, Georgia Infantry. December 5, 1862 transferred to Co. E, 46th Georgia Infantry. April 26, 1865 surrendered at Greensboro, North Carolina. May 1, 1865 paroled at Greensboro, North Carolina. He was born June 21, 1869 and died June 11, 1917. He is buried in Union Cemetery at Ozark, Dale County, Alabama. (find a grave # 8162755)

BLACKWELL, J. H.: Company H, private. 1862 enlisted as a private in Co. F, 54th Regiment, Georgia Infantry.

BLAIR, EDWARD F.: Company F, sergeant. May 17, 1861 enlisted as a private in Chisholm's Company, Georgia State Troops. May 1862 mustered out. May 13, 1862 enlisted as a private in Co. F, 54th Regiment, Georgia Infantry at Savannah, Georgia and received bounty $50.00. May 13, 1862 detailed as Ordinance Sergeant. September, October, November and December 1862 rolls show him as ordinance sergeant. December 31, 1862 received pay. January – February 1863 roll shows him absent detailed as Ordinance Sergeant. December 22, 1864 captured near Columbia, Tennessee and sent to Nashville, Tennessee. January 2, 1865 received at Military Prison at Louisville, Kentucky. January 4, 1865 sent to Camp Chase Prison, Ohio. January 6, 1865 received at Camp Chase Ohio, Prison. February 24, 1865 took the Oath of Allegiance at Camp Chase, Ohio. He is shown on parole papers as: a resident of Chatham County, Georgia, 20 years of age, fair complexion, dark hair, light whiskers, brown eyes and was 5 feet 4 inches high. He was born March 12, 1844 and died July 8, 1867. He is buried in Laurel Grove Cemetery at Savannah, Chatham

County, Georgia. (find a grave # 44293143)

BLAKE, LEVI S.: Company H, private. May 23, 1861 enlisted in Co. I, 20th Regiment, Georgia Infantry. June 23, 1861 discharged at Richmond, Virginia due to disability. July 26, 1861 reenlisted. November 1, 1861 discharged due to disability. January 20, 1863 enlisted as a private in Co. H, 54th Regiment, Georgia Infantry at Columbus, Georgia. January – February 1863 roll shows him present. January – February 1863 roll shows him present. November – December 1863 roll shows him absent on Picket duty. December 31, 1863 received pay. January 1864 and June 2, 1864 issued clothing. January – February 1864 roll shows him present on picket duty.

BLAKE, R. G.: Company H, private. 1862 enlisted as a private in Co. F, 54th Regiment, Georgia Infantry.

BLAKE, R. J. G.: Company F, private. January 20, 1863 enlisted as a private in Co. F, 54th Regiment, Georgia Infantry at Savannah, Georgia and received bounty $50.00. February 25, 1862 through March 31, 1862 received $.25 per day for extra duty at Camp Tattnall near Savannah, Georgia. April 1, 1862 through April 30, 1862 received $.25 per day for extra duty at Camp Young near Savannah, Georgia. July 1, 1862 through July 31, 1862 received $.25 per day for extra duty at Causton Bluff near Savannah, Georgia. August 1, 1862 through August 31, 1862 received $.25 per day for extra duty at Savannah, Georgia. September 1, 1862 through October 31, 1862 received $.25 per day for extra duty as a wagon master at Causton Bluff near Savannah, Georgia. December 1, 1862 through December 31, 1862 received $.25 per day for extra duty at Camp Young near Savannah, Georgia. January 1, 1863 through January 31, 1863 received $.25 per day for extra duty at Savannah, Georgia. January – February 1863 roll shows him present. February 1, 1863 through February 28, 1863 received $.25 per day for extra duty at Camp Young near Savannah, Georgia. February 28, 1863 received $4.00 for commutation of rations while on wagon master duty. March 1, 1863 through March 9, 1863 received $.25 per day for extra duty at Camp Young near Savannah, Georgia. May 1, 1863 received pay. May 1, 1863 through June 30, 1863 received $.25 per day for extra duty as a wagon master at Savannah, Georgia and Vernon Mills. July 1, 1863 through July 31, 1863 received $.25 per day for extra duty as a wagon master at Morton, Mississippi. November – December 1863 roll shows him present in arrest. July 1, 1863 through January 31, 1864 received $.25 per day for extra duty as a wagon master. January 1864 issued clothing. January 23, 1864 he applied for habeas corpus for a discharge from military service due to his youth.

BLAKE, SAMUEL L.: Company H, private. He was captured in Muscogee County, Georgia. July 1864 took the Oath of Allegiance at Military Prison, Louisville, Kentucky. July 28, 1864 shown on roll of deserters from the "Rebel Army" and took oath and was released north of the Ohio River. July 31, 1864 shown on release papers as being a resident of Muscogee County, Georgia, dark complexion, dark hair, hazel eyes and was 5 feet 8 inches high. Captor's statement says he was on picket duty and swam the river to desert. He gave up quite a large amount of information about troop locations, numbers, movements and fortifications upon his desertion.

BLAKER, CHARLES: Company A, private. October 17, 1861 enlisted as a private in Co. C, 1st Independent Battalion, Georgia State Troops. April 16, 1862 roll shows him present. April 1862 mustered out. April 26, 1862 enlisted as a private in Co. A, 54th Regiment, Georgia Infantry at Macon, Georgia. April 30, 1862 received pay. June 30, 1862 roll shows him present. October 31, 1863 received pay. November – December 1863 roll shows him present. January 1, 1864 received pay. January – February 1864 roll shows him present. March 31, 1864 issued clothing. April 29, 1864 transferred to Barnwell's Light Artillery. December 1864 he deserted to enemy.

BLASSINGAME, JAMES, S.: Company I, private. May 6, 1862 enlisted as a private in Co. I, 54th Regiment, Georgia Infantry at Guyton, Georgia and received bounty $50.00. October 31, 1862 received pay. January – February 1863 roll shows him absent sick. August 31, 1863 received pay. November – December 1863 roll shows him absent sick. January 1864 issued clothing. Pension records show; He was in the hospital at Augusta, Georgia with a fever at the close of the war. He was born in Walton County, Georgia December 2, 1836 and died in Georgia March 25, 1913. He is buried in Roberta City Cemetery at Roberta, Crawford County, Georgia. (find a grave #42686903)

BLASSINGAME (BLASINGAME) (BLASENGAME) (BLAZENGAME) (BLAZEGAME), JOHN W.: Company I (F), private. May 6, 1862 enlisted as a private in Co. I, 54th Regiment, Georgia Infantry at Guyton, Georgia and received bounty $50.00. October 22, 1862 attached to Bethesda Hospital as a nurse at Beaulieu Battery (near Savannah, Georgia). October, November and December 1862 rolls show him at the hospital as a nurse. January – February 1863 roll shows him attached to the hospital as a nurse. April 30, 1863 and May 1, 1863 received pay. November – December 1863 roll shows him absent at hospital, nurse for 54th Georgia Regiment. May 1, 1863 through October 31 1863 rolls for Bethesda Hospital show him absent on duty as a nurse in Charleston, South Carolina. November – December 1863 roll of Bethesda Hospital shows him absent on duty as a nurse in Charleston, South Carolina. January 1864 issued clothing. April 26, 1865 surrendered at Greensboro, North Carolina. May 1, 1865 paroled at Greensboro, North Carolina. He was born in Upson County, Georgia September 17, 1834 and died in Upson County, Georgia May 11, 1921. He is buried in Culloden City Cemetery at Culloden, Monroe County, Georgia. (find a grave # 25526655)

BLITCH, BENJAMIN: Company I, private. September 18, 1861 enlisted as a private in Co. C, 1st Regiment, 1st Brigade, Georgia State Troops. March 18, 1862 mustered out. May 6, 1862 enlisted as a private in Co. I, 54th Regiment, Georgia Infantry at Guyton, Georgia and received bounty

$50.00. December 24, 1862 detailed as a cook at Bethesda Hospital at Beaulieu Battery (near Savannah, Georgia). December 31, 1862 received pay. January – February 1863 roll shows him present. August 31, 1863 received pay. May 1, 1863 to October 31, 1863 roll for Bethesda Hospital at Beaulieu Battery (near Savannah, Georgia) shows him as a cook since December 24, 1862. October 1863 detailed as a cook at hospital, Rose Dew Post (near Savannah, Georgia). November – December 1863 roll shows him present as a hospital cook. December 31, 1863 received pay. January 1864 issued clothing. January – February 1864 roll of Hospital, Rose Dew Post shows him returned to his company February 7, 1864 with extra duty pay due him for 1 month 7 days.

BLITCH, HENRY: Employed as a hospital cook. December 31, 1863 received pay. January – February 1863 roll shows him employed as a hospital cook.

BLITCH (BLICH), THOMAS LUKE: Company I, private. May 6, 1862 enlisted as a private in Co. I, 54th Regiment, Georgia Infantry at Guyton, Georgia and received bounty $50.00. December 31, 1862 received pay. January – February 1863 roll shows him absent without leave for 2 days. August 31, 1863 received pay. November – December 1863 roll shows him present. January 1864 issued clothing. August 31, 1864 captured at Jonesboro, Georgia. Register from Military Prison, Louisville Kentucky shows he was received from Nashville, Tennessee on October 28, 1864 and was sent to Camp Douglas, Illinois on October 29, 1864. January 19, 1865 he died of Pneumonia at Camp Douglas, Illinois. He was born in Effingham County, Georgia July 31, 1831 and died at Chicago, Cook County, Illinois January 19, 1865. He is buried in grave #528, Block 2, Chicago City Cemetery. (find a grave # 25796511)

BLITCH, WILLIS (WILLIE) STEPHEN: Company I, private. November 4, 1863 enlisted as a private in Co. I, 54th Regiment, Georgia Infantry at Rose Dew, Georgia. November – December 1863 roll shows him present. January 1864, April 25, 1864 and June 2, 1864 issued clothing. September 12, 1864 admitted to Ocmulgee Hospital at Macon, Georgia with Diarrhoea. September 13, 1864 transferred to Augusta, Georgia. He was a resident of Effingham County, Georgia. He was born November 6, 1846 and died November 16, 1883. He is buried in Union Cemetery at Newington, Screven County, Georgia. (find a grave # 24769003)

BLOIS, JAMES F. H.: Company F, private. May 17, 1861 enlisted as a private and appointed 4th corporal in Chisholm's Company, Georgia State Troops. May 1862 mustered out. May 1862 enlisted as a private in Co. F, 54th Regiment, Georgia Infantry. 1862 he was appointed 2nd corporal of Co. F, 54th Regiment, Georgia Infantry. September 3, 1862 transferred from Co. F, 54th Regiment, Georgia Infantry to Co. C, 18th Battalion, Georgia Infantry. December 4, 1864 he deserted. December 5, 1864 he was received at Bermuda Hundred and took the Oath of Allegiance. December 6, 1864 he was transferred to Wilmington, Delaware.

BLOODWORTH, J. M.: Company B, private. He enlisted as a private in

Co. B, 54th Regiment, Georgia Infantry and received bounty $50.00.
BLOODWORTH, W. M.: Company B, private. He enlisted as a private in Co. B, 54th Regiment, Georgia Infantry and received bounty $50.00.
BLOUNT, GEORGE: Company F, private. May 13, 1863 enlisted as a private in Co. F, 54th Regiment, Georgia Infantry at Guyton, Georgia and received bounty $50.00. September 7, 1862 discharged at Beaulieu, near Savannah, Georgia. September 1862 roll reflects his discharge.
BLUE, J. C.: Company B, private. May 8, 1862 enlisted as a private in Co. B, 54th Regiment, Georgia Infantry at Savannah, Georgia and received bounty $50.00. December 31, 1862 received pay. January – February 1863 roll shows him present. January 1864 issued clothing. May 22, 1864 died in Columbus, Georgia. He is buried in Linwood Cemetery at Columbus, Muscogee County, Georgia. (find a grave #117009090)
BOATRIGHT, B.: Company C, private. April 22, 1862 enlisted as a private in Co. C, 54th Regiment, Georgia Infantry.
BOATRIGHT, DANIEL D.: Company G (C), private. May 6, 1862 enlisted as a private in Co. G, 54th Regiment, Georgia Infantry at Savannah, Georgia and received bounty $50.00. September 1, 1862 transferred to Co. C, 54th Regiment, Georgia Infantry at Beaulieu, near Savannah, Georgia by Special order No. 6. September 1862 roll reflects his transfer. December 31, 1862 received pay. January – February 1863 roll shows him present. January 1, 1864 received pay. January – February 1864 roll shows him present. April 28, 1864 issued clothing. June 15, 1864 wounded near Marietta, Georgia. He was born in Emanuel County, Georgia September 28, 1827 and died in Emanuel County, Georgia December 21, 1884. He is buried in Old Canoochee Cemetery at Twin City, Emanuel County, Georgia. (find a grave #10600945)
BOATRIGHT, JOHN D.: Company C, private. May 6, 1862 enlisted as a private in Co. G, 54th Regiment, Georgia Infantry at Savannah, Georgia and received bounty $50.00. December 31, 1862 received pay. January – February 1863 roll shows him present. January 1, 1864 received pay. January – February 1864 roll shows him present. November 1, 1864 furloughed from hospital at Columbia, Mississippi for 60 days according to pension records. November 17, 1864 issued clothing at Newsom Hospital at Cassville, Georgia. He was unfit for further duty. May 26, 1865 surrendered and paroled at Augusta, Georgia. He was born in Emanuel County, Georgia in November 3, 1838 and died in Emanuel County, Georgia January 27, 1913. He is buried in Hawhammock Cemetery at Canoochee, Emanuel County, Georgia. (find a grave #10529170).
BOATRIGHT, JOSIAH: Company B, private. April 17, 1864 enlisted as a private in Co. G, 54th Regiment, Georgia Infantry at Red Bluff, South Carolina. April 26, 1865 surrendered at Greensboro, North Carolina. May 1, 1865 paroled at Greensboro, North Carolina. He was born in Georgia in 1846.
BOATRIGHT, WILLIAM: Company C, private. May 6, 1862 enlisted as a private in Co. G, 54th Regiment, Georgia Infantry at Savannah, Georgia

and received bounty $50.00. December 31, 1862 received pay. January – February 1863 roll shows him present (absent without leave for 12 days). January 1, 1864 received pay. January – February 1864 roll shows him present. April 28, 1864 issued clothing. He died in service.

BOLAN, THOMAS: Company H, private. May 12, 1862 enlisted as a private in Co. H, 54th Regiment, Georgia Infantry at Columbus, Georgia.

BOLES, CORNELIUS J.: Company H, private. November 6, 1862 enlisted as a private in Co. H, 54th Regiment, Georgia Infantry at Columbus, Georgia and received bounty $50.00. November 1862 roll shows him present. December 31, 1862 received pay. January – February 1863 roll shows him present.

March 10, 1863 through July 10, 1863 on special detail at a rate of $.40 per day. October 31, 1863 received pay. November – December 1863 roll shows him present (absent on picket). January 1864 issued clothing. January – February 1864 roll shows him present detailed as a hewer. July 1864 received pay $49.20. April 26, 1865 surrendered at Greensboro, North Carolina. May 1, 1865 paroled at Greensboro, North Carolina.

BOLTON, JOHN WESLEY, SR.: Company D, private. April 30, 1862 enlisted as a private in Co. D, 54th Regiment, Georgia Infantry at Savannah, Georgia and received bounty $50.00. December 31, 1862 received pay. January – February 1863 roll shows him present detailed as camp guard. January 1864 and April 25, 1864 issued clothing. May 20, 1865 surrendered and paroled at Augusta, Georgia. He was born November 7, 1836 and died October 2, 1916. He is buried in Zeagler Cemetery in Screven County, Georgia. (find a grave # 22662436)

BOLTON, REUBEN: Company D, private. October 7, 1861 enlisted as a private in Co. I, 5th Regiment, Georgia State Troops. April 1862 mustered out. April 30, 1862 enlisted as a private in Co. D, 54th Regiment, Georgia Infantry at Savannah, Georgia and received bounty $50.00. December 31, 1862 received pay. January – February 1863 roll shows him present detailed as camp guard. January 1864 issued clothing. Pension records show he was sent to hospital at Columbus, Mississippi in January 1865. He was furloughed home for 60 days in 1865. He was born in Georgia in 1835.

BOLTON, RICHARD: Company D, private. April 30, 1862 enlisted as a private in Co. D, 54th Regiment, Georgia Infantry at Savannah, Georgia and received bounty $50.00. December 31, 1862 received pay. January – February 1863 roll shows him present. January 1864 and April 25, 1864 issued clothing.

May 20, 1865 surrendered and paroled at Augusta, Georgia. (Pension records show he was at home on May 20, 1865) He was born in Georgia in 1844.

BONE, E. F.: Company H, corporal. He enlisted as a corporal in Co. H, 54th Regiment, Georgia Infantry.

BONHAM, M.: Company D, private. He enlisted as a private in Co. D, 54th Regiment, Georgia Infantry. December 20, 1862 discharged by order.

December 1862 roll indicates his discharge.

BONHAM, M.: Company H, private. He enlisted as a private in Co. H, 54th Regiment, Georgia Infantry.

BONHART, JAMES E.: Company H (A), private. April 22, 1862 enlisted as a private in Co. H, 54th Regiment, Georgia Infantry at Macon, Georgia. September 1, 1862 transferred from Co. H, 54th Regiment, Georgia Infantry at Beaulieu near Savannah, Georgia by Special Order No. 6. September 1862 roll reflects the transfer. April 30, 1863 received pay. June 30, 1863 roll shows him absent on furlough. October 1863 detailed as courier. October 31, 1863 received pay. November – December 1863 roll shows him present (courier to Headquarters). January 1, 1864 received pay. January – February 1864 roll shows him present (courier to headquarters). March 31, 1864, April 29, 1864 and May 8, 1864 issued clothing. February 15, 1865 admitted to Ocmulgee Hospital at Macon, Georgia with Cephalalgia (pain in the head). March 25, 1865 returned to duty as a painter at the Confederate States Armory in Macon, Georgia. April 2, 1865 admitted to Ocmulgee Hospital at Macon, Georgia with Ulcus. April 1865 captured at Macon, Georgia. April 18, 1865 transferred. Pension records shows April 26, 1865 surrendered at Greensboro, North Carolina. May 1, 1865 paroled at Greensboro, North Carolina.

He was a resident of Bibb County, Georgia. He was born in Putnam County, Georgia in 1834 and died in Bibb County, Georgia November 1, 1906. He is buried in Fort Hill Cemetery at Macon, Bibb County, Georgia.

BONNARD (BONARD), CHARLES C.: Company H, private. October 5, 1862 enlisted as a private in Co. H, 54th Regiment, Georgia Infantry at Columbus, Georgia. December 1862 roll at Beaulieu near Savannah, Georgia shows he joined but not before reported (Colonel's Orderly). December 31, 1862 received pay. January – February 1863 roll shows him present. October 31, 1863 received pay. November – December 1863 roll shows him present. December 31, 1863 received pay. January 1864 issued clothing. January 18, 1864 he returned to his regiment. January – February 1864 roll shows him present (Detailed as Colonel Way's orderly by order of General Mercer. Pay due from September 1 to October 31, 1863). October 14, 1864 captured at Dalton, Georgia and sent to Nashville, Tennessee. October 26, 1864 roll of prisoners of War at Louisville, Kentucky, Military Prison shows he arrived there October 24, 1864. October 27, 1864 sent to Camp Douglas, Illinois. October 29, 1864 received at Camp Douglas, Illinois. June 17, 1865 discharged from Camp Douglas, Illinois after taking Oath of Allegiance. He is described on his Prisoner of War document as being a resident of Muscogee County, Georgia, fair complexion, brown hair, blue eyes, 5 feet 7 inches high and was a resident of Columbus City, Georgia.

BOOKER, T. J.: Company K, private. He enlisted as a private in Co. K, 54th Regiment, Georgia Infantry.

BOURQUIN, FRANCES (FRANK) EDWIN: Company I, lieutenant. September 18, 1861 enlisted and elected Jr. 2nd lieutenant of Co. C, 1st

Regiment, 1st Brigade, Georgia State Troops. March 18, 1862 mustered out.

May 6, 1862 enlisted as a private in Co. I, 54th Regiment, Georgia Infantry at Guyton, Georgia and received bounty $50.00. May 16, 1862 appointed 2nd lieutenant of Co. I, 54th Regiment, Georgia Infantry in Savannah, Georgia. July 1862 roll shows the company is stationed in Savannah, Georgia. August 1862 roll shows him present at Beaulieu near Savannah, Georgia. September 1862 roll shows him absent with leave (the regiment is at Beaulieu). October 1862 roll shows him absent sick on sick furlough since October 10. November 1862 and December 1862 roll shows him present at Beaulieu. January – February 1863 roll shows him present. March 3, 1863 received pay $80.00. April 2, 1863 received pay $80.00. September 18 through September 28, 1863 he is shown as absent with leave approved by General Mercer. November 27, 1863 to November 28, 1863 on approved leave of absence. December 3, 1863 received pay $80.00. November – December 1863 roll shows him present. January 19, 1864 received pay $80.00. February 25, 1864 15 days leave granted. April 1864 received pay $240.00. June 2, 1864 received pay $100.00. July 2, 1864 received pay $80.00. July 6, 1864 shown as sick in Convalescent Camp in Macon, Georgia. August 25, 1864 he is shown on report of Mercer's Brigade as being sick in Macon, Georgia (Regiment in camp near Atlanta, Georgia). September 14, 1864 he is shown on roll as sick in the Medical Board Division Hospital (the regiment is near Jonesboro, Georgia). He was killed December 20, 1864 at Columbia Tennessee when a tree fell on him.

BOWEN, HEZEKIAH: Company K, private. May 5, 1862 enlisted as a private in Co. K, 54th Regiment, Georgia Infantry at Savannah, Georgia and received bounty $50.00. January 1, 1863 received pay. January – February 1863 roll shows him present. March 18, April 18 and April 25, 1864 issued clothing. Pension records show; he was at home on sick furlough at the close of the war. He was born March 6, 1843 and died September 20, 1930. He is buried in Bethesda Primitive Baptist Church Cemetery in Wayne County, Georgia. (find a grave # 38916776)

BOWEN, MALACHI: Company K, private. May 5, 1862 enlisted as a private in Co. K, 54th Regiment, Georgia Infantry at Savannah, Georgia and received bounty $50.00. January 1, 1863 received pay. January – February 1863 roll shows him present. March 18, 1864 issued clothing. Pension records show; he was at home on sick furlough at the close of the war. He could not reach his command at the close of the war. He was born in Bulloch County, Georgia April 18, 1829 and died July 8, 1903. He is buried in Ben James Cemetery in Pierce County, Georgia. (find a grave # 17866507)

BOWEN, ZACHARIAH D.: Company K, private. February 1, 1863 enlisted as a private in Co. C, 20th Regiment, Georgia infantry. September 28, 1864 he transferred as a private to Co. K, 54th Regiment, Georgia Infantry. May 24, 1865 surrendered and paroled at Augusta, Georgia.

BOWERS, BENJAMIN: Company A, private. He enlisted as a private in Co. A, 54th Regiment, Georgia Infantry.

BOWERS, JAMES A.: Company A, private. October 17, 1861 enlisted as a private in Co. C, 1st Independent Battalion, Georgia State Troops. April 16, 1862 roll shows him present. April 1862 mustered out. May 5, 1862 enlisted as a private in Co. A, 54th Regiment, Georgia Infantry at Macon, Georgia and received bounty $50.00. July 30, 1862 transferred to 1st Georgia Sharpshooters by Special Order No. 259. August 1862 roll reflects transfer. February 13, 1863 discharged (under age). He was born in 1847 and died August 4, 1871. He is buried in an unmarked grave in Rose Hill Cemetery at Macon, Bibb County, Georgia.

BOWLES, NEELY: Company H, private. January 28, 1863 enlisted as a private in Co. H, 54th Regiment, Georgia Infantry at Columbus, Georgia.

BOWLES (BOLIN)(BOWLING), V.: Company H, private. January 28, 1863 enlisted as a private in Co. H, 54th Regiment, Georgia Infantry at Columbus, Georgia and received bounty $50.00. January – February 1863 roll shows him present. March 18, 1863 deserted from "Rebel Army". April 18, 1863 admitted to U. S. A. General Hospital, Ladies Home, New York City, New York. April 20, 1863 paroled from U. S. A. General Hospital, Ladies Home, New York City, New York. April 20, 1863 admitted to U. S. A. Convalescent Hospital, Ft. Wood, Bedloe's Island, New York Harbor, New York (reason Convalescent). April 21, 1863 transferred to 51st Hospital.

BOYED,____; Company G, private. July 2, 1862 died of fever in Savannah, Georgia. July 1862 roll shows his death.

BOYD, SAMUEL F.: Company G, private. May 12, 1862 enlisted as a private in Co. G, 54th Regiment, Georgia Infantry at Columbus, Georgia and received bounty $50.00. July 27, 1862 died in Savannah, Georgia. August 1862 roll shows his death.

BOYD, W. A.: May 12, 1862 enlisted as a private in Co. G, 54th Regiment, Georgia Infantry at Columbus, Georgia and received bounty $50.00.

BRADEN, JAMES: Company E, private. He enlisted as a private in Co. E. 54th Regiment, Georgia Infantry. May 10, 1865 surrendered at Tallahassee, Florida. May 12, 1865 paroled at Thomasville, Georgia.

BRADFORD, RICHARD: Company E, private. May 6, 1862 enlisted as a private in Co. E, 54th Regiment, Georgia Infantry at Savannah, Georgia and received bounty $50.00. December 31, 1862 received pay. January 1, 1863 transferred to Co. G, 29th Regiment, Georgia Infantry. January – February 1863 roll shows he transferred to Co. G, 29th Regiment, Georgia Infantry.

BRADFORD, RICHARD: Company F, private. He enlisted in Co. F, 54th Regiment, Georgia Infantry.

BRADLEY, WILLIAM H.; Company F, private. May 6, 1862 enlisted as a private in Co. F, 54th Regiment, Georgia Infantry at Savannah, Georgia and received bounty $50.00. September, October and December 1862 rolls show him detailed as the Major's Orderly. December 31,

1862 received pay. January – February 1863 roll shows him present. November 1, 1863 received pay. November – December 1863 roll shows him present. January 1864 issued clothing. December 18, 1864 deserted near Nashville, Tennessee. January 14, 1865 report of Provost Marshal U. S. forces shows; a resident of Chatham County, Georgia, fair complexion, light hair, grey eyes, 5 feet 6 inches high and had no family. He took Oath of Allegiance.

BRAGG, B.: Company F, private. November 20, 1862 enlisted as a private in Co. F, 54th Regiment, Georgia Infantry at Savannah, Georgia and received bounty $50.00. May 1, 1863 received pay. November – December 1863 roll shows him absent sick in Screven County, Georgia.

BRAGG, DANIEL: Company D, private. He enlisted as a private in Co. D, 54th Regiment, Georgia Infantry. September 10, 1863 he died in Charleston, South Carolina. He is buried in the confederate section of Magnolia Cemetery at Charleston, South Carolina. (find a grave # 20713777)

BRAGG, DAVID: Company D, private. October 7, 1861 enlisted as a private in Co. I, 5th Regiment, Georgia State Troops. April 1862 mustered out December 13, 1862 enlisted and elected 3rd sergeant in Co. D, 54th Regiment, Georgia Infantry at Savannah, Georgia and received bounty $50.00. December 31, 1862 received pay. December 1862 roll shows he joined on December 13 and was stationed at Beaulieu near Savannah, Georgia. January - February 1863 roll shows him present. April 25, 1864 and May 8, 1864 issued clothing. January 19, 1865 admitted to Way Hospital at Meridian, Mississippi with Debilitas. He was born November 17, 1842 and died in Georgia November 10, 1910. He is buried in Oak Hill Baptist Church Cemetery in Jenkins County, Georgia. (find a grave #24425170)

BRAGG, DAVID L.: Company D, sergeant. April 30, 1862 enlisted as a private in Co. D, 54th Regiment, Georgia Infantry at Savannah, Georgia and received bounty $50.00. He was elected 1st sergeant of Co. D, 54th Regiment, Georgia Infantry. December 31, 1862 received pay. January - February 1863 roll shows him present. January 1864 issued clothing. April 26, 1865 surrendered at Greensboro, North Carolina. May 1, 1865 paroled at Greensboro, North Carolina. He was born in 1826 and died in 1866 He is buried in the Lewis Family Cemetery in Jenkins County, Georgia. (find a grave # 25144301)

BRAGG, HENRY: Company D, private. April 30, 1862 enlisted as a private in Co. D, 54th Regiment, Georgia Infantry at Savannah, Georgia and received bounty $50.00. December 31, 1862 received pay. January - February 1863 roll shows him present. January 1864 and April 25, 1864 issued clothing. July 22, 1864 killed in Atlanta, Georgia.

BRAGG, HOWELL: Company D, private. April 30, 1862 enlisted as a private in Co. D, 54th Regiment, Georgia Infantry at Savannah, Georgia and received bounty $50.00. December 31, 1862 received pay. January - February 1863 roll shows him present. January 1864 issued clothing.

Pension records show he was at home sick February 1865. He was born in Screven County, Georgia in 1838 and died January-February 1905.

BRAGG, JASPER: Company D, sergeant. October 14, 1861 enlisted as a private in Co. I, 5th Regiment, Georgia State Troops. April 1862 mustered out. April 30, 1862 enlisted as a 4th sergeant in Co. D, 54th Regiment, Georgia Infantry at Savannah, Georgia and received bounty $50.00. December 31, 1862 received pay. January - February 1863 roll shows him present. January 1864 and April 25, 1864 issued clothing. Pension records show he was at home on sick furlough from February 1, 1865 to the close of the war. He was born in Georgia December 18, 1842 and died November 11, 1845. He is buried in the Bragg Family Cemetery in Jenkins County, Georgia. (find a grave # 30394422)

BRAGG, L.: Company D, private. April 30, 1862 enlisted as a 4th sergeant in Co. D, 54th Regiment, Georgia Infantry at Savannah, Georgia and received bounty $50.00. September, October and November 1862 rolls show him detailed as a butcher. December 31, 1862 received pay. January 15, 1863 received pay which included $.25 per day for being a butcher. January - February 1863 roll shows him present. January 1864 and April 25, 1864 issued clothing.

BRAGG, L: Company F, private. April 29, 1863 enlisted as a private in Co. F, 54th Regiment, Georgia Infantry. June 19, 1864 wounded near Marietta, Georgia.

BRAGG, WILLIAM B.: Company D, private. November 28, 1862 enlisted as a 4th sergeant in Co. D, 54th Regiment, Georgia Infantry at Beaulieu near Savannah, Georgia and received bounty $50.00. December 1862 roll shows he joined at Beaulieu on November 28. December 31, 1862 received pay. January - February 1863 roll shows him present. January 1864 issued clothing. May 18, 1865 surrendered and paroled at Augusta, Georgia. He was born in 1827 and died in 1866. He is buried in Bragg Family Cemetery at Sylvania, Screven County, Georgia. (find a grave #24486498)

BRAKEFIELD, H. M.: Company G, private. May 12, 1862 enlisted as a private in Co. G, 54th Regiment, Georgia Infantry at Columbus, Georgia and received bounty $50.00. May 12, 1862 deserted. August 1862 roll reflects his desertion.

BRAMLETTE, T. P.: Company E, private. April 25, 1864 enlisted as a private in Co. E, 54th Regiment, Georgia Infantry at Dalton, Georgia. April 26, 1865 surrendered at Greensboro, North Carolina. May 1, 1865 paroled at Greensboro, North Carolina.

BRANCH, HAMILTON MCDEVIT.: Company F, lieutenant. May 21, 1861 enlisted as a private in Co. B, 8th Regiment, Georgia Infantry. He was wounded at Dam No. 1 and sent to Richmond, Virginia and then later to Savannah, Georgia. May 13, 1862 enlisted as 2nd lieutenant in Co. F, 54th Regiment, Georgia Infantry in Savannah, Georgia. August 1862 absent with leave. September 1862 roll shows him absent from Beaulieu on Special Service. October 1862 roll shows him absent sick from Beaulieu since October 26. November 1862 roll shows him present. December 14, 1862 report shows him sick in the Hospital. December 1862 roll shows him absent sick from Beaulieu since November 28, 1862. January – February 1863 roll shows him present. March 9, 1863 received pay $80.00. September 24 and September 25, 1863 shown as absent with leave by order of General Mercer. He was elected 1st lieutenant in Co. F, 54th Regiment, Georgia Infantry. July 9, 1863 granted 15 days leave by order of General Mercer. July 1863 roll shows him in Savannah. September 22, 1863 elected 1st lieutenant of Co. F, 54th Regiment, Georgia Infantry. October 13, October 14, October 21 and November 11, 1863 issued clothing. December 3, 1863 received pay $90.00. December 17, 1863 leave granted. November – December 1863 roll shows him absent without leave. January 6, 1864 received pay $90.00. January 19 through January 23, 1864 granted leave as a witness in a General Court Marshal at Savannah, Georgia. February 1, 1864 received pay $90.00. July 2, 1864 received pay $90.00. July 24, 1864 wounded near Atlanta, Georgia. August 25, 1864 report of Mercer's Brigade in the field near Atlanta, Georgia shows him wounded on sick furlough Medical Examining Board, Savannah, Georgia. September 14, 1864 report of Mercer's Brigade near Jonesboro, Georgia shows him on sick furlough from the Medical Board. April 1865 returned to his command and being unfit for field duty he was detailed to collect absentees. He was born in Savannah, Chatham County, Georgia March 17, 1843 and died in Savannah, Chatham County, Georgia February 24, 1899. He is buried in Bonaventure Cemetery at Savannah, Chatham County, Georgia. (find a grave # 12958675)

BRANCH, MICHAEL: Company B, lieutenant. April 21, 1862 enlisted as a private in Co. B, 54th Regiment, Georgia Infantry in Savannah, Georgia. July 28, 1862 appointed 2nd lieutenant of Co. B, 54th Regiment, Georgia Infantry. July 1862 roll shows him present. August 1862 roll from Beaulieu shows him absent with leave from August 10, 1862. September 1862 and October 1862 rolls at Beaulieu near Savannah, Georgia show him present. November 24, 1862 report shows him present. November 1862 roll shows him present at Beaulieu. December 1862 roll shows him present. January – February 1863 roll shows him present. April 2, 1863 received pay $160.00. October 21, 1863 report shows him present at Legare's Point, Johns Island, South Carolina. December 1, 1863 Special order 96/1 granted him leave. July 3, 1864 received pay $80.00. August 2, 1864 wounded near Atlanta, Georgia. August 8, 1864 admitted to Floyd House Hospital at Macon, Georgia with a Gunshot Wound of left leg Gastrochne Minus region (knee). August 25, 1864 report of Mercer's Brigade in the field near Atlanta, Georgia shows him wounded and sent to General Hospital by the Brigade Surgeon. September 14, 1864 report of Mercer's Brigade in camp near Jonesboro, Georgia shows him wounded on furlough by the Medical Board. He developed gangrene in the wound and was sent home where he remained until the close of the war. He was from Holmesville, Appling County, Georgia. He was born April 14, 1831 and died September 28, 1810 in Appling County, Georgia. He is buried in the Baxley Graveyard (Friendship Church Cemetery) in Appling County, Georgia. (find a grave #6665596))

BRANHAM, MATTHEW: Field, Staff Band, musician. May 10, 1862 enlisted as a private in Co. D (K), 54th Regiment, Georgia Infantry in Macon, Georgia and received bounty $50.00. December 19, 1862 transferred from Co. D (K), as a musician in the 54th Regiment, Georgia Infantry in Savannah, Georgia. January 1, 1863 received pay. February 19, 1863 received pay $17.96. January – February 1863 roll shows him present.

BRANNEN (BRANNON) (BRAMAN), WALTER: Company H, private. May 12, 1862 enlisted as a private in Co. H, 54th Regiment, Georgia Infantry in Columbus, Georgia. July 1862 roll shows he was discharged July 18, 1862 at Savannah, Georgia. December 31, 1862 received pay. January – February 1863 roll shows him present. October 31, 1863 received pay. November – December 1863 roll shows him present. November – December 1863 roll shows him present. January 1864 issued clothing. January – February 1864 roll shows him present. June 18, 1864 captured near Marietta, Georgia. June 24, 1864 in Nashville, Tennessee and sent to Military prison at Louisville, Kentucky. June 23, 1864 received at Military Prison at Louisville, Kentucky. July 6, 1864 sent to Camp Morton, Indiana. July 7, 1864 received at Camp Morton at Indianapolis, Indiana. February 26, 1865 transferred for exchange to City Point, Virginia. February 26, 1865 he died at Martinsburg, Virginia.

BRANNER, JAMES HENRY: Company H, private. January 28, 1863 enlisted as a private in Co. H, 54th Regiment, Georgia Infantry at Columbus, Georgia. He contracted severe cold, resulting in hemorrhage of lungs and deafness in 1863. He was discharged due to disability. He was born in Georgia July 3, 1825.

BRANTLEY, A. J.: Company A, sergeant. January 17, 1862 enlisted as a private in Co. C, 1st Independent Battalion, Georgia State Troops. April 16, 1862 roll shows him present. April 1862 mustered out. May 3, 1862 enlisted as 3rd sergeant in Co. A, 54th Regiment, Georgia Infantry in Macon, Georgia. April 30, 1863 received pay. June 30, 1863 roll shows him present. May 8, 1864 issued clothing.

BRANTLEY, F. W.: Company A, lieutenant. January 7, 1863 dropped from the rolls.

BRANTLEY, G. T.: Company K, private. November 15, 1862 enlisted as a private in Co. K, 54th Regiment, Georgia Infantry at Beaulieu near Savannah, Georgia and received bounty $50.00. November 1862 roll shows him joining on November 15. January 1, 1863 received pay. January – February 1863 roll shows him present. March 18, 1864 and June 2, 1864 issued clothing.

BRANTLEY, H. A.: Company A, private. He enlisted as a private in Co. A, 54th Regiment, Georgia Infantry.

BRANTLEY, H. T.: Company A, private. May 3, 1862 enlisted as a private in Co. F, 54th Regiment, Georgia Infantry at Macon, Georgia and received bounty $50.00. January 1, 1864 received pay. January – February 1864 roll shows him absent on detached service. April 30, 1863 received pay. June 30, 1863 roll shows him present. October 31, 1863 received pay. November – December 1863 roll shows him present. April 29, 1864 issued clothing. January 15, 1865 admitted to Way Hospital at Meridian, Mississippi.

BRANTLEY, HORATIO S.: Company F (A), private. May 3, 1862 enlisted as a private in Co. F, 54th Regiment, Georgia Infantry at Macon Georgia and received bounty $50.00. September 1, 1862 transferred from Co. F, 54th Regiment, Georgia Infantry to Co. A, 54th Regiment, Georgia Infantry at Beaulieu near Savannah, Georgia by Special Order No. 6. September 1862 roll shows his transfer. April 30, 1863 received pay. June 30, 1863 roll shows him present. October 31, 1863 received pay. November – December 1863 roll shows him present. January 1, 1864 received pay. January – February 1864 roll shows him present. March 31, 1864 issued clothing. He was born in Georgia in 1828 and died in 1867 of disease contracted in service.

BRANTLEY, MARTIN L.: Company A, private. February 19, 1861 enlisted and appointed 2nd sergeant of Co. M, 1 st Regiment, Georgia Regulars. May 3, 1862 enlisted as a private in Co. A, 54th Regiment, Georgia Infantry at Macon, Georgia. October 18, 1862 elected 3nd lieutenant in Co. A, 54th Regiment, Georgia Infantry to fill vacancy caused by Lt. Dunlap's resignation. October 1862 roll shows him present at Beaulieu, near Savannah, Georgia. November 1862 roll shows him absent with leave since November 26, 1862 from Beaulieu. December 12, 1862 shown as having deserted. December 1862 roll at Beaulieu shows he was dropped December 20, 1862 as his transfer to this regiment has not been effected yet. He was changed back to a private. 1864 reenlisted as a private in in Co. A, 54th Regiment, Georgia Infantry. July 3, 1864 captured at Kennesaw Mountain, Georgia and sent to Nashville, Tennessee. He was transferred to Military Prison at Louisville, Kentucky. July 13, 1864 he was received at Military Prison at Louisville, Kentucky and sent to Camp Morton, Indiana. July 14, 1864 received at Camp Morton, Indiana. March 4, 1865 transferred for exchange to City Point, Virginia. March 15, 1865 exchanged at James River, Virginia.

BRANTLEY, M. V.: Company A, private. May 3, 1862 enlisted as a private in Co. A, 54th Regiment, Georgia Infantry at Macon, Georgia. He died at Macon, Georgia March 15, 1896. He is buried in Rose Hill Cemetery at Macon, Bibb County, Georgia. (find a grave # 100403344)

BRANTLEY, R. E.: Company F (A), private. November 26, 1862 enlisted as a private in Co. D, 2nd Battalion, Georgia Cavalry. January 20, 1863 transferred to Co A, 2nd Battalion, Georgia Cavalry. September 1, 1863 transferred to Co F, 54th Regiment, Georgia Infantry. July 22, 1864 wounded in Atlanta, Georgia. November – December 1864 roll of Co. E, 1st Regiment, Troops and Defenses at Macon, Georgia stationed at Camp

Wright shows him present. He was detailed as clerk for Camp Wright Convalescent Hospital.

BRANTLEY, THOMAS M.: Field and Staff, captain (adjutant). Company C, captain. July 16, 1862 appointed adjutant 54th Regiment, Georgia Infantry. July 1862 roll indicates him. August, September, October, November and December 1862 rolls show him present at Beaulieu, near Savannah, Georgia. January – February 1863 roll shows him present at Beaulieu, near Savannah, Georgia. March 4, 1863 received pay $100.00. April 2, 1863 received pay $100.00. May 1, 1863 (July 16, 1863) elected captain of Co. C, 54th Regiment, Georgia Infantry. May 3, 1863 report shows him absent since April 25, 1863 on a 72 hour leave of absence approved April 18, 1864 by General Mercer. June 21, 1863 to July 1, 1863 he was on furlough approved by General Mercer. October 21, 1863 list of officers in the 54th Georgia includes his name at Legare's Point, John's Island, South Carolina. January – February 1864 roll shows him present. August 19, 1864 received pay $260.00. August 25, 1864 report of Mercer's Brigade in the field near Atlanta, Georgia shows him without leave since June 5, 1864. April 21-22, 1865 captured in Macon, Georgia. He was a resident of Monroe County, Georgia.

BRANTLEY, THOMAS W.: Company A, captain. October 17, 1861 elected captain of Co. C, 1st Independent Battalion, Georgia State Troops. April 18, 1862 elected captain of Co. A, 54th Regiment, Georgia Infantry at Guyton, Georgia. July 2, 1862 roll indicates him present. August 1862 and September 1862 rolls show him present at Beaulieu near Savannah, Georgia. October 1862 roll shows him absent with leave. November 1862 and December 1862 rolls show him present. January 28, 1863 detailed Enrolling Officer, 4th Congressional District. He was granted leave by General Mercer from January 28, 1863 until August 29, 1863 for this task. December 5, 1863 received pay $30.00. November – December 1863 roll shows him present. January 2, 1864 received pay $130.00. February 1, 1864 received pay $130.00. January – February 1864 roll shows him present. March 4, 1864 received pay $130.00. June 7, 1864 received pay $200.00. July 2, 1864 received pay $130.00. August 1, 1864 promoted to major of the 54th Regiment, Georgia Infantry. August 15, 1864 received pay $520.00. August 25, 1864 report of Mercer's Brigade in the field near Atlanta shows him without leave left on 3 days leave from Army Headquarters. September 14, 1864 report of Mercer's Brigade in camp near Jonesboro, Georgia shows him absent with certification from Medical Board since August 14, 1864. September 14, 1864 report of Mercer's Brigade shows him sick according to the Medical Board since September 11, 1864. He is buried in Rose Hill Cemetery at Macon, Georgia.

BRANTLEY, W. J. W.: Company A, private. October 17, 1861 enlisted as a private in Co. C, 1st Independent Battalion, Georgia State Troops. January 17, 1862 appointed 5th sergeant in Co. C, 1st Independent Battalion, Georgia State Troops. April 16, 1862 roll shows him present. April 1862 mustered out. May 3, 1862 enlisted as a private in Co. A, 54th Regiment,

Georgia Infantry at Macon, Georgia and received bounty $50.00. April 30, 1863 received pay. June 30, 1863 roll shows him present.

BRANTLY, ROBERT M.: Company F, private. November 26, 1862 enlisted as a private in Co. F, 54th Regiment, Georgia Infantry at Savannah, Georgia and received bounty $50.00. November 1, 1863 received pay. November 1863 received commutations for rations from October 6, 1863 to November 6, 1863. November – December 1863 roll shows him present. January 1864 issued clothing. July 22, 1864 wounded near Kolb's Farm. July 25, 1864 admitted to Ocmulgee Hospital with a gunshot wound. August 27, 1864 deserted. October 31, 1864 received pay. November – December 1864 roll shows him present at Camp Wright near Macon, Georgia detailed as clerk at Camp Wright Hospital. He was a resident of Macon, Bibb County, Georgia.

BRANTLY, T. W.: Company A, lieutenant. April 30, 1863 detailed as enrolling officer for Co. A, 54th Regiment, Georgia Infantry. January 7, 1863 dropped from the rolls. February 28, 1863 attached to the 20th Infantry. March 1, 1863 was the subject of a report.

BRANNER (BRAWNER), JAMES HENRY: Company H, private. May 12, 1862 enlisted as a private in Co. H, 54th Regiment, Georgia Infantry at Columbus, Georgia and received bounty $50.00.

BRAWNER (BRAUNER), JAMES LEMUEL: Company H, private. November 5, 1862 enlisted as a private in Co. H, 54th Regiment, Georgia Infantry at Columbus, Georgia and received bounty $50.00. November 1862 roll shows him present. December 31, 1862 received pay. January – February 1863 roll shows him present.

BRAWNER, M. L.: Company H, sergeant. May 12, 1862 enlisted as 3rd sergeant in Co. H, 54th Regiment, Georgia Infantry at Columbus, Georgia and received bounty $50.00. December 31, 1862 received pay. January – February 1863 roll shows him present. October 31, 1863 received pay. November – December 1863 roll shows him absent on picket duty. December 31, 1863 received pay. January 1864 issued clothing. January – February 1864 roll shows him present. December 6, 1864 received pay $85.13. April 26, 1865 surrendered at Greensboro, North Carolina. May 1, 1865 paroled at Greensboro, North Carolina. He was born in Georgia July 17, 1839 and died in Harris County, Georgia October 17, 1925. He is buried in Mountain Hill Baptist Church Cemetery at Hamilton, Harris County, Georgia. (find a grave # 17677203)

BRAY, GEORGE W.: Company I, corporal. He enlisted as a private in Co. I, 54th Regiment, Georgia Infantry.

BRAY, WILLIAM: Company F, private. September 7, 1861 enlisted as a private in Co. A, 2nd Battalion, Georgia Cavalry. September 7, 1862 enlisted as a private in Co. F, 54th Regiment, Georgia Infantry at Savannah, Georgia and received bounty $50.00. August, September, October, November and December 1863 detailed as a teamster at a rate of $.25 extra per day. November 1, 1863 received pay. December 31, 1863 received pay. November – December 1863 roll shows him present detailed as post teamster (driving a 4 mule wagon). January 1864 issued clothing. July 3, 1864 captured near Marietta, Georgia. July 12, 1864 appears on roll of Provost Marshal at Nashville, Tennessee to be forwarded to Louisville, Kentucky. July 13, 1864 appears on the roll of Military Prison at Louisville, Kentucky as being transferred to Camp Morton, Indiana. July 14, 1864 received at Camp Morton, Indianapolis, Indiana as a prisoner of war. June 12, 1865 released from Camp Morton, Indiana on oath of allegiance. Description on release papers: resident of Savannah, Georgia, dark complexion, dark hair, dark eyes and 5 feet 7 inches high. He was born March 28, 1836 and died October 9, 1909. He is buried in Bethel Lutheran Church Cemetery at Springfield, Effingham County, Georgia. (find a grave # 67966190)

BRAYNARD, S.: Company H, private. May 12, 1862 enlisted as a private in Co. H, 54th Regiment, Georgia Infantry. July 18, 1862 discharged at Savannah, Georgia. December 1862 indicates his discharge.

BREEN, J.: Company F, private. June 1, 1861 enlisted as a private in Co. F, 54th Regiment, Georgia. Infantry at Savannah, Georgia and received bounty $50.00. October 31, 1863 received pay. August 1864 issued clothing. December 28, 1864 captured at Egypt Station, Mississippi. January 17, 1865 arrived at Military Prison at Alton, Illinois. February 21, 1865 sent to Point Lookout, Maryland for exchange. March 2, 1865 admitted to Jackson Hospital at Richmond, Virginia with Debilitas. March 8, 1865 furloughed from Jackson Hospital at Richmond, Virginia for 30 days and received pay at General Hospital, Camp Winder at Richmond, Virginia.

BREEN, JOHN: Company F, private. February 12, 1863 enlisted as a private in Co. F, 54th Regiment, Georgia Infantry at Savannah, Georgia and received bounty $50.00. January – February 1863 roll shows him present. November 1, 1863 received pay. November – December 1863 roll shows him present. January 1864, April 25, 1864 and August 5, 1864 issued clothing. December 28, 1864 captured at Egypt Station, Mississippi. He was sent to Alton, Illinois. February 1865 sent to James River, Virginia for exchange. March 6-9, 1865 received at Boulware and Cox's Wharves, James River, Virginia. March 30, 1865 took oath of allegiance in Savannah, Georgia. Description shows: dark complexion, dark hair, blue eyes, 50 years of age and 5 feet 7 inches high.

BREWER, J. L.: Company H, private. November 8, 1862 enlisted as a private in Co. H, 54th Regiment, Georgia Infantry at Columbus, Georgia and received bounty $50.00. He died in 1936 and is buried in Grey Hill Cemetery, Commerce, Jackson County, Georgia. (find a grave #43053048)

BREWER, JOSEPH W.: Company I, lieutenant. September 18, 1861 enlisted and elected 2nd lieutenant of Co. C, 1st Regiment, 1st Brigade, Georgia State Troops. March 18, 1862 mustered out. May 6, 1862 enlisted as a private in Co. I, 54th Regiment, Georgia Infantry at Guyton, Georgia and received bounty $50.00. May 16, 1862 elected 1st lieutenant in Co. I,

54th Regiment, Georgia Infantry. July 1862 his name is shown on roll at Savannah, Georgia. August 1862 roll shows him present and sick in quarters at Beaulieu near Savannah, Georgia. September, October, November and December 1862 rolls show him present at Beaulieu. February 27, 1863 died. January – February 1863 roll shows his death. He was born November 21, 1833 and died February 27, 1863. He is buried in Little Ogeechee Baptist Church Cemetery at Oliver, Screven County, Georgia. (find a grave # 24971419)

BREWER, THOMAS A.: Company I (F), private. September 1, 1862 enlisted as a private in Co. I, 54th Regiment, Georgia Infantry at Beaulieu near Savannah, Georgia and received bounty $50.00. August 1862 and September 1862 rolls show him present at Beaulieu and that he joined in September. October 1862 roll shows his name. November 1862 and December 1862 rolls show him as Lt. Colonel's Orderly. December 31, 1862 received pay. January – February 1863 roll shows him absent with leave. October 31, 1863 received pay. November – December 1863 roll shows him present. January 1864 issued clothing. April 26, 1865 surrendered at Greensboro, North Carolina as a member of Co. F, 54th Regiment, Georgia Infantry. May 1, 1865 paroled at Greensboro, North Carolina. He was born October 10, 1844 and died March 25, 1898. He is buried in Little Ogeechee Baptist Church Cemetery at Oliver, Screven County, Georgia. (find a grave # 24972624)

BREWER, WILLIAMSON (WILLIAM) T.: Company I (F), sergeant. September 18, 1861 enlisted as a private in Co. C, 1st Regiment, 1st Brigade, Georgia State Troops. March 18, 1862 mustered out.

September 1, 1862 enlisted as a private in Co. I, 54th Regiment, Georgia Infantry at Guyton, Georgia and received bounty $50.00. September 5, 1862 promoted to 1st corporal in Co. I, 54th Regiment, Georgia Infantry. December 31, 1862 received pay. January – February 1863 roll shows him absent with leave. October 31, 1863 received pay. November 12, 1863 promoted to 5th sergeant in Co. I, 54th Regiment, Georgia Infantry. November – December 1863 roll shows him present and promoted to 5th sergeant. January 1864 and April 25, 1864 issued clothing. April 26, 1865 surrendered at Greensboro, North Carolina as a member of Co. F, 54th Regiment, Georgia Infantry. May 1, 1865 paroled at Greensboro, North Carolina. He was born December 10, 1836 and died August 22, 1907. He is buried in Little Ogeechee Baptist Church Cemetery at Oliver, Screven County, Georgia. (find a grave # 24972750)

BREWSTER, TOMLINSON FORT.: Company H, lieutenant. May 12, 1862 enlisted as a private in Co. H, 54th Regiment, Georgia Infantry at Columbus, Georgia and received bounty $50.00. May 12, 1862 appointed 1st lieutenant in Co. H, 54th Regiment, Georgia Infantry. July 1862 and August 1862 rolls show him present at Beaulieu near Savannah, Georgia. September 1862 roll shows him absent from Beaulieu with leave. October 1862 roll shows him absent from Beaulieu with leave since October 24 for 10 days. November 1862 roll shows him present. December 1862 roll shows him absent with leave since December 26 for 15 days. January 1863 he is shown on leave. January – February 1863 roll shows him present. March 7, 1863 received pay $90.00. April 3, 1863 received pay $75.00. June 11, 1863 to June 26, 1863 he was on furlough. October 1, 1863 and October 21, 1863 issued clothing. December 1, 1863 received pay $90.00. December 13, 1863 dismissed from service by sentence of General Court Marshal December 13, 1863. November 21, 1863 report of General Mercer shows him absent in arrest in Savannah, Georgia. November – December 1863 roll shows him dismissed December 13. December 20, 1863 enlisted as a private in Co. H, 54th Regiment, Georgia Infantry at Beaulieu near Savannah, Georgia. November – December 1863 2nd roll shows him assigned to company at his request under General Order #42. December 31, 1863 received pay. January 1, 1864 received pay. January 1864 issued clothing. January – February 1864 roll shows him absent (detailed by order of General Gilmer as hospital Steward on February 26, 1864). January – February 1863 roll of Jo Thompson Artillery shows him present attached to hospital as steward January 1, 1864 (detailed from Co. H, 54th regiment, Georgia infantry for 53 days at a rate of $.25 per day). November 27, 1864 on roll of Walker Hospital at Columbus, Georgia as Acting Assistant Surgeon (Appointed on board to examine all convalescents on duty in this hospital and return to duty all such as are fit for field service). He was born in Cherokee County, Georgia June 1834 and died in Atlanta; Fulton County, Georgia May 1, 1910. He is buried in Oakland Cemetery at Atlanta, Fulton County, Georgia. (find a grave # 69348540)

BRICE, WILLIAM: Company A, private. He enlisted as a private in Co. A, 54th Regiment, Georgia Infantry.

BRIGMAN, ISAAC: Company H, private. November 10, 1862 enlisted as a private in Co. H, 54th Regiment, Georgia Infantry at Columbus, Georgia and received bounty $50.00. November 1862 roll shows him joining on November 10. December 31, 1862 received pay. January – February 1863 roll shows him present. October 31, 1863 received pay. November – December 1863 roll shows him absent with leave since December 22, 1863. December 31, 1863 received pay. January – February 1864 roll shows him present. January, 1864 and June 2, 1864 issued clothing.

BRIGMAN (BRIDGEMAN), THOMAS: Company H, private. November 7, 1862 enlisted as a private in Co. H, 54th Regiment, Georgia Infantry at Columbus, Georgia and received bounty $50.00. November 1862 roll shows him joining on November 7. December 31, 1862 received pay. January – February 1863 roll shows him present. October 31, 1863 received pay. November – December 1863 roll shows him present. December 31, 1863 received pay. January – February 1864 roll shows him present. January 1864 and June 2, 1864 issued clothing. June 15, 1864 report of Medical Examining Board at Dalton Georgia shows he had been in Cannon Hospital for 60 days with Chronic Diarrhoea with Emaciation and Extreme Debility for 3 months. He was a resident of Crawford, Alabama. December 31, 1864 took Oath of Allegiance at Nashville Tennessee. He is shown on report as; a resident of Russell County, Alabama, dark complexion, brown hair, grey eyes 5 feet 10 inches high and has family.

BRINSON (BRONSON), DAVID M.: Company D, private. October 7, 1861 enlisted as a private in Co. I, 5th Regiment, Georgia State Troops. April 1862 mustered out. April 30, 1862 enlisted as a private in Co. D, 54th Regiment, Georgia Infantry at Savannah, Georgia and received bounty $50.00. December 31, 1862 received pay. January – February 1863 roll shows him present. January 1864 issued clothing. Pension records show he was discharged on account of a hernia in January 1865. He was born in Burke County, Georgia September 19, 1843.

BRITT, H. N.: Company A (D), corporal. May 5, 1862 enlisted as a private in Co. A, 54th Regiment, Georgia Infantry at Macon, Georgia and received bounty $50.00. April 30, 1863 received pay. June 30, 1863 roll shows him present. October 31, 1863 received pay. November – December 1863 roll shows him present. January 1, 1864 received pay. January 1864 issued clothing. January – February 1864 roll shows him present. March 31, 1864 and April 29, 1864 issued clothing. June 28, 1864 report of Medical Examining Board at Dalton Georgia shows he had been in Oliver Hospital for 60 days with Extreme Emaciation and Debility as a result of Febris Typhoid, brain sick for 2 months. April 26, 1865 surrendered at Greensboro, North Carolina as a member of Co. D, 54th Regiment, Georgia Infantry. May 1, 1865 paroled at Greensboro, North Carolina. He was a resident of Fort Valley, Georgia.

BRITT, ISAIAH D.: Company A, private. May 12, 1862 enlisted as a private in Co. A, 54th Regiment, Georgia Infantry at Macon, Georgia and received bounty $50.00. June 22, 1864 he died. August 23, 1864 death claim was iled by his widow, Martha A. E. Britt.

BRITT, J. D.: Company A, private. May 12, 1862 enlisted as a private in Co. A, 54th Regiment, Georgia Infantry at Macon, Georgia and received bounty $50.00. April 30, 1863 received pay. June 30, 1863 roll shows him present (2 months' pay deducted by order of Brigadier General Mercer). October 31, 1863 received pay. November – December 1863 and January – February 1864 rolls show him absent (in arrest in barracks in Savannah, Georgia since December 24, 1863). March 1, 1864 he is shown on report of General Mercer as a prisoner. March 31, 1864, April 29, 1864 and May 8, 1864 issued clothing. June 20, 1864 wounded in the hand near Marietta, Georgia. June 21, 1864 he died in hospital at Atlanta, Georgia.

BRITT, JAMES J.: Company A (D), private. April 9, 1865 enlisted as a private in Co. A, 54th Regiment, Georgia Infantry at Smithfield, North Carolina. April 26, 1865 surrendered in Company D. at Greensboro, North Carolina. May 1, 1865 paroled at Greensboro, North Carolina.

BRITT, JOHN J.: Company A (D), private. May 5, 1862 enlisted as a private in Co. A, 54th Regiment, Georgia Infantry at Macon, Georgia and received bounty $50.00. September 1862 roll shows him as the company cook. April 30, 1863 received pay. June 30, 1863 roll shows him present. October 31, 1863 received pay. November – December 1863 roll shows him present. January – February 1863 roll shows him present. April 29, 1864 issued clothing. April 26, 1865 surrendered in Company D at Greensboro, North Carolina. May 1, 1865 paroled at Greensboro, North Carolina. He was born in Crawford County, Georgia December 6, 1832 and died in Crawford County, Georgia December 8, 1910 he is buried in Providence Cemetery at Roberta, Crawford County, Georgia. (find a grave # 42739360)

BRITT, L.H.: Company A (D), private. May 3, 1862 enlisted as a private in Co. A, 54th Regiment, Georgia Infantry at Macon, Georgia and received bounty $50.00. April 30, 1863 received pay. June 30, 1863 roll shows him present. October 31, 1863 received pay. November – December 1863 roll shows him present. January 1, 1864 received pay. January – February 1864 roll shows him present. April 29, 1864 and May 8, 1864 issued clothing. April 26, 1865 surrendered in Company D at Greensboro, North Carolina. May 1, 1865 paroled at Greensboro, North Carolina.

BRITT, O. D: Company A, private. May 3, 1862 enlisted as a private in Co. A, 54th Regiment, Georgia Infantry. April 30, 1863 received pay. June 30, 1863 roll shows him present (sick in company hospital). August 31, 1863 received pay. November – December 1863 roll shows him present. January 1, 1864 received pay. January – February 1864 roll shows him present. March 21, 1864 issued clothing. Pension records show he was on detail in Government Shoe Shop at Girard, Alabama at close of war. He was born at Knoxville, Georgia January 27, 1836 and died at Columbus, Georgia August 1900.

BRITT, RICE W.: Company C, private. He enlisted as a private in Co. C, 54th Regiment, Georgia Infantry. May 16, 1864 captured at Resacca, Georgia and sent to military Prison at Louisville, Kentucky. May 21, 1864 released from Military Prison at Louisville, Kentucky.

BROADWAY, J.: Company H, private. October 1862 enlisted as a private in Co. H, 54th Regiment, Georgia Infantry. October 31, 1862 discharged from Beaulieu near Savannah, Georgia. October 1862 roll shows him discharged at Beaulieu near Savannah, Georgia. He is buried in Linwood Cemetery at Columbus, Muscogee County, Georgia. (find a grave # 9580150)

BROGDEN (BRADEN), JAMES: Company E, private. August 31, 1862 enlisted as a private in Co. E, 54th Regiment, Georgia Infantry at Coffee Bluff, Georgia. December 31, 1862 received pay. January – February 1863 roll shows him present. January 1864 and April 25, 1864 issued clothing.
May 26, 1865 surrendered and paroled at Thomasville, Georgia. He was born February 17, 1846 and died November 19, 1927. He is buried in Brogdon Cemetery at Alapaha, Berrien County, Georgia. (find a grave # 62973076)

BROGDEN, WILLIAM: Company E, private. February 11, 1863

enlisted as a private in Co. E, 54th Regiment, Georgia Infantry at Coffee Bluff, Georgia. January – February 1863 roll shows him present. January 1864 and April 25, 1864 issued clothing. Pension records show he was discharged at the close of the war. He was born in Wilkinson County, Georgia in 1828.

BRONSON (BRUNSON), LEWIS R. M.: Company A, private. November 30, 1862 enlisted as a private in Co. A, 54th Regiment, Georgia Infantry at Macon, Georgia. November 1862 roll shows he joined November 30. April 20, 1863 received pay. June 30, 1863 roll shows him present. October 31, 1863 received pay. November 14, 1863 received pay for commutation for rations. November – December 1863 roll shows him present. January 1, 1864 received pay. January – February 1864 roll shows him present. April 29, 1864 and May 8, 1864 issued clothing. January 13, 1865 admitted to St. Mary's Hospital at West Point, Mississippi with Diarrhoea. He was born in South Carolina in 1836 and died November 8, 1866. He is buried in an unmarked grave in Rose Hill Cemetery at Macon, Bibb County, Georgia.

BROOKER, JOHN: Company G, musician - private. May 10, 1862 enlisted as a musician in Co. G, 54th Regiment, Georgia Infantry at Macon, Georgia and received bounty $50.00. January – February 1863 roll shows him (colored man – dropped from the roll January 31, 1863).

BROOKS, JAMES P.: Company A (F), private. May 10, 1862 enlisted as a private in Co. A, 54th Regiment, Georgia Infantry at Macon, Georgia and received bounty $50.00. April 20, 1863 received pay. June 30, 1863 roll shows him present. October 31, 1863 received pay. November – December 1863 roll shows him present. January 1, 1864 received pay. January – February 1864 roll shows him present. April 29, 1864 issued clothing. Pension records show April 26, 1865 surrendered in Company F at Greensboro, North Carolina. May 1, 1865 paroled at Greensboro, North Carolina. He was born in Bibb County, Georgia in 1843 and died at Macon, Bibb County, Georgia August 5, 1909. He is buried in Fort Hill Cemetery at Macon, Bibb County, Georgia. (find a grave # 121461747)

BROWN, ALEX J.: Company G (F), private. He enlisted as a private in Co. G, 54th Regiment, Georgia Infantry. April 25, 1864 and May 8, 1864 issued clothes. April 26, 1865 surrendered in Company F at Greensboro, North Carolina. May 1, 1865 paroled at Greensboro, North Carolina. He was born February 21, 1826 and died in Terrell County, Georgia December 1, 1910. He is buried in Oak Grove Church Cemetery at Dover, Terrell County, Georgia. (find a grave # 18501158)

BROWN, EDMUND (ERNEST) WADE: Company F, corporal. May 17, 1861 enlisted as a private in Chisholm's Company, Georgia State Troops. May 1862 mustered out. May 13, 1862 enlisted as a corporal in Co. F, 54th Regiment, Georgia Infantry at Savannah, Georgia and received bounty $50.00. December 31, 1862 received pay. January – February 1863 roll shows him present. November 1, 1863 received pay. November – December 1863 roll shows him present. January 1864, April 25, 1864 and July 29, 1964 issued clothing. October 1864 appointed 3rd corporal of Co. F, 54th Regiment, Georgia Infantry. Pension records show; December 8, 1864 he was sent home on 60 day sick furlough. His furlough was extended. He was unfit for duty at the close of the war. He was born in Georgia August 6, 1847.

BROWN, J. S.: Company C, private. He enlisted as a private in Co. C, 54th Regiment, Georgia Infantry.

BROWN, JAMES: Company F, private. September 10, 1862 enlisted as a private in Co. C, 54th Regiment, Georgia Infantry at Beaulieu near Savannah, Georgia. September 1862 roll shows him joining. October 2, 1862 deserted from Beaulieu near Savannah, Georgia. October 1862 roll shows him deserting.

BROWN, JOHN M.: Company H, private. January 18, 1863 enlisted as a private in Co. H, 54th Regiment, Georgia Infantry at Beaulieu near Savannah, Georgia. January – February 1863 roll shows him present (detailed as a teamster in Quartermaster Department). November – December 1863 and January – February 1864 roll shows him absent (detailed in Engineer Department December 22, 1863 by order of General Mercer). He was born November 20, 1820 and died October 23, 1892. He is buried in County Line Cemetery in Stewart County, Georgia. (find a grave # 44003886)

BROWN, JOHN R.: Company H, private. May 30, 1862 enlisted as a private in Co. A, 54th Regiment, Georgia Infantry at Savannah, Georgia and received bounty $50.00. December 31, 1862 received pay. January – February 1863 roll shows him present. October 31, 1863 received pay. November – December 1863 roll shows him present. December 31, 1863 received pay. January 1864 issued clothing. January – February 1864 roll shows him present (on picket duty). June 2, 1864 issued clothing. Pension record shows; He was detailed to build pontoon bridges at the close of the war. He was born in Tattnall County, Georgia in 1816.

BROWN, R. D.: Company H, sergeant. He enlisted as a sergeant in Co. A, 54th Regiment, Georgia Infantry.

BROWN, W. A. J.: Company I, private. He enlisted as a private in Co. A, 54th Regiment, Georgia Infantry.

BROWN, W. F.: Company A, private. August 16, 1862 enlisted as a private in Co. A, 54th Regiment, Georgia Infantry at Savannah, Georgia. August 1862 roll shows he joined. October, November and December 1862 rolls show he was detailed as the Adjutant's Clerk. May 5, 1863 discharged furnished substitute Thomas Flinn.

BROWN, WILLIAM: Company G, private. October 1, 1862 enlisted as a private in Co. G, 54th Regiment, Georgia Infantry at Savannah, Georgia and received bounty $50.00. October 1862 roll shows he was present at Beaulieu near Savannah, Georgia and became the colonel's orderly (joined by transfer). November 1862 roll shows he was the Colonel's orderly. December 31, 1862 received pay. January – February 1863 roll shows him absent (detached as Orderly of Colonel Charlton H. Way beginning

October 1, 1862). He was born in Georgia in 1842 and died in Russell County, Alabama. He is buried in Crawford Cemetery at Crawford, Russell County, Alabama. (find a grave # 53750249)

BROWNELL, GEORGE W.: Company F, private. May 17, 1861 enlisted as a private in Chisholm's Company, Georgia State Troops. May 1862 mustered out. May 13, 1862 enlisted as a private in Co. F, 54th Regiment, Georgia Infantry at Savannah, Georgia and received bounty $50.00. December 31, 1862 received pay. January – February 1863 roll shows him present. November 1, 1863 received pay. November – December 1863 roll shows him present (detailed as ambulance driver). January 1864 and May 8, 1864 issued clothing. May 18, 1865 surrendered and paroled at Augusta, Georgia.

BRUCE, CHARLES: Company H, private. He enlisted as a private in Co. A, 54th Regiment, Georgia Infantry.

BRUCE, JOEL L.: Company G, private. January 22, 1863 He enlisted as a private in Co. G, 54th Regiment, Georgia Infantry at Columbus, Georgia and received bounty pay $50.00. January – February 1863 roll shows him present. March 30, 1864 returned to his command from Walker Hospital at Columbus, Georgia. June 18, 1864 found "unfit for duty' by the Medical Examining Board of the Confederate States Arsenal at Columbus, Georgia. August 22, 1864 he was Commanding Confederate States Arsenal at Columbus, Georgia. He was born in Greene County, Georgia September 18, 1829.

BRUCE, WILLIAM: Company G, private. September 13, 1862 enlisted as a private in Co. F, 54th Regiment, Georgia Infantry at Savannah, Georgia and received bounty $50.00. September 1862 roll shows he joined. October, November and December 1862 rolls show him detailed as a butcher. October 13, 1862 to November 30, 1862 detailed as a butcher and was paid $.25 extra per day. December 31, 1862 received pay. January 15, 1863 received pay. February 1863 received pay. January – February 1863 roll shows him present (returned to the company for duty from special service, as a butcher on February 21, 1863). September 1, 1863 to September 30, 1863 was detailed as a carpenter on James Island, South Carolina and was paid $.25 extra per day. October 1, 1863 to November 30, 1863 was detailed as a laborer at St. Andrews near Charleston, South Carolina and was paid $.25 extra per day. January 1864 issued clothing. January 1, 1864 to January 31, 1864 was detailed as a laborer at Charleston, South Carolina and was paid $.25 extra per day. January 21, 1864 detail revoked by Special Order No. 16/3.

BRYAN, JESSE: Company G, private. January 22, 1863 He enlisted as a private in Co. G, 54th Regiment, Georgia Infantry at Columbus, Georgia and received bounty pay $50.00. January – February 1863 roll shows him present. January 1964 issued clothing. June 27, 1864 killed at Kennesaw Mountain, Georgia. He died June 27, 1864. He is buried in Stonewall Cemetery at Griffin, Spalding County, Georgia. (find a grave # 90938705)

BRYANT, BENJAMIN: Company H (F), private. May 12, 1862 enlisted as a private in Co. H, 54th Regiment, Georgia Infantry at Columbus, Georgia and received bounty $50.00. October 1862 discharged due to disability. December 31, 1862 received pay. January 17, 1863 transferred from Co. H, 54th Regiment, Georgia Infantry to Co. F, 54th Regiment, Georgia Infantry by order of Colonel Way. January – February 1863 roll of Co. H, 54th Regiment, Georgia Infantry shows him transferred to Co. F, 54th Regiment, Georgia Infantry. January – February 1863 roll of Co. F shows him present and transferred from Co. H, 54th Regiment, Georgia Infantry to Co. F, 5th Regiment, Georgia Reserve Infantry. March – April 1865 roll shows him on detail to guard bridges in South Carolina. He was born in Muscogee County, Georgia July 5, 1845.

BRYANT, BENJAMIN F.: Company F, private. May 12, 1862 enlisted as a private in Co. F, 54th Regiment, Georgia Infantry at Columbus, Georgia and received bounty $50.00. October 1862 discharged due to disability. May, 1864 enlisted as a private in Co. F, 5th Georgia Reserves. March – April 185 on detailed to guard bridges in South Carolina. He was born in Muscogee County, Georgia July 5, 1845.

BRYANT, D. J.: Company F, private. January 28, 1863 enlisted as a private in Co. F, 54th Regiment, Georgia Infantry at Savannah, Georgia and received bounty $50.00. January – February 1863 roll shows him present. November 1, 1863 received pay. November – December 1863 roll shows him present.

BRYANT, E. H.: Company C, sergeant. April 22, 1862 enlisted as a private in Co. C, 54th Regiment, Georgia Infantry at Savannah, Georgia and received bounty $50.00. December 31, 1862 received pay. January – February 1863 roll shows him present (note: absent without leave 10 days). December 1863 appointed 5th sergeant of Co. C, 54th Regiment, Georgia Infantry. January 1, 1864 received pay. January – February 1864 roll shows him present. July 20, 1864 wounded at Peachtree Creek near Atlanta, Georgia. August 3, 1864 died of gunshot wounds at Oliver Hospital at La Grange, Georgia.

BRYANT, NEEDHAM W.: Company C, private. May 6, 1862 enlisted as a private in Co. C, 54th Regiment, Georgia Infantry at Savannah, Georgia and received bounty $50.00. June 30, 1862 received pay. January – February 1863 roll shows him present. January 1, 1864 received pay. January – February 1864 roll shows him absent (detached as a picket at Purysburg, South Carolina by order of Colonel Way dated February 20, 1864). 1864 he was wounded. Pension records show he was at home on sick furlough at the close of the war. He was born December 9, 1836 and died in Emanuel County, Georgia June 10, 1888. He is buried in Old Canoochee Cemetery at Twin City, Emanuel County, Georgia. (find a grave #53966162)

BUCE, COLUMBUS C.: Company H, private. February 11, 1863 enlisted as a private in Co. H, 54th Regiment, Georgia Infantry at Columbus, Georgia and received bounty $50.00. January – February 1863 roll shows him present. October 31, 1863 received pay. November – December 1863 roll shows him present. December 31, 1863 received pay. January – February 1864 roll shows him present (on Picket). January 1864 and June 2, 1864 issued clothing. May 18, 1865 signed Oath of Allegiance and was paroled in Montgomery, Alabama. Description on parole papers: 5 feet 2 inches high, light hair, grey eyes and fair complexion.

BUCKALEW, T. J.: Company B, private. He enlisted as a private in Co. B, 54th Regiment, Georgia Infantry.

BULLARD, E.: Company H, private. May 12, 1862 enlisted as a private in Co. H, 54th Regiment, Georgia Infantry at Columbus, Georgia. May 20, 1862 deserted at Savannah, Georgia.

BULLARD, ELIAS: Company B, private. April 28, 1862 enlisted as a private in Co. B, 54th Regiment, Georgia Infantry at Savannah, Georgia and received bounty $50.00. December 31, 1862 received pay. January – February 1863 roll shows him absent without leave since February 27 - 1 day. January 1864, April 25, 1864 and May 8, 1864 issued clothing. March 16, 1865 admitted to C. S. A. General Hospital, No. 11 at Charlotte, North Carolina with Intermittent Fever (Malaria).

BULLARD, IRVING: Company B, private. April 28, 1862 enlisted as a private in Co. B, 54th Regiment, Georgia Infantry at Savannah, Georgia and received bounty $50.00. Pension records show he was ordered "to go home until further orders". He was born in Appling County, Georgia November 28, 1846.

BULLARD, JASPER S.: Company G, private. January 22, 1863 enlisted as a private in Co. G, 54th Regiment, Georgia Infantry at Columbus, Georgia and received bounty $50.00. January – February 1863 roll shows him present.

BURGER, A.: Company G, private. September 13, 1862 enlisted as a private in Co. G, 54th Regiment, Georgia Infantry at Savannah, Georgia and received bounty $50.00. September 1862 roll at Beaulieu near Savannah, Georgia shows he joined. December 31, 1862 received pay. December 1862 detached as a teamster. January – February 1863 roll shows him absent (detached and sent to Savannah as a teamster with the Quartermaster Department on February 18, 1863). He requested a transfer to the Engineers (date not known).

BURGER, HENRY: Company G, private. May 12, 1862 enlisted as a private in Co. G, 54th Regiment, Georgia Infantry at Columbus, Georgia and received bounty $50.00.

BURGSTEINER, J. I.: Company I, private. He enlisted as a private in Co. I, 54th Regiment, Georgia Infantry.

BURGSTINER, JOHN R.: Company I, private. September 18, 1861 enlisted as a private in Co. C, 1st Regiment, 1st Brigade, Georgia State Troops. March 18, 1862 mustered out. May 6, 1862 enlisted as a private in Co. I, 54th Regiment, Georgia Infantry at Guyton, Georgia and received bounty $50.00. July 29, 1862 died at Savannah, Georgia. July and August 1862 rolls reflect his death.

BURGSTINER, LAWRENCE E.: Field and Staff acting sergeant major. (Company I, private). September 18, 1862 enlisted as a private in Co. C, 1st Regiment, 1st Brigade, Georgia State Troops. March 18, 1862 mustered out. May 6, 1862 enlisted as a private in Co. I, 54th Regiment, Georgia Infantry at Guyton, Georgia and received bounty $50.00. December 31, 1862 received pay. January – February 1863 roll shows him present. May 1864, June 1864 and July 1864 on detached service at the Rose Dew Post as Headquarters Clerk at a rate of pay of $.25 per day. July 31, 1863 to October 31, 1863 he was on detached service as acting Sergeant Major at Savannah at a rate of pay of $.25 per day. October 31, 1863 received pay. October 31, 1863 to December 31, 1863 he was on detached service as acting Sergeant Major at Savannah at a rate of pay of $.25 per day. November – December 1863 roll shows him present (Acting Sergeant Major). January 1, 1864 issued clothing. January 18, 1865 admitted to Ross Hospital at Mobile, Alabama with Excoriation. January 29, 1865 returned to duty. February 6, 1865 sent to General Hospital at Greenville, North Carolina. April 21-22, 1865 captured in Macon, Georgia. He was born July 23, 1844 and died January 20, 1905. He is buried in Springfield City Cemetery at Springfield, Effingham County, Georgia. (find a grave # 36635158)

BURKE, H. S.: Company D, private. August 26, 1862 enlisted as a private in Co. D, 54th Regiment, Georgia Infantry at Beaulieu near Savannah, Georgia and received bounty $50.00. August 1862 roll at Savannah shows he joined. October 1862 roll shows him present. December 31, 1862 received pay. January – February 1863 roll shows him present. May 10, 1865 surrendered at Tallahassee, Florida. May 19, 1865 paroled at Thomasville, Georgia. He is described on his parole papers as: 5 feet 7 inches high, dark hair, blue eyes and dark complexion.

BURKE, J. D.: Company D, private. August 30, 1862 enlisted as a private in Co. D, 54th Regiment, Georgia Infantry at Savannah, Georgia and received bounty $50.00. September 1862 roll shows him discharged September 10, 1862 at Beaulieu near Savannah, Georgia. .

BURKE, THOMAS A.: Field, Staff, Quartermaster (major). October 20, 1861 appointed captain and quartermaster in 1st Regiment, 1st Brigade, Georgia State Troops. April 1862 mustered out. April 30, 1862 enlisted in the 54th Regiment, Georgia Infantry at Savannah, Georgia. July 16, 1862 appointed Assistant Quartermaster and promoted to captain of the 54th Regiment, Georgia Infantry. July 1862 roll shows him at Savannah, Georgia. August, September, October, November and December 1862 rolls show him present at Beaulieu near Savannah, Georgia. November 8, 1862 received pay $58.00 for mileage from Savannah, to Atlanta. . January – February 1863 roll shows him present at Beaulieu near Savannah, Georgia as Regimental Quartermaster. March 1, 1863 his name appears on a list of Quartermasters on Duty with regiments in the Department of South Carolina, Georgia and Florida. April 9, 1863 (August 19, 1863) appointed Quartermaster for the Regiment and promoted to the rank of major. January 12, 1865 was serving as Quartermaster at the rank of major in Charleston, South Carolina.

BURKE, W. D. S.: Company D, private. April 30, 1862 enlisted as a private in Co. D, 54th Regiment, Georgia Infantry at Savannah, Georgia and received bounty $50.00. December 31, 1862 received pay. January – February 1863 roll shows him present. August 31, 1863 received pay. September 3, 1863 received pay $44.00. October 31, 1863 roll of General Hospital No. 2 (also called Hospital Encampment) at Summerville, South Carolina shows him present. December 31, 1863 received pay. December 31, 1863 roll of General Hospital No. 2 (also called Hospital Encampment) at Summerville, South Carolina shows him present. January 1864 issued clothing. January – February 1864 roll of General Hospital No. 2 (also called Hospital Encampment) at Summerville, South Carolina shows him present. He was a resident of Screven County, Georgia. He was born in North Carolina March 8, 1826 and died in Georgia May 8, 1891. He is buried in Big Horse Creek Cemetery in Jenkins County, Georgia. (find a grave # 66942662)

BURKETT, ROBERT: Company A, private. He enlisted as a private in Co. A, 54th Regiment, Georgia Infantry.

BURNS, STEWART: Company E, private. May 6, 1862 enlisted as a private in Co. E, 54th Regiment, Georgia Infantry at Savannah, Georgia and received bounty $50.00. December 31, 1862 received pay. January – February 1863 roll shows him present. January 1864 issued clothing. March 27, 1864 died. June 21, 1864 death benefit claim was filed by Hugh A. Burns.

BURT, A. S.: Company B, private. He enlisted as a corporal in Co. B, 54th Regiment, Georgia Infantry at Savannah, Georgia and received bounty $50.00.

BURT, T. W.: Company B, private. He enlisted as a private in Co. B, 54th Regiment, Georgia Infantry at Savannah, Georgia and received bounty $50.00. He was born in Georgia June 7, 1845 and died in Mississippi December 21, 1921. He is buried in Pearidge Cemetery in Grenada County, Mississippi. (find a grave # 28917496)

BUTLER, HENRY W.; Company F, private. May 17, 1861 enlisted as a private in Chisholm's Company, Georgia State Troops. May 1862 mustered out. May 13, 1862 enlisted as a private in Co. F, 54th Regiment, Georgia Infantry at Savannah, Georgia and received bounty $50.00. November 4, 1862 discharged by civil authority. November 1862 roll shows his discharge. He died in Rincon, Effingham County, Georgia July 14, 1917. He is buried in Laurel Grove Cemetery at Savannah, Chatham County, Georgia. (find a grave # 79562425)

BUTLER, ROBERT M.: Company F, lieutenant. May 17, 1861 enlisted and appointed 3rd sergeant in Chisholm's Company, Georgia State Troops. May 1862 mustered out. May 13, 1862 enlisted as a private in Co. F, 54th Regiment, Georgia Infantry at Savannah, Georgia and received bounty $50.00. He was elected 2nd sergeant of Co. F, 54th Regiment, Georgia

Infantry. December 31, 1862 received pay. January – February 1863 roll shows him present. September 22, 1863 he was elected 1st sergeant of Co. F, 54th Regiment, Georgia Infantry. November 1, 1863 received pay including commutation for rations from July 22, 1863 to September 22, 1863. November – December 1863 roll shows him present. January 1864. February 1, 1864 to February 28, 1864 and April 1, 1864 to April 30, 1864 detailed as Acting Commissary Sergeant for the Oglethorpe Barracks in Savannah, Georgia at a rate of pay of $.25 per day. August 15, 1864 and December 28, 1864 issued clothing. He was elected lieutenant of Co. F, 54th Regiment, Georgia Infantry. April 26, 1865 surrendered as 2nd sergeant of Company D 54th Regiment, Georgia Infantry at Greensboro, North Carolina. May 1, 1865 paroled at Greensboro, North Carolina.

BUTLER, WILLIAM J.: Company I, private. October 1, 1863 enlisted as a private in Co. I, 54th Regiment, Georgia Infantry at Rosedew near Savannah, Georgia and received bounty $50.00. October 31, 1863 received pay. November – December 1863 roll shows him present (sick in post hospital). January 1864 and April 25, 1864 issued clothing. June 24, 1864 he appears on a register of Ocmulgee Hospital at Macon, Georgia with a Gunshot Wound through the left hand. June 25, 1864 was furloughed for 60 days. February 3, 1865 admitted to Way Hospital at Meridian, Mississippi with a Gunshot Wound and was furloughed. He was a resident of Emanuel County, Georgia.

BYRD (BIRD), CLEMENT C.: Company K, private. October 3, 1861 enlisted as a private in Co. A, 1st Regiment, 1st Brigade, Georgia State Troops. April 1862 mustered out. April 18, 1862 enlisted as a private in Co. K, 54th Regiment, Georgia Infantry at Savannah, Georgia and received bounty $50.00. January 1, 1863 received pay. January – February 1863 roll shows him present. March 18, 1864 issued clothing. May 10, 1865 surrendered at Tallahassee, Florida. May 16, 1865 paroled at Thomasville, Georgia. He is described on his parole papers as; 5 feet 7 inches high, sandy hair, grey eyes and dark complexion. He was born in Emanuel County, Georgia July 22, 1843 and died in Appling County, Georgia October 8, 1921.

BYRD (BIRD), HENRY J.: Company F, private. April 4, 1863 enlisted as a private in Co. F, 54th Regiment, Georgia Infantry at Savannah, Georgia and received bounty $50.00. November 1, 1863 received pay. November – December 1863 roll shows him present. January 1864 and April 25, 1864 issued clothing. December 16, 1864 received pay $44.00. He was born in Georgia.

CAESAR, D. ROBERT: Company F, cook. January 1, 1863 enlisted as a private in Co. F, 54th Regiment, Georgia Infantry at Savannah, Georgia and received bounty $50.00. January – February 1863 roll shows him present.

CAESAR, D. ROBERT: Company F, private January 1, 1863 enlisted as a private in Co. F, 54th Regiment, Georgia Infantry at Savannah, Georgia and received bounty $50.00. January – February 1863 roll shows him present.

1864 detailed at the Arsenal at Macon, Georgia. 1864 he transferred to the Confederate Navy. He served on the gunboat Isondiga. 1864 captured at Savannah, Georgia. He was sent to Drewry's Bluff, Virginia. At the fall of Richmond, Virginia he marched toward Appomattox Courthouse, Virginia. April 8, 1865 he was captured. He was born in Savannah, Georgia May 7, 1846.

CALDER, JOHN: Company F, private. He enlisted in Co. F, 54th Regiment, Georgia Infantry.

CALDER, T.: Company F, private. He enlisted in Co. F, 54th Regiment, Georgia Infantry.

CALLINGS, C. C.: Company H, private. He enlisted as a private in Co. H, 54th Regiment, Georgia Infantry.

CALLOWAY, J. J.: Field, Staff, assistant surgeon. He enlisted as assistant surgeon in the 54th Regiment, Georgia Infantry

CAMEL, W. H.: Company B, private. He enlisted as a private in the 4th Georgia Sharpshooters
February 28, 1865 enlisted as a private in Co. B, 54th Regiment, Georgia Infantry at Barnesville, Georgia and received bounty $50.00. April 26, 1865 surrendered at Greensboro, North Carolina. May 1, 1865 paroled at Greensboro, North Carolina.

CAMPBELL, ABNER B.: Field, Staff, chaplain. June 6, 1861 enlisted as a private in Co. H, 9th Regiment, Georgia Infantry. January 27, 1863 appointed chaplain of the 54th Regiment, Georgia infantry. January – February 1863 roll shows him present. April 30, 1863 he is shown absent without leave. July 1, 1863 and August 17, 1863 leave granted. September 19, 1863 resigned his commission. He was born May 23, 1840 and died August 18, 1909. He is buried in Oak Grove Cemetery at Americus, Sumter County, Georgia. (find a grave # 86297550)

CAMPBELL, SAMUEL T.: Company A, private. October 17, 1861 enlisted as a private in Co. C, 1st Independent Battalion, Georgia State Troops. April 16, 1862 roll shows him present. April 1862 mustered out. April 29, 1862 enlisted as a private in Co. A, 54th Regiment, Georgia Infantry at Macon, Georgia and received bounty $50.00. September, October, November and December 1862 rolls show him present detailed as a butcher. September 1, 1862 through February 28, 1863 on special detail as a butcher at Beaulieu near Savannah, Georgia at an extra $.25 per day pay rate. April 30, 1863 received pay. June 30, 1863 roll shows him present. October 31, 1863 received pay. November – December 1863 roll shows him present. January 1, 1864 received pay. January – February 1864 roll shows him present. April 29, 1864 issued clothing. March 3, 1865 admitted to Ocmulgee hospital at Macon, Georgia with Ulcus. April 20-21, 1865 captured at Macon, Georgia. He was a resident of Bibb County, Georgia. He was born in Macon, Bibb County, Georgia April 12, 1824 and died in Macon, Bibb County, Georgia in 1872. He is buried in Jones Chapel Cemetery at Macon, Bibb County, Georgia. (find a grave # 59887147)

CANNADY, DANIEL BERIAN: Company G (C), private. May 6, 1862 enlisted as a private in Co. G, 54th Regiment, Georgia Infantry at Savannah, Georgia and received bounty $50.00. September 1, 1862 transferred from Co. G to Co. C 54th Regiment, Georgia Infantry at Beaulieu near Savannah, Georgia by Special Order No. 6. September 1862 roll reflects his transfer. December 31, 1862 received pay. January – February 1863 roll shows him present. January 1, 1864 received pay. January – February 1864 roll shows him present. July 12, 1864 appears on a register of St. Mary's Hospital at La Grange, Georgia as being furloughed for 30 days (sickness: Diarrhoea and Pneumonia; Extreme Emaciation and Debility). July 16, 1864 issued clothing at St. Mary's Hospital at La Grange, Georgia. July 31, 1864 his name appears on a report of St. Mary's Hospital at La Grange, Georgia. February 14, 1865 admitted to Way Hospital at Meridian, Mississippi. He was a resident of Canoochee, Emanuel County, Georgia. He was born in Emanuel County, Georgia July 26, 1831 and died in Emanuel County, Georgia in 1879. He is buried in Daniel B. Cannady Grave (solitary grave) in Emanuel County, Georgia. (find a grave # 86629007)

CAPE, D. L.: Company H, private. He enlisted as a private in Co. H, 54th Regiment, Georgia Infantry.

CAREY, CHARLES P.: Company F, corporal. May 17, 1861 enlisted as a private in Chisholm's Company, Georgia State Troops. May 1862 mustered out. May 13, 1862 enlisted as 3rd corporal in Co. F, 54th Regiment, Georgia Infantry at Savannah, Georgia and received bounty $50.00. September 5, 1862 discharged at Beaulieu near Savannah, Georgia. September 1862 roll indicates his discharge. (January 1, 1863 enlisted as a private in Co. F, 54th Regiment, Georgia Infantry at Savannah, Georgia and received bounty $50.00. January – February 1863 roll shows him present. July 22, 1863 enlisted as a private in Co. A, 5th Regiment, Georgia Cavalry.

CARITHERS, B. T.: Company I, private. He enlisted as a private in Co. I, 54th Regiment, Georgia Infantry.

CARLTON, D. J.: Company E, private. February 4, 1863 enlisted as a private in Co. E, 54th Regiment, Georgia Infantry at Coffee Bluff near Savannah, Georgia. January – February 1863 roll shows him present. January 1864 issued clothing.

CARR, B.: Company F, private. October 9, 1862 enlisted as a private in Co. F, 54th Regiment, Georgia Infantry at Beaulieu near Savannah, Georgia and received bounty $50.00. October 1862 roll reflects his joining. November 5, 1862 transferred. November 1862 roll shows his transfer.

CARR, JESSE: Company C, private. June 1862 enlisted as a private in Co. C, 54th Regiment, Georgia Infantry. Pension records show: April 26, 1865 surrendered at Greensboro, North Carolina. May 1, 1865 paroled at Greensboro, North Carolina. He died in Hancock County, Georgia October 28, 1907.

CARR, S.: Company F, private. October 9, 1862 enlisted as a private in Co. F, 54th Regiment, Georgia Infantry at Beaulieu near Savannah, Georgia and received bounty $50.00.

CARROLL, D. B.: Company E, private. May 6, 1862 enlisted as a private in Co. E, 54th Regiment, Georgia Infantry at Savannah, Georgia and received bounty $50.00. December 31, 1862 received pay. January – February 1863 roll shows him present. May 14, 1863 detailed as a teamster for the Ordinance Department at Savannah, Georgia. October 31, 1863 list shows him detailed as a teamster on James Island, South Carolina. December 21, 1863 to December 31, 1863 shown on detached service as a carpenter. January 20, 1864 received pay. January 1864 and April 25, 1864 issued clothing.

CARTER, DAVID, JR.: Company B, private. April 28, 1862 enlisted as a private in Co. B, 54th Regiment, Georgia Infantry at Savannah, Georgia and received bounty $50.00. December 31, 1862 received pay. January – February 1863 roll shows him present. January 1864, April 25, 1864 and May 8, 1864 issued clothing. He was a resident of Appling County, Georgia. He was born in Georgia February 23, 1834 and died June 25, 1912. He is buried in Ten Mile Baptist Church Cemetery in Appling County, Georgia

CARTER, DAVID, SR.: Company B, private. October 10, 1861 enlisted as a private in Co. K, 2nd Regiment, 1st Brigade, Georgia State Troops. April 1862 mustered out. April 21, 1862 enlisted as a private in Co. B, 54th Regiment, Georgia Infantry at Savannah, Georgia and received bounty $50.00. December 31, 1862 received pay. January – February 1863 roll shows him present. January 1864 issued clothing. He was a resident of Appling County, Georgia. He was born in 1812 and died in 1880. He is buried in Ten Mile Baptist Church Cemetery in Appling County, Georgia. (find a grave #47124047)

CARTER, DAVID, JEFFERSON: Company B, private. October 10, 1861 enlisted as a private in Co. K, 2nd Regiment, 1st Brigade, Georgia State Troops. April 10, 1862 mustered out. May 16, 1862 enlisted as a private in Co. B, 54th Regiment, Georgia Infantry at Savannah, Georgia and received bounty $50.00. December 31, 1862 received pay. January – February 1863 roll shows him present. January 1864 issued clothing. He was a resident of Appling County, Georgia. May 10, 1865 surrendered at Tallahassee, Florida. May 23 (21), 1865 paroled at Thomasville, Georgia. (find a grave # 12178565)

CARTER, DAVID S.: Company B, private. April 21, 1862 enlisted as a private in Co. B, 54th Regiment, Georgia Infantry at Savannah, Georgia and received bounty $50.00. He was born August 9, 1861 and died December 30, 1904. He is buried in Moody-Tillman Cemetery, Appling County, Georgia. (find a grave # 37261453)

CARTER, GEORGE MARION: Company B, private. April 28, 1862 enlisted as a private in Co. B, 54th Regiment, Georgia Infantry at Savannah, Georgia and received bounty $50.00. June 30, 1862 received pay. January – February 1863 roll shows him absent sick since August 1, 1862. June 15, 1863 discharged. He is described on discharge document:

born in Appling County, Georgia, 24 years of age, 5 feet 7 inches high, dark complexion, black eyes, black hair and by occupation was a farmer (reason for discharge: Vascular Disease of the Heart and Dropsical Effusion of Liver and Spine). January 9, 1864 received pay $112.13. March 18, 1864 issued clothing. May 10, 1865 surrendered at Tallahassee, Florida. May 23 (21), 1865 paroled at Thomasville, Georgia. He is described on Parole papers as 6 feet high, black eyes, black hair and dark complexion. He was a resident of Appling County, Georgia. He was born in Appling County, Georgia August 1, 1838 and died in Thomasville, Thomas County, Georgia. August 11, 1919. He is buried in Evergreen Cemetery at Pavo, Brooks County, Georgia. (find a grave # 125896852)

CARTER, ISAAC D.: Company B, corporal. October 10, 1861 enlisted as a private in Co. K, 2nd Regiment, 1st Brigade, Georgia State Troops. April 1862 mustered out. April 21, 1862 enlisted as 4th corporal in Co. B, 54th Regiment, Georgia Infantry at Savannah, Georgia and received bounty $50.00. December 31, 1862 received pay. January – February 1863 roll shows him present. January 1864 issued clothing. He was a resident of Appling County, Georgia. He was born in Appling County, Georgia May 17, 1832 and died in Pierce County, Georgia August 10, 1927. He is buried in Friendship Methodist Church Cemetery in Bacon County, Georgia. (find a grave # 42138325)

CARTER, ISAAC, JR.: Company B, private. October 10, 1861 enlisted as a private in Co. K, 2nd Regiment, 1st Brigade, Georgia State Troops. April 1862 mustered out. April 28, 1862 enlisted as a private and was appointed 4th corporal in Co. B, 54th Regiment, Georgia Infantry at Savannah, Georgia and received bounty $50.00. December 31, 1862 received pay. January – February 1863 roll shows him present. January 1864 issued clothing. He was a resident of Appling County, Georgia.

CARTER, ISAAC, SR.: Company B, private. April 21, 1862 enlisted as a private in Co. B, 54th Regiment, Georgia Infantry at Savannah, Georgia and received bounty $50.00. December 31, 1862 received pay. January – February 1863 roll shows him present. January 1864 issued clothing. He was a resident of Appling County, Georgia.

CARTER, ISHAM: Company B, private. April 28, 1862 enlisted as a private in Co. B, 54th Regiment, Georgia Infantry at Savannah, Georgia and received bounty $50.00. September 1862 roll shows him detailed as a butcher. December 31, 1862 received pay. January – February 1863 roll shows him present. January 1864, April 25, 1864, May 8, 1864 and June 2, 1864 issued clothing. July 22, 1864 wounded at Kolb's Farm near Atlanta, Georgia. July 25, 1864 admitted to Ocmulgee Hospital at Macon, Georgia with a Gunshot Wound. July 30, 1864 transferred from Ocmulgee Hospital at Macon, Georgia. May 10, 1865 surrendered at Tallahassee, Florida. May 21, 1865 paroled at Thomasville, Georgia. He was a resident of Appling County, Georgia. He was born November 20, 1837 and died October 25, 1898 both in Appling County, Georgia. He is buried in Carter Cemetery in Appling County, Georgia. (find a grave # 70720513)

CARTER, J. C.: Company B, private. He enlisted as a private in Co. B, 54th Regiment, Georgia Infantry. He was wounded, date and location not known.

CARTER, J. W.: Company B, private. October 16, 1863 enlisted as a private in Co. B, 54th Regiment, Georgia Infantry at Macon, Georgia and received bounty $50.00. April 26, 1865 surrendered at Greensboro, North Carolina as a part of Co. A, 4th Georgia Sharpshooters. May 1, 1865 paroled at Greensboro, North Carolina. He was a resident of Appling County, Georgia.

CARTER, J. W.: Company B, private. He enlisted as a private in Co. B, 54th Regiment, Georgia Infantry. May 18, 1865 surrendered and paroled at Augusta, Georgia. He was a resident of Appling County, Georgia.

CARTER, JACKSON: Company B, private. April 28, 1862 enlisted as a private in Co. B, 54th Regiment, Georgia Infantry at Savannah, Georgia and received bounty $50.00. December 31, 1862 received pay. January – February 1863 roll shows him absent without leave 5 days. January 1864 issued clothing. He was a resident of Appling County, Georgia.

CARTER, JAMES H.: Company B, private. April 28, 1862 enlisted as a private in Co. B, 54th Regiment, Georgia Infantry at Savannah, Georgia and received bounty $50.00. December 31, 1862 received pay. January – February 1863 roll shows him present. January 1864 issued clothing. May 23, 1864 admitted to Ocmulgee Hospital at Macon, Georgia with Catarrhus. May 28, 1864 shows him transferred from Ocmulgee Hospital at Macon, Georgia. (On one report his residence is shown as Green County, Mississippi. May 10, 1865 surrendered at Tallahassee, Florida. May 20, 1865 paroled at Thomasville, Georgia. He was a resident of Appling County, Georgia. He was born in Pierce County, April 18, 1845.

CARTER, JEFFERSON: Company B, private. He enlisted as a private in Co. B, 54th Regiment, Georgia Infantry. April 25, 1864 issued clothing. Pension records show he was at home sick with chills and fever on furlough beginning November 1864 and was unable to rejoin his command. He was a resident of Appling County, Georgia. He was born in South Carolina.

CARTER, JESSE: Company B, private. October 10, 1861 enlisted as a private in Co. K, 2nd Regiment, 1st Brigade, Georgia State Troops. April 1862 mustered out. April 21, 1862 enlisted as a private in Co. B, 54th Regiment, Georgia Infantry at Savannah, Georgia and received bounty $50.00. December 31, 1862 received pay. January – February 1863 roll shows him present. January 1864 issued clothing. He was a resident of Appling County, Georgia. He was born in Appling County, Georgia November 30, 1836 and died in Appling County, Georgia May 12, 1906. He was buried in the Old Bum Carter Cemetery. find a grave # 33722541)

CARTER, PAUL: Company B, private. April 21, 1862 enlisted as a private in Co. B, 54th Regiment, (Georgia Infantry at Savannah, Georgia and received bounty $50.00. December 31, 1862 received pay. January – February 1863 roll shows him absent sick since October 25, 1862. January

1864 issued clothing. He was a resident of Appling County, Georgia.

CARTER, PAUL ANDERSON: Company B, private. October 10, 1861 enlisted as a private in Co. K, 2nd Regiment, 1st Brigade, Georgia State Troops. April 1862 mustered out. April 21, 1862 enlisted as a private in Co. B, 54th Regiment, Georgia Infantry. He was a resident of Appling County, Georgia. 1863 he was discharged due to disability. He was born in Georgia May 13, 1842. He is buried in Midway Baptist Church Cemetery in Appling County, Georgia. (find a grave # 125916907)

CARTER, PHILLIP MARION: Company B, corporal. October 10, 1861 enlisted as a private and appointed 1st corporal in Co. K, 2nd Regiment, 1st Brigade, Georgia State Troops. April 1862 mustered out. April 21, 1862 enlisted as a corporal in Co. B, 54th Regiment, Georgia Infantry at Savannah, Georgia and received bounty $50.00. December 31, 1862 received pay. January – February 1863 roll shows him present. January 1864 and April 25, 1864 issued clothing. May 10, 1865 surrendered at Tallahassee, Florida. May 21, 1865 paroled at Thomasville, Georgia. He was a resident of Appling County, Georgia. He was born in Appling County, Georgia January 19, 1844 and died January 10, 1912 in Appling County, Georgia. He is buried in Overstreet Cemetery in Appling County, Georgia. (find a grave # 43863911)

CARTER, STEPHEN W.: Company B, private. April 21, 1862 enlisted as a private in Co. B, 54th Regiment, Georgia Infantry at Savannah, Georgia and received bounty $50.00. December 31, 1862 received pay. January – February 1863 roll shows him present. January 1864 and April 25, 1864 issued clothing. He was a resident of Appling County, Georgia. He was born 1829 and died September 20, 1862 in Savannah, Georgia. He is buried in Ten Mile Cemetery in Bacon County, Georgia. (find a grave # 12178518)

CARTER, THOMAS H.: Company B, private. October 10, 1861 enlisted as a private and appointed 3rd corporal in Co. K, 2nd Regiment, 1st Brigade, Georgia State Troops. April 1862 mustered out. April 21, 1862 enlisted as a private in Co. B, 54th Regiment, Georgia Infantry at Savannah, Georgia and received bounty $50.00. December 31, 1862 received pay. January – February 1863 roll shows him present. January 1864 issued clothing. He was a resident of Appling County, Georgia. He was born August 24, 1838 and died April 17, 1907 in Appling County, Georgia. He is buried in Midway Church Cemetery in Appling County, Georgia. (find a grave # 129209395)

CARTER, THOMAS RAZOR: Company B, private. October 10, 1861 enlisted as a private in Co. K, 2nd Regiment, 1st Brigade, Georgia State Troops. April 1862 mustered out. April 28, 1862 enlisted as a private in Co. B, 54th Regiment, Georgia Infantry at Savannah, Georgia and received bounty $50.00. December 31, 1862 received pay. January – February 1863 roll shows him present. January 1864 and April 25, 1864 issued clothing. January 25, 1865 admitted to Way Hospital at Meridian, Mississippi with a Gunshot Wound. May 10, 1865 surrendered at Tallahassee, Florida. May

20, 1865 paroled at Thomasville, Georgia. He was a resident of Appling County, Georgia. He was born February 7, 1839 and died November 15, 1914. He is buried in Friendship Baptist Church Cemetery in Wayne County, Georgia. (find a grave # 109911344)

CARTER, WILEY: Company B, private. He enlisted as a private in Co. B, 54th Regiment, Georgia Infantry. August 27 (23-30)1863 shown on list from Charleston, South Carolina as being wounded in the head (both eyes out) on Morris Island. He was a resident of Appling County, Georgia.

CARTER, WILEY, JR.: Company B, private. April 21, 1862 enlisted as a private in Co. B, 54th Regiment, Georgia Infantry at Savannah, Georgia and received bounty $50.00. December 31, 1862 received pay. January – February 1863 roll shows him present. January 1864 issued clothing. January 10, 1865 admitted to St. Mary's Hospital at West Point, Mississippi with Ulcus. He was a resident of Appling County, Georgia. He was born in Appling County, Georgia November 8, 1838 and died in Appling County, Georgia July 18, 1880. He is buried in Ten Mile Cemetery in Bacon County, Georgia. (find a grave # 12178473)

CARTER, WILEY, SR.: Company B, private. October 10, 1861 enlisted as a private in Co. K, 2nd Regiment, 1st Brigade, Georgia State Troops. April 1862 mustered out. April 28, 1862 enlisted as a private in Co. B, 54th Regiment, Georgia Infantry at Savannah, Georgia and received bounty $50.00. December 31, 1862 received pay. January – February 1863 roll shows him present (sick in regimental hospital). January 1864 and May 8, 1864 issued clothing. October 15, 1864 issued clothing at Buckner and Gamble Hospital at Fort Valley, Georgia. January 10, 1865 admitted to St. Mary's Hospital at West Point, Mississippi with a Gunshot Wound.

CARTER, WILLIAM B.: Company B, private. He enlisted as a private in Co. B, 54th Regiment, Georgia Infantry. September 1, 1864 wounded at Jonesboro, Georgia. September 19, 1864 admitted to Ocmulgee Hospital at Macon, Georgia with a Gunshot Wound (flesh wound - small shot to the left shoulder). September 25, 1864 transferred to hospital at Augusta, Georgia. He was a resident of Appling County, Georgia.

CARTER, WILLIAM J.: Company B, corporal. April 28, 1862 enlisted as 3rd corporal in Co. B, 54th Regiment, Georgia Infantry at Savannah, Georgia and received bounty $50.00. December 31, 1862 received pay. January – February 1863 roll shows him present. January 1864 and April 25, 1864 issued clothing. He was a resident of Appling County, Georgia. He was born in Appling County, Georgia September 3, 1834 and died in Appling County, Georgia May 8, 1916. He is buried in Ten Mile Creek Baptist Church Cemetery in Appling County, Georgia. (find a grave # 74301148)

CARTER, WILLIAM R., JR.: Company B, private. April 21, 1862 enlisted as a private in Co. B, 54th Regiment, Georgia Infantry at Savannah, Georgia and received bounty $50.00. December 31, 1862 received pay. January – February 1863 roll shows him present. September 21, 1863 received pay $44.00. January 1864 issued clothing. May 10, 1865 surrendered at Tallahassee, Florida. May 21, 1865 paroled at Thomasville, Georgia. Pension records show he was at home on 30 day furlough, ill with chills and fever beginning February 1, 1865 and was unable to return to his command. (Other records show that on May 21, 1865 surrendered and paroled at Augusta, Georgia.) He was a resident of Appling County, Georgia.

CARTER, WILLIAM R., SR.: Company B, sergeant. October 10, 1861 enlisted as a private in Co. K, 2nd Regiment, 1st Brigade, Georgia State Troops. April 1862 mustered out. April 21, 1862 enlisted as a private and appointed 3rd sergeant in Co. B, 54th Regiment, Georgia Infantry at Savannah, Georgia and received bounty $50.00. December 31, 1862 received pay. January – February 1863 roll shows him present. January 1864 and May 8, 1864 issued clothing. July 4, 1864 admitted to St. Mary's Hospital at La Grange, Georgia with Diarrhoea. July 5, 1864 issued clothing at St. Mary's Hospital at La Grange, Georgia. July 31, 1864 appears on a list of St. Mary's Hospital at La Grange, Georgia. May 10, 1865 surrendered at Tallahassee, Florida. May 21, 1865 paroled at Thomasville, Georgia. He was a resident of Appling County, Georgia. He was born in (Pierce) Baxley, Appling County, Georgia (April 25, 1830) May 31, 1837 and died November 19 (18), 1908. He is buried in Sellers Cemetery in Appling County, Georgia. (find a grave # 37518701)

CARTER, WILSON: Company B, private. August 24, 1862 enlisted as a private in Co. B, 54th Regiment, Georgia Infantry at Savannah, Georgia and received bounty $50.00. December 31, 1862 received pay. January – February 1863 roll shows him present. January 1864 issued clothing. He was a resident of Appling County, Georgia. He was born June 14, 1845 and died March 18, 1912. He is buried in Satilla Freewill Baptist Church Cemetery in Jeff Davis County, Georgia. (find a grave #73915240)

CARTIN, J. B.: Company G, private. February 16, 1863 enlisted as a private in Co. G, 54th Regiment, Georgia Infantry at Columbus, Georgia and received bounty $50.00. January – February 1863 roll shows him present.

CARTLIDGE (CARTLEDGE), JOSEPH: Company G, private. May 1, 1863 enlisted as a private in Co. G, 54th Regiment, Georgia Infantry at Savannah, Georgia and received bounty $50.00. August 1862 roll shows he joined. September 1862 roll shows him detailed as Color Guard. He was discharged and furnished substitute.

CARY, CHARLES P.: Company F, private. He enlisted as a private in Co. F, 54th Regiment, Georgia Infantry.

CASH, HENRY: Company H, private. August 9, 1862 enlisted as a private in Co. H, 54th Regiment, Georgia Infantry at Columbus, Georgia and received bounty $50.00. May 1, 1863 received pay. November – December 1863 roll shows him absent on sick furlough since June 12, 1863. January – February 1864 roll shows him present but sick. January 1864 issued clothing.

CAULEY, R. M.: Company B, private. He enlisted as a private in Co. B,

54th Regiment, Georgia Infantry.

CAUSEY, J: Company A, private. He enlisted as a private in Co. A, 54th Regiment, Georgia Infantry. July 21, 1862 died of fever in Savannah, Georgia. July 1862 roll indicates his death.

CAWWELL, H.: Company C, private. He enlisted as a private in Co. C, 54th Regiment, Georgia Infantry May 19, 1865 surrendered and paroled at Hartwell, Georgia.

CHALKER, J. TAYLOR: Company H, private. March 2, 1863 enlisted as a private in Co. H, 54th Regiment, Georgia Infantry at Beaulieu near Savannah, Georgia and received bounty $50.00. October 31, 1863 received pay. November – December 1863 roll shows him present. December 31, 1863 received pay. January 1864 issued clothing. January – February 1864 roll shows him present on picket duty. June 18, 1864 wounded in the right arm and disabled near Marietta, Georgia. He was born in Georgia May 3, 1844.

CHAMBERS, J. E.: Company H, private. He enlisted as a private in Co. H, 54th Regiment, Georgia Infantry.

CHAMBERS, R. G.: Company H, lieutenant. He enlisted as 1st lieutenant in Co. H, 54th Regiment, Georgia Infantry.

CHAPLAIN, JAMES P.: Company F, private. May 17, 1861 enlisted as a private in Chisholm's Company, Georgia State Troops. May 1862 mustered out. May 13, 1862 enlisted as a private in Co. F, 54th Regiment, Georgia Infantry at Savannah, Georgia and received bounty $50.00. November 14, 1862 he was discharged by civil authority. November 1862 roll indicates his discharge.

CHARLES, (Servant): Company I, chief cook. November 1, 1863 enlisted as a private in Co. F, 54th Regiment, Georgia Infantry at Rose Dew near Savannah, Georgia. November – December 1863 roll shows him present (he was chief cook for the company).

CHEEK, F.: Company C, private. November 1, 1862 enlisted as a private in Co. C, 54th Regiment, Georgia Infantry at Savannah, Georgia and received bounty $50.00. December 31, 1862 received pay. January – February 1863 roll shows him present. May 1, 1863 received pay. January – February 1864 roll shows he deserted January 25, 1864.

CHERRY, J. H.: Company A, private. September 16, 1862 enlisted as a private in Co. A, 54th Regiment, Georgia Infantry at Beaulieu near Savannah, Georgia and received bounty $50.00. September 1862 roll indicates he joined.

CHISHOLM, WALTER S.: Company F, captain. May 17, 1861 elected captain of Chisholm's Company, Georgia State Troops. May 1862 mustered out. May 13, 1862 appointed captain of Co. F, 54th Regiment, Georgia Infantry. July 1862 roll shows him stationed at Savannah, Georgia since July 16, 1862. August 1862 roll shows him absent on sick leave from Beaulieu near Savannah, Georgia. September 7, 1862 detailed on Examining Board. September 1862 roll shows him absent on Special Service. October 3, 1862 received pay $57.00. October 1862 roll shows him absent on detached service. November 24, 1862 his name appears on a list of officers at Headquarters, District Georgia, Savannah, Georgia. November 29, 1862 received pay $63.00 for commutation of quarters. November 1862 roll shows him on Examining Board absent by Special Order 48b. December 31, 1862 received pay $63.00 for commutation of quarters. December 1862 roll shows him absent detailed on Board of Examination. January 2, 1863 he is shown as absent on Special Duty. January 31, 1863 received pay $63.00 for commutation of quarters. February 28, 1863 received pay $63.00 for commutation of quarters January – February 1863 roll shows him present. March 2, 1863 received pay $130.00. May 30, 1863, July 31, 1863 and August 30, 1863 appears on list of officers shown as absent with leave with Board of Examiners since April 4, 1863. July 31, 1863 received pay $72.00 for commutation of quarters. August 31, 1863 received pay $51.30 and $27.00 for commutation of quarters. September 23, 1863 resigned his commission due to bad health and the fact he was elected judge of Savannah City Court. September 26, 1863 he is shown on list of officers as being sick in Savannah, Georgia. He was born in Georgia November 17, 1836 and died December 5, 1890. He is buried in Bonaventure Cemetery at Savannah, Chatham County, Georgia. (find a Grave # 75657030)

CHITTIE, WILLIAM: Company I, private. May 6, 1862 enlisted as a private in Co. I, 54th Regiment, Georgia Infantry and received bounty $50.00. November 17, 1862 discharged from service by civil authority at Beaulieu near Savannah, Georgia. November 1862 roll shows his discharge.

CHURCHILL, JOSEPH J.: Company A, private. March 4, 1863 enlisted as a private in Co. A, 54th Regiment, Georgia Infantry at Savannah, Georgia and received bounty $50.00. April 30, 1863 received pay. June 30, 1863 roll shows him present. October 31, 1863 received pay. November – December 1863 roll shows him present. January 1, 1864 received pay. January – February 1864 roll shows him present. March 31, 1864 issued clothing. June 27, 1864 wounded in the head (lost sight in right eye) at Kennesaw Mountain, Georgia . July 20, 1864 captured at Peachtree Creek near Atlanta, Georgia. July 27, 1864 sent from Nashville, Tennessee to Military Prison at Louisville, Kentucky. July 28, 1864 received at Military Prison at Louisville, Kentucky. July 30, 1864 sent from Military Prison at Louisville, Kentucky to Camp Douglas, Illinois. August 1, 1864 received at Camp Douglas Prison, Illinois. June 16, 1865 discharged from Camp Douglas Prison, Illinois. He is described on the Oath of Allegiance as: a resident of Bibb County, Georgia, dark complexion, grey hair, hazel eyes, 5 feet 10 inches high and was from Macon, Georgia.

CLARK, GEORGE: Company F, private. October 2, 1862 enlisted as a private in Co. F, 54th Regiment, Georgia Infantry at Beaulieu near Savannah, Georgia and received bounty $50.00. October 1862 roll indicates he joined. December 31, 1862 received pay. January – February 1863 roll shows him present.

CLARK, JAMES C.: Company I, private. He enlisted as a private in Co. I, 54th Regiment, Georgia Infantry. April 25, 1864 and June 2, 1864 issued clothing. September 29, 1864 died in Walker Hospital at Columbus, Georgia of Chronic Diarrhoea.

CLARK, PICKENS: Company B, private. He enlisted as a private in Co. B, 54th Regiment, Georgia Infantry.

CLARKE, GEORGE J.: Company F, private. October 2, 1862 enlisted as a private in Co. F, 54th Regiment, Georgia Infantry. January – February 1863 roll shows him present.

CLARKE, JOHN G.: Field Staff, quartermaster. January 27, 1862 transferred to the 54th Regiment, Georgia Infantry as regimental commissary at Beaulieu near Savannah, Georgia by Special Order No. 22. April 30, 1862 assigned assistant commissary sergeant of the 54th Regiment, Georgia Infantry by Special Order No. 227-64. July 1862 roll shows him present at Savannah, Georgia. August 1862, September 1862, October 1862, November 1862 and December 1862 rolls show him present at Beaulieu with the rank of captain as the regimental commissary. November 24, 1862 list of officers for the 54th Georgia Regiment includes his name at Savannah, Georgia. January – February 1863 roll shows him present. April 3, 1863 he appears as acting commissary sergeant on a list of absent officers in Savannah, District of Georgia – absent since March 26, 1863. April 9, 1863 received pay $140.00. July 21, 1863 appointed assistant quartermaster of the 54th Georgia Regiment. August 1, 1863 appointed quartermaster of the 54th Regiment, Georgia Infantry. October 21, 1863 list of officers for the 54th Georgia Regiment includes his name as quartermaster at Legare's Point, South Carolina. January 31, 1864 he was relieved of duty by Special Order 25/1. July 20, 1864 his name appears on a list of quartermasters and assistant quartermasters in the Army of Tennessee at Atlanta, Georgia. August 25, 1864 report of officers of Mercer's Brigade at East Point, Georgia includes his name. August 31, 1864 received pay $980.00. He was born in Maine.

CLARKE, WILLIAM S.: Company F, private. May 13, 1862 enlisted as a private in Co. F, 54th Regiment, Georgia Infantry at Savannah, Georgia and received bounty pay $50.00. December 19, 1862 discharged at Beaulieu near Savannah, Georgia by civil authority. December 1862 roll reflects his discharge.

CLAXTON, CHARLES THOMAS JEFFERSON: Company D, private. February 13, 1862 enlisted as a private in Co. F, 54th Regiment, Georgia Infantry at Beaulieu near Savannah, Georgia and received bounty pay $50.00. December 31, 1862 received pay. January 1864, April 25, 1864 and June 2, 1864 issued clothing. May 24, 1865 surrendered and paroled at Augusta, Georgia. He was born in Edgefield County, South Carolina July 25, 1844 and died in Johnson County, Georgia September 28, 1905. He is buried in Gumlog Primitive Baptist Church Cemetery at Kite, Johnson County, Georgia. (find a grave # 70151929)

CLAXTON, JAMES C.: Company H, private. January 23, 1864 enlisted as a private in Co. H, 54th Regiment, Georgia Infantry at Beaulieu near Savannah, Georgia. January 1864 issued clothing. January – February 1864 roll shows him present.

CLAXTON (CLAYSTONE), W.: Company D, private. July 25, 1862 enlisted as a private in Co. F, 54th Regiment, Georgia Infantry at Savannah, Georgia and received bounty pay $50.00. August 1862 roll shows him present.

CLAXTON, WILLIAM I.: Company D, private. July 25, 1862 enlisted as a private in Co. F, 54th Regiment, Georgia Infantry at Savannah, Georgia and received bounty pay $50.00. July 1862 roll indicates his enlistment. August 1862 roll shows him present. December 31, 1862 received pay. January – February 1863 roll shows him present. January 1864 issued clothing. May 30, 1865 surrendered and paroled at Augusta, Georgia. He was born in Edgefield County, South Carolina April 16, 1832 and died in Kite, Johnson County, Georgia April 14, 1900. He is buried in the Kersey Family Cemetery at Kite, Johnson County, Georgia. (find a grave # 93750612)

CLAYTON, JOSEPH: Field Staff, chief musician. May 10, 1862 enlisted as lead musician, 54th Regiment, Georgia Infantry at Macon, Georgia (transferred from Company A). January 1, 1863 received pay. January – February 1863 roll shows him present.

CLEGG, JAMES A.: Company G, private. May 12, 1862 enlisted as a private in Co. F, 54th Regiment, Georgia Infantry at Columbus, Georgia and received bounty pay $50.00. He was appointed chief musician. December 31, 1862 received pay. January – February 1863 roll shows him present. August 8, 1863 received pay $22.00. January 1864, May 8, 1864 and June 25, 1864 issued clothing. July 22, 1864 captured at Oxford, Georgia (near Stone Mountain, Georgia) and sent to Nashville, Tennessee. August 2, 1864 sent to Military Prison at Louisville, Kentucky. August 3, 1864 sent to Camp Chase prison in Columbus, Ohio and received August 4, 1864. March 4, 1865 he was paroled and transferred to City Point, Virginia. March 10-12, 1865 received at Boulware & Cox's Wharves, James River, Virginia. He was born in South Carolina June 13, 1825 and died in Columbus, Muscogee County, Georgia June 25, 1901. He is buried in the Girard Cemetery at Girard, Russell County, Alabama. (find a grave # 59646004)

CLIFTON, THOMAS C.: Company D, private. March 17, 1862 enlisted as a private in Co. D, 54th Regiment, Georgia Infantry at Savannah, Georgia and received bounty pay $50.00. December 31, 1862 received pay. January – February 1863 roll shows him absent detailed to guard. January 1864 and April 25, 1864 issued clothing. April 26, 1865 surrendered at Greensboro, North Carolina. May 1, 1865 paroled at Greensboro, North Carolina. He was born January 7, 1845 and died August 30, 1908. He is buried in Oak Hill Baptist Cemetery at Paramour Hill, Jenkins County, Georgia. (find a grave # 123904801)

COBB, J. W.: Company A, private. September 1, 1863 enlisted as a private in Co. D, 54th Regiment, Georgia Infantry at Macon, Georgia. October 31, 1863 received pay. November – December 1863 roll shows him present. January 1, 1864 received pay. January – February 1864 roll shows him present. April 29, 1864 issued clothing.

COBB, THOMAS A.: Company F, private. November 23, 1863 enlisted as a private in Co. F, 54th Regiment, Georgia Infantry at Savannah, Georgia and received bounty pay $50.00. October 13, 1863 shown on register and assigned to General Hospital No. 1, (General Hospital, Oglethorpe Barracks), Savannah, Georgia. October 15, 1863 detailed as druggist at General Hospital No. 1, Savannah, Georgia. October 31, 1863 received pay with an additional $.25 per day. November 6, 1863 shown on the register of General Hospital No. 1, Savannah, Georgia as being detailed there with a Hernia and Stricture of the Urethra. November 16, 1863 detailed as acting steward of General Hospital No. 1, Savannah, Georgia. November 1863 roll of General Hospital No. 1, Savannah, Georgia shows him present. December 1, 1863 register of General Hospital No. 1, Savannah, Georgia shows him as acting steward. November 30, 1863 received pay with an additional $.25 per day as steward. December 31, 1863 received pay with an additional $.25 per day as steward. December 1863 roll of General Hospital No. 1, Savannah, Georgia shows him present. January 1, 1864 register of General Hospital No. 1, Savannah, Georgia shows he had been filling the position of acting steward and was relieved by the hospital steward who returned to work. January 13, 1864 appears on register of General Hospital No. 1, Savannah, Georgia as being diagnosed with an Oblique Inguinal Hernia right side and Stricture of Urethra. January 1864 roll of General Hospital No. 1, Savannah, Georgia shows him detailed as a druggist there. February 1864 roll of General Hospital No. 1, Savannah, Georgia shows him present and due 3 months 7 days' pay since enlistment. March 2, 1864 issued clothing. March 17, 1864 he appears on a register of General Hospital No. 1, (General Hospital, Oglethorpe Barracks) Savannah, Georgia. August 14, 1864 deserted from Savannah (at Fort Pulaski) and took Oath of Allegiance. He was forwarded to New York City, New York. He is described as blue eyes, light hair, fair complexion, 32 years of age, 5 feet 11 ½ inches high, occupation physician, born in Augusta, Georgia and a resident of Savannah, Georgia.

COCHRAN, JAMES A.: Company H (F), private. May 12, 1862 enlisted as a private in Co. H, 54th Regiment, Georgia Infantry at Savannah (Columbus), Georgia and received bounty $50.00. December 31, 1862 received pay January – February 1863 roll shows him absent from Co. F, 54th Regiment, Georgia Infantry having been transferred from Co. H, 54th Regiment, Georgia Infantry on January 17, 1863.

COKER, B. P.: Company C, private. He enlisted as a private in Co. C, 54th Regiment, Georgia Infantry.

COLDER (CALDER), JOHN: Company F, private. April 20, 1862 enlisted as a private in Chisholm's Company, Georgia State Troops. May 1862 mustered out.

COLDER (CALDER), T.: Company F, private. 1862 enlisted as a private in Co. F, 54th Regiment, Georgia Infantry. October 30, 1862 discharged at Beaulieu near Savannah, Georgia. October 1862 roll shows his discharge.

COLEMAN, ANDREW J.: Company C (F), private. May 5, 1862 enlisted as a private in Co. C, 54th Regiment, Georgia Infantry at Hancock County, Georgia and received bounty $50.00. January 1, 1863 transferred from Co. C, 54th Regiment, Georgia Infantry to Co. F, 54th Regiment, Georgia Infantry. January – February 1863 roll of Co. C, 54th Regiment, Georgia Infantry shows him transferred to Co, F, 54th Regiment, Georgia Infantry by order of Colonel Charlton H. Way. December 31, 1863 received pay. January – February 1863 roll of Co. F, 54th Regiment, Georgia Infantry shows him present. November 1, 1863 received pay. November – December 1863 roll shows him present. January 1864 and May 8, 1864 issued clothing. April 12, 1865 captured at Salisbury, North Carolina (near Greensboro, North Carolina). May 1, 1865 received at Military Prison at Louisville, Kentucky from Nashville, Tennessee. May 1, 1865 sent from Military prison at Louisville, Kentucky to Camp Chase at Columbus, Ohio. May 4, 1865 received at Camp Chase, Columbus, Ohio from Military Prison at Louisville, Kentucky. June 13, 1865 took the Oath of Allegiance at Camp Chase, Ohio. He is described in P. O. W. record as; a resident of Hancock County, Georgia, dark complexion, dark hair, blue eyes, 5 feet 9 inches high and 30 years of age. He was born in Hancock County, Georgia January 12, 1831.

COLEMAN, CAMILLUS T.: Field Staff, assistant surgeon. August 16, 1862 appointed assistant surgeon for the 54th Regiment, Georgia Infantry. October 1862 roll shows him present at Beaulieu near Savannah, Georgia (transferred by order of General Pemberton). November 1862 and December 1862 rolls show him present as assistant surgeon at Beaulieu near Savannah, Georgia. His rank was Captain. January – February 1863 roll shows him present. March 31, 1863 received pay $110.00. November 19, 1863 he was granted leave. March 31, 1865 he was serving as assistant surgeon at Tupelo, Mississippi.

COLEMAN, WILLIAM T.: Company C (F), private. May 5, 1862 enlisted as a private in Co. C, 54th Regiment, Georgia Infantry at Savannah, Georgia and received bounty $50.00. December 31, 1862 received pay. January 1, 1863 transferred from Co. C, 54th Regiment, Georgia Infantry to Co, F, 54th Regiment, Georgia Infantry. January – February 1863 roll of Co. C, 54th Regiment, Georgia Infantry shows him transferred to Co, F, 54th Regiment, Georgia Infantry by order of Colonel Charlton H. Way. January – February 1863 roll of Co. F, 54th Regiment, Georgia Infantry shows him present (transferred from Co. C, 54th Regiment, Georgia Infantry). November 1, 1863 received pay. November – December 1863 roll shows him present. January 1864 issued clothing. January 20, 1864 received pay $18.34 in Charleston, South Carolina. June 18, 1864 shows him captured at Marietta, Georgia. June 26, 1864 received at Military

Prison at Louisville, Kentucky from Nashville, Tennessee. June 27, 1864 sent from Military Prison at Louisville, Kentucky to Camp Morton at Indianapolis, Indiana. June 28, 1864 appears on roll at Camp Morton, Indianapolis, Indiana. March 15, 1865 transferred from Camp Morton, Indiana for exchange. March 22, 1865 died at Point Lookout, Maryland. (Record also shows March 10-12, 1865 received at Boulware & Cox's Wharves, James River, Virginia. March 1865 shown as died in Richmond of Dysentery. He was buried at sea.)

COLLIER, HENRY: Company E, private. May 6, 1862 enlisted as a private in Co. E, 54th Regiment, Georgia Infantry at Savannah, Georgia and received bounty $50.00. December 31, 1862 received pay. January – February 1863 roll of Co. E, 54th Regiment, Georgia Infantry shows him present. January 1864 and April 25, 1864 issued clothing.

COLLIER, VINES H.: Company G, sergeant. He enlisted as a sergeant in Co. G, 54th Regiment, Georgia Infantry. He was born in Georgia May 1, 1806 and died in Stroud, Chambers County, Alabama May 3, 1887. He is buried in Bethel Baptist Church Cemetery in Chambers County, Alabama. (find a grave # 53777636)

COLLINS (CALLINS), C. COLUMBUS: Company H, private. March 4, 1862 enlisted as a private in Co. K, 46th Regiment, Georgia infantry. August 6, 1862 discharged due to being under age. January 28, 1863 enlisted as a private in Co. H, 54th Regiment, Georgia Infantry at Columbus, Georgia and received bounty $50.00. January – February 1863 roll shows him present.

COLLINS, J. C. W.: Company D, private. January 26, 1863 enlisted as a private in Co. D, 54th Regiment, Georgia Infantry at Beaulieu near Savannah, Georgia and received bounty $50.00. December 31, 1862 received pay. January – February 1863 roll shows him present on picket.

COMBS (COOMBS), TALBOT (TALBERT): Company A, private. April 18, 1862 enlisted as a private in Co. A, 54th Regiment, Georgia Infantry at Macon, Georgia and received bounty $50.00. October 22, 1862 detailed as a nurse. October 1862, November 1862 and December 1862 rolls show him detailed as a hospital nurse. January 1, 1863 received pay. January – February 1863 roll shows his name. April 30, 1863 received pay. June 30, 1863 roll shows him absent detailed as a nurse in the Hospital of the 54th Regiment, Georgia Infantry. May 1, 1863 received pay. July 26, 1863 received pay and returned to duty with the regiment from Bethesda Hospital, Beaulieu Battery near Savannah, Georgia. October 31, 1863 roll of Bethesda Hospital, Beaulieu Battery near Savannah, Georgia shows he returned to his company. October 31, 1863 received pay. November – December 1863 roll shows him present. January 1, 1864 received pay. January – February 1864 roll shows him present. March 31, 1864 issued clothing. July 3, 1864 captured at Marietta, Georgia after the battle of Kennesaw Mountain, Georgia. July 3(12), 1864 sent from Nashville, Tennessee to Military Prison at Louisville, Kentucky. July 13, 1864 received and sent from Louisville, Kentucky to Camp Morton, Indiana.

May 20, 1865 took the Oath of Allegiance at Camp Morton at Indianapolis, Indiana and is described therein as; being a resident of Macon, Bibb County, Georgia, florid complexion, light hair, grey eyes and 5 feet 5 ½ inches high.

CONAWAY, CHARLES CHRISTOPHER: Company I, private. September 18, 1861 enlisted as a private in Co. C, 1st Regiment, 1st Brigade, Georgia State Troops. March 18, 1862 mustered out. May 6, 1862 enlisted as a private in Co. I, 54th Regiment, Georgia Infantry at Guyton, Georgia and received bounty $50.00. December 31, 1862 received pay. January – February 1863 roll shows him present. June 1, 1863 attached to Hospital at Rose Dew Post near Savannah as a nurse. January – February 1864 roll of Hospital at Rose Dew Post near Savannah shows him present detailed as a nurse at an additional $.25 per day. August 31, 1863 received pay. November – December 1863 roll shows him present detailed as a nurse. January 1864 issued clothing. He was born in Georgia December 25, 1843 and died December 30, 1928. He is buried in Douglas Cemetery in Bloomingdale, Chatham County, Georgia. (find a grave # 62894399)

CONNER (CONNOR), WILLIAM: Company F, private. February 26, 1863 enlisted as a private in Co. F, 54th Regiment, Georgia Infantry at Savannah, Georgia and received bounty $50.00. January – February 1863 roll shows him present. September 1, 1863 received pay. December 17, 1863 transferred from Co. F, 54th Regiment, Georgia Infantry to Co. B, 8th Georgia Volunteers (Special Order No. 299/17). November – December 1863 roll shows he deserted December 5, 1863.

CONNERAT, WILLIAM H.: Company F, private. May 17, 1861 enlisted as a private in Chisholm's Company, Georgia State Troops. May 1862 mustered out. May 13, 1862 enlisted as a private in Co. F, 54th Regiment, Georgia Infantry at Savannah, Georgia and received bounty $50.00. August 23, 1862 discharged at Savannah. December 1862 roll indicates his discharge.

CONWELL, J. D.: Company C (G), private. June 29, 1864 enlisted as a private in Co. G, 54th Regiment, Georgia Infantry at Elberton, Georgia. April 26, 1865 surrendered at Greensboro, North Carolina as a private in Co. C, 54th Regiment, Georgia Infantry. May 1, 1865 paroled at Greensboro, North Carolina.

COOK, G. W.: Company A, private. March 7, 1863 enlisted as a private in Co. A, 54th Regiment, Georgia Infantry at Savannah, Georgia and received bounty $50.00. April 30, 1863 received pay. June 30, 1863 roll shows him present (absent without leave from June 20, 1862 to June 27, 1862 – in arrest).

COOK, JAMES: Company H, private. January 28, 1862 enlisted as a private in Co. H, 54th Regiment, Georgia Infantry at Columbus, Georgia. He was born June 8, 1823 and died May 2, 1901. He is buried in Linwood Cemetery at Columbus, Muscogee County, Georgia. (find a grave # 33971273)

COOK, SAMUEL S.: Company H, private. January 28(22), 1862 enlisted as a private in Co. H, 54th Regiment, Georgia Infantry at Columbus, Georgia. January – February 1863 roll shows him present. October 31, 1863 received pay. November – December 1863 roll shows him present. December 31, 1863 received pay. January – February 1864 roll shows him present on picket. April 26, 1865 surrendered at Greensboro, North Carolina. May 1, 1865 paroled at Greensboro, North Carolina.

COOK, T.: Company F, private. November 27, 1863 enlisted as a private in Co. F, 54th Regiment, Georgia Infantry at Savannah, Georgia and received bounty $50.00. November – December 1863 roll shows him absent detailed at Hospital No. 1 at Savannah, Georgia.

COOK, WILLIAM W.: Company H, private. January 28, 1863 enlisted as a private in Co. H, 54th Regiment, Georgia Infantry at Columbus, Georgia and received bounty $50.00. January – February 1863 roll shows him present. October 31, 1863 received pay. November – December 1863 roll shows him absent on picket. December 31, 1863 received pay. January 1864 issued clothing. January – February 1864 roll shows him present on picket. March 19-21, 1865 he was wounded at the battle of Bentonville, North Carolina. March 30, 1865 admitted to C. S. A. General Hospital, No. 11 at Charlotte, North Carolina with a Gunshot wound to the Upper Extremities left. April 14, 1865 furloughed.

COOK, WILLIAM: Company B, private. He enlisted as a private in Co. B, 54th Regiment, Georgia Infantry.

COOMBS, TALBOT: Company A, private. He enlisted in as a private in Co. A, 54th Regiment, Georgia Infantry.

COOPER, C. F.: Company F, private. May 13, 1862 enlisted as a private in Co. F, 54th Regiment, Georgia Infantry at Savannah, Georgia and received bounty $50.00. August 23, 1862 discharged at Savannah, Georgia. August 1862 roll indicates his discharge. November 27, 1862 enlisted as a private in Co. C, 63rd Regiment, Georgia Infantry. February 1863 appointed corporal. November – December 1863 roll shows him present.

COOPER, EDWARD (EDMOND): Company F, private. January 1, 1863 enlisted as a private in Co. F, 54th Regiment, Georgia Infantry at Savannah, Georgia and received bounty $50.00. February 3, 1863 deserted. January – February 1863 roll shows he deserted.

COOPER, JOHN: Company F, private. September 29, 1863 enlisted as a private in Co. F, 54th Regiment, Georgia Infantry at Savannah, Georgia and received bounty $50.00. December 13, 1863 detailed to Lieutenant A. T. Cunningham's detachment of detailed men at Savannah, Georgia. November – December 1863 roll shows him absent detailed in the Ordinance Department by order of General Mercer (Special Order 335/1). January 1864 issued clothing. August 14, 1864 deserted, turned himself in at Fort Pulaski near Savannah, Georgia. August 26, 1864 appears on a list of deserters and refugees forwarded from Hilton head, South Carolina to New York City via the Steamer Fulton. He is described as dark eyes, brown hair, dark complexion, 30 years of age, detailed as a clerk, a resident of Savannah and was born in Baltimore, Maryland.

COOPER, WILLIAM: Company G, private. January 22, 1863 enlisted as a private in Co. G, 54th Regiment, Georgia Infantry at Columbus, Georgia and received bounty $50.00. January – February 1863 roll shows him present. January 1864 and April 25, 1864 issued clothing.

CORBITT, NOAH: Company H, private. February 10, 1863 enlisted as a private in Co. H, 54th Regiment, Georgia Infantry at Columbus, Georgia and received bounty $50.00. January – February 1863 roll shows him present. October 31, 1863 received pay. November – December 1863 roll shows him present. December 31, 1863 received pay. January 1864 and June 2, 1864 issued clothing. January – February 1864 roll shows him present.

CORRELL, GEORGE: Company C, private. He enlisted as a private in Co. C, 54th Regiment, Georgia Infantry. June 22, 1864 captured at Kolb's Farm near Marietta, Georgia. July 13, 1864 received at Military Prison, Louisville, Kentucky from Nashville, Tennessee and sent to Camp Morton, Indiana.

COSGROVE, WILLIAM: Company D, private. 1862 he enlisted as a private in Co. D, 54th Regiment, Georgia Infantry. September 10, 1862 deserted. September 1862 roll shows he deserted.

COURSON, J. F.: Company A, private. He enlisted as a private in Co. A, 54th Regiment, Georgia Infantry.

COWART, ERWIN: Company E, private. October 6, 1861 enlisted as a private in Co. K, 5th Regiment, Georgia State Troops. April 1862 mustered out. May 6, 1862 enlisted as a private in Co. E, 54th Regiment, Georgia Infantry at Savannah, Georgia and received bounty $50.00. December 31, 1862 received pay. January – February 1863 roll shows him present. January 1864 and April 25, 1864 issued clothing. June 1864 he was killed near Marietta, Georgia. (He may have been wounded and died July 29, 1864 in Hospital in Macon, Georgia). He is buried in Rose Hill Cemetery in Macon, Bibb County, Georgia. (find a grave # 100445762)

COWART, JOSHUA S.: Company B, private. January 24, 1863 enlisted as a private in Co. B, 54th Regiment, Georgia Infantry at Savannah, Georgia and received bounty $50.00. January – February 1863 roll shows him present on picket duty. May 17, 1864 issued: 1 coat, 1pair pants, 1 pair shoes and 1 hat at Covington, Georgia by the surgeon at the hospital as he is about to go into the field. He was born in Tattnall County, Georgia in 1838.

COWART, WILLIAM: Company K, private. May 5, 1862 enlisted as a private in Co. K, 54th Regiment, Georgia Infantry at Savannah, Georgia and received bounty $50.00. October 13, 1862 to October 31, 1862 detailed as a teamster at Beaulieu near Savannah, Georgia and was paid $.25 per day extra. October 1862 roll shows him detailed as a teamster. January 1, 1863 received pay. January – February 1863 roll shows him present. November 1863 detailed as a teamster at Beaulieu near Savannah, Georgia and was paid $.25 extra per day. March 18, 1864, April 25, 1864 and June 2, 1864 issued clothing. April 21-22, 1865 captured at Macon, Georgia.

COX, F. A.: Company K, private. He enlisted as a private in Co. K, 54th Regiment, Georgia Infantry.

COX, JOHN: Company K, private. He enlisted as a private in Co. K, 54th Regiment, Georgia Infantry.

CRANSON, D.: Company F, private. 1862 enlisted as a private in Co. F, 54th Regiment, Georgia Infantry at Savannah, Georgia. October 10, 1862 he was discharged at Beaulieu near Savannah, Georgia. October 1862 roll shows his discharge.

CRAWFORD, GEORGE: Company F, chief cook. May 18, 1862 enlisted as a private in Co. F, 54th Regiment, Georgia Infantry at Savannah, Georgia and received bounty $50.00. October 1862, November 1862 and December 1862 rolls show him as the company cook. January – February 1863 roll shows him present as chief cook for the company. November 1, 1863 received pay. November – December 1863 roll shows him present. January 1864 and April 25, 1864 issued clothing.

CRAWFORD, J. M.: Company B, private. January 8, 1864 enlisted as a private in Co. B, 54th Regiment, Georgia Infantry at Barnesville, Georgia and received bounty $50.00. April 26, 1865 surrendered at Greensboro, North Carolina. May 1, 1865 paroled at Greensboro, North Carolina.

CRAWFORD, JAMES M.: Company A, private. April 18, 1862 enlisted as a private in Co. B, 54th Regiment, Georgia Infantry at Savannah, Georgia and received bounty $50.00. July 30, 1862 transferred to the Georgia Sharpshooters by Special Order No. 259. August 1862 roll shows his transfer.

CRAWFORD, WILLIAM: Company E, corporal. May 6, 1862 enlisted as a 2nd corporal in Co. E, 54th Regiment, Georgia Infantry at Savannah, Georgia and received bounty $50.00. December 31, 1862 received pay. January – February 1863 roll shows him present. January 1864 issued clothing.

CROOK, ISAIAH: Company K, private. He enlisted as a private in Co. K, 54th Regiment, Georgia Infantry.

CROOMS, A. D.: Company C, private. March 2, 1863 enlisted as a private in Co. B, 54th Regiment, Georgia Infantry at Savannah, Georgia. September 1863 wounded at Battery Wagner on Morris Island near Charleston, South Carolina. January 1, 1864 received pay. January – February 1864 roll shows him absent sick in the hospital at Hardeeville since February 24, 1864. April 28, 1864 issued clothing.

CROSBY, ABRAHAM TAYLOR: Company B, private. April 28, 1862 enlisted as a private in Co. B, 54th Regiment, Georgia Infantry at Savannah, Georgia and received bounty $50.00. Pension records show he surrendered near Atlanta, Georgia in 1865. (One records shows he was born in Tattnall County, Georgia in 1841). He was born in Appling County, Georgia May 1844 and died in Appling County, Georgia May 28, 1917. He is buried in Baxley Graveyard in Appling County, Georgia.

(find a grave # 77007648)
CROSBY, BERRY W.: Company B, private. April 28, 1862 enlisted as a private in Co. B, 54th Regiment, Georgia Infantry at Savannah, Georgia and received bounty $50.00. June 30, 1862 received pay. January – February 1863 roll shows him present. January 1864 and May 8, 1864 issued clothing. He was born in 1836 and died in 1916. He is buried in Johnson Memorial (AKA Corinth) Cemetery in Appling County, Georgia. (find a grave # 77007744)
CROSBY, DAVID: Company B, private. April 28, 1862 enlisted as a private in Co. B, 54th Regiment, Georgia Infantry at Savannah, Georgia and received bounty $50.00. December 31, 1862 received pay. January – February 1863 roll shows him present. January 1864 issued clothing.
CROSBY (CROSBEY), FRANCIS M.: Company I (F), private. September 18, 1861 enlisted as a private in Co. C, 1st Regiment, 1st Brigade, Georgia State Troops. March 18, 1862 mustered out. May 6, 1862 enlisted as a private in Co. I, 54th Regiment, Georgia Infantry at Guyton, Georgia and received bounty $50.00. December 31, 1862 received pay. January – February 1863 roll shows him present. October 31, 1863 received pay. November – December 1863 roll shows him present. January 1864 and April 25, 1864 issued clothing. April 26, 1865 surrendered in Co. F, 54th Regiment, Georgia Infantry at Greensboro, North Carolina. May 1, 1865 paroled at Greensboro, North Carolina. He was born in Bulloch County, Georgia September 8, 1841.
CROSBY, ISHAM: Company B, private. April 28, 1862 enlisted as a private in Co. B, 54th Regiment, Georgia Infantry at Savannah, Georgia and received bounty $50.00. September 19, 1862 detailed as a butcher at $.25 extra pay per day. October 1862, November 1862 and December 1862 rolls show him detailed as a butcher at an additional $.25 per day pay. December 31, 1862 received pay. January 15, 1863 and February 26, 1863 received pay. January – February 1863 roll shows him present on camp guard (note: he returned to the company from the commissary September 21, 1862 through February 1863 where he was detailed as a beef butcher). March 12, 1863 received pay. November 25, 1863 died in the Wayside Hospital at Charleston, South Carolina. January 25, 1864 appears on a register of diseased soldiers at Wayside Hospital at Charleston, South Carolina (effects: $52.30). He was born in Holmesville, Appling County, Georgia in 1832 and died in Wayside Hospital at Charleston, South Carolina November 25, 1863. He is buried in Memorial Church Cemetery in Appling County, Georgia. (find a grave # 77007831)
CROSBY, JAMES, SR.: Company B, private. January 26, 1863 enlisted as a private in Co. B, 54th Regiment, Georgia Infantry at Savannah, Georgia and received bounty $50.00. January – February 1863 roll shows him present on picket duty. January 1864, April 25, 1864 and May 8, 1864 issued clothing. He was born in South Carolina August 23, 1829 and died in Appling County, Georgia May 8, 1895.
CROSBY, JOHN: Company E, private. January 28, 1863 enlisted as

a private in Co. E, 54th Regiment, Georgia Infantry at Coffee Bluff near Savannah, Georgia and received bounty $50.00. January – February 1863 roll shows him present. January 1864 issued clothing. December 15, 1863 admitted to Floyd House and Ocmulgee Hospitals in Macon, Georgia with Ulcus. April 25, 1864 appears on a register of Floyd House and Ocmulgee Hospitals in Macon, Georgia as being furloughed for 60 days. Pension records show; January 1864 he was at home on sick furlough at the close of the war and was unable to rejoin his command. May 10, 1865 surrendered at Tallahassee, Florida. May 25, 1865 paroled at Thomasville, Georgia. He was born in the Barnwell District, South Carolina in 1832 and died in Berrien County, Georgia March 15, 1903.

CROSBY, MATTHEW E.: Company I, private. September 18, 1861 enlisted as a private in Co. C, 1st Regiment, 1st Brigade, Georgia State Troops. March 18, 1862 mustered out. May 6, 1862 enlisted as a private in Co. I, 54th Regiment, Georgia Infantry at Savannah, Georgia and received bounty $50.00. August 25, 1862 died at Savannah, Georgia. August 1862 roll shows his death.

CROSBY, SAMUEL M.: Company B, sergeant. April 28, 1862 enlisted as 5th sergeant in Co. B, 54th Regiment, Georgia Infantry at Savannah, Georgia and received bounty $50.00. December 31, 1862 received pay. January – February 1863 roll shows him present. September 6, 1863 killed in the evacuation of Morris Island (Battery Wagner) at Charleston, South Carolina.

CROSBY, SAMUEL: Company B, private. April 21, 1862 enlisted as a private in Co. B, 54th Regiment, Georgia Infantry at Savannah, Georgia and received bounty $50.00. December 31, 1862 received pay. January – February 1863 roll shows him present. January 1864 issued clothing. He was born in Appling County, Georgia March 15, 1842 and died there.

CROW, M. M.: Company H, private. He enlisted as a private in Co. H, 54th Regiment, Georgia Infantry. May 20, 1865 captured at Hartwell, Georgia.

CROW, T. J.: Company H, private. He enlisted as a private in Co. H, 54th Regiment, Georgia Infantry.

CROZIER, E. B.: Company F, private. February 12, 1863 enlisted as a private in Co. F, 54th Regiment, Georgia Infantry at Savannah, Georgia and received bounty $50.00. January – February 1863 roll shows him absent sick. April 7, 1863 shown at General Hospital No. 1 at Savannah, Georgia transferred to Whitesville with Acute Dysentery. November 1, 1863 received pay. November – December 1863 roll shows him absent, picket at Whitesville No. 3 Railroad. January 1864 issued clothing.

CRUMB, E. P.: Company G, sergeant. May 12, 1862 enlisted as 4th sergeant in Co. G, 54th Regiment, Georgia Infantry at Columbus, Georgia and received bounty pay $50.00. November 3, 1862 transferred from Columbus, Georgia and enlisted as sergeant in Co. G, 54th Regiment, Georgia Infantry. November 1862 roll indicates his transfer.

CRUMMEY (CRUMLEY), JESSE HIRAM: Company B, private.

October 3, 1861 enlisted as a private in Co. A, 1st Regiment, 1st Brigade, Georgia State Troops. April 1862 mustered out. April 28, 1862 enlisted as a private in Co. B, 54th Regiment, Georgia Infantry at Savannah, Georgia and received bounty $50.00. September 1, 1862 transferred from Co. B, 54th Regiment, Georgia Infantry to the 1st Regiment, Georgia Sharpshooters at Beaulieu near Savannah, Georgia by Special Order No. 6. He was born in 1846 and died in 1890. He is buried in Oldfield Cemetery in Appling County, Georgia. (find a grave # 77008260)

CRUMMEY, ELIAS: Company B, private. October 10, 1861 enlisted as a private in Co. K, 2nd Regiment, 1st Brigade, Georgia State Troops. April 1862 mustered out. April 28, 1862 enlisted as 5th sergeant in Co. B, 54th Regiment, Georgia Infantry at Savannah, Georgia and received bounty $50.00. Pension records show he surrendered at Columbus, Georgia in 1865. He was born in May 6, 1845 and died September 26, 1917. He is buried in the Crummey Cemetery in Wayne County, Georgia. (find a grave # 29503735). The Southern Cross of Honor was bestowed on him by the Jesup Chapter United Daughters of the Confederacy in 1903.

CRUTCHFIELD, J.: Company H, private. He enlisted as a private in Co. H, 54th Regiment, Georgia Infantry at Columbus, Georgia and received bounty pay $50.00. January 18, 1863 detached to the Ordinance Department of General Taliaferro's Brigade by Special Order No. 93.

CRUTCHFIELD, THOMAS: Company H, private. December 9, 1862 enlisted as a private in Co. H, 54th Regiment, Georgia Infantry at Columbus, Georgia and received bounty pay $50.00. December 31, 1862 received pay. February 17, 1863 detailed as a blacksmith at Savannah, Georgia by order of General Mercer. January – February 1863 roll shows him absent detailed as a blacksmith by order of General Mercer. January 1, 1863 received pay. November – December 1863 roll shows him present. December 31, 1863 received pay. January – February 1864 roll shows him present on picket duty. January 1864 issued clothing. April 25, 1864 issued clothing.

CULLER, A. M.: Company H, private. He enlisted as a private in Co. H, 54th Regiment, Georgia Infantry. May 10, 1865 surrendered at Tallahassee, Florida. May 19, 1865 paroled at Thomasville, Georgia.

CULPEPPER, JAMES: Company B, private. He enlisted as a private in Co. B, 54th Regiment, Georgia Infantry. January 1864 and May 8, 1864 issued clothing. October 13, 1864 captured near Resacca, Georgia. November 22, 1864 received at Military Prison at Louisville, Kentucky from Nashville, Tennessee. November 24, 1864 sent to Camp Douglas, Illinois. November 26, 1864 received at Camp Douglas, Illinois. June 17, 1865 discharged from Camp Douglas, Chicago, Illinois. He took the oath of Allegiance and is shown as a resident of Musgrove County, Georgia. He is also shown as: fair complexion, light hair, blue eyes, 5 feet 10 inches high and was from Columbus, Georgia.

CULPEPPER, JOHN: Company E, private. He merged with the 54th Regiment, Georgia Infantry from the 37th Georgia Volunteer Infantry.

April 26, 1865 surrendered in Co. E, 54th Regiment, Georgia Infantry at Greensboro, North Carolina. May 1, 1865 paroled at Greensboro, North Carolina.

CUMMINGS, OWEN: Company H, private. He enlisted as a private in Co. H, 54th Regiment, Georgia Infantry at Columbus, Georgia and received bounty pay $50.00. September 1, 1862 transferred from Co. H, 54th Regiment, Georgia Infantry to Co. A, 54th Regiment, Georgia Infantry at Beaulieu near Savannah, Georgia by Special Order No. 6. September 1862 roll shows the transfer. March 14, 1863 died of Pneumonia at General Hospital No.1 at Savannah, Georgia.

CUNNINGHAM, J.: Company A, private. He enlisted as a private in Co. A, 54th Regiment, Georgia Infantry.

CUNNINGHAM, PHILLIP B.: Company G, private. He enlisted as a private in Co. G, 54th Regiment, Georgia Infantry.

CUINNINGHAM, WILLIAM: Company A, private. He enlisted as a private in Co. A, 54th Regiment, Georgia Infantry.

DALTON, WILLIAM: Company G, private. He enlisted as a private in Co. G, 54th Regiment, Georgia Infantry.

DANIEL, Y. A.: Company I, lieutenant. He enlisted as a 1st lieutenant in Co. I, 54th Regiment, Georgia Infantry.

DASHER, LEWIS B.: Company I, private. May 6, 1862 enlisted as a private in Co. I, 54th Regiment, Georgia Infantry at Guyton, Georgia and received bounty $50.00. December 31, 1862 received pay. January – February 1863 roll shows him present (sick in regimental hospital). October 31, 1863 received pay. November – December 1863 roll shows him present. January 1864 issued clothing. He was born in Effingham County, Georgia March 12, 1829 and died in Effingham County, Georgia August 19, 1887. He is buried in Zion Lutheran Church Cemetery at Guyton, Effingham County, Georgia. (find a grave # 67402367)

DASHER, RICHARD A.: Company I, private. September 18, 1861 enlisted as a private in Co. C, 1st Regiment, 1st Brigade, Georgia State Troops. March 18, 1862 mustered out. May 6, 1862 enlisted as a private in Co. I, 54th Regiment, Georgia Infantry at Guyton, Georgia and received bounty $50.00. December 31, 1862 received pay. January – February 1863 roll shows him present. October 31, 1863 received pay. November – December 1863 roll shows him present (detailed to go after lumber at Ogeechee Bridge). January 1864 and June 2, 1864 issued clothing. He was born October 24, 1841 and died September 12, 1906. He is buried in Zion Lutheran Church Cemetery at Guyton, Effingham County, Georgia. (find a grave # 67402376)

DAVID, W. G.: Company I, sergeant. He enlisted as a sergeant in Co. I, 54th Regiment, Georgia Infantry.

DAVIDSON, JOHN E.: Company G (F), private. January 22, 1863 enlisted as a private in Co. G, 54th Regiment, Georgia Infantry at Columbus, Georgia and received bounty pay $50.00. January – February 1863 roll shows him present. April 26, 1865 surrendered in Co. F, 54th Regiment,

Georgia Infantry at Greensboro, North Carolina. May 1, 1865 paroled at Greensboro, North Carolina.

DAVIDSON, JOSEPH: Company A, private. He enlisted in as a private in Co. A, 54th Regiment, Georgia Infantry.

DAVIS, CHARLES: Company F, private. April 29, 1863 enlisted as a private in Co. F, 54th Regiment, Georgia Infantry.

DAVIS, H. C.: Company A, corporal. October 17, 1861 enlisted as a private in Co. C, 1st Independent Battalion, Georgia State Troops. April 16, 1862 roll shows him present. April 1862 mustered out. April 24, 1862 enlisted as a private and appointed 4th corporal in Co. A, 54th Regiment, Georgia Infantry at Macon, Georgia and received bounty $50.00. April 30, 1863 received pay. June 30, 1863 roll shows him present. October 1863 he was appointed 1st corporal of Co. A, 54th Regiment, Georgia Infantry. October 31, 1863 received pay. November – December 1863 roll shows him present. January 1, 1864 received pay. January – February 1864 roll shows him present. April 29, 1864 issued clothing.

DAVIS, J. BENJAMIN: Company F, private. March 17, 1863 enlisted as a private in Co. F, 54th Regiment, Georgia Infantry at Savannah, Georgia and received bounty pay $50.00. September 3, 1863 he is shown as dieting. November 1, 1863 received pay. November – December 1863 roll shows him absent without leave. January 1864 and May 6, 1864 issued clothing. June 28, 1864 issued clothing at Direction Hospital at Griffin, Georgia. Pension records show; September 10, 1864 left his command on sick furlough. He was in the hospital at Whitesville, Georgia when the hospital was abandoned to the enemy. He could not reach his command due to the intervention of the enemy. He was born in Georgia.

DAVIS, J. M.: Company A, private. He enlisted in as a private in Co. A, 54th Regiment, Georgia Infantry.

DAVIS, JAMES BENJAMIN: Company I, private. September 18, 1861 enlisted as a private in Co. C, 1st Regiment, 1st Brigade, Georgia State Troops. March 18, 1862 mustered out. November 9, 1862 enlisted in Co. I, 54th Regiment, Georgia Infantry at Savannah, Georgia and received bounty pay $50.00. Company I, private. November 24, 1862 discharged by Civil Authority at Beaulieu near Savannah, Georgia. November 1862 roll shows his discharge. He was born in 1845 and died October 2, 1921. He is buried in Guyton Cemetery at Guyton, Effingham County, Georgia. (find a grave # 57094165)

DAVIS, JAMES CHRISTOPHER COLUMBUS "TIGER JIM": Company K, private. October 3, 1861 enlisted as a private in Co. A, 1st Regiment, 1st Brigade, Georgia State Troops. April 1862 mustered out. April 28, 1862 enlisted as a private in Co. B, 54th Regiment, Georgia Infantry at Savannah, Georgia and received bounty $50.00. September 1, 1862 transferred from Co. H, 54th Regiment, Georgia Infantry to the 1st Regiment, Georgia Sharpshooters at Beaulieu near Savannah, Georgia by Special Order No. 6. He was born in Coffee, Appling County, Georgia

February 1, 1838 and died in Mershon, Pierce County, Georgia August 6, 1923. He is buried in Ramah Cemetery, Mershon, Pierce County, Georgia. (find a grave # 55602530)

DAVIS, J. M.: Company E, private. May 5, 1862 enlisted as a private in Co. B, 37th Regiment, Georgia Infantry at Macon, Georgia. April 26, 1865 surrendered in Co. E, 54th Regiment, Georgia Infantry at Greensboro, North Carolina. May 1, 1865 paroled at Greensboro, North Carolina.

DAVIS, JAMES M.: Company K, private. April 18, 1862 enlisted as a private in Co. K, 54th Regiment, Georgia Infantry at Savannah, Georgia and received bounty pay $50.00. January 1, 1863 received pay. January – February 1863 roll shows him present. September 2, 1863 received pay $44.00. March 18, 1864, April 25, 1864 and June 2, 1864 issued clothing. November 8, 1864 admitted to 1st Mississippi C. S. A. Hospital at Jackson, Mississippi with Diarrhoea. January 23, 1865 returned to duty.

DAVIS, JOSEPH J.: Company K, private. October 14, 1861 enlisted as a private and appointed 4th corporal of Co. H, 5th Regiment, Georgia State Troops. April 25, 1862 mustered out. May 5, 1862 enlisted as a private in Co. K, 54th Regiment, Georgia Infantry at Savannah, Georgia and received bounty pay $50.00. January 1, 1863 received pay. January – February 1863 roll shows him present. August 22, 1863 received pay $33.00. March 18, 1864 issued clothing.

DAVIS, JOSEPH W.: Company K, private. October 3, 1861 enlisted as a private in Co. A, 1st Regiment, 1st Brigade, Georgia State Troops. April 1862 mustered out April 18, 1862 enlisted as a private in Co. K, 54th Regiment, Georgia Infantry at Savannah, Georgia and received bounty pay $50.00. April 25, 1864 issued clothing. He was on detailed service at Macon, Georgia at the close of the war. He was born in Ware County, Georgia January 7, 1842 and died in Pierce County, Georgia July 3, 1915. He is buried in Mill Creek Cemetery at Patterson, Pierce County, Georgia. (find a grave # 14806386)

DAVIS, T. L.: Company E, private. He enlisted as a private in Co. E, 54th Regiment, Georgia Infantry.

DAVIS, W.: Company C, private. October 10, 1862 enlisted in Co. C, 54th Regiment, Georgia Infantry at Beaulieu near Savannah, Georgia. October 1862 roll shows he joined.

DAVIS, WILLIAM A.: Company E, sergeant. He enlisted as a sergeant in Co. E, 54th Regiment, Georgia Infantry.

DAWKINS, A. J.: Company G (F), private. He enlisted in Co. G, 54th Regiment, Georgia Infantry. April 26, 1865 surrendered in Co. F, 54th Regiment, Georgia Infantry at Greensboro, North Carolina. May 1, 1865 paroled at Greensboro, North Carolina.

DAWKINS, RUFUS L.: Company G, private. February 24, 1863 enlisted in Co. G, 54th Regiment, Georgia Infantry at Columbus, Georgia and received bounty pay $50.00. January – February 1863 roll shows him present. January 1864 issued clothing. January 28, 1865 admitted to Way Hospital at Meridian, Mississippi with Pneumonia and was transferred to Quintard Hospital. February 10, 1865 admitted to Way Hospital at Meridian, Mississippi with Pneumonia and was furloughed for 60 days to Meadow Valley, Alabama. He was born in Georgia October 19, 1844 and died June 12, 1924. He is buried in McDaniel Cemetery in Clay County, Alabama. (find a grave # 48701428)

DAWKINS, THOMAS J.: Company G (F), private. January 27, 1863 enlisted in Co. G, 54th Regiment, Georgia Infantry at Columbus, Georgia and received bounty pay $50.00. January – February 1863 roll shows him present. January 1864 and May 8, 1864 issued clothing. April 26, 1865 surrendered in Co. F, 54th Regiment, Georgia Infantry at Greensboro, North Carolina. May 1, 1865 paroled at Greensboro, North Carolina. He was born September 6, 1818 and died August 6, 1886. He is buried in McDaniel Cemetery in Clay County, Alabama. (find a grave # 48758911)

DEASON, WILLIAM: Company D, private. August 8, 1861 enlisted in Co. D, 1st Regiment Georgia infantry (Olmstead's). He was discharged due to disability. October 15, 1862 enlisted in Co. D, 54th Regiment, Georgia Infantry at Beaulieu near Savannah, Georgia and received bounty pay $50.00. October 1862 roll shows his enlistment (that he joined by transfer). December 31, 1862 received pay. January – February 1863 roll shows him present. June 14, 1863 discharged due to disability and received pay. May 18, 1865 surrendered and paroled at Augusta, Georgia. He was born in South Carolina September 15, 1842.

DEEN, JOSEPH: Company B, private. April 21, 1862 enlisted as a private in Co. B, 54th Regiment, Georgia Infantry at Savannah, Georgia and received bounty pay $50.00. December 31, 1862 received pay. January – February 1863 roll shows him present. January 1864 issued clothing. July 22, 1864 wounded in the right eye resulting in loss of sight in Atlanta, Georgia. January 31, 1865 left thigh crushed in train wreck en route from Nashville, Tennessee to Columbus, Georgia. He was in Columbus Georgia hospital wounded at the close of the war. May 10, 1865 surrendered at Tallahassee, Florida. May 19, 1865 paroled at Albany, Georgia. He was born in Appling County, Georgia May 1, 1830 and died in Georgia November 13, 1913. He is buried in Live Oak Cemetery in Colquitt County, Georgia. (find a grave # 78806451)

DEEN, T. W.: Company B, private. April 28, 1862 enlisted as a private in Co. B, 54th Regiment, Georgia Infantry at Savannah, Georgia and received bounty pay $50.00. January – February 1863 roll shows him present.

DELANEY, HENRY: Company G, private. August 9, 1862 enlisted in Co. G, 54th Regiment, Georgia Infantry at Savannah, Georgia and received bounty pay $50.00. August 1862 roll shows his enlistment. January – February 1863 roll shows he deserted February 1, 1863.

DELOACH, SAMUEL: Company G, private. He enlisted in Co. G, 54th Regiment, Georgia Infantry.

DENNARD (DENARB) JAMES ELKIN: Company F, private. July 22, 1863 enlisted in Co. B, 2nd Battalion Troops and Defenses of Macon, Georgia at Gordon, Georgia. August 1, 1863 enlisted as a private in Co.

F, 54th Regiment, Georgia Infantry at Savannah, Georgia and received bounty pay $50.00. November 1, 1863 received pay. December 31, 1863 received pay. November – December 1863 roll shows him present. January 1864 and April 25, 1864 issued clothing. July 24, 1864 admitted to Ocmulgee Hospital at Macon, Georgia with a gunshot wound to the lid of the right eye with severe contusion. August 9, 1864 was furloughed for 30 days. August 30, 1864 admitted to Ocmulgee Hospital at Macon, Georgia with Neuralgia. December 31, 1864 roll of Camp Wright at Macon, Georgia shows him absent without leave. He was a resident of Gordon in Wilkinson County, Georgia. He was born August 6, 1822 and died December 19, 1901. He is buried in Ramah Baptist Church Cemetery at Gordon, Wilkinson County, Georgia. (find a grave # 39397406)

DENNIS, A. C.: Company A, private. October 17, 1861 enlisted as a private in Co. C, 1st Independent Battalion, Georgia State Troops. April 16, 1862 roll shows him present. April 1862 mustered out.
May 1, 1862 enlisted as a private in Co. A, 54th Regiment, Georgia Infantry at Macon, Georgia and received bounty pay $50.00. April 30, 1863 received pay. June 30, 1863 roll shows him present sick in the company hospital.

DENT, T. W.: Company B, private. April 28, 1862 enlisted as a private in Co. B, 54th Regiment, Georgia Infantry at Savannah, Georgia and received bounty pay $50.00. August 31, 1862 received pay. January – February 1863 roll shows him present (February 17, 1863 he returned to the company from a detail beginning on November 8, 1862 to make shoes). January 1864 issued clothing. He was born in 1829. He is buried in Friendship Baptist Church Cemetery in Wayne County, Georgia. (find a grave #53755821)

DEVEREAUX, D.: Company C, private. January 1, 1863 enlisted as a private in Co. C, 54th Regiment, Georgia Infantry at Savannah, Georgia and received bounty pay $50.00. January – February 1863 roll shows him absent on special service since January 19, 1863.

DEVEREAUX, L.: Company C, private. January 1, 1863 enlisted as a private in Co. C, 54th Regiment, Georgia Infantry at Savannah, Georgia and received bounty pay $50.00. January – February 1863 roll shows him absent on special service since January 19, 1863.

DICKEY, ENOS B.: Company D, private. April 30, 1862 enlisted as a private in Co. D, 54th Regiment, Georgia Infantry at Savannah, Georgia and received bounty pay $50.00. December 31, 1862 received pay. January – February 1863 roll shows him present. January 1864, April 25, 1864 and May 8, 1864 issued clothing. April 26, 1865 surrendered at Greensboro, North Carolina. May 1, 1865 paroled at Greensboro, North Carolina. He died of Typhoid Fever in 1872.

DICKEY, JAMES L. (A.): Company D, private. April 30, 1862 enlisted as a private in Co. D, 54th Regiment, Georgia Infantry at Savannah, Georgia and received bounty pay $50.00. October 22, 1862 discharged from Beaulieu near Savannah, Georgia. October 1862 roll shows his discharge.

Records show January 1864 issued clothing (May have reentered service). He was born in Screven County, Georgia October 9, 1813 and died in Screven County, Georgia December 11, 1893. He is buried in Big Horse Creek Cemetery in Jenkins County, Georgia. (find a grave # 66946120)

DICKEY, MADISON (M. M.): Company D, private. December 1863 enlisted as a private in Co. D, 54th Regiment, Georgia Infantry. May 15, 1865 he surrendered at Augusta, Georgia. He is described as: 5 feet 7 inches high, sandy hair, grey eyes and fair complexion. He was born in 1847 and died in 1891. He is buried in Big Horse Creek Cemetery in Jenkins County, Georgia. (find a grave # 13377839)

DICKEY, SAMUEL CALHOUN MADISON MONROE: Company D, private. April 30, 1862 enlisted as a private in Co. D, 54th Regiment, Georgia Infantry at Savannah, Georgia and received bounty pay $50.00. December 31, 1862 received pay. January – February 1863 roll shows him present. August 5, 1863 he was discharged from the Confederate General Hospital at Columbia, South Carolina. September 3, 1863 returned to duty from Citadel Square Hospital at Charleston, South Carolina. April 25, 1864 issued clothing. July 13, 1864 report of Medical Examining Board at Dalton, Georgia shows he was furloughed from Cannon Hospital due to Chronic Diarrhoea and Extreme Emaciation and Debility (sick for 2 months). May 15, 1865 he surrendered at Augusta, Georgia. He is described as: 5 feet 6 inches high, sandy hair, blue eyes and fair complexion. He was a resident of Millen, Screven County, Georgia. He was born September 4, 1824 and died July 6, 1888. He is buried in Big Horse Creek Cemetery in Jenkins County, Georgia. (find a grave # 13402977)

DICKSON (DIXON), JEPTHA: Company H, private. He enlisted as a private in Co. H, 54th Regiment, Georgia Infantry.

DILLON, EDWARD: Company K, private. He enlisted as a private in Co. K, 54th Regiment, Georgia Infantry

DIXON (DICKSON), ELIJAH: Company K, private. October 3, 1861 enlisted as a private in Co. A, 1st Regiment, 1st Brigade, Georgia State Troops. April 1862 mustered out. April 18, 1862 enlisted as a private in Co. K, 54th Regiment, Georgia Infantry at Savannah, Georgia and received bounty pay $50.00. January 1, 1863 received pay. January – February 1863 roll shows him present. August 16, 1863 died. November 4, 1864 death benefit claim was filed by his widow Kesiah Dickson.

DIXON (DICKSON) ELISHA: Company K, private. October 3, 1861 enlisted as a private in Co. A, 1st Regiment, 1st Brigade, Georgia State Troops. April 1862 mustered out. April 18, 1862 enlisted as a private in Co. K, 54th Regiment, Georgia Infantry at Savannah, Georgia and received bounty pay $50.00. January 1, 1863 received pay. January – February 1863 roll shows him present. March 18, 1864 and April 25, 1864 issued clothing. May 10, 1865 surrendered at Tallahassee, Florida. May 19, 1865 paroled at Thomasville, Georgia. Parole describes him: 5 feet 5 inches high, dark hair, hazel eyes and dark complexion.

DIXON (DICKSON), JAMES JERFFERSON: Company K, private.

October 3, 1861 enlisted as a private in Co. A, 1st Regiment, 1st Brigade, Georgia State Troops. April 1862 mustered out. April 18, 1862 enlisted as a private in Co. K, 54th Regiment, Georgia Infantry at Savannah, Georgia and received bounty pay $50.00. January 1, 1863 received pay. January – February 1863 roll shows him present. March 18, 1864 and June 2, 1864 issued clothing. July 4, 1864 captured at the battle of Pace's Ferry near Marietta, Georgia. February 26, 1865 paroled from Camp Morton, Indiana and forwarded to City Point, Virginia via Baltimore for exchange. He was born May 8, 1845 and died October 7, 1909. He is buried in Shiloh Primitive Baptist Church Cemetery at Blackshear, Pierce County, Georgia. (find a grave # 17693306)

DIXON (DICKSON), JAMES K.: Company K, private. April 18, 1862 enlisted as a private in Co. K, 54th Regiment, Georgia Infantry at Savannah, Georgia and received bounty pay $50.00. January 1, 1863 received pay. January – February 1863 roll shows him present. July 3, 1864 captured at the battle of Pace's Ferry near Marietta, Georgia. July 12, 1864 received at Nashville, Tennessee and sent to the Military Prison at Louisville, Kentucky. July 13, 1864 received at the Military Prison at Louisville, Kentucky from Nashville, Tennessee. July 13, 1864 forwarded to Camp Morton, Indiana from the Military Prison at Louisville, Kentucky. July 14, 1864 received at Camp Morton, Indiana. February 26, 1865 transferred for exchange.

DIXON (DICKSON), JOHN: Company K, private. October 3, 1861 enlisted as a private in Co. A, 1st Regiment, 1st Brigade, Georgia State Troops. April 1862 mustered out. April 18, 1862 enlisted as a private in Co. K, 54th Regiment, Georgia Infantry at Savannah, Georgia and received bounty pay $50.00. August 1862, September 1862 and October 1862 rolls show him detailed as a courier. November 1862 roll shows him detailed as the major's orderly. January 1, 1863 received pay. January – February 1863 roll shows him present. March 18, 1864 and April 25, 1864 issued clothing. August 31, 1864 killed at Jonesboro, Georgia.

DIXON (DICKSON), WILLIAM JACKSON: Company K, private. October 3, 1861 enlisted as a private in Co. A, 1st Regiment, 1st Brigade, Georgia State Troops. April 1862 mustered out. April 18, 1862 enlisted as a private in Co. K, 54th Regiment, Georgia Infantry at Savannah, Georgia and received bounty pay $50.00. January 1, 1863 received pay. January – February 1863 roll shows him present (he was absent without leave for 8 days). January 1864 issued clothing. Pension records show; April 1865 he surrendered at Marietta, Georgia. He was born in Bulloch County, Georgia February 6, 1839 and died in Appling County, Georgia June 6, 1907. He is buried in Old Dixon Cemetery near Bristol in Appling County, Georgia. (find a grave # 122048736)

DOBSON, HOWELL B.: Company E, private. May 6, 1862 enlisted as a private in Co. E, 54th Regiment, Georgia Infantry at Savannah, Georgia and received bounty pay $50.00. August 1, 1862 transferred to Sharpshooters by Special Order No. 259 (in Savannah, Georgia). August 1862 roll indicates his transfer. August 1864 roll shows him sick in the General Hospital. He is buried in Poplarville Cemetery at Poplarville, Pearl River County, Mississippi. (find a grave # 77014420)

DOGGETT, THOMAS J.: Company H, private. March 15, 1863 enlisted in Co. H, 54th Regiment, Georgia Infantry at Columbus, Georgia and received bounty pay $50.00. October 31, 1863 received pay. November – December 1863 roll shows him absent (detailed in Engineer Department on December 22, 1863 by order of General Mercer). January – February 1864 roll shows him absent (detailed in Engineer Department on December 22, 1863 by order of General Mercer). He was born in Choctaw County, Alabama May 10, 1836 and died July 24, 1919 in Chidester, Quachita County, Arkansas. He is buried in Missouri Cemetery at Chidester, Quachita County, Arkansas. (find a grave # 8642038)

DOGGETT, W. J.: Company F, private. February 1, 1862 enlisted as a private in Co. E, 54th Regiment, Georgia Infantry at Savannah, Georgia and received bounty pay $50.00. December 31, 1862 received pay. January – February 1863 roll shows him present. November 1, 1863 received pay. November – December 1863 roll shows him absent sick in the General Hospital at Savannah, Georgia. December 31, 1863 received pay. January 1864 issued clothing. November 3, 1864 issued clothing at Hood Hospital at Cuthbert, Georgia. December 16, 1864 issued clothing at Convalescent Camp Wright near Macon, Georgia. November – December 1864 roll of Co. E, 1st Regiment will looking over ideas. November – December 1864 Roll of Confederate Troops and Defences, Macon, Georgia shows him present at Camp Wright near Macon, Georgia. April 21-22, 1865 captured at Macon, Georgia.

DONALDSON, J.: Company G, private. May 12, 1862 enlisted in Co. G, 54th Regiment, Georgia Infantry at Columbus, Georgia and received bounty pay $50.00.

DOROUGH, JOSEPH T.: Company H, private. January 28, 1863 enlisted in Co. H, 54th Regiment, Georgia Infantry at Columbus, Georgia and received bounty pay $50.00. January – February 1863 roll shows him present. October 31, 1863 received pay. December 1, 1863 detailed as a nurse. November – December 1863 roll shows him absent (detailed as a nurse in Bethesda Hospital since December 1, 1863 by order of Captain Haututer). November – December 1863 roll of Bethesda Hospital, Beaulieu Battery (near Savannah, Georgia) shows him present since December 1, 1863 (due 31 days extra pay). January 1, 1864 received pay. January 1864 issued clothing. January – February 1864 hospital muster roll of Jo Thompson Artillery shows him present. January 10, 1865 admitted to St. Mary's Hospital at West Point, Mississippi with Diarrhoea. He was born April 30, 1825 and died July 11, 1907. He is buried in New Hope Cemetery at Hamilton, Harris County, Georgia. (find a grave # 21843197)

DORTCH, DAVID: Company G, private. He enlisted in Co. G, 54th Regiment, Georgia Infantry.

DOTY, J. M.: Company F, corporal. May 17, 1862 enlisted as a corporal in Co. F, 54th Regiment, Georgia Infantry at Savannah, Georgia and received bounty pay $50.00. August 31, 1862 received pay. December 16, 1862 detached to Engineer Department. January – February 1863 roll shows him absent (bounty $50.00 paid – Reduced to rank January 1, 1863 – Detailed in Engineer Department December 16, 1862 – pay due to December 31, 1862).

DOTY, WILLIAM W.: Company F, private. May 17, 1861 enlisted as a private in Captain Calaghorn's Company, Georgia State Troops. May 1862 mustered out. May 13, 1862 enlisted as a private in Co. F, 54th Regiment, Georgia Infantry at Savannah, Georgia and received bounty pay $50.00. September 2, 1862 discharged. September 1862 roll shows his discharge.

DOUGHERTY, JAMES D.: Company H (A), private. October 17, 1861 enlisted as a private in Co. C, 1st Independent Battalion, Georgia State Troops. April 16, 1862 roll shows him present. April 1862 mustered out. April 23, 1862 enlisted as a private in Co. H, 54th Regiment, Georgia Infantry at Macon, Georgia and received bounty pay $50.00. September 1, 1862 transferred from Co. H, 54th Regiment, Georgia Infantry to Co. A, 54th Regiment, Georgia Infantry by Special Order No. 6 at Beaulieu near Savannah, Georgia. September 1862 roll shows his transfer. April 7, 1863 transferred from General Hospital No. 1 at Savannah, Georgia to Whitesville (convalescent from Rubeola). April 30, 1863 received pay. June 30, 1863 roll shows him present sick in quarters. June 30, 1863 received pay. October 31, 1863 received pay. November – December 1863 roll shows him present. January – February 1864 roll shows him present. March 31, 1864 and May 8, 1864 issued clothing. Pension records show: April 26, 1865 surrendered at Greensboro, North Carolina. May 1, 1865 paroled at Greensboro, North Carolina.

DOWDELL, LUTHER M.: Company H, lieutenant. July 18, 1863 enlisted as a private in Co. H, 54th Regiment, Georgia Infantry at Beaulieu near Savannah, Georgia. October 31, 1863 received pay. December 31, 1863 received pay. November – December 1863 roll shows him present. January 1864 issued clothing. January – February 1864 roll shows him absent (absent sick at Bethesda Hospital since February 6, 1864). He was appointed 2nd lieutenant of Co. H, 54th Regiment, Georgia Infantry. April 26, 1865 surrendered at Greensboro, North Carolina. May 1, 1865 paroled at Greensboro, North Carolina. He was born July 28, 1843 and died August 28, 1916. He is buried in Little Texas Cemetery at Little Texas, Macon County, Alabama. (find a grave # 39383408)

DOWNS (DOUNS), BENJAMIN: Company A, private. November 7, 1861 enlisted as a private in Co. C, 1st Independent Battalion, Georgia State Troops. April 16, 1862 roll shows him present. April 1862 mustered out. April 23, 1862 enlisted in Co. A, 54th Regiment, Georgia Infantry at Macon, Georgia. August 1862 to December 1862 rolls show him detailed as a teamster. August 28, 1862 to February 1863 detailed as a teamster at Beaulieu near Savannah, Georgia at a rate of $.25 per day. April 30,

1863 received pay. June 30 1863 roll shows him present (two month's pay deducted by order of General Mercer). December 16, 1863 deserted. January 4, 1864 listed as a prisoner. May 8, 1864 issued clothing. April 20-21, 1865 captured at Macon, Georgia.

DOWNS, HENRY T.: Company C. private. April 1864 enlisted as a private in Co. C, 54th Regiment, Georgia Infantry. April 26, 1865 surrendered at Greensboro, North Carolina. May 1, 1865 paroled at Greensboro, North Carolina. He was born in Georgia and died in Washington County, Georgia December 29, 1919.

DOWNS, THOMAS J.: Company G (F), private. May 12, 1862 enlisted as a private in Co. G, 54th Regiment, Georgia Infantry at Columbus, Georgia and received bounty $50.00. June 30, 1862 received pay. January – February 1863 roll shows him present (returned to Company for duty February 4, 1863 from absence on sick furlough since October 28, 1862). January 1864 and May 8, 1864 issued clothing. April 26, 1865 surrendered in Co. F, 54th Regiment, Georgia Infantry at Greensboro, North Carolina. May 1, 1865 paroled at Greensboro, North Carolina. He was born in Harris County, Georgia July 5, 1838 and died there January 1, 1915.

DOWSE, SAMUEL: Company F (D), private. March 17, 1863 enlisted as a private in Co. F, 54th Regiment, Georgia Infantry at Savannah, Georgia and received bounty $50.00. June 7, 1863 to December 31, 1863 detailed as acting commissary sergeant issuing rations for the post at Rose-dew Post near Savannah, Georgia at an additional rate of $.25 per day. November 1, 1863 received pay. November – December 1863 roll shows him present (detailed as regimental Quartermaster sergeant). January 1864 and April 25, 1864 issued clothing. April 26, 1865 surrendered in Co. D, 54th Regiment, Georgia Infantry at Greensboro, North Carolina. May 1, 1865 paroled at Greensboro, North Carolina. He was born May 17, 1846 and died June 16, 1900. He is buried in Cleburne Memorial Cemetery at Cleburne, Johnson County, Texas. (find a grave # 19582526)

DOYLE, E. J.: Company F, private. May 13, 1862 enlisted as a private in Co. F, 54th Regiment, Georgia Infantry at Savannah, Georgia and received bounty $50.00. December 31, 1862 received pay.
January – February 1863 roll shows him present.

DOYLE, JAMES S.: Company K, private. He enlisted as a private in Co. K, 54th Regiment, Georgia Infantry.

DREESE, HARRY (HENRY) S.: Company F, private. May 17, 1861 enlisted as a private in Chisholm's Company, Georgia State Troops. May 1862 mustered out. May 13, 1862 enlisted as a private in Co. F, 54th Regiment, Georgia Infantry at Savannah, Georgia and received bounty $50.00. May 15, 1864 transferred to the 22nd Battalion, Georgia Heavy Artillery. (Not found in this Battalion) August 2, 1864 transferred to Captain Wheaton's Company Chatham Siege Artillery. February 1865 roll shows him present. He was born in Saint Augustine, St. Johns County, Florida July 11, 1845 and died in Savannah, Chatham County, Georgia September 5, 1914. He is buried in Bonaventure Cemetery at Savannah,

Georgia. (find a grave # 84984656)

DREESE (DRESS), T.: Company F, private. He enlisted as a private in Co. F, 54th Regiment, Georgia Infantry. October 1862 discharged at Beaulieu near Savannah, Georgia. October 1862 roll shows his discharge.

DREW, NEWTON: Company C, private. December 11, 1861 enlisted as a private in Co. B, 8th Regiment, Georgia State Troops. He mustered out in 1862. April 22, 1862 enlisted as a private in Co. C, 54th Regiment, Georgia Infantry at Emanuel County, Georgia and received bounty $50.00. October 31, 1862 received pay. November 30, 1862 deserted. January – February 1863 roll shows him present (note: absent without leave for 60 days).

DUDLEY, J. L.: Company H, private. He enlisted as a private in Co. H, 54th Regiment, Georgia Infantry.

DUDLEY, L.: Company I, private. He enlisted as a private in Co. I, 54th Regiment, Georgia Infantry.

DUKES, J. H.: Company B, private. April 28, 1862 enlisted as a private in Co. B, 54th Regiment, Georgia Infantry at Savannah, Georgia and received bounty $50.00. December 31, 1862 received pay. January – February 1863 roll shows him present. January 1864 issued clothing. He was born July 10, 1840 and died October 23, 1895. He is buried in Council Cemetery at Medart, Wakulla County, Florida. (find a grave # 8033133)

DUKES, JOHN W.: Company B, private. October 10, 1861 enlisted as a private and appointed 4th sergeant in Co. K, 2nd Regiment, 1st Brigade, Georgia State Troops. April 1862 mustered out. April 21, 1862 enlisted as a 4th sergeant in Co. B, 54th Regiment, Georgia Infantry at Savannah, Georgia and received bounty $50.00. December 31, 1862 received pay. January – February 1863 roll shows him present. January 1864 and June 2, 1864 issued clothing. Pension records show he was at home on 30 day furlough beginning January 25, 1865 and was cut off from his command at the close of the war. He was born February 14, 1834 and died January 30, 1910. He is buried in Ten Mile Creek Baptist Church Cemetery in Appling County, Georgia. (find a grave # 20352744)

DUKES, T. D.: Company B, private. He enlisted as a private in Co. B, 54th Regiment, Georgia Infantry.

DULLER, W. C.: private. He enlisted as a private in the 54th Regiment, Georgia Infantry. May 10, 1865 surrendered at Tallahassee, Florida. May 29, 1865 paroled at Albany, Georgia.

DUMAS, JEFERSON: Company A, private. He enlisted as a private in Co. A, 54th Regiment, Georgia Infantry. He is buried in Riverside Cemetery at Macon, Bibb County, Georgia. (find a grave # 56866176)

DUNAWAY, A. J.: Company K, corporal. He enlisted as a private in Co. K, 54th Regiment, Georgia Infantry.

DUNAWAY, GEORGE W.: Company H, private. February 24, 1864 enlisted as a private in Co. B, 54th Regiment, Georgia Infantry at Hardeeville,

South Carolina and received bounty $50.00. January – February 1864 roll shows him present on picket duty. January 1864 issued clothing. June 8, 1864 furloughed for 60 days to Washington, Georgia from law Hospital at Dalton, Georgia due to Chronic Diarrhoea with Extreme Emaciation and Debility. He was a resident of Washington, Georgia. He was born in Warren County, Georgia August 28, 1838.

DUNAWAY (DUNNAWAY), LEW CURTIS: Company H, private. May 20, 1862 enlisted as a private in Co. H, 54th Regiment, Georgia Infantry at Savannah, Georgia and received bounty $50.00. December 31, 1862 received pay. January – February 1863 roll shows him present. October 31, 1863 received pay. November – December 1863 roll shows him present. December 31, 1863 received pay. January – February 1864 roll shows him present. January 1864 and October 11, 1864 issued clothing.

DUNAWAY (DUNNAWAY), THOMAS: Company H, private. May 20, 1862 enlisted as a private in Co. H, 54th Regiment, Georgia Infantry at Savannah, Georgia and received bounty $50.00. June 2, 1862 issued clothing. December 31, 1862 received pay. January – February 1863 roll shows him present. October 31, 1863 received pay. November – December 1863 roll shows him present. December 31, 1863 received pay. January – February 1864 roll shows him present. January 1864 issued clothing. April 26, 1865 surrendered at Greensboro, North Carolina. May 1, 1865 paroled at Greensboro, North Carolina.

DUNAWAY (DUNNAWAY), WILLIAM: Company H, private. August 13, 1863 enlisted as a private in Co. H, 54th Regiment, Georgia Infantry at Beaulieu near Savannah, Georgia and received bounty $50.00. October 31, 1863 received pay. November – December 1863 roll shows him present. December 31, 1863 received pay. January – February 1864 roll shows him present on picket. January 1864 and June 2, 1864 issued clothing. April 26, 1865 surrendered at Greensboro, North Carolina. May 1, 1865 paroled at Greensboro, North Carolina.

DUNCAN, JOHN D.: Company G, private. January 22, 1863 enlisted as a private in Co. G, 54th Regiment, Georgia Infantry at Columbus, Georgia and received bounty $50.00. January 1864 issued clothing. January – February 1863 roll shows him present. July 2, 1864 captured near Marietta, Georgia. July 4, 1864 sent to Nashville, Tennessee. July 6, 1864 admitted to No. 2 U. S. A. General Hospital at Chattanooga, Tennessee from the field with Chronic Diarrhoea. July 26, 1864 placed in prison at Chattanooga, Tennessee (age 28 years). August 2, 1864 sent from Nashville, Tennessee to Military Prison at Louisville, Kentucky. August 3, 1864 arrived at Military Prison at Louisville, Kentucky sent to Camp Chase, Ohio. August 4, 1864 arrived at Camp Chase, Ohio. October 13, 1864 died of Small Pox at Camp Chase, Ohio. He is buried in grave # 310 (1/3 mile S. C. C. O.) (find a grave # 6408870)

DUNLAP, JOHN H.: Company A, lieutenant. October 17, 1861 elected 2nd lieutenant of Co. C, 1st Independent Battalion, Georgia State Troops. April 1862 roll shows him present. April 1862 mustered out. April 18,

1862 enlisted as 2nd lieutenant in Co. A, 54th Regiment, Georgia Infantry at Savannah, Georgia and received bounty $50.00. July 1862 roll shows him stationed at Savannah, Georgia. August 1862 and September 1862 rolls at Beaulieu near Savannah, Georgia show him absent with leave since July 23, 1862. September 25, 1862 resigned his commission.

DUNLAP, WILLIAM: Company A, private. October 17, 1861 enlisted as a private in Co. C, 1st Independent Battalion, Georgia State Troops. April 16, 1862 roll shows him present. April 1862 mustered out April 18, 1862 enlisted as a private in Co. A, 54th Regiment, Georgia Infantry at Macon, Georgia and received bounty $50.00. April 30, 1863 received pay. June 30, 1863 roll shows him present. October 31, 1863 received pay. November 1863 received pay for commutation of rations. January – February 1864 roll shows him absent on detached service since December 27, 1863. April 29, 1864 issued clothing. July 20, 1864 captured at Peachtree Creek near Atlanta, Georgia. July 27, 1864 sent from Nashville, Tennessee to Military Prison at Louisville, Kentucky. July 28, 1864 received at Military Prison at Louisville, Kentucky. July 30, 1864 sent from Military Prison at Louisville, Kentucky to Camp Douglas (Chase), Illinois. August 1, 1864 received at Camp Douglas, Illinois. June 13, 1865 discharged from Camp Douglas, Indiana. He was born in Pickens' District, South Carolina September 13, 1833.

DUNN, AUGUSTUS H. K.: Company C, private. May 6, 1862 enlisted as a private in Co. C, 54th Regiment, Georgia Infantry at Savannah, Georgia and received bounty $50.00. December 14, 1862 to December 31, 1862 detailed as a teamster at Beaulieu near Savannah, Georgia at an additional $.25 per day. December 31, 1862 received pay. December 1862 roll shows him detailed as a teamster. January – February 1863 roll shows him present (detailed as a teamster). January 1, 1864 received pay. January – February 1864 roll shows him present. He was a resident of Hancock County, Georgia. Pension records show: April 26, 1865 surrendered at Greensboro, North Carolina. May 1, 1865 paroled at Greensboro, North Carolina. He was born in Baldwin County, Georgia October 3, 1842.

DUNN, J. G.: Company G, private. He enlisted as a private in Co. G, 54th Regiment, Georgia Infantry.

DUNN, MARTIN: Company G, private. February 23, 1863 enlisted as a private in Co. G, 54th Regiment, Georgia Infantry in Columbus, Georgia and received bounty $50.00. January – February 1863 roll shows him present. August 20, 1864 received pay $33.00. January 1864 and April 25, 1864 issued clothing. May 19, 1864 captured at Calhoun, Georgia. May 24, 1864 received at Military Prison at Louisville, Kentucky from Nashville, Tennessee. May 25, 1864 sent to Rock Island Prison, Illinois from Military Prison at Louisville, Kentucky. May 27, 1864 received at Rock Island Prison, Illinois. June 10, 1864 transferred to U. S. Navy.

DURDEN (DIRDEN), J.: Company C, private. He enlisted as a private in Co. C, 54th Regiment, Georgia Infantry at Savannah, Georgia and received bounty pay $50.00. October 1862 roll shows him detailed as a butcher.

DURDEN, L. H.: Company C, private. May 6, 1862 enlisted as a private in Co. C, 54th Regiment, Georgia Infantry at Savannah, Georgia and received bounty $50.00. December 31, 1862 received pay. January – February 1863 roll shows him present (in hospital at Bethesda). January 1, 1864 received pay. January – February 1864 roll shows him absent detached as a picket at Purysburg, South Carolina by order of Colonel Way February 20, 1864. April 25, 1864, April 28, 1864 and May 8, 1864 issued clothing. He was a resident of Hancock County.

DURDEN, W. R.: Company C, sergeant. May 6, 1862 enlisted as a 2nd corporal in Co. C, 54th Regiment, Georgia Infantry at Savannah, Georgia and received bounty $50.00. December 31, 1862 received pay. January – February 1863 roll shows him present. January 1, 1864 received pay. January – February 1864 roll shows him present. He was elected 4th sergeant of Co. C, 54th Regiment, Georgia Infantry. February 29, 1864 received pay. November 20, 1864 issued clothing at Convalescent Camp Wright near Macon, Georgia. November – December 1864 roll of Co. A, 2nd Battalion Troops and Defences, Macon, Georgia shows him present at Camp Wright. Pension records show: April 26, 1865 surrendered at Greensboro, North Carolina. May 1, 1865 paroled at Greensboro, North Carolina. He was a resident of Hancock County. He was born in Washington County, Georgia December 1, 1837.

DUTTON, THOMAS A.: Company I, private. May 6, 1862 enlisted as a private in Co. I, 54th Regiment, Georgia Infantry at Guyton, Georgia and received bounty $50.00. December 31, 1862 received pay. January – February 1863 roll shows him present. October 31, 1863 received pay. November – December 1863 roll shows him present. January 1864 and June 2, 1864 issued clothing. He was born June 28, 1846 and died August 30, 1867. He is buried in Elam-Egypt Baptist Church Cemetery at Egypt, Effingham County, Georgia. (find a grave # 68004533)

DUTTON, WILLIAM H.: Company I, private. May 6, 1862 enlisted as a private in Co. I, 54th Regiment, Georgia Infantry at Savannah, Georgia and received bounty $50.00. December 3, 1862 discharged due to disability. December 1862 roll shows his discharge. November 9, 1863 enlisted as a private in Co. I, 54th Regiment, Georgia Infantry at Rose Dew, near Savannah, Georgia. November – December 1863 roll shows him present. December 31, 1863 received pay. January 1864 issued clothing. November 4, 1864, November 20, 1864 and December 15, 1864 issued clothing at Convalescent Camp Wright near Macon, Georgia. November – December 1864 roll of Co. H, 1st Regiment, Troops and Defences, Macon, Georgia shows him present at Camp Wright. He was born in Bulloch County, Georgia April 11, 1831 and died November 30, 1875. He is buried in Elam-Egypt Baptist Church Cemetery at Egypt, Effingham County, Georgia. (find a grave # 68004588)

DUTTON, ZEDEKIAH EAMES: Company I, private. May 6, 1862 enlisted as a private in Co. I, 54th Regiment, Georgia Infantry at Savannah, Georgia and received bounty $50.00. September, October, November and

December 1862 rolls show him detailed as a butcher. September 19, 1862 to February 19, 1863 detailed as a butcher at an additional $.25 per day. December 31, 1862 received pay. January 15, 1863 received pay. February 1863 received pay. March 1863 received pay. October 31, 1863 received pay. January – February 1863 roll shows him present detailed as wagoner for regiment. November – December 1863 roll shows him absent with leave. January 1864 and June 2, 1864 issued clothing. He was born November 28, 1822 and died April 23, 1887. He is buried in New Hope United Methodist Church Cemetery at Leefield, Bulloch County, Georgia. (find a grave # 15864349)

DYAL, D. D.: Company K, private. He enlisted as a private in Co. K, 54th Regiment, Georgia Infantry at Savannah, Georgia and received bounty $50.00. October 27, 1862 discharged at Beaulieu near Savannah, Georgia. October 1862 roll shows his discharge.

DYAL, GEORGE WASHINGTON: Company B (D), private. April 1, 1864 enlisted as a private in Co. B, 54th Regiment, Georgia Infantry at Savannah, Georgia and received bounty $50.00. April 25, 1864 issued clothing. April 26, 1865 surrendered in Co. D, 54th Regiment, Georgia Infantry at Greensboro, North Carolina. May 1, 1865 paroled at Greensboro, North Carolina. He was born in Appling County, Georgia June 10, 1844 and died in Bradford County, Florida May 2, 1923. He is buried in Dyal Cemetery at Raiford, Bradford County, Florida. (find a grave # 77579644)

DYAL, J. D.: Company H (K), private. April 19, 1862 enlisted as a private in Co. K, 54th Regiment, Georgia Infantry at Savannah, Georgia and received bounty $50.00. August 12, 1862 joined Co. K, 54th Regiment, Georgia Infantry at Savannah, Georgia and accounted for in their muster roll. August 1862 roll shows him in Co. K, 54th Regiment, Georgia Infantry. September 1, 1862 transferred from Co. H, 54th Regiment, Georgia Infantry to Co. K, 54th Regiment, Georgia Infantry at Beaulieu near Savannah, Georgia by Special Order No. 6. September 12, 1862 discharged at Beaulieu near Savannah, Georgia. September 1862 roll shows his discharge.

DYE, L. B.: Company G (C), private. April 13, 1864 enlisted as a private in Co. I, 54th Regiment, Georgia Infantry at Elberton, Georgia. April 26, 1865 surrendered in Co. C, 54th Regiment, Georgia Infantry at Greensboro, North Carolina. May 1, 1865 paroled at Greensboro, North Carolina.

DYER, J.: Company A, private. He enlisted as a private in Co. A, 54th Regiment, Georgia Infantry.

DYES (DYER), Z.: Company A (F), private. May 10, 1862 enlisted as a private in Co. F, 54th Regiment, Georgia Infantry at Savannah, Georgia and received bounty $50.00. September 1, 1862 transferred from Co. F, 54th Regiment, Georgia Infantry to Co A, 54th Regiment, Georgia Infantry at Beaulieu near Savannah, Georgia by Special Order No. 6. September 1862 roll shows his transfer. September 16, 1862 discharged at Beaulieu near Savannah, Georgia. September 1862 roll shows transfer and discharge.

EASON, ABRAHAM: Company B, private. April 28, 1862 enlisted as a private in Co. B, 54th Regiment, Georgia Infantry at Savannah, Georgia and received bounty $50.00. December 31, 1862 received pay. January – February 1863 roll shows him on sick leave since February 1, 1863. February 23, 1865 died of Chronic Dysentery. He was born in 1831 and died in Dalton, Whitfield County, Georgia February 23, 1865. He is buried in West Hill Cemetery at Dalton, Whitfield, Georgia. (find a grave # 78188727)

EASON, ABRAHAM MOLTON: Company B, private. October 10, 1861 enlisted as a private in Co. K, 2nd Regiment, 1st Brigade, Georgia State Troops. April 1862 mustered out. April 21, 1862 enlisted as a private in Co. B, 54th Regiment, Georgia Infantry at Savannah, Georgia and received bounty $50.00. December 31, 1862 received pay. January – February 1863 roll shows him sick in the regimental hospital – absent without leave 3 days. May 8, 1864 issued clothing. June 21, 1864 wounded in the right arm above the elbow necessitating amputation near Marietta, Georgia. He was discharged in 1864 due to disability. He was born August 15, 1838 in Appling County, Georgia died December 2, 1904 in Appling County, Georgia. He is buried in Bethel United Methodist Cemetery in Appling County, Georgia. (find a grave # 59725408)

EASON, FELEX KENYON: Company B, lieutenant. October 10, 1861 enlisted and elected as 2nd lieutenant of Co. K, 2nd Regiment, 1st Brigade, Georgia State Troops. April 1862 mustered out. April 21, 1862 enlisted as a private in Co. B, 54th Regiment, Georgia Infantry at Savannah, Georgia and received bounty $50.00. December 20, 1862 elected Jr. 2nd lieutenant of Co. B, 54th Regiment, Georgia Infantry at Beaulieu near Savannah, Georgia (due to J. J. Robinson being cashiered by sentence of General Court Martial). December 1862 roll shows his election. January – February 1863 roll shows him present. March 4, 1863 received pay $80.00. April 2, 1863 received pay $80.00. April 30, 1863 received pay $80.00. October 21, 1863 appears on list of officers at Legare's Point, South Carolina. February 25, 1864 leave granted 15 days by Special Order No, 5/3. July 2, 1864 received pay $160.00. January 9, 1865 leave granted for 30 days by Special Order No. 4/1 at Tupelo, Mississippi. He was born January 24, 1830 in Appling County, Georgia and died January 18, 1903 in Appling County, Georgia. He is buried in Bethel United Methodist Church Cemetery in Appling County, Georgia. (find a grave #65294905)

EASON, GEORGE W.: Company K, captain. October 8, 1861 enlisted as a private and appointed 1st sergeant in Co. A, 1st Regiment, 1st Brigade, Georgia State Troops. April 1862 mustered out. April 19, 1862 enlisted as a private in Co. K, 54th Regiment, Georgia Infantry at Savannah, Georgia and received bounty $50.00. April 19, 1862 elected captain of Co. K, 54th Regiment, Georgia Infantry at Savannah, Georgia. July 1862 roll shows him absent in Savannah, Georgia. August 1862 roll shows him present in arrest at Beaulieu near Savannah, Georgia. September 1862 roll shows him present at Beaulieu near Savannah, Georgia. October 1862 roll shows him present in arrest at Beaulieu near Savannah, Georgia. November 1862 roll shows he was dismissed by General Order No. 82. Record shows he was dismissed by Court Martial. He was born in Appling County, Georgia April 22, 1834 and died in Waycross, Ware County, Georgia October 9, 1903. He is buried in the Waresboro Cemetery in Wayne County, Georgia. (find a grave # 19098723)

EASON, JAMES TILLMAN: Company B, private. April 28, 1862 enlisted as a private in Co. B, 54th Regiment, Georgia Infantry at Savannah, Georgia and received bounty $50.00. December 31, 1862 received pay. January – February 1863 roll shows him present. August 25, 1863 wounded between the eyes at Battery Wagner, Morris Island near Charleston, South Carolina. October 4, 1863 report shows he was wounded in the head (between the eyes) at Battery Wagner near Charleston, South Carolina between August 23 and August 30, 1863. January 1864, April 25, 1864 and June 2, 1864 issued clothing. He was home on furlough at the close of the war. He was born in Appling County, Georgia October 26, 1832 and died in Clinch County, Georgia February 26, 1905. He is buried in North Cemetery at Du Pont, Clinch County, Georgia. (find a grave # 44836609)

EASON, MOSES LEONARD PEEK: Company B, private. April 28, 1862 enlisted as a private in Co. B, 54th Regiment, Georgia Infantry at Savannah, Georgia and received bounty $50.00. December 31, 1862 received pay. January – February 1863 roll shows him present. January 1864 and April 25, 1864 issued clothing. He was born August 1, 1843 in Appling County, Georgia died February 18, 1902 in Appling County, Georgia. He is buried in Bethel United Methodist Cemetery in Appling County, Georgia. (find a grave # 65295403)

EASON, SILAS O.: Company K, private. 1864 he enlisted as a private in Co. K, 54th Regiment, Georgia Infantry. (According to pension records) May 1865 discharged at Screven, Georgia. He was born in Screven, Georgia in 1846.

EASON, WILLIAM HENRY: Company B, private. April 21, 1862 enlisted as a private in Co. B, 54th Regiment, Georgia Infantry at Savannah, Georgia and received bounty $50.00. October 6, 1862 died from accident at Beaulieu near Savannah, Georgia. October 1862 roll reflects his death. He was born March 12, 1841 in Appling County, Georgia died October 6, 1862 in Savannah, Georgia. He is buried in Bethel United Methodist Cemetery in Appling County, Georgia. (find a grave # 65388702)

EASTERS MALACHI: Company E, private. May 6, 1862 enlisted as a private in Co. E, 54th Regiment, Georgia Infantry at Savannah, Georgia and received bounty $50.00. November 2, 1862 died at Beaulieu near Savannah, Georgia. November 1862 roll reflects his death. February 6, 1863 death benefit claim was filed by his father Iley Easters.

EASTERS, WILLIAM B.: Company E, private. May 6, 1862 enlisted as a private in Co. E, 54th Regiment, Georgia Infantry at Savannah,

Georgia and received bounty $50.00. December 31, 1862 received pay. January – February 1863 roll shows him present. January 1864 issued clothing. May 10, 1865 surrendered at Tallahassee, Florida. May 18, 1865 paroled at Albany, Georgia. May 29, 1865 listed on Post Register, Albany, Georgia. (Pension records show: April 26, 1865 surrendered at Greensboro, North Carolina. May 1, 1865 paroled at Greensboro, North Carolina.) He was born in Irwin County, Georgia April 17, 1836 and died in Tift County, Georgia November 17, 1919. He is buried in Pineview Holiness Baptist Church Cemetery at Tifton, Tift County, Georgia. (find a grave # 30282457)

EBERHART, GEORGE: Company C, lieutenant. He enlisted as a private and was elected lieutenant in Co. C, 54th Regiment, Georgia Infantry.

EDENFIELD, HENRY GREENE: Company D, private. April 30, 1862 enlisted as a private in Co. D, 54th Regiment, Georgia Infantry at Savannah, Georgia and received bounty $50.00. September 10, 1862 discharged at Beaulieu near Savannah, Georgia. September 1862 roll reflects his discharge. November 11, 1863 enlisted as a private in Co. F, 5th Regiment, Georgia Cavalry. Pension records state he was cut off from his command while on scout duty near Bentonville, North Carolina in 1865. He was born in Allendale County, South Carolina November 5, 1845 and died in Millen, Jenkins County, Georgia July 15, 1919. He is buried in Oak Hill Baptist Church Cemetery at Paramour Hill, Jenkins County, Georgia. (find a grave # 24429231)

EDWARDS, LEVI DE LYONS: Company I, private. May 6, 1862 enlisted as a private in Co. I, 54th Regiment, Georgia Infantry at Savannah, Georgia and received bounty $50.00. September 24, 1862 discharged at Beaulieu near Savannah, Georgia. September 1862 roll reflects his discharge. October 19, 1863 enlisted as a private in Co. I, 5th Regiment, Georgia Cavalry. May 16, 1864 transferred to Co K, 7th Regiment, Georgia Cavalry. April 9, 1865 surrendered at Appomattox Courthouse, Virginia. He was born October 31, 1845 and died June 25, 1919. He is buried in Laurel Grove Cemetery at Savannah, Chatham County, Georgia. (find a grave # 44329219)

EDWARDS, WILLIAM: Company E, private. He enlisted as a private in Co. E, 54th Regiment, Georgia Infantry.

ELKINS, HARRISON C.: Company I, sergeant. September 18, 1861 enlisted as a private in Co. C, 1st Regiment, 1st Brigade, Georgia State Troops. March 18, 1862 mustered out. May 6, 1862 enlisted as 5th sergeant in Co. I, 54th Regiment, Georgia Infantry at Savannah, Georgia and received bounty $50.00. He was elected 1st sergeant in Co. I, 54th Regiment, Georgia Infantry. December 31, 1862 received pay. January – February 1863 roll shows him present sick. October 31, 1863 received pay. November – December 1863 roll shows him present. January 1864 issued clothing. He was killed at Lost Mountain, Georgia June 16, 1864. He was born about 1841 and died in 1864. He is memorialized in Veterans Park of Effingham County in Springfield, Effingham County, Georgia. (find a grave # 42392543)

ELKINS, LEANDER LAFAYETTE (LUCIUS): Company I, captain. September 18, 1861 elected 1st lieutenant of Co. C, 1st Regiment, 1st Brigade, Georgia State Troops. March 18, 1862 mustered out of Co. C, 1st Regiment, 1st Brigade, Georgia State Troops. May 16, 1862 elected captain of Co. I, 54th Regiment, Georgia Infantry. July 1862 roll indicates him at Savannah, Georgia. August 1862 roll shows him sick in quarters at Beaulieu near Savannah, Georgia. September 1862 roll shows him absent with leave with Chronic Diarrhoea and Jaundice. October 1862 roll shows him absent with leave since October 27, 1862. November 1862 roll shows him absent sick. December 1862 roll shows him absent with leave since November 30, 1862 (he is shown on sick furlough since December 3, 1862). January 3, 1863 he is shown sick on report. January – February 1863 roll shows him present. April 14, 1863 received pay $260.00. April 30, 1863 he is shown as absent sick. July 3, 1863 to July 31, 1863 he is shown on sick furlough. July 5, 1863 to August 30, 1863 he is shown on list of officers as being absent sick at Guyton Hospital by authority of Surgeon's Certificate. December 3, 1863 received pay $130.00. November – December 1863 roll shows him present. January 4, 1864 received pay $130.00. August 25, 1864 report of Mercer's Brigade shows him sick in the hospital at Guyton, Georgia since May 18, 1864. August 29, 1864 received pay $780.00. October 12, 1864 issued clothing. He was born in Guyton, Effingham County, Georgia in June 10, 1837 and died in St. Augustine, St Johns County, Florida October 29, 1904. He is buried in Evergreen Cemetery, at St, Augustine, St Johns County, Florida. (find a grave # 60728689)

ELLIOTT, J. M.: Company F, private. April 29, 1863 enlisted as a private in Co. F, 54th Regiment, Georgia Infantry.

ELLIOTT, J. M.: Company F, private. February 27, 1863 enlisted as a private in Co. F, 54th Regiment, Georgia Infantry at Savannah, Georgia and received bounty $50.00. January – February 1863 roll shows him present. April 7, 1863 admitted to General Hospital No. 1 at Savannah, Georgia with Acute Diarrhoea and was transferred to Whitesville. He received commutation for rations from March 2, 1863 to June 30, 1863. September 3, 1863 received pay $22.00. January 1864, April 25, 1864 and May 8, 1864 issued clothing.

ELLIOTT (ELLETT)(ELLIOT), JOHN M.: Company F, private. February 12, 1863 enlisted as a private in Co. F, 54th Regiment, Georgia Infantry at Savannah, Georgia and received bounty $50.00. February 28, 1863 shown as in detached service with the signal corps. January – February 1863 roll shows him present. March 1, 1863 to July 31, 1863 on detached service and received $3.00 per day. August 1, 1863 to August 31, 1863 on detached service and received $3.00 per day for a total of $90.00. September 1, 1863 to September 30, 1863 on detached service and received $3.00 per day for a total of $90.00. October 1, 1863 to October

31, 1863 on detached service and received $3.00 per day. November 1, 1863 received pay. December 1, 1863 to December 31, 1863 on detached service and received $3.00 per day. November – December 1863 roll shows him present. January 1864 and February 1, 1864 issued clothing. January 1, 1864 to February 29, 1864 on detached service and received $3.00 per day. March 1, 1864 to May 31, 1864 detailed on Telegraph and Signal Duty. June 1, 1864 to June 30, 1864 on detached service and received $3.00 per day. June 30, 1864 received pay. July 1, 1864 to October 31, 1864 on detached service with the signal and telegraph service as a telegraph and signal operator. October 31, 1864 roll shows him absent.

ELLIOTT, JOHN WASHINGTON: Company F, private. February 27, 1863 enlisted as a private in Co. F, 54th Regiment, Georgia Infantry at Savannah, Georgia and received bounty $50.00. December 27, 1863 he was detailed to duty with the Signal Corps at Savannah, Georgia. October 31, 1864 roll shows him absent, telegraph operator at Savannah, Georgia. May 28, 1864 he died in the hospital at Macon, Georgia. He was born near Alexander, Georgia in 1832 and died in the Hospital at Macon, Georgia in May 28, 1864. He is buried in Rose Hill Cemetery at Macon, Georgia. (find a grave # 105095405))

ELLIOTT, ROBERT: Company C, private. May 6, 1862 enlisted as a private in Co. C, 54th Regiment, Georgia Infantry at Savannah, Georgia and received bounty $50.00. June 19, 1864 wounded at Kennesaw Mountain (the date is for Marietta) Georgia. He was born in Georgia September 2, 1820.

ELLIOTT (ELIOTT), S.: Company A, private. February 1, 1864 enlisted as a private in Co. A, 54th Regiment, Georgia Infantry at Savannah, Georgia. January – February 1864 roll shows him present.

ELLIS, ANDREW J. (P.): Company G, private. January 22, 1863 enlisted as a private in Co. G, 54th Regiment, Georgia Infantry at Columbus, Georgia and received bounty $50.00. January – February 1863 roll shows him present. August 23-30, 1863, report shows he was wounded in the head (hand) at Battery Wagner near Charleston, South Carolina between August 23 and August 30, 1863. January 1864 and May 8, 1864 issued clothing. April 26, 1865 surrendered at Greensboro, North Carolina. May 1, 1865 paroled at Greensboro, North Carolina. He was born in Emanuel County, Georgia November 14, 1835 and died in Worth County, Georgia March 31, 1904. He is buried in Hillcrest Cemetery at Sylvester, Worth County, Georgia. (find a grave # 15865168)

ELLIS, J. G.: Company C, private. He enlisted as a private in Co. C, 54th Regiment, Georgia Infantry. August 25, 1863 wounded (right hand – several fingers blown off) at Battery Wagner, Morris Island near Charleston, South Carolina. He was admitted to Citadel Hospital at Charleston, South Carolina.

ELLISON, J. M. B.: Company A, private. He enlisted in as a private in Co. A, 54th Regiment, Georgia Infantry.

ELLISON, RICHARD LANE (LANG): Company G, private. January 22, 1863 enlisted as a private in Co. G, 54th Regiment, Georgia Infantry at Columbus, Georgia and received bounty $50.00. January – February 1863 roll shows him present. August 31, 1863 received pay. September 4, 1863 received pay $44.00. January 1864 and April 25, 1864 issued clothing. July 3, 1864 captured at Kennesaw Mountain near Marietta, Georgia. July 12, 1864 transferred from Nashville, Tennessee to Military Prison at Louisville, Kentucky. July 13, 1864 received from Nashville, Tennessee at Military Prison at Louisville, Kentucky and sent to Camp Morton, Indiana. July 14, 1864 received at Camp Morton, Indianapolis, Indiana. February 19, 1865 transferred for exchange from Camp Morton, Indianapolis, Indiana to City Point, Virginia via Baltimore, Maryland. March 7, 1865 admitted to Receiving and Wayside Hospital or General Hospital No. 9 at Richmond, Virginia and was transferred to Jackson Hospital at Richmond, Virginia on March 10, 1865. March 11, 1865 admitted to Jackson Hospital at Richmond, Virginia with Chronic Diarrhoea and shown on roll as present. March 20, 1865 transferred from Jackson Hospital at Richmond, Virginia to Small Pox Hospital. March 21, 1865 admitted to General Hospital, Howard's Grove at Richmond, Virginia with Variola (Small Pox). May 30, 1865 reached home. He died from inflammatory Rheumatism contracted in service, at Columbus, Muscogee County, Georgia.

ELY, A. JUDSON: Company H, sergeant. March 4, 1862 enlisted as a private in Co. E, 46th Regiment, Georgia Infantry at Hamilton, Georgia. December 15, 1862 transferred to Co. H, 54th Regiment, Georgia Infantry. December 31, 1862 received pay. January – February 1863 roll shows him present. October 31, 1863 received pay. He was elected 3rd corporal in Co. H, 54th Regiment, Georgia Infantry. November – December 1863 roll shows him present. December 31, 1863 received pay. January 1864 issued clothing. January – February 1864 roll shows him present on picket. He was elected sergeant in Co. H, 54th Regiment, Georgia Infantry. April 26, 1865 surrendered at Greensboro, North Carolina. May 1, 1865 paroled at Greensboro, North Carolina. He was born in Muscogee County, Georgia in 1840 and died January 26, 1911. He is buried in Woodbury Cemetery at Woodbury, Meriwether County, Georgia. (find a grave # 38263699).

ELY, GEORGE W.: Company H, private. March 13, 1862 enlisted as a private in Co. H, 54th Regiment, Georgia Infantry at Columbus, Georgia. December 31, 1863 received pay. January 1864 issued clothing. January – February 1864 roll shows him present. January 14, 1865 admitted to Way Hospital at Meridian, Mississippi with Gunshot Wounds. April 26, 1865 surrendered at Greensboro, North Carolina. May 1, 1865 paroled at Greensboro, North Carolina.

ELY, GEORGE W.: Company H, private. April 6, 1862 1862 enlisted as a private in Co. C, 46th Regiment, Georgia Infantry. October 13, 1862 discharged in Charleston, South Carolina due to under age. March 1, 1864 enlisted as a private in Barnwell's Battery, Georgia Light Artillery. June

1864 transferred to Co. H, 54th Regiment, Georgia Infantry. April 26, 1865 surrendered at Greensboro, North Carolina. May 1, 1865 paroled at Greensboro, North Carolina.

ELY, JAMES D.: Company H, private. August 2, 1862 enlisted as a private in Co. H, 54th Regiment, Georgia Infantry at Savannah, Georgia and received bounty $50.00. August 1862 and September 1862 rolls show he joined. December 31, 1862 received pay. January – February 1863 roll shows him present. October 31, 1863 received pay. November – December 1863 roll shows him present. December 31, 1863 received pay. January 1864 issued clothing. January – February 1864 roll shows him present. April 25, 1864 and June 2, 1862 issued clothing. July 22, 1864 wounded in the right necessitating amputation at Atlanta, Georgia. November 25, 1864 received pay $ 49.13. February 1865 roll of Post of Columbus, Georgia shows him present. He was born in 1836 and died in 1892. He is buried in Hamilton Cemetery at Hamilton, Harris County, Georgia. (find a grave # 32829207)

ELY, MARCUS B.: Company H, lieutenant. May 12, 1862 enlisted as a private in Co. H, 54th Regiment, Georgia Infantry at Columbus, Georgia. September, October, November and December 1862 rolls show him as the adjutant's clerk. January 10, 1863 elected Jr. 2nd lieutenant of Co. H, 54th Regiment, Georgia Infantry. January – February 1863 roll shows him present. March 4, 1863 received pay $80.00. March 31, 1863 received pay $80.00. April 30, 1863 received pay $80.00. December 15, 1863 promoted to 2nd lieutenant by order of General Walker. November 19, 1863 to December 9, 1863 he is shown on a leave of absence approved by General Mercer. December 29, 1863 received pay $80.00. November – December 1863 roll shows him but does not indicate present or absent. January 5, 1864 received pay $80.00. February 2, 1864 received pay $80.00. January – February 1864 roll shows him. May 18, 1864 he was sick in Hospital in Columbus, Georgia. August 25, 1864 he is shown on Report of Mercer's Brigade, in the field near Atlanta, Georgia as being sick in Columbus, Georgia. January 15, 1865 admitted to Way Hospital at Meridian, Mississippi with a gunshot wound. April 6, 1865 admitted to Ocmulgee Hospital at Macon, Georgia with Chronic Diarrhoea and was transferred April 18, 1865 to Harris County. April 23, 1865 admitted to Ocmulgee Hospital at Macon, Georgia with Phthisis (Tuberculosis). April 28, 1865 paroled at Ocmulgee Hospital at Macon, Georgia. He was born in 1833 and died April 5, 1880. He is buried in Linwood Cemetery at Columbus, Muscogee County, Georgia. (find a grave # 33391392)

ELY, MARY: Company H, cook (slave). January – February 1864 shown on roll as cook at Hospital of Jo Thompson Artillery as present (hired by consent of owner at $25.00 per month – property of Lieutenant Ely).

ENNIS, W. R.: Company C, private. January 1, 1863 enlisted as a private in Co. C, 54th Regiment, Georgia Infantry at Savannah, Georgia and received bounty $50.00. January – February 1863 roll shows him present. June, July and August 1863 detailed as Wagon Master at

Charleston, South Carolina at an additional $.25 per day. September 1, 1863 received pay. September 1863 detailed as Wagon Master on James Island, South Carolina. October 31, 1863 list from James Island, South Carolina shows him as wagon master for the Quartermasters Department by order of Colonel Way since April 15, 1863. January – February 1864 roll shows him absent on detached as regimental teamster by order of Colonel Way June1, 1863. February 1864 detailed as Wagon Master at Savannah, Georgia. March 1864 detailed as Wagon Master at Hardeeville, South Carolina. April 25, 1864 issued clothing. April 1864 detailed as Wagon Master at Savannah, Georgia. Pension records show: April 26, 1865 surrendered at Greensboro, North Carolina. May 1, 1865 paroled at Greensboro, North Carolina. He is buried in Memory Hill Cemetery at Milledgeville, Baldwin County, Georgia. (find a grave # 16232909)

EPPERLY, CALVIN: private. He enlisted as a private in the 54th Regiment, Georgia Infantry.

ESKEW, W. J.: Company H, private. He enlisted as a private in Co. H, 54th Regiment, Georgia Infantry.

ESTELL, THOMAS: Company F, private. February 2, 1863 enlisted as a private in Co. I, 5th Regiment, Georgia Cavalry. February 1863 transferred from Co. K, 5th Regiment, Georgia Cavalry to Co. F, 54th Regiment, Georgia Infantry at Savannah, Georgia. (He was a substitute for J. F. Mays.) February 2, 1863 He deserted.

ETHRIDGE, S. C.: Company F, private. January 23, 1863 enlisted as a private in Co. F, 54th Regiment, Georgia Infantry.

ETTINGER (ETTLINGER) (ELLINGER), HENRY: Company F, private. January 25, 1863 enlisted as a private in Co. F, 54th Regiment, Georgia Infantry at Savannah, Georgia and received bounty $50.00. January – February 1863 roll shows his transfer and desertion. January – February 1863 roll shows him absent sick. February 10, 1863 transferred from General Hospital No. 1 at Savannah to hospital at Macon, Georgia disease – Secy Syphilis. November 1, 1863 received pay. November – December 1863 roll shows him absent sick in General Hospital No. 1 at Savannah, Georgia. January 1864 and May 8, 1864 issued clothing. June 14, 1864 deserted. June 15, 1864 captured at Golgotha, Cobb County, Georgia (roll states he deserted). June 21, 1864 forwarded to Military Prison at Louisville, Kentucky from Nashville, Tennessee. June 22, 1864 received at Military Prison at Louisville, Kentucky and forwarded to Rock Island, Illinois. June 24, 1864 received at Rock Island Barracks, Illinois. July 6, 1864 transferred to the U. S. Navy from Rock Island Barracks, Illinois.

EVANS, JONATHAN D.: Company E, captain. May 6, 1862 enlisted in Co. E, 54th Regiment, Georgia Infantry at Savannah, Georgia, received bounty $50.00 and was elected captain. July 1862 roll shows his name at Savannah, Georgia. August, September, October, November and December 1862 rolls show him present at Beaulieu near Savannah, Georgia. November 24, 1862 his name appears on list of officers located in Savannah, Georgia. January – February 1863 roll shows him present – on special duty commanding post. March 5, 1863 received pay $130.00. April 2, 1863 received pay $130.00. April 30, 1863 received pay $130.00. October 23, 1863 his name appears on a list at Legare's Point, South Carolina of officers October 29, 1863 dropped from the rolls due to prolonged absence from duty without leave by Special Order No. 257/16. He was born July 1, 1833 and died April 10, 1911. He is buried in Ousley Baptist Church Cemetery in Lowndes County, Georgia. (find a grave # 43507417)

EVERETT, HORACE WASHINGTON: Company I, private. April 9, 1864 enlisted in Co. I, 54th Regiment, Georgia Infantry. Pension records show; April 1865 he was captured in South Carolina. He was born September 26, 1846 and died at Guyton, Effingham County, Georgia September 11, 1905. He is buried in the Springfield City Cemetery at Springfield, Effingham County, Georgia. (find a grave # 50572904)

EVERETT, J. J.: Company I, private. 1864 he enlisted in Co. I, 54th Regiment, Georgia Infantry. January 1864, April 25, 1864 and June 2, 1864 issued clothing. December 24, 1864 admitted to 20th Army of the Columbia, 1st Division Hospital with Chronic Diarrhoea at the age of 15. January 15, 1865 admitted to 20th Army of the Columbia, 2nd Division Hospital with Chronic Diarrhoea. January 19, 1865 admitted to 20th Army of the Columbia, 1st Division Hospital with Chronic Diarrhoea at Savannah, Georgia.

EVERIDGE, ANDERSON: Company H, private. November 28, 1862 enlisted as a private in Co. H, 54th Regiment, Georgia Infantry at Beaulieu near Savannah, Georgia and received bounty $50.00. December 31, 1862 received pay. January – February 1863 roll shows him present. October 31, 1863 received pay. November – December 1863 roll shows him present. December 31, 1863 received pay. January – February 1864 roll shows him present. January 1864 issued clothing.

EYLES (EYLESS), JAMES: Company G, private. May 12, 1862 enlisted as a private in Co. H, 54th Regiment, Georgia Infantry at Columbus, Georgia and received bounty $50.00. February 1, 1863 deserted. January – February 1863 roll shows he deserted.

FAGAN, ELBERT: Company A, private. August 25, 1863 enlisted as a private in Co. A, 54th Regiment, Georgia Infantry at Macon, Georgia. November – December 1863 roll shows him present sick in company hospital (pay due since enlistment). January 1864 issued clothing. January – February 1864 roll shows him present. March 31, 1864 and April 29, 1864 issued clothing. He was born November 10, 1826 and died June 19, 1889. He is buried in Oaklawn Cemetery at Fort Valley, Crawford County, Georgia. (find a grave # 74396073)

FAIN, W. B.: Company H, sergeant. He enlisted as a private in Co. H, 54th Regiment, Georgia Infantry and was elected sergeant.

FAIRCLOTH, J.: Company C, private. He enlisted as a private in Co. H, 54th Regiment, Georgia Infantry. June 18, 1863 issued clothing valued at

$11.00 at Fair Ground Hospital No. 1 at Atlanta, Georgia.

FAIRCLOTH, JOHN T.: Company C, private. May 6, 1862 enlisted as a private in Co. H, 54th Regiment, Georgia Infantry at Savannah, Georgia and received bounty $50.00. November 21, 1862 he died in Fair Grounds Hospital No. 1 at Atlanta, Georgia. He is buried in Oakland Cemetery in Atlanta, Georgia. Death benefit claim filed February 21, 1863. (Find a grave # 40657636)

FALLIGANT, PHILLIP R.: Company C, lieutenant. May 17, 1861 enlisted and appointed 1st sergeant of Chisholm's Company, Georgia State Troops. May 1862 mustered out. May 13, 1862 enlisted as a private in Co. C, 54th Regiment, Georgia Infantry at Savannah, Georgia and received bounty $50.00. May 13, 1862 he was elected 1st sergeant of Co. C, 54th Regiment, Georgia Infantry. December 31, 1862 received pay. January – February 1863 roll shows him present. He was elected Jr. 2nd lieutenant of Co. C, 54th Regiment, Georgia Infantry. November 21, 1863, December 21, 1863 issued clothing. December 7, 1863 received pay $80.00. November – December 1863 roll shows him present. He was elected 2nd lieutenant of Co. C, 54th Regiment, Georgia Infantry. January 1, 1864 received pay $80.00. January 26, 1864 issued clothing. February 1, 1864 received pay $80.00. March 15, 1864 issued clothing. June 19, 1864 wounded in the leg near Marietta, Georgia. July 2, 1864 received pay $80.00. August 25, 1864 report of Mercer's Brigade in camp near Atlanta, Georgia shows him on sick furlough by the examining board at Forsythe, Georgia since July 24, 1864. September 14, 1864 report of Mercer's Brigade in camp near Jonesboro, Georgia shows him on sick furlough by the Examining Board since August 16, 1864. He was born in 1844 and died in Louisville, Jefferson County, Georgia September 18, 1864. He is buried in Laurel Grove Cemetery at Savannah, Chatham County, Georgia. (find a grave # 67003745)

FALVEY, C.: Company A, private. November 21, 1861 enlisted as a private in Co. C, 1st Independent Battalion, Georgia State Troops. April 16, 1862 roll shows him present. April 1862 mustered out. April 18, 1863 enlisted as a private in Co. A, 54th Regiment, Georgia Infantry at Macon, Georgia. June 30, 1863 roll shows he deserted.

FARMER, D. M.: Company C, private. May 6, 1862 enlisted as a private in Co. G, 54th Regiment, Georgia Infantry at Savannah, Georgia and received bounty $50.00. January – February 1863 roll shows him absent without leave. Pension records show: April 26, 1865 surrendered at Greensboro, North Carolina. May 1, 1865 paroled at Greensboro, North Carolina. He was born in Jefferson County, Georgia in 1841.

FARMER, ISAAC V.: Company C, private. He enlisted as a private in Co. C, 54th Regiment, Georgia Infantry. He was born in 1840 and died in 1914. He is buried in Coleman's Chapel Cemetery at Wadley, Jefferson County, Georgia. (find a grave # 73554420)

FARMER, J. M. (V.): Company G (C), private. May 6, 1862 enlisted as a private in Co. G, 54th Regiment, Georgia Infantry at Columbus, Georgia and received bounty $50.00. September 1, 1862 transferred to Company C, 54th Regiment, Georgia Infantry at Beaulieu near Savannah, Georgia by Special Order No. 6. September 1862 roll indicates transfer. December 31, 1862 received pay. January – February 1863 roll shows him present (absent without leave for 9 days). January 1, 1864 received pay. January – February 1864 roll shows him absent (detached as a picket at Purysburg, South Carolina by order of Colonel Way, February 21, 1864). April 25, 1864 and May 8, 1864 issued clothing. May 18, 1865 surrendered and paroled at Augusta, Georgia.

FARMER, JOHN: Company K, private. November 15, 1862 enlisted as a private in Co. K, 54th Regiment, Georgia Infantry at Beaulieu near Savannah, Georgia and received bounty $50.00. November 1862 roll reflects his joining. January 1, 1863 received pay. January – February 1863 roll shows him present (on guard). December 31, 1863 received pay. March 18, 1864 and April 18, 1864 issued clothing. May 27, 1864 captured at Dallas, Georgia. June 5, 1864 sent from Nashville, Tennessee to Military Prison at Louisville, Kentucky. June 6, 1864 received at Military Prison at Louisville, Kentucky from Nashville, Tennessee. June 6, 1864 forwarded to Rock Island Barracks, Illinois. June 9, 1864 received at Rock Island Barracks, Illinois. February 25, 1865 transferred from Rock Island Barracks to City Point, Virginia and exchanged. March 2, 1865 admitted to Jackson Hospital at Richmond, Virginia with Debilitas. March 5, 1865 received at Boulware & Cox's Wharves, James River, Virginia.
 March 7, 1865 received pay from 3rd Division, General Hospital Camp Winder at Richmond, Virginia. March 8, 1865 furloughed for 30 days.

FARROW, GEORGE W.: Company K, private. He enlisted as a private in Co. K, 54th Regiment, Georgia Infantry.

FAULK, HENRY: Company A, private. October 17, 1861 enlisted as a private in Co. C, 1st Independent Battalion, Georgia State Troops. April 16, 1862 roll shows him present. April 1862 mustered out.
 He enlisted as a private in Co. A, 54th Regiment, Georgia Infantry. July 30, 1864 transferred to Sharpshooters by Special Order No. 259 at Savannah, Georgia. September 1864 roll at Savannah, Georgia shows his transfer.

FAULK, ROBERT JAMES: Company A, private. April 29, 1862 enlisted as a private in Co. K, 54th Regiment, Georgia Infantry at Macon, Georgia and received bounty pay $50.00. April 30, 1863 received pay. May 1, 1863 through October 31, 1863 detailed as a teamster at a rate of an additional $.25 per day. June 30, 1863 roll shows him present detailed as teamster in the company. August 1, 1863 received pay. November 1863 received commutation for rations from September 9, 1863 to September 14, 1863. October 31, 1863 received pay. November – December 1863 roll shows him present (teamster for the company). January 1, 1864 received pay. January – February 1864 roll shows him present (teamster for the company). April 29, 1864 issued clothing. He was born in 1838 and died in 1917. He is buried in Liberty Baptist Church Cemetery at Brookfield, Tift County, Georgia. (find a grave # 37275842)

FAULKNER, JAMES LUCIUS: Company E, private. May 6, 1862 enlisted as a private in Co. E, 54th Regiment, Georgia Infantry at Savannah, Georgia and received bounty $50.00. October 31, 1862 received pay. January – February 1863 roll shows him absent without leave since January 27, 1863. January 1864 issued clothing. He was born in Georgia September 2, 1837 and died in Irwin County, Georgia December 3, 1888. He is buried in the Ben Griffin Cemetery in Irwin County, Georgia. (find a grave # 71624474)

FAULKNER, WILLIAM B.: Company E, private. May 6, 1862 enlisted as a private in Co. E, 54th Regiment, Georgia Infantry at Savannah, Georgia and received bounty $50.00. December 31, 1862 received pay. January – February 1863 roll shows him present. August 21, 1863 received pay $33.00. January 1864 issued clothing.

FELTS, ROBERT LEWIS: Company A, private. May 3, 1862 enlisted as a private in Co. A, 54th Regiment, Georgia Infantry at Macon, Georgia and received bounty $50.00. October 31, 1862 received pay. January – February 1863 roll shows him present. April 30, 1863 received pay. June 30, 1863 roll shows him present. January 1, 1864 received pay. January – February 1864 roll shows him present. March 31, 1864 and April 29, 1864 issued clothing. May 20, 1865 surrendered and paroled at Montgomery, Alabama. He is described on his parole: 6 feet 1 inch high, dark hair, hazel eyes and fair complexion. He was born in Putnam County, Georgia August 26, 1841 and died November 28, 1898. He is buried in the Hudson/Felts Cemetery at Gray, Jones County, Georgia. (find a grave # 96346123)

FELVER, GEORGE W.: Company I, corporal. May 6, 1862 enlisted as a private in Co. I, 54th Regiment, Georgia Infantry at Savannah, Georgia and received bounty $50.00. October 16, 1862 discharged. October 1862 roll shows his discharge.

FELZER,___: Company H, corporal. May 12, 1862 enlisted as a private in Co. H, 54th Regiment, Georgia Infantry. He was appointed corporal. October 31, 1862 he was discharged.

FENNELL, G. T.: Company A, private. June 19, 1863 enlisted as a private in Co. A, 54th Regiment, Georgia Infantry at Savannah, Georgia and received bounty $50.00. June 30, 1863 roll shows him present. October 31, 1863 received pay. January – February 1863 roll shows him present. January 1, 1864 received pay. January – February 1864 roll shows him present.

FERRELL, P. H.: Company C (D), private. November 28, 1862 enlisted as a private in Co, E, 63rd Regiment, Georgia Infantry. January 1, 1863 transferred and enlisted as a private in Co. C, 54th Regiment, Georgia Infantry at Savannah, Georgia and received bounty $50.00. January – February 1863 roll shows him present. June 10, 1863 detailed as clerk for Ordinance Department on James Island, South Carolina by Colonel Way. October 31, 1863 roll of detailed men on James Island, South Carolina shows him present. January 1, 1864 received pay. January – February

1864 roll shows him absent (detached as regimental Commissary by order of Colonel Way on July 11, 1863). January 1, 1864 to February 29, 1864 detailed on extra duty as a laborer in Savannah, Georgia. March 1, 1864 to March 31, 1864 detailed at Hardeeville, South Carolina as acting commissary sergeant. April 25, 1864 issued clothing. April 1, 1864 to April 30, 1864 detailed at Savannah, Georgia as acting commissary sergeant. April 26, 1865 surrendered in Co. D, 54th Regiment, Georgia Infantry at Greensboro, North Carolina. May 1, 1865 paroled at Greensboro, North Carolina.

FERRILL, FRANCIS S.: Company F, private. May 17, 1861 enlisted as a private in Chisholm's Company, Georgia State Troops. May 1862 mustered out. May 13, 1862 enlisted as a private in Co. F, 54th Regiment, Georgia Infantry at Savannah, Georgia and received bounty $50.00. September and October 1862 roll shows him as Quartermaster's clerk. September 1, 1862 to October 31, 1862 detailed on extra duty as Quarter Masters Clerk at Beaulieu near Savannah, Georgia at a rate of an additional $.25 per day. October 31, 1862 received pay. December 6, 1862 received pay $22.00. December 31, 1862 received pay $22.00 plus $18.60 commutation of rations. January – February 1863 roll shows him absent detailed in the Quartermasters Department. February 28, 1863 received pay $22.00. March 18, 1863 to August 31, 1863 detailed to the Signal and Telegraph Service, paid an additional $3.00 per day and paid commutation for rations. July 1, 1863 received commutations for rations at Savannah, Georgia for the months of March and April 1863. April 1, 1863 to October 31, 1863 detailed to the Signal and Telegraph Service at Savannah, Georgia paid an additional $3.00 per day. September 4, 1863 received pay $22.00 plus $228.00 for extra duty. November 23, 1863 issued clothing. December 1, 1863 to December 31, 1863 detailed to the Signal and Telegraph Service at Savannah, Georgia. November – December 1863 roll shows him absent detailed in the Signal Corps since May 19, 1863. January 1864 issued clothing. January 1, 1864 to August 31, 1864 detailed to the Signal and Telegraph Service at Savannah, Georgia. June 30, 1864 received pay. October 31, 1864 roll of Signal Corps in Savannah.

FETZER, GEORGE WASHINGTON: Company I, private. September 18, 1861 enlisted as a private and appointed 1st corporal in Co. C, 1st Regiment, 1st Brigade, Georgia State Troops. March 18, 1862 mustered out. May 6, 1862 enlisted in Co. I, 54th Regiment, Georgia Infantry. He was appointed corporal. October 15, 1865 he was discharged at Beaulieu near Savannah, Georgia. November 7, 1862 enlisted as a private in Co. I, 5th Regiment, Georgia Cavalry. April 26, 1865 surrendered at Hillsboro, North Carolina. He was born in Georgia December 29, 1844 and died May 17, 1930. He is buried in Zion Lutheran Church Cemetery at Guyton, Effingham County, Georgia. (find a grave # 51401238)

FIELDS, JAMES J.: Company C, private. December 11, 1861 enlisted as a private in Co. B, 8th Regiment, Georgia State Troops. He mustered out in 1862. April 22, 1862 enlisted as a private in Co. C, 54th Regiment, Georgia Infantry at Savannah, Georgia and received bounty $50.00. December 31, 1862 received pay. January – February 1863 roll shows him present. September 7, 1863 received pay $44.00. January 1, 1864 received pay. January – February 1864 roll shows him present. July 15 through 25, 1864 his name appears on a roll of Floyd House Hospital at Macon, Georgia with a Gunshot Wound (over centre of frontis). May 18, 1865 surrendered and paroled at Augusta, Georgia. He was a resident of Burton, Georgia.

FINNEY, SAMUEL B.: Company A, private. June 13, 1863 enlisted as a private in Co. A, 54th Regiment, Georgia Infantry at Savannah, Georgia and received bounty $50.00. June 30, 1863 roll shows him present. October 31, 1863 received pay. November – December 1863 roll shows him present. January 1, 1864 received pay. January – February 1864 roll shows him present. March 31, 1864 issued clothing. June 18, 1864 wounded near Marietta, Georgia. September 22, 1864 admitted to Ocmulgee Hospital at Macon, Georgia with a gunshot wound (fracture of left tibia – mini ball). October 22, 1864 returned to duty. December 20, 1864 captured at Stones River, Tennessee. January 4, 1865 sent from Nashville, Tennessee to Military Prison at Louisville, Kentucky. January 5, 1865 arrived at Military Prison at Louisville, Kentucky. January 9, 1865 sent to Camp Chase, Ohio. January 11, 1865 arrived at Camp Chase, Ohio. February 16, 1865 died of pneumonia in the Hospital at Camp Chase, Ohio. He was a resident of Jones County, Georgia. He was born in Georgia December 4, 1823 and died at Camp Chase Ohio February 16, 1865. He is buried at Camp Chase, Ohio in grave No. 1297 (1/3 mile south of Camp Chase). (find a grave # 46628512)

FLAKE, R. W.: Company F, private. May 6, 1862 enlisted as a private in Co. F, 54th Regiment, Georgia Infantry at Savannah, Georgia and received bounty $50.00. November 4, 1862 discharged at Beaulieu near Savannah, Georgia. November 1862 roll reflects his discharge.

FLEMING, W. D.: Company C, private. He enlisted as a private in Co. C, 54th Regiment, Georgia Infantry.

FLETCHER, W. W.: private. He enlisted as a private in the 54th Regiment, Georgia Infantry.
May 10, 1865 surrendered at Tallahassee, Florida. May 21, 1865 paroled at Thomasville, Georgia.

FLINN, THOMAS: Company A, private. May 5, 1863 enlisted as a private in Co. A, 54th Regiment, Georgia Infantry at Savannah, Georgia and received bounty $50.00. June 30, 1863 roll shows he was a substitute for W. F. Brown and he deserted.

FLOWERS, WILLIAM R.: Company A, private. October 17, 1861 enlisted as a private in Co. C, 1st Independent Battalion, Georgia State Troops. April 16, 1862 roll shows him present. April 1862 mustered out. April 29, 1862 enlisted as a private in Co. A, 54th Regiment, Georgia Infantry at Macon, Georgia and received bounty $50.00. April 30, 1863 received pay. June 30, 1863 roll shows him present. October 31, 1863 received pay. November – December 1863 roll shows him present. January 1, 1864 received pay. January – February 1864 roll shows him present. April 29, 1864 and May 8, 1864 issued clothing. April 21-22, 1865 captured at Macon, Georgia. He was born in Alabama in 1844 and died April 27, 1908. He is buried in Jones Chapel Cemetery at Macon, Bibb County, Georgia.

FLOYD, STEPHEN: Company B, corporal. October 10, 1861 enlisted as a private in Co. K, 2nd Regiment, 1st Brigade, Georgia State Troops. April 1862 mustered out. April 21, 1862 enlisted as a private in Co. B, 54th Regiment, Georgia Infantry at Savannah, Georgia and received bounty $50.00. December 31, 1862 received pay. January – February 1863 roll shows him present. September 7, 1863 received pay $44.00. January 1864, April 25, 1864 and May 8, 1864 issued clothing. He was elected corporal in Co. B, 54th Regiment, Georgia Infantry. December 20, 1864 received pay $26.00. May 10, 1865 surrendered at Tallahassee, Florida. May 21, 1865 paroled at Thomasville, Georgia.

FOLKS, WILLIAM J.: Company C, lieutenant. May 5, 1862 signed up for service in Jefferson County, Georgia. May 6, 1862 enlisted as a private in Co. C, 54th Regiment, Georgia Infantry at Savannah, Georgia and received bounty $50.00. December 31, 1862 received pay. January – February 1863 roll shows him present (absent without leave 1 day). February 23, 1864 Major Mann established him as his courier. January 1, 1864 received pay. January – February 1864 roll shows him present (established as Major Mann's courier). He was elected 2nd lieutenant of Co. C, 54th Regiment, Georgia Infantry. April 25, 1864 and April 28, 1864 issued clothing. May 18, 1865 surrendered and paroled at Augusta, Georgia. He was a resident of Jefferson County, Georgia. He was born in Jefferson County, Georgia in 1827 and died in 1903. He is buried in Coleman Chapel Cemetery at Wadley, Jefferson County, Georgia. (find a grave # 73554488)

FOLLENDORE (FOLLENDER), CHARLES: Company A, private. January 23, 1864 enlisted as a private in Co. A, 54th Regiment, Georgia Infantry at Savannah, Georgia and received bounty $50.00. January – February 1864 roll shows him present. March 31, 1864 and April 29, 1864 issued clothing. April 20-21, 1865 captured in Macon, Georgia. He was born in the Rutland District, Bibb County, Georgia June 1846 and died in Bibb County, Georgia January 14, 1930. He is buried in New Elm Baptist Church Cemetery at Macon, Bibb County, Georgia. (find a grave # 51359627)

FOLLENDORE (FOLLENDERE), JOSEPH: Company A, private. November 22, 1862 enlisted as a private in Co. A, 54th Regiment, Georgia Infantry at Macon, Georgia. November 1862 roll shows his enlistment. April 30, 1863 received pay. June 30, 1863 roll shows him present. June 30, 1863 received pay. July 1, 1863 received pay. November – December 1863 roll shows him absent sick since November 26, 1863. January – February

1864 roll shows him present. May 4, 1864 admitted to Ocmulgee hospital at Macon, Georgia with a Double Hernia. November 12, 1864 deserted from the hospital. February 13, 1865 admitted to Ocmulgee Hospital at Macon, Georgia. February 20, 1865 register of Floyd House Hospital at Macon, Georgia shows him as a patient with Double Reducible Inguinal hernia also Injury of the Back caused by lifting siege artillery. February 21, 1865 furloughed. He was a resident of Bibb County. He was born in Baden-Wurttemberg, Germany and died in the Rutland District, Bibb County, Georgia August 2, 1882. He is buried in New Elm Baptist Church Cemetery at Macon, Bibb County, Georgia. (find a grave # 24102274)

FORBES, LEMUEL RHODES: Company B, private. June 9, 1862 enlisted as a private in Co. B, 54th Regiment, Georgia Infantry at Savannah, Georgia and received bounty $50.00. June 9, 1862 appointed Commissary clerk (sergeant) at Beaulieu near Savannah, Georgia at a rate of an additional $.25 per day. July, August, September, October, November and December 1862 rolls show him as Commissary clerk (sergeant). December 31, 1862 received pay. January – February 1863 roll shows him present detailed as Commissary Clerk (sergeant). January 1, 1863 to April 30, 1863 detailed as commissary clerk. February 26, 1863 and March 12, 1863 received pay for January 1863 and February 1863 as Commissary Clerk. April and May 1863 received pay. He was born August 21, 1821 and died in Henry County, Georgia June 5, 1906. He is buried in Snapping Shoals Cemetery in Henry County, Georgia. (find a grave # 31953409)

FORD, JAMES D. G.: Company G, private. He enlisted as a private in Co. G, 54th Regiment, Georgia Infantry.

FORD, LEONIDAS ALEXANDER: Company F (A), private. Company A, private. May 2, 1862 enlisted as a private in Co. F, 54th Regiment, Georgia Infantry at Macon, Georgia. May 10, 1862 received bounty $50.00. September 1862 transferred from Co. F, 54th Regiment, Georgia Infantry to Co A, 54th Regiment, Georgia Infantry by Special Order No. 6. September 1862 roll shows the transfer. April 30, 1863 received pay. June 30, 1863 roll shows him present. October 31, 1863 received pay. November – December 1863 roll shows him present. January 1, 1864 received pay. January – February 1864 roll shows him present. April 29, 1864, May 8, 1864, May 25, 1864 and May 26, 1864 issued clothing. He was wounded in the left hip (date and place unknown). April 26, 1865 surrendered as a member of Co. D, 54th Regiment, Georgia Infantry at Greensboro, North Carolina. May 1, 1865 paroled at Greensboro, North Carolina. He was born in Monroe County, Georgia January 18, 1840 died in Cherokee County, Georgia January 29, 1919.

FOREHAND, JOHN A.: Company D, private. October 14, 1861 enlisted as a private in Co. I, 5th Regiment, Georgia State Troops. April 1862 mustered out. April 30, 1862 enlisted as a private in Co. D, 54th Regiment, Georgia Infantry at Savannah, Georgia and received bounty $50.00. September 10, 1862 discharged at Beaulieu near Savannah, Georgia. September 1862 roll reflects his discharge.

FOREHAND, WILLIAM ROAN: Company D, private. November 28, 1862 enlisted as a private in Co. D, 54th Regiment, Georgia Infantry at Beaulieu near Savannah, Georgia and received bounty $50.00. December 1862 roll indicates he joined on November 28, 1862. December 31, 1862 received pay. January – February 1863 roll shows him present. (August 29, 1863 to September 3, 1863) killed at Battery Wagner on Morris Island, South Carolina.

FOUNTAIN, JAMES M.: Company A, private. December 8, 1863 enlisted as a private in Co. A, 54th Regiment, Georgia Infantry at Savannah, Georgia and received bounty $50.00. November – December 1863 roll shows him present. January 1, 1864 received pay. January – February 1864 roll shows him present. April 26, 1865 surrendered as a member of Co. D, 54th Regiment, Georgia Infantry at Greensboro, North Carolina. May 1, 1865 paroled at Greensboro, North Carolina. He was born in Georgia December 9, 1845 and died March 26, 1923. He is buried in Snow Hill Cemetery at Ivey, Wilkinson County, Georgia. (find a grave # 15675963)

FOUNTAIN, WILLIAM T.: Company A, private. June 19, 1863 enlisted as a private in Co. A, 54th Regiment, Georgia Infantry at Savannah, Georgia and received bounty $50.00. June 30, 1863 roll shows him present. October 31, 1863 received pay. November – December 1863 roll shows him present (sick in company hospital). January 1, 1864 received pay. January – February 1864 roll shows him present. March 31, 1864 issued clothing. April 3, 1865 an extension of furlough was granted by medical examining board in Macon, Georgia. He was a resident of Wilkinson County, Georgia. He was born February 22, 1823 and died June 8, 1881. He is buried in Snow Hill Cemetery at Ivey, Wilkinson County, Georgia. (find a grave # 15688958)

FOX, FRANK J., JR.: Company F, private. May 17, 1861 enlisted as a private in Chisholm's Company, Georgia State Troops. May 1862 mustered out. May 13, 1862 enlisted as a private in Co. F, 54th Regiment, Georgia Infantry at Savannah, Georgia and received bounty $50.00. November 14, 1862 discharged by Civil Authority. November 1862 roll reflects his discharge.

FOY, E. C.: Company I, private. He enlisted as a private in Co. I, 54th Regiment, Georgia Infantry.

FOY, EDWARD E.: Company I, sergeant. September 18, 1861 enlisted as a private and appointed 4th sergeant in Co. C, 1st Regiment, 1st Brigade, Georgia State Troops. March 18, 1862 mustered out. May 6, 1862 enlisted as 4th sergeant in Co. I, 54th Regiment, Georgia Infantry at Guyton, Georgia and received bounty $50.00. December 31, 1862 received pay. January – February 1863 roll shows him present (camp guard). He was elected 3rd sergeant in Co. I, 54th Regiment, Georgia Infantry. October 31, 1863 received pay. November – December 1863 roll shows him present. January 1864, April 25, 1864 and June 2, 1864 issued clothing. July 22, 1864 he is shown in Atlanta, Georgia hospital (may have been wounded that day). He was in the hospital at Fort Valley, Georgia until the close of the war. He was born May 2, 1842 and died May 3, 1907. He is buried in Elam-Egypt Baptist Church Cemetery at Egypt, Effingham County, Georgia. (find a grave # 61905035)

FREEBORN, A.: Company F, private. He enlisted as a private in Co. F, 54th Regiment, Georgia Infantry. October 22, 1862 discharged at Beaulieu near Savannah, Georgia. October 1862 roll reflects his discharge.

FREEBORN, JAMES: Company F, private. May 17, 1861 enlisted as a private in Chisholm's Company, Georgia State Troops. May 1862 mustered out. May 17, 1862 enlisted as a private in Co. F, 54th Regiment, Georgia Infantry. May 18, 1864 transferred to Co. F, 22nd Battalion, Georgia Heavy Artillery. June 3, 1864 transferred to Captain Wheaton's Company, Chatham Siege Artillery. February 28, 1865 roll shows him present.

FREEMAN, HENRY: Company H, private. He enlisted as a private in Co. H, 54th Regiment, Georgia Infantry.

FREEMAN, HENRY: Field Staff, musician. May 10, 1862 enlisted as a private in Co. F, 54th Regiment, Georgia Infantry at Macon. January 29, 1863 transferred to Field and Staff by order of Colonel Way. January 1, 1863 received pay. January 29, 1863 he transferred to the regimental band. January – February 1863 roll shows him transferred to field and staff. January – February 1863 roll of Field, Staff and Band shows him present. July 1, 1863 received pay $50.00 (bounty).

FREEMAN, JOHN WESLEY: Company D, private. January 27, 1863 enlisted as a private in Co. D, 54th Regiment, Georgia Infantry at Beaulieu near Savannah, Georgia and received bounty $50.00. December 31, 1862 received pay. January – February 1863 roll shows him present (on picket). January 1864 and May 8, 1864 issued clothing. May 18, 1865 surrendered and paroled at Augusta, Georgia. He is described on parole: 5 feet 8 inches high, light hair, blue eyes and light complexion. Pension records show he was at home quarantined; family had Small Pox on sick furlough at the close of the war. He was born in Georgia September 15, 1844 and died September 10, 1927. He is buried in Little Horse Creek Cemetery at Rocky Ford, Screven County, Georgia. (find a grave # 52164573)

FREEMAN, WILLIAM RANDALL (RANDOLPH): Company D, private. April 30, 1862 enlisted as a private in Co. D, 54th Regiment, Georgia Infantry at Savannah, Georgia and received bounty $50.00. December 31, 1862 received pay. January – February 1863 roll shows him present. January 1864 issued clothing. He was in the hospital at Savannah, Georgia at the close of the war. May 18, 1865 surrendered and paroled at Augusta, Georgia. He was born November 16, 1837 and died December 13, 1919. He is buried in Sylvania Cemetery at Sylvania, Screven County, Georgia. (find a grave # 32278164)

FREENY, THOMAS: Company A, private. He enlisted in as a private in Co. A, 54th Regiment, Georgia Infantry.

FULLER, J. D.: Company A, private. He enlisted in as a private in Co.

A, 54th Regiment, Georgia Infantry.

FULSON, J. M.: Company E, private. He enlisted as a private in Co. E, 54th Regiment, Georgia Infantry.

FUTCH, ELI A.: Company E, private. May 6, 1862 enlisted as a private in Co. E, 54th Regiment, Georgia Infantry at Savannah, Georgia and received bounty $50.00. June 30, 1862 received pay. January – February 1863 roll shows him present. January 1864 and April 25, 1864 issued clothing. Pension records show he "served until the war closed". He was born in Lowndes County, Georgia March 19, 1840 and died July 18, 1913. He is buried in Futch Cemetery in Cook County, Georgia. (Find a grave # 49756128).

FUTCH, MALCOLM C.: Company E, private. May 6, 1862 enlisted as a private in Co. E, 54th Regiment, Georgia Infantry at Savannah, Georgia and received bounty $50.00. December 31, 1862 received pay. January – February 1863 roll shows him present. January 1864 and June 2, 1864 issued clothing. He was born in Lowndes County, Georgia August 20, 1835 and died October 23, 1919. He is buried in Hard Scramble Cemetery in Clinch County, Georgia. (find a grave # 33305487)

FUTCH, THOMAS DUGGER: Company E, private. May 6, 1862 enlisted as a private in Co. E, 54th Regiment, Georgia Infantry at Savannah, Georgia and received bounty $50.00. December 31, 1862 received pay. January – February 1863 roll shows him present. January 1864 and April 25, 1864 issued clothing. He was born in Lowndes County, Georgia April 5, 1833 and died in Berrien County, Georgia March 18, 1901. He is buried in Futch Cemetery in Cook County, Georgia. (Find a grave # 47712323)

FUTRELLE, ABRAHAM JOINER: Company I, private. September 18, 1861 enlisted as a private in Co. C, 1st Regiment, 1st Brigade, Georgia State Troops. March 18, 1862 mustered out. May 6, 1862 enlisted as a private in Co. I, 54th Regiment, Georgia Infantry at Savannah, Georgia and received bounty $50.00. December 31, 1862 received pay. January – February 1863 roll shows him present (sick in the regimental hospital). October 31, 1863 received pay. November – December 1863 roll shows him present (boat hand). January 1864 and June 2, 1864 issued clothing. He was born February 5, 1842 and died September 9, 1920. He is buried in Guyton Cemetery at Guyton, Effingham County, Georgia. (find a grave # 54158182)

FUTRELL, MICAJAH BENJAMIN: Company I, corporal. September 18, 1861 enlisted as a private in Co. C, 1st Regiment, 1st Brigade, Georgia State Troops. March 18, 1862 mustered out. May 6, 1862 enlisted as 2nd corporal in Co. I, 54th Regiment, Georgia Infantry at Savannah, Georgia and received bounty $50.00. December 31, 1862 received pay. January – February 1863 roll shows him present. October 31, 1863 received pay. November 15, 1863 appointed 1st corporal in Co. I, 54th Regiment, Georgia Infantry. November – December 1863 roll shows him present. January 1864 and June 2, 1864 issued clothing. June 24, 1864 issued clothing at Cannon Hospital at LaGrange, Georgia. Pension records show; February 4, 1865 he was furloughed for 60 days. He was born in Effingham County, Georgia April 29, 1839 and died in Effingham County, Georgia October 20, 1924. He is buried in Guyton Cemetery at Guyton, Effingham County, Georgia. (find a grave # 51566319)

GAFFNEY, JOHN: Company A, private. October 17, 1861 enlisted as a private in Co. C, 1st Independent Battalion, Georgia State Troops. April 16, 1862 roll shows him present. April 1862 mustered out. April 23, 1862 enlisted as a private in Co. A, 54th Regiment, Georgia Infantry at Savannah, Georgia and received bounty $50.00. September 1862 roll shows him as the Captain's orderly. October 1862 roll shows him as the captain's cook. April 30, 1863 received pay. June 30, 1863 roll shows him present. August 31, 1863 received pay. November 1863 received commutation for rations pay. November – December 1863 roll shows him present. January 1, 1864 received pay. January – February 1864 roll shows him present. March 31, 1864 and May 8, 1864 issued clothing. January 17, 1865 admitted to Way Hospital at Meridian, Mississippi with Debility.

GAINES, T. M.: Company C, lieutenant. He enlisted as 2nd lieutenant in Co. A, 54th Regiment, Georgia Infantry.

GAINES, W. M.: Company C, private. He enlisted as a private in Co. C, 54th Regiment, Georgia Infantry.

GALLIGANT, PHILLIP R.: Company F, private. He enlisted in Co. F, 54th Regiment, Georgia Infantry.

GANANN, GEORGE M.: Company I, sergeant. September 18, 1861 enlisted as a private and appointed 3rd sergeant in Co. C, 1st Regiment, 1st Brigade, Georgia State Troops. March 18, 1862 mustered out. May 6, 1862 enlisted as a private in Co. I, 54th Regiment, Georgia Infantry at Guyton, Georgia and received bounty $50.00. December 31, 1862 received pay. January – February 1863 roll shows him present. He was appointed 3rd sergeant of Co. I, 54th Regiment, Georgia Infantry. April 30, 1863 received pay. November 12, 1863 reduced from rank of 3rd sergeant and appointed sub Enrolling Officer. November – December 1863 roll shows his reduction in rank. January 1864 issued clothing. He was born October 13, 1832 and died August 8, 1892. He is buried in Scarboro Cemetery in Jenkins County, Georgia. (find a grave # 65631705)

GANANN, J. H.: Company B, private. June 3, 1863 received pay $24.20.

GANANN, JOSEPH HANIN: Company I, lieutenant. May 21, 1861 enlisted as a private in Co. B, 8th Regiment, Georgia State Troops. He mustered out in 1862. May 6, 1863 enlisted as a private in Co. I, 54th Regiment, Georgia Infantry at Beaulieu near Savannah, Georgia and received bounty $50.00. March 7, 1863 elected 2nd lieutenant in Co. I, 54th Regiment, Georgia Infantry. April 2, 1863 received pay $66.66. August 17, 1863 granted a leave of absence by General Mercer. September 18, 1863 detailed to recruiting service. September 21, 1863 to October 1, 1863 he was on recruiting service. December 19, 1863 received pay $90.00. November – December 1863 roll shows him acting adjutant for the post. January 5, 1864 received pay $90.00. February 1, 1864 received pay $90.00. March 12, 1864 received pay. March 14, 1864 issued clothing. June 7, 1864 received pay $80.00. July 2, 1864 received pay $80.00. July 22, 1864 killed at Atlanta, Georgia. He died July 22, 1864 and is memorialized in Effingham County Veterans Park in Springfield, Effingham County, Georgia. (find a grave # 42393168)

GARLAND, JOHN N.: Company A, private. He enlisted as a private in Co. A, 54th Regiment, Georgia Infantry. He is buried in the Garland Cemetery in Jones County, Georgia. (find a grave # 112851539)

GARLAND, JAMES W.: Company A, private. February 25, 1863 enlisted as a private in Co. A, 54th Regiment, Georgia Infantry at Savannah, Georgia and received bounty $50.00. April 30, 1863 received pay. June 20, 1863 to June 27, 1863 absent without leave in arrest. June 30, 1863 roll shows him present. June 30, 1863 received pay. August 1, 1863 received pay. November 26, 1863 admitted to Floyd House and Ocmulgee Hospitals at Macon, Georgia with Ulcus (Stationed at Charleston, South Carolina). November – December 1863 roll shows him absent sick in hospital at Savannah, Georgia. January 15, 1864 granted a 30 day furlough from Floyd House and Ocmulgee Hospitals at Macon, Georgia. January – February 1864 roll shows him absent sick in hospital at Macon, Georgia since November 26, 1863. April 28, 1864 admitted to Ocmulgee Hospital at Macon, Georgia with Ulcus Chronic. May 16, 1864 transferred from Ocmulgee Hospital at Macon, Georgia. Pension records shows he was detailed with Siege Artillery. He was born in Hancock County, Georgia March 3, 1827 and died May 10, 1912. He is buried in Mount Hope Church Cemetery at Shoulderbone, Hancock County, Georgia. (find a grave # 19358300)

GASKINS, WILLIAM: Company E, private. May 6, 1862 enlisted as a private in Co. E, 54th Regiment, Georgia Infantry at Guyton, Georgia and received bounty $50.00. December 31, 1862 received pay. January – February 1863 roll shows him present. August 23 – 30, 1863 wounded in the head at Battery Wagner on Morris Island near Charleston, South Carolina. January 1864 and May 8, 1864 issued clothing. May 16, 1865 paroled at Thomasville, Georgia. He is described on his parole as: 5 feet 5 inches high, black hair, blue eyes and dark complexion. He was born March 5, 1833 and died August 27, 1910. He is buried in the Empire Primitive Baptist Church Cemetery at Lakeland, Lanier County, Georgia. (find a grave # 38845639)

GATELEY, PATRICK: Company D, private. April 30, 1862 enlisted as a private in Co. D, 54th Regiment, Georgia Infantry. August 1, 1862 transferred to the Sharpshooters by Special Order No. 259. August 1862 roll shows his transfer. He was born in County Galway, Ireland in 1821 and died in Savannah, Chatham County, Georgia December 17, 1886. He is buried in Catholic Cemetery at Savannah, Chatham County, Georgia. (find a grave # 131475640)

GATLIN, JAMES W.: Company G, private. He enlisted as a private in

Co. G, 54th Regiment, Georgia Infantry.

GAVIN (GAVAN), WILLIAM S.: Company F (D), private. May 17, 1861 enlisted as a private in Chisholm's Company, Georgia State Troops. May 1862 mustered out. May 6, 1862 enlisted as a private in Co. F, 54th Regiment, Georgia Infantry at Savannah, Georgia and received bounty $50.00. October 1862 roll shows him company cook. December 31, 1862 received pay. January – February 1863 roll shows him present. He was captured at Jackson, Mississippi in 1863 and paroled. November 1, 1863 received pay $90.00. November – December 1863 roll shows him absent on picket at Little Ogeechee Bridge. January 1864 issued clothing. April 26, 1865 surrendered in Co. D, 54th Regiment, Georgia Infantry at Greensboro, North Carolina. May 1, 1865 paroled at Greensboro, North Carolina.

GEORGE P. D.: Company I, private. He enlisted as a private in Co. I, 54th Regiment, Georgia Infantry. August 1862 transferred (command unknown). August 1862 roll shows his transfer.

GEORGES, W.: Company G, private. December 24, 1862 enlisted as a private in Co. G, 54th Regiment, Georgia Infantry. December 1862 roll shows his enlistment.

GERMAN, W. T.: Company C (H), private. May 6, 1862 enlisted as a private in Co. C, 54th Regiment, Georgia Infantry at Savannah, Georgia and received bounty $50.00. He transferred from Co. C, 54th Regiment, Georgia Infantry to Company H, 54th Regiment, Georgia Infantry.

GIBSON, JOSHUA C.: Company G, corporal. He enlisted as a corporal in Co. G, 54th Regiment, Georgia Infantry.

GILES, D. J.: Company A, private. He enlisted as a private in Co. A, 54th Regiment, Georgia Infantry.

GILL, J. J.: Company A, private. March 4, 1862 enlisted as a private in Co. I, 44th Regiment, Georgia Infantry. 1864 transferred to Co. A, 54th Regiment, Georgia Infantry. Pension records show: April 26, 1865 surrendered at Greensboro, North Carolina. May 1, 1865 paroled at Greensboro, North Carolina.
He was born in Meriwether County, Georgia.

GILL, W. J.: Company K, corporal. He enlisted as a corporal in Co. K, 54th Regiment, Georgia Infantry.

GLAZE, A. N.: Company K, lieutenant. He enlisted as a 2nd lieutenant in Co. K, 54th Regiment, Georgia Infantry.

GLISSON, WILLIAM W.: Company C, private. September 25, 1863 enlisted as a private in Co. C, 54th Regiment, Georgia Infantry at Savannah, Georgia and received bounty $50.00. January 1, 1864 issued clothing. April 25, 1864 issued clothing. May 8, 1864 issued clothing. May 21, 1864 admitted to Ocmulgee Hospital with a Gunshot Wound. June 6, 1864 report of Floyd House and Ocmulgee Hospital at Macon, Georgia shows he had severe wound of the left buttock involving extensively the muscles of that region. June 7, 1864 furloughed for 60 days to Burke County. He was a resident of Burke County, Georgia.

GLOER, J. A.: Company I, lieutenant. He enlisted as a 2nd lieutenant in Co. I, 54th Regiment, Georgia Infantry.

GLOBLE, WILLIAM D.: Company G, private. He enlisted as a private in Co. G, 54th Regiment, Georgia Infantry.

GODFREY, JAMES ERWIN, JR: Field Staff, Surgeon. April 27, 1861 appointed surgeon for the C. S. A. May 4 (10), 1862 appointed surgeon of the 54th Regiment, Georgia Infantry at Beaulieu near Savannah, Georgia. July 1862 roll shows his name. August 22, 1862 he is shown as serving as surgeon in the 54th Regiment, Georgia infantry. August, September, October, November and December 1862 rolls show him present at Beaulieu near Savannah, Georgia. October 21, 1862 roll at Legare's Point near Charleston, South Carolina shows him present. January – February 1863 roll shows him present. March 1863 received pay $162.00. November 24, 1863 roll at Savannah, Georgia shows him present. August 22 and 27, 1864 report from 54th Georgia Hospital at Red Bluff, South Carolina shows him as the Medical Officer. He was born in South Carolina. January 17, 1865 served as Senior Surgeon of Smith Brigade. April 26, 1865 surrendered at Greensboro, North Carolina. May 1, 1865 paroled at Greensboro, North Carolina.

GODFREY, JAMES ERWIN, SR: Field Staff, Chaplin. May 10, 1862 he was appointed Chaplin of the 54th Regiment, Georgia Infantry at Beaulieu near Savannah, Georgia. July 1862 roll shows his name. August, September, October, November and December 1862 rolls show him present at Beaulieu near Savannah, Georgia. November 24, 1862 roll at Savannah, Georgia show his name. November 19, 1862 He resigned his commission due to disability. He was born in South Carolina.

GODFREY, NICKERSON: Field and Staff, cook. December 31, 1862 received pay. January – February 1863 roll shows him present employed as a cook.

GOENS, BOSWELL: Company G, private. December 20, 1862 enlisted as a private in Co. G, 54th Regiment, Georgia Infantry at Savannah, Georgia and received bounty $50.00. December 31, 1862 received pay. January – February 1863 roll shows him present. August 20, 1863 received pay $33.00. January 1864 and April 25, 1864 issued clothing. June 27, 1864 wounded at Kennesaw Mountain, Georgia. July 14, 1864 died at Flewellen Hospital at Barnesville, Georgia. He is buried in Greenwood Cemetery at Barnesville, Lamar County, Georgia. (find a grave # 75069883)

GOGGANS, J. M.: Company B, private. He enlisted as a private in Co. B, 54th Regiment, Georgia Infantry.

GOINS, DAVID F.: Company F, private. September 10, 1861 enlisted as a private in Co. A, 60th Regiment, Georgia Infantry. He was discharged due to disability. February 19, 1863 enlisted as a private in Co. F, 54th Regiment, Georgia Infantry at Savannah, Georgia and received bounty $50.00. January – February 1863 roll shows him present. October 1, 1863 to December 31, 1863 detailed as a teamster at a rate of $.25 extra per day. November 1, 1863 received pay. November – December 1863 roll shows him absent detailed as post teamster (driving a 4 mule wagon). January 1864 issued clothing. January 1, 1864 appears on roll of Floyd House and Ocmulgee Hospital at Macon, Georgia as having furlough extended for 30 days. April 30, 1865 captured at Macon, Georgia. He died in Columbus, Georgia August 5, 1895.

GOODMAN, JASPER: Company H, private. May 12, 1862 enlisted as a private in Co. H, 54th Regiment, Georgia Infantry.

GOODMAN, JOSEPH G.: Company H, private. January 27, 1863 enlisted as a private in Co. H, 54th Regiment, Georgia Infantry at Columbus, Georgia and received bounty $50.00. January – February 1863 roll shows him present. October 31, 1863 received pay. November – December 1863 roll shows him present. December 31, 1863 issued clothing. January – February 1864 roll shows him present. January 1864 and June 2, 1864 issued clothing. July 22, 1864 captured in the Battle of Atlanta, Georgia. July 29, 1864 sent from Nashville, Tennessee to Military Prison at Louisville, Kentucky. July 30, 1864 arrived at military Prison at Louisville, Kentucky and was sent to Camp Chase, Ohio. August 1, 1864 arrived at Camp Chase, Ohio. March 1865 sent to City Point, Virginia for exchange. March 10-12, 1865 received at Boulware & Cox's Wharves, James River, Virginia. March 12, 1865 admitted to Receiving and Wayside Hospital or General Hospital No. 9 at Richmond, Virginia and transferred to Jackson Hospital at Richmond, Virginia. March 13, 1865 admitted to Jackson Hospital at Richmond, Virginia with Pneumonia. March 14, 1865 transferred to Camp Lee. He was born in Mitchell County, Georgia September 2, 1843.

GOODWIN, THOMAS W.: Company C, sergeant. December 11, 1861 enlisted as a private in Co. B, 8th Regiment, Georgia State Troops. He mustered out in 1862. April 22, 1862 enlisted as 2nd sergeant in Co. C, 54th Regiment, Georgia Infantry at Savannah, Georgia and received bounty $50.00. December 31, 1862 received pay. January – February 1863 roll shows him absent on special duty. May 26, 1863 transferred to Co. K, 28th Regiment, Georgia Infantry Special Order No. 125/12. April 26, 1865 surrendered at Greensboro, North Carolina. May 1, 1865 paroled at Greensboro, North Carolina.

GORDON, J. F.: Company B, private. He enlisted as a private in Co. B, 54th Regiment, Georgia Infantry.

GORMAN, CHARLES: Company H, private (musician). May 10, 1862 enlisted as a private in Co. H, 54th Regiment, Georgia Infantry at Macon, Georgia and received bounty $50.00. January 29, 1863 transferred to the Field Staff (regimental band) by order of Colonel Way. January – February 1863 roll shows him transferred.

GOULDING, THOMAS EDWARDS: Company G, private. June 23, 1862 enlisted as a private in Co. G, 54th Regiment, Georgia Infantry at Savannah, Georgia and received bounty $50.00. December 31, 1862 received pay. January – February 1863 roll shows him present. January 1864, April 25, 1864 and May 8, 1864 issued clothing. June 18, 1864 captured near Marietta, Georgia. June 26, 1864 arrived at Military Prison at Louisville, Kentucky from Nashville, Tennessee. June 27, 1864 sent to Camp Morton, Indiana, June 28, 1864 received at Camp Morton, Indianapolis, Indiana. March 15, 1865 transferred to Point Lookout, Maryland for exchange. March 28, 1865 received at Boulware & Cox's Wharves, James River, Virginia. He was born May 7, 1838 and died September 25, 1902. He is buried in Linwood Cemetery at Columbus, Muscogee County, Georgia. (find a grave # 26619098)

GRADY, JOHN H.: Company I, private. September 18, 1861 enlisted as a private in Co. C, 1st Regiment, 1st Brigade, Georgia State Troops. March 18, 1862 mustered out. May 6, 1862 enlisted as a private in Co. I, 54th Regiment, Georgia Infantry at Guyton, Georgia and received bounty $50.00. December 31, 1862 received pay. January – February 1863 roll shows him present. October 31, 1863 received pay. November – December 1863 roll shows him present on picket guard. January 1864 issued clothing. June 7, 1864 issued clothing at Marshall Hospital at Columbus, Georgia. He was appointed corporal of Co. I, 54th Regiment, Georgia Infantry. April 26, 1865 surrendered at Greensboro, North Carolina. May 1, 1865 paroled at Greensboro, North Carolina.

GRADDY, J. H.: Company A, private. February 23, 1864 enlisted as a private in Co. A, 4th Regiment, Georgia Sharpshooters at Macon, Georgia. April 26, 1865 surrendered in Co. B, 54th Regiment, Georgia Infantry at Greensboro, North Carolina. May 1, 1865 paroled at Greensboro, North Carolina.

GRAHAM, B. R.: Company G (C), private. May 6, 1862 enlisted as a private in Co. G, 54th Regiment, Georgia Infantry at Savannah, Georgia and received bounty $50.00. September 1, 1862 transferred from Co. G, 54th Regiment, Georgia Infantry at Savannah, Georgia to Co. C, 54th Regiment, Georgia Infantry at Beaulieu near Savannah, Georgia Special Order No. 6. September 1862 roll reflects his transfer. December 31, 1862 received pay. January – February 1863 roll shows him present (pay retained for 1 Enfield rifle lost). January 1, 1864 received pay. January – February 1864 roll shows him present. May 15, 1864 wounded at Resaca, Georgia. March 23, 1864 admitted to Way Hospital at Meridian, Mississippi with a Gunshot Wound and was transferred. April 25, 1864 and May 8, 1864 issued clothing. He was born in Georgia June 4, 1839.

GRACEN, THOMAS J.: Company C, private. May 6, 1862 enlisted as a private in Co. C, 54th Regiment, Georgia Infantry at Savannah, Georgia and received bounty $50.00. August and September 1862 roll show him detailed as a mechanic in the quartermaster's department. October 16, 1862 transferred from Co. C, 54th Regiment, Georgia Infantry to Co. D, 2nd Regiment, Engineer Troops as an artificer. December 1863 roll shows him present. Pension records show he was in South Carolina rebuilding bridges over Broad River, and surrendered at Alston, South Carolina. He died in Effingham County, Georgia September 8, 1918. He was born in Beaufort County, South Carolina September 1840.

GRANDBERRY, GEORGE L.: Company G (F), private. May 12, 1862 enlisted as a private in Co. G, 54th Regiment, Georgia Infantry at Columbus, Georgia and received bounty $50.00. September 1862 roll shows him detailed at the company commissary. December 1862 roll shows him detailed in the Engineer department. December 31, 1862 received pay. January – February 1863 roll shows him present. January 1864 and April 25, 1864 issued clothing. June 2, 1864 admitted to Ocmulgee Hospital at Macon, Georgia with Chronic Diarrhoea. June 5, 1864 returned to duty. April 26, 1865 surrendered in Co. F, 54th Regiment, Georgia Infantry at Greensboro, North Carolina. May 1, 1865 paroled at Greensboro, North Carolina. He was a resident of Harris County, Georgia.

GRANDBERRY, THOMAS J.: Company G (F), lieutenant. May 12, 1862 enlisted as a private in Co. G, 54th Regiment, Georgia Infantry at Columbus, Georgia and received bounty $50.00. May 12, 1862 he was elected 1st sergeant Co. G, 54th Regiment, Georgia Infantry. December 31, 1862 received pay. January – February 1863 roll shows him present. January 1864 and May 8, 1864 issued clothing. July 27, 1864 he was elected 2nd lieutenant Co. F, 54th Regiment, Georgia Infantry. April 26, 1865 surrendered in Co. F, 54th Regiment, Georgia Infantry at Greensboro, North Carolina. May 1, 1865 paroled at Greensboro, North Carolina.

GRAVES, R. N.: Company K, private. He enlisted as a private in Co. K, 54th Regiment, Georgia Infantry.

GRAY, J. A.: Company C, private. He enlisted as a private in Co. C, 54th Regiment, Georgia Infantry.

GRAYSON, THOMAS J.: Company D, private. April 30, 1862 enlisted as a private in Co. C, 54th Regiment, Georgia Infantry. August 1862 and September 1862 shown as a mechanic in the quartermasters Department at Beaulieu near Savannah, Georgia at a rate of an additional $.40 per day extra. September 1862 he is shown as a carpenter at Beaulieu near Savannah, Georgia. October 1862 roll shows him transferred on October 16, 1862 to 2nd Engineer troops as an artificer.

GREEN, BARTLETT (BARTLEY) WYLEY: Company G, private. May 12, 1862 enlisted as a private in Co. G, 54th Regiment, Georgia Infantry at Columbus, Georgia and received bounty $50.00. December 1862 roll shows him as a teamster. December 31, 1862 received pay. February 18, 1863 detached and assigned to the Quartermaster's Department as a Teamster. January 1863 received pay $8.75 from The Engineer Department as a teamster. January – February 1863 roll shows him detached and sent to Savannah, Georgia as a teamster on February 18, 1863. June 2, 1863 received pay $22.50 from The Engineer Department as a teamster. November 11, 1863 issued clothing. December 1, 1863 received pay $66.00. December 2, 1863 issued clothing. January 1864 issued clothing. April 24, 1864 died in General Hospital No. 1 at Savannah, Georgia of Pneumonia. He is buried in Laurel Grove Cemetery at Savannah, Georgia. (find a grave # 65119846)

GREEN, DANIEL A.: Company C, captain. December 11, 1861 elected captain of Co. B, 8th Regiment, Georgia State Troops. April 22, 1862 elected captain of Co. C, 54th Regiment, Georgia Infantry at Savannah, Georgia. July 1862 appears on roll. August 1862 roll shows him as present at Beaulieu near Savannah, Georgia. September 1862 roll shows him absent without leave from Beaulieu near Savannah, Georgia. October, November and December 1862 rolls show him present at Beaulieu. November 24, 1862 appears on list of officers in the Savannah District. January – February 1863 roll shows him absent detached on Special Service. March 10, 1863 received pay $360.00. April 2, 1863 received pay $130.00. April 30, 1863 dropped from the roll of the regiment Special Order No. 10/15 for desertion. He was born in Georgia February 22, 1840 and died in Georgia May 25, 1912. He is buried in Westview Cemetery at Atlanta, Fulton County, Georgia. (find a grave # 35412406)

GREEN, G. A.: Company H, sergeant. He enlisted as a sergeant in Co. H, 54th Regiment, Georgia Infantry.

GREEN, JAMES: Company E, private. May 6, 1862 enlisted as a private in Co. E, 54th Regiment, Georgia Infantry at Savannah, Georgia and received bounty $50.00. December 31, 1862 received pay. January – February 1863 roll shows him present. January 1864 issued clothing.

GREEN, MARSHALL: Company E, private. May 6, 1862 enlisted as a private in Co. E, 54th Regiment, Georgia Infantry at Savannah, Georgia and received bounty $50.00. December 31, 1862 received pay. January – February 1863 roll shows him present. January 1864 and June 2, 1864 issued clothing. Pension records show; he was on detail at Fort Valley, Georgia and could not reach command before surrender. May 10, 1865 surrendered at Tallahassee, Florida. May 24, 1865 paroled at Thomasville, Georgia. He was born in Georgia and died in Berrien County, Georgia June 1910.

GREEN, NATHANIEL J.: Company K, private. October 3, 1861 enlisted as a private in Co. A, 1st Regiment, 1st Brigade, Georgia State Troops. April 1862 mustered out. April 18, 1862 enlisted as a private in Co. E, 54th Regiment, Georgia Infantry at Savannah, Georgia and received bounty $50.00. May 19, 1862 placed on extra duty as wagoner for Quartermaster's Department. July 1862 roll shows him as wagoner. August 1862 roll shows him as a teamster. September 1862 through December 1862 he is shown on rolls as a teamster. September 1862 received pay (an additional $.25 per day) as a teamster. October 1862 received pay (an additional $.25 per day) as a teamster. December 1862 received pay (an additional $.25 per day) as a teamster. January 1, 1863 received pay. He was injured in a railroad collision. January – February 1863 roll shows him present (on extra duty as wagoner in Quartermaster's Department). April 1863 he is shown as a teamster in Savannah, Georgia. June 1863 he is shown as a teamster at Beaulieu near Savannah, Georgia. July and August 1863 he is shown as a teamster at Charleston, South Carolina. September and October 1863 he is shown as a teamster. October 1863 list of men detailed as teamster for the Quartermaster's Department at James Island, South

Carolina. November 16, 1863 received pay (an additional $.25 per day) as a teamster. November and December 1863 he is shown detailed as a teamster. January and February 1864 shown detailed as a teamster at Savannah, Georgia. April 18, 1864 and March 18, 1864 issued clothing. Pension records show: April 26, 1865 surrendered at Greensboro, North Carolina. May 1, 1865 paroled at Greensboro, North Carolina. He was born in the Beaufort District, South Carolina March 29, 1842 and died June 19, 1928. He is buried in the Screven City Cemetery at Screven, Wayne County, Georgia. (find a grave # 60036786). The Southern Cross of Honor was bestowed on him by the Jesup Chapter United Daughters of the Confederacy in 1904.

GREEN, WILLIAM HIRAM: Company E, private. May 6, 1862 enlisted as a private in Co. E, 54th Regiment, Georgia Infantry at Savannah, Georgia and received bounty $50.00. November 9, 1862 discharged at Beaulieu near Savannah, Georgia. November 1862 shows his discharge.

GREENWAY, G. W.: Company C, private. He enlisted as a private in Co. C, 54th Regiment, Georgia Infantry.

GRESHAM, J. T.: Company K, private. He enlisted as a private in Co. K, 54th Regiment, Georgia Infantry.

GRIFFETH, J. W.: Company I, corporal. He enlisted as a private in Co. I, 54th Regiment, Georgia Infantry.

GRIFFETH, O. P.: Company I, sergeant. He enlisted as a sergeant in Co. I, 54th Regiment, Georgia Infantry.

GRIFFIN, JAMES: Company F, private. October 2, 1862 enlisted as a private in Co. F, 54th Regiment, Georgia Infantry at Savannah, Georgia and received bounty $50.00. October 1862 roll shows his enlistment. December 1, 1862 deserted. December 1862 roll shows he deserted. January – February 1863 roll shows him present (absent without leave from November 20, 1862 to January 30, 1863 – 2 months and 10 days).

GRIFFIN, JAMES H.: Company E, lieutenant. May 6, 1862 enlisted as a private in Co. E, 54th Regiment, Georgia Infantry at Savannah, Georgia and received bounty $50.00. May 6, 1862 appointed 2nd lieutenant of Co. E, 54th Regiment, Georgia Infantry. May 24, 1862 shown on list of officers in the Savannah Headquarters. July 1862 through December 1862 rolls show him present at Beaulieu near Savannah, Georgia. January – February 1863 roll shows him present. March 10, 1863 received pay $80.00. October 21, 1863 shown on list of officers at Legare's Point, South Carolina. October 29, 1863 appointed 1st lieutenant of Co. E, 54th Regiment, Georgia Infantry. March 12, 1864 issued clothing. May 15, 1864 wounded at Resaca, Georgia. August 25, 1864 report of Mercer's Brigade in the field Near Atlanta, Georgia shows him wounded- at home on furlough by the medical board (May 15, 1864). He was born April 18, 1829 and died December 10, 1896. He is buried in Fletcher Cemetery at Alapaha, Berrien County, Georgia. (find a grave # 131696675)

GRIFFIN, LEWIS LODGE: Company E, private. May 6, 1862 enlisted as a private in Co. E, 54th Regiment, Georgia Infantry at Savannah, Georgia and received bounty $50.00. December 31, 1862 received pay. January – February 1863 roll shows him present. January 1864 and April 25, 1864 issued clothing. July 22, 1864 wounded at Atlanta, Georgia. Pension records show; he was on special detail at the close of the war He was born in Irwin County, Georgia May 12, 1833 and died in Adel, Cook County, Georgia February 21, 1905. He is buried in Woodlawn City Cemetery at Adel, Cook County, Georgia. (find a grave # 15017618)

GRIFFIN, LEWIS MOSES: Company E, private. May 6, 1862 enlisted as a private in Co. E, 54th Regiment, Georgia Infantry at Savannah, Georgia and received bounty $50.00. December 31, 1862 received pay. January – February 1863 roll shows him present as a blacksmith. June 14, 1863 through July 31, 1863 detailed as a carpenter at Rose Dew Post repairing and building headquarters at the post. September 8, 1863 received pay. January 1864 and April 25, 1864 issued clothing. April 1864 through May 1864 detailed as a mechanic at Savannah, Georgia. June 1864 received pay at an additional $.40 per day as a mechanic. September 1864 he is shown as a mechanic. October 1864 received extra pay as a mechanic ($12.00). He was born in Irwin County, Georgia October 10, 1829 and died in Calhoun County, Florida May 3, 1914. He is buried in Camps Head Cemetery in Calhoun County, Florida. (find a grave # 55989858)

GRIFFIN, LUCIUS (colored): Company G (Field Staff), private (musician). May 10, 1862 enlisted as a private in Co. G, 54th Regiment, Georgia Infantry at Macon (Columbus), Georgia and received bounty $50.00. January 1, 1863 received pay. January – February 1863 roll shows him (colored man dropped from the rolls January 31, 1863 and transferred to Field Staff (regimental band) as a musician. January – February 1863 Field Staff roll shows him present.

GRIFFIN, SOLOMON: Company E, corporal. May 6, 1862 enlisted as a private and was appointed 2nd corporal in Co. E, 54th Regiment, Georgia Infantry at Savannah, Georgia and received bounty $50.00. December 31, 1862 received pay. January – February 1863 roll shows him present. January 1864, April 25, 1864 and May 8, 1864 issued clothing. Pension records show; June 9, 1865 he was discharged at Albany, Georgia. He was born in Lowndes County, Georgia June 26, 1837 and died at Nashville, Berrien County, Georgia November 11, 1907. He is buried in the Griffin Cemetery in Berrien County, Georgia. (find a grave # 51831018)

GRIFFIN, WILLIAM HENRY HARRISON: Company E, private. May 6, 1862 enlisted as a private in Co. E, 54th Regiment, Georgia Infantry at Savannah, Georgia and received bounty $50.00. December 31, 1862 received pay. January – February 1863 roll shows him present. January 1864 and April 25, 1864 issued clothing. July 15 through July 25, 1864 register of Ocmulgee Hospital at Macon, Georgia with Gunshot Wounds in scalp, above left ear, in chin (flesh) and furloughed for 30 days. November 1864 wounded at Nashville, Tennessee. He was born December 22, 1813 and died March 29, 1893. He is buried in Shady Grove Community Cemetery at Opelika, Lee County, Alabama. (find a grave # 13695460)

GRIFFIN, WILLIAM THOMAS: Company C, private. May 6, 1862 enlisted as a private in Co. C, 54th Regiment, Georgia Infantry at Savannah, Georgia and received bounty $50.00. December 31, 1862 received pay. January – February 1863 roll shows him present. January 1, 1864 received pay. January – February 1864 roll shows him present. April 28, 1864 issued clothing. Pension records show: April 26, 1865 surrendered at Greensboro, North Carolina. May 1, 1865 paroled at Greensboro, North Carolina. He was born in Georgia in 1844 and died in Washington County, Georgia August 18, 1914. He is buried in Friendship Baptist Church Cemetery at Deepstep, Washington County, Georgia. (find a grave # 102766558)

GRIFFIS (GRIFFIN), DAVID: Company K, corporal. May 5, 1862 enlisted as a private in Co. K, 54th Regiment, Georgia Infantry at Savannah, Georgia and received bounty $50.00. January 1, 1863 received pay. January – February 1863 roll shows him present on guard. March 18, 1864, April 18, 1864 and April 25, 1864 issued clothing. November 7, 1864 admitted to Ocmulgee Hospital at Macon, Georgia with Ascites. November 18, 1864 transferred to Appling County, Georgia. He was a resident of Appling County, Georgia. May 10, 1865 surrendered at Tallahassee, Florida. May 21, 1865 paroled at Thomasville, Georgia.

GRIFFIS, ELIJAH: Company K, private. October 3, 1861 enlisted as a private in Co. A, 1st Regiment, 1st Brigade, Georgia State Troops. April 1862 mustered out. April 18, 1862 enlisted as a private in Co. K, 54th Regiment, Georgia Infantry at Savannah, Georgia and received bounty $50.00. January 1, 1863 received pay. January – February 1863 roll shows him present. March 18, 1864, April 25, 1864 and June 2, 1864 issued clothing. May 10, 1865 surrendered at Tallahassee, Florida. May 21, 1865 paroled at Thomasville, Georgia.

GRIFFIS, JOEL C.: Company K, private. October 14, 1861 enlisted as a private in Co. H, 5th Regiment, Georgia State Troops. April 25, 1862 mustered out. May 5, 1862 enlisted as a private in Co. K, 54th Regiment, Georgia Infantry at Savannah, Georgia and received bounty $50.00. January 1, 1863 received pay. January – February 1863 roll shows him present. March 18, 1864, April 25, 1864 and June 2, 1864 issued clothing. July 22, 1864 killed at Atlanta, Georgia.

GRIFFIS (GRIFFIN), J. G.: Company K, corporal. October 3, 1861 enlisted as a private in Co. A, 1st Regiment, 1st Brigade, Georgia State Troops. April 1862 mustered out. April 18, 1862 enlisted as a private in Co. K, 54th Regiment, Georgia Infantry at Savannah, Georgia and received bounty $50.00. January 1, 1863 received pay. January – February 1863 roll shows him absent in hospital. March 18, 1864, April 25, 1864, October 13, 1864 and October 31, 1864 issued clothing. He was promoted to corporal. May 10, 1865 surrendered at Tallahassee, Florida. May 21, 1865 paroled at Thomasville, Georgia.

GRIFFITH, J. W.: Company I, private. He enlisted as a private in Co. I, 54th Regiment, Georgia Infantry.

GRIFFITH, O. P.: Company I, private. He enlisted as a private in Co. I, 54th Regiment, Georgia Infantry.

GRIMES, JACKSON: Company G, private. July 15, 1861 enlisted as a private in Co. G, 20th Regiment, Georgia Infantry. November 10, 1861 discharged at Richmond, Virginia due to disability. May 12, 1862 enlisted as a private in Co. G, 54th Regiment, Georgia Infantry at Columbus, Georgia and received bounty $50.00. June 30, 1862 received pay. July 6, 1862 detailed as a nurse in the medical department. July 1862, August 1862 and September 1862 rolls show him detailed as a hospital nurse. October 3, 1862 detailed in the government shoe factory at Columbus, Georgia. January – February 1863 roll shows him absent on detached service at Columbus, Georgia in government shoe factory. July 31, 1863 issued clothes form the Columbus, Georgia Quartermaster's Department. November 1863 received $ 3.00 extra pay ($.10 per pair for 30 pairs of shoes) at the government shoe factory at Columbus, Georgia. July 1864 received pay $32.00 for extra work ($.08 per pair for 400 pairs of shows in June and July 1864). April 21, 1864 shown on list of men detailed as having a stiff leg. August 20, 1864 report shows he was employed as a shoemaker at Columbus, Georgia and that he was 31 years of age and able bodied (date of detail October 9, 1862). January 1865 report shows he worked as a shoemaker and was sick 7 days at Columbus, Georgia.

GRIMES, W.: Company G, private. December 24, 1862 enlisted as a private in Co. G, 54th Regiment, Georgia Infantry.

GRINER, WILLIAM, JR.: Company D, private. October 14, 1861 enlisted as a private in Co. I, 5th Regiment, Georgia State Troops. April 1862 mustered out. April 30, 1862 enlisted as a private in Co. D, 54th Regiment, Georgia Infantry at Beaulieu near Savannah, Georgia and received bounty $50.00. December 31, 1862 received pay. January – February 1863 roll shows him present. January 1864 and April 25, 1864 issued clothing. July 22, 1864 pension records show he was wounded in the head at Atlanta, Georgia. He was sent to the hospital and remained two weeks. Pension records show he was at home on sick furlough at the close of the war. He was born in Screven County, Georgia January 12, 1846 and died in Augusta, Richmond County, Georgia May 22, 1922. He is buried in McDonald Baptist Church Cemetery at Sylvania, Screven County, Georgia. (find a grave #55040621)

GRIST, FREDERICK: Company A, private. He enlisted as a private in Co. A, 54th Regiment, Georgia Infantry. July 20, 1864 captured at Peachtree Creek near Atlanta, Georgia. July 28, 1864 arrived at Military Prison at Louisville from Nashville, Tennessee. July 30, 1864 sent to Camp Douglas, Illinois. August 1, 1864 received at Camp Douglas, Illinois. June 20, 1865 discharged from Camp Douglas, Illinois. He was a resident of Macon, Bibb County, Georgia.

GROOMS, B.: Company A, private. July 25, 1863 enlisted as a private in Co. A, 54th Regiment, Georgia Infantry at Savannah, Georgia and received bounty $50.00. April 30, 1863 received pay. November – December

1863 roll shows him absent (sick in the hospital at Savannah, Georgia).

GROOMS, BURRELL B.: Company A, private. February 25, 1863 enlisted as a private in Co. A, 54th Regiment, Georgia Infantry at Savannah, Georgia and received bounty $50.00. April 30, 1863 received pay. June 30, 1863 roll shows him absent sick in the hospital at Savannah, Georgia. April 29, 1864 issued clothing.

GROOMS, JOSEPH C.: Company I, private. May 6 1862 enlisted as a private in Co. I, 54th Regiment, Georgia Infantry at Guyton, Georgia and received bounty $50.00. October 31, 1862 received pay. December 31, 1862 received pay. January – February 1863 roll shows him present (sick in regimental hospital). May 1, 1863 received pay. November – December 1863 roll shows him present (fisherman for major). January 1864 issued clothing. January – February 1864 roll shows him present (shown absent without leave for seven months and a half). May 13, 1864 wounded at Resaca, Georgia by a shell. August 20, 1864 admitted to Ocmulgee Hospital at Macon Georgia with a Gunshot Wound – shell (lower 1/3 left leg). August 23, 1864 transferred to and admitted to Floyd House Hospital at Macon Georgia with a Gunshot Wound in the lower left leg. September 1864 sent to hospital in Macon, Georgia with gangrene in his left foot. October 5, 1864 admitted to Floyd House Hospital at Macon Georgia with a Gunshot Wound (flesh) instep of the left foot (Phagedema). He remained there for 3 months he was furloughed home for 60 days and was unable to rejoin his command. He was a resident of Bulloch County, Georgia. He was born May 10, 1841 in Georgia and died in Bulloch County, Georgia. October 12, 1928. He is buried in Lanes Primitive Baptist Church Cemetery at Brooklet, Bulloch County, Georgia. (find a grave # 52610797)

GROVES (GROVER), S. H.: Company K. private. He enlisted as a private in Co. K, 54th Regiment, Georgia Infantry. April 25, 1864 issued clothing. May 10, 1865 surrendered at Tallahassee, Florida. May 25, 1865 paroled at Thomasville, Georgia.

GRUBBS, D. J.: Company C. private. He enlisted as a private in Co. C, 54th Regiment, Georgia Infantry.

GUNN, J. A.: Company B. corporal. He enlisted as a private in Co. B, 54th Regiment, Georgia Infantry. He was elected corporal.

GUNN, W. C.: Company B. private. He enlisted as a private in Co. B, 54th Regiment, Georgia Infantry.

GUTHRIE, G. W.: Company A, private. February 23, 1863 enlisted as a private in Co. A, 54th Regiment, Georgia Infantry at Savannah, Georgia and received bounty $50.00. April 30, 1863 received pay. June 30, 1863 roll shows him present.

GUTHRIE (GUTHERY), SAMUEL: Company E. private. May 6, 1862 enlisted as a private in Co. E, 54th Regiment, Georgia Infantry at Savannah, Georgia and received bounty $50.00. December 31, 1862 received pay. January – February 1863 roll shows him present. January 1864, April 25, 1864 and June 2, 1864 issued clothing. May 10, 1865 surrendered at Tallahassee, Florida. May 24, 1865 paroled at Thomasville, Georgia. (Pension records show: April 26, 1865 surrendered at Greensboro, North Carolina. May 1, 1865 paroled at Greensboro, North Carolina.) He died in Berrien County, Georgia February 19, 1910. He was born in Lowndes County Georgia November 10, 1831 and died February 17, 1910. He is buried in Guthrie Cemetery at Lakeland, Lanier County, Georgia. (find a grave # 30400806)

GUYTON (GUITON), ROBERT HABERSHAM: Company I, private. He enlisted as a private in Co. I, 54th Regiment, Georgia Infantry. January 1864 issued clothing. April 26, 1865 surrendered at Greensboro, North Carolina. May 1, 1865 paroled at Greensboro, North Carolina (shown as absent sick). He was born July 28, 1845 and died in Guyton, Effingham County, Georgia April 3, 1904. He is buried in Guyton Cemetery at Guyton, Effingham County, Georgia. (find a grave # 59435120)

HABERSHAM, WILLIAM W.: Company F, private. April 29, 1863 enlisted as a private in Co. F, 54th Regiment, Georgia Infantry.

HABERSHAM, WILLIAM N., JR.: Company F, private. December 9, 1861 enlisted as a private in Co. D, 2nd Battalion, Georgia Cavalry. August 13, 1862 discharged and furnished substitute W. T. Hannan. He enlisted as a private in Co. F, 54th Regiment, Georgia Infantry. July 22, 1864 he was killed in Atlanta, Georgia. He is buried in Laurel Grove Cemetery at Savannah, Chatham County, Georgia. (find a grave # 43456302)

HAGIN, D.: Company I, private. He enlisted as a private in Co. I, 54th Regiment, Georgia Infantry. January 1864 issued clothing.

HAGIN (HAGINS), H.: Company I (F), private. October 8, 1863 enlisted as a private in Co. I, 54th Regiment, Georgia Infantry at Rose Dew, South Carolina and received bounty $50.00. November – December 1863 roll shows him present on picket guard. January 1864, April 25, 1864 and June 2, 1864 issued clothing. April 26, 1865 surrendered in Co. F, 54th Regiment, Georgia Infantry at Greensboro, North Carolina. May 1, 1865 paroled at Greensboro, North Carolina.

HALL, A. M.: Company F, private. May 6, 1862 enlisted as a private in Co. F, 54th Regiment, Georgia Infantry.

HALL, HOUSTON HENRY (HENRY HOUSTON): Company C, corporal. December 11, 1861 enlisted as a private in Co. B, 8th Regiment, Georgia State Troops. He mustered out in 1862. April 22, 1862 enlisted as 3rd corporal in Co. C, 54th Regiment, Georgia Infantry at Savannah, Georgia and received bounty $50.00. December 31, 1862 received pay. January – February 1863 roll shows him present. January 1, 1864 received pay. January – February 1864 roll shows him present. April 25, 1864 and May 8, 1864 issued clothing. May 27, 1865 surrendered and paroled at Augusta, Georgia. (Pension records show he was at home on furlough at the close of the war.) He was born October 20, 1830 and died February 13, 1914. He is buried in Hall Cemetery at Modoc, Emanuel County, Georgia. (find a grave #10437719)

HALL, J. R.: Company C, private. He enlisted as a private in Co. C, 54th

Regiment, Georgia Infantry.

HALL, JAMES J.: Company C, private. May 6, 1862 enlisted as a private in Co. C, 54th Regiment, Georgia Infantry at Savannah, Georgia and received bounty $50.00. December 31, 1862 received pay. January – February 1863 roll shows him present. January 1, 1864 received pay. January – February 1864 roll shows him present. He was born July 20, 1830 and died December 20, 1907. He is buried in Hines Cemetery in Emanuel County, Georgia. (find a grave # 61361524)

HALL, JOHN B.: Company C, private. He enlisted as a private in Co. C, 54th Regiment, Georgia Infantry. July 20, 1864 captured at Peachtree Creek near Atlanta, Georgia. July 31, 1865 roll of Camp Douglas, Illinois shows he was admitted to the General Hospital on July 9, 1865 being unable to travel after being released.

HALL, JOHN K.: Company C, private. May 6, 1862 enlisted as a private in Co. C, 54th Regiment, Georgia Infantry at Savannah, Georgia and received bounty $50.00. December 31, 1862 received pay. January – February 1863 roll shows him present. January 1, 1864 received pay. January – February 1864 roll shows him absent sick in Hospital at Hardeeville, South Carolina since February 24, 1864. July 20, 1864 captured at Peachtree Creek near Atlanta, Georgia. July 29, 1864 received at Military Prison at Louisville, Kentucky from Nashville, Tennessee. July 30, 1864 sent to Camp Douglas, Illinois. July 14, 1865 admitted to U. S. A. General Hospital at Camp Douglas near Chicago, Illinois from the General Hospital U. S. Prison Hospital for convalescent. July 30, 1865 discharged from service. He was born in Burke County, Georgia in 1836.

HALL, R. M.: Company D, private. April 30, 1862 enlisted as a private in Co. D, 54th Regiment, Georgia Infantry at Savannah, Georgia and received bounty $50.00. December 31, 1862 received pay. January – February 1863 roll shows him present (absent without leave 5 days). March 12, 1863 placed on detached service at the government salt works. January 1864 and April 25, 1864 issued clothing. May 19, 1865 surrendered and paroled at Augusta, Georgia. He was born in Jefferson County, Georgia May 22, 1826.

HAMBY, CHARLES: Company F (A), private. He enlisted as a private in Co. F, 54th Regiment, Georgia Infantry.

HAMER, JAMES T.: Company H, corporal. May 12, 1862 enlisted as 4th corporal in Co. H, 54th Regiment, Georgia Infantry at Columbus, Georgia and received bounty $50.00. December 31, 1862 received pay. January – February 1863 roll shows him present. October 31, 1863 received pay. November – December 1863 roll shows him present. December 31, 1863 received pay. January 1864 issued clothing. January – February 1864 roll shows him absent (detailed by order of Major W. H. Mann on February 16, 1864). June 18, 1864 wounded in the right eye resulting in loss of sight in operations near Marietta, Georgia (Powder Springs, Georgia). December 29, 1864 admitted to Floyd House and Ocmulgee Hospital at Macon,

Georgia with a Gunshot wound to the right eye (ball entered frontal sinus passed upwards and downwards fracturing frontal bone and destroying globe of the eye). March 6, 1865 admitted to Ocmulgee Hospital at Macon, Georgia with Gunshot wound to the right eye (mini ball) on June 18, 1864 in battle. March 27, 1865 appears on register of Floyd House and Ocmulgee Hospital at Macon, Georgia with a Gunshot wound to the right eye destroying it and lodging. March 28, 1865 he was furloughed for 60 days. He was a resident of Harris County, Georgia. He was born in Georgia August 9, 1843 and died March 23, 1922. He is buried in Salem Cemetery in Troup County, Georgia. (find a grave # 100831818).

HAMIL, A. F.: Company B, sergeant. He enlisted as a sergeant in Co. B, 54th Regiment, Georgia Infantry.

HAMMACK, J. B.: Company G, private. January 22, 1863 enlisted as a private in Co. G, 54th Regiment, Georgia Infantry at Columbus, Georgia and received bounty $50.00. January – February 1863 roll shows him present. January 1864 and April 25, 1864 issued clothing.

HAMMOCK, JAMES B.: Company G (F), sergeant. November 6, 1862 enlisted as a private in Co. G, 54th Regiment, Georgia Infantry at Columbus, Georgia and received bounty $50.00. November 1862 roll shows his enlistment. December 31, 1862 received pay. January – February 1863 roll shows him present. September 5, 1863 received pay $44.00. January 1864 and April 25, 1864 issued clothing. He was elected 1st sergeant of Co. F, 54th Regiment, Georgia Infantry. April 26, 1865 surrendered in Co. F, 54th Regiment, Georgia Infantry at Greensboro, North Carolina. May 1, 1865 paroled at Greensboro, North Carolina.

HAMMOND, R. P.: Company A, private. May 10, 1862 enlisted as a private in Co. A, 54th Regiment, Georgia Infantry at Macon, Georgia and received bounty $50.00. September 1, 1862 transferred from Co. A to Co. F by Special Order No. 6. September 1862 rolls of Co. A and Co. F reflect the transfer and show him as the company cook. December 31, 1862 received pay. January – February 1863 roll shows him present in Co. F, 54th Regiment, Georgia Infantry (transferred from Co. A). February 8, 1863 discharged by civil authority.

HAMMOND, R. P.: Company G, sergeant. May 10, 1862 enlisted as a private in Co. G, 54th Regiment, Georgia Infantry. He was appointed 1st sergeant of Co. G, 54th Regiment, Georgia Infantry. Pension records show: April 26, 1865 surrendered at Greensboro, North Carolina. May 1, 1865 paroled at Greensboro, North Carolina.

HANCOCK, CADER: Company E, private. May 6, 1862 enlisted as a private in Co. E, 54th Regiment, Georgia Infantry at Macon, Georgia and received bounty $50.00. December 31, 1862 received pay. January – February 1863 roll shows him present. July 1, 1863 detailed for extra duty as a mechanic at Savannah, Georgia to August 31, 1863 at a rate of $.40 extra per day for a total of $24.80. September 1, 1863 through January 31, 1864 detailed as a mechanic in Savannah, Georgia. January 1864 issued clothing. February 1, 1864 through April 27, 1864 detailed as a mechanic in Savannah, Georgia. May 1, 1864 received pay and clothing allowance $110.13. May 8, 1864 issued clothing. January 30, 1865 admitted to Way Hospital at Meridian, Mississippi with a Gunshot Wound. Pension records show he lost sight of right eye due to fever. January 1865 furloughed home. May 10, 1865 surrendered at Tallahassee, Florida. May 29, 1865 paroled at Thomasville (Albany), Georgia. He was born in Irwin County, Georgia February 29, 1828 and died December 5, 1902. He is buried in Brushy Creek Cemetery at Adel, Cook County, Georgia. (find a grave # 33566447).

HANCOCK (HANDCOCK), DANIEL J.: Company E, private. May 6, 1862 enlisted as a private in Co. E, 54th Regiment, Georgia Infantry at Macon, Georgia and received bounty $50.00. December 31, 1862 received pay. January – February 1863 roll shows him present. July 1, 1863 detailed for extra duty as a mechanic at Savannah, Georgia to August 31, 1863 at a rate of $.40 extra per day for a total of $24.80. September 1, 1863 to October 31, 1863 detailed as a mechanic in Savannah, Georgia at a rate of an extra #.40 per day. November 1, 1863 through February 29, 1864 detailed as a mechanic in Savannah, Georgia. January 1864 issued clothing. March 1, 1864 to April 27, 1864 detailed as a mechanic in Savannah, Georgia. May 1, 1864 received pay and clothing allowance $103.13. September 30, 1864 he died of Pneumonia at Macon, Georgia. He was born March 27, 1836 in Lowndes County, Georgia and died at Macon, Bibb County, Georgia September 30, 1864. He is buried at Rose Hill Cemetery in Macon, Bibb County, Georgia. (find a grave # 62575785)

HANCOCK, JOHN MARK: Company E, private. He enlisted as a private in Co. E, 54th Regiment, Georgia Infantry. May 10, 1865 surrendered at Tallahassee, Florida. May 29, 1865 paroled at Albany, Georgia. He was born in 1836 and died in Berrien County, Georgia in 1899.

HANCOCK, WILLIAM: Company H, corporal. May 20, 1862 enlisted as a private in Co. H, 54th Regiment, Georgia Infantry at Columbus, Georgia and received bounty $50.00. December 31, 1862 received pay. January – February 1863 roll shows him present. October 31, 1863 received pay. November – December 1863 roll shows him present. December 31, 1863 received pay. January 1864 issued clothing. January – February 1864 roll shows him present detailed as a hewer. He was appointed corporal. April 26, 1865 surrendered at Greensboro, North Carolina. May 1, 1865 paroled at Greensboro, North Carolina.

HAND, J.: Company B, private. He enlisted as a private in Co. B, 54th Regiment, Georgia Infantry.

HANNAH, W. B.: Company I, private. February 25, 1863 enlisted as a private in Co. I, 54th Regiment, Georgia Infantry at Beaulieu near Savannah, Georgia and received bounty $50.00. December 31, 1862 received pay. January – February 1863 roll shows him present. October 31, 1863 received pay. November – December 1863 roll shows him present (color corporal).

January 1864 issued clothing. 1864 died in service at Covington, Georgia and is buried there in the Covington Confederate Cemetery at Covington, Newton County, Georgia. Plot: Row 3 No. 5 (effects receipt No. 6455). (find a grave # 15884558)

HANNON, JAMES H.: Company K, lieutenant. October 8, 1861 enlisted as a private and elected 1st lieutenant in Co. A, 1st Regiment, 1st Brigade, Georgia State Troops. April 1862 mustered out. April 18, 1862 enlisted as a private in Co. K, 54th Regiment, Georgia Infantry at Savannah, Georgia and received bounty $50.00. April 18, 1862 appointed 1st lieutenant of Co. K, 54th Regiment, Georgia Infantry. July 18, 1862 resigned his commission at Savannah, Georgia. July 1862 roll shows his resignation due to being unfit for service (kidney problem). August 1862 roll shows he resigned due to disability on July 18, 1862 and J. T. Mann, corporal in Jeff Davis legion elected in his place.

HANNAN, WILLIAM T.: Company F, private. April 13, 1862 enlisted as a private in Co. D, 2nd Battalion, Georgia Cavalry. June 30, 1863 transferred as a private to Co. F, 54th Regiment, Georgia Infantry. August 13, 1863 was furnished as a substitute for W. N. Habersham.

HANSLEY, CHARLES: Company A (F), private. May 10, 1862 enlisted as a private in Co. A, 54th Regiment, Georgia Infantry. February 8, 1863 transferred from Co. A, 54th Regiment, Georgia Infantry to Co. F, 54th Regiment, Georgia Infantry. February 8, 1863 he was discharged by civil authority, due to dropsy. He was born in Bibb County, Georgia in 1843.

HARDEE, J. C.: Company A, private. September 1, 1863 enlisted as a private in Co. A, 54th Regiment, Georgia Infantry at Macon, Georgia. December 31, 1864 roll of Co. B, 2nd Battalion Troops and Defences, Macon, Georgia show him stationed at Camp Wright and absent as Provost Guard at Macon, Georgia.

HARDEN, STEPHEN: Company B, private. He enlisted as a private in Co. B, 54th Regiment, Georgia Infantry.

HARDEN, WILLIAM: Company F, private. May 17, 1861 enlisted as a private and appointed 4th sergeant of Chisholm's Company, Georgia State Troops. May 1862 mustered out. May 13, 1862 enlisted as a private in Co. F, 54th Regiment, Georgia Infantry at Savannah, Georgia and received bounty $50.00. December 16, 1862 detailed on extra duty with the Signal Corps. December 31, 1862 received pay. January – February 1863 roll shows him present. January 6, 1863 received pay $22.00. March 7, 1863 received pay $22.00. January 1, 1863 to September 30, 1863 on extra duty as a Signal and Telegraph Operator in Savannah, Georgia at a rate of $3.00 additional a day. September 30, 1863 received pay $90.00 at Savannah, Georgia. October 1, 1863 to December 31, 1863 on extra duty as a Signal and Telegraph Operator in Savannah, Georgia at a rate of $3.00 additional a day. December 25, 1863 issued clothing. January 1864 issued clothing. January 1, 1864 to August 31, 1864 he is shown on extra duty with Signal and Telegraph Service in Savannah, Georgia at a rate of $3.00 additional a day. June 30, 1864 received pay. October 31, 1864 he is shown absent detailed as a telegraph operator at the Atlantic and Gulf Railroad at $3.00 extra per day. He was born in Georgia November 11, 1844.

HARDY, THOMAS C.: Company A, private. September 1, 1862 enlisted as a private in Co. A, 54th Regiment, Georgia Infantry. January – February 1864 roll shows him absent (detailed on fortifications at Savannah, Georgia as an overseer).

HARDY (HARDEE), WILLIAM: Company C, private. June 1, 1863 enlisted as a private in Co. C, 54th Regiment, Georgia Infantry at Savannah, Georgia. January – February 1864 roll shows he deserted January 25, 1864. He was born in Washington County, Georgia May 15, 1828.

HARGROVE, D. C.: Company A, private. He enlisted as a private in Co. A, 54th Regiment, Georgia Infantry. May 23, 1865 paroled at Talladega, Alabama.

HARGROVES (HARGROVE), SAMUEL: Company K, private. October 3, 1861 enlisted as a private in Co. A, 1st Regiment, 1st Brigade, Georgia State Troops. April 1862 mustered out. April 18, 1862 enlisted as a private in Co. K, 54th Regiment, Georgia Infantry at Savannah, Georgia and received bounty $50.00. January 1, 1863 received pay. January – February 1863 roll shows him present on guard. March 18, 1864 issued clothing.

HARMON, ABRAHAM WILLIAM.: Company F, private. May 17, 1861 enlisted as a private and appointed 1st corporal of Chisholm's Company, Georgia State Troops. May 1862 mustered out. October 10, 1862 enlisted as a private in Co. F, 54th Regiment, Georgia Infantry. November 20, 1862 discharged by civil authority. November 1862 roll reflects his discharge. November 13, 1863 enlisted as a private in Captain Wheaton's Company, Chatham Siege Artillery. February 28, 1865 roll shows him present. He was born in Savannah, Chatham County, Georgia January 21, 1845 and died in Savannah, Chatham County, Georgia April 27, 1922. He is buried in Laurel Grove Cemetery (North) at Savannah, Chatham County, Georgia. (find a grave # 21691529)

HARMON, HYDE A. (H.): Company K, private. October 3, 1861 enlisted as a private in Co. A, 1st Regiment, 1st Brigade, Georgia State Troops. April 1862 mustered out. April 18, 1862 enlisted as a private in Co. K, 54th Regiment, Georgia Infantry at Savannah, Georgia and received bounty $50.00. September 15, 1862 discharged at Beaulieu near Savannah, Georgia. September 1862 roll reflects his discharge.

HARNED, SAMUEL B.: Company G, sergeant. May 12, 1862 enlisted as a private and was elected 2nd sergeant of Co. G, 54th Regiment, Georgia Infantry at Columbus, Georgia and received bounty $50.00. December 31, 1862 received pay. January – February 1863 roll shows him present. January 1864 and April 25, 1864 issued clothing. June 27, 1864 appointed 1st sergeant of Co. G, 54th Regiment, Georgia Infantry.

HARNESBURGER, J. T.: Company K, private. He enlisted as a private in Co. K, 54th Regiment, Georgia Infantry.

HARPER, ANDREW: Company G, private. September 8, 1861 enlisted as a private in Co. C, 37th Regiment, Georgia Infantry at Lynchburg, Virginia. April 26, 1865 surrendered in Co. G, 54th Regiment, Georgia Infantry at Greensboro, North Carolina. May 1, 1865 paroled at Greensboro, North Carolina.

HARPER, J. G.: Company G, private. January 31, 1863 enlisted as a private in Co. G, 54th Regiment, Georgia Infantry at Columbus, Georgia and received bounty $50.00. January – February 1863 roll shows him present. September 8, 1863 admitted to General Hospital at Guyton, Georgia. August 8, 1863 received pay $22.00. October 31, 1863 received pay. November – December 1863 roll of General Hospital at Guyton, Georgia shows him present as a patient. January 1864 issued clothing. January – February 1864 roll of General Hospital at Guyton, Georgia shows him present as a patient. He is buried in Buffington Cemetery at Castleberry, Conecuh County, Alabama. (find a grave # 50765658)

HARRELL, JOHN B.: Company G, private. January 22, 1863 enlisted as a private in Co. G, 54th Regiment, Georgia Infantry. May 15, 1864 wounded in the right shoulder and the left arm at Resaca, Georgia. He was born in Georgia February 9, 1845.

HARRELL, M. F.: Company G, private. He enlisted as a private in Co. G, 54th Regiment, Georgia Infantry. January 1864 and April 25, 1864 issued clothing. May 10, 1865 surrendered at Tallahassee, Florida. May 20, 1865 paroled at Bainbridge, Georgia.

HARRELL, MOSES, JR.: Company G, private. January 22, 1863 enlisted as a private in Co. G, 54th Regiment, Georgia Infantry.

HARRELL, MOSES, SR.: Company G, private. January 22, 1863 enlisted as a private in Co. G, 54th Regiment, Georgia Infantry.

HARRIGAN (HARRINGTON), HUGH H.: Company F, corporal. May 17, 1861 enlisted as a private in Chisholm's Company, Georgia State Troops. May 1862 mustered out. May 13, 1862 enlisted as a private in Co. F, 54th Regiment, Georgia Infantry at Savannah, Georgia and received bounty $50.00. December 31, 1862 received pay. January – February 1863 roll shows him present. November 1, 1863 received pay. November – December 1863 roll shows him absent on picket duty at Little Ogeechee Bridge. January 1864, April 25, 1864 and May 8, 1864 issued clothing. March 11, 1865 he deserted and took oath at Savannah, Georgia. March 16, 1865 transferred to Hilton Head, South Carolina. March 20, 1865 arrived at Hilton Head, South Carolina. March 22, 1865 transferred from Hilton Head, South Carolina to New York City, New York by Steamer Fulton. He was a resident of Savannah, Georgia. He was born in Westchester, New York. He is described as 5 feet 8 inches high, light complexion, light hair, grey eyes, 20 years of age and by occupation a clerk.

HARRINGTON, J. A.: Company H (A), private. May 10, 1862 enlisted as a private in Co. H, 54th Regiment, Georgia Infantry at Savannah, Georgia and received bounty $50.00. September 1, 1862 transferred from Co. H,

54th Regiment, Georgia Infantry to Co. A 54th Regiment, Georgia Infantry at Beaulieu near Savannah, Georgia by Special Order No. 6.

HARRIS, ELI: Company H, private. He enlisted as a private in Co. H, 54th Regiment, Georgia Infantry. May 19, 1865 surrendered and paroled at Augusta, Georgia.

HARRIS, F.: Company A, private. April 18, 1862 enlisted as a private in Co. A, 54th Regiment, Georgia Infantry at Macon, Georgia and received bounty $50.00. April 30, 1863 received pay. June 30, 1863 roll shows him present (sick in the company hospital). October 31, 1863 received pay. November – December 1863 roll shows him present. January 1, 1864 received pay. January – February 1864 roll shows him present. April 29, 1862 issued clothing.

HARRIS, H. C.: Company B, private. He enlisted as a private in Co. B, 54th Regiment, Georgia Infantry.

HARRIS, JAMES N.: Company A, sergeant. November 14, 1861 enlisted as a private in Co. C, 1st Independent Battalion, Georgia State Troops. April 16, 1862 roll shows him present. April 1862 mustered out. April 18, 1862 enlisted as a private in Co. A, 54th Regiment, Georgia Infantry at Macon, Georgia and received bounty $50.00. April 30, 1863 received pay. June 30, 1863 roll shows him present. October 31, 1863 received pay. November – December 1863 roll shows him present. January 1, 1864 received pay. January – February 1864 roll shows him present. April 29, 1864 issued clothing. June 19, 1864 captured near Marietta, Georgia. June 26, 1864 received at Military Prison at Louisville, Kentucky from Nashville, Tennessee. June 27, 1864 sent to Camp Morton, Indiana from Military Prison at Louisville, Kentucky. March 4, 1865 transferred from Camp Morton, Indiana for exchange. March 4, 1865 paroled at Camp Morton, Indiana and forwarded to City Point, Virginia via Baltimore, Maryland for exchange. March 10-12, 1865 received at Boulware & Cox Wharves, James River, Virginia. He was born February 4, 1846 and died October 24, 1894. He is buried in Salem Primitive Baptist Church Cemetery at Musella, Crawford County, Georgia. (find a grave # 25703708)

HARRIS, JOSEPH J.: Company A, private. April 28, 1862 enlisted as a private in Co. A, 54th Regiment, Georgia Infantry at Macon, Georgia and received bounty $50.00. December 13, 1862 deserted.

HARRIS, JOSEPH JACKSON: Company A, corporal. October 17, 1861 enlisted as 2nd corporal in Co. C, 1st Independent Battalion, Georgia State Troops. April 16, 1862 roll shows him present. April 1862 mustered out. April 18, 1862 enlisted as a private in Co. A, 54th Regiment, Georgia Infantry at Macon, Georgia and received bounty $50.00. April 30, 1863 received pay. June 30, 1863 roll shows him present (one month's pay deducted by order of General Mercer). Pension records show: April 26, 1865 surrendered at Greensboro, North Carolina. May 1, 1865 paroled at Greensboro, North Carolina. He was born in 1839 in Macon, Bibb County, Georgia and died in Macon, Bibb County, Georgia April 24, 1885. He is buried in Jones Chapel Cemetery at Macon, Bibb County, Georgia.

(find a grave # 70757601)

HARRIS, STOGNER RILEY: Company K, sergeant. October 3, 1861 enlisted as a private in Co. A, 1st Regiment, 1st Brigade, Georgia State Troops. April 1862 mustered out. April 18, 1862 enlisted as a private in Co. K, 54th Regiment, Georgia Infantry at Savannah, Georgia and received bounty $50.00. January 1, 1863 received pay. January – February 1863 roll shows him present. January 1864 and April 18, 1864 issued clothing. He was appointed sergeant of Co. K, 54th Regiment, Georgia Infantry. May 23, 1865 surrendered and paroled at Thomasville, Georgia. He died at Milledgeville, Georgia August 10, 1909. He was born in Georgia February 16, 1842 and died in Wayne County, Georgia August 10, 1909. He is buried in Stogner Family Cemetery at Ritch, Wayne County, Georgia. (find a grave # 71960062). The Southern Cross of Honor was bestowed on him by the Jesup Chapter United Daughters of the Confederacy in 1904.

HARRIS, WILLIAM: Company F, private (cook). October 1, 1862 enlisted as a private in Co. F, 54th Regiment, Georgia Infantry at Savannah, Georgia and received bounty $50.00. October, November and December 1862 rolls show him as the company cook. January – February 1863 roll shows him present. November 1, 1863 received pay. November – December 1863 roll shows him present. January 1864 and April 25, 1864 issued clothing. May 11, 1864 he was given the order to proceed to Dalton, Georgia as the cook of Co. F by Special Order No. 105/1.

HARRISON, J. E.: Company E, private. He enlisted as a private in Co. E, 54th Regiment, Georgia Infantry. April 1, 1864.

HART, WILLIAM J.: Company H, sergeant. May 12, 1862 enlisted as 4th sergeant in Co. H, 54th Regiment, Georgia Infantry at Columbus, Georgia and received bounty $50.00. December 31, 1862 received pay. January – February 1863 roll shows him present. November – December 1863 roll shows him present. December 31, 1863 received pay. January 1864 issued clothing. January – February 1864 roll shows him present. April 25, 1864 issued clothing. April 26, 1865 surrendered at Greensboro, North Carolina. May 1, 1865 paroled at Greensboro, North Carolina. He was born in Harris County, Georgia March 11, 1837.

HARTLEY, H. T.: Company D, private. April 30, 1862 enlisted as a private in Co. D, 54th Regiment, Georgia Infantry. He died in service.

HARTLEY, J. W.: Company D, private. April 30, 1862 enlisted as a private in Co. D, 54th Regiment, Georgia Infantry. He died at Lexington, Kentucky.

HARVEY, E. W.: Company H (A) (D), private. April 24, 1862 enlisted as a private in Co. H, 54th Regiment, Georgia Infantry at Macon, Georgia and received bounty $50.00. September 1, 1862 transferred from Co. H, 54th Regiment, Georgia Infantry to Co. A, 54th Regiment, Georgia Infantry by Special Order No. 6. September 1862 rolls reflect the transfer. April 30, 1863 received pay. June 30, 1863 roll shows him present. October 31, 1863 received pay. November – December 1863 roll shows him present. January 1, 1864 received pay. January – February 1864 roll shows him absent on furlough. March 19, 1864 transferred to Co. D, 54th Regiment, Georgia Infantry by Special Order No. 54/1. March 31, 1864 issued clothing. April 1, 1864 he deserted.

HARVEY, WILLIAM H.: Company H, private. March 14, 1862 enlisted as a private in Co. H, 54th Regiment, Georgia Infantry at Columbus, Georgia and received bounty $50.00. October 31, 1863 received pay. November – December 1863 roll shows him present. December 31, 1863 received pay. January 1864 issued clothing. January – February 1864 roll shows him present. June 2, 1864 issued clothing.

HASSETT, WILLIAM B.: Company F, private. May 17, 1861 enlisted as a private in Chisholm's Company, Georgia State Troops. May 1862 mustered out. May 13, 1862 enlisted as a private in Co. F, 54th Regiment, Georgia Infantry at Savannah, Georgia and received bounty $50.00. November 1862 detailed with the Quartermaster's Department. November and December 1862 rolls show him with the Quartermaster's Department. December 31, 1862 received pay. January – February 1863 roll shows him present. April 24, 1863 detailed as clerk for the brigade surgeon. July 31, 1863 received pay $44.00. September 30, 1863 received pay for extra duty $180.00. October 1, 1863, October 7, 1863 and December 24, 1863 issued clothing (detailed). November 1863 received pay $245.90. December 2, 1863 received pay $23.60 and $12.25. October 1, 1863 to February 13, 1864 detailed for extra duty as a clerk at (headquarters Colston's Brigade) Savannah, Georgia at a rate of $3.00 additional pay per day (paid $168.00). February 14, 1864 transferred to District headquarters by Special Order No. 35/3. March 22, 1864 received pay $30.00 for the purchase of a copying book. March 1, 1864 to April 30, 1864 detailed for extra work as a clerk at Savannah, Georgia at a rate of $3.00 additional pay per day. April 27, 1864 and September 22, 1864 issued clothing.

HAYNES, JOHN: Company H, private. He enlisted as a private in Co. H, 54th Regiment, Georgia Infantry.

HAYS, ___: Company H, private. July 26, 1862 enlisted as a private in Co. H, 54th Regiment, Georgia Infantry at Savannah, Georgia and received bounty $50.00. July 1862 roll shows his enlistment.

HEATH, W. M.: Company A, private. He enlisted as a private in Co. A, 54th Regiment, Georgia Infantry.

HEATH, E. R.: Company A, private. He enlisted as a private in Co. A, 54th Regiment, Georgia Infantry.

HEDRICK, GEORGE GUSTAVAS: Company F, private. May 17, 1861 enlisted as a private in Chisholm's Company, Georgia State Troops. May 1862 mustered out. May 13, 1862 enlisted as a private in Co. F, 54th Regiment, Georgia Infantry at Savannah, Georgia and received bounty $50.00. He was born February 11, 1845 and died May 11, 1876. He is buried in Bonaventure Cemetery at Savannah, Chatham County, Georgia. (find a grave # 75782935)

HEDRICK, J. J.: Company F, private. October 10, 1862 enlisted as a private in Co. F, 54th Regiment, Georgia Infantry. December 2, 1862 discharged by civil authority. December 1862 roll shows his discharge.

HEIDT, ISAIAH: Company I, private. January 1, 1863 enlisted as a private in Co. I, 54th Regiment, Georgia Infantry at Savannah, Georgia and received bounty $50.00. December 31, 1862 received pay. January – February 1863 roll shows him present. October 31, 1863 received pay. November – December 1863 roll shows him present. October 31, 1863 received pay. November – December 1863 roll shows him absent (detailed to guard commissary stores at No. 3 C. R. R. on December 15, 1863). February 1, 1864 to February 29, 1864 detailed as a teamster at Savannah, Georgia. March 1, 1864 to March 31, 1864 detailed as a teamster at Hardeeville, South Carolina. April 25, 1864 issued clothing. He was born in Georgia in 1826 and died in Georgia in 1889. He is buried in Old Providence Cemetery in Guyton, Effingham County, Georgia. (find a grave # 49434331)

HEIDT, JAMES JEREMIAH: Company I, private. May 6, 1862 enlisted as a private in Co. I, 54th Regiment, Georgia Infantry at Guyton, Georgia and received bounty $50.00. December 31, 1862 received pay. January – February 1863 roll shows him present. January 1, 1863 to February 26, 1863 detailed at Beaulieu near Savannah, Georgia at a rate of $.25 per day extra. June 1, 1863 to June 30, 1863 detailed at Beaulieu near Savannah, Georgia at a rate of $.25 per day extra. October 31, 1863 received pay. July 1, 1863 to December 31, 1863 detailed as post teamster at Rose Dew Post near Savannah, Georgia. November – December 1863 roll shows him present (wagoner for post). January 1864 issued clothing. January 1, 1864 received pay. March 1, 1864 to March 31, 1864 detailed as a teamster at Hardeeville, South Carolina. April 1, 1864 to April 30, 1864 detailed on extra duty as a laborer at Savannah, Georgia. April 25, 1864 issued clothing. June 30, muster roll for Texas Hospital at Auburn, Alabama shows him present. April 26, 1865 surrendered at Greensboro, North Carolina. May 1, 1865 paroled at Greensboro, North Carolina. He was born in Georgia April 19, 1835 and died in Effingham County, Georgia February 26, 1899. He is buried in Bethel Lutheran Church Cemetery in Springfield, Effingham County, Georgia. (find a grave # 49082017)

HELMY (HELMEY), BENJAMIN J.: Company F, private. September 18, 1861 enlisted as a private in Co. C, 1st Regiment, 1st Brigade, Georgia State Troops. May 1862 mustered out. May 6, 1862 enlisted as a private in Co. F, 54th Regiment, Georgia Infantry at Savannah, Georgia and received bounty $50.00. December 31, 1862 received pay. January – February 1863 roll shows him present. November 1, 1863 received pay. November – December 1863 roll shows him present. January 1864, April 25, 1864 and May 8, 1864 issued clothing. December 13, 1864 captured at Triune, Tennessee. January 5, 1865 received at Military Prison at Louisville, Kentucky from Nashville, Tennessee. January 9, 1865 sent to Camp Chase, Ohio. January 11, 1865 arrived at Camp Chase Military Prison at Columbus, Ohio from Military Prison at Louisville, Kentucky. January 22, 1865 died of Pneumonia in Camp Chase Military Prison at

Columbus, Ohio (grave # 852 1/3 mile south of Camp Chase). (find a grave under Helmy # 55115750))

HELTON, JOHN: Company E, private. He enlisted as a private in Co. E, 54th Regiment, Georgia Infantry.

HENDERSON, GEORGE W.: Company A, private. He enlisted as a private in Co. A, 54th Regiment, Georgia Infantry. June 19, 1864 captured at Marietta, Georgia. June 26, 1864 received at Military Prison at Louisville, Kentucky from Nashville, Tennessee. June 27, 1864 transferred from Military Prison at Louisville, Kentucky to Camp Morton, Indiana. June 28, 1864 received at Camp Morton, Indiana. March 4, 1865 transferred for exchange.

HENDERSON, ISAAC T.: Company B, private. He enlisted as a private in the 54th Regiment, Georgia Infantry. May 10, 1865 surrendered at Tallahassee, Florida. May 15, 1865 paroled at Thomasville, Georgia. He was born June 2, 1844 and died December 7, 1929 in Jeff Davis County, Georgia. He is buried in Hazlehurst City Cemetery at Hazlehurst, Jeff Davis County, Georgia (find a grave # 90278980).

HENDERSON, JAMES W.: Company H (A), private. April 20, 1862 enlisted as a private in Co. A, 54th Regiment, Georgia Infantry at Macon, Georgia and received bounty $50.00. September 1, 1862 transferred from Co. H, 54th Regiment, Georgia Infantry to Co. A, 54th Regiment, Georgia Infantry by Special Order No. 6. September 1862 rolls show the transfer. April 30, 1863 received pay. June 30, 1863 roll shows him present. August 31, 1863 received pay. November 1863 received commutation for rations. November – December 1863 roll shows him absent (on detached service since December 27, 1863). January 1, 1864 received pay. January – February 1864 roll shows him present. April 29, 1864 issued clothing. June 19, 1864 captured near Marietta, Georgia. March 4, 1865 paroled at Camp Morton, Indiana and sent to City Point, Virginia via Baltimore, Maryland for exchange. March 10-12, 1865 received at Boulware & Cox's Wharves, James River, Virginia. He was a resident of Carroll County, Georgia.

HENGRAW, L. O.: Company A, private. He enlisted as a private in Co. A, 54th Regiment, Georgia Infantry. May 28, 1865 surrendered and paroled at Selma, Alabama.

HENSEL, R. M.: private. He enlisted as a private in the 54th Regiment, Georgia Infantry. May 10, 1865 surrendered at Tallahassee, Florida. May 10, 1865 paroled at Thomasville, Georgia. He is described as: 5 feet 10 inches high, light hair, blue eyes and fair complexion.

HERNANDEZ, EDWIN RANDOLPH: Company F, private. May 17, 1861 enlisted as a private in Chisholm's Company, Georgia State Troops. May 1862 mustered out. May 13, 1862 enlisted as a private in Co. F, 54th Regiment, Georgia Infantry at Savannah, Georgia and received bounty $50.00. September 10, 1862 discharged at Beaulieu near Savannah, Georgia. September 1862 rolls show his discharge. He died September 7, 1899. He is buried in Laurel Grove Cemetery at Savannah, Chatham

County, Georgia. (find a grave # 28260229)

HERNDON, E.: Company B, private. December 20, 1862 enlisted as a private in Co. B, 54th Regiment, Georgia Infantry. December 1862 shows his enlistment.

HERNDON G. W.: Company I, private. He enlisted as a private in Co. I, 54th Regiment, Georgia Infantry. January 1863 died in Institute Hospital.

HERNDON G. W.: Company B, private. March 14, 1864 enlisted in Co. A., 4th Georgia Sharpshooters in Macon, Georgia. Transferred to Co. B, 54th Regiment, Georgia Infantry. April 26, 1865 surrendered at Greensboro, North Carolina. May 1, 1865 paroled at Greensboro, North Carolina.

HERNDON, GEORGE WILLIS: Company B, private. April 28, 1862 enlisted as a private in Co. B, 54th Regiment, Georgia Infantry at Savannah, Georgia and received bounty $50.00. December 31, 1862 received pay. January – February 1863 roll shows him present (sick in the regimental hospital). January 1864 issued clothing. April 26, 1865 surrendered at Greensboro, North Carolina. May 1, 1865 paroled at Greensboro, North Carolina. He was born January 1, 1834 in Appling County, Georgia and died August 1, 1910 in Appling County, Georgia. He is buried at Pleasant Grove Cemetery in Appling County, Georgia. (find a grave # 25716046)

HERNDON, ISAAC: Company B, private. December 20, 1862 enlisted as a private in Co. B, 54th Regiment, Georgia Infantry at Savannah, Georgia and received bounty $50.00. December 31, 1862 received pay. January – February 1863 roll shows him present. November 13, 1863 he died of wounds received at Battery Wagner near Charleston, South Carolina. May 25, 1864 Death Benefit Claim filed by his father, James Herndon. He was born in 1842 in Appling County, Georgia. He is most likely buried in unmarked grave at Magnolia Cemetery at Charleston, South Carolina.

HERNDON, WILEY (WILLIAM) L.: Company K, private. October 3, 1861 enlisted as a private in Co. A, 1st Regiment, 1st Brigade, Georgia State Troops. April 28, 1862 enlisted as a private in Co. K, 54th Regiment, Georgia Infantry at Savannah, Georgia and received bounty $50.00. January 1, 1863 received pay. January – February 1863 roll shows him present on picket. June 17, 1864 admitted to Ocmulgee, Hospital at Macon, Georgia with a Gunshot Wound of the left hand, ball passing through and fracturing metacarpal bone on the ring finger. March 18, 1864, April 25, 1864 and June 2, 1864 issued clothing. June 20, 1864 furloughed for 60 days to Appling, County, Georgia. May 4, 1865 surrendered at Citronella, Alabama. May 16, 1865 paroled at Meridian, Mississippi. He was born in 1839 in Appling County, Georgia and died circa 1865 in Appling County, Georgia. He was buried in Appling County, Georgia and his marker is in Milikin Cemetery (across Georgia 121 from where he was buried in Appling County, Georgia). (find a grave # 129212827)

HERRINGTON, JAMES: Company B, private. He enlisted as a private in Co. B, 54th Regiment, Georgia Infantry.

HERRINGTON, JOHN: Company A, private. April 3, 1862 enlisted as a private in Co. A, 54th Regiment, Georgia Infantry at Macon, Georgia and received bounty $50.00. April 30, 1863 received pay. June 30, 1863 roll shows him absent on furlough. October 31, 1863 received pay. November – December 1863 roll shows him present. January 1, 1864 received pay. January – February 1864 roll shows him present. April 29, 1864 and May 8, 1864 issued clothing. He was born in Emanuel County, Georgia in 1832 and died in Emanuel County, Georgia in 1898. He is buried in Herrington Cemetery at Nunez, Emanuel County, Georgia. (find a grave # 78022764)

HERRINGTON (HARRINGTON), JOHN: Company B, private. He enlisted as a private in Co. B, 54th Regiment, Georgia Infantry. January 1864 issued clothing. June 8, 1864 shown on list of Oliver Hospital at Dalton, Georgia as being furloughed for 60 days (Chronic Diarrhoea with extreme emaciation and debility – sick 3 months) May 18, 1865 surrendered and paroled at Augusta, Georgia. He was a resident of Swainsboro, Georgia.

HERRINGTON (HARRINGTON), RILEY A.: Company F (A), private. October 17, 1861 enlisted as a private in Co. C, 1st Independent Battalion, Georgia State Troops. April 16, 1862 roll shows him present. April 1862 mustered out. April 16, 1862 roll shows him present. April 1862 mustered out at Camp Lee near Savannah, Georgia. April 18, 1862 enlisted as a private in Co. F, 54th Regiment, Georgia Infantry at Macon, Georgia and received bounty $50.00. September 1, 1862 transferred from Co. F, 54th Regiment, Georgia Infantry to Co. A, 54th Regiment, Georgia Infantry at Beaulieu near Savannah, Georgia by Special Order No. 6. April 30, 1863 received pay. September 1862 rolls reflect the transfer. June 30, 1863 roll shows him present. October 31, 1863 received pay. November 1863 received commutation for rations. November – December 1863 roll shows him present (sick in company hospital). January 1, 1864 received pay. January – February 1864 roll shows him present. April 29, 1864 issued clothing. June 19, 1864 captured at Marietta, Georgia. June 26, 1864 received at Military Prison at Louisville, Kentucky from Nashville, Tennessee. June 27, 1864 sent to Camp Morton, Indiana from Military Prison at Louisville, Kentucky. June 28, 1864 received at Camp Morton, Indianapolis, Indiana. March 4, 1865 transferred from Camp Morton, Indiana for exchange. March 4, 1865 paroled at Camp Morton, Indiana and forwarded to City Point, Virginia via Baltimore, Maryland for exchange. March 10-12, 1865 received at Boulware & Cox's Wharves, James River, Virginia.

HEWETT, JOSEPH ADKIN: Company H, private. January 28, 1863 enlisted as a private in Co. H, 54th Regiment, Georgia Infantry at Columbus, Georgia and received bounty $50.00. January – February 1863 roll shows him present. October 31, 1863 received pay. November – December 1863 roll shows him present. December 31, 1863 received pay. January 1864 issued clothing. January – February 1864 roll shows him absent (on ten days furlough since February 28, 1864). July 9, 1864 admitted to Ocmulgee Hospital at Macon, Georgia with a Gunshot Wound (ball entering just above the left ear). July 11, 1864 furloughed for 60 days to Cusseta, Chattahoochee County, Georgia.

HICKS, ALFORD: Company A, private. November 14, 1861 enlisted as a private in Co. C, 1st Independent Battalion, Georgia State Troops. April 16, 1862 roll shows him present. April 1862 mustered out. April 23, 1862 enlisted as a private in Co. A, 54th Regiment, Georgia Infantry at Macon, Georgia and received bounty $50.00. April 30, 1863 received pay. June 30, 1863 roll shows him present. October 31, 1863 received pay. November – December 1863 roll shows him present sick in company hospital. December 31, 1863 received pay. January 1864 issued clothing. January – February 1864 roll shows him present. April 29, 1864 issued clothing. April 21-22, 1865 captured at Macon, Georgia. He was born in Chattahoochee County, Georgia in 1843.

HICKS, H.: Company H (A), private. He enlisted as a private in Co. H, 54th Regiment, Georgia Infantry. September 1, 1862 transferred from Co. H, 54th Regiment, Georgia Infantry to Co. A, 54th Regiment, Georgia Infantry by Special Order No. 6. September 1862 rolls show the transfer.

HIGHTOWER, J. G.: Company B, private. He enlisted as a private in Co. B, 54th Regiment, Georgia Infantry.

HIGHTOWER, SEABORN JOHNSON: Company H, private. May 12, 1862 enlisted as a private in Co. H, 54th Regiment, Georgia Infantry at Columbus, Georgia and received bounty $50.00. October 1862 shows him detailed to the company commissary. December 1862 roll shows him detailed as an ambulance driver. December 31, 1862 received pay. January – February 1863 roll shows him present. October 31, 1863 received pay. November – December 1863 roll shows him absent on sick furlough. December 1, 1863 to December 31, 1863 detailed for extra duty at Beaulieu near Savannah, Georgia at a rate of an additional $.25 per day. December 31, 1863 received pay. January 1864 issued clothing. January – February 1864 roll shows him present. June 2, 1864 issued clothing. July 9, 1864 accidentally wounded in the left arm at Atlanta, Georgia resulting in arm amputation near the shoulder. November 28, 1864 received pay $49.73. He was born in Greene County, Georgia November 24, 1835 and died at the Confederate Soldiers Home in Atlanta, Georgia August 29, 1910. He is buried in Westview Cemetery at Atlanta, Fulton County, Georgia. (find a grave # 50763608)

HIGHTOWER, WILLIAM J.: Company H, lieutenant. May 12, 1862 enlisted as a private in Co. H, 54th Regiment, Georgia Infantry at Columbus, Georgia and received bounty $50.00. May 16, 1862 appointed 2nd lieutenant of Co. H, 54th Regiment, Georgia Infantry. June 2, 1862 he is shown as absent without leave. July 1862 roll shows him present at Savannah, Georgia. August 1862 roll shows him present at Beaulieu near Savannah, Georgia. September and October 1862 rolls show him absent sick since September 19, 1862. November 24, 1862 list shows him in the Savannah Area. November and December 1862 rolls at Beaulieu near Savannah, Georgia show him absent without leave since November 12,

1862. January 7, 1863 dropped from the rolls due to ill health by order of General Beauregard (Special Order No. 47). January – February 1863 roll shows him dropped from the rolls.

HINELY, EDWIN JEFFERSON: Company I, private. September 18, 1861 enlisted as a private in Co. C, 1st Regiment, 1st Brigade, Georgia State Troops. March 18, 1862 mustered out. May 6, 1862 enlisted as a private in Co. I, 54th Regiment, Georgia Infantry at Guyton, Georgia and received bounty $50.00. December 31, 1862 received pay. January – February 1863 roll shows him present. October 31, 1863 received pay. November – December 1863 roll shows him absent in arrest. January 1864 issued clothing. He was born in Effingham County, Georgia October 27, 1843 and died in Georgia December 13, 1898. He is buried in the Springfield City Cemetery in Springfield, Effingham County, Georgia. (find a grave # 38152435)

HINELY, JAMES ANDREW: Company I (F), corporal. May 6, 1862 enlisted as a private in Co. I, 54th Regiment, Georgia Infantry at Guyton, Georgia and received bounty $50.00. December 31, 1862 received pay. January – February 1863 roll shows him present. October 31, 1863 received pay. November – December 1863 roll shows him present. He was elected 4th corporal of Co. F, 54th Regiment, Georgia Infantry. January 1864 and September 23, 1864 issued clothing. January 13, 1865 admitted to St. Mary's Hospital at West Point, Mississippi with Diarrhoea. April 26, 1865 surrendered in Co. F, 54th Regiment, Georgia Infantry at Greensboro, North Carolina. May 1, 1865 paroled at Greensboro, North Carolina. He was born June 11, 1840 and died June 11, 1865. He is buried in Ganann Cemetery in Stillwell, Effingham County, Georgia. (find a grave # 63527446)

HINELY, JAMES W.: Company I, private. May 6, 1862 enlisted as a private in Co. I, 54th Regiment, Georgia Infantry at Guyton, Georgia and received bounty $50.00. December 31, 1862 received pay. January – February 1863 roll shows him present. October 31, 1863 received pay. November – December 1863 roll shows him present. January 1864 and April 25, 1864 issued clothing. He was born in Effingham County, Georgia January 14, 1834 and died in Effingham County, Georgia August 22, 1896. He is buried in Jerusalem Lutheran Church Cemetery at Rincon, Effingham County, Georgia. (find a grave # 66660964)

HINELY, JOHN MATTHEW: Company I, private. September 18, 1861 enlisted as a private in Co. C, 1st Regiment, 1st Brigade, Georgia State Troops. March 18, 1862 mustered out. May 6, 1862 enlisted as a private in Co. I, 54th Regiment, Georgia Infantry at Guyton, Georgia and received bounty $50.00. December 31, 1862 received pay. January – February 1863 roll shows him present sick in regimental hospital. August 27, 1863 to December 31, 1863 on detached duty as courier to Brigade headquarters in Savannah, Georgia at a rate of an additional $.25 per day. October 31, 1863 received pay. November – December 1863 roll shows him present (courier for post). January 20, 1864 received pay. January

1864 and April 28, 1864 issued clothing. Pension records show; He was in the hospital at the close of the war. He was born March 25, 1829 and died October 19, 1896. He is buried in Burgsteiner Family Cemetery at Springfield, Effingham County, Georgia. (find a grave # 32561858)

HINELY, THOMAS HARMON: Company F, corporal. September 18, 1861 enlisted as a private in Co. C, 1st Independent Battalion, Georgia State Troops. March 18, 1862 mustered out. May 6, 1862 enlisted as a private in Co. F, 54th Regiment, Georgia Infantry at Savannah, Georgia and received bounty $50.00. December 31, 1862 received pay. January – February 1863 roll shows him present. November 1, 1863 received pay. November – December 1863 roll shows him present. September 1863 received commutation of rations. December 31, 1863 received pay. January 1864 and May 8, 1864 issued clothing. June 19, 1864 wounded near Marietta, Georgia. August 20, 1864 admitted to Hospital at Shelby Springs, Alabama. July – August 1864 roll of Hospital at Shelby Springs, Alabama shows him present as a patient. August 20, 1864 admitted to 1st Mississippi C. S. A. Hospital at Jackson Mississippi with Irritilatis Spinalis. September 18, 1864 returned to duty. September 22, 1864 issued clothing. October 23, 1864 admitted to Ocmulgee Hospital at Macon, Georgia with Neuralgia. October 26, 1864 transferred from Ocmulgee Hospital at Macon, Georgia. He was a resident of Guyton, Effingham County, Georgia. He was born in Effingham County, Georgia September 25, 1842 and died at Rincon, Effingham County, Georgia December 1, 1912. He is buried in Jerusalem Lutheran Church Cemetery at Rincon, Emanuel County, Georgia. (find a grave # 26519860)

HINGES, MARTIN: Company F, private. January 20, 1863 enlisted as a private in Co. F, 54th Regiment, Georgia Infantry at Savannah, Georgia and received bounty $50.00. January – February 1863 roll shows him present. November 1, 1863 received pay. November – December 1863 roll shows him present (in arrest). January 1864 issued clothing. July 22, 1864 wounded in Atlanta, Georgia. September 7, 1864 shown on a roll of Floyd House Hospital at Macon, Georgia with a Gunshot Wound left thigh, lower 3rd, flesh wound.

HOBBY, WENSLEY H.: Company D, lieutenant. October 28, 1861 enlisted and was elected 2nd lieutenant of Co. I, 5th Regiment, Georgia State Troops. April 1862 mustered out.

October 4, 1862 enlisted as a private in Co. D, 54th Regiment, Georgia Infantry at Beaulieu near Savannah, Georgia and received bounty $50.00. October 1862 roll shows him as captain's clerk. November 1, 1862 to November 30, 1862 shown as detailed as a butcher at Beaulieu near Savannah, Georgia. November and December 1862 rolls show him detailed as commissary clerk. December 31, 1862 received pay. January 15, 1863 received pay (with an additional $.25 per day in payment for detailed duty). January 1, 1863 to February 19, 1863 detailed as a butcher. February 26, 1863 received pay (with an additional $.25 per day in payment for detailed duty). January – February 1863 roll shows him present (detailed in the commissary department). March 1, 1863 to March 31, 1863 detailed as a clerk. March 12, 1863 received pay (with an additional $.25 per day in payment for detailed duty). March 24, 1864 appointed 2nd lieutenant of Co. D, 54th Regiment, Georgia Infantry. He was a resident of Screven County, Georgia. He was born in Augusta, Richmond County, Georgia April 23, 1831 and died in Screven County, Georgia May 6, 1892. He is buried in Sylvania Cemetery at Sylvania, Screven County, Georgia. (find a grave # 32278273)

HODGE, JOHN R.: Company A (F), private. May 6, 1862 enlisted as a private in Co. A, 54th Regiment, Georgia Infantry at Savannah, Georgia and received bounty $50.00. December 31, 1862 received pay. January 1, 1863 transferred from Co. A, 54th Regiment, Georgia Infantry to Co. F, 54th Regiment, Georgia Infantry. January – February 1863 roll shows him present. April 30, 1863 received pay. June 30, 1863 roll shows him present. October 1, 1864 received pay at Savannah, Georgia (additional $.25 per day in payment for detailed duty). October 31, 1863 received pay. November – December 1863 roll of Co. A, 54th Regiment, Georgia Infantry shows him absent (teamster for company and absent on furlough since December 27, 1863). January – February 1864 roll shows him present (teamster for the company). March 31, 1864 and April 29, 1864 issued clothing. May 19, 1864 captured at Kingston, Georgia. May 24, 1864 arrived at Military Prison at Louisville, Kentucky from Nashville, Tennessee. May 28, 1864 sent to Rock Island, Illinois. May 29, 1864 received at Rock Island Barracks, Illinois. October 15, 1864 enlisted at Rock Island Barracks, Illinois in the U. S. Army for frontier service.

HODGES, JAMES K. POLK: Company I, private. April 1863 enlisted as a private in Co. I, 54th Regiment, Georgia Infantry. March – April 1865 he was sick in the hospital in Nashville, Tennessee. He was born in Effingham County, Georgia May 21, 1846 and died in Effingham County, Georgia February 16, 1918. He is buried in Little Ogeechee Baptist Church Cemetery at Oliver, Screven County, Georgia. (find a grave # 24321686)

HODGES, JAMES P.: Company I, private. January 25, 1863 enlisted as a private in Co. I, 54th Regiment, Georgia Infantry. September 13, 1864 died in C. S. A. Hospital at Jackson, Mississippi of Chronic Diarrhoea.

HODGES, JONATHAN G.: Company I, private. January 22, 1863 enlisted as a private in Co. I, 54th Regiment, Georgia Infantry at Beaulieu near Savannah, Georgia. December 31, 1862 received pay. January – February 1863 roll shows him present. October 31, 1863 received pay. November – December 1863 roll shows him present on picket guard. December 31, 1863 received pay. January 1864 issued clothing. April 28, 1864 admitted to Hospital at Shelby Springs, Alabama. July – August 1864 roll of Hospital at Shelby Springs, Alabama shows him present. August 20, 1864 admitted to 1st Mississippi C. S. A. Hospital at Jackson, Mississippi with Chronic Diarrhoea. September 13, 1864 he died in 1st Mississippi C. S. A. Hospital at Jackson, Mississippi of Chronic Diarrhoea (also shown: September 14, 1864 he died in General Hospital at Shelby

Springs, Alabama).

HODGES, R. E.: Company I, private. July 30, 1863 enlisted as a private in Co. I, 54th Regiment, Georgia Infantry at Rose Dew near Savannah, Georgia. October 31, 1863 received pay. November – December 1863 roll shows him present on picket guard. January 1864 and June 2, 1864 issued clothing.

HOFFMAN, JOHN J.: Company E, sergeant. He enlisted as a sergeant in Co. E, 54th Regiment, Georgia Infantry.

HOGAN, JAMES: Company K, sergeant. He enlisted as a sergeant in Co. K, 54th Regiment, Georgia Infantry.

HOLLOMAN, FRANKLIN: Company A, private. May 6, 1862 enlisted as a private in Co. A, 54th Regiment, Georgia Infantry at Savannah, Georgia and received bounty $50.00. April 30, 1863 received pay. June 30, 1863 roll shows him present. October 31, 1863 received pay. November 1863 received commutation for rations. November – December 1863 roll shows him present. January 1, 1864 received pay. January – February 1864 roll shows him present. March 31, 1864 and April 29, 1864 issued clothing. February 20, 1865 admitted to Way Hospital at Meridian, Mississippi with a Gunshot Wound and was transferred to Macon, Georgia. April 20 (21), 1865 captured at Macon, Georgia. He was born June 23, 1831 and died June 3, 1917. He is buried in Holliman Cemetery in Jones County, Georgia. (find a grave # 130442296)

HOLLOWAY (HALLOWAY), D. W.: Company H, private. February 24, 1863 enlisted as a private in Co. H, 54th Regiment, Georgia Infantry at Columbus, Georgia and received bounty $50.00. December 31, 1862 received pay. January – February 1863 roll shows him present. October 31, 1863 received pay. November – December 1863 roll shows him present. December 31, 1863 received pay. January 1864 issued clothing. January – February 1864 roll shows him present. June 2, 1864 issued clothing. February 8, 1865 admitted to Way Hospital at Meridian, Mississippi with a Gunshot Wound and was furloughed. May 10, 1865 surrendered at Tallahassee, Florida. May 19, 1865 paroled at Albany, Georgia.

HOLLOWAY, EDWARD S.: Company G, private. May 18, 1864 enlisted in Co. C, 37th Regiment, Georgia Infantry in Macon, Georgia. April 26, 1865 surrendered in Co. G, 54th Regiment, Georgia Infantry at Greensboro, North Carolina. May 1, 1865 paroled at Greensboro, North Carolina.

HOLLOWAY, JOSEPH B.: Company G, sergeant. He enlisted as 1st sergeant in Co. G, 54th Regiment, Georgia Infantry.

HOLSTEAD, WILLIAM H.: Company E, private. February 28, 1862 enlisted in Co. K, 37th Regiment, Georgia Infantry in Columbus, Georgia. April 26, 1865 surrendered in Co. E, 54th Regiment, Georgia Infantry at Greensboro, North Carolina. May 1, 1865 paroled at Greensboro, North Carolina.

HOOD, W. C.: Company B, private. He enlisted as a private in Co. B, 54th Regiment, Georgia Infantry.

HOOKER, GEORGE W. (H.): Company B, private. April 28, 1862 enlisted as a private in Co. B, 54th Regiment, Georgia Infantry at Savannah, Georgia and received bounty $50.00. December 31, 1862 received pay. January – February 1863 roll shows him present. January 1864, April 25, 1864 and May 8, 1864 issued clothing. April 21-22, 1865 captured and paroled in Macon, Georgia in 1865. He was born in Appling County July 16, 1840.

HORNE (HORN), L. J.: Company H, private. November 5, 1862 enlisted as a private in Co. H, 54th Regiment, Georgia Infantry at Columbus, Georgia and received bounty $50.00. Pension records show; he was discharged August 1863. 1864 he enlisted in Co. C, 9th Regiment, Georgia Militia. He was paroled in 1865. He was born in Harris County August 1847 and died there July 4, 1930.

HORN (HORNE), THOMAS JEFFERSON: Company H, private. November 5, 1862 enlisted as a private in Co. H, 54th Regiment, Georgia Infantry at Columbus, Georgia and received bounty $50.00. Pension records show; he was discharged August 1863. 1864 he enlisted in Co. I, 9th Regiment, Georgia Militia. He was paroled in 1865. January – February 1864 roll shows him present.

HORNE (HORN), THOMAS JEFFERSON: Company H, private. November 5, 1862 enlisted as a private in Co. H, 54th Regiment, Georgia Infantry at Columbus, Georgia and received bounty $50.00. November 1862 roll shows his enlistment. December 31, 1862 received pay. January – February 1863 roll shows him present. October 31, 1863 received pay. November – December 1863 roll shows him present. December 31, 1863 received pay. January 1864 issued clothing. January – February 1864 roll shows him present on guard. June 26, 1864 died of Febris Continuing Commumis in Cannon Hospital at LaGrange, Georgia. His effects were $5.00 in cash. He was born in Harris County, Georgia August 1847 and died in La Grange, Troup County, Georgia June 26, 1864. He is buried in Stonewall Confederate Cemetery at La Grange, Troup County, Georgia. (find a grave # 63274945)

HORTON, J. W.: Company H (A), private. May 4, 1862 enlisted as a private in Co. H, 54th Regiment, Georgia Infantry at Macon, Georgia and received bounty $50.00. September 1, 1862 transferred from Co. H, 54th Regiment, Georgia Infantry to Co. A, 54th Regiment, Georgia Infantry at Beaulieu near Savannah, Georgia by Special Order No. 6. September rolls show his transfer. June 30, 1863 roll shows he deserted.

HOTALING (HOTELLING), A.: Company A, private. December 17, 1861 enlisted as a private in Co. C, 1st Independent Battalion, Georgia State Troops. April 16, 1862 roll shows him present. April 1862 mustered out May 4, 1862 enlisted as a private in Co. A, 54th Regiment, Georgia Infantry at Macon, Georgia and received bounty $50.00. June 13, 1862 appointed wagoner for the quartermaster's department. July through December 1862 rolls at Beaulieu near Savannah, Georgia reflect his appointment as wagoner (teamster) at a rate of an additional $.25 per day. January 1 to

February 28, 1863 on detached service at a rate of an additional $.25 per day. April 30, 1863 received pay June 30, 1863 roll shows him absent (teamster in the 54th Georgia Regiment). June 1, 1863 to August 31, 1863 detached at Charleston, South Carolina as forage master at a rate of an additional $.25 per day. September 21, 1863 received pay $22.00. October 31, 1863 received pay. November – December 1863 roll shows him present. January 1, 1864 received pay. January – February 1864 roll shows him present. March 31, 1864 and May 8, 1864 issued clothing.

HOUSE, DANIEL S.: Company A, private. November 14, 1862 enlisted as a private in Co. A, 54th Regiment, Georgia Infantry at Macon, Georgia and received bounty $50.00. April 30, 1863 received pay. June 30, 1863 roll shows him present as an ambulance driver. May 1, 1863 to June 30, 1863 detailed as an ambulance driver at Savannah, Georgia. October 31, 1863 received pay. November 1863 received commutation for rations. November – December 1863 roll shows him present. January 1, 1864 received pay. January – February 1864 roll shows him present. February 21, 1864 transferred to Captain McAlpin's Engineer Department by Special Order No. 1/13. He died in 1892.

HOUSE, W.: Company A, private. November 30, 1862 enlisted as a private in Co. A, 54th Regiment, Georgia Infantry at Beaulieu near Savannah, Georgia and received bounty $50.00. November 1862 roll reflects his enlistment.

HOUSTON, EDWIN A.: Company H, private. January 28, 1863 enlisted as a private in Co. H, 54th Regiment, Georgia Infantry at Columbus, Georgia and received bounty $50.00. January – February 1863 roll shows him present. October 31, 1863 received pay. November – December 1863 roll shows him present. December 31, 1863 received pay. January 1864 issued clothing. January – February 1864 roll shows him present on guard. January 10, 1865 admitted to St. Mary's Hospital at West Point, Mississippi with Catarrhus. January 11, 1865 admitted to Way Hospital at Meridian, Mississippi with a Gunshot Wound and was furloughed. He was born October 13, 1844 and died March 22, 1875. He is buried in Salem Cemetery at Salem, Lee County, Alabama. (find a grave # 13924238)

HOWARD, ABNER: Company G, sergeant. May 12, 1862 enlisted as a private in Co. G, 54th Regiment, Georgia Infantry at Columbus, Georgia and received bounty $50.00. December 31, 1862 received pay. January 15, 1863 elected 5th sergeant of Co. G, 54th Regiment, Georgia Infantry. January – February 1863 roll shows him present (elected 5th sergeant to replace Sergeant F. Roberts who resigned – January 15, 1863). He was born in 1830 and died in 1880. He is buried in Ellerslie United Methodist Church Cemetery at Ellerslie, Harris County, Georgia. (find a grave # 50819105)

HOWARD, J. W.: Company B, private. He enlisted as a private in Co. B, 54th Regiment, Georgia Infantry.

HOWARD, WESLEY L.: Company A, private. April 18, 1862 enlisted as a private in Co. A, 54th Regiment, Georgia Infantry. July 22, 1864 killed in the battle of Atlanta, Georgia.

HOWARD, WILLIAM LAFAYETTE (J.): Company H, private. January 28, 1863 enlisted as a private in Co. H, 54th Regiment, Georgia Infantry at Columbus, Georgia and received bounty $50.00. January – February 1863 roll shows him present. October 31, 1863 received pay. November – December 1863 roll shows him present. December 31, 1863 received pay. January 1864 issued clothing. January – February 1864 roll shows him absent on ten (10) days furlough since February 28, 1864). July 22, 1864 killed at Atlanta, Georgia.

HOWELL (HEWELL), JOSEPH ADKIN: Company H, private. January 28, 1863 enlisted as a private in Co. H, 54th Regiment, Georgia Infantry. November – December roll shows him present. Pension records show; June 25 (27), 1864 he was wounded in the head resulting in deafness and loss of left eye at Kennesaw Mountain, Georgia. He was born in Georgia December 2, 1826.

HOWELL (HEWELL), JOSEPH C.: Company H, private. He enlisted as a private in Co. H, 54th Regiment, Georgia Infantry.

HOYT, WILLIAM: Company A, private. He enlisted in as a private in Co. A, 54th Regiment, Georgia Infantry.

HUBBARD, A. J.: Company H, corporal. May 12, 1862 enlisted as a private in Co. H, 54th Regiment, Georgia Infantry at Columbus, Georgia and received bounty $50.00. December 31, 1862 received pay. January – February 1863 roll shows him present. October 31, 1863 received pay. November – December 1863 roll shows him present. December 31, 1863 received pay. January 1864 issued clothing. January – February 1864 roll shows him present on picket. April 25, 1864 issued clothing. April 26, 1865 surrendered at Greensboro, North Carolina. May 1, 1865 paroled at Greensboro, North Carolina. He was born in Henry County, Georgia August 1831.

HUBBARD, ERASMUS: Company H, private. February 25, 1864 enlisted as a private in Co. H, 54th Regiment, Georgia Infantry at Hardeeville, South Carolina. January 1864 issued clothing. January – February 1864 roll shows him present on guard. April 25, 1864 issued clothing. 1864 he died leaving effects of $6.00. He was born in 1843 and died July 6, 1864. He is buried in Madison Historic Cemetery at Madison, Morgan County, Georgia. (find a grave # 60074075)

HUBBARD, RICHARD JACKSON: Company H, private. January 28, 1863 enlisted as a private in Co. H, 54th Regiment, Georgia Infantry at Columbus, Georgia and received bounty $50.00. January – February 1863 roll shows him present. October 31, 1863 received pay. November – December 1863 roll shows him absent on picket. December 31, 1863 received pay. January 1864 issued clothing. January – February 1864 roll shows him present on guard. June 1864 issued clothing. Pension records show; he was at home on sick furlough at the close of the war. He was born in Harris County, Georgia September 15, 1840. He was born September 15, 1842 and died July 23, 1929. He is buried in Getzen Memorial Baptist

Church Cemetery at Fortson, Muscogee County, Georgia. (find a grave # 89993340)

HUCKABY, J. CARTER: Company H, private. May 12, 1862 enlisted as a private in Co. H, 54th Regiment, Georgia Infantry at Columbus, Georgia and received bounty $50.00. December 31, 1862 received pay. January – February 1863 roll shows him present. October 31, 1863 received pay. November – December 1863 roll shows him absent on picket. December 31, 1863 received pay. January 1864 issued clothing. January – February 1864 roll shows him present. August 31, 1864 captured near Jonesboro, Georgia. September 3, 1864 sent to Nashville, Tennessee. September 19-22, 1864 exchanged at Rough and Ready, Georgia. October 27, 1864 he died at Macon, Georgia. He is buried in Rose Hill Cemetery at Macon, Bibb County, Georgia. (find a grave # 105242952)

HUCKABY, OLIVER B.: Company H, private. May 12, 1862 enlisted as a private in Co. H, 54th Regiment, Georgia Infantry at Columbus, Georgia and received bounty $50.00. December 31, 1862 received pay. January – February 1863 roll shows him present. October 31, 1863 received pay. November – December 1863 roll shows him absent on picket. December 31, 1863 received pay. January 1864 issued clothing. January – February 1864 roll shows him present.

HUDGEONS, FRANCIS L.: Company G, private. April 22, 1864 enlisted in Co. C, 37th Regiment, Georgia Infantry in Macon, Georgia. April 26, 1865 surrendered in Co. G, 54th Regiment, Georgia Infantry at Greensboro, North Carolina. May 1, 1865 paroled at Greensboro, North Carolina.

HUDSON, DAVID BISHOP: Company A, private. May 6, 1862 enlisted as a private in Co. A, 54th Regiment, Georgia Infantry at Macon, Georgia and received bounty $50.00. April 30, 1863 received pay. June 30, 1863 roll shows him present. August 1, 1863 to August 31, 1863 detailed as teamster at an additional rate of $.25 per day at Savannah, Georgia. October 1, 1863 to October 31, 1863 detailed as teamster at an additional rate of $.25 per day at Isle of hope near Savannah, Georgia. October 31, 1863 received pay. November – December 1863 roll shows him present. December 1863 received pay. January 1, 1864 received pay. January – February 1864 roll shows him present. March 31, 1864 issued clothing. April 26, 1865 surrendered Co. D, 54th Regiment, Georgia Infantry at Greensboro, North Carolina. May 1, 1865 paroled at Greensboro, North Carolina. He was born April 19, 1840 and died March 20, 1900. He is buried in the Hudson /Felts Cemetery at Gray, Jones County, Georgia. (find a grave # 96346569)

HUDSON, JOHN WESLEY: Company A, private. May 5, 1862 enlisted as a private in Co. A, 54th Regiment, Georgia Infantry at Macon, Georgia and received bounty $50.00. April 30, 1863 received pay. June 30, 1863 roll shows him present (sick in company hospital). October 31, 1863 received pay. November – December 1863 roll shows him present as teamster (sick in company hospital). December 1863 received pay.

January 1, 1864 received pay. January – February 1864 roll shows him present (teamster for company). March 31, 1864 issued clothing. April 26, 1865 surrendered Co. D, 54th Regiment, Georgia Infantry at Greensboro, North Carolina. May 1, 1865 paroled at Greensboro, North Carolina. He was born August 30, 1831 and died in Jones County, Georgia July 11, 1900. He is buried in Hudson/Felts Cemetery at Gray, Jones County, Georgia. (find a grave # 80197878)

HUDSON, WILLIAM J.: Company A, private. May 3, 1862 enlisted as a private in Co. A, 54th Regiment, Georgia Infantry at Macon, Georgia and received bounty $50.00. April 30, 1863 received pay. June 30, 1863 roll shows him present. October 31, 1863 received pay. November – December 1863 roll shows him present. January 1, 1864 received pay. January – February 1864 roll shows him present. March 31, 1864 issued clothing.

HUGHES (HUGHS), ISHAM: Company B, private. October 10, 1861 enlisted as a private in Co. K, 2nd Regiment, 1st Brigade, Georgia State Troops. April 1862 mustered out. April 21, 1862 enlisted as a private in Co. B, 54th Regiment, Georgia Infantry at Savannah, Georgia and received bounty $50.00. December 31, 1862 received pay. January – February 1863 roll shows him present. January 1864 issued clothing.

HUGHES, M. H.: Company B, private. April 21, 1862 enlisted as a private in Co. B, 54th Regiment, Georgia Infantry at Savannah, Georgia and received bounty $50.00. Pension records show he was at home on sick furlough at the close of the war. He was born in Appling County, Georgia July 31, 1837 and died May 29, 1915 in Appling (Jeff Davis) County, Georgia. He is buried in Oak View Cemetery in Jeff Davis County, Georgia. (find a grave # 61879043)

HUGHES (HUGHS), WILLIAM: Company B, private. April 28, 1862 enlisted as a private in Co. B, 54th Regiment, Georgia Infantry at Savannah, Georgia and received bounty $50.00. December 31, 1862 received pay. January – February 1863 roll shows him present. January 1864 and April 25, 1864 issued clothing. July 25, 1864 died of Fever near Atlanta, Georgia.

HUGHEY, JOHN: Company B, private. He enlisted as a private in Co. B, 54th Regiment, Georgia Infantry.

HUGHEY, JOHN W.: Company B, lieutenant. October 10, 1861 enlisted in and appointed 2nd lieutenant of Co. K, 2nd Regiment, 1st Brigade, Georgia State Troops. April 1862 mustered out. April 21, 1862 enlisted as 1st sergeant of Co. B, 54th Regiment, Georgia Infantry. July 28, 1862 elected 1st lieutenant of Co. B, 54th Regiment, Georgia Infantry at Savannah, Georgia. July 1862 roll shows his election to 1st lieutenant. August and September 1862 rolls show him present at Beaulieu near Savannah, Georgia. October 1862 roll at Beaulieu near Savannah, Georgia shows him absent with leave for 10 days since October 25, 1862. November 24, 1862 his name appears on a list of officers at Savannah, Georgia. November and December 1862 rolls show him present at Beaulieu near Savannah, Georgia. October 21, 1862 he appears on a list of officers at Legare's Point, South Carolina. January – February 1863 roll shows him present. March 5, 1863 received pay $90.00. April 2, 1863 received pay $90.00. June 25, 1863 to June 28, 1863 he was on furlough approved by General Mercer. June 30, 1863 his name appears on a list of officers absent. September 14, 1863 received pay $180.00. December 14, 1863 requested a leave of absence to visit his home. December 22, 1863 detailed for special duty (Special Order No. 112/2). June 7, 1864 received pay $180.00. January 24, 1864 granted a leave of absence for 50 days at Tupelo, Mississippi (Special Order No. 19/1). Pension records show he was at home on furlough at the close of the war. He was born September 1, 1837 and died October 31, 1916. He is buried in the Reidsville City Cemetery at Reidsville, Tattnall County, Georgia. (find a grave # 67567899)

HUGULEY W. W.: Company K, sergeant. He enlisted as a sergeant in Co. K, 54th Regiment, Georgia Infantry.

HUNT, A.: Company F, private. He enlisted as a private in Co. F, 54th Regiment, Georgia Infantry.

HUNT, ALBERT R.: Company F, private. April 29, 1863 enlisted as a private in Co. F, 54th Regiment, Georgia Infantry. April 20-21, 1865 captured at Macon, Georgia. January 1864 and April 25, 1864 issued clothing.

HUNT, J. L.: Company B, private. He enlisted as a private in Co. B, 54th Regiment, Georgia Infantry.

HUNTER, CHARLES C.: Company F, lieutenant. May 21, 1861 enlisted as a private in Co. B, 8th Regiment, Georgia State Troops. January 1, 1862 he was discharged. May 13, 1862 enlisted as 2nd lieutenant in Co. F, 54th Regiment, Georgia Infantry at Savannah, Georgia. July 1862 roll shows his name. August 1862 roll at Beaulieu near Savannah, Georgia shows him present. September 1862 roll shows him absent with leave. October 1862 roll shows him absent sick since October 24, 1862. November 24, 1862 he appears on a list of officers at Savannah, Georgia. November 1862 roll shows him absent with leave since November 25, 1862. December 1862 roll shows him present at Beaulieu near Savannah, Georgia. January – February 1863 roll shows him present. March 9, 1863 received pay $80.00. March 31, 1863 received pay $80.00. July 2, 1863 received pay $90.00. July 24, 1863 to July 28, 1863 he was on furlough approved by General Mercer. December 1, 1863 received pay $80.00. December 24, 1863 to December 26, 1863 he was on a leave of absence approved by General Mercer. November - December 1863 roll shows him present. January 23, 1864 appears on a list of officers absent (witness at General Court Marshal in Savannah, Georgia). January 1, 1864 received pay $80.00. February 3, 1864 received pay $80.00. February 29, 1864 his name appears on Inspectors Report No. 107 of a General Court Martial. March 2, 1864 issued clothing. April 29, 1864 received pay $240.00. June 19, 1864 wounded in the leg near Marietta, Georgia. July 2, 1864 received pay $80.00. He was elected 1st lieutenant. April 26, 1865 surrendered Co. D, 54th Regiment, Georgia Infantry at Greensboro, North Carolina. May 1, 1865 paroled at Greensboro, North Carolina.

HUNTER, G. F.: Company G, private. He enlisted as a private in Co. G, 54th Regiment, Georgia Infantry.

HUNTER, GEORGE S.: Company G, private. January 23, 1863 enlisted as a private in Co. G, 54th Regiment, Georgia Infantry at Columbus, Georgia and received bounty $50.00. January – February 1863 roll shows him present. September 1, 1863 to September 30, 1863 detailed on extra duty as a carpenter at James Island, South Carolina at a rate of $.25 per day extra. October 1, 1863 to January 31, 1864 detailed on extra duty as a laborer at Charleston, South Carolina at a rate of an additional $.25 per day. January 1864 issued clothing. February 1, 1864 to February 29, 1864 detailed on extra duty as a harness maker at Savannah, Georgia. March 1, 1864 to March 31, 1864 detailed on extra duty as a mechanic at Hardeeville, South Carolina. April 1, 1864 to April 30, 1864 detailed on extra duty as a mechanic at Savannah, Georgia. May 8, 1864 issued clothing.

HUNTER, SIMON PETER: Company G, private. January 22, 1863 enlisted as a private in Co. G, 54th Regiment, Georgia Infantry at Columbus, Georgia and received bounty $50.00. January – February 1863 roll shows him present. January 1864 and May 8, 1864 issued clothing. June 27, 1864 severely wounded at Kennesaw Mountain, Georgia. June 28, 1864 admitted to St. Mary's Hospital at La Grange, Georgia. June 30, 1864 transferred to Columbus, Georgia hospital where he stayed until the close of the war. He was born in Talbot County, Georgia May 1, 1840.

HURST, ____: Company D, private. 1862 enlisted as a private in Co. D, 54th Regiment, Georgia Infantry. July 24, 1862 died in Savannah, Georgia. July 1862 roll shows his death.

HURST, EMANUEL: Company I, private. September 18, 1861 enlisted as a private in Co. C, 1st Regiment, 1st Brigade, Georgia State Troops. March 18, 1862 mustered out. May 6, 1862 enlisted as a private in Co. I, 54th Regiment, Georgia Infantry at Guyton, Georgia and received bounty $50.00. December 31, 1862 received pay. January – February 1863 roll shows him present. April 30, 1863 received pay. November – December 1863 roll shows him present on picket guard. January 1864 issued clothing. June 9, 1864 died of Typhoid Fever in Oliver Hospital at La Grange, Georgia. He is buried in Stonewall Confederate Cemetery at La Grange, Troup County, Georgia. (find a grave # 67461213)

HURST, FELIX M.: Company I, corporal. September 18, 1861 enlisted as a private and appointed 4th corporal in Co. C, 1st Regiment, 1st Brigade, Georgia State Troops. March 18, 1862 mustered out May 6, 1862 enlisted as 4th corporal in Co. I, 54th Regiment, Georgia Infantry at Guyton, Georgia and received bounty $50.00. December 31, 1862 received pay. January – February 1863 roll shows him present. October 31, 1863 received pay. November – December 1863 roll shows him present (detailed to go after lumber at Ogeechee Bridge). January 1864 issued clothing.

HURST, J. L.: Company I, sergeant. May 6, 1862 enlisted as 4th sergeant in Co. I, 54th Regiment, Georgia Infantry at Guyton, Georgia and received bounty $50.00. December 31, 1862 received pay. January – February 1863 roll shows him present. October 31, 1863 received pay. November – December 1863 roll shows him absent (detailed to guard commissary at No, 3 railroad on December 15, 1863). January 1864 issued clothing.

HURST, J. S.: Company I, sergeant. May 6, 1862 enlisted as 5th sergeant in Co. I, 54th Regiment, Georgia Infantry at Guyton, Georgia and received bounty $50.00.

HURST, JAMES ANDREW: Company D, private. May 6, 1862 enlisted as a private in Co. D, 54th Regiment, Georgia Infantry. October 1862 pension records show he was discharged due to heart disease. He then enlisted in the Militia. He was born in Screven County, Georgia January 3, 1836 and died April 13, 1905. He is buried in Green Fork Cemetery at Millen, Jenkins County, Georgia. (find a grave # 102642951)

HURST, JOSEPH W.: Company D, private. December 13, 1862 enlisted as a private in Co. D, 54th Regiment, Georgia Infantry at Beaulieu near Savannah, Georgia and received bounty $50.00. December 1862 roll shows his enlistment. December 31, 1862 received pay. January – February 1863 roll shows him present. September 13, 1863 received pay $44.00. January 1864 issued clothing. July 22, 1864 wounded in the left arm and was permanently disabled at Atlanta, Georgia. Pension records show he was furloughed home and was unable to return to his command. He was born in Georgia March 8, 1825 and died in Screven County, Georgia August 1906.

HUSON, SAMUEL: Field and Staff, musician. May 10, 1862 enlisted as a private in Co. K, 54th Regiment, Georgia Infantry at Guyton, Georgia and received bounty $50.00. He transferred to the band as a musician. January 1, 1863 received pay. January – February 1863 roll shows him present as a musician.

HUTCHINSON, RAYMOND R.: Company H, private. August 25, 1862 enlisted as a private in Co. H, 54th Regiment, Georgia Infantry at Columbus, Georgia and received bounty $50.00. August 1862 roll at Beaulieu near Savannah, Georgia shows his enlistment. September 1862 roll shows him present. December 31, 1862 received pay. January – February 1863 roll shows him present. October 31, 1863 received pay. November – December 1863 roll shows him present. December 31, 1863 received pay. January – February 1864 roll shows him present. April 26, 1865 surrendered at Greensboro, North Carolina. May 1, 1865 paroled at Greensboro, North Carolina. January 1864 issued clothing. He was born in Warren County, Georgia October 27, 1817. He is buried in Macedonia Baptist Church Cemetery at Manchester, Meriwether County, Georgia. (find a grave # 116442060)

HYSLER, WILLIAM: Company A, private. April 22, 1862 enlisted as a private in Co. A, 54th Regiment, Georgia Infantry at Macon, Georgia and received bounty $50.00. April 30, 1863 received pay. June 30, 1863 roll shows him present. October 31, 1863 received pay. November – December 1863 roll shows him present. January 1, 1864 received pay. January – February 1864 roll shows him present. March 31, 1864 issued clothing. He was born in 1828 and died April 28, 1888. He is buried in Fort Hill Cemetery at Macon, Bibb County, Georgia.

ISABELL, A. D.: Company H, private. He enlisted as a private in Co. H, 54th Regiment, Georgia Infantry.

ISABELL, J. J.: Company H, corporal. He enlisted as a corporal in Co. H, 54th Regiment, Georgia Infantry.

ISABELL, R. M.: Company H, private. He enlisted as a private in Co. H, 54th Regiment, Georgia Infantry.

ISOM, DANIEL: Company H, private. March 4, 1862 enlisted in Co. D, 37th Regiment, Georgia Infantry in Hartwell, Georgia. June 23, 1863 to June 30, 1863 detailed as a nurse at Buckner Hospital at Cherokee Springs, Georgia and received $2.00 extra pay. June 30, 1863 received pay. July 1, 1863 to July 31, 1863 detailed as a nurse at Buckner Hospital at Cherokee Springs, Georgia and received $7.75 extra pay. August 24, 1863 received pay. November – December 1863 roll of Bragg hospital at Newnan, Georgia shows him present. April 26, 1865 surrendered in Co. H, 54th Regiment, Georgia Infantry at Greensboro, North Carolina. May 1, 1865 paroled at Greensboro, North Carolina.

JACKSON, A.: private. He enlisted as a private in the 54th Regiment, Georgia Infantry. May 10, 1865 surrendered at Tallahassee, Florida. May 21, 1865 paroled at Thomasville, Georgia.

JACKSON, ANDREW: Company G, sergeant. May 12, 1862 enlisted as 4th corporal in Co. G, 54th Regiment, Georgia Infantry at Columbus, Georgia and received bounty $50.00. December 31, 1862 received pay. January – February 1863 roll shows him present. He was elected 5th sergeant of Co. G, 54th Regiment, Georgia Infantry. January 1864 and May 8, 1864 issued clothing. March 18, 1865 wounded at Bentonville, North Carolina. He was in the hospital at the close of the war. April 29, 1865 surrendered at Garrett House, Greensboro, North Carolina. May 2, 1865 paroled at Greensboro, North Carolina. He was born in Georgia in 1838 and died in Muscogee County, Georgia October 19, 1913.

JACKSON, MONK L.: Company F, private. January 22, 1863 enlisted as a private in Co. F, 54th Regiment, Georgia Infantry at Savannah, Georgia and received bounty $50.00. January – February 1863 roll shows him present. November 1, 1863 received pay. November 22, 1863 to December 31, 1863 detailed as a timber cutter (carpenter) for the post at Rose Dew Point at a rate of $.20 extra per day. November – December 1863 roll shows him absent (detailed as timber cutter for post). January 1864 issued clothing. January 20, 1864 received pay. July 3, 1864 wounded in the left hip near Marietta, Georgia. July 5, 1864 admitted to Ocmulgee Hospital at Macon, Georgia with a Gunshot Wound (between the Trochanter and Sacrum – hip). July 8, 1864 furloughed from Ocmulgee Hospital at

Macon, Georgia to Burke County, Georgia. Pension records show; he was at home in Burke County, Georgia wounded at the close of the war. He was a resident of Alexander, Burke County, Georgia. He was born in Sampson County, North Carolina October 28, 1835 and died in Millen, Jenkins County, Georgia December 21, 1921. He is buried in Big Horse Creek Cemetery in Jenkins County, Georgia. (find a grave # 41663503).

JACKSON, P. W.: Company A, private. August 31, 1863 enlisted as a private in Co. A, 54th Regiment, Georgia Infantry at Savannah, Georgia and received bounty $50.00. November 27, 1863 admitted to Floyd House and Ocmulgee Hospitals at Macon with Chronic Bronchitis, Georgia. November – December 1863 roll shows him absent sick at Macon Hospital. January – February 1864 roll shows him absent detailed as assistant enrolling officer in Macon, Georgia. He was a resident of Knoxville, Georgia. He died October 18, 1908. He is buried at Sardis Church Cemetery in Bibb County, Georgia.

JACKSON, ROBERT T.: Company G, corporal. He enlisted as a corporal in Co. G, 54th Regiment, Georgia Infantry.

JACKSON, W. A.: Company B, private. He enlisted as a private in Co. B, 54th Regiment, Georgia Infantry. Pension records show he was at home on sick furlough at the close of the war. He was born September 7, 1844 in Georgia and died in Wayne County, Georgia April 8, 1902. He is buried in Piney Grove Church Cemetery in Wayne County, Georgia. (find a grave #76743560)

JACKSON, WILLIAM W.: Company G, lieutenant. He enlisted as 1st lieutenant in Co. G, 54th Regiment, Georgia Infantry.

JACOBS, B.: private. He enlisted as a private in the 54th Regiment, Georgia Infantry.

JACOBS, JOHN: Company C, private. September 25, 1862 enlisted as a private in Co. C, 54th Regiment, Georgia Infantry at Beaulieu near Savannah, Georgia and received bounty $50.00. September 1862 roll shows his enlistment.

JAMES, WILLIAM: Company A, private. August 31, 1863 enlisted as a private in Co. A, 54th Regiment, Georgia Infantry at Savannah, Georgia and received bounty $50.00. October 31, 1863 received pay. November – December 1863 roll shows him present. January 1, 1864 received pay. January – February 1864 roll shows him present. February 29, 1864 received pay. March 31, 1864 and May 8, 1864 issued clothing. May – June 1864 roll of Polk Hospital at Atlanta, Georgia shows him present June 30, 1864 received pay. April 21, 1865 captured at Macon, Georgia. He died April 22, 1892.

JARRELL, J. D.: Company F, private. February 22, 1863 enlisted as a private in Co. F, 54th Regiment, Georgia Infantry at Savannah, Georgia and received bounty $50.00. November 1, 1863 received pay. November – December 1863 roll shows him absent without leave.

JARRELL, JOHN E.: Company F, private. February 26, 1863 enlisted as a private in Co. F, 54th Regiment, Georgia Infantry at Savannah, Georgia and received bounty $50.00. January – February 1863 roll shows him present. November – December 1863 roll shows him absent without leave. January 1864 issued clothing. January 10, 1865 admitted to St. Mary's Hospital at West Point, Mississippi with Diarrhoea.

JEFFERS, J. M.: Company D, private. October 12, 1861 enlisted as a private in Co. E, 2nd Regiment, 1st Brigade, Georgia State Troops. April 1862 mustered out. April 30, 1862 enlisted as a private in Co. D, 54th Regiment, Georgia Infantry at Savannah, Georgia and received bounty $50.00. December 31, 1862 received pay. January – February 1863 roll shows him present. January 1864, April 25, 1864 and May 8, 1864 issued clothing. Pension records show: May 2, 1865 surrendered and paroled at Augusta, Georgia. He was born in Burke County, Georgia July 13, 1840.

JEFFERS, WILLIAM W.: Company D, corporal. October 12, 1861 enlisted as a private in Co. E, 2nd Regiment, 1st Brigade, Georgia State Troops. April 1862 mustered out. April 30, 1862 enlisted as a private in Co. D, 54th Regiment, Georgia Infantry at Savannah, Georgia and received bounty $50.00. September 1862 roll shows him as color guard. December 31, 1862 received pay. January – February 1863 roll shows him present. January 1864, April 25, 1864 and May 8, 1864 issued clothing. He was elected corporal of Co. D, 54th Regiment, Georgia Infantry. December 5, 1864 captured at Brown County, Georgia. January 28, 1865 admitted to Provost Guard, U. S. A. Hospital at Hilton Head, South Carolina with Acute Bronchitis. March 4, 1865 returned to duty. March 6, 1865 took oath of allegiance at Hilton Head, South Carolina. March 12, 1865 name appears on roll of prisoners received at Fort Delaware, Delaware from Hilton Head, South Carolina.

JENKINS, C. J.: Company I, private. May 6, 1862 enlisted as a private in Co. I, 54th Regiment, Georgia Infantry at Guyton, Georgia and received bounty $50.00. August 13, 1862 discharged at Savannah, Georgia.

JENKINS, CHARLES J.: Company I, private. April 30, 1862 enlisted as a private in Co. I, 54th Regiment, Georgia Infantry at Savannah, Georgia and received bounty $50.00. October 1862 detailed to the commissary department. December 31, 1862 received pay. January – February 1863 roll shows him present. December 31, 1863 received pay. January 1864 issued clothing. August 20, 1864 admitted to Hospital at Shelby Springs, Alabama. July – August 1864 roll of Hospital at Shelby Springs, Alabama shows him present. December 27, 1864 issued clothing at Hood Hospital at Cuthbert, Georgia. He was born October 11, 1847 and died August 19, 1924. He is buried in Brewton Cemetery at Hagan, Evans County, Georgia. (find a grave # 72080348)

JENKINS, DANIEL TWIGGS: Company D, private. April 30, 1862 enlisted as a private in Co. D, 54th Regiment, Georgia Infantry at Savannah, Georgia and received bounty $50.00. August 20, 1864 admitted to 1st Mississippi C. S. A. Hospital at Jackson, Mississippi with Diarrhoea. August 31, 1864 appears on the hospital roll of hospital at Shelby Springs, Alabama. Pension records show he was on detail at Chester, South

Carolina from April 15, 1865 to the close of the war. He was born in Screven County, Georgia July 16, 1837 and died in Georgia July 25, 1911. He is buried in Antioch Christian Church Cemetery at Sylvania, Screven County, Georgia. (find a grave # 24719341).

JENKINS, ELIAS: Company C, private. May 6, 1862 enlisted as a private in Co. I, 54th Regiment, Georgia Infantry at Guyton, Georgia and received bounty $50.00. July 15, 1862 appointed as wagoner for the Quartermaster's Department. July 15, 1862 to January 31, 1864 detailed as a teamster at a rate of an additional $.25 per day. July, August, September, October 1862 roll shows him detailed in Quartermaster's Department. December 31, 1862 received pay. January – February 1863 roll shows him present sick in quarters. October 20, 1863 to December 31, 1863 detailed as a driver on James Island, South Carolina at a rate of an additional $.25 per day. October 31, 1863 shown on list of men detailed on James Island, South Carolina (driver). November 1, 1863 received pay. January – February 1864 roll shows him present. May 8, 1864 issued clothing.

JENKINS, J. T.: Company D, private. April 30, 1862 enlisted as a private in Co. D, 54th Regiment, Georgia Infantry at Savannah, Georgia and received bounty $50.00. He was in the hospital at Macon, Georgia at the close of the war.

JENKINS, K.: Company C, private. February 9, 1863 enlisted as a private in Co. C, 54th Regiment, Georgia Infantry at Savannah, Georgia and received bounty $50.00. January – February 1863 roll shows him present. January 1, 1864 received pay. January – February 1864 roll shows him present.
May 8, 1864 issued clothing.

JENKINS, LEVI: Company C, private. May 23, 1862 enlisted as a private in Co. C, 54th Regiment, Georgia Infantry at Savannah, Georgia and received bounty $50.00. October 1, 1862 to December 31, 1862 detailed as a teamster in Beaulieu near Savannah, Georgia at a rate of $.25 extra per day. November 1862 roll shows him as a teamster. December 31, 1862 received pay. January – February 1863 roll shows him present detailed as a teamster. January 1, 1863 to February 28, 1863, detailed as a butcher in Savannah, Georgia at a rate of $.25 extra per day. February 26, 1863 received pay. March 12, 1863 received pay. June 1, 1863 to June 30, 1863 detailed as a teamster in Beaulieu near Savannah, Georgia at a rate of $.25 extra per day. November 1, 1863 received pay. October 31, 1863 he is shown on list of detailed men at James Island, South Carolina. November 16, 1863 received pay. July 1, 1863 to January 31, 1864 detailed as a teamster in Charleston, South Carolina at a rate of $.25 extra per day. January – February 1864 roll shows him present (on extra or daily duty as company teamster by order of Colonel Way January 25, 1864). February 1, 1864 to April 30, 1864 detailed as a teamster in Savannah, Georgia and Hardeeville, South Carolina at a rate of $.25 extra per day. May 8, 1864 issued clothing.

JENKINS, MCKIBBER (MCKIBBOW): Company C, private.

February 9, 1863 enlisted as a private in Co. C, 54th Regiment, Georgia Infantry. May 15, 1864 he was wounded at Resaca, Georgia. Pension records show: April 26, 1865 surrendered at Greensboro, North Carolina. May 1, 1865 paroled at Greensboro, North Carolina. He was born in Hancock County, Georgia in 1826.

JENKINS, MICHAEL: Company D, lieutenant. October 7, 1861 enlisted and elected Jr. 2nd lieutenant in Co. I, 5th Regiment, Georgia State Troops. April 1862 mustered out. April 30, 1862 appointed 2nd lieutenant in Co. D, 54th Regiment, Georgia Infantry. July 1862 roll bears his name. August and September 1862 roll shows him present at Beaulieu near Savannah, Georgia. October 1862 roll shows him present, sick, at Beaulieu near Savannah, Georgia. November 24, 1862 roll of officers shows him present at Savannah, Georgia. November and December 1862 rolls show him present at Beaulieu near Savannah, Georgia. January – February 1864 roll shows him present. March 10, 1863 received pay $80.00. April 2, 1863 received pay $80.00. October 21, 1863 list of officers at Legare's Point, South Carolina shows him present. October 27, 1863 admitted to Bethesda Hospital at Savannah, Georgia. November 4, 1863 resigned his commission for health reasons (disability).

JENKINS, PAUL: Company D, private. October 14, 1861 enlisted as a private in Co. I, 5th Regiment, Georgia State Troops. April 1862 mustered out. April 30, 1862 enlisted as a private in Co. D, 54th Regiment, Georgia Infantry at Savannah, Georgia and received bounty $50.00. December 31, 1862 received pay. January – February 1863 roll shows him present (absent without leave 9 days). September 21, 1863 received pay $44.00. January 1864 issued clothing.

JENKINS, PEYTON H.: Company D, private. April 30, 1862 enlisted as a private in Co. D, 54th Regiment, Georgia Infantry at Savannah, Georgia and received bounty $50.00. December 31, 1862 received pay. January – February 1863 roll shows him present. January 1864 issued clothing. Pension records show he was furloughed home from a Mississippi hospital on account of Chronic Diarrhoea. May 18, 1865 surrendered and paroled at Augusta, Georgia. He was born in Screven County, Georgia February 18, 1830.

JENKINS, WILLIAM E.: Company A, lieutenant. October 17, 1861 elected 1st sergeant of Co. C, 1st Independent Battalion, Georgia State Troops. April 16, 1862 roll shows him present. April 1862 mustered out. April 28, 1862 enlisted as a private in Co. A, 54th Regiment, Georgia Infantry at Macon, Georgia and received bounty $50.00. July 1862 roll shows him present at Savannah, Georgia. August 1862 roll shows him absent without leave since August 28, 1862. October 18, 1862 appointed 2nd lieutenant of Co. A, 54th Regiment, Georgia Infantry. September, October, November and December rolls show him present at Beaulieu near Savannah, Georgia. November 24, 1862 shown on list of officers at Savannah, Georgia. April 30, 1863 absent with leave. June 20, 1863 to June 27, 1863 shown as a witness in a habeas corpus case. June 25,

1863 to July 28, 1863 absence approved by General Mercer, (witness in Habeas Corpus case and Surgeon's Certificate). June 30, 1863 roll shows him absent with leave on surgeon's certificate. December 11, 1863 leave granted. December 10, 1863 to December 26, 1863 on sick leave approved by General Beauregard. December 31, 1863 30 days sick leave granted. November – December 1863 roll shows him absent on sick furlough since December 17, 1863. December 17, 1863 to January 23, 1864 on sick leave approved by General Beauregard. January 15, 1864 admitted to Floyd House and Ocmulgee Hospitals at Macon, Georgia (extension of furlough recommended). February 29, 1864 shown on report as sick. January – February 1864 roll shows him sick, absent on sick leave, since September 3, 1863. July 18, 1864 received pay $160.00. August 22, 1864 received pay $410.00. August 25, 1864 report of Mercer's Brigade, near Atlanta, Georgia shows him absent without leave. September 14, 1864 report of Mercer's Brigade, near Jonesboro, Georgia, shows him absent without leave. Surgeon's Certificate states he suffered with Chronic Rheumatism. Pension records show he was returning to his company at the close of the war. He was born in Georgia February 16, 1838 and died in Macon, Bibb County, Georgia May 10, 1906. He is buried in Jones Chapel Cemetery at Macon, Bibb County, Georgia. (find a grave # 73988984)

JENNINGS, WILLIAM J.: Company G, private. He enlisted as a private in Co. G, 54th Regiment, Georgia Infantry. He transferred to Co. C, 54th Regiment, Georgia Infantry. He was born in 1842 and died in 1921. He is buried in Alpine Community Church Cemetery at Menlo, Chattooga County, Georgia. (find a grave # 41607065)

JESSUP, JAMES J.: Company A, private. October 17, 1861 enlisted as a private in Co. C, 1st Independent Battalion, Georgia State Troops. April 16, 1862 roll shows him present. April 1862 mustered out. October 1, 1863 enlisted as a private in Co. A, 54th Regiment, Georgia Infantry at Savannah, Georgia and received bounty $50.00. November – December 1863 roll shows him present. January 1, 1864 received pay. January – February 1864 roll shows him present (sick in company hospital). March 31, 1864 issued clothing. April 20, 1864 captured at Macon, Georgia. Pension records show: April 26, 1865 surrendered at Greensboro, North Carolina. May 1, 1865 paroled at Greensboro, North Carolina. He died in Bibb County, Georgia August 4, 1891.

JILES, D. J.: Company A, private. October 1, 1863 enlisted as a private in Co. A, 54th Regiment, Georgia Infantry at Savannah, Georgia and received bounty $50.00. June 30, 1863 roll shows him present. October 31, 1863 received pay. November – December 1863 roll shows him present. January 1, 1864 received pay. January – February 1864 roll shows him present. April 29, 1864 issued clothing.

JIM (NEGRO): Field and Staff Musician. August 1, 1862 he enlisted as a musician in the 54th Regiment, Georgia Infantry.

JOHNSON, BENJAMIN LLOYD: Company G (C) private. May 12, 1862 enlisted as a private in Co. G, 54th Regiment, Georgia Infantry at

Columbus, Georgia and received bounty $50.00. September 1, 1862 transferred from Co. G, 54th Regiment, Georgia Infantry to Co. A, 54th Regiment, Georgia Infantry by Special Order No. 6. September 1862 rolls reflect his transfer. November 21, 1862 detailed as hospital duty at Confederate Medical College Hospital at Savannah, Georgia by Special Order No. 273 at a rate of an extra $.25 per day. November and December 1862 rolls show him detailed as a hospital nurse. January – February 1863 roll shows him absent (detailed as a nurse in city hospital). July 18, 1863 issued clothing. October 31, 1863 report from James Island, South Carolina shows him detailed as a nurse. October 31, 1863 received pay $44.00. November 30, 1863 and December 31, 1863 received pay. November 1863, December 1863, January 1864 and February 1864 rolls of General Hospital No. 2 at Savannah, Georgia show him present. January 31, 1864 received pay (shown as hospital ward master). February 15, 1864 issued clothing. January – February 1864 roll shows him absent (detached as nurse in hospital at Savannah, Georgia by order of General Mercer on July 10, 1862). May 18, 1865 surrendered and paroled at Augusta, Georgia. He was a resident of Emanuel County, Georgia. He was born in Georgia May 22, 1842 and died near Thrift, Georgia September 10, 1904. He is buried in Lewis Primitive Baptist Church Cemetery in Jenkins County, Georgia. (find a grave # 60815962)

JOHNSON, BENJAMIN W.: Company C, private. December 11, 1861 enlisted as a private in Co. B, 8th Regiment, Georgia State Troops. He mustered out in 1862. April 22, 1862 enlisted as a private in Co. D, 54th Regiment, Georgia Infantry at Savannah, Georgia and received bounty $50.00. October 31, 1862 received pay. January – February 1863 roll shows him present. May 1, 1863 received pay. September 4, 1863 received pay $44.00. January – February 1864 roll shows him absent (absent sick since August 3, 1863 surgeon's certificate received monthly). May 26, 1865 surrendered and paroled at Augusta, Georgia. He was born in Emanuel County, Georgia in 1833 and died in Emanuel County, Georgia 1876. He is buried in Johnson Cemetery at Summertown, Emanuel County, Georgia. (find a grave # 52908137)

JOHNSON, D. R.: Company K, corporal. October 3, 1861 enlisted as a private in Co. K, 1st Regiment, Georgia State Troops. April 1862 mustered out. April 18, 1862 enlisted as a private in Co. K, 54th Regiment, Georgia Infantry at Savannah, Georgia and received bounty $50.00. January 1, 1863 received pay. January – February 1863 roll shows him present. October 7, 1863 received pay $26.00. March 18, 1864 and April 25, 1864 issued clothing. He was appointed corporal of Co. K, 54th Regiment, Georgia Infantry. May 10, 1865 surrendered at Tallahassee, Florida. May 19, 1865 paroled at Thomasville, Georgia. He is described as; 5 feet 9 inches high, dark hair, grey eyes and dark complexion. He was born in Appling County, Georgia October 25, 1843. The Southern Cross of Honor was bestowed on him by the Jesup Chapter United Daughters of the Confederacy in 1903.

JOHNSON, F. W.: Company A, private. He enlisted as a private in Co. A, 54th Regiment, Georgia Infantry.

JOHNSON, J. C.: Company C, private. September 24, 1862 enlisted as a private in Co. F, 54th Regiment, Georgia Infantry at Savannah, Georgia and received bounty $50.00. December 31, 1862 received pay. January – February 1863 roll shows him present. May 3, 1864 detailed as captain's cook. January 1, 1864 received pay. January – February 1864 roll shows him present detailed as the captain's cook. April 25 and 28, 1864 issued clothing. July 20, 1864 wounded in the right wrist and permanently disabled at Peachtree Creek near Atlanta, Georgia. July 29, 1864 roll of Floyd House and Ocmulgee Hospitals at Macon, Georgia with a Gunshot Wound to the hand. May 26, 1865 surrendered and paroled at Augusta, Georgia. He was a resident of Midville, Burke County, Georgia. He was born in Georgia February 2, 1836.

JOHNSON, JAMES HAMPTON: Company F (K), private. October 3, 1861 enlisted as a private in Co. A, 1st Regiment, 1st Brigade, Georgia State Troops. April 1862 mustered out. April 18, 1862 enlisted as a private in Co. F, 54th Regiment, Georgia Infantry at Savannah, Georgia and received bounty $50.00. September 1, 1862 transferred from Co. F, 54th Regiment, Georgia Infantry to Co. K, 54th Regiment, Georgia Infantry by Special Order No. 6. September 1862 roll reflects the transfer. January 1863 received pay. January – February 1863 roll shows him present. April 25, 1864, May 18, 1864 and June 2, 1864 issued clothing. July 3, 1864 admitted to St. Mary's Hospital at La Grange, Georgia with Dysenteria. May 10, 1865 surrendered at Tallahassee, Florida. May 19, 1865 paroled at Thomasville, Georgia. He is described as; 5 feet 6 inches high, dark hair, dark eyes and dark complexion.

JOHNSON, JOHN: Company G (C) private. December 11, 1861 enlisted as a private in Co. B, 8th Regiment, Georgia State Troops. He mustered out in 1862. April 22, 1862 enlisted as a private in Co. G, 54th Regiment, Georgia Infantry at Savannah, Georgia and received bounty $50.00. September 1, 1862 transferred from Co. G, 54th Regiment, Georgia Infantry to Co. C, 54th Regiment, Georgia Infantry at Beaulieu near Savannah, Georgia by Special Order No. 6. October 31, 1862 received pay. January – February 1863 roll shows him present. January 1, 1864 received pay. January – February 1864 roll shows him present. April 25, 1864 and May 8, 1864 issued clothing. Pension records show he was at home on sick furlough at the close of the war. May 24, 1865 surrendered and paroled at Augusta, Georgia. He was born in Georgia. He was born in 1841 and died May 1911. He is buried in Porterdale Cemetery at Columbus, Muscogee County, Georgia. (find a grave # 73782511)

JOHNSON, JOHN D.: Company C, private. December 11, 1861 enlisted as a private in Co. B, 8th Regiment, Georgia State Troops. He mustered out in 1862. April 22, 1862 enlisted as a private in Co. C, 54th Regiment, Georgia Infantry at Savannah, Georgia and received bounty $50.00. January 1, 1864 received pay. January – February 1864 roll shows him present. He was born in Emanuel County, Georgia in 1834 and died in Jenkins County, Georgia July 2, 1897. He is buried in Elam Church Cemetery at Four Points, Jenkins County, Georgia. (find a grave # 47059195)

JOHNSON, JOSIAH C.: Company C, private. May 12, 1862 enlisted as a private in Co. G, 54th Regiment, Georgia Infantry and received bounty $50.00. He was discharged in May 1862. He was born February 2, 1836 and died November 14, 1898. He is buried in Johnson Cemetery at Summertown, Emanuel County, Georgia. (find a grave # 52908150)

JOHNSON, S. A.: Company A, private. October 17, 1861 enlisted as a private in Co. C, 1st Independent Battalion, Georgia State Troops. April 16, 1862 roll shows him present. April 1862 mustered out. April 21, 1862 enlisted as a private in Co. A, 54th Regiment, Georgia Infantry at Macon, Georgia and received bounty $50.00. December 31, 1862 received pay. June 30, 1863 roll shows him absent detailed to work for Major R. M. Cuyler at the Macon Arsenal. July 1, 1863 to August 31, 1863 detailed at the Macon Arsenal at a rate of $2.75 extra per day. August 31, 1863 received pay. August 10, 1863 to October 31, 1863 detailed as a blacksmith at a rate of $.40 per day. October 31, 1863 received pay. November – December 1863 roll shows him present (blacksmith for the company). January 1, 1864 received pay. January – February 1864 roll shows him present (blacksmith h for the company). March 31, 1864 issued clothing.

JOHNSON, T.: Company E, private. October 31, 1862 enlisted as a private in Co. E, 54th Regiment, Georgia Infantry at Beaulieu near Savannah, Georgia and received bounty $50.00. October 1862 roll shows his enlistment.

JOHNSON, WILLIAM R.: Company C, private. November 15, 1862 enlisted as a private in Co. C, 54th Regiment, Georgia Infantry. Pension records show he was at home on sick furlough at the close of the war. May 24, 1865 surrendered and paroled at Augusta, Georgia. He was born February 2, 1846 in Georgia and died August 9, 1919 in Emanuel County, Georgia. He is buried in Hebron Primitive Baptist Church Cemetery at Garfield, Emanuel County, Georgia. (find a grave #40159402)

JOHNSON, WILLIAM T.: Company A, private. May 3, 1862 enlisted as a private in Co. A, 54th Regiment, Georgia Infantry at Macon, Georgia and received bounty $50.00. August 1, 1862 appointed teamster. August, September, October, November and December 1862 rolls show him being detailed as a teamster at a rate of $.25 extra per day. January 1, 1863 to February 28, 1863 detailed as a teamster at a rate of $.25 extra per day. April 30, 1863 received pay. May 1, 1863 to July 31, 1863 detailed as a harness repairer at a rate of $.25 extra per day. June 30, 1863 roll shows him present. August 1863 received pay. August 1, 1863 to October 31, 1863 detailed as harness repairer at a rate of $.40 extra per day. October 31, 1863 received pay. November 1863 received commutation for rations. November – December 1863 roll shows him present (harness maker and repair). January 1, 1864 received pay. January – February 1864 roll shows him present (harness maker and repair). April 29, 1864 issued clothing. May 27, 1864 wounded in the hip at Pickett's Mill, Georgia. August 22, 1864 admitted to Ocmulgee Hospital at Macon, Georgia with a Gunshot Wound in the left hip. August 28, 1864 furloughed. October 24, 1864 admitted to Ocmulgee Hospital at Macon, Georgia with a Gunshot Wound in the left hip (old wound). October 26, 1864 transferred. November 4, 1864 admitted to Ocmulgee Hospital at Macon, Georgia with a Gunshot Wound in the left hip (old wound). November 16, 1864 report of admitted to Ocmulgee Hospital at Macon, Georgia describes Gunshot Wound in the left hip (ball entering anterior surface up 3 degrees left thigh out the left gluteal region involving femur, still suppurating). November 17, 1864 furloughed. February 14, 1865 admitted to Ocmulgee Hospital at Macon, Georgia with a Gunshot Wound in the left hip (old wound). March 3, 1865 returned to duty. He was a resident of Macon, Bibb County.

JOHNSON, WILLIAM T.: Company H, private. He enlisted as a private in Co. H, 54th Regiment, Georgia Infantry. June 29, 1864 admitted to Ocmulgee Hospital at Macon, Georgia with a Gunshot Wound. November 29, 1864 returned to duty.

JOINER, JAMES: Company B, private. He enlisted as a private in Co. B, 54th Regiment, Georgia Infantry.

JOINER, JAMES L.: Company A, private. March 15, 1861 enlisted as a private in Co. A, 1st Regiment, Georgia Infantry. 1861 contracted Chronic Diarrhoea. April 1862 was discharged due to disability. April 21, 1862 enlisted as a private in Co. A, 54th Regiment, Georgia Infantry at Macon, Georgia and received bounty $50.00. February 28, 1863 received pay. May 1, 1863 to August 31, 1863 detailed as a teamster at Savannah, Georgia at a rate of $.25 extra per day. June 30, 1863 roll shows him present (teamster for company). October 31, 1863 received pay. November – December 1863 roll shows him present. January 1, 1864 received pay. January – February 1864 roll shows him present. March 31, 1864 issued clothing. April 21, 1865 captured at Macon, Georgia. Pension records state he was sent home on furlough six months before the close of the war. He died of disease contracted in service January 30, 1879.

JOINER, THOMAS: Company F, private. He enlisted as a private in Co. F, 54th Regiment, Georgia Infantry. December 19, 1862 received pay $60.00.

JONES, GEORGE: Field and Staff, musician. January 27, 1863 enlisted as a musician in the 54th Regiment, Georgia Infantry at Savannah, Georgia and received bounty $50.00. January – February 1863 roll shows him present.

JONES, J. J.: Company A, private. November 5, 1862 enlisted as a private in Co. A, 54th Regiment, Georgia Infantry at Macon, Georgia and received bounty $50.00. November 1862 roll shows his enlistment. October 31, 1864 roll shows him present.

JONES, JAMES J.: Company G, private. May 12, 1862 enlisted as a private in Co. G, 54th Regiment, Georgia Infantry at Columbus, Georgia and received bounty $50.00. December 31, 1862 received pay. January – February 1863 roll shows him present. January 1864 issued clothing. September 4, 1864 wounded in the thigh and ankle near Lovejoy Station, Georgia. He was born in Putnam County, Georgia March 1835 and died in Troup County, Georgia in November 7, 1921. He is buried in Shiloh Cemetery at Double Churches, Muscogee County, Georgia. (find a grave # 58725269)

JONES, JOHN J.: Company A (F), sergeant. May 3, 1862 enlisted as a private in Co. A, 54th Regiment, Georgia Infantry at Macon, Georgia and received bounty $50.00. April 30, 1863 received pay. June 30, 1863 roll shows him present. November 11, 1863 transferred to Co. E, Phillips Legion Special Order No. 268/24. November – December 1863 roll shows him transferred. He returned to Co. F, 54th Regiment, Georgia Infantry and was elected 4th sergeant. April 26, 1865 surrendered at Greensboro, North Carolina. May 1, 1865 paroled at Greensboro, North Carolina.

JONES, JOSEPH P.: Company C, private. May 5, 1862 enlisted as a private in Co. C, 54th Regiment, Georgia Infantry at Savannah, Georgia and received bounty $50.00. December 31, 1862 received pay. January – February 1863 roll shows him present. January 1, 1864 received pay. January – February 1864 roll shows him present. April 25 and 28, 1864 issued clothing. May 18, 1865 surrendered and paroled at Augusta, Georgia.

JONES, N. S.: Company A, private. April 21, 1862 enlisted as a private in Co. A, 54th Regiment, Georgia Infantry at Macon, Georgia and received bounty $50.00. April 7, 1863 transferred to Whitesville Hospital from General Hospital No. 1 at Savannah, Georgia with Rheumatism. June 30, 1863 roll shows he was discharged June 29, 1863 since the roll was made out. July 1, 1863 received pay.

JONES, PHILLIP: Company I, private. May 5, 1862 enlisted as a private in Co. I, 54th Regiment, Georgia Infantry at Savannah, Georgia and received bounty $50.00. December 31, 1862 received pay. January – February 1863 roll shows him present. August 31, 1863 received pay. October 1, 1863 to December 31, 1863 detailed to the Macon Arsenal on extra duty at a rate of $3.00 extra per day. November – December 1863 roll shows him absent (detailed to work in the Macon Arsenal on October 1, 1863). January 1, 1864 to February 29, 1864 detailed to the Macon Arsenal on extra duty at a rate of $2.00 extra per day. January 1864 received pay $174.00 (Macon Arsenal) and issued clothing. February 29, 1864 received pay. March 1864 received pay $102.00 (Macon Arsenal). March 17, 1864 admitted to Ocmulgee Hospital at Macon, Georgia with Ulceration of Cornea. April 1, 1864 to April 30, 1864 detailed to the Macon Arsenal on extra duty at a rate of $2.00 extra per day. April 1864 received pay. May 5, 1864 returned to duty. May 1864 received pay $207.35 (Macon Arsenal). June 1864 received pay $212.00 (Macon

Arsenal). July 1864 received pay $200.15 (Macon Arsenal). February 1865 received pay as a machinist $164.50 (Macon Arsenal $7.00 per day). March 1865 received pay as a machinist $194.25 (Macon Arsenal $7.00 per day).

JONES, RUSSELL B.: Company B, private. He enlisted as a private in Co. C, 54th Regiment, Georgia Infantry.

JONES, SEABORN L.: Company H, private. March 18, 1861 enlisted and appointed 2nd corporal of Co. B, 1st Regiment, Georgia Infantry (Ramsey's). March 18, 1862 mustered out at Augusta, Georgia. August 13, 1863 enlisted as a private in Co. H, 54th Regiment, Georgia Infantry at Macon, Georgia and received bounty $50.00. October 31, 1863 received pay. November – December 1863 roll shows him present. December 31, 1863 received pay. January – February 1864 roll shows him present. January 1864 issued clothing. He was born July 26, 1826 and died July 31, 1904. He is buried in Harmony Cemetery at Cataula, Harris County, Georgia. (find a grave # 25169009)

JONES, THOMAS: Company C, sergeant. He enlisted as a sergeant in Co. C, 54th Regiment, Georgia Infantry.

JONES, W. S.: Company A, private. April 21, 1862 enlisted as a private in Co. A, 54th Regiment, Georgia Infantry at Macon, Georgia and received bounty $50.00. December 31, 1862 received pay. June 30, 1863 roll shows he was discharged since roll was made out.

JONIER, JAMES L.: Company A, private. He enlisted as a private in Co. A, 54th Regiment, Georgia Infantry.

JORDAN, J.: Company A, private. He enlisted as a private in Co. A, 54th Regiment, Georgia Infantry. August 18, 1862 he died at home. August 1862 roll reflects his death.

JORDAN, JAMES J.: Company A, private. May 5, 1862 enlisted as a private in Co. A, 54th Regiment, Georgia Infantry at Macon, Georgia and received bounty $50.00. June 30, 1863 roll shows he deserted. April 29, 1864 issued clothing. October 15, 1864 he died in Jones County, Georgia.

JORDAN, JAMES R.: Company G, private. He enlisted as a private in Co. G, 54th Regiment, Georgia Infantry.

JORDAN, RICHARD: Company A, private. He enlisted in as a private in Co. A, 54th Regiment, Georgia Infantry.

JOYNER, JOHN A.: Company D, private. October 14, 1861 enlisted as a private and appointed 1st corporal in Co. I, 5th Regiment, Georgia State Troops. April 1862 mustered out. April 30, 1862 enlisted as a private in Co. D, 54th Regiment, Georgia Infantry at Savannah, Georgia and received bounty $50.00. December 31, 1862 received pay. January – February 1863 roll shows him present. Pension records show; February 15, 1865 he was sent to Columbus, Mississippi hospital. February 20, 1865 he was furloughed for 60 days sick with Malarial Fever. He was born in Screven County, Georgia December 18, 1841 and died in Savannah, Chatham County, Georgia April 8, 1930. He is buried in Bay Branch

Baptist Church Cemetery at Sylvania, Screven County, Georgia. (find a grave # 90166518).

JOYNER (JOINER), WILLIAM B.: Company D, private. April 30, 1862 enlisted as a private in Co. D, 54th Regiment, Georgia Infantry at Savannah, Georgia and received bounty $50.00. December 31, 1862 received pay. January – February 1863 roll shows him present. January 1864 issued clothing. Pension records show: April 26, 1865 surrendered at Greensboro, North Carolina. May 1, 1865 paroled at Greensboro, North Carolina. He was born in Georgia September 23, 1842.

KEANE, JAMES F.: Company K, private. He enlisted as a private in Co. K, 54th Regiment, Georgia Infantry.

KEANE, JAMES J.: Company F, private. May 13, 1862 enlisted as a private in Co. F, 54th Regiment, Georgia Infantry at Savannah, Georgia and received bounty $50.00. December 31, 1862 received pay. January – February 1863 roll shows him present. November 1, 1863 received pay. November – December 1863 roll shows him present (present in arrest). January 1864 and May 8, 1864 issued clothing. May 18, 1864 captured at Kingston, Georgia. May 24, 1864 forwarded to Military Prison at Louisville, Kentucky from Nashville, Tennessee. May 25, 1864 received at Military Prison at Louisville, Kentucky and forwarded to Rock Island, Illinois (Alton, Illinois). May 27, 1864 received at Rock Island, Illinois. June 10, 1864 enlisted in the U. S. Navy at Rock Island Barracks, Illinois. He was buried in Catholic Cemetery at Savannah, Chatham County, Georgia. (find a grave # 79867420)

KEARNEY, J. F.; Company I, private. May 6, 1862 enlisted as a private in Co. I, 54th Regiment, Georgia Infantry at Guyton, Georgia and received bounty $50.00. December 31, 1862 received pay. January – February 1863 roll shows him present. October 31, 1864 received pay. November – December 1863 roll shows him absent sick. January 1864 issued clothing. April 2, 1864 transferred to Captain Matthew Artillery by Special Order No. 92/8.

KEARNEY, JAMES: Company I, private. May 6, 1862 enlisted as a private in Co. I, 54th Regiment, Georgia Infantry at Guyton, Georgia and received bounty $50.00. December 31, 1862 received pay. January – February 1863 roll shows him present.

KEEN, JAMES C.: Company C, private. May 6, 1862 enlisted as a private in Co. C, 54th Regiment, Georgia Infantry at Savannah, Georgia and received bounty $50.00. December 31, 1862 received pay. January – February 1863 roll shows him present. January 1, 1864 received pay. January – February 1864 roll shows him present. May 20, 1865 surrendered and paroled at Augusta, Georgia. He was a resident of Emanuel County, Georgia.

KEENE, KINDRED L.: Company B, private. He enlisted as a private in Co. B, 54th Regiment, Georgia Infantry. December 22, 1862 received pay.

KEIFER, A. N.: Company F, private. May 6, 1862 enlisted as a private in Co. C, 54th Regiment, Georgia Infantry at Savannah, Georgia and received bounty $50.00. June 1, 1862 discharged at Savannah, Georgia. August 1862 roll shows his discharge.

KELLY, JOHN: Company C, private. He enlisted as a private in Co. C, 54th Regiment, Georgia Infantry.

KELLY (KELLEY), LAWRENCE: Company F, private. May 17, 1861 enlisted as a private in Chisholm's Company, Georgia State Troops. May 1862 mustered out. May 13, 1862 enlisted as a private in Co. F, 54th Regiment, Georgia Infantry at Savannah, Georgia and received bounty $50.00. December 31, 1862 received pay. January – February 1863 roll shows him present.

KELLY (KELLEY), WILLIAM: Company F, private. July 10, 1863 enlisted as a private in Co. F, 54th Regiment, Georgia Infantry at Savannah, Georgia and received bounty $50.00. September 1, 1863 received pay. October 31, 1863 received pay. November – December 1863 roll shows him absent sick in General Hospital at Savannah, Georgia. December 1863 roll of General Hospital No. 2 at Savannah, Georgia shows him present as a patient. December 31, 1863 received pay. February 23, 1864 admitted to General Hospital at Guyton, Georgia. January 1864 and February 11, 1864 issued clothing. January – February 1864 roll of General Hospital at Guyton, Georgia shows him present as a patient. March 8, 1864 furloughed. March 11, 1864 issued clothing. July 22, 1864 wounded at Atlanta, Georgia. July 15, 1864 issued clothing. August 31, 1864 issued clothing. December 17, 1864 admitted to 1st Mississippi C. S. A. Hospital at Jackson, Mississippi with a Gunshot Wound. February 20, 1865 furloughed to Montgomery, Alabama. February 28, 1865 admitted to Ocmulgee Hospital at Macon, Georgia with a Gunshot Wound in the left leg resulting in a fracture. May 10, 1865 surrendered at Tallahassee, Florida. May 25, 1865 paroled at Albany, Georgia. He was a resident of Chatham County, Georgia.

KEMP, JOHN S.: Company C, private. February 18, 1863 enlisted as a private in Co. C, 54th Regiment, Georgia Infantry at Savannah, Georgia and received bounty $50.00. January – February 1863 roll shows him present. January 1, 1864 received pay. January – February 1864 roll shows him present. May 18, 1865 surrendered and paroled at Augusta, Georgia. He was born February 8, 1845 and died March 7, 1904. He is buried in Antioch Primitive Baptist Church Cemetery at Twin City, Emanuel County, Georgia. (find a grave # 50676885)

KEMP, WILLIAM WESLEY: Company D, private. April 30, 1862 enlisted as a private in Co. D, 54th Regiment, Georgia Infantry at Savannah, Georgia and received bounty $50.00. September 4, 1862 to September 18, 1862 detailed as a laborer on extra duty at Beaulieu near Savannah, Georgia at a rate of an extra $.25 per day. October 1863 he was discharged and furnished a substitute, Hilliard Mincey. Pension records show; 1864 he enlisted in the Georgia Militia. 1865 surrendered in Atlanta, Georgia. He died in Screven County January 21, 1888. He is buried in the Kemp Family Cemetery at Sylvania in Screven County, Georgia. (find a grave

31618924)

KENDRICK, C. B.: Company H, private. July 24, 1861 enlisted in Co. C, 2nd Regiment, Georgia Infantry. October 21, 1861 discharged due to disability. May 12, 1862 enlisted as a private in Co. H, 54th Regiment, Georgia Infantry at Columbus, Georgia and received bounty $50.00. December 31, 1862 received pay. January – February 1863 roll shows him present. October 31, 1863 received pay. November – December 1863 roll shows him present. December 31, 1863 received pay. January 1864 issued clothing. January – February 1864 roll shows him present. June 2, 1864 and September 27, 1864 issued clothing.

KENDRICK, NATHANIEL O.: Company G, private. He enlisted as a private in Co. G, 54th Regiment, Georgia Infantry.

KENDRICK, WILLIAM: Company H, private. May 12, 1862 enlisted as a private in Co. H, 54th Regiment, Georgia Infantry.

KENNEDY, WILLIAM: Company C, private. April 5, 1862 enlisted as a private in Co. C, 54th Regiment, Georgia Infantry. December 15, 1862 discharged at Beaulieu near Savannah, Georgia. December 1862 roll shows his discharge.

KENNON, HENRY A. J. (G.): Company H, corporal. May 12, 1862 enlisted as a private in Co. H, 54th Regiment, Georgia Infantry at Columbus, Georgia and received bounty $50.00. December 31, 1862 received pay. January – February 1863 roll shows him present. October 31, 1863 received pay. November – December 1863 roll shows him present. December 31, 1863 received pay. January – February 1864 roll shows him present. January 1864 issued clothing. He was elected corporal of Co. H, 54th Regiment, Georgia Infantry. April 26, 1865 surrendered at Greensboro, North Carolina. May 1, 1865 paroled at Greensboro, North Carolina. He was born in Upson County, Georgia February 5, 1837.

KERBY (KIRBY), W. L.: Company I, private. He enlisted as a private in Co. I, 54th Regiment, Georgia Infantry. December 2, 1862 he was discharged by civil authority at Beaulieu near Savannah, Georgia.

KERSEY, G. H.: Company K, private. October 3, 1861 enlisted as a private in Co. A, 1st Regiment, 1st Brigade, Georgia State Troops. April 1862 mustered out. April 18, 1862 enlisted as a private in Co. K, 54th Regiment, Georgia Infantry at Savannah, Georgia and received bounty $50.00. January 1, 1863 received pay. January – February 1863 roll shows him present (absent without leave 8 days). March 18, 1864 and April 18, 1864 issued clothing.

KERSEY, GENERAL M.: Company K, private. September 18, 1861 enlisted as a private in Co. C, 1st Regiment, 1st Brigade, Georgia State Troops. March 18, 1862 mustered out. May 5, 1862 enlisted as a private in Co. K, 54th Regiment, Georgia Infantry at Savannah, Georgia and received bounty $50.00. January 1, 1863 received pay. January – February 1863 roll shows him present. March 18, 1864 and April 18, 1864 issued clothing. May 30, 1864 captured near Dallas, Georgia. June 5, 1864 forwarded to Military Prison at Louisville, Kentucky from Nashville, Tennessee. June

6, 1864 received at Military Prison at Louisville, Kentucky and forwarded to Rock Island, Illinois (Alton, Illinois). June 9, 1864 received at Rock Island Barracks, Illinois. October 6, 1864 enlisted in the U. S. Army for frontier service. He was born in Georgia September 1839 and died in Bradford County, Florida. (find a grave # 11535037)

KESSLER (KESLER), JAMES ALBERT: Company I, corporal. September 18, 1861 enlisted as a private in Co. C, 1st Regiment, 1st Brigade, Georgia State Troops. March 18, 1862 mustered out. May 6, 1862 enlisted as a private in Co. I, 54th Regiment, Georgia Infantry at Guyton, Georgia and received bounty $50.00. December 31, 1862 received pay. January – February 1863 roll shows him present. October 31, 1863 received pay. November 12, 1863 promoted from private to 4th corporal of Co. I, 54th Regiment, Georgia Infantry. November – December 1863 roll shows him present. January 1864 issued clothing. June 15, 1864 wounded in the hand and face at Lost Mountain, Georgia. Pension records show he was discharged in 1865. He was born in Effingham County, Georgia August 9, 1849 and died in Effingham County, Georgia June 10, 1916. He is buried in Zion Lutheran Church Cemetery at Guyton, Effingham County, Georgia. (find a grave # 65113941)

KESSLER (KESLER), W. V.: Company I, private. August 11, 1863 enlisted as a private in Co. I, 54th Regiment, Georgia Infantry Rose Dew near Savannah, Georgia. October 31, 1863 received pay. December 15, 1863 detailed to guard commissary stores at No. 3 C. R. R. November – December 1863 roll shows him present (detailed to guard commissary stores). January 1864 and April 25, 1864 issued clothing.

KETCHUM, CHRISTOPHER C.: Company A, private. December 25, 1861 enlisted as a private in Co. D, 1st Independent Battalion, Georgia State Troops. April 16, 1862 roll shows him present. April 1862 mustered out. April 23, 1862 enlisted as a private in Co. A, 54th Regiment, Georgia Infantry. July 30, 1862 transferred to Sharpshooters by Special Order No. 259. August 1862 roll shows the transfer. August 16, 1864 deserted. August 23, 1864 took the Oath of Allegiance at Chattanooga, Tennessee.

KILCHRIST (KILCREASE), HICKERSON: Company H, private. He enlisted as a private in Co. H, 54th Regiment, Georgia Infantry. April 25, 1864 issued clothing. June 18, 1864 captured near Marietta, Georgia. June 26, 1864 received at Military Prison at Louisville, Kentucky from Nashville, Tennessee. June 27, 1864 sent from Military Prison at Louisville, Kentucky to Camp Morton, Indiana. July 22, 1864 he died of Chronic Diarrhoea at Camp Morton, Indiana. He is buried in grave No. 974 Crown Hill Cemetery, Indianapolis, Indiana. (find a grave # 14736072)

KILCREASE, D. G.: Company H, private. February 9, 1864 enlisted as a private in Co. H, 54th Regiment, Georgia Infantry at Columbus, Georgia and received bounty $50.00. April 25, 1864 issued clothing. December 6, 1864 received pay $41.43. April 26, 1865 surrendered at Greensboro, North Carolina. May 1, 1865 paroled at Greensboro, North Carolina. He was born February 15, 1845 and died May 18, 1931. He is buried in Joy

Cemetery at Joy, Clay County, Texas. (find a grave # 60010134)

KILCRESE, JAMES A.: Company H, private. January 28, 1864 enlisted as a private in Co. H, 54th Regiment, Georgia Infantry at Columbus, Georgia and received bounty $50.00. January – February 1863 roll shows him present. October 31, 1863 received pay. November – December 1863 roll shows him present. February 1, 1864 transferred to Co. F, 63rd Regiment, Georgia Infantry by order of General Beauregard. January – February 1864 roll shows him transferred to Co. F, 63rd Regiment, Georgia Infantry on February 1, 1864 by order of General Beauregard Special Order No. 25/4.

KILCREASE, WILLIAM; Company H, private. January 28, 1864 enlisted as a private in Co. H, 54th Regiment, Georgia Infantry at Columbus, Georgia and received bounty $50.00.

KILGORE, T. H.: Company B, private. He enlisted in 4th Georgia Sharpshooters – consolidated with Co. B, 54th Regiment, Georgia Infantry. April 26, 1865 surrendered at Greensboro, North Carolina. May 1, 1865 paroled at Greensboro, North Carolina.

KIMBREW (KIMBROUGH), BENJAMIN: Company A, private. He enlisted as a private in Co. A, 54th Regiment, Georgia Infantry.

KIMBREW (KIMBROUGH), BENJAMIN F.: Company F, private. February 21, 1863 enlisted as a private in Co. F, 54th Regiment, Georgia Infantry at Savannah, Georgia. January – February 1863 roll shows him present. April 6, 1863 he died in Savannah, Georgia. September 26, 1863 death benefit claim was filed by his father John H. Kimbrough of Bibb County, Georgia.

KIMBREW (KIMBROUGH), E. S.: Company A, private. May 3, 1862 enlisted as a private in Co. A, 54th Regiment, Georgia Infantry at Macon, Georgia and received bounty $50.00. December 30, 1862 received pay. June 30, 1863 roll shows him absent on furlough. October 31, 1863 received pay. November – December 1863 roll shows him present. January 1, 1864 received pay. January – February 1864 roll shows him present. April 29, 1864 issued clothing. January 13, 1865 admitted to St. Mary's Hospital at West Point, Mississippi with Pneumonia.

KIMBREW, THOMAS M.: Company A, private. May 3, 1862 enlisted as a private in Co. A, 54th Regiment, Georgia Infantry at Macon, Georgia and received bounty $50.00. December 30, 1862 received pay. June 30, 1863 roll shows him present. October 31, 1863 received pay. November – December 1863 roll shows him present (carpenter for company). January 1, 1864 received pay. January – February 1864 roll shows him present (carpenter for company). May 8, 1864 issued clothing. He was born in Bibb County, Georgia November 15, 1837 and died June 22, 1901. He is buried in Thunderpond Family Cemetery at Macon, Bibb County, Georgia. (find a grave # 51002189)

KINARD, E. (A.) J.: Company E, private. May 6, 1862 enlisted as a private in Co. E, 54th Regiment, Georgia Infantry at Savannah, Georgia and received bounty $50.00. December 31, 1862 received pay. January

– February 1863 roll shows him present. January 1864 and April 25, 1864 issued clothing.

KINERT, JAMES B.: private. He enlisted as a private in the 54th Regiment, Georgia Infantry. May 10, 1865 surrendered at Tallahassee, Florida. May 26, 1865 paroled at Albany, Georgia.

KING, THOMAS DUAUGN: Company A, corporal. July 1, 1863 enlisted as a private in Co. A, 54th Regiment, Georgia Infantry at Macon, Georgia and received bounty $50.00. October 1863 appointed 4th corporal in Co. A, 54th Regiment, Georgia Infantry. October 31, 1863 received pay. November – December 1863 roll shows him present. January 1, 1864 received pay. January – February 1864 roll shows him present. March 31, 1864 issued clothing.

KIRBY, JOHN: Company A, private. He enlisted as a private in Co. A, 54th Regiment, Georgia Infantry.

KIRBY (KERBY), WILLIAM L.: Company I, private. May 6, 1862 enlisted as a private in Co. I, 54th Regiment, Georgia Infantry at Savannah, Georgia and received bounty $50.00. September 4, 1862 to September 17, 1862 detailed as a laborer at Beaulieu near Savannah, Georgia at a rate of $.25 extra per day. September 1862 roll shows him detailed as a teamster. October 13, 1862 to November 30, 1862 detailed as a teamster at a rate of $.25 extra per day. December 2, 1862 discharged by civil authority. December 1862 roll shows his discharge.

KIRKLAND, ABRAHAM L.: Company C, corporal. May 6, 1862 enlisted as a private in Co. C, 54th Regiment, Georgia Infantry at Savannah, Georgia and received bounty $50.00. December 31, 1862 received pay. January – February 1863 roll shows him present. January 1, 1864 received pay. January – February 1864 roll shows him present. He was elected corporal of Co. C, 54th Regiment, Georgia Infantry. August 1, 1864 died in Filmer Hospital at Forsyth, Georgia of a Gunshot Wound. He is buried in the Forsythe City Cemetery at Forsythe, Monroe County, Georgia. (find a grave # 18512753)

KIRKLAND, EDWARD LEWIS: Company C, private. May 6, 1862 enlisted as a private in Co. C, 54th Regiment, Georgia Infantry at Savannah, Georgia and received bounty $50.00. December 31, 1862 received pay. January – February 1863 roll shows him present. January 1, 1864 received pay. January – February 1864 roll shows him present. 1864 he was elected clerk of Superior Court of Emanuel County, Georgia and was discharged by civil authority. He was a resident of Emanuel County, Georgia. He was born in Emanuel County, Georgia November 28, 1830 and died April 7, 1919. He is buried in Kirkland Cemetery at Summertown, Emanuel County, Georgia. (find a grave # 66411575).

KIRKLAND, HENRY C. C.: Company C, sergeant. May 6, 1862 enlisted as a private in Co. C, 54th Regiment, Georgia Infantry at Savannah, Georgia and received bounty $50.00. December 31, 1862 received pay. January – February 1863 roll shows him present. January 1, 1864 received pay. January – February 1864 roll shows him present. He was elected sergeant of Co. C, 54th Regiment, Georgia Infantry. Pension records show he was at home on sick furlough at the close of the war. May 26, 1865 surrendered and paroled at Augusta, Georgia. He was a resident of Emanuel County, Georgia. He was born in Emanuel County, Georgia January 9, 1843 and died in Emanuel County, Georgia May 31, 1906. He is buried in Summertown Cemetery at Summertown, Emanuel County, Georgia. (find a grave # 66262810)

KIRKLAND, HEBRY THOMAS: Company C, private. May 6, 1862 enlisted as a private in Co. C, 54th Regiment, Georgia Infantry at Savannah, Georgia and received bounty $50.00. December 31, 1862 received pay. January – February 1863 roll shows him present. January 1, 1864 received pay. January – February 1864 roll shows him present. April 25, 1864 issued clothing. June 19, 1864 he was wounded at Kennesaw Mountain (date is for near Marietta), Georgia. Pension records show he was at home on sick furlough at the close of the war. May 20, 1865 surrendered and paroled at Augusta, Georgia. He was born in Georgia April 3, 1840 and died January 16, 1929. He is buried in Connors Baptist Church Cemetery at Cobbtown, Tattnall County, Georgia. (find a grave # 93043895)

KIRKLAND, H. T.: Company G, private. May 3, 1862 enlisted as a private in Co. G, 54th Regiment, Georgia Infantry at Columbus, Georgia and received bounty $50.00.

KIRKLAND (KIRTLAND), N. G.: Company G (C), private. May 12, 1862 enlisted as a private in Co. G, 54th Regiment, Georgia Infantry. September 1, 1862 transferred from Co. G, 54th Regiment, Georgia Infantry to Co. C, 54th Regiment, Georgia Infantry at Beaulieu near Savannah, Georgia by Special Order No. 6. September 1862 roll shows the transfer.

KIRKLAND (KIRKLIN), RICHARD: Company K, private. He enlisted as a private in Co. K, 54th Regiment, Georgia Infantry.

KIRKMAN, CHARLES: Company G, private. He enlisted as a private in Co. G, 54th Regiment, Georgia Infantry. January 1864 issued clothing. December 25, 1864 captured at Pulaski, Tennessee. January 2, 1865 received at Military prison at Louisville, Kentucky from Nashville, Tennessee. January 4, 1865 sent to Camp Chase, Ohio. January 6, 1865 received at Camp Chase, Ohio. June 13, 1865 took the oath of allegiance at Camp Chase, Ohio. He is described as: a resident of Talladega, Alabama, fair complexion, dark hair, blue eyes, 5 feet 8 ½ inches high, and 18 years of age.

KITCHENS, C. M.: Company A, private. May 8, 1863 enlisted as a private in Co. A, 54th Regiment, Georgia Infantry.

KITCHENS, MILES W.: Company A, private. September 4, 1863 enlisted as a private in Co. A, 54th Regiment, Georgia Infantry at Macon, Georgia and received bounty $50.00. October 31, 1863 received pay. November – December 1863 roll shows him present. January 1, 1864 received pay. January – February 1864 roll shows him present. April 29, 1864 and May 8, 1864 issued clothing. July 20, 1864 wounded in the thigh at Peachtree Creek near Marietta, Georgia. Pension records show he was in the hospital, wounded, at the close of the war. He was born in Georgia November 28, 1844 (1846) and died in Gray, Jones County, Georgia July 31, 1928. He is buried in the Kitchens Family Cemetery at Gray, Jones County, Georgia. (find a grave # 54994277)

KITCHENS, ORREN WILLIAM; Company A, private. May 8, 1862 enlisted as a private in Co. A, 54th Regiment, Georgia Infantry at Macon, Georgia and received bounty $50.00. December 30, 1862 received pay. June 30, 1863 roll shows him present. October 31, 1863 received pay. November – December 1863 roll shows him present. January 1, 1864 received pay. January – February 1864 roll shows him present. April 29, 1864 issued clothing. (One source indicates: He was born in Jones County, Georgia in 1839 and died there in 1917.) He was born in Jones County, Georgia August 2, 1825 and died in Sumter County, Georgia March 19, 1899. He is buried in the Kitchens Family Cemetery at Andersonville, Sumter County, Georgia. (find a grave # 44116874)

KITCHENS, URIAS K. JR.: Company A, private. November 14, 1862 enlisted as a private in Co. A, 54th Regiment, Georgia Infantry at Beaulieu near Savannah, Georgia, Georgia and received bounty $50.00. December 30, 1862 received pay. June 30, 1863 roll shows him present. October 31, 1863 received pay. November – December 1863 roll shows him present. January 1, 1864 received pay. January – February 1864 roll shows him present. April 29, 1864 issued clothing. March 29, 1865 admitted to Ocmulgee Hospital at Macon, Georgia with Chronic Diarrhoea. April 7, 1865 returned to duty. He was a resident of Jones County, Georgia. Pension records state; November 1864 he was sent to Odell Springs, Mississippi Hospital with Dysentery and remained there until the close of the war. He was born in Twiggs County, Georgia November 13, 1841 and died in Jones County, Georgia April (March) 19, 1926. He is buried in New Salem Cemetery at Gray, Jones County, Georgia. (find a grave # 6967634)

KITCHENS, WILLIAM HENRY: Company A, private. February 6, 1864 enlisted as a private in Co. A, 54th Regiment, Georgia Infantry at Savannah, Georgia, and received bounty $50.00. January – February 1864 roll shows him present. April 29, 1864 issued clothing. May 28, 1864 he was wounded in the left temple near Marietta, Georgia. June 1, 1864 admitted to Ocmulgee Hospital at Macon, Georgia with a Gunshot Wound. July 3, 1864 returned to duty. June 4, 1864 deserted. June 22, 1864 admitted to Ocmulgee Hospital at Macon, Georgia with a Gunshot Wound March 29, 1865 admitted to Ocmulgee Hospital at Macon, Georgia with Chronic Diarrhoea. April 7, 1865 returned to duty. Pension records state he was in the hospital at Macon, Georgia at the close of the war. He was a resident of Jones County, Georgia. He was born in Jones County, Georgia August 30, 1845 and died in Twiggs County, Georgia July 22, 1925. He is buried in the William Henry Kitchens Cemetery in Twiggs County, Georgia. (find a grave # 35899635)

KNIGHT, E. J.: Company K, private. May 5, 1862 enlisted as a private in

Co. K, 54th Regiment, Georgia Infantry at Savannah, Georgia and received bounty $50.00.

KNIGHT, EZEKIEL STAFFORD: Company K, private. May 5, 1862 enlisted as a private in Co. K 54th Regiment, Georgia Infantry at Savannah, Georgia and received bounty $50.00. January 1, 1863 received pay. January – February 1863 roll shows him present. March 18, 1864, April 25, 1864 and June 2, 1864 issued clothing. July 22, 1864 killed at Atlanta, Georgia.

KNIGHT, GEORGE D.: Company A, sergeant. October 17, 1861 enlisted as a private and appointed 3rd corporal in Co. C, 1st Independent Battalion, Georgia State Troops. April 16, 1862 roll shows him present. April 1862 mustered out. April 19, 1862 enlisted as a private in Co. A, 54th Regiment, Georgia Infantry at Macon, Georgia, Georgia and received bounty $50.00. October 31, 1862 received pay. January – February 1863 roll shows him present. January 1, 1864 received pay. January – February 1864 roll shows him present. March 16, 1864, March 31, 1864 and May 25, 1864 issued clothing. June 17 (18), 1864 captured near Marietta, Georgia. June 26, 1864 received at Military Prison at Louisville, Kentucky from Nashville, Tennessee. June 27, 1864 sent to Camp Morton, Indiana from Military Prison at Louisville, Kentucky. June 28, 1864 received at Camp Morton, Indiana. March 4, 1865 transferred for exchange and forwarded to City Point, Virginia via Baltimore, Maryland. March 10-12, 1865 received at Boulware & Cox's Wharves, James River, Virginia. March 13, 1865 admitted to Jackson Hospital at Richmond, Virginia with Chronic Diarrhoea. March 22, 1865 furloughed for 60 days to Charlotte, North Carolina.

KNIGHT, GEORGE WALTON: Company G, captain. May 14, 1862 enlisted and elected captain of Co. G, 54th Regiment, Georgia Infantry at Savannah, Georgia. July 1862 roll shows him present at Savannah, Georgia. August 1862 roll shows him present at Beaulieu near Savannah, Georgia. September 1862 roll at Beaulieu near Savannah, Georgia shows him absent sick. October 1862 roll shows him absent with leave since October 25, 1862 (for 10 days). November 24, 1862 list of officers in the Savannah, Georgia area includes his name. November and December 1862 rolls show him present at Beaulieu near Savannah, Georgia. January – February 1863 roll shows him absent sitting on Court Martial at Savannah, Georgia. February 28, 1863 detailed to Court Martial. March 1, 1863 detailed to Court Martial. April 3, 1863 received pay $260.00. April 3, 1863 his name is on list of officers absent. May 2, to May 12 1863 granted a leave of absence granted by General Mercer. June 5, 1863 resigned his commission due to ill health. He was born May 7, 1823 and died April 19, 1869 at Atlanta, Fulton County, Georgia. He is buried in Oakland Cemetery at Atlanta, Fulton County, Georgia. (find a grave # 40621171)

KNIGHT, GEORGE WASHINGTON: Company E, corporal. May 6, 1862 enlisted as a private in Co. E, 54th Regiment, Georgia Infantry at Savannah, Georgia and received bounty $50.00. December 30, 1862 received pay. June 30, 1863 roll shows him present. January 1864, April 25, 1864 and June 2, 1864 issued clothing. He was appointed corporal of Company E, 54th Regiment, Georgia Infantry. August 22, 1864 wounded near Jonesboro, Georgia. August 24, 1864 admitted to Ocmulgee Hospital at Macon, Georgia with a Gunshot Wound (left foreleg middle 3rd flesh - calf). August 27, 1864 furloughed. Pension records show he was at home on sick furlough at the close of the war. May 10, 1865 surrendered at Tallahassee, Florida. May 18, 1865 paroled at Thomasville, Georgia. He was a resident of Milltown, Berrien County, Georgia. He was born in Lowndes County, Georgia September 8, 1845 and died in Berrien County, Georgia February 8, 1913. He is buried in Empire Primitive Baptist Church Cemetery at Lakeland, Lanier County, Georgia. (find a grave # 53325056)

KNIGHT, HAMPTON: Company K, corporal. May 5, 1862 enlisted as 4th corporal in Co. K, 54th Regiment, Georgia Infantry at Savannah, Georgia and received bounty $50.00. January 1, 1863 received pay. January – February 1863 roll shows him present. March 18, 1864 and April 18, 1864 issued clothing. May 10, 1865 surrendered at Tallahassee, Florida. May 20, 1865 paroled at Thomasville, Georgia. He was born in Georgia May 14, 1835 and died in Florida January 5, 1899. He is buried in Corinth Methodist Church Cemetery at Lake City, Columbia County, Florida. (find a grave # 40255320)

KNIGHT, ISHAM REDDISH): Company K, private. November 9, 1862 enlisted as a private in Co. K, 54th Regiment, Georgia Infantry at Beaulieu near Savannah, Georgia and received bounty $50.00. November 1862 roll shows his enlistment. January 1, 1863 received pay. January – February 1863 roll shows him present. March 18, 1864 and June 2, 1864 issued clothing. July 22, 1864 killed at Atlanta, Georgia.

KNIGHT, J. R.: Company K, private. He enlisted as a private in Co. K, 54th Regiment, Georgia Infantry.

KNIGHT, J. W.: Company E, private. He enlisted as a private in Co. E, 54th Regiment, Georgia Infantry.

KNIGHT, JAMES: Company K, private. He enlisted as a private in Co. K, 54th Regiment, Georgia Infantry.

KNIGHT, JAMES M.: Company K, private. September 18, 1861 enlisted as a private in Co. C, 1st Regiment, 1st Brigade, Georgia State Troops. March 18, 1862 mustered out. April 18, 1862 enlisted as a private in Co. K, 54th Regiment, Georgia Infantry at Beaulieu near Savannah, Georgia and received bounty $50.00. November 1862 roll shows his enlistment. January 1, 1863 received pay. January – February 1863 roll shows him present. March 18, 1864 issued clothing. May 10, 1865 surrendered at Tallahassee, Florida. May 19, 1865 paroled at Thomasville, Georgia. He is described as: 5 feet 6 inches high, light hair, blue eyes and dark complexion. He was born April 89, 1841 and died November 9, 1916. He is buried in the Drawdy - Knight Cemetery in Wayne County, Georgia. (find a grave # 84071852). The Southern Cross of Honor was bestowed on (a James Knight) him by the Jesup Chapter United Daughters of the Confederacy in 1902.

KNIGHT, JAMES MCGILLIS: Company K, private. September 18, 1861 enlisted as a private in Co. C, 1st Regiment, 1st Brigade, Georgia State Troops. March 18, 1862 mustered out. April 18, 1862 enlisted as a private in Co. K, 54th Regiment, Georgia Infantry at Beaulieu near Savannah, Georgia and received bounty $50.00. November 1862 roll shows his enlistment. January 1, 1863 received pay. January – February 1863 roll shows him present. March 18, 1864 issued clothing. July 22, 1864 wounded, right arm broken at Atlanta, Georgia. Pension records show; he was at home wounded at the close of the war. He was born in Georgia April 9, 1841 and died November 9, 1916. He is buried in the Drawdy-Knight Cemetery in Wayne County, Georgia. (find a grave # 84071852). The Southern Cross of Honor was bestowed on (a James Knight) him by the Jesup Chapter United Daughters of the Confederacy in 1902.

KNIGHT, JONATHAN N.: Company E, private. May 6, 1862 enlisted as a private in Co. E, 54th Regiment, Georgia Infantry at Savannah, Georgia and received bounty $50.00. December 31, 1862 received pay. January – February 1863 roll shows him present. January 1864 issued clothing. He was wounded in action. May 10, 1865 surrendered at Tallahassee, Florida. May 19, 1865 paroled at Thomasville, Georgia. He was born December 25, 1836 and died August 14, 1865 (4). He is buried in Empire Primitive Baptist Church Cemetery at Lakeland, Lanier County, Georgia. (find a grave # 125081376)

KNIGHT, JONATHAN N.: Company K, private. He enlisted as a private in Co. K, 54th Regiment, Georgia Infantry. May 30, 1864 a list from St. Mary's hospital at LaGrange, Georgia shows him unfit for field service, yet able for light duty in Convalescent Camp. He was born April 29, 1847 and died February 14, 1895. He is buried in the Drawdy-Knight Cemetery in Wayne County, Georgia. (find a grave # 84105513)

KNIGHT, JONATHAN W.: Company E, private. He enlisted as a private in Co. E, 54th Regiment, Georgia Infantry. January 1864 issued clothing. July 29, 1864 he is furloughed for 60 days from Floyd House Hospital at Macon, Georgia (Gunshot Wound to the left shoulder and back, producing simple fracture of spine and scapula). He was a resident of Nashville, Berrien County, Georgia.

KNIGHT, NATHANIEL STAFFORD: Company K, corporal. September 18, 1861 enlisted as a private in Co. C, 1st Regiment, 1st Brigade, Georgia State Troops. March 18, 1862 mustered out. April 18, 1862 enlisted as a private in Co. K, 54th Regiment, Georgia Infantry at Savannah, Georgia and received bounty $50.00. April 22, 1862. January 1, 1864 received pay. January – February 1864 roll shows him present (absent on 12 hour pass to visit Savannah, Georgia). March 18, 1864 issued clothing. He was promoted to corporal of Co. K, 54th Regiment, Georgia Infantry. January 1865 to the close of the war, pension records show he was on detail duty. May 10, 1865 surrendered at Tallahassee, Florida. May 19, 1865 paroled at Thomasville, Georgia. He is described: 6 feet high, light hair, blue eyes and light complexion. He was born in Georgia December 15, 1839 and died December 5, 1924. He is buried in Palmetto Cemetery at Brunswick, Glynn County, Georgia. (find a grave # 35842705)

KNIGHT, R. B.: Company C, captain. April 18, 1862 enlisted as a private in Co. C, 54th Regiment, Georgia Infantry at Savannah, Georgia and received bounty $50.00. April 22, 1862 appointed 1st lieutenant of Co. K, 54th Regiment, Georgia Infantry. July 1862 roll shows him present. August 1862 roll shows him absent on sick leave of 30 days since August 5. September 10, 1862 received pay $180.00. September 1862 roll shows him absent sick without leave. October 1862 roll shows him present. November 3, 1862 he was on furlough from headquarters. November 24, 1862 list of officers in the Savannah, Georgia area includes his name. November 1862 roll shows him absent with leave for 30 days since November 2, 1862 in State Senate (clerk). December 1862 roll shows him absent without leave since December 18, 1862. January – February 1863 roll shows him present. March 17, 1863 received pay $360.00. April 2, 1863 received pay $90.00. April 7, 1863 absent by authority of General Mercer to be with the State Legislature. April 25, 1863 elected captain Co. C, 54th Regiment, Georgia Infantry. May 3, 1863 list of officers absent notes his absence. July 16, 1863 resigned his commission due to have been appointed tax assessor for the 29th District of the State of Georgia (General Order No. 48, Government Service).

KNIGHT, RUFUS T.: Company C, private. May 6, 1862 enlisted as a private in Co. K, 54th Regiment, Georgia Infantry at Savannah, Georgia and received bounty $50.00. December 31, 1862 received pay. January – February 1863 roll shows him present. January 1, 1864 received pay. January – February 1864 roll shows him present. May 8, 1864 issued clothing. August 24, 1864 issued clothing at Marshall Hospital at Columbus, Georgia. April 26, 1865 surrendered in Co. D, 54th Regiment, Georgia Infantry at Greensboro, North Carolina. May 1, 1865 paroled at Greensboro, North Carolina.

KRENSON, ALEXANDER D.: Company F, private. He enlisted as a private in Co. F, 54th Regiment, Georgia Infantry. June 15, 1864 transferred to Co. F, 22nd Battalion, Georgia heavy Artillery. August 2, 1864 transferred to Captain Wheaton's Company, Chatham Siege Artillery. February 28, 1865 roll shows him present. He was born July 26, 1845 and died August 15, 1874. He is buried in Bonaventure Cemetery at Savannah, Chatham County, Georgia. (find a grave # 110796687)

KUHLMAN, CHRISTAIN: Company C, lieutenant. December 11, 1861 enlisted as a private in Co. B, 8th Regiment, Georgia State Troops. He mustered out in 1862. April 22, 1862 enlisted as 2nd lieutenant in Co. C, 54th Regiment, Georgia Infantry at Savannah, Georgia and received bounty $50.00. July 1862 roll at Beaulieu near Savannah, Georgia shows him on roll. August 1862 roll at Beaulieu near Savannah, Georgia shows him absent on ten days leave since August 28, 1862. September and October 1862 rolls at Beaulieu near Savannah, Georgia show him present. November 24, 1862 list of officers in the Savannah, Georgia area includes him. November 1862 roll at Beaulieu near Savannah, Georgia shows him in arrest for 2 weeks beginning November 23, 1862 by General Order No. 97. December 1862 roll at Beaulieu near Savannah, Georgia shows him present. January 2, 1863 he is shown as being sick. January – February 1863 roll shows him present. March 4, 1863 received pay $80.00. April 2, 1863 received pay $80.00. May 21, 1863 to May 31, 1863 he was on leave of absence approved by General Mercer. October 10, 1863 appointed 1st lieutenant Co. C, 54th Regiment, Georgia Infantry. October 21, 1863 list of officers at Legare's Point, South Carolina includes him. January – February 1864 roll shows him present. April 26, 1865 surrendered at Greensboro, North Carolina. May 1, 1865 paroled at Greensboro, North Carolina.

LACHILSON (LACKSION) (LACKLEYSON), K.: Company F, private. April 23, 1863 enlisted as a private in Co. F, 54th Regiment, Georgia Infantry.

LACHILSON (LACKSION) (LACKLEYSON), ROBERT, JR.: Company F, private. May 13, 1862 enlisted as a private in Co. F, 54th Regiment, Georgia Infantry at Savannah, Georgia and received bounty $50.00. May 13, 1862 detailed by order of General Lawton (working in government machine shop). October 1862 roll shows him detailed for government work. December 31, 1862 received pay. January – February 1863 roll shows him detailed by General Lawton. October 1, 1863 detailed by order of General Mercer. November – December 1863 roll shows him absent, detailed by General Mercer. January 1864 and July 7, 1864 issued clothing. January 17, 1865 admitted to Way Hospital at Meridian, Mississippi with a Gunshot Wound. April 12, 1865 captured at Salisbury, North Carolina. April 29, 1865 sent from Nashville, Tennessee to Military Prison at Louisville, Kentucky. May 1, 1865 received at Military Prison at Louisville, Kentucky from Nashville Tennessee. May 2, 1865 sent from Military Prison at Louisville, Kentucky to Camp Chase, Ohio. May 3, 1865 received at Camp Chase, Ohio. June 18, 1865 took the Oath of Allegiance at Camp Chase, Ohio. He is described as: fair complexion, black hair, grey eyes 5 feet 11 ½ inches high and 20 years of age. He was a resident of Chatham County, Georgia.

LAMB, EDWIN J.: Company E (C), private. December 7, 1861 enlisted as a private in Co. G, 29th Regiment, Georgia Infantry. January 1, 1863 transferred to Co. E, 54th Regiment, Georgia Infantry. December 31, 1862 received pay. January – February 1863 roll shows him present. April 25, 1863 transferred form General Hospital No. 1 at Savannah, Georgia to General Hospital at Augusta, Georgia with Tertian Fever (Malaria). January 1864 issued clothing.

LAMB, E.R.: Company C, private. May 6, 1862 enlisted as a private in

Co. C, 54th Regiment, Georgia Infantry at Savannah, Georgia and received bounty $50.00. January 1, 1864 received pay. January – February 1864 roll shows him present. Pension records show he was at home on January through April 1865. May 30, 1865 surrendered and paroled at Augusta, Georgia.

LAMB, EATONTON W.: Company G, private. January 25, 1863 enlisted as a private in Co. G, 54th Regiment, Georgia Infantry at Columbus, Georgia and received bounty $50.00. January – February 1863 roll shows him absent sick in the regimental Hospital since February 23, 1863. April 30, 1863 received pay. September 22, 1863 he died in Confederate General Hospital No. 1 at Columbia, South Carolina. December 28, 1863 death benefit claim was filed by his father, Green E. Lamb. He is described as being: 39 years of age, 5 feet 8 inches high, fair complexion, dark hair, blue eyes and was by occupation a farmer. He was a resident of Russell County, Alabama.

LAMB, F. M.: Company C, private. May 6, 1862 enlisted as a private in Co. C, 54th Regiment, Georgia Infantry at Savannah, Georgia and received bounty $50.00. October 31, 1862 received pay. January – February 1863 roll shows him present (absent without leave for 23 days). January 1, 1864 received pay. January – February 1864 roll shows him present.

LAMB, H. B: Company C, private. He enlisted as a private in Co. C, 54th Regiment, Georgia Infantry. June 2, 1865 surrendered and paroled at Augusta, Georgia.

LAMB, ISAAC BRINSON: Company C, private. February 18 (26), 1863 enlisted as a private in Co. C, 54th Regiment, Georgia Infantry at Savannah, Georgia and received bounty $50.00. January – February 1863 roll shows him present. October 25, 1863 discharged due to disability by Board of Examination. January – February 1864 roll shows he was discharged October 25, 1863 (not before reported). He was born in 1826 and died in 1905. He is buried in Lambs Chapel Cemetery, Emanuel County, Georgia. (find a grave # 73383451)

LAMB, ISAAC D. G.: Company C, lieutenant. December 11, 1861 appointed 1st sergeant of Co. B, 8th Regiment, Georgia State Troops. April 22, 1862 elected Jr. 2nd lieutenant of Co. C, 54th Regiment, Georgia Infantry. July 1862 roll shows him on roll. August, September and October 1862 rolls at Beaulieu near Savannah, Georgia show him present. November 24, 1862 list of officers in the Savannah, Georgia area shows him on list. November and December 1862 rolls show him absent sick since November 25, 1862. January 2, 1863 Inspectors Report No. 22 shows him sick. March 3, 1863 received pay $80.00. April 8, 1863 received pay $80.00. July 16, 1863 elected 2nd lieutenant of Co. C, 54th Regiment, Georgia Infantry. October 21, 1863 list of officers at Legare's Point, South Carolina shows him on list. He was elected 1st lieutenant of Co. C, 54th Regiment, Georgia Infantry. January – February 1864 roll shows him present. February 25, 1864 granted 15 days leave by Special Order No. 5/13. June 1, 1864 received pay $80.00. June 19, 1864 sent to General

Hospital by Brigade Surgeon. June 24, 1864 furloughed for 30 days from Floyd House and Ocmulgee Hospitals at Macon, Georgia due to Chronic Diarrhoea. August 25, 1864 report of Mercer's Brigade shows him sick, sent to General Hospital by Brigade Surgeon on June 19, 1864. May 18, 1865 surrendered and paroled at Augusta, Georgia. He is buried in the Kirkland Cemetery at Summertown, Emanuel County, Georgia. (find a grave # 66411585)

LAMB, ISAAC M.: Company C, private. February 25, 1863 enlisted as a private in Co. C, 54th Regiment, Georgia Infantry at Savannah, Georgia and received bounty $50.00. January – February 1864 roll shows him present. Pension records show he was at home on 30 days furlough at the close of the war. He was born in Jefferson County, Georgia October 26, 1841 and died in Laurens County, Georgia May 15, 1912. He is buried in Union Springs Baptist Church Cemetery in Laurens County, Georgia. (find a grave # 131141611)

LAMB, J. B.: Company C, private. February 15, 1863 enlisted as a private in Co. C, 54th Regiment, Georgia Infantry at Savannah, Georgia and received bounty $50.00. August 25, 1863 he was wounded, right thigh broken on Morris Island, South Carolina, Battery Wagner. Certificate of Disability for Discharge (November 16, 1863 at Charleston, South Carolina) states he was born in Emanuel County, Georgia, 35 years of age, 5 feet 8 inches high, fair complexion, blue eyes, light hair and by occupation was a farmer.

LAMB, J. M.: Company C, private. February 25, 1863 enlisted as a private in Co. C, 54th Regiment, Georgia Infantry at Savannah, Georgia and received bounty $50.00. January – February 1863 roll shows him present. January 1, 1864 received pay. January – February 1864 roll shows him present. April 25, 1864 and May 8, 1864 issued clothing. He was a resident of Emanuel County, Georgia.

LAMB, SIMEON S.: Company C, private. May 6, 1862 enlisted as a private in Co. C, 54th Regiment, Georgia Infantry at Savannah, Georgia and received bounty $50.00. December 31, 1862 received pay. January – February 1863 roll shows him present. April 1865 he was furloughed for 10 days sick with Pneumonia. May 1865 surrendered and paroled at Macon, Georgia. He was born in Georgia August 24, 1841 and died in Emanuel County, Georgia November 16, 1911. He is buried in Joiner-Bunn Cemetery at Canoochee, Emanuel County, Georgia. (find a grave # 61683311)

LAMB, THOMAS G.: Company C, private. December 11, 1862 enlisted as a private in Co. B, 8th Regiment, Georgia State Troops. April 22, 1862 enlisted as a private in Co. C, 54th Regiment, Georgia Infantry at Savannah, Georgia and received bounty $50.00. November 13, 1862 shown as deserted. October 31, 1862 received pay. January – February 1863 roll shows him present (absent without leave for 22 days). January 1, 1864 received pay. January – February 1864 roll shows him present.

LAMB, THOMAS L.: Company E, private. August 1, 1861 enlisted as a private in Co. C, 29th Regiment, Georgia Infantry. October 31, 1861 received pay. May 6, 1862 enlisted as a private in Co. E, 54th Regiment, Georgia Infantry at Savannah, Georgia and received bounty $50.00. December 31, 1862 received pay. January – February 1863 roll shows him absent as a teamster. June 1, 1863 to July 31, 1863 detailed for extra duty as an ambulance driver for the post at Beaulieu and Rose Dew near Savannah, Georgia at a rate of $.25 extra per day. September 8, 1863 received pay. October 31, 1863 list of detailed men at James Island, South Carolina shows him as a teamster for the medical department. January 1864 issued clothing. October 29, 1864 issued clothing at Convalescent Camp Wright. May 10, 1865 surrendered at Tallahassee, Florida. May 18, 1865 paroled at Thomasville, Georgia. He is described as; 5 feet 6 inches high, light hair, blue eyes and with a dark complexion.

LAMB, WILLIAM JOSEPH: Company E, sergeant. August 1, 1861 enlisted and appointed 2nd corporal of Co. C, 29th Regiment, Georgia Infantry. October 31, 1861 appears on roll. May 6, 1862 enlisted as 3rd sergeant in Co. E, 54th Regiment, Georgia Infantry at Savannah, Georgia and received bounty $50.00. December 31, 1862 received pay. January – February 1863 roll shows him present. January 1864 issued clothing. September 10, 1864 wounded in the leg near Atlanta, Georgia. September 16, 1864 and September 24, 1864 he appears on registers of Floyd House and Ocmulgee Hospitals at Macon, Georgia with a Gunshot Wound in the right leg (upper 1/3, ball cutting through anterior apex, 1/3 tibia). September 25, 1864 furloughed home for 60 days. He was unable to return to his command. He was a resident of Milltown, Georgia. He was born in North Carolina April 20, 1837 and died in Lowndes County, Georgia June 13, 1908. He is buried in Beaver Dam Cemetery at Ray City, Berrien County, Georgia. (find a grave # 49103397)

LAMBERT, JOSEPH: Company E, private. He enlisted as a private in Co. E, 54th Regiment, Georgia Infantry.

LAND, AARON: Company H, lieutenant. May 12, 1862 enlisted as 1st sergeant in Co. H, 54th Regiment, Georgia Infantry at Columbus, Georgia and received bounty $50.00. December 31, 1862 received pay. January – February 1863 roll shows him present. October 31, 1863 received pay. November – December 1863 roll shows him present. December 31, 1863 received pay. January 1864 issued clothing. January – February 1864 roll shows him present. April 14, 1864 board of examination was convened due to him claiming a grade higher than first sergeant. He was elected 1st lieutenant of Co. H, 54th Regiment, Georgia Infantry. June 2, 1864 issued clothing. January 12, 1865 admitted to St. Mary's Hospital at West Point, Mississippi with Chilblains. April 26, 1865 surrendered at Greensboro, North Carolina. May 1, 1865 paroled at Greensboro, North Carolina. He was born in Coweta County, Georgia February 24, 1834 and died in Muscogee County, Georgia October 11, 1901. He is buried at Double Churches Cemetery at Columbus, Muscogee County, Georgia. (find a grave # 16468078)

LAND, HARVEY MONROE: Company H, private. September 15, 1863 enlisted as a private in Co. E, 54th Regiment, Georgia Infantry at Columbus, Georgia and received bounty $50.00. October 31, 1863 received pay. November – December 1863 roll shows him present. December 31, 1863 received pay. January 1864 issued clothing. January – February 1864 roll shows him present. November 30, 1864 wounded at Franklin, Tennessee. December 25, 1864 captured at Pulaski, Tennessee. June 13, 1865 he was released from Camp Chase, Ohio. (Another record shows February 14, 1865 admitted to Way Hospital at Meridian, Mississippi with Rilusuia.) He was born in Muscogee County, Georgia August 20, 1844 and died in Cottonton, Russell County, Alabama. He is buried in Mount Lebanon Baptist Church Cemetery at Cottonton, Russell County, Alabama. (find a grave # 41997496)

LAND, JOHN HENRY: Company H, private. May 12, 1862 enlisted as a private.in Co. H, 54th Regiment, Georgia Infantry at Columbus, Georgia and received bounty $50.00. December 31, 1862 received pay. January – February 1863 roll shows him present. October 31, 1863 received pay. November – December 1863 roll shows him present. December 31, 1863 received pay. January 1864 issued clothing. January – February 1864 roll shows him present. April 26, 1865 surrendered at Greensboro, North Carolina. May 1, 1865 paroled at Greensboro, North Carolina. He was born December 10, 1845 and died October 16, 1926. He is buried Vivian Cemetery in Vivian, Caddo Parrish, Louisiana. (find a grave # 10504094)

LAND, WILLIAM J.: Company A, private. January 7, 1863 enlisted as a private Co. A, 54th Regiment, Georgia Infantry at Beaulieu near Savannah, Georgia and received bounty $50.00. June 30, 1863 roll shows him absent detailed in Medical Laboratory at Charleston, South Carolina. August 10, 1863 received pay $63.80. November – December 1863 roll shows him absent detailed in Medical Laboratory at Columbia, South Carolina. January 1864 issued clothing. January 15, 1864 received pay $22.00. January – February 1864 roll shows him absent detailed in Medical Laboratory at Columbia, South Carolina. February 29, 1864 received pay. February 29, 1864 roll shows him absent detailed in Medical Laboratory at Columbia, South Carolina. March 2, 1864 received pay $22.00. November 30, 1864 roll of men detailed at Medical Purveying Laboratory and Distilling Department at Columbia, South Carolina shows him present since March 31, 1863.

LANDERS, JOHN: Company K, private. November 15, 1861 enlisted in Co. E, 7th Texas Infantry. Transferred to Co. K, 54th Regiment, Georgia Infantry. April 26, 1865 surrendered at Greensboro, North Carolina. May 1, 1865 paroled at Greensboro, North Carolina.

LANE, A.: Company C, private. He enlisted as a private in Co. C, 54th Regiment, Georgia Infantry. February 1, 1864 died.

LANE, ALFRED: Company B, private. October 10, 1861 enlisted as a private in Co. K, 2nd Regiment, 1st Brigade, Georgia State Troops.

April 1862 mustered out. April 21, 1862 enlisted as a private Co. B, 54th Regiment, Georgia Infantry at Savannah, Georgia and received bounty $50.00. July 31, 1862 transferred to Co. C, 1st Georgia Sharpshooters at Savannah, Georgia by Special Order No. 259. July 1862 roll shows his transfer. August 1864 roll shows him absent sick.

LANE, D. P.: Company E, private. September 10, 1861 originally enrolled as a private in the Confederate States Army in Virginia. He enlisted as a private in Co. E, 54th Regiment, Georgia Infantry. October 30, 1863 received pay. November – December 1864 roll of Co. D, 1st Regiment Troops and Defences Macon, Georgia stationed at Camp Wright, Macon, Georgia shows him present.

LANGFORD, GEORGE W.: Company F, corporal. He enlisted as a private Co. F, 54th Regiment, Georgia Infantry. He was promoted to 3rd corporal. January 1864 and April 25, 1864 issued clothing. April 26, 1865 surrendered at Greensboro, North Carolina. May 1, 1865 paroled at Greensboro, North Carolina. He died October 1, 1936. He is buried in Bonaventure Cemetery at Savannah, Chatham County, Georgia. (find a grave # 123018974)

LANGFORD, GEORGE W.: Company G, private. He enlisted as a private Co. G, 54th Regiment, Georgia Infantry. Pension records show: April 26, 1865 surrendered at Greensboro, North Carolina. May 1, 1865 paroled at Greensboro, North Carolina.

LANGFORD, W. PIERCE: Company H, private. He enlisted as a private in Co. H, 54th Regiment, Georgia Infantry. He was born June 6, 1846 and died March 29, 1924. He is buried in Bass Family Cemetery in Troup County, Georgia. (find a grave # 94890788)

LANGSTON, W. J.: Company A, private. April 26, 1862 enlisted as a private in Co. A, 54th Regiment, Georgia Infantry at Macon, Georgia, Georgia and received bounty $50.00. September 1862 roll shows him as company cook. December 13, 1862 he is shown as deserted. December 30, 1862 received pay. May 1, 1863 to October 31, 1863 detailed as a carpenter (company mechanic) around Savannah, Georgia at a rate of $.25 extra per day. June 30, 1863 roll shows him present detailed as a carpenter. October 31, 1863 received pay. November 1863 received commutation for rations. November – December 1863 roll shows him present detailed as company carpenter. January 1, 1864 received pay. January – February 1864 roll shows him present detailed as company carpenter. March 31, 1864 and May 8, 1864 issued clothing.

LANIER, ISAAC J.: Company I, private. September 8, 1863 enlisted as a private Co. I, 54th Regiment, Georgia Infantry at Rose Dew near Savannah, Georgia and received bounty $50.00. October 25, 1863 admitted to General Hospital at Guyton, Georgia. November – December 1863 roll of General Hospital at Guyton, Georgia shows him present as a patient. November – December 1863 roll shows him absent sick. January – February 1864 roll of General Hospital at Guyton, Georgia shows him present as a patient (pay due since enlistment). January 1864 and April 25,

1864 issued clothing. May 20, 1864 captured at Cassville, Georgia. May 27, 1864 sent from Nashville, Tennessee to Military Prison at Louisville, Kentucky. May 29, 1864 received at Military Prison at Louisville, Kentucky from Nashville, Tennessee. May 30, 1864 sent from Military Prison at Louisville, Kentucky to Rock Island Barracks, Illinois. June 1, 1864 received at Rock Island Barracks, Illinois. October 31, 1864 took the oath of allegiance at Rock Island Barracks, Illinois (note: volunteered in the U. S. A. for frontier service but was rejected). He is described as fair complexion, light hair, blue eyes, 5 feet 10 inches high and 20 years of age. He was born August 18, 1843 and died December 29, 1902. He is buried in Little Ogeechee Baptist Church Cemetery at Oliver, Screven County, Georgia. (find a grave # 24969999)

LANIER, T. J.: Company G (C), private. May 12, 1862 enlisted as a private.in Co. G, 54th Regiment, Georgia Infantry at Columbus, Georgia and received bounty $50.00. September 1, 1862 transferred from Co. G, 54th Regiment, Georgia Infantry to Co. C, 54th Regiment, Georgia Infantry at Beaulieu near Savannah, Georgia by Special Order No. 6. September 1862 rolls show his transfer. August 23, 1862 died in Savannah, Georgia. August 1862 roll reflects his death.

LANKFORD (LANGFORD), W. PIERCE: Company H, private. May 12, 1862 enlisted as a private in Co. H, 54th Regiment, Georgia Infantry at Columbus, Georgia and received bounty $50.00. December 31, 1862 received pay. January – February 1863 roll shows him present. October 31, 1863 received pay. November – December 1863 roll shows him absent on picket. December 31, 1863 received pay. January 1864 issued clothing. January – February 1864 roll shows him present sick. April 26, 1865 surrendered at Greensboro, North Carolina. May 1, 1865 paroled at Greensboro, North Carolina. He was born in Georgia June1846.

LARISCY, ALLEN: Company D, private. October 14, 1861 enlisted as a private in Co. I, 5th Regiment, Georgia State Troops. April 1862 mustered out. April 30, 1864 enlisted as a private Co. D, 54th Regiment, Georgia Infantry at Savannah, Georgia and received bounty $50.00. December 31, 1862 received pay. January – February 1863 roll shows him present. January 1864 and May 6, 1864 issued clothing. May 18, 1865 surrendered and paroled at Augusta, Georgia.

LARISCY, JACKSON: Company D, sergeant. October 14, 1861 enlisted as a private in Co. I, 5th Regiment, Georgia State Troops. April 1862 mustered out. April 30, 1862 enlisted as 2nd sergeant Co. D, 54th Regiment, Georgia Infantry at Savannah, Georgia and received bounty $50.00. December 31, 1862 received pay. January – February 1863 roll shows him present. January 1864, April 25, 1864 and June 2, 1864 issued clothing. May 18, 1865 surrendered and paroled at Augusta, Georgia.

LARISCY, MOSES LAMAR, JR.: Company D, private. October 15, 1862 enlisted as a private in Co. D, 54th Regiment, Georgia Infantry at Beaulieu near Savannah, Georgia and received bounty $50.00. October 1862 roll indicates he joined by transfer. December 31, 1862 received pay. February 25, 1863 detailed on detached service with the Engineer Department at Savannah, Georgia. January – February 1863 roll shows him absent (absent without leave 5 days). March 15, 1863 attached to the Ordinance Department by order of General Mercer. October 31 shown on list of men detailed at James Island, South Carolina shows him attached to the Ordinance Department (getting or cutting shingles. January 1864 issued clothing. July 13, 1864 detail was extended by Special Order No. 164/4. He was born April 26, 1841 and died in Georgia February 16, 1913. He is buried in McDonald Baptist Church Cemetery at Sylvania, Screven County, Georgia. (find a grave #115258060)

LARISEY, MOSES, SR.: Company D, private. June 28, 1862 enlisted as a private in Co. D, 54th Regiment, Georgia Infantry at Savannah, Georgia and received bounty $50.00. September 1, 1862 to December 31, 1862 detailed as a butcher at Beaulieu near Savannah, Georgia at a rate of $.25 extra per day. September, October, November and December 1862 rolls show him detailed as a butcher. December 31, 1862 received pay. January 1, 1863 to February 19, 1863 detailed as a butcher at Beaulieu near Savannah, Georgia at a rate of $.25 extra per day. February 26, 1863 received pay. January – February 1863 roll shows him present. March 12, 1863 received pay. January 1864 issued clothing. July 13, 1864 detail extended.

LARISCY, WILLIAM M.: Company D, sergeant. October 7, 1861 enlisted and elected 3rd corporal in Co. I, 5th Regiment, Georgia State Troops. April 1862 mustered out. April 30, 1864 enlisted as 3rd sergeant Co. D, 54th Regiment, Georgia Infantry at Savannah, Georgia and received bounty $50.00. December 31, 1862 received pay. January – February 1863 roll shows him present. January 1864 issued clothing. Pension records show he was on the road sick at the close of the war. He was born March 25, 1837 in Georgia and died in Screven County April 7, 1912. He is buried in McDonald Baptist Church Cemetery at Sylvania, Screven County, Georgia. (find a grave # 22606045)

LARRISSAY, MOSES: Company H, private. May 12, 1862 enlisted as a private in Co. H, 54th Regiment, Georgia Infantry at Warrenton, Georgia and received bounty $50.00.

LAW, W. S.: Company F, private. He enlisted as a private in Co. F, 54th Regiment, Georgia Infantry. November 20, 1862 discharged by civil authority at Beaulieu near Savannah, Georgia. November 1862 roll reflects his discharge.

LAWES, WILLIAM A.: Company G (F), private. May 12, 1862 enlisted as a private in Co. G, 54th Regiment, Georgia Infantry at Columbus, Georgia and received bounty $50.00. October 31, 1862 received pay. January – February 1863 roll shows him present (returned to company February 10, 1863 from absence on sick furlough since November 20, 1862. September 1, 1863 to September 30, 1863 detailed as Forage Master on James Island, South Carolina at a rate of $.25 extra per day. October 1, 1863 to December 31, 1863 detailed as Forage Master at St. Andrews near

Charleston, South Carolina at a rate of $.25 extra per day. November 3, 1863 received pay $22.00. January 1864 issued clothing. January 1, 1864 to April 30, 1864 detailed as Forage Master at Charleston, South Carolina at a rate of $.25 extra per day. April 25, 1864 and May 20, 1864 issued clothing (April and May shows he was detailed). Transferred to Co. F, 54th Regiment, Georgia Infantry. April 26, 1865 surrendered at Greensboro, North Carolina. May 1, 1865 paroled at Greensboro, North Carolina.

LAWRENCE, F. M.: Company A, private. September 1, 1863 he enlisted as a private in Co. A, 54th Regiment, Georgia Infantry at Macon, Georgia and received bounty $50.00. He was detailed to the Macon Arsenal at a rate of an extra $3.00 per day. November – December 1863 roll shows him absent detailed at the Macon Arsenal. December 31, 1863 received pay at the Macon Arsenal. January 31, 1864 received pay at the Macon Arsenal. January – February 1864 roll shows him absent detailed at the Macon Arsenal. February 29, 1864 received pay at the Macon Arsenal. March 1864 received pay. April 1864 received pay at the Macon Arsenal. May 1864 received pay $236.50 (at the Macon Arsenal). June 30, 1864 received pay $93.00 ($3.00 per day). June 1864 he was still detailed at the Macon Arsenal. December 1, 1864 appears on the roll of Floyd House Hospital at Macon, Georgia with Irritation Spinalis (preceded by an attack 4 years since – general health bad). April 12, 1865 extension of the detail recommended for 60 days (Unfit for service for that time). April 30, 1865 he was captured in Macon, Georgia.

LAWRENCE, F. M.: Company A, private. He enlisted as a private in Co. A, 54th Regiment, Georgia Infantry at Macon, Georgia and received bounty $50.00. June 5, 1863 he was Detailed Conscript. July 1863 he was shown at the Macon Arsenal. August 1863 he was detailed at the Macon Arsenal as a carpenter. November 1863 records show he was a carpenter with the Ordinance Department at the Macon Arsenal. December 29, 1863 records show he was detailed by Special Order No. 288/1. Records show he was detailed as a carpenter. January 31, 1864 received pay at the Macon Arsenal. March 1864 received pay. May 17, 1864 captured near Calhoun, Georgia. May 21, 1864 forwarded to Resaca. He was born in Bibb County, Georgia in 1845 and died in Crisp County, Georgia. He is buried in Sunnyside Cemetery at Cordele, Crisp County, Georgia. (find a grave # 60227680)

LAWRENCE, W. D.: Company C, private. He enlisted as a private in Co. C, 54th Regiment, Georgia Infantry. May 20, 1865 surrendered and paroled at Augusta, Georgia.

LAWRENCE, W. S.: Company D, private. April 30, 1864 enlisted as a private Co. D, 54th Regiment, Georgia Infantry at Savannah, Georgia and received bounty $50.00. August 19, 1862 transferred to 1st Georgia Sharpshooters by Special Order No. 259.

LAWS, WILLIAM A.: Company G, private. May 12, 1862 enlisted as a private in Co. G, 54th Regiment, Georgia Infantry at Columbus, Georgia and received bounty $50.00. 1862 appointed 1st corporal of Co.

G, 54th Regiment, Georgia Infantry. Pension records show: April 26, 1865 surrendered at Greensboro, North Carolina. May 1, 1865 paroled at Greensboro, North Carolina.

LAWSON, FRANCIS M.: Company A, private. February 23, 1863 enlisted as a private in Co. A, 54th Regiment, Georgia Infantry at Savannah, Georgia and received bounty $50.00. April 30, 1863 received pay. June 30, 1863 roll shows him present. October 31, 1863 received pay. November – December 1863 roll shows him present. January 1, 1864 received pay. January – February 1864 roll shows him present (due pay for September and October 1863). April 29, 1864 issued clothing. May 17, 1864 captured near Calhoun, Georgia. May 24, 1864 received at Military Prison at Louisville, Kentucky from Nashville Tennessee. May 25, 1864 forwarded to Rock Island, Illinois from Military Prison at Louisville, Kentucky. May 27, 1864 received at Rock island, Illinois from Military Prison at Louisville, Kentucky.

LAYFIELD, JAMES N.: Company G (C), private. May 12, 1862 enlisted as a private in Co. G, 54th Regiment, Georgia Infantry at Savannah, Georgia and received bounty $50.00. September 1, 1862 transferred from Co. G, 54th Regiment, Georgia Infantry to Co. C, 54th Regiment, Georgia Infantry by Special Order No. 6 at Beaulieu near Savannah, Georgia. September 1862 both company rolls show him transferred. December 31, 1862 received pay. January – February 1863 roll shows him present. January 1, 1864 received pay. January – February 1864 roll shows him present. June 19, 1864 wounded left leg and captured near Marietta, Georgia. June 24, 1864 sent from Nashville, Tennessee to Military Prison at Louisville, Kentucky. June 26, 1864 received at Military Prison at Louisville, Kentucky from Nashville Tennessee. June 27, 1864 sent from Military Prison at Louisville, Kentucky to Camp Morton, Indiana. June 28, 1864 received at Camp Morton, Indiana. March 15, 1865 transferred for exchange from Camp Morton, Indiana. He was forwarded to Point Lookout, Maryland via Baltimore & Ohio Railroad. He was born in Georgia in 1840. He died July 27, 1887. He is buried in Antioch Baptist Church Cemetery in Harris County, Georgia. (find a grave # 63724226)

LAYFIELD, LUNDY: Company C, private. February 9, 1863 enlisted as a private in Co. C, 54th Regiment, Georgia Infantry at Savannah, Georgia and received bounty $50.00. January – February 1863 roll shows him present. January 1, 1864 received pay. January – February 1864 roll shows him present. April 28, 1864 issued clothing. June 27, 1864 he was wounded at Kennesaw Mountain, Georgia. He transferred to Co. D, 54th Consolidated Regiment, Georgia Infantry. April 26, 1865 surrendered at Greensboro, North Carolina. May 1, 1865 paroled at Greensboro, North Carolina. He was born in Hancock County, Georgia 1827.

LEE, DAVID JESSE: Company G (C), private. December 11, 1861 enlisted as a private in Co. B, 8th Regiment, Georgia State Troops. He mustered out in 1862. April 22, 1862 enlisted as a private in Co. G, 54th Regiment, Georgia Infantry at Savannah, Georgia and received bounty

$50.00. September 1, 1862 transferred from Co. G, 54th Regiment, Georgia Infantry to Co. C, 54th Regiment, Georgia Infantry by Special Order No. 6 at Beaulieu near Savannah, Georgia. December 31, 1862 received pay. January – February 1863 roll shows him present. August 8, 1863 received pay $22.00. January 1, 1864 received pay. January – February 1864 roll shows him absent (absent sick in Hospital at Hardeeville, South Carolina since February 24, 1864). May 8, 1864 issued clothing. He was born October 8, 1843 and died October 30, 1905. He is buried in Douglas Branch Baptist Church Cemetery in Screven County, Georgia. (find a grave # 32256219)

LEE, GILFORD J.: Company E, private. October 6, 1861 enlisted as a private in Co. K, 5th Regiment, Georgia State Troops. April 1862 mustered out. May 6, 1862 enlisted as a private in Co. E, 54th Regiment, Georgia Infantry at Savannah, Georgia and received bounty $50.00. December 31, 1862 received pay. January – February 1863 roll shows him present. January 1864 issued clothing. He was born September 6, 1840 and died in 1918. He is buried in O'Brian Cemetery at O'Brian, Suwannee County, Florida (find a grave # 16943016)

LEE, HENRY G.: Company C, private. December 2, 1862 enlisted as a private in Co. C, 54th Regiment, Georgia Infantry at Savannah, Georgia and received bounty $50.00. December 1862 roll shows he joined the company on December 3, 1862 at Beaulieu near Savannah, Georgia. December 31, 1862 received pay. January – February 1863 roll shows him present. He was captured near Newton, North Carolina. April 19, 1865 he was paroled at Newton, North Carolina. January 1, 1864 received pay. January – February 1864 roll shows him present. Pension records show he served until the end of the war. He was born in Putnam County, Georgia in 1829.

LEE, JAMES L.: Company E, private. May 6, 1862 enlisted as a private in Co. E, 54th Regiment, Georgia Infantry at Savannah, Georgia and received bounty $50.00. December 31, 1862 received pay. January – February 1863 roll shows him present. August 21, 1863 received pay $33.00. January 1864 issued clothing. May 28, 1864 Medical Examining Board at St. Mary's Hospital, Dalton, Georgia found him unfit and furloughed him for 60 days (Chronic Diarrhoea with extreme emaciation and Debility – sick since July 1863). May 25, 1865 surrendered and paroled at Thomasville, Georgia. He was a resident of Milltown, Georgia. He was born in Georgia February 4, 1846 and died in Georgia January 1, 1935. He is buried in Liberty Baptist Church Cemetery at Bickley, Ware County, Georgia. (find a grave # 64207605)

LEE, JESSE: Company E, private. May 6, 1862 enlisted as a private in Co. E, 54th Regiment, Georgia Infantry at Savannah, Georgia and received bounty $50.00. December 31, 1862 received pay. January – February 1863 roll shows him present. January 1864 and April 25, 1864 issued clothing. May 25, 1865 surrendered and paroled at Thomasville, Georgia.

LEE, JOHN: Company E, private. October 6, 1861 enlisted as a private in Co. K, 5th Regiment, Georgia State Troops. April 1862 mustered out. May 6, 1862 enlisted as a private in Co. E, 54th Regiment, Georgia Infantry at Savannah, Georgia and received bounty $50.00. December 31, 1862 received pay. January – February 1863 roll shows him present. August 21, 1863 received pay $33.00. January 1864 issued clothing. He was born March 31, 1842 and died May 24, 1902. He is buried in Union Primitive Baptist Church Cemetery at Lakeland, Lanier County, Georgia. (find a grave # 59634453)

LEE, R. H.: Company I, private. He enlisted as a private in Co. I, 54th Regiment, Georgia Infantry. April 25, 1864 issued clothing. July 1, 1864 died at Walker Hospital at Columbus, Georgia of Pneumonia. He is buried in Linwood Cemetery at Columbus, Muscogee County, Georgia in Plot; Section L, Row 7. (find a grave # 97936594)

LEGGETT, BERRY A.: Company K, private. October 3, 1861 enlisted as a private in Co. A, 1st Regiment, 1st Brigade, Georgia State Troops. April 1862 mustered out. April 19, 1862 enlisted as a private in Co. K, 54th Regiment, Georgia Infantry at Savannah, Georgia and received bounty $50.00. January 1, 1863 received pay. January – February 1863 roll shows him present. March 18, 1864 issued clothing. May 10, 1865 surrendered at Tallahassee, Florida. May 23, 1865 paroled at Thomasville, Georgia.

LEGGETT, BRYANT (BRIANT): Company B, private. April 28, 1862 enlisted as a private in Co. B, 54th Regiment, Georgia Infantry at Savannah, Georgia and received bounty $50.00. December 31, 1862 received pay. January – February 1863 roll shows him present. January 1864 issued clothing. He was born March 10, 1834 and died June 23, 1898 and is buried in Crosby Chapel Cemetery in Appling County, Georgia. (find a grave # 18702416)

LEROY, CHARLES: Company I, private. November 1, 1863 enlisted as a private in Co. I, 54th Regiment, Georgia Infantry. December 1863 appointed cook.

LESNEUR, J. B.: Company B, private. He enlisted as a private in Co. B, 54th Regiment, Georgia Infantry.

LESTER, F. C.: Company A, private. April 26, 1862 enlisted as a private in Co. A, 54th Regiment, Georgia Infantry at Macon, Georgia and received bounty $50.00. June 30, 1863 roll shows him deserted. November 25, 1863 enlisted as a private in Co. A, 54th Regiment, Georgia Infantry at Savannah, Georgia. November – December 1863 roll shows him present. January 1, 1864 received pay. January – February 1864 roll shows him absent without leave since February 26, 1864. April 2, 1864 transferred from Co. A, 54th Regiment, Georgia Infantry to Co. K, 54th Regiment, Georgia Infantry by Special order No. 67.

LESTER, F. C.: Company D, private. He enlisted as a private in Co. D, 54th Regiment, Georgia Infantry. September 6, 1864 shown as a deserter.

LESTER, R. F.: Company B, private. April 21, 1862 enlisted as a private in Co. B, 54th Regiment, Georgia Infantry at Savannah, Georgia and received bounty $50.00. December 31, 1862 received pay. January – February 1863 roll shows him present (absent without leave 5 days).

LEWIS, D. HENRY: Company D, private. October 10, 1861 enlisted as a private in Co. K, 2nd Regiment, 1st Brigade, Georgia State Troops. April 1862 mustered out. April 30, 1862 enlisted as a private in Co. D, 54th Regiment, Georgia Infantry at Savannah, Georgia and received bounty $50.00. December 31, 1862 received pay. January – February 1863 roll shows him present. January 1864 issued clothing. August 20, 1864 admitted to 1st Mississippi C. S. A. Hospital at Jackson, Mississippi with Diarrhoea. October 17, 1864 transferred. July – August 1864 roll of Hospital at Shelby Springs, Alabama shows him present as a patient. April 26, 1865 surrendered at Greensboro, North Carolina. May 1, 1865 paroled at Greensboro, North Carolina.

LEWIS, DANIEL: Company C, private. December 11, 1861 enlisted as a private in Co. B, 8th Regiment, Georgia State Troops. He mustered out in 1862. April 22, 1862 enlisted as a private in Co. C, 54th Regiment, Georgia Infantry at Savannah, Georgia and received bounty $50.00. December 31, 1862 received pay. January – February 1863 roll shows him present (in hospital at Bethesda). January 1, 1864 received pay. January – February 1864 roll shows him present. April 25, 1864 issued clothing. May 16, 1864 he was wounded in the left arm at Resaca, Georgia. He was furloughed for 60 days. May 18, 1865 surrendered and paroled at Augusta, Georgia. He was born in Butts, County, Georgia August 7, 1842 and died November 19, 1924. He is buried in Lewis Primitive Baptist Church Cemetery in Jenkins County, Georgia. (find a grave #60832647)

LEWIS, E. G.: Company C, private. February 24, 1864 enlisted as a private in Co. C, 54th Regiment, Georgia Infantry at Savannah, Georgia and received bounty $50.00. January – February 1863 roll shows him present. January 1, 1864 detached acting sutler at Hardeeville by order of Colonel Charlton Way. January 1, 1864 received pay. January – February 1864 roll shows him absent detached as sutler. April 28, 1864 issued clothing. He is buried in Memory Hill Cemetery at Milledgeville, Baldwin County, Georgia. (find a grave # 17202633)

LEWIS, HENRY SEABORN: Company D, private. April 30, 1862 enlisted as a private in Co. D, 54th Regiment, Georgia Infantry at Savannah, Georgia and received bounty $50.00. December 31, 1862 received pay. January – February 1863 roll shows him present. January 1864 issued clothing. July 22, 1864 killed at Atlanta, Georgia. He was born October 9, 1833 and died in Atlanta, Georgia July 22, 1864. He is buried in the Lewis Family Cemetery in Jenkins County, Georgia

LEWIS, JOHN GREEN: Company E, private. January 23, 1863 enlisted as a private in Co. E, 54th Regiment, Georgia Infantry at Coffee Bluff near Savannah, Georgia and received bounty $50.00. January – February 1863 roll shows him present. May 1, 1863 to December 31, 1863 detailed in Headquarters Department at Rose Dew near Savannah,

Georgia as a teamster (driving a 2 mule wagon) at a rate of $.25 extra per day. September 8, 1863 received pay. October 31, 1863 he is shown on list of detailed men at James Island, South Carolina as a driver for the Headquarters Department. January 9, 1864 received pay $22.00. January 1864 issued clothing. January 17, 1864 received pay $22.00. January 20, 1864 received pay. May 8, 1864 issued clothing. May 10, 1865 surrendered at Tallahassee, Florida. May 24, 1865 paroled at Thomasville, Georgia. He was born in Georgia February 24, 1836 and died October 19, 1922. He is buried in Empire Primitive Baptist Church Cemetery at Lakeland, Lanier County, Georgia. (find a grave # 125029868)

LEWIS, ROBERT HENRY: Company A, private. April 26, 1862 enlisted as a private in Co. A, 54th Regiment, Georgia Infantry at Macon, Georgia and received bounty $50.00. December 30, 1862 received pay. June 30, 1863 roll shows him absent (absent on furlough since December 27, 1863). October 31, 1863 received pay. November – December 1863 roll shows him present. January – February 1864 roll shows him present (carpenter for company). March 31, 1864, May 8, 1864 and June 10, 1864 issued clothing. November 19, 1864 issued clothing at Convalescent Camp Wright in Macon, Georgia. Pension records show: April 26, 1865 surrendered at Greensboro, North Carolina. May 1, 1865 paroled at Greensboro, North Carolina. He was born in Greene County, Georgia September 5, 1831 and died in Bibb County, Georgia January 14, 1902. He is buried in Fort Hill Cemetery at Macon, Bibb County, Georgia. (find a grave # 120679911)

LEWIS, S.: Company D, private. April 30, 1862 enlisted as a private in Co. D, 54th Regiment, Georgia Infantry at Savannah, Georgia and received bounty $50.00. December 31, 1862 received pay. January – February 1863 roll shows him present.

LEWIS, S.: Company D, private. April 30, 1862 enlisted as a private in Co. D, 54th Regiment, Georgia Infantry at Savannah, Georgia and received bounty $50.00. October 16, 1862 he died at Beaulieu near Savannah, Georgia. October 1862 roll reflects his death.

LEWIS, THOMAS M.: Company D, private. April 30, 1862 enlisted as a private in Co. D, 54th Regiment, Georgia Infantry at Savannah, Georgia and received bounty $50.00. December 31, 1862 received pay. January – February 1863 roll shows him present. August 29, 1863 to September 3, 1863 killed at Battery Wagner on Morris Island, South Carolina.

LIGHTBOURNE (LIGHTBURN), JOHN L.: Company F, private. July 1, 1862 enlisted as a private in Co. F, 54th Regiment, Georgia Infantry at Savannah, Georgia and received bounty $50.00. August 1862 roll shows he joined July 1, 1862. December 31, 1862 received pay. January – February 1863 roll shows him discharged by civil authority January 1, 1863. April 1, 1863 enlisted in Co. F, 63rd Regiment, Georgia infantry. July 3, 1864 captured near Marietta, Georgia. July 16, 1864 received at Military Prison at Louisville, Kentucky from Nashville, Tennessee. July 16, 1864 sent to Camp Douglas, Illinois from Military Prison at Louisville, Kentucky.

July 18, 1864 received at Camp Douglas, Illinois from Military Prison at Louisville, Kentucky. July 14, 1865 admitted to U. S. A. General Hospital at Camp Douglas, Illinois. July 20, 1865 discharged from the hospital. August 1, 1865 admitted to post Hospital at Camp Douglas, Illinois for Convalescence. August 31, 1865 discharged from the hospital.

LIGHTFOOT, THOMAS J.: Company D, private. April 30, 1862 enlisted as a private in Co. D, 54th Regiment, Georgia Infantry at Savannah, Georgia and received bounty $50.00. December 31, 1862 received pay. January – February 1863 roll shows him present. January 1864 and April 25, 1864 issued clothing. February 6, 1864 admitted to Ocmulgee Hospital at Macon, Georgia with Bronchitis. Pension records show; May 12, 1865 he was discharged from Macon, Georgia hospital He was a resident of Burke County. He was born in Burke County, Georgia May 10, 1838 and died October 20, 1902. He is buried in Oak Hill Baptist Church Cemetery at Paramore Hill, Jenkins County, Georgia. (find a grave # 43361875)

LIGHTSEY, ALFRED: Company K, private. May 5, 1862 enlisted as a private in Co. K, 54th Regiment, Georgia Infantry at Savannah, Georgia and received bounty $50.00. January 1, 1863 received pay. January – February 1863 roll shows him present. November 16, 1863 transferred from Co. K, 54th Regiment, Georgia Infantry to Co. K, 4th Regiment, (Clinch's) Georgia Cavalry by Special Order No. 240/1. May 10, 1865 surrendered at Tallahassee, Florida. May 21, 1865 paroled at Thomasville, Georgia. He was born in Appling County, Georgia December 17, 1832.

LINDSEY, WILLIAM C.: Company E, private. May 6, 1862 enlisted as a private in Co. E, 54th Regiment, Georgia Infantry at Savannah, Georgia and received bounty $50.00. December 31, 1862 received pay. January – February 1863 roll shows him present. January 1864 and April 25, 1864 issued clothing. Pension records show; winter of 1864 he contracted Typhoid Fever at Corinth, Mississippi. January 10, 1865 admitted to St. Mary's Hospital at West Point, Mississippi with Rheumatism. February 15, 1865 admitted to Way Hospital at Meridian, Mississippi with Chronic Diarrhoea and was furloughed. He was born in 1830 and died May 7, 1865. He is buried in Wilkes Cemetery in Cook County, Georgia. (find a grave # 49547750)

LLOYD, E. D.: Company I, corporal. September 18, 1861 enlisted as a private in Co. C, 1st Regiment, 1st Brigade, Georgia State Troops. March 18, 1862 mustered out. May 6, 1862 enlisted as a private and appointed 3rd corporal in Co. I, 54th Regiment, Georgia Infantry at Savannah, Georgia and received bounty $50.00. December 31, 1862 received pay. January – February 1863 roll shows him present. October 31, 1863 received pay. November 1863 appointed 1st corporal of Co. I, 54th Regiment, Georgia Infantry. November – December 1863 roll shows him present. January 1864 and June 2, 1864 issued clothing.

LOUKIE (LODKIE), W.: Company D, private. April 30, 1862 enlisted as a private in Co. D, 54th Regiment, Georgia Infantry at Savannah, Georgia and received bounty $50.00. August 17, 1862 he died of disease

in Savannah, Georgia. August 1862 roll reflects his death.
LONES, W. S.: Company A, private. He enlisted as a private in Co. A, 54th Regiment, Georgia Infantry.
LONG, R.: Company B, private. October 15, 1862 enlisted as a private in Co. B, 54th Regiment, Georgia Infantry at Beaulieu near Savannah, Georgia and received bounty $50.00. October 1862 roll shows his enlistment.
LONG, ROBERT ALBERT: Company B, private. 1861 he enlisted in Co. I, Clinch's 4th Georgia Cavalry. April 17, 1862 enlisted as a private in Co. B, 54th Regiment, Georgia Infantry at Savannah, Georgia and received bounty $50.00. December 31, 1862 received pay. January – February 1863 roll shows him present. January 1864 and April 25, 1864 issued clothing. Pension records show he was on picket duty at Fort Valley, Georgia beginning in February 1865. April 1865 could not reach his command. He was born in Georgia April 12, 1844 and died in Wayne County, Georgia May 31, 1923. He is buried in the Ritch Baptist Church Cemetery at K'Ville, Wayne County, Georgia. (find a grave # 24962286)
LONG, THOMAS: Company B, private. October 10, 1861 enlisted as a private in Co. K, 2nd Regiment, 1st Brigade, Georgia State Troops. April 1862 mustered out. April 21, 1862 enlisted as a private in Co. B, 54th Regiment, Georgia Infantry at Savannah, Georgia and received bounty $50.00. December 31, 1862 received pay. January – February 1863 roll shows him present. October 7, 1863 received pay $44.00. Pension records show he was at home on sick furlough from August 1864 to the close of the war. He was born in Georgia.
LOOKER, JAMES: Company F, private. He enlisted as a private in Co. F, 54th Regiment, Georgia Infantry.
LOVETT, EDWARD T.: Company F, private. April 29, 1863 enlisted as a private in Co. F, 54th Regiment, Georgia Infantry.
LOWE, ANDREW J.: Company G, sergeant. May 12, 1862 enlisted as 1st sergeant in Co. G, 54th Regiment, Georgia Infantry at Columbus, Georgia and received bounty $50.00. July 21, 1862 received $3.00 in commutation for rations. September 25, 1862 discharged at Beaulieu near Savannah, Georgia. September 1862 roll reflects his discharge.
LOUKIE, W.: Company D, private. He enlisted as a private in Co. D, 54th Regiment, Georgia Infantry.
LOWREY, J. A.: Company B, private. He enlisted as a private in Co. B, 54th Regiment, Georgia Infantry.
LUCAR (LOOKER), JAMES: Company F, private. September 4, 1862 enlisted as a private in Co. K, 54th Regiment, Georgia Infantry at Savannah, Georgia and received bounty $50.00. January – February 1863 roll shows him present. September 1, 1863 received pay. November – December 1863 roll shows he deserted December 12, 1863.
LUCAR (LOOKER), WILLIAM: Company F, private. September 10, 1862 enlisted as a private in Co. K, 54th Regiment, Georgia Infantry at Savannah, Georgia and received bounty $50.00. September 1862 roll reflects his enlistment.

LUKE, JAMES J.: Company E, private. May 6, 1862 enlisted as a private in Co. E, 54th Regiment, Georgia Infantry at Savannah, Georgia and received bounty $50.00. December 31, 1862 received pay. January – February 1863 roll shows him present. January 1864, April 25, 1862 and June 2, 1864 issued clothing. Pension records show he was at home on sick furlough February 1865 to the close of the war. He was born in Laurens County, Georgia in 1837 and died in Lowndes County, Georgia in 1899. He was born December 28, 1838 and died April 8, 1918. He is buried in Saint Luke Baptist Church Cemetery in Berrien County, Georgia. (find a grave # 51914471)

LUKE, JOHN G.: Company E, private. May 6, 1862 enlisted as a private in Co. E, 54th Regiment, Georgia Infantry at Savannah, Georgia and received bounty $50.00. December 31, 1862 received pay. January – February 1863 roll shows him present. January 1864, and April 25, 1864 issued clothing. May 10, 1865 surrendered at Tallahassee, Florida. May 29, 1865 paroled at Albany, Georgia. May 29, 1865 his name appears on the Post Register at Albany, Georgia. He was born in Georgia March 23, 1831 and died in Lowndes County, Georgia January 24, 1897. He is buried in Joe Howell Cemetery in Lowndes County, Georgia. (find a grave # 104344984)

LUKE, J. P.: Company E, private. May 6, 1862 enlisted as a private in Co. E, 54th Regiment, Georgia Infantry at Savannah, Georgia and received bounty $50.00. December 31, 1862 received pay. January – February 1863 roll shows him present. January 1864 and April 25, 1864 issued clothing.

LUKE, WILLIAM H.: Company E, private. May 6, 1862 enlisted as a private in Co. E, 54th Regiment, Georgia Infantry at Savannah, Georgia and received bounty $50.00. December 31, 1862 received pay. January – February 1863 roll shows him present. January 1864, April 25, 1864 and June 2, 1864 issued clothing. October 13, 1864 issued clothing at May Hospital, Augusta, Georgia. May 10, 1865 surrendered at Tallahassee, Florida. May 29, 1865 paroled at Albany, Georgia. May 29, 1865 his name appears on the Post Register at Albany, Georgia He was born in Laurens County, Georgia November 13, 1841 and died in Berrien County, Georgia November 13, 1910. He is buried in Rowetown Cemetery at Alapaha, Berrien County, Georgia. (find a grave # 54106813)

LYLES, JOHN C.: Company A, private. September 1, 1863 enlisted as a private in Co. A, 54th Regiment, Georgia Infantry at Macon, Georgia and received bounty $50.00. October 31, 1863 received pay. November – December 1863 roll shows him present (sick in company hospital). January 1, 1864 received pay. January – February 1864 roll shows him present. March 29, 1865 admitted to Ocmulgee Hospital at Macon, Georgia with Chronic Diarrhoea. April 7, 1865 he is shown as deserting from Ocmulgee Hospital at Macon, Georgia. He was a resident of Wilkinson County, Georgia.

LYNN, DANIEL: Company K, private. November 9, 1862 enlisted as a private in Co. K, 54th Regiment, Georgia Infantry at Beaulieu near Savannah, Georgia and received bounty $50.00. November 1862 roll reflects his enlistment. January 1, 1863 received pay. January – February 1863 roll shows him present. March 18, 1864 and April 18, 1864 issued clothing. He was born October 30, 1825 and died February 9, 1904 in Appling County, Georgia. He is buried in the Lynn Cemetery in Jeff Davis County, Georgia. (find a grave # 130588860)

LYNN, GEORGE W.: Company K, private. May 5, 1862 enlisted as a private in Co. K, 54th Regiment, Georgia Infantry at Savannah, Georgia and received bounty $50.00. January 1, 1863 received pay. January – February 1863 roll shows him present. January 24, 1864 detailed as a teamster for Quartermaster's Department at Tupelo, Mississippi. March 18, 1864 and April 18, 1864 issued clothing. He was born in Tattnall County, Georgia in 1830.

LYNN, H. B.: Company K, private. May 5, 1862 enlisted as a private in Co. K, 54th Regiment, Georgia Infantry at Savannah, Georgia and received bounty $50.00. September 20, 1862 he died at Beaulieu near Savannah, Georgia. September 1862 roll reflects his death.

LYNN, JOHN J.: Company G, captain. April 26, 1865 surrendered at Greensboro, North Carolina. May 1, 1865 paroled at Greensboro, North Carolina.

LYON, THOMAS B.: Company G, sergeant. He enlisted as a sergeant in Co. G, 54th Regiment, Georgia Infantry.

LYSTER, J. C.: Company A, private. April 30, 1862 enlisted as a private in Co. A, 54th Regiment, Georgia Infantry at Macon, Georgia and received bounty $50.00. February 28, 1863 received pay. June 30, 1863 roll shows him present (absent without leave May 2, 1863 to June 24, 1863 – in arrest). October 31, 1863 received pay. November – December 1863 roll shows him present. January 1, 1864 received pay. January – February 1864 roll shows him present. April 29, 1864 issued clothing. November 20, 1864 and December 15, 1864 issued clothing at Convalescent Camp Wright near Macon, Georgia. November – December 1864 roll of Co. H, 1st Regiment Troops and Defenses, Macon, Georgia stationed at Camp Wright near Macon, Georgia shows him absent without leave (ordered to be replaced).

LYSTER, THOMAS: Company F, private. February 26, 1863 enlisted as a private in Co. F, 54th Regiment, Georgia Infantry at Savannah, Georgia and received bounty $50.00. January – February 1863 roll shows him present. June 14, 1863 to July 31, 1863 detailed at extra duty as a carpenter (repairing and building quarters at post) at a rate of $.40 extra per day. September 8, 1863 received pay. November 1, 1863 received pay. November – December 1863 roll shows him present. January 1864, April 25, 1864 and May 8, 1864 issued clothing. Pension records show; he was at home on sick furlough at the close of the war. He was born in 1830 and died in Wilkinson County, Georgia in 1878. He is buried in Lyster Cemetery at Gordon, Wilkinson County, Georgia. (find a grave #

28095616)

LYSTER, W. L.: Company A, private. April 30, 1862 enlisted as a private in Co. A, 54th Regiment, Georgia Infantry at Macon, Georgia and received bounty $50.00. October 20, 1862 discharged at Beaulieu near Savannah, Georgia. October 1862 roll reflects his discharge.

MADDOX, W. C.: Company B, private. He enlisted as a private in Co. B, 54th Regiment, Georgia Infantry.

MAINOR, B. F.: Company E, private. He enlisted as a private in Co. E, 54th Regiment, Georgia Infantry.

MANDETLE, JOSEPH: Company A, private. He enlisted as a private in Co. A, 54th Regiment, Georgia Infantry. April 20-21, 1865 captured in Macon, Georgia.

MANN, JOHN: Company A (F), private. May 10, 1862 enlisted as a private in Co. A, 54th Regiment, Georgia Infantry at Macon, Georgia and received bounty $50.00. December 31, 1862 received pay. February 23, 1863 transferred from Co. A, 54th Regiment, Georgia Infantry to Co. F, 54th Regiment, Georgia Infantry. January – February 1863 roll shows him discharged by civil authority.

MANN, JOHN T.: Company K, lieutenant. September 17, 1861 enlisted as a private in 1st Company E, 6th Regiment, Virginia Cavalry. This company transferred into Jeff Davis' Legion, Mississippi Cavalry and became Co. F, of that unit. He was discharged and on September 15, 1862 enlisted as a private in Co. K, 54th Regiment, Georgia Infantry at Savannah, Georgia and received a bounty $50.00. July 27, 1862 appointed Jr. 2nd lieutenant in Co. K, 54th Regiment, Georgia Infantry. September 1862 roll shows him absent not yet reported for duty at Beaulieu near Savannah, Georgia. October 1862 roll shows him absent (he reported for duty but was absent on furlough since October 25, 1862). November 24, 1862 list of officers in the Savannah, Georgia area includes his name. November 1862 roll shows him present at Beaulieu near Savannah, Georgia. December 20, 1862 he was promoted to senior 2nd lieutenant. December 1862 roll shows him present and reflects his promotion. January 1, 1863 received pay. January – February 1863 roll shows him present. April 25, 1863 appointed 1st lieutenant of Co. K, 54th Regiment, Georgia Infantry. October 23, 1863 list of officers at Legare's Point, South Carolina includes his name. February 29, 1864 he was on picket duty in the Charleston, South Carolina area. March 4, 1863 received pay $80.00. April 8, 1863 received pay $80.00. July 2, 1864 received pay $90.00. July 3, 1864 received pay $260.00. July 4, 1864 he was killed at Vining Station near Atlanta, Georgia. November 4, 1864 death benefit claim was filed by his father William Mann. He is buried at Oakland Cemetery at Atlanta, Georgia. (find a grave #20924282)

MANN, WILLIAM H.: Field and Staff, major. October 3, 1861 elected captain of Co. A, 1st Regiment, 1st Brigade, Georgia State Troops. April 1862 mustered out of the Georgia State Troops into the 54th Regiment, Georgia Infantry. May 16, 1862 elected major of the 54th Regiment, Georgia

Infantry at Beaulieu near Savannah, Georgia. July 1862 roll includes his name. August 1862 roll shows him present at Beaulieu near Savannah, Georgia. September 1862 roll shows him absent with leave. October, November and December 1862 rolls show him present at Beaulieu near Savannah, Georgia. November 24, 1862 list of officers in the Savannah, Georgia area includes his name. January – February 1863 roll shows him present. April 3, 1863 he is shown on list of officers absent from Savannah, Georgia (absent with leave since March 4, 1863), April 30, 1863 received pay $300.00. October 23, 1863 list of officers at Legare's Point, South Carolina includes his name. December 8, 1863 received pay $150.00. February 25, 1864 Assigned Special Command by General Walker Special Order No. 33/1. March 5, 1864 detailed for Council by Special Order 38/1. June 7, 1864 received pay $300.00. July 2, 1864 received pay $300.00. July 22, 1864 killed in battle at Atlanta, Georgia November 4, 1864 death benefit claim was filed by his widow, L. Joanna Mann. He was born in Georgia in 1837 and died in Atlanta, Georgia July 22, 1864. He is buried in Greenwood Cemetery at Atlanta, Fulton County, Georgia. (find a grave # 84166471)

MANSFIELD, WILLIAM H.: Field and Staff, quartermaster sergeant. May 13, 1862 enlisted as a private in Co. F, 54th Regiment, Georgia Infantry at Savannah, Georgia and received bounty $50.00. May 16, 1862 elected quartermaster sergeant of the 54th Regiment, Georgia Infantry at Beaulieu near Savannah, Georgia. January 1, 1863 received pay. January – February 1863 roll shows him present.

MARSHALL, J. F.: Company A, private. May 3, 1862 enlisted as a private in Co. A, 54th Regiment, Georgia Infantry at Macon, Georgia and received bounty $50.00. April 30, 1863 received pay. May 1, 1863 to July 31, 1863 detailed as a carpenter (company Mechanic) near Savannah, Georgia. June 30, 1863 roll shows him present (carpenter). July 1863 received pay. October 31, 1863 received pay. November – December 1863 roll shows him present. January 1, 1864 received pay. January – February 1864 roll shows him present. April 29, 1864 issued clothing. He was born December 1, 1832 and died July 21, (year unknown). He is buried in Grace and Truth Baptist Church Cemetery in Bibb County, Georgia. (find a grave # 52786477)

MARSHALL, M. A. (BABE): Company H, private. May 17, 1862 enlisted as a private in Co. H, 54th Regiment, Georgia Infantry at Columbus, Georgia and received bounty $50.00. December 31, 1862 received pay. January – February 1863 roll shows him present. October 31, 1863 received pay. November – December 1863 roll shows him present. December 31, 1863 received pay. January 1864 issued clothing. January – February 1864 roll shows him present. April 26, 1865 surrendered at Greensboro, North Carolina. May 1, 1865 paroled at Greensboro, North Carolina. He was born in Harris County, Georgia November 8, 1841 and died in Harris County, Georgia July 12, 1900. He is buried in Old Hopewell Cemetery in Harris County, Georgia. (find a grave # 112056198)

MARTIN, J. B.: Company G, private. November 15, 1862 enlisted as a private in Co. G, 54th Regiment, Georgia Infantry at Columbus, Georgia and received bounty $50.00. November 1862 roll shows his enlistment. December 15, 1862 deserted. January – February 1863 roll shows he deserted.

MARTIN LA FAYETTE: Company G (F), private. January 28, 1863 enlisted as a private in Co. G, 54th Regiment, Georgia Infantry at Columbus, Georgia and received bounty $50.00. January 1864 issued clothing. January – February 1863 roll shows him present. May 8, 1864 issued clothing. He transferred to Co. F, Consolidated 54th Regiment, Georgia Infantry. April 26, 1865 surrendered in Co. F, Consolidated 54th Regiment, Georgia Infantry at Greensboro, North Carolina. May 1, 1865 paroled at Greensboro, North Carolina. He died September 7, 1900. He is buried in Bethel Mission Cemetery in Lee County, Alabama. (find a grave # 75121522)

MARTIN, W. H.: Company C, private. April 22, 1862 enlisted as a private in Co. C, 54th Regiment, Georgia Infantry at Savannah, Georgia and received bounty $50.00. December 31, 1862 received pay. January – February 1863 roll shows him present. He died of disease in 1863. He was a resident of Emanuel County, Georgia.

MASON, D.: Company A (F), private. October 17, 1861 enlisted as a private in Co. C, 1st Independent Battalion, Georgia State Troops. April 16, 1862 roll shows him present. April 1862 mustered out. May 10, 1862 enlisted as a private in Co. A, 54th Regiment, Georgia Infantry at Macon, Georgia and received bounty $50.00. September 1, 1862 transferred from Co. A, 54th Regiment, Georgia Infantry to Co. F, 54th Regiment, Georgia Infantry by Special Order No. 6 at Beaulieu near Savannah, Georgia. September 1862 roll reflects his transfer. December 31, 1862 received pay. February 23, 1863 transferred from Co. A, 54th Regiment, Georgia Infantry to Co. F, 54th Regiment, Georgia Infantry. January – February 1863 roll shows him present.

MASON, DANIEL M.: Company A, private. October 17, 1861 enlisted as a private in Co. C, 1st Independent Battalion, Georgia State Troops. April 16, 1862 roll shows him present. April 1862 mustered out. March 1, 1863 enlisted as a private in Co. A, 54th Regiment, Georgia Infantry at Macon, Georgia and received bounty $50.00. April 30, 1863 received pay. June 30, 1863 roll shows him present. October 31, 1863 received pay. November – December 1863 roll shows him present. December 31, 1863 received pay. January – February 1864 roll shows him present. April 29, 1864 issued clothing. He is buried in Catholic Cemetery at Savannah, Chatham County, Georgia. (find a grave # 65119983)

MASON, JOHN: Company A, private. May 10, 1862 enlisted as a private in Co. F, 54th Regiment, Georgia Infantry at Savannah, Georgia and received bounty $50.00. September 1, 1862 transferred from Co. F, 54th Regiment, Georgia Infantry to Co. A, 54th Regiment, Georgia Infantry by Special Order No. 6 at Beaulieu near Savannah, Georgia. September

1862 rolls reflect the transfer.

MASON, JOHN B.: Company A, private. June 19, 1863 enlisted as a private in Co. A, 54th Regiment, Georgia Infantry at Savannah, Georgia and received bounty $50.00. June 30, 1863 roll shows him present. June 30, 1863 received pay. November 1, 1863 received pay. November – December 1863 roll shows him absent sick in Macon, Georgia hospital. January 1, 1864 detailed at Macon, Georgia hospital. January – February 1864 roll shows him absent detailed at Macon, Georgia hospital. March 10, 1864 he appears on a register of Floyd House and Ocmulgee Hospitals at Macon, Georgia on detail. March 18, 1864 he appears on a register of Floyd House and Ocmulgee Hospitals at Macon, Georgia with General Debility and on detail. January 1, 1864 to November 30, 1864 detailed as watchman for Central Laboratory at Macon, Georgia at a rate of an additional $18.00 per month Special Order 9/4. March 10, 1864 register of Floyd House and Ocmulgee Hospitals at Macon, Georgia shows him detailed, (shows him suffering from effects of a leg fracture causing a limp that was suffered 12 years ago according to Surgeon's Certificate). March 18, 1864 register of Floyd House and Ocmulgee Hospitals at Macon, Georgia shows General Debility (detailed). April 9, 1864 detailed to the Central Laboratory from the 54th Regiment, Georgia Infantry for 60 days by surgeons order Special Order No. 99/2. April 29, 1864 issued clothing. June 17, 1864 detail extended to the Central Laboratory from the 54th Regiment, Georgia Infantry for 60 days by surgeons order (shown as unfit for field duty) Special Order No. 141/14. September 12, 1864 list of Guards at the Central Laboratory list him as night watchman at warehouse. A roll of men detailed and employed at the C. S. Central Laboratory at Macon, Bibb County, Georgia list him: 42 years of age, unfit for duty, as night watchman at the warehouse (appears to be a part of a letter to General Howell Cobb dated October 24, 1864). November 30, 1864 received pay $290.00. He was a resident of Jones County, Georgia.

MASON, JOHN MARTIN: Company A, private. April 26, 1862 enlisted as a private in Co. A, 54th Regiment, Georgia Infantry at Macon, Georgia and received bounty $50.00. September 19, 1862 to December 31, 1862 detailed as a butcher at a rate of $.25 extra per day. October, November and December 1862 rolls show him detailed as a butcher at a rate of $.25 extra per day. January 15, 1863 received pay. April 30, 1863 received pay. June 30, 1863 roll shows him present (two month's pay deducted by order of General Mercer). August 31, 1863 received pay. November – December 1863 roll shows him present. January 1, 1864 received pay. January – February 1864 roll shows him present. April 29, 1864 issued clothing.

MASON, S. O.: Company A, private. He enlisted as a private in Co. A, 54th Regiment, Georgia Infantry

MASSETTE, ROBERT: Company A, private. May 1, 1863 enlisted as a private in Co. A, 54th Regiment, Georgia Infantry at Savannah, Georgia and received bounty $50.00. June 30, 1863 roll shows him present.

October 31, 1863 received pay. November – December 1863 roll shows him present. January 1, 1864 received pay. January – February 1864 roll shows him present. April 29, 1864 issued clothing.

MASSEY, JOHN S.: Company K, private. October 3, 1861 enlisted as a private in Co. A, 1st Regiment, 1st Brigade, Georgia State Troops. April 1862 mustered out. April 19, 1862 enlisted as a private in Co. K, 54th Regiment, Georgia Infantry at Savannah, Georgia and received bounty $50.00. January – February 1863 roll shows him present. May 10, 1865 surrendered at Tallahassee, Florida. May 19, 1865 paroled at Thomasville, Georgia. He was born May 12, 1844 and died August 24, 1906. He is buried in the Jesup City Cemetery at Jesup, Wayne County, Georgia. (find a grave #54584721)

MASSEY, JOHN S.: Company K, private. April 18, 1862 enlisted as a private in Co. A, 54th Regiment, Georgia Infantry at Savannah, Georgia and received bounty $50.00. January 1, 1863 received pay. January – February 1863 roll shows him present. March 18, 1864, April 18, 1864 and June 2, 1864 issued clothing. May 10, 1865 surrendered at Tallahassee, Florida. May 19, 1865 paroled at Thomasville, Georgia. He is described as 5 feet 10 inches high, light hair, gray eyes and fair complexion.

MASSEY, JOHN J.: Company H, private. December 8, 1862 enlisted as a private in Co. H, 54th Regiment, Georgia Infantry at Beaulieu near Savannah, Georgia and received bounty $50.00. December 1862 roll shows his enlistment. December 31, 1862 received pay. January – February 1863 roll shows him present. June 16, 1863 received commutation for rations. October 31, 1863 received pay. November – December 1863 roll shows him absent (on picket). December 31, 1863 received pay. January 1864 issued clothing. January – February 1864 roll shows him present (detailed as hewer). He was born May 13, 1846 and died November 27, 1907. He is buried in Cedar Grove Cemetery in Walker County, Georgia. (find a grave # 32026503)

MATHIS, ELBERT: Company E, private. May 2, 1862 enlisted as a private in Co. E, 54th Regiment, Georgia Infantry. August 1, 1862 transferred to 1st Georgia Sharpshooters by Special Order No. 259. September 19, 1863 captured at Chickamauga, Georgia. April 1864 he was exchanged. June 15, 1864 he was captured near Marietta, Georgia. February 25, 1865 he was paroled at Rock Island, Illinois and sent for exchange. March 15, 1865 received at Boulware & Cox's Wharves, James River, Virginia. He was born in Lowndes County, Georgia October 4, 1836 and died in Cook County, Georgia November 11, 1915. He is buried in Cat Creek Cemetery at Valdosta, Lowndes County, Georgia. (find a grave # 54876008)

MATHIS, JOHN J.: Company E, private. May 6, 1862 enlisted as a private in Co. E, 54th Regiment, Georgia Infantry. August 1, 1862 transferred to 1st Georgia Sharpshooters by Special Order No. 259. August 1864 roll shows him absent sick. He was born September 17, 1835 and died January 2, 1917. He is buried in Manntown Cemetery at Glen Saint Mary, Baker County, Florida. (find a grave # 48102710)

MATTHEWS, P. F.: Company B, private. He enlisted as a private in Co. B, 54th Regiment, Georgia Infantry.

MAXWELL, J.: Company F, private. May 18, 1862 enlisted as a private in Co. F, 54th Regiment, Georgia Infantry at Savannah, Georgia and received bounty $50.00. November 1, 1863 received pay. November – December 1863 roll shows him present on special service. January 1864 issued clothing.

MAXWELL, JAMES A.: Company F, private. May 18, 1862 enlisted as a private in Co. F, 54th Regiment, Georgia Infantry at Savannah, Georgia and received bounty $50.00. December 31, 1862 received pay. January – February 1863 roll shows him absent sick. May 8, 1864 issued clothing.

MAY, BATON (BATEN): Company E, corporal. May 6, 1862 enlisted as a private and was appointed 1st corporal in Co. E, 54th Regiment, Georgia Infantry at Savannah, Georgia and received bounty $50.00. December 31, 1862 received pay. January – February 1863 roll shows him present. January 1864 issued clothing. May 10, 1865 surrendered at Tallahassee, Florida. May 10, 1865 paroled at Thomasville, Georgia. He is described as 5 feet 9 inches high, dark hair, hazel eyes and dark complexion. He died in Berrien County, Georgia November 1906.

MAY, JEREMIAH M. (JERRY): Company E, corporal. September 17, 1861 enlisted as a private in Co. A, 18th Battalion, Georgia Infantry for 6 months. March 1862 mustered out at Savannah, Georgia. May 6, 1862 enlisted as 1st corporal in Co. E, 54th Regiment, Georgia Infantry at Savannah, Georgia and received bounty $50.00. December 31, 1862 received pay. January – February 1863 roll shows him present. January 1864 issued clothing. Pension records show; February 2, 1865 he was on detail and could not reach his command before surrender. May 10, 1865 surrendered at Tallahassee, Florida. May 24, 1865 paroled at Thomasville, Georgia. He was born in Warren County, Georgia September 2, 1834 and died in 1928. He is buried in Empire Primitive Baptist Church Cemetery at Lakeland, Lanier County, Georgia. (find a grave # 33073435)

MAY, S. D.: Company A, corporal. April 25, 1862 enlisted as a private in Co. A, 54th Regiment, Georgia Infantry at Macon, Georgia and received bounty $50.00. April 30, 1863 received pay. June 30, 1863 roll shows him present. October 1863 appointed 2nd corporal of Co. A, 54th Regiment, Georgia Infantry. October 31, 1863 received pay. November – December 1863 roll shows him absent on furlough since December 23, 1863. January – February 1864 roll shows him present. April 29, 1864 issued clothing.

MAY, WILLIAM F.: Company F, private. January 21, 1863 enlisted as a private in Co. F, 54th Regiment, Georgia Infantry at Savannah, Georgia and received bounty $50.00. September 1, 1863 received pay. November – December 1863 roll shows him present (present on special service – company clerk). January 1864 and April 25, 1864 issued clothing. May 11, 1864 Special Order No. 105/1 (proceed to Dalton, Georgia). April 20-21, 1865 he was captured in Macon, Georgia.

MCABEE, GEORGE W.: Company B, private. September 1, 1861 enlisted in Co. C, 4th Georgia Battalion Sharpshooters. Transferred to Co. B, 54th Regiment, Consolidated Georgia infantry. April 26, 1865 surrendered at Greensboro, North Carolina. May 1, 1865 paroled at Greensboro, North Carolina.

MCADAMS, BARNEY: Company H (A), private. May 22, 1862 enlisted as a private in Co. H, 54th Regiment, Georgia Infantry at Macon, Georgia and received bounty $50.00. September 1, 1862 transferred from Co. H, 54th Regiment, Georgia Infantry to Co. A, 54th Regiment, Georgia Infantry by Special Order No. 6 at Beaulieu near Savannah, Georgia. September 1862 rolls reflect the transfer. April 30, 1863 received pay. June 30, 1863 roll shows him present (absent without leave from June 20, 1863 to June 23, 1863 - in arrest. October 31, 1863 received pay. November – December 1863 roll shows him present. January 1, 1864 received pay. January – February 1864 roll shows him present. April 29, 1864 issued clothing. July 4, 1864 wounded in the ankle near Marietta, Georgia. Pension records show: he was wounded July 4, 1864 and discharged due to disability in July 1864. He was born in Georgia October 13, 1839 and died March 19, 1923. He is buried in Lyster Cemetery at Gordon, Wilkinson County, Georgia. (find a grave # 28096472)

MCARDIE, FRANCIS: Company E, sergeant. He enlisted as 1st sergeant in Co. E, 54th Regiment, Georgia Infantry.

MCARTHY, L. E.: Company F, corporal. May 17, 1861 enlisted as a private in Chisholm's Company, Georgia State Troops. May 1862 mustered out. May 6, 1862 enlisted as corporal in Co. F, 54th Regiment, Georgia Infantry at Savannah, Georgia and received bounty $50.00. 1862 appointed corporal in Co. F, 54th Regiment, Georgia Infantry. November 14, 1862 discharged by civil authority at Beaulieu near Savannah, Georgia. November 1862 roll shows his discharge.

MCBRIDE, JAMES F.: Company C, private. March 18, 1864 enlisted as a private in Co. C, 54th Regiment, Georgia Infantry. December 21, 1864 captured while home on sick furlough in Emanuel County, Georgia. February 1, 1865 arrived at Hilton Head, South Carolina and was sent to Point Lookout, Maryland. June 29, 1865 took oath of allegiance at Point Lookout, Maryland. He is described as being a resident of Emanuel County, Georgia, light complexion, dark hair, hazel eyes and was 5 feet 6 inches high. He was born in Jefferson County, Georgia July 4, 1844 and died in Emanuel County, Georgia January 7, 1911. He is buried in Oak Chapel Cemetery in Emanuel County, Georgia. (find a grave #78244386)

MCCALL, JAMES GEORGE: Company E, private. March 18, 1864 enlisted as a private in Co. E, 54th Regiment, Georgia Infantry.

MCCALL, GEORGE J., JR.: Company B, sergeant. April 21, 1862 enlisted as a sergeant in Co. B, 54th Regiment, Georgia Infantry at Savannah, Georgia and received bounty $50.00. December 31, 1862 received pay. January – February 1863 roll shows him present. He was born November 26, 1843 and died August 11, 1900. He is buried in McCall Cemetery in Wayne County, Georgia. (find a grave # 17327231)

MCCANTS, WILLIAM ALBERT: Company H, private. September 15, 1864 enlisted as a private in Co. H, 54th Regiment, Georgia Infantry at Columbus, Georgia and received bounty $50.00. September 1862 roll shows his enlistment. December 31, 1862 received pay. January – February 1863 roll shows him present. October 31, 1863 received pay. November – December 1863 roll shows him present. December 31, 1863 received pay. January 1864 issued clothing. January – February 1864 roll shows him absent (sick in Bethesda Hospital since February 6, 1864). May 16, 1864 captured at Resaca, Georgia. May 20, 1864 sent from Nashville, Tennessee to Military Prison at Louisville, Kentucky.
May 21, 1864 received at Military Prison at Louisville, Kentucky from Nashville Tennessee. May 31, 1864 died in the hospital at Military Prison at Louisville, Kentucky of Typhoid Malarial Fever. He is buried at Cave Hill Cemetery, Louisville, Kentucky – range 1, grave #89. (Section O, Lot 267, Grave #56). (find a grave #3292778)
MCCLARY, SAMUEL B.: Company G, lieutenant. May 12, 1862 appointed Jr. 2nd lieutenant of Co. G, 54th Regiment, Georgia Infantry. July 1862 roll shows him present at Savannah, Georgia. August, September and October 1862 roll show him present at Beaulieu near Savannah, Georgia. November 24, 1862 he appears on list of officers at Savannah, Georgia. November and December 1862 rolls show him present at Beaulieu near Savannah, Georgia. January – February 1863 roll shows him present. March 21, 1863 received pay $160.00. August 10, 1863 received pay $80.00 (in the hospital). October 21, 1863 he appears on list of officers at Legare's Point, South Carolina. June 1864 he was wounded near Marietta, Georgia. June 18, 1864 died at Receiving Hospital at Marietta, Georgia. He is buried in Linwood Cemetery at Columbus, Muscogee County, Georgia. (find a grave # 34557805)
MCCLURE, W. J.: Company K, private. He enlisted as a private in Co. K, 54th Regiment, Georgia Infantry.
MCCONNELL, JOHN E.: Company E, private. May 6, 1862 enlisted as a private in Co. E, 54th Regiment, Georgia Infantry. August 1, 1862 transferred to 1st Georgia Sharpshooters by Special Order No. 259. September 20, 1864 died of Chronic Diarrhoea at Fair Grounds Hospital No. 1 at Atlanta, Georgia.
MCCORKLE, HEZEKIAH: Company K, lieutenant. He enlisted as 1st lieutenant in Co. K, 54th Regiment, Georgia Infantry.
MCCORMICK (MCCOMMICK), JOHN: Company F (D), private. January 18, 1863 enlisted as a private in Co. F, 54th Regiment, Georgia Infantry at Savannah, Georgia and received bounty $50.00. January – February 1863 roll shows him present. November 1, 1863 received pay. November – December 1863 roll shows him present. January 1864 and May 8, 1864 issued clothing. April 26, 1865 surrendered in Co. D, 54th Regiment, Consolidated Georgia Infantry at Greensboro, North Carolina. May 1, 1865 paroled at Greensboro, North Carolina.
MCCOY, A. J.: Company D, private. April 30, 1862 enlisted as a

private in Co. D, 54th Regiment, Georgia Infantry at Savannah, Georgia and received bounty $50.00. December 31, 1862 received pay. January – February 1863 roll shows him present. January 1864 issued clothing. May 18, 1865 surrendered and paroled at Augusta, Georgia. He was born in Burke County, Georgia in 1835.

MCCOY, CLAY M.: Company H, sergeant. May 12, 1862 enlisted as a sergeant in Co. H, 54th Regiment, Georgia Infantry at Columbus, Georgia and received bounty $50.00. December 31, 1862 received pay. January – February 1863 roll shows him present. October 31, 1863 received pay. November – December 1863 roll shows him present. December 31, 1863 received pay. January 1864 issued clothing. January – February 1864 roll shows him present. May 23 (24), 1865 surrendered and paroled at Thomasville, Georgia.

MCCOY, J: Company C, private. He enlisted as a private in Co. C, 54th Regiment, Georgia Infantry. He died in Macon, Georgia September 1, 1864. He is buried in Rose Hill Cemetery at Macon, Bibb County, Georgia. (find a grave #105193478)

MCCOY, SAMUEL: Company D, private. April 30, 1862 enlisted as a private in Co. D, 54th Regiment, Georgia Infantry at Savannah, Georgia and received bounty $50.00. July 15, 1862 detailed as a teamster (wagoner) for the Quartermaster's Department. July, August, September, October, November and December 1862 rolls show him detailed as teamster (wagoner) at a rate of $.25 extra per day. October 1862 received pay. December 31, 1862 received pay. January 1, 1863 to February 28, 1863 detailed as a teamster in Savannah, Georgia at a rate of $.25 extra per day. January – February 1863 roll shows him present (detailed as a teamster). June 1, 1863 to December 31, 1863 detailed as a teamster (in Savannah and Charleston) at a rate of $.25 extra per day. November 16, 1863 received pay. January 1864 issued clothing. January 1, 1864 to April 30, 1864 detailed as a teamster (in Savannah and Charleston) at a rate of $.25 extra per day. He was born April 2, 1838 and died April 16, 1904. He is buried in Green Park Cemetery Millen, Jenkins County, Georgia. (find a grave # 103396354)

MCCOY, SEABORN: Company D, private. April 30, 1862 enlisted as a private in Co. D, 54th Regiment, Georgia Infantry at Savannah, Georgia and received bounty $50.00. December 31, 1862 received pay. January – February 1863 roll shows him present. January 1864 issued clothing. Pension records show: he was discharged at the close of the war. He was born in Screven County, Georgia May 8, 1830. He is buried in Fellowship Baptist Church Cemetery at Cecil, Cook County, Georgia. (find a grave # 22894646)

MCCRANIE, DANIEL J.: Company E, private. May 6, 1862 enlisted as a private in Co. E, 54th Regiment, Georgia Infantry at Savannah, Georgia and received bounty $50.00. December 31, 1862 received pay. January – February 1863 roll shows him present. January 1864 and April 25, 1864 issued clothing. May 10, 1865 surrendered at Tallahassee, Florida.

May 12, 1865 paroled at Thomasville, Georgia. He was born December 19, 1832 and died February 18, 1877. He is buried in Woodlawn City Cemetery at Adel, Cook County, Georgia. (find a grave # 61902750)

MCCRARY, ROBERT A.: Company E, private. August 1862 enlisted as a private in Co. E, 54th Regiment, Georgia Infantry. December 18, 1864 captured at Franklin Tennessee. December 21, 1864 received and sent to Camp Douglas, Illinois from Military Prison at Louisville, Kentucky. December 24, 1864 received at Camp Douglas, Illinois from Military Prison at Louisville, Kentucky. May 9, 1865 took Oath of Allegiance at Camp Douglas, Illinois. He is described as a resident of Muscogee County, Georgia, dark complexion, brown hair, grey eyes and 6 feet 1 inch high. He was a resident of Muscogee County, Georgia.

MCCRAW, B. B.: Company H, private. May 12, 1862 enlisted as a private in Co. H, 54th Regiment, Georgia Infantry at Columbus, Georgia and received bounty $50.00. December 31, 1862 received pay. January – February 1863 roll shows him absent without leave since February 26, 1863.

MCCRAY (MCCRARY), DAVID M.: Company I, private. January 31, 1863 enlisted as a private in Co. I, 54th Regiment, Georgia Infantry at Beaulieu near Savannah, Georgia and received bounty $50.00. December 31, 1862 received pay. January – February 1863 roll shows him present (sick in regimental hospital). February 28, 1863 received pay. November – December 1863 roll shows him absent (absent sick). January 1864 issued clothing. May 10, 1865 surrendered at Tallahassee, Florida. May 10, 1865 paroled at Thomasville, Georgia. He is described as 5 feet 8 inches high, auburn hair, grey eyes and light complexion.

MCCULLAR, ALFRED M.: Company K, private. October 3, 1861 enlisted as a private in Co. A, 1st Regiment, 1st Brigade, Georgia State Troops. April 1862 mustered out. April 18, 1862 enlisted as a private in Co. K, 54th Regiment, Georgia Infantry at Savannah, Georgia and received bounty $50.00. October and December 1862 rolls show him Color Corporal. January 1, 1863 received pay. January – February 1863 roll shows him present (absent without leave 8 days). March 18, 1864 issued clothing. May 10, 1865 surrendered at Tallahassee, Florida. May 19, 1865 paroled at Thomasville, Georgia. He is described as 5 feet 4 inches high, light hair, blue eyes and light complexion.

MCCULLAR (MCCULLER), M. CALVIN (M. C.): Company K, private. October 3, 1861 enlisted as a private in Co. A, 1st Regiment, 1st Brigade, Georgia State Troops. April 1862 mustered out. April 18, 1862 enlisted as a private in Co. K, 54th Regiment, Georgia Infantry at Savannah, Georgia and received bounty $50.00. July 1, 1862 detailed as a nurse in the medical department at a rate of $.25 extra per day. July, August and September 1862 rolls show he was detailed as a nurse. August 31, 1862 received pay $18.50. September 1862 roll of Medical College Hospital at Savannah, Georgia shows him present as a nurse. January 1, 1863 received pay. January – February 1863 roll shows him present (absent without leave 8 days). March 18, 1864 and June 2, 1864 issued clothing. May 10, 1865 surrendered at Tallahassee, Florida. May 19, 1865 paroled at Thomasville, Georgia. He is described as 6 feet 1 inch high, dark hair, dark eyes and dark complexion.

MCCULLAR (MCCULLOUGH), PERRY H.: Company K, sergeant. October 3, 1861 enlisted as a private in Co. K, 1st Regiment, Georgia State Troops. April 1862 mustered out. April 18, 1862 enlisted as a private and appointed 5th sergeant in Co. K, 54th Regiment, Georgia Infantry at Savannah, Georgia and received bounty $50.00. August, September, October and November 1862 rolls show him detailed as a mail carrier (courier). January 1, 1863 received pay. January – February 1863 roll shows him present. March 18, 1864 issued clothing. May 10, 1865 surrendered at Tallahassee, Florida. May 18, 1865 paroled at Thomasville, Georgia. He is described as 5 feet 6 inches high, dark hair, grey eyes and dark complexion. He was born May 3, 1835 and died March 17, 1886. He is buried in Pellicer Creek Cemetery in Saint Johns County, Florida. (find a grave #44498208)

MCDERMID, JOHN: Company E, private. May 6, 1862 enlisted as a private in Co. E, 54th Regiment, Georgia Infantry at Savannah, Georgia and received bounty $50.00. December 31, 1862 received pay. January – February 1863 roll shows him present. January 1864 issued clothing. January 16, 1864 received pay $22.00. January 28, 1864 received pay $22.00. He was born in 1835. He is buried in the McDermid Cemetery at Sparks, Cook County, Georgia. (find a grave #111410005)

MCDONALD, JAMES: Company G, private. November 15, 1862 enlisted as a private in Co. G, 54th Regiment, Georgia Infantry at Columbus, Georgia and received bounty $50.00. November 1862 roll shows his enlistment.

MCDONALD, LA FAYETTE: Company G, private. May 12, 1862 enlisted as a private in Co. G, 54th Regiment, Georgia Infantry at Columbus, Georgia and received bounty $50.00. December 31, 1862 received pay. January – February 1863 roll shows him present. January 1864 issued clothing. June 18, 1864 captured near Marietta, Georgia. June 26, 1864 received at Military Prison at Louisville, Kentucky from Nashville, Tennessee. June 27, 1864 sent from Military Prison at Louisville, Kentucky to Camp Morton, Indiana. June 28, 1864 received at Camp Morton, Indiana from Military Prison at Louisville, Kentucky. March 4, 1865 paroled and transferred for exchange at Camp Morton, Indiana. March 10-12, 1865 received at Boulware & Cox's Wharves, James River, Virginia.

MCDONALD, SAMUEL H.: Company G, private. May 12, 1862 enlisted as a private in Co. G, 54th Regiment, Georgia Infantry at Columbus, Georgia and received bounty $50.00. December 31, 1862 received pay. January – February 1863 roll shows him present. January 1864 issued clothing. December 20, 1864 his right leg was Frostbitten at Murphysboro, Tennessee. December 26, 1864 captured at Nashville,

Tennessee (near Pulaski, Tennessee). January 12, 1865 received at Military Prison at Louisville, Kentucky from Nashville, Tennessee. January 14, 1865 sent from Military Prison at Louisville, Kentucky to Camp Chase, Ohio. January 15, 1865 received at Camp Chase, Ohio from Military Prison at Louisville, Kentucky. March 2, 1865 leg amputated at Camp Chase, Ohio. May 16, 1865 took the oath of allegiance at Camp Chase, Ohio. He is described as resident of Meriwether County, Georgia, dark complexion, black hair, black eyes, 5 feet 10 inches high and age 23. He was born in Georgia May 2, 1842.

MCDONALD, WILLIAM H.: Company G (F), sergeant. May 12, 1862 enlisted as a private in Co. G, 54th Regiment, Georgia Infantry at Columbus, Georgia and received bounty $50.00. December 31, 1862 received pay. January – February 1863 roll shows him present. He was elected 4th corporal of Co. G, 54th Regiment, Georgia Infantry. January 1864 issued clothing. June 28, 1864 issued clothing at Direction Hospital at Griffin, Georgia. He was elected 3rd sergeant of Co. F, 54th Regiment, Georgia Infantry. April 26, 1865 surrendered at Greensboro, North Carolina. May 1, 1865 paroled at Greensboro, North Carolina. He was born in Georgia January 22, 1841 and died in Harris County, Georgia February 11, 1908. He is buried in Ellerslie United Methodist Church Cemetery at Ellerslie, Harris County, Georgia. (find a grave # 50788655)

MCDUFFIE, BENJAMIN F.: Company G, lieutenant. He enlisted in Co. G, 54th Regiment, Georgia Infantry at Columbus, Georgia. He was born in Georgia June 12, 1844 and died in Georgia March 2, 1900. He is buried in Oakland Cemetery at Atlanta, Fulton County, Georgia. (find a grave # 35318974)

MCELROY, JAMES M.: Company G, private. January 22, 1863 enlisted as a private in Co. G, 54th Regiment, Georgia Infantry. Pension records show: April 26, 1865 surrendered at Greensboro, North Carolina. May 1, 1865 paroled at Greensboro, North Carolina. He was born in Georgia.

MCGAR, E. D. (J.): Company C, corporal. May 4, 1862 enlisted as a 4th corporal in Co. C, 54th Regiment, Georgia Infantry at Savannah, Georgia and received bounty $50.00. December 31, 1862 received pay. January – February 1863 roll shows him present (in hospital at Bethesda). January 1, 1864 received pay. January – February 1864 roll shows him present (sick since February 27, 1864). He died while on sick furlough. He was a resident of Emanuel County, Georgia.

MCGAR, E. J.: Company C, private. May 4, 1862 enlisted as a private in Co. C, 54th Regiment, Georgia Infantry at Savannah, Georgia and received bounty $50.00. December 31, 1862 received pay. January – February 1863 roll shows him present (in hospital at Bethesda). January 1, 1864 received pay. January – February 1864 roll shows him present (sick since February 27, 1864). 1864 he died of disease in Macon, Georgia. He was a resident of Emanuel County, Georgia.

MCGAR, J. C.: Company C, private. May 6, 1862 enlisted as a private in Co. C, 54th Regiment, Georgia Infantry at Savannah, Georgia and received bounty $50.00. December 31, 1862 received pay. January – February 1863 roll shows him present. 1864 he died of disease at Macon, Georgia. He was a resident of Emanuel County, Georgia.

MCGAULEY (MCCAULEY), DAVID M.: Company B, private. December 11, 1861 enlisted as a private in Co. B, 8th Regiment, Georgia State Troops. He mustered out in 1862. April 28, 1862 enlisted as a private in Co. B, 54th Regiment, Georgia Infantry at Savannah, Georgia and received bounty $50.00. December 31, 1862 received pay. January – February 1863 roll shows him present (sick in regimental hospital). August 20, 1863 received pay $33.00. May 23, 1865 surrendered and paroled at Thomasville, Georgia. He was born in Georgia May 21, 1843 and died in Wayne County, Georgia April 8, 1905. He is buried in Old Bethel Cemetery at Jesup, Wayne County, Georgia. (find a grave # 70697689). The Southern Cross of Honor was bestowed on him by the Jesup Chapter United Daughters of the Confederacy in 1903.

MCGEE, GEORGE C.: Company E, lieutenant. He enlisted in Co. E, 54th Regiment, Georgia Infantry.

MCGEE, W. A.: Company E, private. He enlisted in Co. E, 54th Regiment, Georgia Infantry.

MCGEE, WILLIAM H.: Company H, private. December 6, 1862 enlisted as a private in Co. H, 54th Regiment, Georgia Infantry at Savannah, Georgia and received bounty $50.00. December 1862 roll shows his enlistment. December 31, 1862 received pay. January – February 1863 roll shows him present. October 31, 1863 received pay. November – December 1863 roll shows him present. December 31, 1863 received pay. January 1864 issued clothing. January – February 1864 roll shows him present (on picket).

MCGINTY (MCGENTRY), VALERIUS A.: Company H, private. September 3, 1862 enlisted as a private in Co. H, 54th Regiment, Georgia Infantry at Beaulieu near Savannah, Georgia and received bounty $50.00. September and August 1862 rolls show his enlistment. December 1862 roll shows his enlistment. December 31, 1862 received pay. January – February 1863 roll shows him present. October 31, 1863 received pay. November – December 1863 roll shows him present. December 31, 1863 received pay. January 1864 issued clothing. January – February 1864 roll shows him present. April 25, 1864 issued clothing. April 12, 1865 captured at Salisbury, North Carolina. May 1, 1865 received at Military Prison at Louisville, Kentucky. May 2, 1865 sent to Camp Chase, Ohio from Military Prison at Louisville, Kentucky. May 4, 1865 received at Camp Chase, Ohio from Military Prison at Louisville, Kentucky. June 13, 1865 took the oath of allegiance at Camp Chase, Ohio. He is described as a resident of Warren County, Georgia, fair complexion, dark hair, dark eyes, 5 feet 11 ¼ inches high and was 21 years of age. He was born September 10, 1846 and died December 25, 1908. He is buried in Norwood Cemetery at Norwood, Warren County, Georgia. (find a grave # 121223532)

MCGUIRE, PETER: Company F, private. September 10, 1862 enlisted as a private in Co. F, 54th Regiment, Georgia Infantry at Beaulieu near Savannah, Georgia and received bounty $50.00. September 1862 roll shows his enlistment. October 16, 1862 deserted. October 1862 roll shows his desertion.

MCGUIRK, HORACE: Company E, private. He enlisted as a private in Co. E, 54th Regiment, Georgia Infantry.

MCHALE, ANTONY: Company F, private. May 17, 1861 enlisted as a private in Chisholm's Company, Georgia State Troops. May 1862 mustered out. May 13, 1862 enlisted as a private in Co. F, 54th Regiment, Georgia Infantry at Savannah, Georgia and received bounty $50.00. December 17, 1863 transferred to Co. G, 54th Regiment, Georgia Infantry at Savannah, Georgia. November – December 1863 roll shows him present.

MCHARQUE, WILLIAM: Company G, private. He enlisted in Co. G, 54th Regiment, Georgia Infantry.

MCHUGH, JOHN: Company G (F), private. September 25, 1862 enlisted as a private in Co. G, 54th Regiment, Georgia Infantry at Savannah, Georgia and received bounty $50.00. September 1862 roll shows his enlistment. December 31, 1862 received pay. January – February 1863 roll shows him present. He transferred to Co. F, 54th Regiment, Georgia Infantry. May 8, 1864 issued clothing. April 26, 1865 surrendered at Greensboro, North Carolina. May 1, 1865 paroled at Greensboro, North Carolina.

MCKINNEY, GEORGE M.: Company E, private. He enlisted as a private in Co. E, 54th Regiment, Georgia Infantry.

MCKINNEY, JOSHUA: Company G, corporal. May 12, 1862 enlisted as 4th corporal in Co. G, 54th Regiment, Georgia Infantry at Columbus, Georgia and received bounty $50.00. August 18, 1862 discharged. August 1862 roll shows his discharge.

MCKINNEY, PIESANT: Company G, private. May 12, 1862 enlisted as a private in Co. G, 54th Regiment, Georgia Infantry at Columbus, Georgia and received bounty $50.00. December 31, 1862 received pay. January – February 1863 roll shows him present.

MCKINNEY, WILLIAM: Company G, private. May 12, 1862 enlisted as a private in Co. G, 54th Regiment, Georgia Infantry at Columbus, Georgia and received bounty $50.00. December 31, 1862 received pay. January – February 1863 roll shows him present. January 1864 and May 8, 1864 issued clothing. He was born April 7, 1845 and died August 8, 1921. He is buried in Philadelphia Cemetery at Smith's Station, Lee County, Alabama. (find a grave # 20008972)

MCLENDON, DENNIS: Company C, private. December 11, 1861 enlisted as a private in Co. B, 8th Regiment, Georgia State Troops. He mustered out in 1862. April 22, 1862 enlisted as a private in Co. C, 54th Regiment, Georgia Infantry at Savannah, Georgia and received bounty $50.00. December 31, 1862 received pay. January – February 1863 roll shows him present. January 1, 1864 received pay. January – February 1864 roll shows him absent (sick in hospital at Hardeeville, South Carolina since February 24, 1864). February 29, 1864 received pay. November 15, 1864 roll of Ladies' Hospital at Montgomery, Alabama shows him present as a patient. May 18, 1865 surrendered and paroled at Augusta, Georgia. He was a resident of Emanuel County, Georgia. He was born in 1839 and died January 3, 1901. He is buried in McLendon Family Cemetery at Dublin, Laurens County, Georgia. (find a grave # 47244518)

MCLENDON, JOHN M.: Company C, sergeant. December 11, 1861 enlisted as a private in Co. B, 8th Regiment, Georgia State Troops. He mustered out in 1862. April 22, 1862 enlisted as 4th sergeant in Co. C, 54th Regiment, Georgia Infantry at Savannah, Georgia and received bounty $50.00. December 31, 1862 received pay. January – February 1863 roll shows him present. April 12, 1863 was promoted to 4th sergeant of Co. C, 54th Regiment, Georgia Infantry. December 1863 was promoted to 3rd sergeant of Co. C, 54th Regiment, Georgia Infantry. January 1, 1864 received pay. January – February 1864 roll shows him present. May 18, 1865 surrendered and paroled at Augusta, Georgia. He was a resident of Emanuel County, Georgia. He was born in 1825 and died January 8, 1873. He is buried in Lambs Chapel Cemetery at Swainsboro, Emanuel County, Georgia. (find a grave # 73383767)

MCLEROY, ABRAHAM E.: Company H, private. May 12, 1862 enlisted as a private in Co. H, 54th Regiment, Georgia Infantry at Columbus, Georgia and received bounty $50.00. December 31, 1862 received pay. January – February 1863 roll shows him present. October 31, 1863 received pay. November – December 1863 roll shows him present. December 31, 1863 received pay. January 1864 issued clothing. January – February 1864 roll shows him present. Pension records show: June 5, 1864 (May 25-26, 1864) severely wounded at New Hope Church near Dallas, Georgia. He remained in the Field Hospital until July 15, 1864. July 1864 sent to Distributing Hospital at Atlanta, Georgia. He was then sent to the hospital at Madison, Georgia. August 1864 sent to Columbus, Georgia Hospital where he remained until after April 26, 1865. He was born in Harris County, Georgia November 27, 1836 and died in Columbus, Muscogee County, Georgia June 29, 1911. He is buried in Richardson Cemetery in Harris County, Georgia. (find a grave # 45190723)

MCLEROY, JNO M.: Company G, private. January 22, 1863 enlisted as a private in Co. G, 54th Regiment, Georgia Infantry at Columbus, Georgia and received bounty $50.00. January – February 1863 roll shows him present. January 1864 and April 25, 1864 issued clothing. He transferred to Co. F, 54th Regiment, Georgia Infantry. April 26, 1865 surrendered at Greensboro, North Carolina. May 1, 1865 paroled at Greensboro, North Carolina.

MCLEROY, NATHAN: Company H, private. May 12, 1862 enlisted as a private in Co. H, 54th Regiment, Georgia Infantry at Columbus, Georgia and received bounty $50.00. December 31, 1862 received pay. January – February 1863 roll shows him present. October 31, 1863 received pay. November – December 1863 roll shows him present. December 31, 1863 received pay. January 1864 issued clothing. January – February 1864 roll shows him present (on picket). June 2, 1864 issued clothing.

MCMANUS, JOHN A (H.): Company A, lieutenant. October 17, 1861 elected Jr. 2nd lieutenant of Co. C, 1st Independent Battalion, Georgia State Troops. April 16, 1862 shows him present. April 1862 mustered out. April 18, 1862 elected 1st lieutenant in Co. B, 54th Regiment, Georgia Infantry. April 28, 1862 enlisted as a lieutenant in Co. B, 54th Regiment, Georgia Infantry at Macon, Georgia and received bounty $50.00. June 17, 1862 detached as Enrolling Conscript Officer for the 4th Congressional District by Special Order No. 73, General Hugh D. Mercer. July, August, September, October, November and December 1862 rolls show him absent (detached as Enrolling Conscript Officer for the 2nd Congressional District in Macon, Georgia). November 24, 1862 roll of officers in Savannah, Georgia shows him present. December 27, 1862 received $39.28 for expenses. January 31, 1863 received pay $30.00 for commutation for fuel. June 30, 1863 roll shows him present as 1st lieutenant. November – December 1863 roll shows him absent on detached service since October 15, 1863. February 1, 1864 resigned his commission. January – February 1864 roll shows his resignation. He was born in Camden, Kershaw County, South Carolina December 5, 1833 and died in Macon, Bibb County, Georgia May 18, 1889. He is buried in Riverside Cemetery at Macon, Bibb County, Georgia. (find a grave # 18498668)

MCMILLAN (MACMILLEN), HECTOR: Company F, private. February 1, 1863 enlisted as a private in Co. F, 54th Regiment, Georgia Infantry at Savannah, Georgia and received bounty $50.00. January – February 1863 roll shows him present. He was born November 2, 1827 and died March 24, 1892. He is buried in the Scotland City Cemetery in Wheeler County, Georgia. (find a grave # 35367727)

MCTAQUE, H.: Company A, private. October 29, 1862 enlisted as a private in Co. A, 54th Regiment, Georgia Infantry at Macon, Georgia and received bounty $50.00. November 1862 roll shows he joined on November 15, 1862 at Macon, Georgia. April 30, 1863 received pay. June 30, 1863 roll shows him absent (absent without leave).

MEADOWS, ASA: Company G, private. May 12, 1862 enlisted as a private in Co. G, 54th Regiment, Georgia Infantry at Columbus, Georgia and received bounty $50.00. August 1862 roll shows he deserted on May 12, 1862. He was born in Alabama and died in Marion County, Texas. He is buried in Johnson-Meadows Cemetery in Marion County, Texas. (find a grave # 39224890)

MEDDERS (MEADOWS), JAMES RILEY: Company K, private. October 3, 1861 enlisted as a private in Co. A, 1st Regiment, 1st Brigade, Georgia State Troops. April 1862 mustered out. May 5, 1862 enlisted as a private in Co. K, 54th Regiment, Georgia Infantry at Savannah, Georgia and received bounty $50.00. January 1, 1863 received pay. January – February 1863 roll shows him present. March 18, 1864, April 18, 1864 and June 2, 1864 issued clothing. February 1865 pension records show he was discharged at Tupelo, Mississippi. He was born in Georgia September 13, 1838 and died in Bacon County, Georgia September 21, 1920. He is buried in Big Creek Cemetery in Bacon County, Georgia. (find a grave #47106673)

MEDDERS (MEADOWS), JOHN SMITH: Company K, private. October 3, 1861 enlisted as a private in Co. A, 1st Regiment, 1st Brigade, Georgia State Troops. April 1862 mustered out. April 18, 1862 enlisted as a private in Co. K, 54th Regiment, Georgia Infantry at Savannah, Georgia and received bounty $50.00. January 1, 1863 received pay. January – February 1863 roll shows him present. March 18, 1864 issued clothing. September 1, 1864 wounded in the right arm near Jonesboro, Georgia, necessitating amputation below the elbow (26 years of age). He was born in Appling County, Georgia April 6, 1836 and died in Appling County, Georgia December 9, 1900. He is buried in Big Creek Cemetery in Bacon County, Georgia. (find a grave #59520333)

MEDDERS, W. W.: Company K, private. July 1, 1863 enlisted as a private in Co. K, 54th Regiment, Georgia Infantry at Savannah, Georgia and received bounty $50.00. March 18, 1864 issued clothing. Pension records show; October 1864 he was at home on sick furlough at the close of the war. He was born in Appling County, Georgia August 17, 1845 and died June 20, 1924.

MELL, GEORGE FARIES.: Company F, private. May 17, 1861 enlisted as a private in Chisholm's Company, Georgia State Troops. May 1862 mustered out. May 13, 1862 enlisted as a private in Co. F, 54th Regiment, Georgia Infantry at Savannah, Georgia and received bounty $50.00. May 13, 1862 detailed in the Government Machine Shop by order of General Lawton. October 1, 1862 detailed for Government work by order of General Mercer. October 1862 roll shows him detailed for Government work. January – February 1863 roll shows him absent (detailed by order of General Lawton). November – December 1863 roll shows him absent (absent detailed by General Mercer). January 1864 and February 25, 1864 issued clothing. August 1, 1864 transferred to Engineer Troops by Special Order No. 180/12. He was born in Savannah, Chatham County, Georgia in 1846 and died in Savannah, Chatham County, Georgia December 30, 1873. He is buried in Laurel Grove Cemetery at Savannah, Chatham County, Georgia. (find a gave # 60277971)

MELL, THOMAS B.: Company F, sergeant. May 17, 1861 enlisted and appointed 3rd corporal in Chisholm's Company, Georgia State Troops. May 1862 mustered out. May 13, 1862 enlisted as a private in Co. F, 54th Regiment, Georgia Infantry at Savannah, Georgia and received bounty $50.00. December 31, 1862 received pay. January – February 1863 roll shows him present. October 7, 1863 received pay $34.00. October 31, 1863 received pay $34.00. October 1863 received pay $108.00. November 5, 1863 issued clothing. November 1863 received pay $90.00. December 1, 1863 received pay $34.00. December 31, 1863 received pay $93.00. November – December 1863 roll shows him present (returned to duty).

January 1, 1864 received pay $22.00. January 4, 1864, April 25, 1864 and May 8, 1864 issued clothing. July 23, 1864 captured near Atlanta, Georgia. July 23, 1864 received at Military Prison at Louisville, Kentucky from Nashville, Tennessee. July 31, 1864 sent to Camp Chase, Ohio from Military Prison at Louisville, Kentucky. August 2, 1864 received at Camp Chase, Ohio from Military Prison at Louisville, Kentucky. March 4, 1865 transferred to City Point, Virginia. May 12, 1865 received from U. S. Steamer Mary Powell at U. S. Army General Hospital at Point Lookout, Maryland with Chronic Diarrhoea. July 25, 1865 took oath of allegiance at Point Lookout, Maryland and released at Hammond General Hospital at Point Lookout, Maryland. Shows as; a resident of Chatham County, Georgia, dark complexion, fair hair, grey eyes and 6 feet high. April 14, 1865 admitted to Jackson Hospital at Richmond, Virginia with Chronic Dysentery. May 1, 1865 transferred to 3rd Division Hospital at Richmond, Virginia. He was born in Savannah, Chatham County, Georgia in 1844 and died July 3, 1888. He is buried in Laurel Grove Cemetery at Savannah, Chatham County, Georgia. (find a grave # 60300657)

MERRITT (MERRETT), J. D.: Company I, private. May 6, 1862 enlisted as a private in Co. I, 54th Regiment, Georgia Infantry at Guyton, Georgia and received bounty $50.00. December 31, 1862 received pay. January – February 1863 roll shows him present. October 31, 1863 received pay. November – December 1863 roll shows him present (picket guard). January 1864 and June 2, 1864 issued clothing.

MERRITT, WILLIAM: Company I, private. He enlisted as a private in Co. I, 54th Regiment, Georgia Infantry.

MERRITT, WILLIAM: Company G, private. He enlisted as a private in Co. G, 54th Regiment, Georgia Infantry.

MIDDLETON, GEORGE W.: Company B, private. October 10, 1861 enlisted as a private in Co. K, 2nd Regiment, 1st Brigade, Georgia State Troops. April 1862 mustered out. April 21, 1862 enlisted as a private in Co. B, 54th Regiment, Georgia Infantry. July 30, 1862 transferred from Co. H, 54th Regiment, Georgia Infantry at Beaulieu near Savannah, Georgia to 1st Georgia Sharpshooters by Special Order No. 259. January 6, 1865 he died of pneumonia in General Hospital at Atlanta, Georgia. He is buried in Oakland Cemetery at Atlanta, Fulton County, Georgia. (find a grave #9562345)

MILES, EDWARD: Company K, private. He enlisted as a private in Co. K, 54th Regiment, Georgia Infantry.

MILES, MIDDLETON: Company B, private. April 28, 1862 enlisted as a private in Co. B, 54th Regiment, Georgia Infantry at Savannah, Georgia and received bounty $50.00. December 31, 1862 received pay. January – February 1863 roll shows him present. January 12, 1864 detail revoked by Special Order No. 9/1. January 1864 and June 2, 1864 issued clothing. June 27, 1864 killed on Pigeon Hill at Kennesaw Mountain, Georgia. He was born April 26, 1837 in Appling County, Georgia and died at Kennesaw Mountain, Georgia June 27, 1864. He is buried in the

Confederate Cemetery at Marietta. Georgia. (find a grave #59950736)

MILLER, E. W.: Company D, private. He enlisted as a private in Co. D, 54th Regiment, Georgia Infantry. January 1864 and April 25, 1864 issued clothing.

MILLER, EDWARD W.: Company D, lieutenant. He enlisted in and was appointed 4th sergeant of Co. K, 20th Regiment, Georgia Infantry. November 17, 1863 elected 2nd lieutenant Co. D, 54th Regiment, Georgia Infantry. November 28, 1863 (February 3, 1864) discharged from Co. K, 20th Regiment, Georgia Infantry. November 28, 1863 joined Co. D, 54th Regiment, Georgia Infantry. January 1864 issued clothing. February 29, 1864 Inspection Report #107 shows him in charge of picket duty. April 25, 1864 issued clothing. July 3, 1864 he was wounded at Marietta, Georgia. (Pension records show; He was wounded in the right leg and the left shoulder near Atlanta, Georgia July 1864 and was sent to the hospital in Augusta, Georgia). August 29, 1864 received pay $480.00. October 6, 1864 received pay $80.00. November 21, 1864 received pay $160.0. May 26, 1865 surrendered and paroled at Augusta, Georgia. He was born in Georgia in 1840.

MILLER, EUGENE: Company D, sergeant. He enlisted as a private in Co. D, 54th Regiment, Georgia Infantry. January 1864 and April 25, 1864 issued clothing. July 14, 1864 wounded in the right arm and shoulder broken near Marietta, Georgia. Pension records show he was at home wounded at the close of the war. May 26, 1865 surrendered and paroled at Augusta, Georgia.

MILLER, HENRY A.: Company F, private. February 15, 1863 January – February 1863 roll shows him present. He enlisted as a private in Co. F, 54th Regiment, Georgia Infantry at Savannah, Georgia and received bounty $50.00. March 1864 discharged due to disability. He was born in Georgia and died in Lowndes County, Georgia March 8, 1925.

MILLER, JOHN MILO, JR.: Company D, lieutenant. He enlisted as a private in Co. K, 20th Regiment, Georgia Infantry. He transferred to Co. D, 54th Regiment, Georgia Infantry. June 19, 1863 appointed Jr. 2nd Lieutenant of Co. D, 54th Regiment, Georgia Infantry. October 21, 1863 he appears on a list of Legare's Point, South Carolina. November 18, 1863 granted leave. February 29, 1864 granted leave. June 7, 1864 received pay $360.00 July 2, 1864 received pay $90.00. August 31, 1864 received pay $270.00. May 26, 1865 surrendered and paroled at Augusta, Georgia.

MILLER, JOHN W.: Company H, private. October 14, 1863 enlisted as a private in Co. H, 54th Regiment, Georgia Infantry at Beaulieu near Savannah, Georgia and received bounty $50.00. October 31, 1863 received pay. November – December 1863 roll shows him present. December 31, 1863 received pay. January 1864 issued clothing. January – February 1864 roll shows him present (on guard). April 25, 1864 and June 2, 1864 issued clothing. June 9, 1864 killed at Big Shanty, Georgia near Marietta, Georgia.

MILLER, JOSEPH: Company D, captain. October 7, 1861 enlisted and elected 1st sergeant of Co. I, 5th Regiment, Georgia State Troops. April 1862 mustered out. April 30, 1862 enlisted and was elected 1st lieutenant of Co. D, 54th Regiment, Georgia Infantry. July 1862 roll shows his name. August 1862 roll shows him absent with leave for 10 days beginning August 30, 1862 from Beaulieu near Savannah, Georgia. September, October, November and December 1862 rolls show him present at Beaulieu near Savannah, Georgia. November 24, 1862 his name appears on a list of officers in Savannah, Georgia. January – February 1863 roll shows him present. March 5, 1863 received pay $90.00. April 2, 1863 received pay $90.00. August 25, 1863 appointed captain of Co. D, 54th Regiment, Georgia Infantry. October 21, 1863 his name appears on a list of officers at Legare's Point, South Carolina. March 2, 1864 granted 15 days leave by Special Order No. 11/5. March 16, 1864 granted 15 days leave by Special Order No. 25. June 1, 1864 received pay $260.00. August 3, 1864 received pay $130.00. August 21, 1864 received pay $180.00. August 25, 1864 report of Mercer's Brigade in the field near Atlanta, Georgia shows him sick sent to the hospital at Macon, Georgia by Brigade Surgeon on July 8, 1864. January 24, 1865 granted 30 days leave at Tupelo, Mississippi by Special Order 19/1. May 26, 1865 surrendered and paroled at Augusta, Georgia. He was born in 1843 and died in 1885. He is buried in Little Horse Creek Cemetery at Rocky Ford, Screven County, Georgia. (find a grave # 52163905)

MILLER, MARTIN F.: Company E, private. October 6, 1861 enlisted as a private in Co. K, 5th Regiment, Georgia State Troops. April 1862 mustered out. January 3, 1863 enlisted as a private in Co. E, 54th Regiment, Georgia Infantry at Coffee Bluff near Savannah, Georgia. January – February 1863 roll shows him present. May 4, 1863 to July 31, 1863 detailed as acting ordinance sergeant of the 54th Regiment, Georgia Infantry (in charge of ordinance stores) at a rate of $.25 extra per day. July 1, 1863 received bounty pay $50.00. July 3, 1863 to October 31, 1863 detailed as acting ordinance sergeant (post ordinance sergeant) at a rate of $.25 extra per day. October 31, 1863 his name appears on a list of detailed men at James Island, South Carolina. October 1, 1863 to December 31, 1863 he was detailed as acting ordinance sergeant at Rose Dew Point near Savannah, Georgia at a rate of $.25 extra per day. January 1864 issued clothing. February 8, 1864 received pay $22.00 in Atlanta, Georgia. April 25, 1864 issued clothing.

MILLER, THOMAS A.: Company F, private. February 12, 1863 enlisted as a private in Co. F, 54th Regiment, Georgia Infantry at Savannah, Georgia and received bounty $50.00. January – February 1863 roll shows him present. September 1, 1863 received pay. November – December 1863 roll shows him present. January 1864 issued clothing. Pension records show; he was at home on 10 days furlough at the close of the war. He was born in Irwin County, Georgia in 1841 and died December 26, 1917. He is buried in an unmarked grave in Rose Hill Cemetery at Macon,

Bibb County, Georgia.

MILTON, I.: private. He enlisted as a private in the 54th Regiment, Georgia Infantry. May 10, 1865 surrendered at Tallahassee, Florida. May 15, 1865 paroled at Thomasville, Georgia.

MINCEY, A. S.: Company D, private. April 30, 1862 enlisted as a private in Co. D, 54th Regiment, Georgia Infantry at Beaulieu near Savannah, Georgia and received bounty $50.00. December 1862 roll shows him detailed as a butcher. December 31, 1862 received pay. January 1, 1863 to February 19, 1863 detailed as a butcher at Beaulieu near Savannah, Georgia at a rate of $.25 extra per day. January 15, 1863 received pay. February 15, 1863 detailed with the Engineer Department at Savannah, Georgia at a rate of $.25 extra per day. February 26, 1863 received pay. January – February 1863 roll shows him present. March 12, 1863 received pay. March 15, 1863 detailed cutting shingles for the ordinance department. October 31, 1863 list of detailed men at James Island, South Carolina shows him detailed cutting shingles for the ordinance department at a rate of $.25 extra per day. January 1864 issued clothing.

MINCEY, HILLIARD: Company D, private. October 1863 enlisted as a private in Co. D, 54th Regiment, Georgia Infantry (substitute for W. W. Kemp).

MIMS, ____: Field and Staff, musician. August 1, 1862 he enlisted as a musician in the 54th Regiment, Georgia Infantry.

MINGLEDORFF, GEORGE D.: Company I, private. September 1, 1862 enlisted as a private in Co. I, 54th Regiment, Georgia Infantry at Beaulieu near Savannah, Georgia and received bounty $50.00. August 1862 roll shows his enlistment. December 31, 1862 received pay. January – February 1863 roll shows him present. October 31, 1863 received pay. November – December 1863 roll shows him present (picket guard). January 1864 and April 25, 1863 issued clothing. He was born January 25, 1828 and died November 18, 1896. He is buried in the Springfield City Cemetery in Springfield, Effingham County, Georgia. (find a grave #50573050)

MINGLEDORFF, LEWIS ASBURY: Company I, private. January 1, 1863 enlisted as a private in Co. I, 54th Regiment, Georgia Infantry at Beaulieu near Savannah, Georgia and received bounty $50.00. December 31, 1862 received pay. January – February 1863 roll shows him present. October 31, 1863 received pay. November – December 1863 roll shows him present (picket guard). January 1864 and April 25, 1864 issued clothing. Pension records show; October 1864 he was furloughed on account of Measles. He was never able to rejoin his command. He was born in Georgia November 20, 1844 and died in Springfield, Effingham County, Georgia April 21, 1928. He is buried in the Springfield City Cemetery in Springfield, Effingham County, Georgia. (find a grave #50573056)

MINTON, S. T.: Company C, private. February 18, 1863 enlisted as a private in Co. C, 54th Regiment, Georgia Infantry at Savannah, Georgia and received bounty $50.00. January – February 1863 roll shows him present.

January 1, 1864 received pay. January – February 1864 roll shows him present. April 28, 1864 issued clothing. May 18, 1865 surrendered and paroled at Augusta, Georgia.

MITCHEL, T. C.: Company I, private. He enlisted as a private in Co. I, 54th Regiment, Georgia Infantry.

MITCHELL, J. R.: Company A, private. He enlisted as a private in Co. A, 54th Regiment, Georgia Infantry.

MITCHELL, ROBERT J.: Company A, private. October 1. 1862 enlisted as a private in Co. A, 54th Regiment, Georgia Infantry at Beaulieu near Savannah, Georgia and received bounty $50.00. November 7, 1862 deserted. December 7, 1863 he is described as: 23 years of age, 5 feet 10 inches high, dark eyes, black hair dark complexion and was born in Macon, Bibb County, Georgia. June 30, 1863 roll shows him as having deserted.

MITCHELL, THOMAS SNEAD: Company H, private. He enlisted as a private in Co. H, 54th Regiment, Georgia Infantry. September 1862 roll shows him detailed as a steward. January 7, 1863 received pay $33.00. He was born September 4, 1836 died in Pensacola, Florida June 10, 1911. He is buried in Linwood Cemetery at Columbus, Muscogee County, Georgia. (find a grave #59273209)

MIXION, JAMES: Company A, private. May 3, 1862 enlisted as a private in Co. A, 54th Regiment, Georgia Infantry and received bounty $50.00. April 30, 1863 received pay. June 30, 1863 roll shows him present sick in company hospital (absent without leave May 3 through May 5). October 31, 1863 received pay. November – December 1863 roll shows him present. January 1, 1864 received pay. January – February 1864 roll shows him present. March 31, 1864 and April 29, 1864 issued clothing. June 29, 1864 wounded in the foot at Kennesaw Mountain near Atlanta, Georgia. July 8, 1864 admitted to Ocmulgee Hospital at Macon, Georgia with a Gunshot Wound of the left foot. July 12, 1864 furloughed to Wilkinson County, Georgia. September 9, 1864 admitted to Ocmulgee Hospital at Macon, Georgia with a Gunshot Wound of the left foot. September 16, 1864 he appears on a register of Ocmulgee Hospital at Macon, Georgia with a Gunshot Wound of the left foot requiring amputation of 3rd toe. September 17, 1864 furloughed. He was a resident of Griswold, Jones County, Georgia. He was born in Georgia January 1, 1830 and died in Jones County, Georgia in 1905.

MOBLEY, M. D.: Company C, private. He enlisted as a private in Co. C, 54th Regiment, Georgia Infantry.

MOODY, ALLEN: Company H (K) (F), private. April 19, 1862 enlisted as a private in Co. H, 54th Regiment, Georgia Infantry at Savannah, Georgia and received bounty $50.00. August 1862 roll shows his enlistment. September 1, 1862 transferred from Co. H, 54th Regiment, Georgia Infantry to Co. K, 54th Regiment, Georgia Infantry by Special Order No. 6 at Beaulieu near Savannah, Georgia. September 1862 roll shows his transfer. January 1, 1863 received pay. January 1, 1863 transferred from

Co. K, 54th Regiment, Georgia Infantry to Co. F, 54th Regiment, Georgia Infantry. January – February 1863 rolls show him transferred from Co. K, 54th Regiment, Georgia Infantry to Co. F, 54th Regiment, Georgia Infantry on January 1, 1863.

MOODY, DAVID HENRY: Company B, private. April 28, 1862 enlisted as a private in Co. B, 54th Regiment, Georgia Infantry at Savannah, Georgia and received bounty $50.00. December 31, 1862 received pay. January – February 1863 roll shows him present (absent without leave 3 days). January 1864, April 25, 1864 and May 8, 1864 issued clothing. July 15, 1864 register of Ocmulgee Hospital at Macon, Georgia shows him present with a Gunshot Wound to the right thigh with a compound fracture. May 10, 1865 surrendered at Tallahassee, Florida. May 21, 1865 paroled at Thomasville, Georgia. He was born in Appling County, Georgia November 27, 1844 and died in Lakeland, Polk County, Florida December 16, 1916. He is buried in Lakeview Cemetery at Lakeland, Polk County, Florida. (find a grave #74308392)

MOODY, GEORGE TOBE: Company B, private. December 11(17), 1862 enlisted as a private in Co. B, 54th Regiment, Georgia Infantry at Savannah, Georgia and received bounty $50.00. December 1862 roll shows his enlistment. December 31, 1862 received pay. January – February 1863 roll shows him present. January 1864 issued clothing. May 10, 1865 surrendered at Tallahassee, Florida. May 21, 1865 paroled at Thomasville, Georgia. He was born in Appling County, Georgia December 14, 1844 and died July 19, 1906. He is buried in Martha Memorial Cemetery in Pierce County, Georgia. (find a grave # 17103884)

MOODY, GEORGE W.: Company B, captain. October 10, 1861 elected 1st lieutenant of Co. K, 2nd Regiment, Georgia State Troops. April 1862 mustered out. April 21, 1862 enlisted and elected captain of Co. B, 54th Regiment, Georgia Infantry at Savannah, Georgia. July 1862 roll at Savannah, Georgia shows his name. August, September and October 1862 rolls show him present at Beaulieu near Savannah, Georgia. November 24, 1862 his name appears on a list of officers at Savannah, Georgia. November 1862 roll shows him absent with 15 days leave since November 18, 1862. December 1862 roll shows him absent detailed on General Court Martial in Savannah, Georgia on December 17, 1862. February 10, 1863 received $63.60 in pay for expenses attending Court Martial. January – February 1863 roll shows him present. March 6, 1863 received pay $130.00. April 3, 1863 received pay $130.00. October 21, 1863 his name appears on a list of officers at Legare's Point, South Carolina. April 7, 1864 received pay $130.00. June 7, 1864 received pay $130.00. July 3, 1864 received pay $130.00. He was born March 9, 1814 and died July 17, 1902. He is buried in George Moody Cemetery in Appling County, Georgia. (find a grave #38134064)

MOODY, ISAAC ISHAM: Company B, private. October 10, 1861 enlisted as a private in Co. K, 2nd Regiment, Georgia State Troops. April 1862 mustered out. April 21, 1862 enlisted as a private in Co. B, 54th

Regiment, Georgia Infantry at Savannah, Georgia and received bounty $50.00. He was born February 5, 1847 and died October 27, 1890. He is buried in George Moody Cemetery in Appling County, Georgia. (find a grave # 38134000)

MOODY, ISHAM: Company B, private. October 10, 1861 enlisted as a private in Co. K, 2nd Regiment, Georgia State Troops. April 1862 mustered out. April 21, 1862 enlisted as a private in Co. B, 54th Regiment, Georgia Infantry at Savannah, Georgia and received bounty $50.00. December 31, 1862 received pay. January – February 1863 roll shows him present detailed as company clerk. January 1864 and April 25, 1864 issued clothing. May 10, 1865 surrendered at Tallahassee, Florida. May 21, 1865 paroled at Thomasville, Georgia. May 10, 1865 surrendered at Tallahassee, Florida. May 21, 1865 paroled at Thomasville, Georgia. He was born December 20, 1840 and died September 26, 1936. He is buried in Moody Cemetery in Wayne County, Georgia.

MOODY, JACOB: Company B, private. He enlisted as a private in Co. B, 54th Regiment, Georgia Infantry at Savannah, Georgia. June 27, 1864 killed at Kennesaw Mountain, Georgia. He was born in Holmesville, Appling County, Georgia in 1843 and died at Kennesaw Mountain, Georgia June 27, 1864. He is buried in Marietta Confederate Cemetery at Marietta, Cobb County, Georgia. (find a grave #73582029)

MOODY, JACOB H.: Company B, private. October 10, 1861 enlisted as a private in Co. K, 2nd Regiment, 1st Brigade, Georgia State Troops. April 1862 mustered out. April 21, 1862 enlisted as a private in Co. B, 54th Regiment, Georgia Infantry at Savannah, Georgia and received bounty $50.00. September and October 1862 rolls show him detailed to the company commissary. December 31, 1862 received pay. January – February 1863 roll shows him present. May 10, 1865 surrendered at Tallahassee, Florida. January 1864 and June 2, 1864 issued clothing. May 20, 1865 paroled at Thomasville, Georgia.

MOODY, JAMES L.: Company B, lieutenant. April 21, 1862 enlisted as 2nd lieutenant in Co. B, 54th Regiment, Georgia Infantry at Savannah, Georgia and received bounty $50.00. July 16, 1862 he died in Savannah, Georgia. August 12, 1863 death benefit claim was filed by his father, Jacob Moody. June 15, 1863 death benefit paid $42.66. He is buried in Moody Cemetery on U. S. 1 North in Appling County, Georgia. (find a grave # 37529888)

MOODY, JAMES M.: Company B, private. He enlisted as a private in Co. B, 54th Regiment, Georgia Infantry at Savannah, Georgia. June 27, 1864 killed at Kennesaw Mountain, Georgia. He was born in Holmesville, Appling County, Georgia in 1843 and died at Kennesaw Mountain, Georgia June 27, 1864. He is buried in Marietta Confederate Cemetery at Marietta, Cobb County, Georgia. (find a grave #73581643)

MOODY, WILLIAM B.: Company I, private. September 18, 1861 enlisted as a private in Co. C, 1st Regiment, 1st Brigade, Georgia State Troops. March 18, 1862 mustered out. May 6, 1862 enlisted as a private in Co. I, 54th Regiment, Georgia Infantry at Guyton, Georgia and received bounty $50.00. October 1862 roll shows him detailed as color corporal. December 31, 1862 received pay. January – February 1863 roll shows him present. October 31, 1863 received pay. November – December 1863 roll shows him present (boat hand). January 1864 issued clothing.

MOODY (MOODEY), WILLIAM: Company K, private. October 3, 1861 enlisted as a private and appointed 3rd sergeant in Co. A, 1st Regiment, 1st Brigade, Georgia State Troops. April 1862 mustered out. April 19, 1862 enlisted as a private in Co. K, 54th Regiment, Georgia Infantry at Savannah, Georgia and received bounty $50.00. July 30, 1862 transferred to 1st Georgia Sharpshooters (appointed 3rd corporal) by Special Order No. 259. August 1862 roll shows his transfer. September 19, 1863 killed at Chickamauga, Georgia.

MOORE, A. M.: Company C, private. May 6, 1862 enlisted as a private in Co. C, 54th Regiment, Georgia Infantry at Savannah, Georgia and received bounty $50.00. December 31, 1862 received pay. January – February 1863 roll shows him present. January 1, 1864 received pay. January – February 1864 roll shows him present. May 20, 1865 surrendered and paroled at Augusta, Georgia. He was a resident of Emanuel County, Georgia.

MOORE, ANGUS P.: Company F, private. September 18, 1861 enlisted as a private in Co. C, 1st Regiment, 1st Brigade, Georgia State Troops. March 18, 1862 mustered out. March 30, 1863 enlisted as a private in Co. F, 54th Regiment, Georgia Infantry at Decatur, Georgia and received bounty $50.00. September 1, 1863 received pay. November – December 1863 roll shows him absent (absent sick in Coweta County, Georgia). January 1864, April 25, 1864 and May 8, 1864 issued clothing. April 26, 1865 surrendered in Co. D, 54th Regiment, Consolidated Georgia Infantry at Greensboro, North Carolina. May 1, 1865 paroled at Greensboro, North Carolina. He was born August 22, 1842 and died May 7, 1902. He is buried in Little Ogeechee Baptist Church Cemetery at Oliver, Screven County, Georgia. (find a grave # 24970176)

MOORE, CHARLES: Company F, private. August 1, 1863 enlisted as a private in Co. F, 54th Regiment, Georgia Infantry at Savannah, Georgia and received bounty $50.00. November 1, 1863 received pay. November – December 1863 roll shows him present. January 1864 issued clothing.

MOORE, GEORGE W.: Company F, private. January 3, 1861 enlisted as a private in Captain A. C. Davenport's Company, Independent Cavalry, Georgia State Troops. Term of service was 60 days. May 1, 1862 enlisted as a private in Co. C, 1st Regiment, Georgia Infantry. June 4, 1864 enlisted as a private in Co. G, 1st (Olmstead's) Georgia infantry. December 27, 1862 transferred as a private to Co. F, 54th Regiment, Georgia Infantry at Beaulieu near Savannah, Georgia. December 27, 1862 discharged by order. December 1862 rolls show transfer and discharge.

MOORE, I. V.: Company I, sergeant. He enlisted as a sergeant in Co. I, 54th Regiment, Georgia Infantry.

MOORE (MOON), J. S.: Company A, private. May 3, 1862 enlisted as a private in Co. A, 54th Regiment, Georgia Infantry. July 1, 1862 he died at Atlanta, Georgia. He is buried at Oakland Cemetery in Atlanta, Georgia. (States Company C on the headstone.) (find a grave #22763441)

MOORE (MOON), J. S.: Company C, private. May 6, 1862 enlisted as a private in Co. C, 54th Regiment, Georgia Infantry at Savannah, Georgia and received bounty $50.00. December 31, 1862 received pay. January – February 1863 roll shows him present. August 23 – 30 (25), 1863 wounded in the thigh, thigh broken (crushed by a shell and amputated above the knee) at Battery Wagner, Charleston, South Carolina. September 20, 1863 he died at home of wounds received at Morris Island, South Carolina. January – February 1864 roll shows his death on September 20, 1863. He was a resident of Emanuel County, Georgia. He is buried in Oakland Cemetery at Atlanta, Fulton County, Georgia. (find a grave #22763441)

MOORE, JAMES M.: Company G, private. He enlisted as a private in Co. G, 54th Regiment, Georgia Infantry.

MOORE, JOHN E. (T.): Company C, private. He enlisted as a private in Co. G, 54th Regiment, Georgia Infantry. September 19, 1863 he died in Charleston, South Carolina. He is buried in the confederate section of Magnolia Cemetery at Charleston, South Carolina. (find a grave # 20398513)

MOORE, RICHARD J.: Company G, private. He enlisted as a private in Co. G, 54th Regiment, Georgia Infantry.

MOORE, SAMUEL W.: Company A, private. May 1, 1862 enlisted as a private in Co. A, 54th Regiment, Georgia Infantry. June 30, 1864 died with fever in 2nd Fairgrounds Hospital at Atlanta, Georgia.

MOORE, SEBORN O.: Company A, private. April 19, 1862 enlisted as a private in Co. A, 54th Regiment, Georgia Infantry at Savannah, Georgia and received bounty $50.00. February 21, 1863 he died. May 28, 1864 death benefit claim was filed by his widow Eunecy A. Moore. He was a resident of Bibb County, Georgia.

MOORE, THOMAS STREET.: Company C, private. March 4, 1862 enlisted as a private in Co. K, 28th Regiment, Georgia Infantry. 1864 he transferred from Co. K, 28th Regiment, Georgia Infantry to Co. C, 54th Regiment, Georgia Infantry. January – February 1864 roll shows him present. Pension records show: April 26, 1865 surrendered at Greensboro, North Carolina. May 1, 1865 paroled at Greensboro, North Carolina. He was born in Emanuel County, Georgia January 1, 1844 and died in Jefferson County, Georgia September 23, 1928. He is buried in Coleman's Chapel Cemetery at Wadley, Jefferson County, Georgia. (find a grave # 62995302)

MOORE, THOMAS S.: Company C, private. March 15, 1862 enlisted as a private in Co. C, 54th Regiment, Georgia Infantry at Savannah, Georgia and received bounty $50.00. January 1, 1864 received pay. January – February 1864 roll shows him present.

MOORE, W.: Company H, private. October 8, 1862 enlisted as a private in Co. H, 54th Regiment, Georgia Infantry. October 1862 roll shows his enlistment.

MOORE, WILLIAM B.: Company H, private. September 1, 1862 enlisted as a private in Co. H, 54th Regiment, Georgia Infantry at Columbus, Georgia and received bounty $50.00. December 31, 1862 received pay. January – February 1863 roll shows him present. October 31, 1863 received pay. November – December 1863 roll shows him present. December 31, 1863 received pay. January 1864 issued clothing. January – February 1864 roll shows him present. April 26, 1865 surrendered at Greensboro, North Carolina. May 1, 1865 paroled at Greensboro, North Carolina.

MOORE, WILLIAM W.: Company A, private. May 14, 1862 enlisted as a private in Co. A, 54th Regiment, Georgia Infantry at Macon, Georgia and received bounty $50.00. November 1862 roll shows he joined on November 15, 1862 at Macon, Georgia. April 30, 1863 received pay. June 1, 1863 he died. June 30, 1863 roll shows his death on June 1, 1863. November 23, 1863 death benefit claim was filed by his father Owen W. Moore. He was a resident of Macon, Bibb County, Georgia. He was born in 1842 and died June 1, 1863. He is buried in James Cemetery at James, Jones County, Georgia. (find a grave # 17495661)

MORGAN, A. J. (A. P.): Company H, private. February 1862 enlisted as a private in Co. H, 54th Regiment, Georgia Infantry. Pension records show: April 26, 1865 surrendered at Greensboro, North Carolina. May 1, 1865 paroled at Greensboro, North Carolina. He was born in Warren County, Georgia May 3, 1845.

MORGAN, A. L.: Company C, lieutenant. He enlisted as a lieutenant in Co. C, 54th Regiment, Georgia Infantry.

MORGAN, C. C.: Company C, private. May 6, 1862 enlisted as a private in Co. C, 54th Regiment, Georgia Infantry at Savannah, Georgia and received bounty $50.00. December 31, 1862 received pay. January – February 1863 roll shows him present. January 1, 1864 received pay. January – February 1864 roll shows him absent (absent sick in hospital at Hardeeville, South Carolina). April 25, 1864 issued clothing. July 22, 1864 he was killed in Atlanta, Georgia. He was a resident of Emanuel County, Georgia.

MORGAN, JAMES NATHAN: Company H, private. August 12, 1862 enlisted as a private in Co. H, 54th Regiment, Georgia Infantry at Savannah, Georgia and received bounty $50.00. August and September 1862 rolls show his enlistment. December 31, 1862 received pay. January – February 1863 roll shows him present. October 31, 1863 received pay. November – December 1863 roll shows him present. December 31, 1863 received pay. January – February 1864 roll shows him present (on guard). June 20, 1864 wounded in the left hand and permanently disabled near Marietta, Georgia or June 27, 1864 wounded in the left hand and permanently disabled at Kennesaw Mountain, Georgia. He was born in Harris County, Georgia December 8, 1833 and died in Harris County, Georgia November 17, 1905. He is buried in Union Baptist Church Cemetery at Whitesville,

Harris County, Georgia. (find a grave # 87089374)
MORGAN, JESSE CLEVELAND: Company C, private. May 6, 1862 enlisted as a private in Co. C, 54th Regiment, Georgia Infantry at Savannah, Georgia and received bounty $50.00. December 31, 1862 received pay. January 5, 1863 received pay $77.13. January – February 1863 roll shows him present. January 1, 1864 received pay. January – February 1864 roll shows him present. April 25, 1864 and May 8, 1864 issued clothing. July 22, 1864 wounded and permanently disabled at Atlanta, Georgia. Pension records show he was at home on wounded furlough at the close of the war. He was a resident of Emanuel County, Georgia. He was born in Jackson County, Georgia July 6, 1837 and died in Emanuel County, Georgia July 14, 1923. He is buried in Cool Springs Cemetery in Candler County, Georgia. (find a grave # 62283227)
MORGAN, R. H.: Company H, private. May 12, 1862 enlisted as a private in Co. H, 54th Regiment, Georgia Infantry at Savannah, Georgia and received bounty $50.00. November 6, 1863 issued clothing.
MORGAN, ROBERT J.: Company H, private. May 12, 1862 enlisted as a private in Co. H, 54th Regiment, Georgia Infantry at Columbus, Georgia and received bounty $50.00. June 3, 1863 detailed as a teamster by order of General Taliaferro. September 1, 1863 to September 30, 1863 detailed as a teamster at St. Andrews, South Carolina at a rate of $.25 extra per day. September 1863 received pay. October 1, 1863 to October 31, 1863 detailed as a teamster at Charleston, South Carolina at a rate of $.25 extra per day. October 1863 received pay. November 1, 1863 to November 30, 1863 detailed as a teamster at St. Andrews, South Carolina at a rate of $.25 extra per day. November 1863 received pay. December 1, 1863 to December 31, 1863 detailed as a teamster at Charleston, South Carolina at a rate of $.25 extra per day. December 1863 received pay. November – December 1863 roll shows him absent (detailed as a teamster). January 1, 1864 to February 29, 1864 detailed as a teamster at Charleston, South Carolina at a rate of $.25 extra per day. January and February 1864 received pay. January 25, 1864 issued clothing. January – February 1864 roll shows him absent (detailed as a teamster). Mach 1, 1864 to April 30, 1864 detailed as a teamster at Charleston, South Carolina at a rate of $.25 extra per day. March and April 1864 received pay. April 19, 1864 issued clothing. May 21, 1864 granted furlough by Special Order No. 119/3.
MORRIS, EDMUND (EMANUEL) DARLING: Company E, private. May 6, 1862 enlisted as a private in Co. E, 54th Regiment, Georgia Infantry at Savannah, Georgia and received bounty $50.00. November 1, 1862 to December 31, 1862 detailed on extra duty as a mechanic at Savannah, Georgia at a rate of $.40 extra per day. December 31, 1862 received pay. January – February 1863 roll shows him present. July 1, 1863 to October 31, 1863 detailed on extra duty as a mechanic at Savannah, Georgia at a rate of $.40 extra per day. August 1863 received pay $24.80. January 1864 issued clothing. January 1, 1864 to April 27, 1864 detailed on extra duty as a mechanic at Savannah, Georgia at a rate of $.40 extra per day.

March 26, 1864 issued clothing. May 1, 1864 received pay $109.13 (including clothing payment). May 10, 1865 surrendered at Tallahassee, Florida. May 26, 1865 surrendered at Albany, Georgia. He was born June 16, 1832 and died in Berrien County, Georgia June 20, 1907. He is buried in Old City Cemetery at Nashville, Berrien County, Georgia. (find a grave # 96401733)

MORRIS, J. H.: Company E, private. He enlisted as a private in Co. E, 54th Regiment, Georgia Infantry. June 2, 1863 died at Rose Dew Island 12 miles south of Savannah, Georgia of Congestion of the Brain.

MORRIS, WILLIAM E., JR.: Company E, private. May 6, 1862 enlisted as a private in Co. E, 54th Regiment, Georgia Infantry at Savannah, Georgia and received bounty $50.00. December 31, 1862 received pay. January – February 1863 roll shows him present. July 1, 1863 to August 31, 1863 detailed on extra duty as a mechanic at Savannah, Georgia at a rate of $.40 extra per day. August 1863 received pay $24.80. September 1, 1863 to December 31, 1863 detailed on extra duty as a mechanic at Savannah, Georgia at a rate of $.40 extra per day. October 31, 1863 received pay. January 1864 issued clothing. January 1, 1864 to April 27, 1864 detailed on extra duty as a mechanic at Savannah, Georgia at a rate of $.40 extra per day. February 20, 1864 he is described as being; 28 years of age (born in 1836), blue eyes, light hair, fair complexion, 6 feet high and was born in Pickens District, South Carolina. February 27, 1864 received pay $22.00. March 22, 1864 issued clothing. May 1, 1864 received pay $88.13 (including clothing payment). June 2, 1864 issued clothing. 1864 contracted Chronic Diarrhoea. May 10, 1865 surrendered at Tallahassee, Florida. May 26, 1865 surrendered at Albany, Georgia. He was born in Pickens District, South Carolina July 19, 1834. He died in 1913 and is buried in Old City Cemetery at Nashville, Berrien County, Georgia. (find a grave # 96402911)

MORRISON, JAMES: Company A, private. He enlisted as a private in Co. A, 54th Regiment, Georgia Infantry. He deserted on March 26, 1865 and was discharged March 28, 1865 and instructed to stay north of the Ohio River during the war. March 20, 1865 took oath of allegiance at Military Prison at Louisville, Kentucky and is described as; a resident of Butts County, Georgia, fair complexion, dark hair, gray eyes, 5 feet 8 inches high and was a conscript.

MORRISON, JAMES B.: Company A, private. September 2, 1863 enlisted as a private in Co. A, 54th Regiment, Georgia Infantry at Macon, Georgia and received bounty $50.00. October 31, 1863 received pay. November – December 1863 roll shows him present. January 1, 1864 received pay. January – February 1864 roll shows him present. March 31, 1864 issued clothing. May 19, 1864 captured at Kingston, Georgia. May 24, 1864 received at Military Prison at Louisville, Kentucky from Nashville, Tennessee. May 25, 1864 sent to Rock Island Barracks, Illinois from Military Prison at Louisville, Kentucky. May 27, 1864 received at Rock Island Barracks, Illinois from Military Prison at Louisville, Kentucky.

August 6, 1864 he died of Chronic Diarrhoea at Rock Island Barracks, Illinois (he is buried in grave no. 1380). (find a grave #9121582)

MORROW, G.: Company G, private. He enlisted as a private in Co. G, 54th Regiment, Georgia Infantry. May 12, 1862 he deserted at Savannah, Georgia. August 1862 roll indicates his desertion.

MORROW, J. P.: Company C, private. He enlisted as a private in Co. C, 54th Regiment, Georgia Infantry. October 24, 1862 he died at Fair Ground Hospital at Atlanta, Georgia.

MORTIMER, CHARLES: Company F, private. January 2, 1863 enlisted as a private in Co. I, 5th Regiment, Georgia Cavalry. January 2, 1863 transferred to and enlisted as a private in Co. K, 5th Georgia Cavalry. February 2, 1863 transferred from Co. K, 5th Georgia Cavalry to Co. F, 54th Regiment, Georgia Infantry. February 2 1863 deserted at Savannah, Georgia. January – February 1863 roll shows his transfer and desertion.

MORTON, DAVID MITCHELL: Company I, private. January 9, 1863 enlisted as a private in Co. I, 54th Regiment, Georgia Infantry at Beaulieu near Savannah, Georgia and received bounty $50.00. December 31, 1862 received pay. January – February 1863 roll shows him present. October 31, 1863 received pay. November – December 1863 roll shows him present (sick in post hospital). January 1864 and April 25, 1864 issued clothing. July 22, 1864 wounded at Atlanta, Georgia. July 26, 1864 admitted to Ocmulgee Hospital at Macon, Georgia with a Vulnus Contusion (wound from shell ext. from upper portion right thigh). July 30, 1864 transferred (furloughed for 60 days). December 24, 1864 admitted to 1st Division Hospital, 20th A. C. with a Gunshot Wound in the thigh (flesh) requiring a simple dressing (he was 19 years of age). January 11, 1865 admitted 2nd Division, 20th A. C. Hospital with a Gun Shot wound to the right thigh. January 16, 1865 sent to general headquarters. He was a resident of Egypt, Effingham County, Georgia. He was born in Egypt, Effingham County, Georgia January 19, 1845 and died in Egypt, Effingham County, Georgia October 1912. He is buried in Old Elam Cemetery at Egypt, Effingham County, Georgia. (find a grave #82207281)

MORTON, HENRY O.: Company I, private. September 17, 1863 enlisted as a private in Co. I, 54th Regiment, Georgia Infantry at Rose Dew near Savannah, Georgia and received bounty $50.00. October 31, 1863 received pay. November – December 1863 roll shows him present. January 1864 April 25, 1864 issued clothing. July 8, 1864 admitted to Ocmulgee Hospital at Macon, Georgia. July 15-25, 1864 he appears on a register of Ocmulgee Hospital at Macon, Georgia with Remitting Fever (malaria) and General Debility. July 23, 1864 he was furloughed to Screven County for 30 days. He was a resident of Hassendale, Screven County, Georgia. He was born March 13, 1820 and died October 19, 1884. He is buried in Little Ogeechee Baptist Church Cemetery at Oliver, Screven County, Georgia. (find a grave #24963091)

MORTON, SILAS: Company I, private. September 18, 1861 enlisted as a private in Co. C, 1st Regiment, 1st Brigade, Georgia State Troops.

March 18, 1862 mustered out. August 25, 1863 enlisted as a private in Co. I, 54th Regiment, Georgia Infantry at Rose Dew near Savannah, Georgia and received bounty $50.00. October 31, 1863 received pay. December 15, 1863 detailed to guard commissary stores at #3 C. R. R. November – December 1863 roll shows him absent (detailed to guard commissary stores). January 1864 issued clothing. July 8, 1864 admitted to Ocmulgee Hospital at Macon, Georgia with Remitting Fever (malaria). July 23, 1864 he was furloughed to Effingham County for 30 days. He was born June 13, 1836 and died August 3, 1914. He is buried in the Silas Morton Cemetery in Effingham County, Georgia. (find a grave #19589477)

MOSES, DANIEL L.: Company F, private. January 19, 1863 enlisted as a private in Co. F, 54th Regiment, Georgia Infantry at Savannah, Georgia and received bounty $50.00. January – February 1863 roll shows him present. July 7, 1863 subject of court martial General Order 83/14. September 26, 1863 detailed Ordinance Sergeant by special order. August 31, 1863 received pay. November – December 1863 roll shows him present (detailed ordinance sergeant by Special Order) returned to duty. December 7, 1863 detailed for extra duty for 60 days by Special Order No. 329/2. January 1864 and April 25, 1864 issued clothing. June 18, 1864 detailed for extra duty on account of disability by Special Order No. 142/2. He was born in Charleston, South Carolina March 10, 1830 and died in Savannah, Georgia November 1, 1905. He is buried in Laurel Grove Cemetery at Savannah, Chatham County, Georgia. (find a grave # 90839687)

MOSS, JAMES: Company K, private. August 1, 1864 enlisted in Co. H, 37th Regiment, Georgia Infantry at Washington, Georgia. April 26, 1865 surrendered in Co. K, 54th Regiment, Consolidated Georgia Infantry at Greensboro, North Carolina. May 1, 1865 paroled at Greensboro, North Carolina.

MULARKEY, P. J.: Company F, private. February 2, 1863 enlisted as a private in Co. F, 54th Regiment, Georgia Infantry at Savannah, Georgia and received bounty $50.00. November – December 1863 roll shows him present. January 1864 issued clothing. November 6, 1864 detailed for extra work by Special Field Order No. 141/11.

MULKEY, JOHN J.: Company A, private. March 18, 1861 enlisted as a private in Co. C, 1st Independent Battalion, Georgia State Troops. March 18, 1862 mustered out – discharged by expiration of term of service. August 1, 1863 enlisted as a private in Co. A, 54th Regiment, Georgia Infantry at Savannah, Georgia and received bounty $50.00. October 31, 1863 received pay. November – December 1863 roll shows him present (sick in company hospital). January 1, 1864 received pay. January – February 1864 roll shows him present. April 29, 1864 and May 8, 1864 issued clothing. December 19, 1864 captured near Murfreesboro, Tennessee. January 2, 1865 received at Military Prison at Louisville, Kentucky from Nashville, Tennessee. January 4, 1865 sent to Camp Chase, Ohio from Military Prison at Louisville, Kentucky. January 6, 1865 received at

Camp Chase, Ohio from Military Prison at Louisville, Kentucky. June 12, 1865 took Oath of Allegiance at Camp Chase, Ohio and is described as; a resident of Pike County, Alabama, fair complexion, light hair, gray eyes, 5 feet 1 inch high and was 20 years of age. He was born in Pike County, Georgia in 1843 and died in Travis County, Texas December 15, 1928. He is buried in the Texas State Cemetery at Austin, Travis County, Texas. (find a grave # 65346683)

MULKEY (MULKER), JOHN H.: Company G, private. July 6, 1862 enlisted as a private in Co. F, 54th Regiment, Georgia Infantry at Savannah, Georgia and received bounty $50.00. December 31, 1862 received pay. January – February 1863 roll shows him present. January 1864 and April 25, 1864 issued clothing. July 3, 1864 captured near Marietta, Georgia. July 14, 1864 received at Military Prison at Louisville, Kentucky from Nashville, Tennessee. July 14, 1864 sent to Camp Douglas, Illinois from Military Prison at Louisville, Kentucky. July 16, 1864 received at Camp Douglas, Illinois from Military Prison at Louisville, Kentucky. April 6, 1865 transferred and enlisted in the 6th U. S. Volunteers.

MULKEY, WILLIAM GREEN: Company A, private. November 1, 1863 enlisted as a private in Co. A, 54th Regiment, Georgia Infantry at Macon, Georgia and received bounty $50.00. November – December 1863 roll shows him present. January 1, 1864 received pay. January – February 1864 roll shows him present (sick in company hospital). April 29, 1864 issued clothing. June 19, 1864 captured near Marietta, Georgia. June 26, 1864 received at Military Prison at Louisville, Kentucky from Nashville, Tennessee. June 27, 1864 sent to Camp Morton, Indiana from Military Prison at Louisville, Kentucky. March 4, 1865 paroled at Camp Morton, Indiana and forwarded to City Point, Virginia via Baltimore, Maryland. He was born in Georgia March 28, 1845 and died in Pike County, Alabama February 5, 1910. He is buried in Bethel Cemetery at Banks, Pike County, Alabama. (find a grave # 70149556)

MULLINNIX, H. J.: Company H, private. He enlisted as a private in Co. H, 54th Regiment, Georgia Infantry.

MULLINS, JACKSON A.: Company H, private. October 9, 1863 enlisted as a private in Co. H, 54th Regiment, Georgia Infantry at Beaulieu near Savannah, Georgia and received bounty $50.00. October 31, 1863 received pay. November – December 1863 roll shows him present. December 31, 1863 received pay. January 1864 issued clothing. January – February 1864 roll shows him present (present sick).

MURPHY (MURPHEY), ERASMUS M.: Company G, private. July 18, 1864 enlisted in Co C, 37th Regiment, Georgia Infantry. April 26, 1865 surrendered in Co. G, 54th Regiment, Consolidated Georgia Infantry at Greensboro, North Carolina. May 1, 1865 paroled at Greensboro, North Carolina.

MURPHY (MURPHEY), JAMES C.: Company F, private. September 4, 1862 enlisted as a private in Co. F, 54th Regiment, Georgia Infantry at Savannah, Georgia and received bounty $50.00. September 1862 roll shows his enlistment as September 10, 1862. December 31, 1862 received pay. January – February 1863 roll shows him present. September 1, 1863 received pay. November – December 1863 roll shows he deserted November 1, 1863.

MURPHY, STEPHEN: Company B, private. September 1864 enlisted as a private in Co. B, 54th Regiment, Georgia Infantry at Red Bluff, S. C. December 16, 1864 wounded at Nashville, Tennessee. March 1865 furloughed for 60 days. He was at home on sick furlough at the close of the war. He was born in Georgia June 1845 (1844) and died April 2, 1929. He is buried in Pleasant Grove Cemetery in Appling County, Georgia. (find a grave #86382138)

MURPHY (MURPHEY), TIMOTHY: Company F, private. May 13, 1862 enlisted as a private in Co. F, 54th Regiment, Georgia Infantry at Savannah, Georgia and received bounty $50.00. December 8, 1862 discharged at Beaulieu near Savannah, Georgia by Civil Authority. December 1862 roll shows his discharge.

MURPHY, WILLIAM M.: Company B, private. October 10, 1861 enlisted as a private in Co. K, 2nd Regiment, 1st Brigade, Georgia State Troops. April 1862 mustered out. April 21, 1862 enlisted as a private in Co. B, 54th Regiment, Georgia Infantry at Savannah, Georgia and received bounty $50.00. December 31, 1862 received pay. January – February 1863 roll shows him present. January 1864 issued clothing. January 1, 1864 to January 31, 1864 detailed as a teamster. Pension records show he was on guard duty at Fort Valley, Georgia at the close of the war. He was born in Georgia January 9, 1842 and died January 15, 1922. He is buried in Bethel United Methodist Church Cemetery in Appling County, Georgia. (find a grave #65258402)

NAGLE, PATRICK: Company F, private. May 13, 1862 enlisted as a private in Co. F, 54th Regiment, Georgia Infantry at Savannah, Georgia and received bounty $50.00. September 7, 1862 discharged. September 1862 roll shows his discharge.

NANCE, WILLIAM H.: Company G, private. He enlisted as a private in Co. G, 54th Regiment, Georgia Infantry.

NARRAMORE, HENRY L.: Company H, private. April 11, 1863 enlisted as a private in Co. H, 54th Regiment, Georgia Infantry at Columbus, Georgia and received bounty $50.00. October 31, 1863 received pay. November – December 1863 roll shows him present. December 31, 1863 received pay. January 1864 issued clothing. January – February 1864 roll shows him absent on ten (10) days furlough since February 21, 1864.

NASH, GEORGE W.: Company E, corporal. He enlisted as a corporal in Co. E, 54th Regiment, Georgia Infantry.

NASH, J. H.: Company E, sergeant. He enlisted as a sergeant in Co. E, 54th Regiment, Georgia Infantry.

NEAL, JAMES L.: Company H, private. May 12, 1862 enlisted as a private in Co. H, 54th Regiment, Georgia Infantry at Warrenton, Georgia and received bounty $50.00. September 1862 shows him detailed as captain's orderly. October 1862 roll shows him detailed as captain's clerk.

NEAL, ____: Company H, private. July 26, 1862 enlisted as a private in Co. H, 54th Regiment, Georgia Infantry at Savannah, Georgia and received bounty $50.00. July 1862 roll shows his enlistment.

NEASE, E. J.: Company F, private. He enlisted as a private in Co. F, 54th Regiment, Georgia Infantry **NEASE, E. L.:** Company F, private. January 22, 1864 enlisted as a private in Co. F, 54th Regiment, Georgia Infantry at Savannah, Georgia and received bounty $50.00. January – February 1863 roll shows him present. November 1, 1863 received pay. November – December 1863 roll shows him present. January 1864, April 25, 1864 and May 8, 1864 issued clothing.

NEASE, EDWARD LEONARD: Company I, private. January 22, 1864 enlisted as a private in Co. I, 54th Regiment, Georgia Infantry at Savannah, Georgia and received bounty $50.00. January – February 1863 roll shows him present. November 1, 1863 received pay. November – December 1863 roll shows him present. January 1864, April 25, 1864 and May 8, 1864 issued clothing. He was born in Effingham County, Georgia November 26, 1823 and died in Marlow, Effingham County, Georgia July 6, 1892. He is buried in Zion Lutheran Church Cemetery at Guyton, Effingham County. (find a grave # 51528977)

NEASE, JAMES JEREMIAH: Company I, private. May 6, 1862 enlisted as a private in Co. I, 54th Regiment, Georgia Infantry at Guyton, Georgia and received bounty $50.00. December 31, 1862 received pay. January – February 1863 roll shows him absent sick. June 30, 1863 received pay. November – December 1863 roll shows him present. January 1864 and April 25, 1864 issued clothing. He was born in Effingham County, Georgia October 28, 1827 and died in Effingham County, Georgia January 31, 1911. He is buried in Springfield City Cemetery at Springfield, Effingham County, Georgia. (find a grave # 50573097)

NEASE JOHN N.: Company I, private. September 18, 1861 enlisted as a private in Co. C, 1st Regiment, 1st Brigade, Georgia State Troops. March 18, 1862 mustered out. May 6, 1862 enlisted as a private in Co. I, 54th Regiment, Georgia Infantry at Guyton, Georgia and received bounty $50.00. December 31, 1862 received pay. January – February 1863 roll shows him present. October 31, 1863 received pay. November 22, 1863 to December 31, 1863 detailed for extra duty as a carpenter at Savannah, Georgia at a rate of $.40 extra per day. November – December 1863 roll shows him present (detailed to get shingles for post). January 1864 issued clothing. January 20, 1864 received pay. April 25, 1864 issued clothing. He was born February 9, 1832 and died February 3, 1898. He is buried in Salem Lutheran Church Cemetery in Cocke County, Tennessee. (find a grave # 72044085)

NEASE, JOHN ROBERT: Company I, private. May 6, 1862 enlisted as a private in Co. I, 54th Regiment, Georgia Infantry at Guyton, Georgia and received bounty $50.00. December 31, 1862 received pay. January – February 1863 roll shows him absent sick. December 31, 1863 received pay. January 1864 issued clothing. January – February 1864 roll shows him present. April 25, 1864 issued clothing. December 24, 1864 captured in Savannah, Georgia. January 27, 1865 received at Fort Delaware, Delaware from Effingham County, Georgia. He was born in Effingham County, Georgia October 28, 1827 and died in Effingham County, Georgia January 31, 1911. He is buried in the Springfield City Cemetery in Springfield, Effingham County, Georgia. (find a grave #50573099)

NEASE, JOHN ROBERT, JR.: Company I, private. May 6, 1862 enlisted as a private in Co. I, 54th Regiment, Georgia Infantry at Guyton, Georgia and received bounty $50.00. December 31, 1862 received pay. January – February 1863 roll shows him present. December 31, 1863 received pay. January 1864 issued clothing. January – February 1864 roll shows him present. April 25, 1864 issued clothing. July 22, 1864 wounded at Atlanta, Georgia. December 21, 1864 captured at Savannah, Georgia. March 12, 1865 received at Fort Delaware, Delaware from Hilton Head, South Carolina. June 16, 1865 released, paroled and took the oath of allegiance at Fort Delaware, Delaware by General Order No. 109. He is described as; a resident of Effingham County, Georgia, dark complexion, dark hair, dark eyes and 5 feet 9 inches high, He was born in Georgia March 16, 1844 and died in Effingham County, Georgia February 6, 1926. He is buried in the Springfield City Cemetery in Springfield, Effingham County, Georgia. (find a grave #50573100)

NEASE, LEONARD J.: Company G (I) (D), private. September 18, 1861 enlisted as a private in Co. C, 1st Regiment, 1st Brigade, Georgia State Troops. March 18, 1862 mustered out. May 6, 1862 enlisted as a private in Co. I, 54th Regiment, Georgia Infantry at Guyton, Georgia and received bounty $50.00. April 25, 1863 detailed as nurse in hospital. July 22, 1864 wounded in Atlanta, Georgia. (He appears on all three company rolls but there is no record of transfer.) He was born March 14, 1841. He is buried in the Springfield City Cemetery in Springfield, Effingham County, Georgia. (find a grave #50573103)

NEASE, THOMAS E.: Company I, sergeant. September 18, 1861 enlisted as a private and appointed 2nd sergeant in Co. C, 1st Regiment, 1st Brigade, Georgia State Troops. He served as acting 1st sergeant until October 1, 1861. March 18, 1862 mustered out. May 6, 1862 enlisted as 2nd sergeant in Co. I, 54th Regiment, Georgia Infantry at Guyton, Georgia and received bounty $50.00. December 31, 1862 received pay. January – February 1863 roll shows him present. October 31, 1863 received pay. November – December 1863 roll shows him present. January 1864 and April 25, 1864 issued clothing. He was born September 20, 1841 and died July 22, 1893. He is buried in Zion Lutheran Church Cemetery at Guyton, Effingham County, Georgia. (find a grave #67402626)

NEASE, WILLIAM ALBERT: Company I, private. May 6, 1862 enlisted as a private in Co. I, 54th Regiment, Georgia Infantry at Guyton, Georgia and received bounty $50.00. December 31, 1862 received pay. January – February 1863 roll shows him present (camp guard). October

31, 1863 received pay. November 22, 1863 to December 31, 1863 detailed for extra duty as a carpenter at Savannah, Georgia at a rate of $.40 extra per day. November – December 1863 roll shows him present (detailed to get shingles for post). January 20, 1864 received pay. September 3, 1864 captured near Jonesboro, Georgia. September 22, 1864 exchanged by order of General W. T. Sherman. January 1864 issued clothing. January 1865 he was sent to the hospital at Montgomery, Alabama and was furloughed for 60 days. He was born in Georgia December 28, 1838 and died September 9, 1925. He is buried in the Springfield City Cemetery in Springfield, Effingham County, Georgia. (find a grave #50573116)

NELSON, FRANKLIN: Company E, private. May 6, 1862 enlisted as a private in Co. E, 54th Regiment, Georgia Infantry at Guyton, Georgia and received bounty $50.00. June 7, 1864 appointed quartermaster's department wagoner. July, August, November and December 1862 rolls show his appointment as wagoner (teamster). September 1, 1862 to December 31, 1862 detailed as post teamster (acting as wagon master for post) at a rate of $.25 extra per day. December 31, 1862 received pay. January – February 1863 roll shows him absent detailed as a teamster. September, October, November and December 1862 received pay. June 1, 1863 to October 31, 1863 detailed as post teamster (acting as wagon master for post) at a rate of $.25 extra per day. September 8, 1863 and October 1863 received pay. October 31, 1863 list at James Island, South Carolina includes him as driver for the quartermaster's department since May 18, 1862. January 1864 issued clothing. January 2, 1864 received pay $22.00 + $212.00. May 8, 1864 issued clothing.

NESMITH (NEESMITH), JOHN H. (D.): Company F, private. July 1, 1863 enlisted as a private in Co. F, 54th Regiment, Georgia Infantry at Savannah, Georgia and received bounty $50.00. December 31, 1862 received pay. January – February 1863 roll shows him present. November 1, 1863 received pay. November – December 1863 roll shows him present. January 1864 and May 8, 1864 issued clothing. May 27, 1864 he died in Atlanta, Georgia. He was born in North Carolina in 1824 and died May 27, 1864 in Atlanta, Georgia. He is buried in Oakland Cemetery in Atlanta, Fulton County, Georgia. (find a grave #103425039)

NEWSOME (NEWSOM), C. M.: Company A, private. September 1, 1863 enlisted as a private in Co. A, 54th Regiment, Georgia Infantry at Macon, Georgia and received bounty $50.00. October 31, 1863 received pay. November – December 1863 roll shows him present. January 1, 1864 received pay. January – February 1864 roll shows him present. April 29, 1864 issued clothing.

NEWSOME, H.: Company A, private. He enlisted as a private in Co. A, 54th Regiment, Georgia Infantry.

NEWTON, JAMES B.: Company D, private. July 10, 1862 enlisted as a private in Co. D, 54th Regiment, Georgia Infantry at Savannah, Georgia and received bounty $50.00. August 1862 roll shows his enlistment. December 31, 1862 received pay. January – February 1863 roll shows him present (absent without leave 5 days). January 1864 issued clothing. Wounded in action around Atlanta, Georgia. October 13, 1864 issued clothing at Fairground Hospital at Vineville, Georgia. November 21, 1864 issued clothing. He was born in 1844 and died December 12, 1912. He is buried in Scarboro Cemetery in Jenkins County, Georgia.

NEWTON, M. J.: Company D, private. He enlisted as a private in Co. D, 54th Regiment, Georgia Infantry.

NEWTON, MITCHELL J.: Company D, private. October 7, 1861 enlisted as a private in Co. I, 5th Regiment, Georgia State Troops. April 1862 mustered out. April 30, 1862 enlisted as a private in Co. D, 54th Regiment, Georgia Infantry at Savannah, Georgia and received bounty $50.00. December 31, 1862 received pay. January – February 1863 roll shows him present. January 1864, April 25, 1864 and May 8, 1864 issued clothing. October 14, 1864 captured at Dalton, Georgia. October 24, 1864 received at Military Prison at Louisville, Kentucky from Nashville, Tennessee. October 26, 1864 sent to Camp Douglas, Illinois from Military Prison at Louisville, Kentucky. November 26, 1864 received at Camp Douglas, Illinois from Military Prison at Louisville, Kentucky. June 17, 1865 discharged from Camp Douglas, Illinois. Described as; a resident of St. Mary's, Georgia, fair complexion, dark hair, grey eyes and 5 feet 10 inches high. He was born in Georgia in 1832.

NICHOLAS, JAMES HAMILTON: Company K, private. October 3, 1861 enlisted as a private in Co. A, 1st Regiment, 1st Brigade, Georgia State Troops. April 1862 mustered out. April 18, 1862 enlisted as a private in Co. K, 54th Regiment, Georgia Infantry at Savannah, Georgia and received bounty $50.00. 1862 discharged due to disability. (Another record: He was born January 14, 1843 and died November 13, 1916) He was born August 6, 1862 and died May 13, 1910. He is buried in the Screven Cemetery at Screven, Wayne County, Georgia. (find a grave #59990589)

NICHOLAS (NICHOLS), JOSIAH L.: Company K, private. April 18, 1862 enlisted as a private in Co. K, 54th Regiment, Georgia Infantry at Savannah, Georgia and received bounty $50.00. April 23, 1862 deserted at Savannah, Georgia. August 1862 roll shows his desertion.

NICHOLAS (NICHOLS), WILLIAM REESE: Company K, private. October 3, 1861 enlisted as a private in Co. A, 1st Regiment, 1st Brigade, Georgia State Troops. April 1862 mustered out. April 18, 1862 enlisted as a private in Co. K, 54th Regiment, Georgia Infantry at Savannah, Georgia and received bounty $50.00. October, November and December 1862 rolls show him detailed as a butcher at a rate of $.25 extra per day. January 1, 1863 and January 15, 1863 received pay. January – February 1863 roll shows him present (returned from extra duty in C. M. D. P. February 19, 1863). March 12, 1863 received pay. March 18, 1864 and April 18, 1864 issued clothing. July 22, 1864 wounded in the left shoulder at Atlanta, Georgia. May 10, 1865 surrendered at Tallahassee, Florida. May 21, 1865 paroled at Thomasville, Georgia. He was born in Georgia January

23, 1837 and died July 18, 1898. He is buried in the Patterson Cemetery in Pierce County, Georgia. (find a grave # 67172365)

NIX, V.: Company E, private. May 6, 1862 enlisted as a private in Co. E, 54th Regiment, Georgia Infantry at Savannah, Georgia and received bounty $50.00. August 1, 1862 detailed as a teamster. August 1862 roll shows him being detailed. December 31, 1862 received pay. January – February 1863 roll shows him present. January 1864 and May 8, 1864 issued clothing. Pension records show; May 1864 wounded in the left hip near Marietta, Georgia. He was at home wounded at the close of the war. He was born in Georgia December 25, 1835.

NIXON, JAMES: Company A, private. He enlisted as a private in Co. E, 54th Regiment, Georgia Infantry. June 29, 1864 wounded in the left foot. September 9, 1864 admitted to Ocmulgee Hospital at Macon, Georgia with a Gunshot Wound to the left foot causing 2nd toe to be amputated. September 17, 1864 furloughed to Wilkinson County, Georgia. He was a resident of Griswold, Twiggs County, Georgia.

NOLAND, GEORGE W.: Company A, private. December 20, 1862 enlisted as a private in Co. K, 57th Regiment, Georgia Infantry at Macon, Georgia and received bounty $50.00. January – February 1864 roll shows him present. April 2, 1864 transferred from Co. K, 57th Regiment, Georgia Infantry to Co. A, 54th Regiment, Georgia Infantry. March – April 1864 roll of Co. K, 57th Regiment, Georgia Infantry shows his transfer. November – December 1864 roll of Co. F, 1st Regiment, Troops and Defences, Macon, Georgia shows him present at Camp Wright.

NOLAND, I. T.: Company E, private. He enlisted as a private in Co. E, 54th Regiment, Georgia Infantry.

NOLAND (NOLEN), S. W.: Company A, private. April 26, 1865 surrendered at Greensboro, North Carolina. May 2, 1865 paroled at Greensboro, North Carolina.

NOLAND (NOLAN), W. A.: Company A, private. April 26, 1862 enlisted as a private in Co. A, 54th Regiment, Georgia Infantry at Macon, Georgia and received bounty $50.00. February 28, 1863 received pay. June 30, 1863 roll shows him present. October 31, 1863 received pay. November 1863 received commutation for rations. November – December 1863 roll shows him present. January 1, 1864 received pay. January – February 1864 roll shows him present. March 31, 1864 issued clothing. He was born in Georgia March 4, 1833 and died September 12, 1902. He is buried in Snow Hill Cemetery at Ivey, Wilkinson County, Georgia. (find a grave # 15716842).

NORDETTE, JOHN: Company A, private. April 26, 1862 enlisted as a private in Co. A, 54th Regiment, Georgia Infantry at Macon, Georgia and received bounty $50.00. April 30, 1863 received pay. June 30, 1863 roll shows him present (as a musician in the 54th Regiment, Georgia Infantry). November – December 1863 roll shows him absent (musician in the 54th Regiment, Georgia Infantry).

January – February 1864 roll shows him absent (musician in the 54th

Regiment, Georgia Infantry).

NORMAN, W. B.: Company K, sergeant. He enlisted as sergeant in Co. K, 54th Regiment, Georgia Infantry.

NORRIS, AMOS P.: Company H, private. February 24, 1864 enlisted as a private in Co. H, 54th Regiment, Georgia Infantry at Hardeeville, South Carolina. January 1864 issued clothing. January – February 1864 roll shows him present (on picket). June 2, 1864 issued clothing. May 20, 1865 surrendered and paroled at Augusta, Georgia. He was born in Warren County, Georgia May 3, 1845.

NORRIS, JAMES MARCUS (MONROE): Company H, private. December 6, 1862 enlisted as a private in Co. H, 54th Regiment, Georgia Infantry at Beaulieu near Savannah, Georgia and received bounty $50.00. December 1862 roll shows his enlistment. December 31, 1862 received pay. January – February 1863 roll shows him present. October 31, 1863 received pay. November – December 1863 roll shows him present. December 31, 1863 received pay. January 1864 issued clothing. January – February 1864 roll shows him present (on picket). December 23, 1864 received pay $22.00. April 26, 1865 surrendered at Greensboro, North Carolina. May 1, 1865 paroled at Greensboro, North Carolina. He was born in Warren County, Georgia March 18, 1844.

NORRIS, JOSEPH MARSHALL: Company H, private. May 20, 1862 enlisted as a private in Co. H, 54th Regiment, Georgia Infantry at Savannah, Georgia and received bounty $50.00. December 31, 1862 received pay. January – February 1863 roll shows him present. October 31, 1863 received pay. November – December 1863 roll shows him present. December 31, 1863 received pay. January – February 1864 roll shows him present. December 23, 1864 received pay $22.00. April 26, 1865 surrendered at Greensboro, North Carolina. May 1, 1865 paroled at Greensboro, North Carolina.

NUNEZ, GEORGE W.: Company B, private. October 10, 1861 enlisted as a private in Co. K, 2nd Regiment, 1st Brigade, Georgia State Troops. April 1862 mustered out. April 21, 1862 enlisted as a private in Co. B, 54th Regiment, Georgia Infantry at Savannah, Georgia and received bounty $50.00. December 31, 1862 received pay. January – February 1863 roll shows him present. January 1864 and April 25, 1864 issued clothing. May 10, 1865 surrendered at Tallahassee, Florida. May 24, 1865 paroled at Thomasville, Georgia.

NUNN, E. C.: Company G (F), private. He enlisted as a private in Co. F, 54th Regiment, Georgia Infantry April 26, 1865 surrendered in Co. F, 54th Regiment, Consolidated Georgia Infantry at Greensboro, North Carolina. May 1, 1865 paroled at Greensboro, North Carolina.

NUNNALLY (NUNNERY), LITTLEBURY B.: Company H, private. November 3, 1862 enlisted as a private in Co. H, 54th Regiment, Georgia Infantry at Columbus, Georgia and received bounty $50.00. November 1862 roll shows his enlistment. December 31, 1862 received pay. January – February 1863 roll shows him present. October 31, 1863 received pay.

November – December 1863 roll shows him present. December 31, 1863 received pay. January 1864 issued clothing. January – February 1864 roll shows him present (on picket). April 25, 1864 issued clothing. December 28, 1864 took the oath of allegiance at Nashville, Tennessee. He is described as: a resident of Harris County, Georgia, fair complexion, sandy hair, grey eyes, 6 feet 2 inches high with a wife and two children.

ODOM, BENJAMIN F.: Company G, sergeant. May 12, 1863 enlisted as 4th sergeant in Co. G, 54th Regiment, Georgia Infantry at Columbus, Georgia and received bounty $50.00. December 31, 1862 received pay. January – February 1863 roll shows him absent on recruiting service with Lieutenant Thomas since February 9, 1863. January 1864 issued clothing. May 8, 1864 issued clothing. Pension records show; May 25, 1864 he was wounded and disabled at New Hope Church, Georgia. He was in the hospital at the close of the war.

ODUM, ISAAC M.: Company K, private. November 15, 1862 enlisted as a private in Co. K, 54th Regiment, Georgia Infantry at Beaulieu near Savannah, Georgia and received bounty $50.00. November 1862 roll shows his enlistment. January 1, 1863 received pay. January – February 1863 roll shows him present (in hospital). September 23, 1863 received pay $44.00. March 18, 1864 and June 2, 1864 issued clothing. July 3, 1864 captured near Marietta, Georgia. July 12, 1864 sent to Military Prison at Louisville, Kentucky from Nashville, Tennessee. July 14, 1864 received at Military Prison at Louisville, Kentucky from Nashville, Tennessee. July 14, 1864 sent to Camp Douglas, Illinois from Military Prison at Louisville, Kentucky. July 16, 1864 received at Camp Douglas, Illinois from Military Prison at Louisville, Kentucky. June 16, 1865 discharged at Camp Douglas, Illinois. He is described as light complexion, light hair, blue eyes, 6 feet 3 inches high and was a resident of Stockton, Lowndes County, Georgia.

OGDEN, ISAAC M.: Company B, private. April 21, 1862 enlisted as a private in Co. B, 54th Regiment, Georgia Infantry at Savannah, Georgia and received bounty $50.00. December 31, 1862 received pay. January – February 1863 roll shows him present (absent without leave 3 days). He was born August 15, 1842 and died April 30, 1925. He is buried in Piney Grove Church Cemetery in Wayne County, Georgia. He was born August 15, 1842 and died April 30, 1925. He is buried in Piney Grove Church Cemetery in Wayne County, Georgia.

OGDEN, ISHAM C.: Company B, private. October 10, 1861 enlisted as a private in Co. K, 2nd Regiment, 1st Brigade, Georgia State Troops. He was appointed 2nd corporal of Co. K, 2nd Regiment, 1st Brigade, Georgia State Troops. April 1862 mustered out. April 21, 1862 enlisted as a private and was appointed 2nd corporal in Co. B, 54th Regiment, Georgia Infantry at Savannah, Georgia and received bounty $50.00. December 31, 1862 received pay. January – February 1863 roll shows him absent (on 12 hours leave for the day only). January 1864 and April 25, 1864 issued clothing. May 10, 1865 surrendered at Tallahassee, Florida. May

21, 1865 paroled at Thomasville, Georgia. (Another record shows: He was born April 18, 1848 and died January 18, 1908.) He was born May 8, 1836 and died November 3, 1910. He is buried in Piney Grove Church Cemetery in Wayne County, Georgia. (find a grave #36428482)

OGDEN, JAMES: Company B, private. He enlisted as a private in Co. B, 54th Regiment, Georgia Infantry. August 17, 1863 died in Charleston, South Carolina. He is buried in the confederate section of Magnolia Cemetery at Charleston, South Carolina. (find a grave # 112694959)

OGDEN, JOHN R.: Company B, private. October 10, 1861 enlisted as a private in Co. K, 2nd Regiment, 1st Brigade, Georgia State Troops. April 1862 mustered out. April 21, 1862 enlisted as a private in Co. B, 54th Regiment, Georgia Infantry at Savannah, Georgia and received bounty $50.00. December 31, 1862 received pay. January – February 1863 roll shows him present. January 1864 issued clothing. June 27, 1864 wounded at Kennesaw Mountain near Atlanta, Georgia. He contracted gangrene in the wound. Pension records show he was at home on wounded furlough at the close of the war.

May 10, 1865 surrendered at Tallahassee, Florida. May 20, 1865 paroled at Thomasville, Georgia. He was born December 8, 1841 and died June 17, 1914. He is buried in Piney Grove Church Cemetery in Wayne County, Georgia. (find a grave #68159820)

OGLESBY, A. R.: Company C, private. October 4, 1864 enlisted as a private in Co. C, 54th Regiment, Georgia Infantry at Griffin, Georgia. January 1, 1864 received pay. January – February 1864 roll shows him present. April 25, 1864 issued clothing.

OGLESBY (OGLESBEE), ARCHIBALD: Company D, private. October 7, 1861 enlisted as a private in Co. I, 5th Regiment, Georgia State Troops. April 1862 mustered out. April 30, 1862 enlisted as a private in Co. D, 54th Regiment, Georgia Infantry at Savannah, Georgia and received bounty $50.00. December 31, 1862 received pay. January – February 1863 roll shows him present (sick in hospital). August 23 – 30, 1863 wounded (concussion) at Battery Wagner on Morris Island, South Carolina. January 1864 and April 25, 1864 issued clothing. He was born in Screven County, Georgia February 1844 and died there April 3, 1920.

OGLESBY, B. S.: Company C, private. October 1, 1864 enlisted as a private in Co. C, 54th Regiment, Georgia Infantry at Griffin, Georgia. January 1, 1864 received pay. January – February 1864 roll shows him present. April 25, 1864 and May 8, 1864 issued clothing. May 24, 1865 surrendered and paroled at Augusta, Georgia.

OGLESBY (OGLESBEE), FRANCIS ALLEN (W.): Company D, private. October 7, 1861 enlisted as a private in Co. I, 5th Regiment, Georgia State Troops. April 1862 mustered out. April 30, 1862 enlisted as a private in Co. D, 54th Regiment, Georgia Infantry at Savannah, Georgia and received bounty $50.00. December 31, 1862 received pay. January – February 1863 roll shows him present. January 1864 and April 25, 1864 issued clothing. July 22, 1864 wounded at Atlanta, Georgia. He was at home, wounded at the close of the war.

OGLESBY (OGLESBEE), J. W.: Company C, private. He enlisted as a private in Co. C, 54th Regiment, Georgia Infantry. May 30, 1865 surrendered and paroled at Augusta, Georgia.

OGLESBY, K. T.: Company C, private. October 1, 1862 enlisted as a private in Co. C, 54th Regiment, Georgia Infantry.

OGLESBY, SEABORN, JR.: Company C, private. May 6, 1862 enlisted as a private in Co. C, 54th Regiment, Georgia Infantry at Savannah, Georgia and received bounty $50.00. December 31, 1862 received pay. January – February 1863 roll shows him present. January 1, 1864 received pay. January – February 1864 roll shows him present. April 25, 1864 and May 8, 1864 issued clothing. August 29 – September 3, 1863 killed at Battery Wagner on Morris Island, South Carolina. He was a resident of Emanuel County, Georgia.

OGLESBY, SEABORN ALLEN, SR.: Company C, private. May 6, 1862 enlisted as a private in Co. C, 54th Regiment, Georgia Infantry at Savannah, Georgia and received bounty $50.00. December 31, 1862 received pay. January – February 1863 roll shows him present. Pension records show: April 26, 1865 surrendered at Greensboro, North Carolina. May 1, 1865 paroled at Greensboro, North Carolina.
He was a resident of Emanuel County, Georgia. He was born in Georgia June 5, 1829 and died May 5, 1863 (some records show 1880). He is buried in Deep Creek Baptist Church Cemetery in Jenkins County, Georgia. (find a grave #48402140)

OGLESBY, WILLIAM M.: Company C, private. December 11, 1861 enlisted as a private in Co. B, 8th Regiment, Georgia State Troops. He mustered out in 1862. April 22, 1862 enlisted as a private in Co. C, 54th Regiment, Georgia Infantry at Savannah, Georgia and received bounty $50.00. December 31, 1862 received pay. January – February 1863 roll shows him present. May 1, 1863 received pay. August 27 (23 – 30), 1863 wounded (flesh wound in right shoulder and concussion) at Battery Wagner on Morris Island, South Carolina. January – February 1864 roll shows him present. April 25, 1864 and April 28, 1864 issued clothing. Pension records show he was at home on sick furlough at the close of the war. May 24, 1865 surrendered and paroled at Augusta, Georgia.

OGLETREE, JAMES B.: Company G (F), private. August 8, 1862 enlisted as a private in Co. G, 54th Regiment, Georgia Infantry at Columbus, Georgia and received bounty $50.00. August 1862 roll shows his enlistment. December 31, 1862 received pay. January – February 1863 roll shows him present. September 11, 1863 received pay $44.00. January 1864 and May 8, 1864 issued clothing. April 26, 1865 surrendered in Co. F, 54th Regiment, Consolidated Georgia Infantry at Greensboro, North Carolina. May 1, 1865 paroled at Greensboro, North Carolina. He was born in Wilkes County, Georgia December 3, 1800 and died at Auburn, Lee County, Alabama April 15, 1866. He is buried in Pine Hill Cemetery at Auburn, Lee County, Alabama. (find a grave # 101198208)

OLDHAM, JOSEPH: Company E, private. He enlisted as a private in Co. E, 54th Regiment, Georgia Infantry. He was captured and became a prisoner of war.

OLIVER, D. M.: Company B, private. He enlisted as a private in Co. B, 54th Regiment, Georgia Infantry.

OLIVER, J. R.: Company B, private. He enlisted as a private in Co. B, 54th Regiment, Georgia Infantry.

OLLIFF, JAMES: Company I, private. September 4, 1862 enlisted as a private in Co. I, 54th Regiment, Georgia Infantry at Beaulieu near Savannah, Georgia and received bounty $50.00. December 31, 1862 received pay. January – February 1863 roll shows him present (camp guard). October 31, 1863 received pay. November – December 1863 roll shows him present (sick in post hospital). January 1864, April 25, 1864 and June 2, 1864 issued clothing.

O'CONNER, FRANKLIN G.: Company H, private. March 13, 1863 enlisted as a private in Co. H, 54th Regiment, Georgia Infantry at Columbus, Georgia and received bounty $50.00. August 31, 1863 received pay. November – December 1863 roll shows him absent (sick in General Hospital at Savannah, Georgia). December 31, 1863 received pay. January 1864 issued clothing. January – February 1864 roll shows him present. April 25, 1864 issued clothing. November 30, 1864 roll of provost guard at Columbus, Georgia shows him present.

O'KELLEY, W. F.: Company I, private. He enlisted in Co. E, 37th Regiment, Georgia infantry. January 19, 1865 enlisted in Co. I, 54th Regiment, Georgia Infantry at Tupelo, Mississippi. April 26, 1865 deserted.

O'NEAL, WILLIAM A.: Company G, private. May 12, 1862 enlisted as a private in Co. G, 54th Regiment, Georgia Infantry at Columbus, Georgia and received bounty $50.00. December 31, 1862 received pay. January – February 1863 roll shows him present. January 1864, April 25, 1864 and May 8, 1864 issued clothing.

O'QUINN, FRANCIS: Company B, private. April 21, 1862 enlisted as a private in Co. B, 54th Regiment, Georgia Infantry at Savannah, Georgia and received bounty $50.00. December 31, 1862 received pay. January – February 1863 roll shows him present. January 1864 and May 8, 1864 issued clothing. He was born September 25, 1840 and died May 17, 1916. He is buried in Mt. Vernon Baptist Church Cemetery in Appling County, Georgia. (find a grave #71880868)

O'QUINN, GEORGE W.: Company K, private. October 3, 1861 enlisted as a private in Co. A, 1st Regiment, 1st Brigade, Georgia State Troops. April 1862 mustered out. April 18, 1862 enlisted as a private in Co. K, 54th Regiment, Georgia Infantry at Savannah, Georgia and received bounty $50.00. July 30, 1862 transferred to Co. C, 1st Georgia Sharpshooters by Special Order No. 259. May-June 1863 roll shows him present. He was born December 14, 1849 and died July 4, 1915. He is buried in the O'Quinn Baptist Church Cemetery in Wayne County, Georgia. (find a grave #54205045)

O'QUINN, SILAS, SR.: Company B, private. October 10, 1861 enlisted as a private and appointed 3rd sergeant in Co. K, 2nd Regiment, 1st Brigade, Georgia State Troops. April 1862 mustered out. September 5, 1862 enlisted as a private in Co. B, 54th Regiment, Georgia Infantry. October 15, 1862 transferred to Co. K, Clinch's 4th Regiment, Georgia Cavalry. March 1864 roll shows him present. May 10, 1865 surrendered at Tallahassee, Florida. May 25, 1865 paroled at Thomasville, Georgia. He was born in Georgia. He was born in Sampson County, North Carolina July 24, 1789 and died in Wayne County, Georgia January 6, 1880. He is buried in the Silas O'Quinn Family Cemetery at Odum, Wayne County, Georgia. (find a grave # 72684070)

O'QUINN, SILAS ATKISON: Company B, private. October 10, 1861 enlisted as a private in Co. K, 2nd Regiment, 1st Brigade, Georgia State Troops. April 1862 mustered out. September 5, 1862 enlisted as a private in Co. B, 54th Regiment, Georgia Infantry. March 1864 roll shows him present. May 10, 1865 surrendered at Tallahassee, Florida. May 25, 1865 paroled at Thomasville, Georgia. He was born in Appling County, Georgia May 14, 1827 and died in Georgia April 17, 1907. He is buried in Bachlott Cemetery at Bachlott, Brantley County, Georgia. (find a grave # 9292395)

OSWALT, JOSEPH: Company G, private. February 3, 1863 enlisted as a private in Co. G, 54th Regiment, Georgia Infantry at Columbus, Georgia and received bounty $50.00. January – February 1863 roll shows him present. January 1864 issued clothing. January 25, 1864 detailed as shoemaker at Columbus, Georgia (50 years of age and physically disabled). June 25, 1864 detail extender Special Order No, 148/4. August 20, 1864 he is shown on roll of men employed on extra duty at Columbus, Georgia.

OUSLEY, ANDREW J.: Company G, private. May 12, 1862 enlisted as a private in Co. G, 54th Regiment, Georgia Infantry at Columbus, Georgia and received bounty $50.00. January – February 1863 roll shows him present. December 31, 1863 received pay. January 1864 and April 25, 1864 issued clothing. December 5, 1864 admitted to of Bemiss Hospital at Opelika, Alabama. December 7, 1864 Hospital Muster Roll of Bemiss Hospital at Opelika, Alabama shows him present as a patient.

OUTLAW, WILLIAM H.: Company E, private. October 6, 1861 enlisted as a private in Co. K, 5th Regiment, Georgia State Troops. April 1862 mustered out. May 6, 1862 enlisted as a private in Co. E, 54th Regiment, Georgia Infantry at Savannah, Georgia and received bounty $50.00. December 31, 1862 received pay. January – February 1863 roll shows him present. January 1864 and May 8, 1864 issued clothing. Pension records show; he suffered hernia lifting heavy iron on gun boat. He was at home wounded at the close of the war. He was born in Dade County, Alabama January 29, 1840 and died July 28, 1910. He is buried in Pleasant Cemetery at Ray City, Berrien County, Georgia. (find a grave

123815303)

OVERSTREET, GEORGE M. T.: Company K, sergeant. April 18, 1862 enlisted as a private in Co. K, 54th Regiment, Georgia Infantry at Savannah, Georgia and received bounty $50.00. December 1862 roll shows him color sergeant. He was elected 3rd sergeant of Co. K, 54th Regiment, Georgia Infantry. January 1, 1863 received pay. January – February 1863 roll shows him present. March 18, 1864 issued clothing. May 10, 1865 surrendered at Tallahassee, Florida. May 23, 1865 paroled at Thomasville, Georgia. He was born in Appling County, Georgia July 21, 1824 and died in Surrency, Appling County, Georgia September 11, 1911. He is buried in the Overstreet Cemetery in Appling County, Georgia (find a grave #10405502)

OVERSTREET, HENRY: Company D, private. January 20, 1863 enlisted as a private in Co. D, 54th Regiment, Georgia Infantry at Beaulieu near Savannah, Georgia and received bounty $50.00. December 31, 1862 received pay. January – February 1863 roll shows him present (on picket). July 1, 1863 detailed to the medical department at Savannah, Georgia as a hospital steward at a rate of $.25 extra per day. August 31, 1863 received pay. October 31, 1863 he appears on a list of men detailed at James Island, South Carolina. January – February 1864 roll of hospital at Rose Dew Post near Savannah, Georgia shows him present as a steward.

OVERSTREET, J. H.: Company K, private. He enlisted as a private in Co. K, 54th Regiment, Georgia Infantry at Savannah, Georgia and received bounty $50.00. May 15, 1862 deserted at Savannah, Georgia. August 1862 roll reflects his desertion.

OVERSTREET, MOSES L.: Company B, private. October 10, 1861 enlisted as a private in Co. K, 2nd Regiment, 1st Brigade, Georgia State Troops. April 1862 mustered out. He enlisted as a private in Co. K, 54th Regiment, Georgia Infantry at Savannah, Georgia and received bounty $50.00. June 27, 1864 wounded, necessitating amputating finger on left hand at Kennesaw Mountain near Atlanta, Georgia. May 10, 1865 surrendered at Tallahassee, Florida. May 23, 1865 paroled at Thomasville, Georgia. He was born in Appling County, Georgia August 27, 1825 and died in Baxley, Appling County, Georgia July 26, 1895. He is buried in Bethel United Methodist Church Cemetery in Appling County, Georgia. (find a grave #25379337)

OVERSTREET, WILLIAM H.: Company B, private. October 10, 1861 enlisted as a private in Co. K, 2nd Regiment, Georgia State Troops. April 1862 mustered out. April 21, 1862 enlisted as a private in Co. B, 54th Regiment, Georgia Infantry at Savannah, Georgia and received bounty $50.00. January 19, 1863 discharged by civil authority. January – February 1863 roll shows his discharge. He was born September 17, 1827 and died in Surrency, Appling County, Georgia January 27, 1892. He is buried in the Overstreet Cemetery in Appling County, Georgia. (find a grave #44719639)

PACETTY, ALEXANDER: Company F, private. May 17, 1861

enlisted as a private in Chisholm's Company, Georgia State Troops. May 1862 mustered out. May 13, 1862 enlisted as a private in Co. F, 54th Regiment, Georgia Infantry at Savannah, Georgia and received bounty $50.00. September 5, 1862 he was discharged. September 1862 roll shows his discharge.

PALMER, THOMAS H.: Company H, private. June 5, 1863 enlisted as a private in Co. H, 54th Regiment, Georgia Infantry at Beaulieu near Savannah, Georgia and received bounty $50.00. October 31, 1863 received pay. November – December 1863 roll shows him present. December 31, 1863 received pay. January 1864 issued clothing. January – February 1864 roll shows him present. June 2, 1864 issued clothing. June 18, 1864 captured near Marietta, Georgia. June 26, 1864 received at Military Prison at Louisville, Kentucky from Nashville, Tennessee. June 27, 1864 sent to Camp Morton, Indiana from Military Prison at Louisville, Kentucky. June 28, 1864 received at Camp Morton, Indiana from Military Prison at Louisville, Kentucky. February 19, 1865 transferred for exchange from Camp Morton, Indiana. February 19, 1865 paroled at Camp Morton, Indiana and forwarded to Point Lookout, Maryland via Baltimore, Maryland. March 3, 1865 admitted to Receiving and Wayside Hospital or General Hospital No. 9 at Richmond, Virginia. March 4, 1865 transferred to Howard Grove Hospital at Richmond, Virginia. March 5, 1865 admitted to Jackson Hospital at Richmond, Virginia. March 9, 1865 furloughed for 60 days from Jackson Hospital at Richmond, Virginia.

PALMER, WYCHE J.: Company H, private. February 11, 1863 enlisted as a private in Co. H, 54th Regiment, Georgia Infantry at Columbus, Georgia and received bounty $50.00. January – February 1863 roll shows him present. October 31, 1863 received pay. November – December 1863 roll shows him present. December 31, 1863 received pay. January 1864 issued clothing. January – February 1864 roll shows him present. He died December 7, 1898. He is buried in Moon – David Cemetery at Columbus, Muscogee County, Georgia. (find a grave # 34102217)

PARISH, PETER: Company C, private. May 21, 1863 enlisted as a private in Co. C, 54th Regiment, Georgia Infantry at Savannah, Georgia and received bounty $50.00. January 1, 1864 received pay. January – February 1864 roll shows him present. Pension records show: April 26, 1865 surrendered at Greensboro, North Carolina. May 1, 1865 paroled at Greensboro, North Carolina. He was born in Hancock County, Georgia March 1824.

PARKER, HENRY L.: Company G, private. May 12, 1862 enlisted as a private in Co. G, 54th Regiment, Georgia Infantry at Savannah, Georgia and received bounty $50.00. July 2, 1862 detailed for extra duty with the medical department as an ambulance driver at a rate of $.25 extra per day. July, August, September and October 1862 rolls show him detailed as an ambulance driver. September 1862 received pay. October 31, 1862 died at Beaulieu near Savannah, Georgia. October 1862 roll shows his death.

PARKER, ISRAEL: Company D, corporal. October 7, 1861 enlisted as a private in Co. I, 5th Regiment, Georgia State Troops. April 1862 mustered out. April 30, 1862 enlisted as 4th corporal of Co. D, 54th Regiment, Georgia Infantry at Savannah, Georgia and received bounty $50.00. December 31, 1862 received pay. January – February 1863 roll shows him present. January 1864 and April 25, 1864 issued clothing. He was born October 27, 1841 and died July 27, 1904. He is buried in McDonald Baptist Cemetery at Sylvania, Screven County, Georgia. (find a grave # 115285696)

PARKER, JOHN: Company D, sergeant. April 30, 1862 enlisted as 4th sergeant in Co. D, 54th Regiment, Georgia Infantry at Savannah, Georgia and received bounty $50.00.

PARKER, JOHN: Company D, private. April 30, 1862 enlisted as a private in Co. D, 54th Regiment, Georgia Infantry at Savannah, Georgia and received bounty $50.00. December 31, 1862 received pay. January – February 1863 roll shows him present. January 1864 issued clothing. July 5, 1864 died in Catoosa Hospital at Griffin, Georgia of Febris Congestion.

PARKER, L. H.: Company G, private. He enlisted as a private in Co. G, 54th Regiment, Georgia Infantry.

PARKER, PRESTON: Company G, private. October 18, 1862 enlisted as a private in Co. G, 54th Regiment, Georgia Infantry at Columbus, Georgia and received bounty $50.00. December 31, 1862 received pay. January – February 1863 roll shows him present. January 1864 and May 8, 1864 issued clothing.

PARKER, SAMPSON D.: Company G, corporal. May 12, 1862 enlisted as 2nd corporal in Co. G, 54th Regiment, Georgia Infantry at Columbus, Georgia and received bounty $50.00. December 31, 1862 received pay. January – February 1863 roll shows him present.

PARKMAN, WILLIAM H.: Company G, private. May 12, 1862 enlisted as a private in Co. G, 54th Regiment, Georgia Infantry at Columbus, Georgia and received bounty $50.00. May 25, 1862 deserted at Savannah, Georgia. August 1862 roll shows his desertion. He was born January 8, 1831 and died May 7, 1907. He is buried in Fort Benning Cemetery #2 at Fort Benning, Chattahoochee County, Georgia. (find a grave # 29562290)

PARR, WILLIAM M.: Company E, private. May 6, 1862 enlisted as a private in Co. E, 54th Regiment, Georgia Infantry at Savannah, Georgia and received bounty $50.00. December 31, 1862 received pay. January – February 1863 roll shows him present. June 2, 1864 issued clothing. Pension records show he was at home on furlough at the close of the war. He was born in South Carolina January 30, 1842 and died in Berrien County, Georgia August 8, 1917. He is buried in Flat Creek Cemetery in Berrien County, Georgia. (find a grave # 61946866)

PARRISH, C. A. J.: Company A, private. He enlisted as a private in Co. A, 54th Regiment, Georgia Infantry. September 17, 1862 he died at Beaulieu near Savannah, Georgia. September 1862 roll shows his death. February 9, 1863 death benefit claim was filed by his widow, Sarah Parrish.

He was a resident of Jones, County, Georgia.

PARRISH, C. C.: Company A, private. He enlisted as a private in Co. A, 54th Regiment, Georgia Infantry.

PARRISH, E. C.: Company A, private. September 1, 1863 enlisted as a private in Co. A, 54th Regiment, Georgia Infantry at Macon, Georgia. October 31, 1863 received pay. November – December 1863 roll shows him present. January 1, 1864 received pay. January – February 1864 roll shows him present. March 31, 1864 issued clothing.

PARRISH, PETER: Company C, private. He enlisted as a private in Co. C, 54th Regiment, Georgia Infantry.

PATE, JORDAN P.: Company G, private. January 22, 1863 enlisted as a private in Co. G, 54th Regiment, Georgia Infantry at Columbus, Georgia and received bounty $50.00. January – February 1863 roll shows him present. June 1, 1863 to June 30, 1863 detailed for extra duty at Beaulieu near Savannah, Georgia at a rate of $.25 extra per day. June 1863 received pay. January 1864, April 25, 1864 and May 8, 1864 issued clothing. He was born in Georgia January 6, 1833 and died in Chattahoochee County, Georgia January 9, 1914. He is buried in Johnson Cemetery #44 in Chattahoochee County, Georgia. (find a grave # 19664810)

PATTEN, GEORGE I. (T.): Company I, private. October 13, 1863 enlisted as a private in Co. I, 54th Regiment, Georgia Infantry at Rose Dew near Savannah, Georgia and received bounty $50.00. October 31, 1863 received pay. November – December 1863 roll shows him present (adjutant's clerk).
January 1864 issued clothing.

PATTEN, H. D.: Company I, private. He enlisted as a private in Co. I, 54th Regiment, Georgia Infantry.

PATTON (PATTEN), HENRY: Company G, private. January 22, 1863 enlisted as a private in Co. G, 54th Regiment, Georgia Infantry at Columbus, Georgia and received bounty $50.00. January – February 1863 roll shows him present. January 1864 issued clothing. July 29, 1864 died of Dysentery at Macon, Georgia. He is buried in Rose Hill Cemetery at Macon, Georgia. (Find a grave # 94924942)

PATTEN, JAMES MADISON: Company E, private. May 6, 1862 enlisted as a private in Co. E, 54th Regiment, Georgia Infantry at Savannah, Georgia and received bounty $50.00. December 31, 1862 received pay. January – February 1863 roll shows him present. January 1864, April 25, 1864, June 2, 1864 and August 26, 1864 issued clothing. October 17, 1864 register of Floyd House Hospital at Macon, Georgia shows him as a patient with Chronic Diarrhoea and Emaciation. He was a resident of Milltown, Georgia. He was born September 24, 1832 and died December 20, 1907. He is buried in Union Primitive Baptist Church Cemetery at Lakeland, Lanier County, Georgia. (find a grave # 34693768)

PATTEN, JEHU: Company E, sergeant. October 6, 1861 enlisted as a private in Co. K, 5th Regiment, Georgia State Troops. April 1862 mustered out. May 6, 1862 enlisted as a private in Co. E, 54th Regiment, Georgia

Infantry at Savannah, Georgia and received bounty $50.00. He was elected 4th sergeant of Co. E, 54th Regiment, Georgia Infantry. December 31, 1862 received pay. January – February 1863 roll shows him present. January 1864 and May 8, 1864 issued clothing. Pension records show; November 1864 he was at home on 60 day sick furlough at the close of the war. Furlough was extended. He could not reach his command due to intervention of the enemy. He was born in Irwin County, Georgia August 15, 1839 and died in Berrien County, Georgia July 24, 1907. He is buried in Union Primitive Baptist Church Cemetery at Lakeland, Lanier County, Georgia. (find a grave # 34693842)

PATTEN, WILLIAM C.: Company I, private. He enlisted as a private in Co. I, 54th Regiment, Georgia Infantry. April 25, 1864 issued clothing.

PATTERSON, ABRAHAM E.: Company K (F), private. October 3, 1861 enlisted as a private in Co. A, 1st Regiment, 1st Brigade, Georgia State Troops. April 1862 mustered out. October 3, 1861 enlisted as a private in Co. A, 1st Regiment, 1st Brigade, Georgia State Troops. April 1862 mustered out. April 18, 1862 enlisted as 3rd sergeant in Co. K, 54th Regiment, Georgia Infantry at Savannah, Georgia and received bounty $50.00. January 1, 1863 received pay. January 1, 1863 transferred as a private from Co. K, 54th Regiment, Georgia Infantry to Co. F, 54th Regiment, Georgia Infantry. January – February 1863 rolls show him present (transferred from Co. K, 54th Regiment, Georgia Infantry to Co. F, 54th Regiment, Georgia Infantry). November 1, 1863 received pay. November – December 1863 roll shows him present. January 1864 issued clothing. May 10, 1865 surrendered at Tallahassee, Florida. May 21, 1865 paroled at Thomasville, Georgia. He was born in Appling County, Georgia.

PATTERSON, ALF W.: Company A, private. January 8, 1864 enlisted as a private in Co. A, 54th Regiment, Georgia Infantry at Savannah, Georgia and received bounty $50.00. January – February 1864 roll shows him present (sick in company hospital). May 8, 1864 issued clothing. November 23, 1864 captured at Gordon, Georgia. February 1, 1865 arrived at Point Lookout, Maryland from Hilton Head, South Carolina. June 15, 1865 took the Oath of Allegiance and was released from Point Lookout, Maryland. He is described as: a resident of Wilkinson County, Georgia, light complexion, light hair, blue eyes and 5 feet 7 3/4 inches high.

PATTERSON, ISHAM: Company K, lieutenant. October 3, 1861 enlisted as a private in Co. A, 1st Regiment, 1st Brigade, Georgia State Troops. April 1862 mustered out. April 18, 1862 enlisted as a private in Co. K, 54th Regiment, Georgia Infantry at Savannah, Georgia and received bounty $50.00. January 1, 1863 received pay. January – February 1863 roll shows him present. December 1863 he was promoted to 2nd lieutenant of Co. K, 54th Regiment, Georgia Infantry. June 7, 1864 he received pay $240.00 (as a lieutenant). July 1864 received pay $80.00. October 17, 1864 admitted to Ocmulgee Hospital at Macon, Georgia with Chronic Diarrhoea. October 26, 1864 transferred to Appling County, Georgia.

December 19, 1864 received pay $80.00. He was a resident of Appling County, Georgia. He was born June 4, 1838 and died August 28, 1902. He is buried in Antioch Methodist Church Cemetery at Homerville, Clinch County, Georgia. (find a grave # 24883322)

PATTERSON, JASPER: Company K, private. May 5, 1862 enlisted as a private in Co. K, 54th Regiment, Georgia Infantry at Savannah, Georgia and received bounty $50.00. January 1, 1863 received pay. January – February 1863 roll shows him present. He died at James Island, South Carolina.

PATTERSON, JOHNSON: Company K, lieutenant. May 27, 1863 appointed Jr. 2nd lieutenant. October 21, 1863 his name appears on a list of officers at Legare's Point, South Carolina. July 15, 1865 he was sent to the General Hospital by the Brigade Surgeon. August 25, 1864 report of Mercer's Brigade in the field near Atlanta, Georgia shows him sick and sent to the General Hospital. September 14, 1864 report of Mercer's Brigade in camp at Jonesboro, Georgia shows him sick in the medical board hospital. January 16, 1865 Special order No. 11/5 revoked his leave of absence by surgeon's certificate. May 10, 1865 surrendered at Tallahassee, Florida. May 21, 1865 paroled at Thomasville, Georgia.

PATTERSON, S. L.: Company D, private. May 2, 1862 enlisted as a private in Co. D, 54th Regiment, Georgia Infantry. November 18, 1862 received pay $43.63. April 29, 1864 issued clothing.

PATTERSON, SAMUEL L.: Company A, private. May 3, 1862 enlisted as a private in Co. D, 57th Regiment, Georgia Infantry. July 4, 1863 captured at Vicksburg, Mississippi. July 6, 1863 paroled and exchanged at Vicksburg, Mississippi. April 1, 1864 transferred from Co. D, 57th Regiment, Georgia Infantry to Co. A, 54th Regiment, Georgia Infantry in exchange for E. W. Harvey.

PATTERSON, SOLOMOM R.: Company K, private. October 3, 1861 enlisted as a private in Co. A, 1st Regiment, 1st Brigade, Georgia State Troops. April 1862 mustered out. May 5, 1862 enlisted as 3rd sergeant in Co. K, 54th Regiment, Georgia Infantry at Savannah, Georgia and received bounty $50.00. January 1, 1863 received pay. January – February 1863 rolls show him present. March 18, 1864 issued clothing. May 23, 1864 admitted to Ocmulgee Hospital at Macon, Georgia with Remittent Febris. May 28, 1864 transferred to Green County, Mississippi. June 2, 1864 issued clothing. Pension records show; He was sick in the hospital at the close of the war. May 10, 1865 surrendered at Tallahassee, Florida. May 20, 1865 paroled at Thomasville, Georgia. He was a resident of Appling County, Georgia. He was born in Georgia August 23, 1840 and died in Appling County, Georgia September 22, 1917. He is buried in the Surrency City Cemetery, Surrency, Appling County, Georgia. (find a grave #117625690)

PATTERSON, WILLIAM CRAVEN, SR.: Company A, private. June 17, 1863 enlisted a private in Co. A, 54th Regiment, Georgia Infantry at Macon, Georgia and received bounty $50.00. June 30, 1863 roll shows him present. October 31, 1863 received pay. November – December 1863 roll shows him present. January 1, 1864 received pay. January – February 1864 roll shows him present. March 31, 1864 and April 29, 1864 issued clothing. September 1, 1864 he was killed at Jonesboro, Georgia. He was born in Buncombe County, North Carolina November 5, 1813 and died at Jonesboro, Georgia September 1, 1864. He is buried in the Patterson Family Cemetery at Ivey, Wilkinson County, Georgia. (find a grave # 43308331)

PATTON, S. A.: Company B, private. March 4, 1862 enlisted as a private in Co. B, 54th Regiment, Georgia Infantry at Forsythe, Georgia. April 30, 1864 received pay. December 31, 1864 muster roll of Co. C, 2nd Battalion Troops and Defences, Macon, Georgia shows him present.

PAYNE, GREEN BERRY: Company A, private. October 17, 1863 enlisted as a private in Co. A, 54th Regiment, Georgia Infantry at Savannah, Georgia and received bounty $50.00. October 31, 1863 received pay. November – December 1863 roll shows him present. January 1, 1864 received pay. January – February 1864 roll shows him present. April 29, 1864 issued clothing. December 19, 1864 captured near Murfreesboro, Tennessee. January 2, 1865 received at Military Prison at Louisville, Kentucky from Nashville, Tennessee. January 4, 1865 sent to Camp Chase, Ohio from Military Prison at Louisville, Kentucky. January 6, 1865 received at Camp Chase, Ohio from Military Prison at Louisville, Kentucky. April 22, 1865 enlisted in U. S. Army. He was born in North Carolina August 10, 1835 and died in Swain County, North Carolina August 13, 1901. He is buried in Paynetown Cemetery in Swain County, North Carolina. (find a grave # 35324182)

PAYNE, IRA: Company F, private. July 28, 1862 enlisted as a private in Co. F, 54th Regiment, Georgia Infantry at Savannah, Georgia. November 1, 1863 received pay. November – December 1863 roll shows him present. January 1864, April 25, 1864 and May 8, 1864 issued clothing. June 18, 1864 captured near Marietta, Georgia. June 26, 1864 received at Military Prison at Louisville, Kentucky from Nashville, Tennessee. June 27, 1864 sent to Camp Morton, Indiana from Military Prison at Louisville, Kentucky. June 28, 1864 received at Camp Morton, Indiana from Military Prison at Louisville, Kentucky. July 20, 1864 died of measles at Camp Morton, Indiana. He was buried there in Green Lawn (now Crown Hill) Cemetery, grave No. 969. (find a grave # 14736427)

PEABODY, ELBERT WELLS: Company E, corporal. March 25, 1863 enlisted as a private in Co. H, 3rd Battalion, Georgia Infantry. May 6, 1863 transferred as a corporal in Co. E, 54th Regiment, Georgia Infantry. He was born April 6, 1845 and died March 9, 1904. He is buried in Lakeview Cemetery at Sanford, Seminole County, Florida. (find a grave # 21108984)

PEAVY, MICHAEL: Company C, private. May 6, 1862 enlisted as a private in Co. K, 54th Regiment, Georgia Infantry at Savannah, Georgia and received bounty $50.00. December 31, 1862 received pay. January

– February 1863 roll shows him present. January 1, 1864 received pay. January – February 1864 roll shows him present. April 25 and April 28, 1864 issued clothing. June 27, 1864 he was wounded in the right arm at Kennesaw Mountain, Georgia. He was a resident of Hancock County, Georgia. He was born in Georgia January 13, 1834 and died in Johnson, County, Georgia November 20, 1907. He is buried in Bethany Baptist Church Cemetery at Sandersville, Washington County, Georgia. (find a grave # 65259999)

PEEL, E.: Company D, private. April 30, 1862 enlisted as a private in Co. D, 54th Regiment, Georgia Infantry at Savannah, Georgia and received bounty $50.00. December 31, 1862 received pay. January – February 1863 roll shows him present. January 1864 and May 8, 1864 issued clothing. July 20, 1864 killed at Peachtree Creek near Atlanta, Georgia.

PEEL, HENRY W.: Company D, private. April 29, 1862 enlisted as a private in Co. D, 54th Regiment, Georgia Infantry at Beaulieu near Savannah, Georgia and received bounty $50.00. December 31, 1862 received pay. January – February 1863 roll shows him present. January 1864, April 25, 1864 and May 8, 1864 issued clothing. January 19, 1865 admitted to Way Hospital at Meridian, Mississippi with Debilitas. He was born February 1, 1845 and died September 18, 1887. He is buried in Little Buckhead Cemetery at Millen, Jenkins County, Georgia. (find a grave # 74899843)

PEEL, THOMAS: Company F, private. January 21, 1863 enlisted as a private in Co. F, 54th Regiment, Georgia Infantry at Savannah, Georgia and received bounty $50.00. January – February 1863 roll shows him present. January 1864 issued clothing.

PEELER, ISAAC JOHN: Company C (D), lieutenant. May 5, 1862 enlisted as a private in Co. C, 54th Regiment, Georgia Infantry at Savannah, Georgia and received bounty $50.00. May 6, 1862 was elected 5th sergeant of Co. C, 54th Regiment, Georgia Infantry. December 31, 1862 received pay. January – February 1863 roll shows him present. 1863 was elected 2nd sergeant of Co. C, 54th Regiment, Georgia Infantry. 1863 was elected 2nd lieutenant of Company C, 54th Regiment, Georgia Infantry. January 1, 1864 received pay. January – February 1864 roll shows him present. January 13, 1865 he was admitted to St. Mary's Hospital at West Point, Mississippi with Rheumatism. April 15, 1864 he was elected 2nd lieutenant of Company D, 54th Consolidated Regiment, Georgia Infantry. April 26, 1865 surrendered in Co. D, 54th Regiment, Consolidated Georgia Infantry at Greensboro, North Carolina. May 1, 1865 paroled at Greensboro, North Carolina. He was a resident of Hancock County, Georgia.

PENN, MONROE, JR.: Company G, private. He enlisted as a private in Co. G, 54th Regiment, Georgia Infantry.

PEOPLES, JESSE L.: Company E, sergeant. May 6, 1862 enlisted as 4th sergeant in Co. E, 54th Regiment, Georgia Infantry at Savannah, Georgia and received bounty $50.00. July 17, 1862 died of fever at Savannah, Georgia. July 1862 roll shows his death.

PEPPER, WILLIAM: Company G, private. February 12, 1863 enlisted as a private in Co. G, 54th Regiment, Georgia Infantry at Columbus, Georgia and received bounty $50.00. January – February 1863 roll shows him present. January 1864 and May 8, 1864 issued clothing.

PERDUE, ELIJAH: Company G, corporal. He enlisted as a corporal in Co. G, 54th Regiment, Georgia Infantry.

PERDUE, JAMES M.: Company H, private. February 6, 1863 enlisted as a private in Co. H, 54th Regiment, Georgia Infantry at Columbus, Georgia and received bounty $50.00. January – February 1863 roll shows him present. October 31, 1863 received pay. November – December 1863 roll shows him present. December 31, 1863 received pay. January 1864 issued clothing. January – February 1864 roll shows him present. June 2, 1864 issued clothing. Pension records show; He was paroled at the end of the war. He was born in Chattahoochee County, Georgia in 1844.

PETTINGALE, E.: Company C, private. He enlisted as a private in Co. C, 54th Regiment, Georgia Infantry. January 21, 1864 detailed on detached service.

PETTIGREW (PETTINGILL), E.: Company F, private. March 9, 1863 enlisted as a private in Co. F, 54th Regiment, Georgia Infantry at Savannah, Georgia. November 18, 1863 deserted. January – February 1863 roll shows his desertion. September 7, 1863 brought from jail in Columbus, Georgia to jail in Macon, Georgia.

PEURIFOY, CHARLES HARDY: Company G, sergeant. He enlisted as a sergeant in Co. G, 54th Regiment, Georgia Infantry. He was born in Upson County, Georgia June 30, 1838 and died in Upson County, Georgia October 8, 1900. He is buried in the Peurifoy Family Cemetery at Yatesville, Upson County, Georgia. (find a grave # 66965960)

PHELAN, P. D.: Company F, private. April; 10, 1863 enlisted as a private in Co. F, 54th Regiment, Georgia Infantry at Savannah, Georgia and received bounty $50.00. November 1, 1863 received pay. November – December 1863 roll shows him present. January 1864, April 25, 1864 and May 8, 1864 issued clothing.

PHELPS, GEORGE WASHINGTON: Company G, private. January 22, 1863 enlisted as a private in Co. G, 54th Regiment, Georgia Infantry at Columbus, Georgia and received bounty $50.00. January – February 1863 roll shows him present. April 30, 1863 received pay. November 15, 1864 Hospital Muster Roll of Ladies' Hospital at Montgomery, Alabama shows him present as a patient. January 1864 issued clothing. He was born in 1825 and died in 1898. He is buried in Union primitive Baptist Church Cemetery in Russell County, Alabama. (find a grave # 16522667)

PHILLIPS, LAFAYETTE N.: Company B, lieutenant. October 10, 1861 enlisted in and appointed 1st lieutenant of Co. K, 2nd Regiment, 1st Brigade, Georgia State Troops. April 1862 mustered out.
April 21, 1862 enlisted and elected 1st lieutenant of Co. B, 54th Regiment, Georgia Infantry at Savannah, Georgia and received bounty $50.00. July 15, 1862 he died. August 12, 1863 death benefit claim was filed Joseph

Tillman, administrator of estate. He was a resident of Appling County, Georgia. Death Benefit paid $45.00.

PHILLIPS, WILLIAM P.: Company H, private. March 23, 1863 enlisted as a private in Co. H, 54th Regiment, Georgia Infantry at Columbus, Georgia and received bounty $50.00. October 31, 1863 received pay. November – December 1863 roll shows him present. December 31, 1863 received pay. January 1864 issued clothing. January – February 1864 roll shows him present. February 29, 1864 received pay. April 25, 1864 issued clothing. September 9, 1864 admitted to Marshall Hospital at Columbus, Georgia. November 30, 1864 Hospital Muster Roll of Marshall Hospital at Columbus, Georgia shows him present as a patient. April 26, 1865 surrendered at Greensboro, North Carolina. May 1, 1865 paroled at Greensboro, North Carolina. He was born in Harris County, Georgia in 1842.

PICKLES (PICKLE), JOHN F.: Company B, private. February 7, 1862 enlisted as a private in Co. K, 2nd Regiment, 1st Brigade, Georgia State Troops. April 1862 mustered out. April 21, 1862 enlisted as a private in Co. B, 54th Regiment, Georgia Infantry at Savannah, Georgia and received bounty $50.00. June 5, 1862 detailed as wagoner (teamster) in the quartermaster's department at a rate of $.25 extra per day. July through December 1862 rolls show him detailed as a teamster at a rate of $.25 extra per day. September 1862 received pay. November 1862 received pay. December 31, 1862 received pay. June 1, 1863 to June 30, 1863 detailed as a teamster at a rate of $.25 extra per day at Beaulieu near Savannah, Georgia. July 1, 1863 to October 31, 1863 detailed as a teamster at a rate of $.25 extra per day at Charleston, South Carolina. January – February 1863 roll shows him present (employed as a teamster in the quartermaster's department). October 31, 1863 list of men detailed at James Island, South Carolina shows him as a driver (teamster) for the quartermaster's department. September 1, 1863 to December 31, 1863 detailed as a teamster at a rate of $.25 extra per day on James Island, South Carolina. November 16, 1863 received pay. January 1864 issued clothing. January 1, 1864 to February 29, 1864 detailed as a teamster at a rate of $.25 extra per day in Savannah, Georgia. March 1, 1861 to March 31, 1864 detailed as a teamster at Hardeeville, South Carolina. April 1, 1864 to April 30, 1864 detailed as a teamster in Savannah, Georgia. April 25, 1864 issued clothing. November 10, 1864 took the Oath of Allegiance at Nashville, Tennessee. He is described as a resident of Wilkinson County, Georgia, fair complexion, light hair, blue eyes and 5 feet 7 ½ inches high.

PIERCE, E.: Company D, private. April 30, 1862 enlisted as a private in Co. D, 54th Regiment, Georgia Infantry at Savannah, Georgia and received bounty $50.00. December 31, 1862 received pay. January – February 1863 roll shows him present. January 1864 issued clothing.

PIERCE, E. N.: Company D, private. April 30, 1862 enlisted as a private in Co. D, 54th Regiment, Georgia Infantry at Savannah, Georgia and received bounty $50.00. December 31, 1862 received pay. January

– February 1863 roll shows him present. January 1864 issued clothing.

PIERCE, JOHN: Company F, private. January 21, 1863 enlisted as a private in Co. F, 54th Regiment, Georgia Infantry at Savannah, Georgia and received bounty $50.00. January – February 1863 roll shows him present. November 1, 1863 received pay. November – December 1863 roll shows him present.
January 1864, April 25, 1864 and May 8, 1864 issued clothing.

PIERCE, JOHN ROBERT: Company D, corporal. April 30, 1862 enlisted as 3rd corporal in Co. D, 54th Regiment, Georgia Infantry at Savannah, Georgia and received bounty $50.00. December 31, 1862 received pay. January – February 1863 roll shows him present. January 1864 and May 8, 1864 issued clothing. He was born in Georgia January 11, 1837 and died in Screven County, Georgia August 26, 1908. He is buried in McDonald Baptist Cemetery at Sylvania, Screven County, Georgia. (find a grave # 97073684)

PIGG, GEORGE TILLMAN: Company H, private. January 16, 1863 enlisted as a private in Co. H, 54th Regiment, Georgia Infantry at Savannah, Georgia and received bounty $50.00 as a substitute for R. F. Beal. January – February 1863 roll shows him present. October 31, 1863 received pay. November – December 1863 roll shows him present. December 31, 1863 received pay. January – February 1864 roll shows him present (on picket). January 1864 issued clothing. July 4, 1864 issued clothing at Cannon Hospital at Union Springs, Alabama.

PLATT (PLOTT), JOSEPH JAMES: Company G, private. May 12, 1862 enlisted as a private in Co. G, 54th Regiment, Georgia Infantry at Columbus, Georgia and received bounty $50.00. December 31, 1862 received pay. January – February 1863 roll shows him present. January 1864 issued clothing. April 25, 1864 issued clothing. July 3, 1864 captured near Marietta, Georgia. July 14, 1864 received at Military Prison at Louisville, Kentucky from Nashville, Tennessee. July 16, 1864 sent to Camp Douglas, Illinois from Military Prison at Louisville, Kentucky. July 18, 1864 received at Camp Douglas, Illinois from Military Prison at Louisville, Kentucky. May 4, 1865 forwarded to New Orleans, Louisiana for exchange from Camp Douglas, Illinois. May 11, 1865 received at New Orleans, Louisiana for exchange from Camp Douglas, Illinois. May 23, 1865 exchanged.

PLATT, MARK: Company G, private. May 12, 1862 enlisted as a private in Co. G, 54th Regiment, Georgia Infantry at Columbus, Georgia and received bounty $50.00.

POPE, GEORGE W.: Company E, private. May 6, 1862 enlisted as a private in Co. E, 54th Regiment, Georgia Infantry at Savannah, Georgia and received bounty $50.00. December 31, 1862 received pay. January – February 1863 roll shows him present. January 1864 and April 25, 1864 issued clothing.

POSS, H. T. JR.: Company K, private. He enlisted as a private in Co. K, 54th Regiment, Georgia Infantry.

POSS, H. T. SR.: Company K, private. He enlisted as a private in Co. K, 54th Regiment, Georgia Infantry.

POTTERFIELD, K. W.: Company I, private. He enlisted as a private in Co. I, 54th Regiment, Georgia Infantry.

POTTERFIELD, R. L. T.: Company I, private. He enlisted as a private in Co. I, 54th Regiment, Georgia Infantry.

POWELL, B. F.: Company D, private. July 1862 he enlisted in the Georgia Siege Artillery 9 (command not given). July 1863 he transferred as a private to Co. D, 54th Regiment, Georgia Infantry. January 1864 issued clothing. April 26, 1865 surrendered at Greensboro, North Carolina. May 1, 1865 paroled at Greensboro, North Carolina. He was born in Jefferson County, Florida April 23, 1831.

POWELL, T. W.: Company B, private. He enlisted as a private in Co. B, 54th Regiment, Georgia Infantry.

POWER, S. P.: Company I, private. He enlisted as a private in Co. I, 54th Regiment, Georgia Infantry.

POWER, T. B.: Company I, private. He enlisted as a private in Co. I, 54th Regiment, Georgia Infantry.

POWERS, T.: Company A, private. He enlisted as a private in Co. A, 54th Regiment, Georgia Infantry.

PRESCOTT, HENRY: Company K, private. September 10, 1861 enlisted in Co. I, 27th Regiment, Georgia at Camp Stephens, Spaulding County, Georgia. December 1861 in hospital at Richmond, Virginia. February 24, 1862 furloughed 60 days due to sickness. April 18, 1862 enlisted as a private in Co. K, 54th Regiment, Georgia Infantry at Savannah, Georgia and received bounty $50.00. May 15, 1862 detailed as a teamster at a rate of $.25 extra per day. November and December 1862 rolls show him detailed as a teamster. November 1, 1862 to December 31, 1862 detailed as a teamster at a rate of $.25 extra per day at Beaulieu near Savannah, Georgia. December 1862 received pay. January 1, 1863 received pay. January – February 1863 roll shows him present (detailed as a teamster in quartermaster's department). July 1, 1863 to December 31, 1863 detailed as a teamster at a rate of $.25 extra per day at Legare's Point on James Island, South Carolina. October 31, 1863 list of men detailed at James Island, South Carolina includes him. December 1863 received pay. January 1, 1864 to April 30, 1864 detailed as a teamster at a rate of $.25 extra per day. March 18, 1864, April 18, 1864, April 25, 1864 and June 2, 1864 issued clothing. May 10, 1865 surrendered at Tallahassee, Florida. May 25, 1865 paroled at Thomasville, Georgia.

PRESCOTT, N.: Company K, private. He enlisted as a private in Co. K, 54th Regiment, Georgia Infantry.

PUDER, WILLIAM B.: Company F, private. May 13, 1862 enlisted as a private in Co. F, 54th Regiment, Georgia Infantry at Savannah, Georgia and received bounty $50.00. May 13, 1862 detailed in government machine shop. October 1862 roll shows him detailed for government work. December 31, 1862 received pay. January – February 1863 roll shows him absent (detailed by order of General Lawton). October 1, 1863 detailed by order of General Mercer. November – December 1863 roll shows him absent (detailed by General Mercer). January 1864 and July 6, 1864 issued clothing. November 1864 left command due to sickness, near Franklin, Tennessee. February 15, 1865 admitted to Way Hospital at Meridian, Mississippi with Chronic Diarrhoea and was transferred to Columbus, Georgia. April 11, 1865 admitted to Ocmulgee Hospital at Macon, Georgia with Diarrhoea. April 18, 1865 transferred. April 23, 1865 admitted to Ocmulgee Hospital at Macon, Georgia with Diarrhoea. April 29, 1865 he was captured and paroled at Macon, Georgia. April 30, 1865 returned to duty. (He is shown as a resident of Choctaw County, Alabama.) He was born in Savannah, Georgia in 1844. He is buried in Catholic Cemetery at Savannah, Chatham County, Georgia. (find a grave # 80550632)

PULLIN, J. M.: Company I, private. He enlisted as a private in Co. I, 54th Regiment, Georgia Infantry.

PURVIS, STEPHEN: Company K, private. May 5, 1862 enlisted as a private in Co. K, 54th Regiment, Georgia Infantry at Savannah, Georgia and received bounty $50.00. January 1, 1863 received pay. January – February 1863 roll shows him present.

QUESENBERRY, P.: Company I, ordinance sergeant. December 31, 1862 enlisted as a private in Co. I, 54th Regiment, Georgia Infantry. August 1863 received pay. April 15, 1865 took the oath of allegiance at Louisville, Kentucky (to remain north of the Ohio River during the war). He is described as a resident of Floyd County, Georgia, fair complexion, dark hair, hazel eyes and was 6 feet high.

QUINN, J. A.: Company F, private. November 27, 1862 enlisted as a private in Co. F, 54th Regiment, Georgia Infantry at Beaulieu near Savannah, Georgia and received bounty $50.00. November roll shows his enlistment.

QUINN, PATRICK: Company F, private. July 25, 1861 he enlisted as a private in Captain J. B. Read's Independent Company, Georgia Infantry. November 1862 mustered out. December 1, 1862 enlisted as a private in Co. F, 54th Regiment, Georgia Infantry at Savannah, Georgia and received bounty $50.00. December 1862 roll shows his enlistment. December 31, 1862 received pay. January – February 1863 roll shows him present.

QUINN, WILLIAM: Field and Staff, drum major.

RABURN (RABUN), W.: Company H (A), private. May 3, 1862 enlisted as a private in Co. H 54th Regiment, Georgia Infantry at Macon, Georgia and received bounty $50.00. September 1, 1862 transferred from Co. H, 54th Regiment, Georgia Infantry to Co. A, 54th Regiment, Georgia Infantry by Special Order No. 6 at Beaulieu near Savannah, Georgia. September 1862 roll reflects the transfer. January – February 1864 roll shows him present (absent without leave for 1 year 20 days).

RABURN (RABUN), WILLIAM: Company A, private. June 9, 1861 enlisted as a private in Co. B, 12th Regiment, Georgia Infantry. July 9, 1861 discharged at Richmond, Virginia. May 18, 1862 enlisted as a private in Co. A, 54th Regiment, Georgia Infantry at Macon, Georgia and received bounty $50.00. August 31, 1862 received pay. June 30, 1863 roll shows him absent (absent sick). March 31, 1864 issued clothing.

RACKLEY, JOEL P.: Company F, private. February 1, 1863 enlisted as a private in Co. F, 54th Regiment, Georgia Infantry at Savannah, Georgia and received bounty $50.00. January – February 1863 roll shows him present. November 1, 1863 received pay. November – December 1863 roll shows him present. Pension records show; he was at home on sick furlough March 1865 to the close of the war. He was born in Burke County, Georgia May 29, 1839 and died in Screven County, Georgia December 12, 1921. He was born May 29, 1839 and died December 12, 1920. He is buried in Sylvania Cemetery at Sylvania, Screven County, Georgia. (find a grave # 32278685)

RAHN, CLAUDIUS F.: Company I, sergeant. September 18, 1861 enlisted as a private in Co. C, 1st Regiment, 1st Brigade, Georgia State Troops. March 18, 1862 mustered out. May 6, 1862 enlisted as 1st sergeant in Co. I, 54th Regiment, Georgia Infantry at Savannah, Georgia and received bounty $50.00. August 10, 1862 he died at Savannah, Georgia. August 1862 roll shows his death. He was born December 5, 1841 and died in Savannah, Chatham County, Georgia August 10, 1862. He is buried in the Springfield City Cemetery in Springfield, Effingham County, Georgia. (find a grave #50573181)

RAHN, LEWIS WILLIAM: Company I, private. September 18, 1861 enlisted as a private in Co. C, 1st Regiment, 1st Brigade, Georgia State Troops. March 18, 1862 mustered out. May 6, 1862 enlisted as private in Co. I, 54th Regiment, Georgia Infantry at Savannah, Georgia and received bounty $50.00. December 31, 1862 received pay. January – February 1863 roll shows him present. October 31, 1863 received pay. November – December 1863 roll shows him present (in arrest). January 1864 June 2, and 1864 issued clothing. He was born July 31, 1841 and died June 19, 1915. He is buried in the Springfield City Cemetery in Springfield, Effingham County, Georgia. (find a grave #40485099)

RAHN, WILLIAM O.: Company I, private. October 7, 1863 enlisted as private in Co. I, 54th Regiment, Georgia Infantry at Rose Dew near Savannah, Georgia and received bounty $50.00. October 31, 1863 received pay. November – December 1863 roll shows him absent (detailed to guard commissary at #3 C. R. R. December 15, 1863). January 1864 and April 25, 1864 issued clothing. June 20, 1864 he died of Chronic Diarrhoea in Effingham County, Georgia. He was born January 1, 1819 and died in Effingham County, Georgia June 20, 1864. He is buried in the Springfield City Cemetery in Springfield, Effingham County, Georgia. (find a grave #50573225)

RAIFORD, C. L.: Company H, private. November 3, 1862 enlisted as a private in Co. H, 54th Regiment, Georgia Infantry at Columbus, Georgia and received bounty $50.00. December 31, 1862 received pay. January

– February 1863 roll shows him present. October 31, 1863 received pay. November – December 1863 roll shows him present. December 31, 1863 received pay. January – February 1864 roll shows him present. April 26, 1865 surrendered at Greensboro, North Carolina. May 1, 1865 paroled at Greensboro, North Carolina.

RAILEY, J. H.: Company H, private. He enlisted as a private in Co. H, 54th Regiment, Georgia Infantry. January 1864 issued clothing. April 25, 1864 issued clothing.

RAILEY (RALEY), JAMES: Company A, private. October 17, 1861 enlisted as a private in Co. C, 1st Independent Battalion, Georgia State Troops. April 16, 1862 roll shows him present. April 1862 mustered out. May 1, 1863 enlisted as a private in Co. A, 54th Regiment, Georgia Infantry at Savannah, Georgia and received bounty $50.00. June 30, 1863 roll shows him present. October 31, 1863 received pay. November 1863 received pay for commutation for rations. November – December 1863 roll shows him present. January 1, 1864 received pay. January – February 1864 roll shows him present. March 31, 1863 issued clothing. August 1, 1864 he died at Thomaston, Georgia. October 26, 1864 death benefit claim was filed by his widow, Elizabeth Railey. He died July 31, 1864. He is buried in the Confederate Section of Glenwood Cemetery at Thomaston, Upson County, Georgia. (find a grave #10532222)

RAILEY (RALEY), JEFFERSON WILEY: Company H, private. May 12, 1862 enlisted as a private in Co. H, 54th Regiment, Georgia Infantry at Columbus, Georgia and received bounty $50.00. December 31, 1862 received pay. January – February 1863 roll shows him present. October 31, 1863 received pay. November – December 1863 roll shows him present. December 31, 1863 received pay. January 1864 issued clothing. January – February 1864 roll shows him present. He was born in Georgia in 1833 and died in Cataula, Harris County, Georgia. He is buried in Harmony Cemetery at Cataula, Harris County, Georgia. (find a grave # 43141062)

RAILEY (RALEY), JOHN F.: Company H, private. May 12, 1862 enlisted as a private in Co. H, 54th Regiment, Georgia Infantry at Columbus, Georgia and received bounty $50.00. November 1862 roll shows him detailed as an ambulance driver. December 31, 1862 received pay. January – February 1863 roll shows him present (detailed as an ambulance driver). October 31, 1863 received pay. November – December 1863 roll shows him present. December 31, 1863 received pay. January – February 1864 roll shows him present.

RAILEY, JOHN T.: Company H, private. He enlisted as a private in Co. H, 54th Regiment, Georgia Infantry.

RAINE, W. J.: Company A, private. He enlisted a private in Co. A, 54th Regiment, Georgia Infantry.

RAINEY, H. P.: Company E, private. He enlisted as a private in Co. E, 54th Regiment, Georgia Infantry.

RAMSEY, JOHN: Company H, private. September 1, 1862 enlisted as a private in Co. H, 54th Regiment, Georgia Infantry at Columbus, Georgia and received bounty $50.00. October, November and December 1862 rolls show him detailed as a teamster. October 13, 1862 to December 31, 1862 detailed as a teamster at a rate of $.25 extra per day. December 31, 1862 received pay. January – February 1863 roll shows him present (detailed as a teamster for quartermaster's department). June 1863 received pay at Beaulieu. June 1, 1863 to August 31, 1863 detailed as a teamster at a rate of $.25 extra per day. October 31, 1863 received pay. November 1863 received pay. November – December 1863 roll shows him present (teamster). December 31, 1863 received pay. January 1864 issued clothing. January – February 1864 roll shows him present (wagon master in quartermaster's department since February 14, 1864). February 1, 1864 to April 30, 1864 detailed as a teamster (wagon master) at a rate of $.25 extra per day. June 2, 1864 issued clothing. April 26, 1865 surrendered at Greensboro, North Carolina. May 1, 1865 paroled at Greensboro, North Carolina.

RAMSEY, JOHN: Company H, private. October 19, 1862 enlisted as a private in Co. H, 54th Regiment, Georgia Infantry at Beaulieu near Savannah, Georgia and received bounty $50.00. October 1862 roll shows his enlistment.

RATHBONE, TILLMON: Company K, private. He enlisted as a private in Co. K, 54th Regiment, Georgia Infantry.

RAWLS, JAMES F.: Company I, lieutenant. May 6, 1862 enlisted as a private in Co. I, 54th Regiment, Georgia Infantry at Savannah, Georgia and received bounty $50.00. May 16, 1862 appointed 2nd lieutenant Co. I, 54th Regiment, Georgia Infantry. July 1862 his name appears on a list of officers at Savannah, Georgia. August 1862 roll shows him present at Beaulieu near Savannah, Georgia sick in quarters. September and October 1862 rolls at Beaulieu near Savannah, Georgia show him present. November 24, 1864 his name appears on a list of officers at Savannah, Georgia. November 29, 1862 absent on sick leave. November 1862 roll shows him absent (absent with leave for 12 hours November 30, 1862). December 1862 roll shows him absent sick since December 2, 1862. He was promoted to 1st lieutenant of Co. I, 54th Regiment, Georgia Infantry. January – February 1863 roll shows him absent sick. March 4, 1863 received pay $80.00. April 2, 1863 received pay $88.00. May 22, 1863 on 10 days leave approved by General Mercer. May 30, 1863 appears on list of officers absent on approved leave. August 30, 1863 shown on list of officers on leave (absent August 24, 1863 on private business) approved by General Mercer. December 26, 1863 received pay $180.00. November – December 1863 roll shows him absent sick. December 26, 1863 he was on 30 days sick leave approved by General Beauregard. January 23, 1864 his name appears on list of officers absent (on approved leave). March 8, 1864 issued clothing. July 19, 1864 received pay $180.00. August 1, 1864 received pay. January 18, 1865 admitted to Way Hospital at Meridian, Mississippi with a Gunshot Wound and was furloughed. He was born May 20, 1831 and died May 16, 1903. He is buried in Wilson – Rawls

Cemetery in Bulloch County, Georgia. (find a grave # 97455549)

RAWLS (RAWLES), MORGAN: Field and Staff, lieutenant colonel. September 18, 1861 elected captain of Co. C. 1st Regiment, 1st Brigade, Georgia State Troops. March 1862 mustered out. May 6, 1862 elected captain of Co. I, 54th Regiment, Georgia Infantry at Savannah, Georgia. May 16, 1862 elected lieutenant colonel of 54th Regiment, Georgia Infantry at Savannah, Georgia. July 1862 his name appears on roll. August 1862 roll shows him absent on court martial since August 24, 1862. September, October and November 1862 rolls show him present at Beaulieu near Savannah, Georgia. November 14, 1862 received expense pay $120.00. November 24, 1862 appears on a list of officers at Savannah, Georgia. December 10, 1862 detailed for court martial. December 1862 roll shows him absent detailed to general court martial by special Order No. 666 on December 10, 1862. January – February 1863 roll shows him absent on General Court Martial in Savannah by Special Order No. 42. February 5, 1863 received expense pay $56.20. February 11, 1863 detailed for court martial. March 31, 1863 received pay $240.00. April 3, 1863 his name appears on a list of officers absent from command at Savannah, Georgia. October 21, 1863 his name appears on list of officers present at Legare's Point, South Carolina. October 30, 1863 granted a leave of absence to attend the General Session of the Georgia Legislature as representative from Effingham County. December 19, 1863 received pay $340.00. December 31, 1863 received pay $170.00. July 22, 1864 wounded at Atlanta, Georgia. August 25, 1864 report of Mercer's Brigade in the field near Atlanta, Georgia shows him wounded in the hospital at Guyton, Georgia. September 14, 1864 report of Mercer's Brigade in camp near Jonesboro, Georgia shows him in the Medical Board Division hospital since July 22, 1864. He was born in Statesboro, Bulloch County, Georgia June 29, 1829 and died in Guyton, Effingham County, Georgia October 18, 1906. He is buried in Guyton Cemetery at Guyton, Effingham County, Georgia. (find a grave #7980413)

RAWLS, ZACCHEUS (ZACHEUS) A.: Company I, private. September 18, 1861 enlisted as a private and appointed color sergeant in Co. C, 1st Regiment, 1st Brigade, Georgia State Troops. March 18, 1862 mustered out. May 6, 1862 enlisted as a private in Co. I, 54th Regiment, Georgia Infantry at Guyton, Georgia and received bounty $50.00. October 1862 roll shows him detailed as color bearer. December 31, 1862 received pay. January – February 1863 roll shows him present (camp guard). April 30, 1863 received pay. October 1, 1863 detailed as sub enrolling officer. November – December 1863 roll shows him absent (detailed as sub enrolling officer). January 1864 issued clothing. March 1, 1864 Special Order No. 10/5 shows him as a prisoner. June 16, 1864 released from confinement. He was born September 14, 1841 and died in Bulloch County, Georgia May 12, 1921. He is buried in New Hope United Methodist Church Cemetery at Leefield, Bulloch County, Georgia. (find a grave #75404846)

RAY, JOHN: Company E, private. May 6, 1862 enlisted as a private in

Co. E, 54th Regiment, Georgia Infantry at Savannah, Georgia and received bounty $50.00. December 31, 1862 received pay. January – February 1863 roll shows him present. January 1864 issued clothing. He was born March 13, 1838 and died May 19, 1900. He is buried in Pleasant Cemetery at Ray City, Berrien County, Georgia. (find a grave # 46656170)

RAY, RUFUS: Company E, private. 1862 enlisted as a private in Co. E, 54th Regiment, Georgia Infantry. April 1863 discharged due to disability at Savannah, Georgia. He was born in Barnwell County, South Carolina in 1837 and died in Lowndes County, Georgia in 1897. He is buried in Cat Creek Cemetery at Valdosta, Lowndes County, Georgia. (find a grave # 94036645)

RAYMUR (RAYMER), ALEXANDER J.: Company F, private. May 17, 1861 enlisted as a private in Chisholm's Company, Georgia State Troops. May 1862 mustered out. May 13, 1862 enlisted as a private in Co. F, 54th Regiment, Georgia Infantry at Savannah, Georgia and received bounty $50.00. September and October 1862 rolls show him detailed as captain's orderly. November 20, 1862 discharged by civil authority. November 1862 roll at Beaulieu near Savannah, Georgia shows his discharge. February 29, 1863 enlisted as a private in Co. F, 54th Regiment, Georgia Infantry at Savannah, Georgia. January – February 1863 roll shows him present. May 31, 1863 received commutation for rations $16.20. June 23, 1863 received commutation for rations $13.80. July 31, 1863 received pay $28.00. August 19, 1863 issued clothing. August 1863 received pay $62.00. September 1, 1863 received pay $22.00. September 1863 received pay $60.00. October 3, 1863 issued clothing. October 1863 received pay for extra duty $93.00. November 10 and 28, 1863 issued clothing. November 1863 received pay for extra duty $90.00. December 17, 1863 issued clothing. December 1863 received pay for extra duty $93.00. November – December 1863 roll shows him absent (detailed in Colonel Rockerd's office). January 1864 issued clothing. January 31, 1864 received pay January 1, 1864 to April 30, 1864 detailed orderly and mail carrier. January 4, 1864 received pay $22.00. January 5, 1864 detailed as orderly until February 1, 1864 at a rate of pay of $3.00 per day by Special Order No. 5/2. February 13, 1864 issued clothing. February 29, 1864 received pay $22.00. March 31, 1864 received pay. April 28, 1864 issued clothing. April 30, 1864 received pay. July 30, 1864 issued clothing. September 29, 1864 issued clothing. December 23, 1864 wounded near Pulaski, Tennessee. April 20-21, 1865 captured at Macon, Georgia.

REDDISH, WILLIAM THOMAS: Company B, private. April 21, 1862 enlisted as a private in Co. B, 54th Regiment, Georgia Infantry at Savannah, Georgia and received bounty $50.00. December 31, 1862 received pay. January – February 1863 roll shows him present. January 1864 issued clothing. January 25, 1865 admitted to Way Hospital at Meridian, Mississippi with a Gunshot Wound. May 10, 1865 surrendered at Tallahassee, Florida. May 20, 1865 paroled at Thomasville, Georgia. He was born in Appling County, Georgia December 8, 1842 and died

September 24, 1901. He is buried in Piney Grove Cemetery at Odum, Wayne County, Georgia. (find a grave # 66986445)

REDRICH, G. G.: Company F, private. He enlisted as a private in Co. F, 54th Regiment, Georgia Infantry at Savannah, Georgia and received bounty $50.00. April 8, 1865 reported at Savannah, Georgia as a deserter. He is described as; a resident of Savannah, Georgia, 19 years of age, hazel eyes, black hair, fair complexion, 5 feet 3 inches high and stated he wishes to remain in the city.

REED, THOMAS J.: Company B, private. September 4, 1862 enlisted as a private in Co. B, 54th Regiment, Georgia Infantry at Savannah, Georgia and received bounty $50.00. September to December 1862 rolls show him as Quartermaster's clerk. September 24, 1862 to December 31, 1862 detailed as quartermaster's clerk at Beaulieu near Savannah, Georgia at a rate of $.25 extra per day. October 1862 received pay. November 1862 received pay. December 31, 1862 received pay at Beaulieu near Savannah, Georgia. January 1863 received pay at Beaulieu near Savannah, Georgia. January – February 1863 roll shows him present employed in the quartermaster's department as a clerk. June 1, 1863 to June 30, 1863 detailed with the quartermasters department at a rate of $.25 extra per day. June 1863 received pay. July 1, 1863 to August 31, 1863 detailed as a quartermaster's clerk and teamster at Charleston, South Carolina at a rate of $.25 extra per day. September 1, 1863 to October 31, 1863 detailed as quartermaster's clerk at James Island, South Carolina at a rate of $.25 extra per day. October 31, 1863 list of detailed men at James Island, South Carolina shows him as quartermaster's clerk. November 16, 1863 received pay. January 1864 issued clothing. January 31, 1864 issued clothing and certified by the medical examining board unfit for field service and detailed as a quartermaster's clerk to July 31, 1864 at a rate of $.25 extra per day. February 19, 1864 issued clothing and shown as detailed. March, April, June and July 1864 received pay at Charleston, South Carolina. June 30, 1864 issued clothing and shown as detailed. July 1864 his name appears on a list of men detailed at James Island, South Carolina. August 11, 1864 his detail was extended by Special Order No. 189/11.

REES, GEORGE: Field and Staff, musician. January 27, 1862 enlisted as a musician in the 54th Regiment, Georgia Infantry at Beaulieu near Savannah, Georgia. January – February 1863 roll shows him present. July 1, 1863 received bounty pay $50.00.

REGISTER, REUBIN: Company E, private. May 6, 1862 enlisted as a private in Co. E, 54th Regiment, Georgia Infantry at Savannah, Georgia and received bounty $50.00. December 31, 1862 received pay. January – February 1863 roll shows him present. He was born in Berrien County, Georgia November 25, 1863. September 14, 1863 died of Typhoid Fever at Charleston, South Carolina. He is buried in the Confederate section of Magnolia Cemetery in Charleston, South Carolina (row 7 grave 46). (find a grave #77220865)

REYNOLDS, A. W.: Company D, private. April 30, 1862 enlisted as a private in Co. D, 54th Regiment, Georgia Infantry at Savannah, Georgia and received bounty $50.00. December 31, 1862 received pay. January – February 1863 roll shows him present. January 1864 and April 25, 1864 issued clothing. July 2, 1864 killed near Marietta, Georgia.

REYNOLDS, W. M.: Company D, private. April 30, 1862 enlisted as a private in Co. D, 54th Regiment, Georgia Infantry at Savannah, Georgia and received bounty $50.00. December 31, 1862 received pay. January – February 1863 roll shows him present. 1963 transferred to Prichard's Battery, Georgia Light Artillery. January 1864 and April 25, 1864 issued clothing. October 1864 transferred to Co. D, 1st Regiment, Engineer Troops. April 26, 1865 he was discharged at Newberry District, South Carolina. He was born in South Carolina January 1, 1842 and died August 2, 1906. He is buried in Little Buckhead Cemetery at Millen, Jenkins County, Georgia. (find a grave # 74855342)

RHODES, JOHN M.: Company G, sergeant. April 30, 1862 enlisted as a private in Co. G, 54th Regiment, Georgia Infantry. He was elected sergeant. May 10, 1865 surrendered at Tallahassee, Florida. May 18, 1865 paroled at Albany, Georgia.

RHODES, N. H.: Company D, private. April 30, 1862 enlisted as a private in Co. D, 54th Regiment, Georgia Infantry at Savannah, Georgia and received bounty $50.00. August and September 1862 rolls show him detailed as a mechanic in the quartermaster's department.

RHODES, W. H.: Company D, private. He enlisted as a private in Co. D, 54th Regiment, Georgia Infantry. September 1, 1862 to September 30, 1862 detailed as a carpenter at Beaulieu near Savannah, Georgia at a rate of $.40 extra per day. September 30, 1862 received pay. May 20, 1865 surrendered and paroled at Augusta, Georgia.

RICH, ANDREW JACKSON: Company C, private. February 18, 1864 enlisted in Co. C, 54th Regiment, Georgia Infantry at Camp Rose, South Carolina. January – February 1864 roll shows him present. May 1865 he was in Floyd House and Ocmulgee Hospitals at Macon, Georgia with Mumps and Typhoid Fever. May 27, 1865 surrendered and paroled at Augusta, Georgia. He was born in Emanuel County, Georgia January 25, 1845 and died in Emanuel County, Georgia May 20, 1933. He is buried in Hawhammock Cemetery at Canoochee, Emanuel County, Georgia. (find a grave #10370232)

RICH, S. E.: Company G, private. May 12, 1862 enlisted as a private in Co. G, 54th Regiment, Georgia Infantry at Columbus, Georgia and received bounty $50.00.

RICH, STEPHEN EMANUEL: Company C, private. He enlisted in Co. C, 54th Regiment, Georgia Infantry. August 15, 1864 admitted to Ocmulgee Hospital at Macon, Georgia. August 18, 1864 transferred from Ocmulgee Hospital at Macon, Georgia. August 15, 1864 admitted to Ocmulgee Hospital at Macon, Georgia with Intermittent Febris. August 23, 1864 transferred from Ocmulgee Hospital at Macon, Georgia to Augusta, Georgia. January 13, 1865 admitted to St. Mary's Hospital at

West Point, Mississippi with Rheumatism. May 27, 1865 surrendered and paroled at Augusta, Georgia. He was a resident of Emanuel County, Georgia. He was born in Emanuel County, Georgia September 29, 1831 and died in Emanuel County, Georgia. He is buried in Hall Cemetery at Modoc, Emanuel County, Georgia. (find a grave # 68181472)

RICHARDSON,___: Company C, private. July 1, 1862 enlisted as a private in Co. C, 54th Regiment, Georgia Infantry at Savannah, Georgia and received bounty $50.00. July 1862 roll shows his enlistment.

RICHARDSON, N. L.: Company A, private. He enlisted as a private in Co. A, 54th Regiment, Georgia Infantry.

RICHARDSON, S.: Company C, private. He enlisted as a private in Co. B, 54th Regiment, Georgia Infantry. January 1864 and April 25, 1864 issued clothing.

RICHARDSON, S. W.: Company C, private. May 6, 1862 enlisted as a private in Co. C, 54th Regiment, Georgia Infantry at Savannah, Georgia and received bounty $50.00. December 31, 1862 received pay. January – February 1863 roll shows him present. January 1, 1864 received pay. January – February 1864 roll shows him present.

RICHARDSON, SAMUEL: Company C, private. June 25, 1862 enlisted as a private in Co. C, 54th Regiment, Georgia Infantry at Savannah, Georgia and received bounty $50.00. April 25, 1864 and April 28, 1864 issued clothing. He was wounded in the Atlanta Campaign in 1864. He was a resident of Emanuel County, Georgia. He was born October 17, 1832 and died August 29, 1906. He is buried in Shiloh United Methodist Church Cemetery at Reidsville, Tattnall County, Georgia. (find a grave # 47302284)

RICHARDSON, W. B.: Field and Staff, assistant surgeon. May 10, 1862 appointed assistant surgeon for the 54th Regiment, Georgia Infantry. August 8, 1862 resigned due to disability.

RICHARDSON, W. L.: Company A, private. April 26, 1862 enlisted as a private in Co. A, 54th Regiment, Georgia Infantry at Macon, Georgia and received bounty $50.00. June 1, 1862 appointed as wagoner for quartermaster's department. July, August, September, October, November and December 1862 rolls show him detailed as a teamster (wagoner). September 1, 1862 to December 31, 1862 detailed as a teamster at a rate of $.25 extra per day. October, November and December 1862 received pay. January 1, 1863 to February 19, 1863 detailed as a teamster at Beaulieu near Savannah, Georgia at a rate of $.25 extra per day. January 1863 received pay. February 1863 received pay. March 1, 1863 attached Siege Train Hospital at Savannah, Georgia as a wagoner. May 1, 1863 to June 30, 1863 detailed as a wagoner at a rate of $.25 extra per day. April 30, 1863 received pay. June 30, 1863 roll shows him present as a teamster at the hospital. October 31, 1863 received pay. November – December 1863 roll shows him present (a teamster for Siege Train Hospital at Savannah, Georgia). December 31, 1863 received pay. January 1, 1864 received pay. January – February 1864 roll shows him present (a teamster for Siege

Train Hospital). February 29, 1864 received pay. April 29, 1864 issued clothing. March – April 1864 roll of Siege Train Hospital at Savannah, Georgia shows him present as a teamster.

RICKS, ___: Company A, sergeant. He enlisted as a sergeant in Co. A, 54th Regiment, Georgia Infantry. July 12, 1862 died at Savannah, Georgia. July 1862 roll shows his death.

RITCH, GREEN BERRY: Company K, lieutenant. October 3, 1861 enlisted as a private and elected Jr. 2nd lieutenant in Co. A, 1st Regiment, 1st Brigade, Georgia State Troops. April 1862 mustered out. April 18, 1862 enlisted and elected as 2nd lieutenant in Co. K, 54th Regiment, Georgia Infantry at Savannah, Georgia. July 1862 roll shows him absent. July 27, 1862 appointed rank of 2nd lieutenant. August, September, October and November 1862 rolls show him present at Beaulieu near Savannah, Georgia. November 24, 1862 his name appears on list of officers at Savannah, Georgia. December 20, 1862 he was promoted to 1st lieutenant of Co. K, 54th Regiment, Georgia Infantry at Beaulieu near Savannah, Georgia. December 1862 roll shows him present at Beaulieu near Savannah, Georgia. January 1, 1863 received pay. January – February 1863 roll shows him present April 30, 1863 dropped from the roll by Special Order No. 101/15. March 4, 1863 received pay $180.00. April 3, 1863 received pay $90.00. April 25, 1863 dropped from the rolls for desertion. (One source: He was born February 6, 1843 and died December 12, 1900.) He was born February 1, 1847 and died May 13, 1910 (on tombstone). He is buried in Old Ritch Cemetery in Wayne County, Georgia. (find a grave # 53856897)

RITCH, JOHN G.: Company K, private. February 2, 1862 enlisted as a private in Co. A, 1st Regiment, 1st Brigade, Georgia State Troops. April 1862 mustered out. April 18, 1862 enlisted as a private in Co. K, 54th Regiment, Georgia Infantry at Savannah, Georgia and received bounty $50.00. January 1, 1863 received pay. January – February 1863 roll shows him present. He was born in Appling County, Georgia April 17, 1828 and died in Wayne County, Georgia July 3, 1901. He is buried in Old Ritch Cemetery in Wayne County, Georgia. (find a grave #19079079)

RITCH, THOMAS JEFFERSON: Company G, sergeant. May 12, 1862 enlisted as 3rd sergeant in Co. G, 54th Regiment, Georgia Infantry at Columbus, Georgia and received bounty $50.00. December 31, 1862 received pay. January – February 1863 roll shows him present. 1863 discharged and furnished substitute. August 4, 1863 enlisted and appointed sergeant of Co. K, 12th Regiment, Georgia State Guards Cavalry (Robinson's). February 4, 1864 mustered out at Atlanta, Georgia. He was born in Muscogee County, Georgia November 5, 1840 and died in Atlanta, Fulton County, Georgia December 27, 1921. He is buried in Hollywood Cemetery at Atlanta, Fulton County, Georgia. (find a grave # 14178764)

RITCH, THOMAS JEFFERSON: Company A, private. He enlisted as a private in Co. A, 54th Regiment, Georgia Infantry.

RITCHEY, (RICKEY) (RICHY), EDWARD JEFFERSON: Company A, private. November 1, 1863 enlisted as a private in Co. A, 54th Regiment, Georgia Infantry at Savannah, Georgia. November – December 1863 roll shows him present. January 1, 1864 received pay. January – February 1864 roll shows him present. April 29, 1864 issued clothing. May 1, 1864 admitted to Ocmulgee Hospital at Macon, Georgia with Rubeola. May 9, 1864 deserted from Ocmulgee Hospital at Macon, Georgia. May 18, 1864 admitted to Ocmulgee Hospital at Macon, Georgia with Rheumatism. May 25, 1864 returned to duty. June 6, 1864 wounded in both legs at New Hope Church, Georgia. August 31, 1864 he was wounded in the arm at Jonesboro, Georgia. Pension records show; December 15, 1864 he was wounded in the head at Nashville, Tennessee. He was permanently disabled by his wounds. He was born in Georgia August 10, 1833. He was a resident of Jones County, Georgia.

RITTENBERRY, M. G.: Company A, private. He enlisted as a private in Co. A, 54th Regiment, Georgia Infantry.

ROACH, ELIAS: Company H, private. He enlisted as a private in Co. H, 54th Regiment, Georgia Infantry. May 20, 1865 surrendered and paroled at Augusta, Georgia.

ROBERSON, H. P.: Company K, private. October 3, 1861 enlisted as a private in Co. A, 1st Regiment, 1st Brigade, Georgia State Troops. April 1862 mustered out. April 18, 1862 enlisted as a private in Co. K, 54th Regiment, Georgia Infantry at Savannah, Georgia and received bounty $50.00. January 1, 1864 received pay. January – February 1864 roll shows him present. March 18, 1864, April 18, 1864 and April 25, 1864 issued clothing. 1864 died of disease.

ROBERSON, H. W.: Company K, private. October 15, 1861 enlisted as a private in Co. A, 1st Regiment, 1st Brigade, Georgia State Troops. April 1862 mustered out. April 18, 1862 enlisted as a private in Co. K, 54th Regiment, Georgia Infantry at Savannah, Georgia and received bounty $50.00. January 1, 1864 received pay. January – February 1864 roll shows him present. March 18, 1864, April 18, 1864 and April 25, 1864 issued clothing. July 6, 1864 died of Pneumonia at Fair Grounds Hospital No. 2 at Atlanta, Georgia.

ROBERSON (ROBINSON), JOHN JACKSON: Company B, lieutenant. October 10, 1861 appointed 4th corporal of Co. K, 2nd Regiment, 1st Brigade, Georgia State Troops. April 1862 mustered out. April 21, 1862 enlisted as Jr. 2nd lieutenant in Co. B, 54th Regiment, Georgia Infantry at Savannah, Georgia and received bounty $50.00. July 1862 roll shows him on roll. August, September and October 1862 rolls show him present at Beaulieu near Savannah, Georgia (in arrest). November 1, 1862 cashiered by General Order No. 82. November 1862 roll shows him cashiered. He was born in Georgia.

ROBERSON (ROBINSON), JOSEPH D.: Company B, sergeant. October 10, 1861 appointed 2nd corporal of Co. K, 2nd Regiment, 1st Brigade, Georgia State Troops. April 1862 mustered out. April 21, 1862 enlisted as a private in Co. B, 54th Regiment, Georgia Infantry at Savannah, Georgia and received bounty $50.00. December 31, 1862 received pay. January – February 1863 roll shows him present. He was elected sergeant of Co. B, 54th Regiment, Georgia Infantry. April 25, 1864 issued clothing. February 1865 pension records show he was paroled for 20 days. He was cut off from his command by the Federal Army. May 10, 1865 surrendered at Tallahassee, Florida. May 21, 1865 paroled at Thomasville, Georgia. (another record; He was born in Wayne County, Georgia in February 28, 1838 and died in Jesup, Wayne County, Georgia August 20, 1895) he was born October 29, 1834 and died March 28, 1915. . He is buried in Bethlehem Wesleyan Church Cemetery in Wayne County, Georgia. (find a grave #54005308)

ROBERSON, W. H.: Company K, private. October 3, 1861 enlisted as a private in Co. A, 1st Regiment, 1st Brigade, Georgia State Troops. April 1862 mustered out. April 18, 1862 enlisted as a private in Co. K, 54th Regiment, Georgia Infantry at Savannah, Georgia and received bounty $50.00. January 1, 1864 received pay. January – February 1864 roll shows him present. March 18, 1864, April 18, 1864 and April 25, 1864 issued clothing. He was born in 1841 and died in 1924. (one record shows 1864 he died of disease.) He is buried in old Bethel Cemetery at Jesup, Wayne County, Georgia. (find a grave #79721235)

ROBERSON, T.: Company B, private. He enlisted as a private in Co. B, 54th Regiment, Georgia Infantry.

ROBERTS, AUGUSTUS S.: Company D, captain. October 7, 1861 elected 1st lieutenant of Co. I, 5th Regiment, Georgia State Troops. October 28, 1861 elected captain of Co. I, 5th Regiment, Georgia State Troops. April 1862 mustered out. April 30, 1862 elected captain of Co. D, 54th Regiment, Georgia Infantry. July 1862 he is shown on roll. August and September 1862 rolls show him present at Beaulieu near Savannah, Georgia. October 1862 roll shows him absent with leave since October 24, 1862 (for 10 days). November 24, 1862 list of officers in Savannah, Georgia shows him. November and December 1862 rolls show him present at Beaulieu near Savannah, Georgia. February 11, 1863 detailed for court martial by Special Order No. 42/4. January – February 1863 roll shows him present. March 3, 1863 received pay $130.00. April 2, 1863 received pay $130.00. April 30, 1863 absent with leave. August 20, 1863 to September 6, 1863 he was killed at Battery Wagner, Morris Island, South Carolina. He was born in 1820 and died in Charleston, South Carolina August 27, 1863. He is buried in McDonald Baptist Church Cemetery at Sylvania, Screven County, Georgia. (find a grave # 115486514)

ROBERTS, FRANCIS: Company G, sergeant. May 12, 1862 enlisted as 1st corporal in Co. G, 54th Regiment, Georgia Infantry at Columbus, Georgia and received bounty $50.00. December 31, 1862 received pay. He was elected sergeant in Co. G, 54th Regiment, Georgia Infantry. January – February 1863 roll shows him resigned and discharged by furnishing a substitute Robert P. Anderson on January 15, 1863. He was born January

22, 1842 and died January 7, 1919. He is buried in Clowers Cemetery at Cataula, Harris County, Georgia. (find a grave # 48501564)

ROBERTS, J. L.: Company A, private. July 1, 1863 enlisted as a private in Co. A, 54th Regiment, Georgia Infantry at Savannah, Georgia and received bounty $50.00. October 31, 1862 received pay. January – February 1863 roll shows him absent (on special service since December 19, 1863). January 1, 1864 received pay. January – February 1864 roll shows him present. He died June 6, 1903.

ROBERTS, JOHN: Company A, private. May 6, 1862 enlisted as a private in Co. A, 54th Regiment, Georgia Infantry at Macon, Georgia and received bounty $50.00. June 30, 1863 roll shows him absent (detailed at the Macon, Georgia Arsenal). July 1, 1863 to December 31, 1863, detailed to Macon, Georgia Arsenal as a laborer at a rate of $2.00 to $3.00 per day. August 31, 1863 received pay. September 30, 1863 received pay. October 31, 1863 received pay. November 1863 received pay. December 31, 1863 received pay. November – December 1863 roll shows him absent (detailed at the Macon, Georgia Arsenal). January 1, 1864 to July 31, 1864 detailed at the Macon, Georgia Arsenal as a machinist at a rate of $3.00 per day by Special Order No. 288/1. January – February 1864 roll shows him absent (detailed at the Macon, Georgia Arsenal). January 31, 1864 received pay. February 29, 1864 received pay. March 1864 received pay $123.20. April 1864 received pay (piece work). May 1864 received pay $125.25. June 1864 received pay $ 101.25. July 1864 received pay $131.50. February 1865 received pay as a Machinist at Macon, Georgia Arsenal $70.50 ($6.00 per day). March 1865 received pay as a Machinist at Macon, Georgia Arsenal $135.25 ($6.50 per day). April 20-21, 1865 He was captured at Macon, Georgia. He was born May 30, 1829 and died October 31, 1898. He is buried in Riverside Cemetery at Macon, Bibb County, Georgia. (find a grave # 35963302)

ROBERTS, JOHN J.: Company F (A), private. May 1, 1862 enlisted as a private in Co. F, 54th Regiment, Georgia Infantry. January 1, 1863 transferred from Co. F, 54th Regiment, Georgia Infantry to Co. A, 54th Regiment, Georgia Infantry at Savannah, Georgia and received bounty $50.00. December 31, 1862 received pay. January – February 1863 roll shows him transferred from Co. A, 54th Regiment, Georgia Infantry to Co. F, 54th Regiment, Georgia Infantry. April 20-21, 1865 captured at Macon, Georgia. He was born July 23, 1839 and died June 6, 1903. He is buried in Clinton United Methodist Church Cemetery at Clinton, Jones County, Georgia. (find a grave # 21774931)

ROBERTS, JOHN M.: Company D (F), private. October 7, 1861 enlisted as a private in Co. I, 5th Regiment, Georgia State Troops. April 1862 mustered out. April 30, 1862 enlisted as 5th Sergeant in Co. D, 54th Regiment, Georgia Infantry at Savannah, Georgia and received bounty $50.00. December 31, 1862 received pay. January 7, 1863 reduced in rank to private by Special Order No. 1. January 12, 1863 transferred to Co. F, 54th Regiment, Georgia Infantry. January – February 1863 rolls show him reduced in rank to private January 7, 1863 by Special Order No. 1 and transferred to Co. F, 54th Regiment, Georgia Infantry.

ROBERTS, JOHN S.: Company C, private. October 30, 1862 enlisted as a private in Co. C, 54th Regiment, Georgia Infantry at Savannah, Georgia and received bounty $50.00. January – February 1864 roll shows him absent (sick in hospital at Hardeeville, South Carolina since February 24, 1864). June 27, 1864 wounded in the right wrist and ankle at Kennesaw Mountain, Georgia. April 20-21, 1865 captured at Macon, Georgia. He was born in Georgia August 15, 1831.

ROBERTS, NAP B.: Company G, captain. April 16, 1861 enlisted as a private in Co. G, 2nd Regiment, Georgia Infantry. November 7, 1861 discharged due to disability. May 12, 1862 elected 1st lieutenant of Co. G, 54th Regiment, Georgia Infantry. July 1862 roll shows him present at Savannah, Georgia. August 1862 roll shows him present at Beaulieu near Savannah, Georgia. September 1862 roll shows him absent with leave. October, November and December 1862 rolls show him present at Beaulieu near Savannah, Georgia. November 24, 1862 his name appears on a list of officers present at Savannah, Georgia. January – February 1863 roll shows him present. October 5, 1863 issued clothing. October 21, 1863 his name appears on a list of officers present at Legare's Point, South Carolina. February 10, 1864 "He was examined by the board and found fully competent for promotion". February 15, 1864 appointed captain of Co. G, 54th Regiment, Georgia Infantry by Special Order No. 29/1. January 13, 1865 admitted to St. Mary's Hospital at West Point, Mississippi with Chilblain.

ROBERTS, R.: Company A, private. November 5, 1862 enlisted as a private in Co. A, 54th Regiment, Georgia Infantry at Macon, Georgia and received bounty $50.00. November 1862 roll shows his enlistment.

ROBERTS, REUBEN J.: Company A, private. April 29, 1862 enlisted as a private in Co. A, 54th Regiment, Georgia Infantry at Macon, Georgia and received bounty $50.00. June 30, 1863 roll shows him absent on furlough. October 31, 1863 received pay. November – December 1863 roll shows him present. January 1, 1864 received pay. January – February 1864 roll shows him absent on furlough. March 31, 1864 and April 29, 1864 issued clothing. June 19, 1864 captured near Marietta, Georgia. June 26, 1864 received at Military Prison at Louisville, Kentucky from Nashville, Tennessee. June 27, 1864 sent to Camp Morton, Indiana from Military Prison at Louisville, Kentucky. June 28, 1864 received at Camp Morton, Indianapolis, Indiana from Military Prison at Louisville, Kentucky. July 26, 1864 died of Erysipelas at Camp Morton, Indianapolis, Indiana. He is buried in grave no. 989 at Crown Hill (Green Lawn) Cemetery, Indianapolis, Marion County, Indiana. (find a grave #14736539)

ROBERTS, SIMEON: Company C, private. October 30, 1862 enlisted as a private in Co. C, 54th Regiment, Georgia Infantry at Savannah, Georgia and received bounty $50.00. November 1862 roll shows his enlistment at Coffee Bluff near Savannah, Georgia. December 31, 1862 received pay. January – February 1863 roll shows him present. October 18, 1863 detailed at James Island, South Carolina with the medical department as a nurse. October 31, 1863 list of men detailed at James Island, South Carolina shows him. November 1, 1863 received pay. January – February 1864 roll shows him absent (sick in the hospital at Hardeeville, South Carolina since February 24, 1864). October 29, 1864 and December 16, 1864 issued clothing at Convalescent Camp Wright at Macon, Georgia. April 20-21, 1865 captured at Macon, Georgia.

ROBERTS, SOLOMOM: Company A, private. May 3, 1862 enlisted as a private in Co. A, 54th Regiment, Georgia Infantry at Macon, Georgia and received bounty $50.00. April 30, 1863 received pay. June 30, 1863 roll shows him present. Pension records show he was at home on furlough at the close of the war.

ROBERTS, T.: Company C, private. April 22, 1862 enlisted as a private in Co. C, 54th Regiment, Georgia Infantry at Savannah, Georgia and received bounty $50.00. December 31, 1862 received pay. January – February 1863 roll shows him present. January 1, 1864 received pay. January – February 1864 roll shows him present.

ROBERTS, THOMAS: Company C, private. December 11, 1861 enlisted as a private in Co. B, 8th Regiment, Georgia State Troops. He mustered out in 1862. May 12, 1862 enlisted as 3rd sergeant in Co. G, 54th Regiment, Georgia Infantry at Columbus, Georgia and received bounty $50.00. December 31, 1862 received pay. January – February 1863 roll shows him present. January 1, 1864 received pay. January – February 1864 roll shows him present. April 25, 1864 and April 26, 1864 issued clothing. January 13, 1865 admitted to St. Mary's Hospital at West Point, Mississippi with Rheumatism.

ROBERTS, WILLIAM: Company F, private. May 6, 1862 enlisted as a private in Co. F, 54th Regiment, Georgia Infantry at Savannah, Georgia and received bounty $50.00. July 27, 1862 discharged at Savannah, Georgia. August 1862 shows his discharge.

ROBERTS, WILLIAM H.: Company A, private. April 28, 1862 enlisted as a private in Co. A, 54th Regiment, Georgia Infantry at Macon, Georgia and received bounty $50.00. July 29, 1862 detailed as a nurse. August 1, 1862 detailed as a nurse at Convalescent Camp. August and September 1862 rolls show him detailed as a nurse at Convalescent Camp. October 1862 roll shows him detailed as a teamster. June 30, 1863 roll shows him absent (nurse in hospital at Whiteville, Georgia). October 31, 1863 received pay. November 1863 roll at General Hospital at Guyton, Georgia shows he returned to his command on November 6, 1863. November – December 1863 roll shows him present. January 1, 1864 received pay. January – February 1864 roll shows him present. March 31, 1864 and May 8, 1864 issued clothing. June 18(19), 1864 he was captured near Marietta, Georgia. June 26, 1864 received at Military Prison at Louisville, Kentucky from Nashville, Tennessee. June 27, 1864 sent to Camp Morton, Indianapolis, Indiana from Military Prison at Louisville, Kentucky. June

28, 1864 received at Camp Morton, Indianapolis, Indiana from Military Prison at Louisville, Kentucky. February 26, 1865 transferred for exchange. March 10, 1865 admitted to Receiving and Wayside Hospital or General Hospital No. 9 at Richmond, Virginia and transferred to Jackson, Hospital at Richmond, Virginia. March 11, 1865 admitted to Jackson, Hospital at Richmond, Virginia with Pneumonia. March 12, 1865 transferred to Camp Lee. He was born in Jones County, Georgia September 17, 1829.

ROBERTSON (ROBERSON), G. B.: Company C, private. May 6, 1862 enlisted as a private in Co. C, 54th Regiment, Georgia Infantry at Savannah, Georgia and received bounty $50.00. December 31, 1862 received pay. January – February 1863 roll shows him present (in hospital at Bethesda). January 1, 1864 received pay. January – February 1864 roll shows him present. 1864 wounded in the left leg (Erysipelas developed). April 26, 1865 surrendered in Co. D, 54th Regiment, Consolidated Georgia Infantry at Greensboro, North Carolina. May 1, 1865 paroled at Greensboro, North Carolina. He was born in Upson County, Georgia in 1844. He was a resident of Hancock County, Georgia.

ROBERTSON, GEORGE R.: Company F (D), sergeant. May 17, 1861 enlisted as a private in Chisholm's Company, Georgia State Troops. May 1862 mustered out. May 13, 1862 enlisted as 3rd corporal in Co. F, 54th Regiment, Georgia Infantry at Savannah, Georgia and received bounty $50.00. December 31, 1862 received pay. January – February 1863 roll shows him present. He was elected 3rd sergeant of Co. F, 54th Regiment, Georgia Infantry. October 1863 appointed 4th sergeant of Co. F, 54th Regiment, Georgia Infantry. November 1, 1863 received pay. November – December 1863 roll shows him present. January 1864 and April 25, 1864 issued clothing. April 26, 1865 surrendered in Co. D, 54th Regiment, Consolidated Georgia Infantry at Greensboro, North Carolina. May 1, 1865 paroled at Greensboro, North Carolina.

ROBINSON, DAVID SHANNON: Company E, private. October 10, 1861 enlisted as a private and appointed 2nd corporal in Co. K, 2nd Regiment, 1st Brigade, Georgia State Troops. April 1862 mustered out. May 6, 1862 enlisted as a private in Co. E, 54th Regiment, Georgia Infantry at Savannah, Georgia and received bounty $50.00. December 31, 1862 received pay. January – February 1863 roll shows him present. January 1864 and April 25, 1864 issued clothing. May 10, 1865 surrendered at Tallahassee, Florida. May 16, 1865 paroled at Thomasville, Georgia. He is described as 5 feet 8 inches high, dark hair, black eyes and light complexion. He was born July 30, 1835 and died May 20, 1913. He is buried in Oaky Grove Cemetery at Nashville, Berrien County, Georgia. (find a grave # 66005025)

ROBINSON, J. D.: Company K, private. 1862 enlisted as a private in Co. K, 54th Regiment, Georgia Infantry at Savannah, Georgia. The Southern Cross of Honor was bestowed on him by the Jesup Chapter United Daughters of the Confederacy in 1905.

ROBINSON, WILLIAM A.: Company H, private. August 1, 1862 appointed 3rd sergeant of Captain Whitt's Company (Express Infantry). October 5, 1863 transferred to Co. H, 54th Regiment, Georgia Infantry at Beaulieu near Savannah, Georgia. October 31, 1863 received pay. November – December 1863 roll shows him present. December 31, 1863 received pay. January 1864 issued clothing. January – February 1864 roll shows him present (on picket). April 25, 1864 issued clothing. August 1, 1864 he is shown as in Floyd House Hospital at Macon, Georgia with a Gunshot Wound of the face 1 inch in front of the left ear. September 7, 1864 appears on the Register of Floyd House and Ocmulgee Hospitals at Macon, Georgia as being a patient in Floyd House Hospital with a Gunshot Wound through the face (both superior and inferior max partial anebylosis of lower third.). He was a resident of Thomasville, Georgia.

ROCKMORE, J. T.: Company H (A), private. He enlisted as a private in Co. H, 54th Regiment, Georgia Infantry. September 1, 1862 transferred from Co. H, 54th Regiment, Georgia Infantry to Co. A, 54th Regiment, Georgia Infantry by Special Order No. 6 at Beaulieu near Savannah, Georgia. September 1862 rolls show the transfer.

RODGERS, ADAM CRAIL: Company H, private. May 12, 1862 enlisted as a private in Co. H, 54th Regiment, Georgia Infantry at Columbus, Georgia and received bounty $50.00. December 31, 1862 received pay. January – February 1863 roll shows him present. October 31, 1863 received pay. November – December 1863 roll shows him present. December 31, 1863 received pay. January 1864 issued clothing. January – February 1864 roll shows him present. October 13, 1864 issued clothing in the Fairground Hospital at Vineville, Georgia. November 26, 1864 issued clothing. April 26, 1865 surrendered at Greensboro, North Carolina. May 1, 1865 paroled at Greensboro, North Carolina.
He was born in South Carolina July 25, 1835 and died in Georgia April 1920. He is buried in Nelson Cemetery at Hamilton, Harris County, Georgia. (find a grave # 90266365)

RODGERS, JAMES MCCURDY: Company H, private. May 12, 1862 enlisted as a private in Co. H, 54th Regiment, Georgia Infantry at Columbus, Georgia and received bounty $50.00. December 31, 1862 received pay. January – February 1863 roll shows him present. October 31, 1863 received pay. November – December 1863 roll shows him present. December 31, 1863 received pay. January 1864 issued clothing. January – February 1864 roll shows him absent (absent sick in Bethesda Hospital since January 16, 1864). He was born in South Carolina October 29, 1829 and died in Muscogee County, Georgia September 10, 1908. He is buried in Double Churches Cemetery at Columbus, Muscogee County, Georgia. (find a grave # 82779947)

RODGERS, ROBERT HILL: Company H, private. January 21, 1864 enlisted as a private in Co. H, 54th Regiment, Georgia Infantry at Beaulieu near Savannah, Georgia and received bounty $50.00. January 1864 issued clothing. January – February 1864 roll shows him present. He was born in Muscogee County, Georgia November 7, 1825 and died in Cleburne

County, Arkansas August 9, 1907. He is buried in Good Springs Cemetery in Cleburne County, Arkansas. (find a grave # 116457117)

RODGERS, SAMUEL C.: Company H, private. May 12, 1862 enlisted as a private in Co. H, 54th Regiment, Georgia Infantry at Columbus, Georgia and received bounty $50.00. December 31, 1862 received pay. January – February 1863 roll shows him present. October 31, 1863 received pay. November – December 1863 roll shows him present. December 31, 1863 received pay. January 1864 issued clothing. January – February 1864 roll shows him present. Pension records show: April 26, 1865 surrendered at Greensboro, North Carolina. May 1, 1865 paroled at Greensboro, North Carolina.

He was born in South Carolina July 9, 1836 and died in Muscogee County January 15, 1915. (find a grave # 67581841)

RODGERS, T. J.: Company H, private. November 12, 1862 enlisted as a private in Co. H, 54th Regiment, Georgia Infantry at Columbus, Georgia and received bounty $50.00. December 31, 1862 received pay. January – February 1863 roll shows him present. October 31, 1863 received pay. November – December 1863 roll shows him present. December 31, 1863 received pay. January 20, 1864 discharged by civil authority. January – February 1864 roll shows him present. He was born in Muscogee County, Georgia May 6, 1848 and died June 1907. He is buried in Camp Hill Cemetery at Camp Hill, Tallapoosa County, Alabama. (find a grave # 39945764)

RODGERS, WILLIAM MATTHEW: Company H, corporal. November 12, 1862 enlisted as a private in Co. H, 54th Regiment, Georgia Infantry at Columbus, Georgia and received bounty $50.00. December 31, 1862 received pay. January – February 1863 roll shows him present. October 31, 1863 received pay. November – December 1863 roll shows him present. December 31, 1863 received pay. January 1864 issued clothing. January – February 1864 roll shows him present. April 26, 1865 surrendered at Greensboro, North Carolina. May 1, 1865 paroled at Greensboro, North Carolina. He was born in South Carolina August 24, 1838 and died in Muscogee County, Georgia February 11, 1918. He is buried in Cedarwood Cemetery at Roanoke, Randolph County, Alabama. (find a grave # 38868598)

ROE, NOAH: Company E, private. May 6, 1862 enlisted as a private in Co. E, 54th Regiment, Georgia Infantry at Savannah, Georgia and received bounty $50.00. May 6, 1862 deserted at Savannah, Georgia. August 1862 roll shows his desertion.

ROE, RICHARD: Company C, private. August 25, 1862 enlisted as a private in Co. C, 54th Regiment, Georgia Infantry at Savannah, Georgia and received bounty $50.00. September 25, 1862 died at Beaulieu near Savannah, Georgia. September 1862 roll shows his death.

ROGERS, R. A.: Company H, private. November 12, 1862 enlisted as a private in Co. H, 54th Regiment, Georgia Infantry at Columbus, Georgia and received bounty $50.00. November 1862 roll shows his enlistment.

ROOKS, ZACHARIAH: Company E, private. May 6, 1862 enlisted as a private in Co. E, 54th Regiment, Georgia Infantry at Savannah, Georgia and received bounty $50.00. December 31, 1862 received pay. January – February 1863 roll shows him present. January 1864 issued clothing. September 13, 1864 issued clothing. December 31, 1864 received pay $70.90 and furloughed from hospital at Columbus, Mississippi.

RORIE, W. A.: Company K, private. He enlisted as a private in Co. E, 54th Regiment, Georgia Infantry.

RORY, (ROVY), L. B.: Company G, private. May 12, 1862 enlisted as a private in Co. G, 54th Regiment, Georgia Infantry at Columbus, Georgia and received bounty $50.00. June 23, 1862 discharged and furnished substitute Thomas E. Goulding.

ROSE, GEORGE A.: Company F, private. May 17, 1861 enlisted as a private in Chisholm's Company, Georgia State Troops. May 1862 mustered out. May 13, 1862 enlisted as a private in Co. F, 54th Regiment, Georgia Infantry at Savannah, Georgia and received bounty $50.00. November 20, 1862 discharged by civil authority near Savannah, Georgia. November 1862 roll shows his discharge.

ROSS, G. W.: Company B, private. He enlisted as a private in Co. B, 54th Regiment, Georgia Infantry.

ROSS, J. W.: Company A, corporal. May 3, 1862 enlisted as 3rd corporal in Co. A, 54th Regiment, Georgia Infantry at Macon, Georgia and received bounty $50.00. April 30, 1863 received pay. June 30, 1863 roll shows him present. September 23, 1863 detailed as a nurse in the company hospital. October 31, 1863 received pay. November – December 1863 roll shows him present (nurse in company hospital). November – December 1863 roll of Siege Train Hospital at Savannah, Georgia shows him present employed as a nurse. December 31, 1863 received pay. January 1, 1864 received pay. January – February 1864 roll shows him present (nurse in company hospital). January – February 1864 roll of Siege Train Hospital at Savannah, Georgia shows him present employed as a nurse. March 31, 1864 issued clothing. April 20-21, 1865 captured in Macon, Georgia.

ROVY, L. B.: Company G, private. He enlisted as a private in Co. G, 54th Regiment, Georgia Infantry.

ROWELL, DAVID R.: Company B, private. October 10, 1861 enlisted as a private in Co. K, 2nd Regiment, 1st Brigade, Georgia State Troops. December 28, 1861 discharged. September 23, 1862 enlisted as a private in Co. B, 54th Regiment, Georgia Infantry at Beaulieu near Savannah, Georgia and received bounty $50.00. September 1862 roll shows his enlistment. December 31, 1862 received pay. January 9, 1863 received pay $40.48. January – February 1863 roll shows him present (absent without leave 2 days). October 31, 1863 received pay. November 23, 1863 discharged due to disability on surgeon's certificate. January 9, 1864 received pay. He is described on his discharge as: being born in the Barnwell District South Carolina, 23 years of age, 5 feet 2 inches high, dark complexion, blue eyes, brown hair and by occupation was a cow herdsman. April

24, 1864 enlisted as a private in Clinch's Battery, Georgia Light Artillery. September 5, 1864 sent home with Typhoid Febris. He was unable to rejoin his command.

ROWLAND, J., JR.: Company K, private. He enlisted as a private in Co. K, 54th Regiment, Georgia Infantry. November 29, 1864 captured and sent to Military Prison at Louisville, Kentucky.

ROYISTON, S. W.: Company H, private. He enlisted as a private in Co. H, 54th Regiment, Georgia Infantry.

RUCKER, ___: Company G, private. January 22, 1863 enlisted as a private in Co. G, 54th Regiment, Georgia Infantry.

RUFORD, S.: Company H, private. November 8, 1862 enlisted as a private in Co. H, 54th Regiment, Georgia Infantry at Beaulieu near Savannah, Georgia. November 1862 roll shows his enlistment.

RUMSEY, J. W.: Company B, private. He enlisted as a private in Co. B, 54th Regiment, Georgia Infantry.

RUSSELL, CHARLES R.: Company H, captain. April 16, 1862 enlisted as a private in Co. G, 2nd Regiment, Georgia infantry. July 24, 1861 elected 2nd lieutenant of Co. G, 2nd Regiment, Georgia infantry. April 28, 1862 elected 1st lieutenant of Co. G, 2nd Regiment, Georgia infantry. May 1862 resigned his commission. May 12, 1862 elected captain of Co. H, 54th Regiment, Georgia Infantry. May 30, 1862 and July 1862 roll shows him present at Savannah, Georgia. August 16, 1862 granted 30 days leave. August 1862 roll shows him absent on 30 days leave. September 1862 roll shows him present at Beaulieu near Savannah, Georgia. October 1862 roll shows him absent (10 days) with leave since October 16, 1862. November 24, 1862 his name appears on a list of officers at Savannah, Georgia. November and December 1862 rolls show him present at Beaulieu near Savannah, Georgia. January 19, 1863 detailed as enrolling officer. February 28, 1863 report shows him detailed. January – February 1863 roll shows him absent recruiting and enrolling conscripts. March 1, 1863 report shows him detailed enrolling conscripts. March 17, 1863 received pay $130.00. April 3, 1863 detailed as enrolling officer until April 21, 1863. April 30, 1863 received pay $260.00. May 18, 1863 absent due to being detailed to a General Court Martial. May 30, 1863 shows him absent since May 12, 1863 General Court martial. June 30, 1863 reports of officers absent from the Military District of Georgia list him as being absent since February 28, 1863. October 31, 1863 report shows him sick on surgeon's certificate. October 1, 1863 and November 4, 1863 issued clothing. November – December 1863 roll shows him in arrest awaiting sentence of Court Martial. December 31, 1863 received pay $ 130.00. January – February 1864 roll shows him present. February 17, 1864 received pay $ 130.00. March 26, 1864 he is shown on leave by Special Order 85/1. June 7, 1864 received pay $ 520.00. August 1, 1864 received pay $260.00. August 31, 1864 received pay $ 130.00. December 2, 1864 received pay $390.00. April 26, 1865 surrendered at Greensboro, North Carolina. May 1, 1865 paroled at Greensboro, North Carolina. He died in Muscogee County, Georgia in 1891. He was born May 15, 1837 and died April 7, 1891. He is buried in Linwood Cemetery at Columbus, Muscogee County, Georgia. (find a grave # 34679457)

RUSSELL, DICKERSON GILLESPIE, SR.: Field and Staff, ensign. July 24, 1861 enlisted in Co. C, 2nd Regiment, Georgia infantry (16 years of age, 4 feet 10 inches high, light complexion, black eyes, light hair and by occupation a druggist). October 19, 1861 discharged and paid $18.52. May 12, 1862 enlisted as a private in Co. H, 54th Regiment, Georgia Infantry at Columbus, Georgia and received bounty $50.00. December 31, 1862 received pay. January – February 1863 roll shows him present. November – December 1863 roll shows him present (detailed as regiment adjutant's clerk). January 1864 issued clothing. January 8, 1864 received pay $22.00. January – February 1864 roll shows him present (detailed as adjutant's clerk). March 3, 1864 received pay $22.00. June 2, 1864 issued clothing. July 22, 1864 he was appointed ensign of the 54th Regiment, Georgia infantry. September 14, 1864 report of Mercer's Brigade shows him sick in the division hospital. November 28, 1864 received pay $120.00. He was born September 3, 1841 and died in Louisiana May 5, 1913. He is buried in Liberty Cemetery at Linville, Union Parrish, Louisiana. (find a grave # 41115284)

RUSSELL, JOHN: Company I, private. He enlisted as a private in Co. I, 54th Regiment, Georgia Infantry.

RUSSELL, JOSEPH: Company H, private. He enlisted as a private in Co. H, 54th Regiment, Georgia Infantry. November 21, 1862 received pay $40.70 at Atlanta, Georgia.

RUSSELL, R. A.: Company H, private. August 12, 1862 enlisted as a private in Co. H, 54th Regiment, Georgia Infantry at Beaulieu near Savannah, Georgia.

RUSSELL, R. H.: Company H, private. September 15, 1862 enlisted as a private in Co. H, 54th Regiment, Georgia Infantry at Beaulieu near Savannah, Georgia. September 1862 roll shows his enlistment.

RUSSELL, W. J.: Company I, private. He enlisted as a private in Co. I, 54th Regiment, Georgia Infantry.

RUTLEDGE, A. J.: Company A, private. He enlisted as a private in Co. A, 54th Regiment, Georgia Infantry. July 30, 1862 transferred to 1st Georgia Sharpshooters by Special Order No. 259. August 1862 roll shows his transfer.

RYE, WILLIAM G.: Company A, private. April 22, 1862 enlisted as a private in Co. A, 54th Regiment, Georgia Infantry at Macon, Georgia and received bounty $50.00. April 30, 1863 received pay. June 30, 1863 roll shows him present. October 31, 1863 received pay. November – December 1863 roll shows him present. January 1, 1864 received pay. January – February 1864 roll shows him present. April 23, 1864 transferred from Co. A, 54th Regiment, Georgia Infantry to Co. B, 63rd Regiment, Georgia Infantry by Special Order No. 88.

RYLE (RYAL), FRANCIS M.: Company A, private. May 2, 1862 enlisted as a private in Co. A, 54th Regiment, Georgia Infantry at Macon, Georgia and received bounty $50.00. April 30, 1863 received pay. June 30, 1863 roll shows him present (absent without leave from May 3 to May 13). August 31, 1863 received pay. November – December 1863 roll shows him present. January 1, 1864 received pay. January – February 1864 roll shows him present. March 31, 1864 issued clothing. May 28, 1864 he was wounded in battle near Dallas, Georgia. June 1, 1864 admitted to Ocmulgee Hospital at Macon, Georgia with a Gunshot Wound. June 6, 1864 appears on a register of Floyd House and Ocmulgee Hospitals at Macon, Georgia as being admitted to Ocmulgee Hospital in Macon, Georgia with a Gunshot Wound of the left hand ball passing between the metacarpal bones of the little and forefinger. June 7, 1864 furloughed for 60 days. Pension records show he was at home on furlough at the close of the war. He was born in Wilkinson County, Georgia February 2, 1833.

SAFFOLD, R. B.: Company K, private. He enlisted as a private in Co. K, 54th Regiment, Georgia Infantry.

SAILORS, A. J.: Company I, private. He enlisted as a private in Co. I, 54th Regiment, Georgia Infantry.

SALLAS (SALLIS), A. S.: Company A, corporal. He enlisted as a private in Co. A, 54th Regiment, Georgia Infantry. May 6, 1865 paroled at Charlotte, North Carolina.

SALLAS (SALLIS), DAVID: Company H, private. October 9, 1863 enlisted as a private in Co. H, 54th Regiment, Georgia Infantry at Beaulieu near Savannah, Georgia. October 31, 1863 received pay. November – December 1863 roll shows him present. December 31, 1863 received pay. January 1864 issued clothing. January – February 1864 roll shows him present (on guard). July 4, 1864 he died. November 30, 1864 death benefit claim filed his widow, Louisa Sallas. He was a resident of Dover, Russell County, Alabama.

SALLAS (SALLIS), EPHRAIM S.: Company H, corporal. November 2, 1863 enlisted as a private in Co. H, 54th Regiment, Georgia Infantry at Beaulieu near Savannah, Georgia. October 31, 1863 received pay. November – December 1863 roll shows him present. December 31, 1863 received pay. January 1864 issued clothing. January – February 1864 roll shows him present (on guard). May 23, 1864 issued clothing. He was elected corporal of Co. H, 54th Regiment, Georgia Infantry. April 26, 1865 surrendered at Greensboro, North Carolina. May 1, 1865 paroled at Greensboro, North Carolina. He was born in 1827 and died July 25, 1900. He is buried in Oswichee Cemetery at Oswichee, Russell County, Alabama. (find a grave # 13196473)

SAMMONS, A. J.: Company F, private. April 29, 1863 enlisted as a private in Co. F, 54th Regiment, Georgia Infantry.

SAMMONS, ANDERSON L.: Company C (F) (D), private. May 6, 1862 enlisted as a private in Co. C, 54th Regiment, Georgia Infantry at Savannah, Georgia and received bounty $50.00. December 31, 1862 received pay. January 17, 1863 transferred from Co. C, 54th Regiment,

Georgia Infantry to Co. F, 54th Regiment, Georgia Infantry by order of Colonel Way. January – February 1863 rolls show him present and reflect the transfer. November 1, 1863 received pay. January 1864 issued clothing. January – February 1864 roll shows him present. April 25, 1864 and May 8, 1864 issued clothing. June 30, 1864 issued clothing in Direction Hospital at Griffin, Georgia. April 26, 1865 surrendered in Co. D, 54th Regiment, Consolidated Georgia Infantry at Greensboro, North Carolina. May 1, 1865 paroled at Greensboro, North Carolina. He was a resident of Burke County, Georgia at the time of the war. He was born in Jefferson County, Georgia July 1, 1829 and died in Montgomery County, Georgia June 25, 1913. He is buried in Tarrytown Cemetery at Tarrytown, Montgomery County, Georgia. (find a grave # 28063053)

SAMMONS, BENJAMIN B.: Company C, sergeant. December 11, 1861 enlisted and appointed 1st corporal in Co. B, 8th Regiment, Georgia State Troops. He mustered out in 1862. April 22, 1862 enlisted as 3rd sergeant in Co. C, 54th Regiment, Georgia Infantry at Savannah, Georgia and received bounty $50.00. December 31, 1862 received pay. He was elected 1st sergeant of Co. C, 54th Regiment, Georgia Infantry. January – February 1863 roll shows him present. October 30, 1863 he died. January 25, 1864 his mother received his effects which included; $55.08, watch and chain and sundries (Certificate # 437). He was a resident of Emanuel County, Georgia. He died in Charleston, South Carolina October 30, 1863. He is buried in the confederate section of Magnolia Cemetery at Charleston, Charleston County, South Carolina. (find a grave # 20753390)

SAMMONS, JOHN: Company C (F), private. May 6, 1862 enlisted as a private in Co. C, 54th Regiment, Georgia Infantry at Savannah, Georgia and received bounty $50.00. December 31, 1862 received pay. January 17, 1863 transferred from Co. C, 54th Regiment, Georgia Infantry to Co. F, 54th Regiment, Georgia Infantry by order of Colonel Way. January – February 1863 rolls show him present and reflect the transfer. November 1, 1863 received pay. November 5, 1863 to December 31, 1863 detailed as timber cutter for post at a rate of $.40 extra per day. November – December 1863 roll shows him absent (detailed as carpenter (timber cutter) for post). January 1864 issued clothing. January 20, 1864 received pay. April 25, 1864 issued clothing. He was a resident of Burke County, Georgia.

SAMMONS, WILEY G.: Company C, private. May 6, 1862 enlisted as a private in Co. C, 54th Regiment, Georgia Infantry at Savannah, Georgia and received bounty $50.00. December 31, 1862 received pay. January – February 1863 roll shows him present. September 1, 1863 received pay. January – February 1864 roll shows him present. May 20, 1865 surrendered and paroled at Augusta, Georgia. He was a resident of Hancock, Georgia. (one source: He died in Johnson County, Georgia August 19, 1901.) He was born in Jefferson County, Georgia July 6, 1836 and died in Jefferson County, Georgia August 2, 1897. He is buried in providence Baptist Church Cemetery at Louisville, Jefferson County, Georgia. (find a grave # 32885278)

SANDERS, A. T.: Company A, private. December 25, 1863 enlisted as a private in Co. A, 54th Regiment, Georgia Infantry at Savannah, Georgia and received bounty $50.00. November – December 1863 roll shows him present. January 1, 1864 received pay. January – February 1864 roll shows him present. April 29, 1864 issued clothing.

SANDERS, ALBERRY: Company H, private. He enlisted as a private in Co. H, 54th Regiment, Georgia Infantry.

SANDERS, D.: Company D (F), private. November 7, 1862 enlisted as a private in Co. D, 54th Regiment, Georgia Infantry. January 12, 1863 transferred from Co. D, 54th Regiment, Georgia Infantry to Co. F, 54th Regiment, Georgia Infantry.

SANDERS, D. S.: Company D (F), private. November 7, 1862 enlisted as a private in Co. D, 54th Regiment, Georgia Infantry at Beaulieu near Savannah, Georgia and received bounty $50.00. November 1862 roll shows his enlistment. December 31, 1862 received pay. January 12, 1863 transferred from Co. D, 54th Regiment, Georgia Infantry to Co. F, 54th Regiment, Georgia Infantry. January – February 1863 roll shows him present and transferred.

SANDERS, G. T.: Field and Staff, musician. He enlisted as a private in Co. K, 54th Regiment, Georgia Infantry (originally in Co. K.). He was transferred to Field and Staff as a musician.

SANDERS, R. B.: Company D (F), private. October 1, 1862 enlisted as a private in Co. D, 54th Regiment, Georgia Infantry at Beaulieu near Savannah, Georgia and received bounty $50.00. December 31, 1862 received pay. January 1, 1863 transferred from Co. D, 54th Regiment, Georgia Infantry to Co. F, 54th Regiment, Georgia Infantry. January – February 1863 roll shows him as deserted on January 1, 1863.

SANDERS, SAMUEL GREENBERRY: Company E, private. February 14, 1864 enlisted as a private in Co. E, 54th Regiment, Georgia Infantry. May 23, 1864 admitted to Ocmulgee Hospital at Macon, Georgia with Acute Diarrhoea. June 9, 1864 returned to duty. Pension records show he was at home on sick furlough February 2, 1865 to the close of the war. He was born in Georgia in 1847. May 10, 1865 surrendered at Tallahassee, Florida. May 19, 1865 paroled at Thomasville, Georgia. He is described as: 5 feet 11 inches high, dark hair, black eyes and dark complexion. He was a resident of Tallapoosa County, Alabama. He was born in Georgia April 1847 and died in Georgia October 23, 1918. He is buried in Long Bridge Cemetery at Nashville, Berrien County, Georgia. (find a grave # 24741001)

SAPP, ALLEN: Company K (F), private. October 3, 1861 enlisted as a private in Co. A, 1st Regiment, 1st Brigade, Georgia State Troops. April 1864 mustered out. April 18, 1862 enlisted as a private in Co. K, 54th Regiment, Georgia Infantry at Savannah, Georgia and received bounty $50.00. January 1, 1863 transferred from Co. K, 54th Regiment, Georgia Infantry to Co. F, 54th Regiment, Georgia Infantry. January 1, 1863 received pay. January – February 1863 roll shows his transfer and him present in

Co. F. March 18, 1864 issued clothing. May 10, 1865 surrendered at Tallahassee, Florida. May 21, 1865 paroled at Thomasville, Georgia.

SAPP, JOHN HENRY: Company K, private. October 3, 1861 enlisted as a private in Co. A, 1st Regiment, 1st Brigade, Georgia State Troops. April 1862 mustered out. April 18, 1862 enlisted as a private in Co. K, 54th Regiment, Georgia Infantry at Savannah, Georgia and received bounty $50.00. January 1, 1863 received pay. January – February 1863 roll shows him present. March 10, 1864 issued clothing. Pension records show; he was at home on furlough at the close of the war. May 10, 1865 surrendered at Tallahassee, Florida. May 26, 1865 paroled at Thomasville, Georgia. He was born March 7, 1837 and died in Hoboken, Brantley County, Georgia January 27, 1901. He is buried in Spring Hill Cemetery in Brantley County, Georgia. (find a grave # 33278428)

SAPP, WILLIAM WASHINGTON: Company K, private. May 5, 1862 enlisted as a private in Co. K, 54th Regiment, Georgia Infantry at Savannah, Georgia and received bounty $50.00. January 1, 1863 received pay. January – February 1863 roll shows him present. March 18, 1864 and April 25, 1864 issued clothing. July 4, 1864 wounded near Marietta, Georgia. May 10, 1865 surrendered at Tallahassee, Florida. May 22, 1865 paroled at Thomasville, Georgia. He was born February 1, 1835 and died December 9, 1902. He is buried in Dyal Cemetery at Raiford, Bradford County, Florida. (find a grave # 11305740)

SASSER, ALLEN, Sr.: Company D, private. April 18, 1862 enlisted as a private in Co. D, 54th Regiment, Georgia Infantry at Savannah, Georgia and received bounty $50.00. December 1862 furnished substitute and was discharged. January 1864 enlisted as a private in Co. D, 1st Battalion, Georgia Militia. September 1864 sent to Brigade Hospital at Atlanta, Georgia. September 1864 transferred to Macon, Georgia and furloughed home. He was born in Screven County, Georgia March 1842 and died in Screven County, Georgia September 7, 1925. He is buried in Little Horse Creek Cemetery at Rocky Ford, Screven County, Georgia. (find a grave # 52120533)

SASSER, HENRY: Company D, lieutenant. April 30, 1862 enlisted and elected Jr. 2nd lieutenant of Co. D, 54th Regiment, Georgia Infantry at Savannah, Georgia and received bounty $50.00. July 1862 roll has his name at Savannah. August 1862 roll shows him absent from Beaulieu near Savannah, Georgia (absent with 24 hour leave since August 30, 1862). September 1862 roll shows him absent from Beaulieu on ten days leave. October 1862 roll shows him present at Beaulieu near Savannah, Georgia. November 24, 1862 list of officers at Savannah includes his name. November and December 1862 rolls show him present at Beaulieu near Savannah, Georgia. January – February 1863 roll shows him absent sick. February 28, 1863 he was detailed as enrolling officer. March 1, 1863 list of officers absent from Savannah, Georgia shows him absent sick. April 3, 1863 list of officers absent from Savannah, Georgia shows him detached as enrolling officer till April 21, 1863. May 3, 1863 list of officers absent shows him absent on sick furlough. May 14, 1863 resigned his commission due to disability. He was born in Screven County, Georgia May 28, 1835 and died in Screven County, Georgia January 24, 1871. He is buried in Little Horse Creek Cemetery at Rocky Ford, Screven County, Georgia. (find a grave # 21250133)

SASSER, HOWELL: Company D, private. April 30, 1862 enlisted as a private in Co. D, 54th Regiment, Georgia Infantry at Savannah, Georgia and received bounty $50.00. December 1862 furnished substitute and was discharged. 1864 enlisted as a private in Co. D, 1st Battalion, Georgia Militia He was born in Screven County, Georgia in 1801 and died in Screven County, Georgia June 8, 1871. He is buried in Little Horse Creek Cemetery at Rocky Ford, Screven County, Georgia. (find a grave # 21266540)

SASSER, LITTLETON: Company D, private. April 30, 1862 enlisted as a private in Co. D, 54th Regiment, Georgia Infantry at Savannah, Georgia and received bounty $50.00. He was born in Screven County, Georgia in 1837 and died in Screven County, Georgia in 1919. He is buried in Little Horse Creek Cemetery at Rocky Ford, Screven County, Georgia. (find a grave # 78295706)

SASSER, R. D.: Company F, private. October 10, 1862 enlisted as a private in Co. F, 54th Regiment, Georgia Infantry. December 18, 1862 discharged by civil authority. December 1862 roll shows his discharge.

SASSER, R. D.: Company H, private. He enlisted as a private in Co. H, 54th Regiment, Georgia Infantry.

SATTEAN, S. R.: private. He enlisted as a private in the 54th Regiment, Georgia Infantry. May 10, 1865 surrendered at Tallahassee, Florida. May 20, 1865 paroled at Bainbridge, Georgia.

SAWYER, WILLIAM: Company A, private. April 24, 1862 enlisted as a private in Co. A, 54th Regiment, Georgia Infantry at Macon, Georgia and received bounty $50.00. June 1, 1862 detailed as wagon master for quartermasters department. July through December 1862 rolls show him detailed as wagon master (teamster) for regimental quartermasters department. September 1, 1862 to December 31, 1862 detailed for extra duty as wagon master at a rate of $.25 extra per day. September 30, 1862, October 31, 1862, November 30, 1862 and December 31, 1862 received pay. January 31, 1863 and February 28, 1863 received pay. January 1, 1863 to February 28, 1863 detailed for extra duty as wagon master at a rate of $.25 extra per day. April 30, 1863 received pay. June 30, 1863 shows him absent as a wagon master for the regiment. November – December 1863 roll shows him absent (detailed as wagon master for regiment). January – February 1864 roll shows him absent (detailed as wagon master for regiment). February 16, 1864 and April 29, 1864 issued clothing. June 1, 1864 detail extended Special Order No. 127/14. He was born December 25, 1843 and died September 5, 1885. He is buried in Memory Hill Cemetery at Milledgeville, Baldwin County, Georgia. (find a grave # 17859800)

SCARBOROUGH (SCARBROUGH), S. M.: Company I, private. He enlisted as a private in Co. I, 54th Regiment, Georgia Infantry. April 26, 1865 surrendered at Greensboro, North Carolina. May 6, 1865 paroled at Charlotte, North Carolina. He was born February 24, 1831 and died December 24, 1888. He is buried in Mill Shoal Baptist Church Cemetery in Madison County, Georgia. (find a grave # 52497587)

SCOTT, H. T.: Company C, private. February 1864 enlisted as a private in Co. C, 54th Regiment, Georgia Infantry. July 20, 1864 wounded at Peachtree Creek near Atlanta, Georgia. April 25, 1864 issued clothing. September 9, 1864 shows on a register as being in Ocmulgee Hospital at Macon, Georgia with a Gunshot Wound in the lower 3rd of the left leg. Pension records show he was at home wounded at the close of the war. He was born in Georgia in 1845 and was a resident of Millville, Wilkinson County, Georgia.

SCOTT, WILLIAM B.: Company A, private. October 17, 1861 enlisted as a private in Co. C, 1st Independent Battalion, Georgia State Troops. April 1862 roll shows him present. April 1862 mustered out. April 22, 1862 enlisted as a private in Co. A, 54th Regiment, Georgia Infantry at Macon, Georgia. November 15, 1862 deserted. December 31, 1862 received pay. June 30, 1863 roll shows him absent in arrest at Savannah, Georgia Barracks. November – December 1863 roll shows him absent in arrest at Savannah, Georgia Barracks. February 23, 1864 deserted.

SEAGRAVES, J. P.: Company B, private. He enlisted as a private in Co. B, 54th Regiment, Georgia Infantry.

SECKINGER, VALENTINE M.: Company I, private. September 18, 1861 enlisted as a private in Co. C, 1st Regiment, Georgia State Troops. March 18, 1862 mustered out. September 30, 1863 enlisted as a private in Co. A, 54th Regiment, Georgia Infantry at Rose Dew near Savannah, Georgia. He enlisted as a private in Co. A, 54th Regiment, Georgia Infantry at Macon, Georgia. January 1864 and April 25, 1864 issued clothing. He was born September 13, 1845 and died May 16, 1917. He is buried at Fellowship Baptist Church Cemetery at Fellowship, Marion County, Florida. (find a grave #22911088)

SELVES (SELLS), JOHN: Company C, sergeant. He enlisted as a private in Co. C, 54th Regiment, Georgia Infantry. He was appointed sergeant of Co. C, 54th Regiment, Georgia Infantry. July 20, 1864 captured near Atlanta, Georgia. July 28, 1864 received at Military Prison at Louisville, Kentucky from Nashville, Tennessee. July 30, 1864 sent to Camp Douglas, Illinois from Military Prison at Louisville, Kentucky. August 1, 1864 received at Camp Douglas, Illinois from Military Prison at Louisville, Kentucky. June 13, 1865 discharged.

SEUZE (SEUSE), G. W.: Company I, private. May 6, 1862 enlisted as a private in Co. I, 54th Regiment, Georgia Infantry at Savannah, Georgia and received bounty $50.00. August 19, 1862 discharged at Savannah, Georgia. August 1862 roll shows his discharge.

SHAFFER, S.: Company F, private. May 13, 1862 enlisted as a private in Co. F, 54th Regiment, Georgia Infantry at Savannah, Georgia and received bounty $50.00. October 31(2), 1862 discharged at Beaulieu near Savannah, Georgia. October 1862 roll shows his discharge.

SHAFFER, WILLIAM LEWIS: Company F, private. May 13, 1862 enlisted as a private in Co. F, 54th Regiment, Georgia Infantry at Savannah, Georgia and received bounty $50.00. He was born in 1844 and died January 30, 1865. He is buried in Laurel Grove Cemetery (North) at Savannah, Chatham County, Georgia. (find a grave # 44574958)

SHANKS, W. W.: Company H private. May 12, 1862 enlisted as a private in Co. H, 54th Regiment, Georgia Infantry at Columbus, Georgia and received bounty $50.00. May 14, 1862 deserted at Savannah, Georgia.

SHARPE (SHARP), HENRY JAMES: Company A, private. April 29, 1862 enlisted as a private in Co. A, 54th Regiment, Georgia Infantry at Macon, Georgia and received bounty $50.00. September 1862 roll shows him detailed as the company cook. April 30, 1863 received pay. June 30, 1863 roll shows him present (sick in company hospital). October 31, 1863 received pay. November – December 1863 roll shows him present. January 1, 1864 received pay. January – February 1864 roll shows him present. March 31, 1864 and May 8, 1864 issued clothing. April 20-21, 1865 captured and paroled at Macon, Georgia. He was born in Jones County, Georgia in 1832.

SHARPE, JAMES ALEXANDER: Company B, private. January 24, 1863 enlisted as a private in Co. B, 54th Regiment, Georgia Infantry at Savannah, Georgia and received bounty $50.00. January – February 1863 roll shows him present. July 4, 1863 detailed as a nurse in the medical department at James Island, South Carolina. October 31, 1863 list of men detailed at James Island, South Carolina shows him as a nurse in the medical department. January 1864 and April 25, 1864 issued clothing. He was born in 1840 and died August 8, 1900. He is buried in Mount Moriah Cemetery at Lyons, Toombs County, Georgia. (find a grave #38311965)

SHARPE (SHARP), JOHN T.: Company B, private. February 10, 1863 enlisted as a private in Co. B, 54th Regiment, Georgia Infantry at Savannah, Georgia and received bounty $50.00. January – February 1863 roll shows him present (sick in regimental hospital). January 1864 and June 23, 1864 issued clothing. Pension records show he was home on sick furlough at the close of the war. He was born in Tattnall County, Georgia January 1, 1830.

SHAW, JAMES: Company F, private. May 17, 1861 enlisted as a private in Chisholm's Company, Georgia State Troops. May 1862 mustered out. May 13, 1862 enlisted as a private in Co. F, 54th Regiment, Georgia Infantry.

SHAW, WILLIAM A.: Company F, lieutenant. May 17, 1861 appointed 5th sergeant of Captain Chisholm's Company, Georgia State Troops. May 1862 mustered out. May 13, 1862 enlisted as 3rd sergeant in Co. F, 54th Regiment, Georgia Infantry at Savannah, Georgia and received bounty $50.00. December 31, 1862 received pay. January – February 1863 roll shows him present. September 22, 1863 elected 2nd sergeant in Co. F, 54th Regiment, Georgia Infantry. November 1, 1863 received pay. January – February 1864 roll shows him present. January 1864 and May 8, 1864 issued clothing. He was elected 2nd lieutenant in Co. F, 54th Regiment, Georgia Infantry. January 9, 1865 admitted to St. Mary's Hospital at West Point, Mississippi with Remitting Febris (note: to go on train on January 11, 1865). April 16, 1865 captured at Ft. Tyler, West Point, Georgia.

SHEALY (SHELY), ROBERT W.: Company D, sergeant. April 30, 1862 enlisted as a private in Co. D, 54th Regiment, Georgia Infantry at Savannah, Georgia and received bounty $50.00. He was elected 5th sergeant in Co. D, 54th Regiment, Georgia Infantry. December 31, 1862 received pay. January – February 1863 roll shows him present. January 1864 issued clothing. July 27, 1864 he was captured near Atlanta, Georgia.

SHEAROUSE, WILLIAM JASPER: Company I, private. September 18, 1861 enlisted as a private in Co. C, 1st Regiment, Georgia State Troops. March 18, 1862 mustered out. May 6, 1862 enlisted as a private in Co. I, 54th Regiment, Georgia Infantry at Guyton, Georgia and received bounty $50.00. December 31, 1862 received pay. January – February 1863 roll shows him present. October 31, 1863 received pay. November 5, 1863 to December 31, 1863 detailed for extra work as a carpenter at a rate of $.40 extra per day at Rose Dew near Savannah, Georgia. December 1863 received pay. November – December 1863 roll shows him present (detailed to get shingles for the post). January 1864 and June 2, 1864 issued clothing. October 15, 1864 issued clothing at Buckner and Gamble Hospital at Fort Valley, Georgia. December 19, 1864 captured at Triune, Tennessee. January 5, 1865 received at Military Prison at Louisville, Kentucky from Nashville, Tennessee. January 9, 1865 sent to Camp Chase, Ohio from Military Prison at Louisville, Kentucky. January 11, 1865 received at Camp Chase, Ohio from Military Prison at Louisville, Kentucky. He was a resident of Effingham, County, Georgia. January 20, 1865 died of Pneumonia at Camp Chase, Ohio. He was born in 1840. He is buried in grave 815 (1/3 mile South of C.C.) at Camp Chase Confederate Cemetery. (find a grave #55108381)

SHEPPARD, LORENZO DOW, JR.: Company D, private. April 16, 1864 enlisted as a private in Co. D, 54th Regiment Georgia Infantry at Savannah, Georgia and received bounty $50.00. April 26, 1865 surrendered in Co. D, 54th Regiment, Consolidated Georgia Infantry at Greensboro, North Carolina. May 1, 1865 paroled at Greensboro, North Carolina. He was born February 22, 1847 and died September 28, 1904. He is buried in Guyton Cemetery at Guyton, Effingham County, Georgia. (find a grave # 36305480)

SHERROD (SHERRETT), WILLIAM GOOLEY, JR.: Company C, private. May 6, 1862 enlisted as a private in Co. C, 54th Regiment, Georgia Infantry at Savannah, Georgia and received bounty $50.00. October 31, 1862 received pay. November 6, 1862 shown as deserted. January – February 1863 roll shows him present (absent without leave for 35 days).

He was born in Emanuel County, Georgia in 1835 and died in Emanuel County, Georgia January 3, 1916. He is buried in Hines Cemetery in Emanuel County, Georgia. (find a grave #61360608)

SIKES, J. R.: Company B, private. He enlisted as a private in Co. B, 54th Regiment, Georgia Infantry.

SLIAS, A.: Company H, private. September 4, 1862 enlisted as a private in Co. H, 54th Regiment. June 23, 1862 deserted at Savannah, Georgia. August 1862 roll shows his desertion.

SILVERS, JOHN: Company C, sergeant. He enlisted as a private in Co. C, 54th Regiment, Georgia Infantry. July 20, 1864 captured near Atlanta, Georgia. July 25, 1864 to July 31, 1864 received at Military Prison at Louisville, Kentucky from Nashville, Tennessee.

SILVERS (SIBNERS), RICE D.: Company C, private. He enlisted as a private in Co. C, 54th Regiment, Georgia Infantry. July 20, 1864 captured near Atlanta, Georgia. July 28, 1864 received at Military Prison at Louisville, Kentucky from Nashville, Tennessee. July 30, 1864 sent to Camp Douglas, Illinois from Military Prison at Louisville, Kentucky. August 1, 1864 received at Camp Douglas, Illinois from Military Prison at Louisville, Kentucky.

SIMMONS, A. P.: Company A, private. October 17, 1861 enlisted as a private in Co. C, 1st Independent Battalion, Georgia State Troops. April 1862 mustered out. June 10, 1863 enlisted as a private in Co. A, 54th Regiment, Georgia Infantry at Savannah, Georgia and received bounty $50.00. June 30, 1863 roll shows him present (joined from desertion in arrest). October 31, 1863 received pay. November – December 1863 roll shows him present. January 1, 1864 received pay. January – February 1864 roll shows him present. March 31, 1864 issued clothing.

SIMMONS, ANDREW J.: Company I, private. May 6, 1862 enlisted as a private in Co. I, 54th Regiment, Georgia Infantry at Savannah, Georgia and received bounty pay $50.00. June 15, 1862 to February 28, 1863 detailed as wagoner for quartermaster's department at a rate of $.25 extra per day. July, August, September, November and December 1862 rolls show him detailed as a teamster (wagoner) in the quartermaster's department. September 30, 1862 received pay. October 31, 1862 received pay. November 1862 received pay. December 31, 1862 received pay. January 31, 1863 received pay. February 1863 received pay. January – February 1863 roll shows him present (wagoner for regiment). June 1, 1863 to June 30, 1863 detailed as a teamster at a rate of $.25 extra per day. June 30, 1863 received pay. July 1, 1863 to October 31, 1863 detailed as a teamster at a rate of $.25 extra per day. January 1864 issued clothing. January 1, 1864 to April 30, 1864 detailed as a teamster at a rate of $.25 extra per day. He left command on detail at Tupelo, Mississippi. He was enroute to command at the close of the war. He was born in Georgia January 7, 1844 and died in Effingham County, Georgia April 25, 1917. He is buried in Guyton Cemetery at Guyton, Effingham County, Georgia. (find a grave #50843411)

SIMMONS, D. T.: Company I, private. He enlisted as a private in Co. I, 54th Regiment, Georgia Infantry.

SIMMONS, DAVID: Company B, private. July 28, 1862 enlisted as a private in Co. B, 54th Regiment, Georgia Infantry at Savannah, Georgia and received bounty $50.00. July 1862 roll shows his enlistment. December 1862 roll shows him detailed as a boatman. December 31, 1862 received pay. January – February 1863 roll shows him absent (absent on sick leave since January 18, 1863). January 31, 1864 transferred from Co. B, 54th Regiment, Georgia Infantry at Red Bluff, South Carolina to Co. G, 4th Georgia (Clinch's) Cavalry in exchange for Henry A. Williams.

SIMMONS, H. H. C.: Company G, private. May 12, 1862 enlisted as a private in Co. G, 54th Regiment, Georgia Infantry at Columbus, Georgia and received bounty $50.00.

SIMMONS, HENRY E.: Company C (D), private. February 6, 1864 enlisted as a private in Co. C, 54th Regiment, Georgia Infantry at Camp Rose in Hardeeville, South Carolina. January – February 1864 roll shows him present. April 25, 1864 and May 8, 1864 issued clothing. April 26, 1865 surrendered in Co. D, 54th Regiment, Consolidated Georgia Infantry at Greensboro, North Carolina. May 1, 1865 paroled at Greensboro, North Carolina. He was born in Hancock County, Georgia June 28, 1845 and died there February 8, 1918.

SIMMONS, J. D.: Company I, private. March 3, 1864 enlisted as a private in Co. I, 54th Regiment, Georgia Infantry at Dalton, Georgia (Formerly in Co. E, 37th Regiment, Georgia Infantry. April 26, 1865 shown as deserted. May 18, 1865 surrendered and paroled at Augusta, Georgia.

SIMMONS, J. F.: Company C, private. May 6, 1862 enlisted as a private in Co. C, 54th Regiment, Georgia Infantry at Savannah, Georgia and received bounty $50.00. September 30, 1862 received pay. December 31, 1862 received pay. January – February 1863 roll shows him present (in hospital at Bethesda). January 1, 1864 received pay. January – February 1864 roll shows him present. May 8, 1864 issued clothing.

SIMMONS, JOHN M.: Company I, private. October 8, 1861 enlisted in Co. K, 1st Regiment, 1st Brigade, Georgia State Troops. April 8, 1862 mustered out. May 6, 1862 enlisted as a private in Co. I, 54th Regiment, Georgia Infantry at Savannah, Georgia and received bounty $50.00. December 31, 1862 received pay. January – February 1863 roll shows him present (sick). October 31, 1863 received pay. November – December 1863 roll shows him present (detailed to go after lumber at Ogeechee Bridge). January 1964 issued clothing. October 23, 1864 admitted to Ocmulgee Hospital at Macon, Georgia with Debilitis. He was a resident of Decatur County, Georgia. His pension records show he was home on sick furlough at the close of the war. He was born in Thomas County, Georgia October 18, 1842.

SIMMONS, LACY W.: Company I, private. October 8, 1861 enlisted in Co. K, 1st Regiment, 1st Brigade, Georgia State Troops. April 8, 1862 mustered out. May 6, 1862 enlisted as a private in Co. I, 54th Regiment,

Georgia Infantry at Savannah, Georgia and received bounty $50.00. June 1, 1862 to December 31, 1862 detailed to the quartermaster's department as a wagoner at a rate of $.25 extra per day. July, August, September, October and November 1862 rolls show him detailed to the quartermaster's department as a wagoner. December 31, 1862 received pay. January – February 1863 roll shows him present (picket guard). October 31, 1863 received pay. November – December 1863 roll shows him present. September 1, 1863 to July 1, 1863 detailed as a teamster at a rate of $.25 extra per day. July 1, 1863 to December 31, 1863 detailed as ambulance driver at a rate of $.25 extra per day. January 20, 1864 received pay. January 1864 issued clothing. October 23, 1864 admitted to Ocmulgee Hospital at Macon, Georgia with Chronic Diarrhoea. November 18, 1864 he was transferred from Ocmulgee Hospital at Macon, Georgia. January 19, 1865 he was admitted to Way Hospital at Meridian, Mississippi with Debilitas. He transferred to Co. F, 54th Regiment, Georgia Infantry. April 26, 1865 surrendered at Greensboro, North Carolina. May 1, 1865 paroled at Greensboro, North Carolina. He was a resident of Decatur County, Georgia. He was born in 1844 and died in 1932. He is buried in Foggartyville Cemetery at Bradenton, Manatee County, Florida. (find a grave #25945935)

SIMMONS, R.: Company A, private. November 20, 1862 enlisted as a private in Co. A, 54th Regiment, Georgia Infantry at Macon, Georgia and received bounty $50.00. April 30, 1863 received pay. May 1, 1863 to July 31, 1863 detailed as a blacksmith. June 30, 1863 roll shows him present (detailed as a blacksmith). July 31, 1863 received pay.

SIMMONS, R. G.: Company C, private. May 6, 1862 enlisted as a private in Co. C, 54th Regiment, Georgia Infantry at Savannah, Georgia and received bounty $50.00. November 1862 roll shows his enlistment. September 30, 1862 received pay. December 31, 1862 received pay. January – February 1863 roll shows him present. October 7, 1863 received pay $ 44.00. January 1, 1864 received pay. January – February 1864 roll shows him present. April 28, 1864 and May 8, 1864 issued clothing. He was a resident of Hancock, Georgia.

SIMMONS, THOMAS: Company B, private. July 28, 1862 enlisted as a private in Co. B, 54th Regiment, Georgia Infantry at Savannah, Georgia and received bounty $50.00. December 31, 1862 received pay. January – February 1863 roll shows him present. January 1864 issued clothing. May 10, 1865 surrendered at Tallahassee, Florida. May 25, 1865 paroled at Thomasville, Georgia.

SIMMONS, WILLIAM: Company A, private. He enlisted as a private in Co. A, 54th Regiment, Georgia Infantry at Macon, Georgia and received bounty $50.00. July 30, 1862 transferred to 1st Georgia Sharpshooters by Special Order No. 259. August 1862 roll shows his transfer. February 20, 1863 discharged under age.

SIMMONS, WILLIAM: Company D, private. October 17, 1861 enlisted as a private in Co. C, 1st Independent Battalion, Georgia State

Troops. April 16, 1862 roll shows him present. April 1862 mustered out. December 13, 1862 enlisted as a private in Co. D, 54th Regiment, Georgia Infantry at Beaulieu near Savannah, Georgia and received bounty $50.00. December 1862 roll shows his enlistment. December 31, 1862 received pay. January – February 1863 roll shows him present. January 1864 and May 8, 1864 issued clothing. May 25, 1864 wounded in the right hand at New Hope Church, Georgia (according to pension records). He was at home on wounded furlough at the close of the war. He was born in Screven County, Georgia February 10, 1827 and died there in 1904.

SIMMONS, WILLIAM: Company D, private. October 17, 1861 enlisted as a private in Co. C, 1st Independent Battalion, Georgia State Troops. April 16, 1862 roll shows him present. April 1862 mustered out. April 30, 1862 enlisted as a private in Co. D, 54th Regiment, Georgia Infantry. July 20, 1862 transferred to 1st Georgia Sharpshooters by Special Order No. 259. February 20, 1863 discharged due to being underage

SIMONTON, W. B.: Company B, private. He enlisted as a private in Co. B, 54th Regiment, Georgia Infantry.

SIMPSON, A. C.: Company C (D), private. March 17, 1864 enlisted as a private in Co. C, 54th Regiment, Georgia Infantry at Dawson's Bluff. April 25, 1864 and May 8, 1864 issued clothing. April 26, 1865 surrendered in Co. D, 54th Regiment, Consolidated Georgia Infantry at Greensboro, North Carolina. May 1, 1865 paroled at Greensboro, North Carolina.

SIMPSON, ASA ENOCH: Company C (D), private. July 15, 1863 enlisted as a private in Co. C, 54th Regiment, Georgia Infantry at Beaulieu near Savannah, Georgia and received bounty $50.00. January – February 1864 roll shows him present. April 25, 1864 and May 8, 1864 issued clothing. April 26, 1865 surrendered in Co. D, 54th Regiment, Consolidated Georgia Infantry at Greensboro, North Carolina. May 1, 1865 paroled at Greensboro, North Carolina. He was born in Sparks, Hancock County, Georgia June 10, 1845 and died in Sparks, Hancock County, Georgia March 30, 1928. He is buried in Mount Zion Methodist Church Cemetery at Mount Zion, Hancock County, Georgia. (find a grave # 13693390)

SIMPSON, A. S.: Company C (D), private. May 6, 1862 enlisted as a private in Co. C, 54th Regiment, Georgia Infantry at Savannah, Georgia and received bounty $50.00. December 31, 1862 received pay. January – February 1863 roll shows him present. January 1, 1864 received pay. January – February 1864 roll shows him present. April 26, 1865 surrendered in Co. D, 54th Regiment, Consolidated Georgia Infantry at Greensboro, North Carolina. May 1, 1865 paroled at Greensboro, North Carolina. He was born in Hancock County, Georgia August 19, 1837.

SIMPSON, JAMES T.: Company C (D), private. May 6, 1862 enlisted as a private in Co. C, 54th Regiment, Georgia Infantry at Savannah, Georgia and received bounty $50.00. December 31, 1862 received pay. January – February 1863 roll shows him present. January 1, 1864 received pay. January – February 1864 roll shows him present. May 23, 1864 admitted to Ocmulgee Hospital at Macon, Georgia with Chronic Diarrhoea. May

29, 1864 returned to duty. June 17, 1864 admitted to St, Mary's hospital at La Grange, Georgia. July 6, 1864 issued clothing and returned to duty. April 26, 1865 surrendered in Co. D, 54th Regiment, Consolidated Georgia Infantry at Greensboro, North Carolina. May 1, 1865 paroled at Greensboro, North Carolina. He was a resident of Johnson County, Georgia. He was born in Hancock County, Georgia February 26, 1849.

SIMPSON, JOHN F.: Company C (D), private. May 6, 1862 enlisted as a private in Co. C, 54th Regiment, Georgia Infantry at Savannah, Georgia and received bounty $50.00. December 31, 1862 received pay. January – February 1863 roll shows him present. January 1, 1864 received pay. January – February 1864 roll shows him present. July 20, 1864 wounded at Peachtree Creek near Atlanta, Georgia through the breast and left hand (necessitating the amputation of four fingers). April 26, 1865 surrendered in Co. D, 54th Regiment, Consolidated Georgia Infantry at Greensboro, North Carolina. May 1, 1865 paroled at Greensboro, North Carolina. He was a resident of Hancock County, Georgia. He was born in Georgia July 26, 1846 and died April 15, 1917. He is buried in Memory Hill Cemetery at Milledgeville, Baldwin County, Georgia. (find a grave # 16882646)

SIMPSON, WILLIAM HENRY: Company C (D), private. May 6, 1862 enlisted as a private in Co. C, 54th Regiment, Georgia Infantry at Savannah, Georgia and received bounty $50.00. June 15, 1862 detailed as a teamster. August, September and October 1862 rolls show him as a teamster. September 30, 1862 received pay at Beaulieu near Savannah, Georgia. September 1, 1862 to October 31, 1862 detailed as a teamster at a rate of $.25 extra per day. October 31, 1862 received pay at Beaulieu near Savannah, Georgia. December 31, 1862 received pay. January – February 1863 roll shows him present (detailed as a teamster). January 1, 1864 received pay. January – February 1864 roll shows him present. April 28, 1862 and May 8, 1864 issued clothing. He was appointed 1st corporal of Co. C, 54th Regiment, Georgia Infantry. April 26, 1865 surrendered in Co. D, 54th Regiment, Consolidated Georgia Infantry at Greensboro, North Carolina. May 1, 1865 paroled at Greensboro, North Carolina. He was born in Hancock County, Georgia December 14, 1839 and died in Greene County, Georgia December 1, 1910. He is buried in Siloam Cemetery at Siloam, Greene County, Georgia. (find a grave # 52942873)

SIRMONS (SERMONS), BENJAMIN JONATHAN: Company E, private. May 6, 1862 enlisted as a private in Co. E, 54th Regiment, Georgia Infantry at Savannah, Georgia and received bounty $50.00. November 1862 roll shows him detailed as a boatman. December 31, 1862 received pay. January – February 1863 roll shows him present. August – September 1863 wounded in the right shoulder and permanently disabled at Battery Wagner on Morris Island near Charleston, South Carolina. Unfit for further service. January 1864 issued clothing. He was born in Georgia in 1828 and died in Berrien County, Georgia September 22, 1913.

SIRMONS, JOHN CLEM: Company E, private. May 6, 1862 enlisted as a private in Co. E, 54th Regiment, Georgia Infantry at Savannah, Georgia and received bounty $50.00. December 31, 1862 received pay. January – February 1863 roll shows him present. January 1864 issued clothing. May 10, 1865 surrendered at Tallahassee, Florida. May 25, 1865 paroled at Thomasville, Georgia. He was born April 28, 1839 and died November 30, 1920. He is buried in Empire Primitive Baptist Church at Lakeland, Lanier County, Georgia. (find a grave # 53328664)

SIZEMORE, GEORGE: Company A, private. He enlisted as a private in Co. A, 54th Regiment, Georgia Infantry.

SKELTON, JOHN D.: Company H, corporal. He enlisted as a corporal in Co. H, 54th Regiment, Georgia Infantry. He was born in Franklin County, Georgia January 14, 1820 and died in Hart County Georgia August 12, 1903. He is buried Sardis Baptist Church Cemetery at Hartwell, Hart County, Georgia. (find a grave # 83931460)

SKELTON, W. J.: Company H, private. He enlisted as a private in Co. H, 54th Regiment, Georgia Infantry.

SKINNER, J. J.: Company A, private. He enlisted as a private in Co. A, 54th Regiment, Georgia Infantry.

SLADE, J. F.: Company F, private. February 15, 1863 enlisted as a private in Co. F, 54th Regiment, Georgia Infantry at Savannah, Georgia and received bounty $50.00. January – February 1863 roll shows him present. March 6, 1863 admitted to General Hospital No. 1 at Savannah, Georgia with Acute Bronchitis. April 10, 1863 died in General Hospital No. 1 at Savannah, Georgia of Acute Bronchitis.

SLATON, A. M.: Company G, private. November 7, 1862 enlisted as a private in Co. G, 54th Regiment, Georgia Infantry at Columbus, Georgia and received bounty $50.00. November 1862 roll shows his enlistment. December 31, 1862 received pay. January – February 1863 roll shows him present.

SLAUGHTER, ABNER: Company G, private. May 12, 1862 enlisted as a private in Co. G, 54th Regiment, Georgia Infantry at Columbus, Georgia and received bounty $50.00. December 31, 1862 received pay. January – February 1863 roll shows him present. January 1864 issued clothing. May 30, 1864 his name appears on a report of vaccinations at St. Mary's Hospital at La Grange, Georgia. June 22, 1864 returned to duty from St. Mary's Hospital at La Grange, Georgia. He transferred from Co. G, 54th Regiment, Georgia Infantry to Co. F, 54th Regiment, Georgia Infantry. April 26, 1865 surrendered at Greensboro, North Carolina. May 1, 1865 paroled at Greensboro, North Carolina. He was born in Harris County, Georgia in 1835.

SLAUGHTER, JOHN W.: Company G, corporal. May 12, 1862 enlisted as a private in Co. G, 54th Regiment, Georgia Infantry at Columbus, Georgia and received bounty $50.00. He was elected 4th corporal of Co. G, 54th Regiment, Georgia Infantry. December 31, 1862 received pay. January – February 1863 roll shows him present. September 9, 1863 issued clothing at General Hospital No. 1 at Columbia, South Carolina. January 1864 and May 8, 1864 issued clothing. May 15, 1864 he was wounded in the right leg and ankle crushed at Resaca, Georgia. May 1864 he was sent to hospital at Columbus, Georgia. March 24, 1865 captured at Russellville, Alabama. May 1865 he was paroled at Columbus, Georgia. He was born in Georgia March 24, 1846.

SLAUGHTER, RICHARD J.: Company G, private. 1863 he enlisted as a private in Co. G, 54th Regiment, Georgia Infantry at Columbus, Georgia and received bounty $50.00. March 1865 was sent to the hospital with measles. He was in the hospital at Columbus, Georgia at the close of the war. He was born in Georgia in 1847.

SLOCOMB, F. B.; Company A, private. He enlisted as a private in Co. A, 54th Regiment, Georgia Infantry.

SLOCUMB, WILLIAM F.: Company A, private. November 3, 1863 enlisted as a private in Co. A, 54th Regiment, Georgia Infantry at Macon, Georgia and received bounty $50.00. January – February 1864 roll shows him present (pay due since enlistment). March 31, 1864 issued clothing. July 1, 1864 appears on a register of Floyd House Hospital at Macon, Georgia with General Debility and Anemia following Rubeola and Pneumonia. April 26, 1865 surrendered in Co. D, 54th Regiment, Consolidated Georgia Infantry at Greensboro, North Carolina. May 1, 1865 paroled at Greensboro, North Carolina. He was a resident of Jones County, Georgia. He died In Macon, Bibb County, Georgia March 1890. He is buried in the Slocumb Family Cemetery in Jones County, Georgia.

SLOMAN (SLOWMAN), T. J.: Company G, private. November 11, 1862 enlisted as a private in Co. G, 54th Regiment, Georgia Infantry at Columbus, Georgia and received bounty $50.00. November 1862 roll shows his enlistment. January – February 1863 roll shows him as deserted December 15, 1862. .

SMALEY, JAMES: Company K, private. He enlisted as a private in Co. K, 54th Regiment, Georgia Infantry.

SMITH, A. A.: Company G, private. May 12, 1862 enlisted as a private in Co. G, 54th Regiment, Georgia Infantry at Columbus, Georgia and received bounty $50.00. August 1862 roll shows he deserted May 12, 1862 at Savannah, Georgia.

SMITH, A. R.: Company D, private. He enlisted as a private in Co. D, 54th Regiment, Georgia Infantry.
May 18, 1865 surrendered and paroled at Augusta, Georgia.

SMITH, C.: Company A, private. April 26, 1862 enlisted as a private in Co. A, 54th Regiment, Georgia Infantry at Macon, Georgia and received bounty pay $50.00. April 30, 1863 received pay. June 30, 1863 roll shows him absent (on furlough). October 31, 1863 received pay. November – December 1863 roll shows him present. January 1, 1864 received pay. January – February 1864 roll shows him present. April 29, 1864 and August 8, 1864 issued clothing.

SMITH, CICERO C.: Company A, sergeant. April 24, 1862 enlisted as 2nd corporal in Co. A, 54th Regiment, Georgia Infantry at Macon, Georgia and received bounty pay $50.00. April 30, 1863 received pay. He was elected 2nd corporal of Co. A, 54th Regiment, Georgia Infantry. June 30, 1863 roll shows him present. October 31, 1863 received pay. He was elected 5th sergeant of Co. A, 54th Regiment, Georgia Infantry. November – December 1863 roll shows him present. January 1, 1864 received pay. January – February 1864 roll shows him present. March 31, 1864 issued clothing.

SMITH, GREEN CLARK: Company A, corporal. April 26, 1862 enlisted as a private in Co. A, 54th Regiment, Georgia Infantry at Macon, Georgia and received bounty $50.00. April 30, 1863 received pay. June 30, 1863 roll shows him present. October 1863 was elected 3rd corporal of Co. A, 54th Regiment, Georgia Infantry. October 31, 1863 received pay. November – December 1863 roll shows him present. January 1, 1864 received pay. January – February 1864 roll shows him present. April 29, 1864 issued clothing. April 26, 1865 surrendered in Co. D, 54th Regiment, Consolidated Georgia Infantry at Greensboro, North Carolina. May 1, 1865 paroled at Greensboro, North Carolina. He was born in Georgia October 19, 1844 and died in Jones County, Georgia March 17, 1924. He is buried in Clinton United Methodist Church Cemetery at Clinton, Jones, County, Georgia. (find a grave # 21773879)

SMITH, GEORGE R.: Company F, private. May 13, 1862 enlisted as a private in Co. F, 54th Regiment, Georgia Infantry at Macon, Georgia and received bounty $50.00. November 1862 roll shows him detailed as color corporal. January 7, 1863 detailed as clerk for Brigade Surgeon. July 31, 1863 received pay $22.00. September 1, 1863 to July 1, 1864 detailed for special duty at a rate of pay of $1.25 per day. October 1, 1863 and November 11, 1863 issued clothing. December 31, 1862 received pay. January – February 1863 roll shows him present. November 18, 1863 received pay $44.00. November – December 1863 roll shows him absent (detailed as clerk for Brigade Surgeon since July 7, 1863). January 1864 issued clothing. April 21 and 24, 1864 granted furlough by Special Order No. 94/2. May 13, 1864 granted furlough by Special Order No. 112/2. July 1, 1864 received pay. July 18, 1864 received pay $108.75. He was born in Savannah, Chatham County, Georgia October 20, 1845 and died November 1, 1864. He is buried in Laurel Grove Cemetery at Savannah, Chatham County, Georgia. (find a grave # 96452931)

SMITH, HENRY LUKE: Company A, lieutenant. November 28, 1861 enlisted as a private in Co. C, 1st Independent Battalion, Georgia State Troops. April 16, 1862 roll shows him present. April 17, 1862 mustered out. April 18, 1862 enlisted as a private in Co. A, 54th Regiment, Georgia Infantry at Macon, Georgia and received bounty $50.00. January 13, 1863 he was elected Jr. 2nd lieutenant of Co. A, 54th Regiment, Georgia Infantry. June 30, 1863 roll shows him present. December 1, 1863 received pay $80.00. November – December 1863 roll shows him present. January – February 1864 roll includes his name. July 2, 1864 received pay $80.00. September 16, 1864 admitted to Ocmulgee Hospital at Macon, Georgia with Chronic Diarrhoea. September 21, 1864 appears on a register of Floyd

House Hospital at Macon, Georgia with Chronic Diarrhoea. September 30, 1864 transferred to Milledgeville, Georgia. He was a resident of Jones County, Georgia. He was born in Georgia in 1841. He is buried in Smiths Grove Cemetery in Jefferson County, Georgia. (find a grave # 68597741)

SMITH, J. C.: Company E, private. May 6, 1862 enlisted as a private in Co. E, 54th Regiment, Georgia Infantry at Savannah, Georgia and received bounty $50.00. December 31, 1862 received pay. January – February 1863 roll shows him present.

SMITH, J. J.: Company I, private. He enlisted as a private in Co. I, 54th Regiment, Georgia Infantry.

SMITH, JAMES: Company E, private. January 28, 1863 enlisted as a private in Co. E, 54th Regiment, Georgia Infantry at Coffee Bluff near Savannah, Georgia and received bounty $50.00. January – February 1863 roll shows him present. January 1864 and May 8, 1864 issued clothing. February 13, 1865 died of Chronic Diarrhoea in Columbia, South Carolina at the Hospitals of the Army of Tennessee.

SMITH, JAMES M.: Company K, private. October 3, 1861 enlisted as a private in Co. A, 1st Regiment, 1st Brigade, Georgia State Troops. April 1862 mustered out. April 18, 1862 enlisted as a private in Co. K, 54th Regiment, Georgia Infantry at Savannah, Georgia and received bounty $50.00. August and September 1862 rolls show him detailed as a teamster. September 19, 1862 to October 10, 1862 detailed as a butcher at Savannah, Georgia. January 1, 1863 received pay. January – February 1863 roll shows him present. July 1, 1863 to August 1, 1863 detailed as a teamster at a rate of $.25 extra per day. November 16, 1863 received pay. March 18, 1864 issued clothing. May 10, 1865 surrendered at Tallahassee, Florida. May 21, 1865 paroled at Thomasville, Georgia. (Pension records indicate he surrendered April 26, 1865 at Greensboro, North Carolina.) He was born in South Carolina October 4, 1829 He died in Henry County, Georgia in 1914.

SMITH, JOHN J.: Company A, private. September 1, 1863 enlisted as a private in Co. A, 54th Regiment, Georgia Infantry at Macon, Georgia and received bounty $50.00. October 31, 1863 received pay. November – December 1863 roll shows him present. January 1, 1864 received pay. January – February 1864 roll shows him present. March 31, 1864 issued clothing.

SMITH, JOHN W.: Company A (D), corporal. February 10, 1863 enlisted as a private in Co. A, 54th Regiment, Georgia Infantry at Macon, Georgia and received bounty $50.00. February 28, 1863 received pay. May 5, 1863 transferred from General Hospital No. 1 at Savannah, Georgia to General Hospital at Whitesville, Georgia (Pleurisy Convalescent). June 30, 1863 roll shows him absent (in hospital at Whiteville). October 31, 1863 received pay. November – December 1863 roll shows him present. January 1, 1864 received pay. January – February 1864 roll shows him present. March 31, 1864 issued clothing. He was elected 4th corporal of

Co. A, 54th Regiment, Georgia Infantry. April 26, 1865 surrendered in Co. D, 54th Regiment, Consolidated Georgia Infantry at Greensboro, North Carolina. May 1, 1865 paroled at Greensboro, North Carolina. He was born in Jones County, Georgia August 2, 1842 and died in Jones County, Georgia September 17, 1917. He is buried in the Smith Cemetery at Gray, Jones County, Georgia. (find a grave # 58521009)

SMITH, MEE: Company F, private. August 11, 1862 enlisted as a private in Co. F, 54th Regiment, Georgia Infantry at Beaulieu near Savannah, Georgia and received bounty $50.00. September 1862 roll shows his enlistment.

SMITH, R.: sergeant. He enlisted in the 54th Regiment, Georgia Infantry as a 2nd sergeant.

SMITH, ROBERT WILLIAM: Company A, lieutenant. October 17, 1861 enlisted as a private in Co. C, 1st Independent Battalion, Georgia State Troops. April 16, 1862 roll shows him present. April 1862 mustered out. April 21, 1862 enlisted as a sergeant in Co. A, 54th Regiment, Georgia Infantry at Macon, Georgia and received bounty $50.00. April 30, 1863 received pay. June 30, 1863 roll shows him present as 1st sergeant. October 31, 1863 received pay. November – December 1863 roll shows him present. January 1, 1864 received pay. January – February 1864 roll shows him present. September 7, 1864 admitted to Ocmulgee Hospital at Macon, Georgia with a Gunshot Wound to the right hip in the flesh (Batt. C. L. B). September 14, 1864 report of Mercers Brigade (in camp near Jonesboro, Georgia) shows him wounded and sent to division hospital. September 21, 1864 transferred. February 24, 1865 admitted to Ocmulgee Hospital at Macon, Georgia with a Gunshot Wound. He was transferred to hospital at Vineville. August 31, 1864 discharged due to wounds. He was a resident of Bibb County, Georgia. He died in Macon, Bibb County, Georgia April 1886.

SMITH, RODDEN JR.: Company A, lieutenant. He enlisted as 3rd lieutenant in Co. A, 54th Regiment, Georgia Infantry. December 23, 1862 resigned due to disability.

SMITH, S. T.: Company B, private. February 16, 1865 enlisted in Co. B, 4th Georgia Sharpshooters at Macon, Georgia. April 26, 1865 surrendered in Co. B, 54th Regiment, Consolidated Georgia Infantry at Greensboro, North Carolina. May 1, 1865 paroled at Greensboro, North Carolina.

SMITH, SAMUEL J.: Company F, private. He enlisted in Co. G, 54th Regiment, Georgia Infantry. September 14, 1863 received pay $44.00. He transferred from Co. G, 54th Regiment, Georgia Infantry to Co. F, 54th Regiment, Georgia Infantry. April 26, 1865 surrendered at Greensboro, North Carolina. May 1, 1865 paroled at Greensboro, North Carolina.

SMITH, SEABORN: Company B, private. April; 28, 1862 enlisted as a private in Co. B, 54th Regiment, Georgia Infantry at Savannah, Georgia and received bounty $50.00. December 31, 1862 received pay. January – February 1863 roll shows him present. January 1864 issued clothing. May 10, 1865 surrendered at Tallahassee, Florida. May 21, 1865 paroled at Thomasville, Georgia. He was born October 28, 1835 and died October 25, 1876. He is buried in Antioch Baptist Church Cemetery in Bacon, County, Georgia. (find a grave # 16135648)

SMITH, STEPHEN: Company I, private. He enlisted as a private in Co. I, 54th Regiment, Georgia Infantry.

SMITH, T.: Company C (F), private. January 31, 1862 enlisted as a private in Co. C, 54th Regiment, Georgia Infantry at Savannah, Georgia and received bounty pay $50.00. January 1, 1863 transferred from Co. C, 54th Regiment, Georgia Infantry to Co. F, 54th Regiment, Georgia Infantry. January – February 1863 rolls show his transfer and him present. March 16, 1863 admitted to General Hospital No. 1 at Savannah, Georgia with Congestive Febris. March 17, 1863 he died at General Hospital No. 1 at Savannah, Georgia with Congestive Febris.

SMITH, T. A.: Company B, private. He enlisted as a private in Co. B, 54th Regiment, Georgia Infantry.

SMITH, THOMAS: Company B, private. October 10, 1861 enlisted as a private in Co. K, 2nd Regiment, 1st Brigade, Georgia State Troops. April 1862 mustered out. April 21, 1862 enlisted as a private in Co. B, 54th Regiment, Georgia Infantry at Savannah, Georgia and received bounty $50.00. December 31, 1862 received pay. January – February 1863 roll shows him present. January 1864 issued clothing. October 17, 1864 issued clothing at Augusta, Georgia.

SMITH, W. D.: Company A, private. September 1, 1863 enlisted as a private in Co. A, 54th Regiment, Georgia Infantry at Macon, Georgia and received bounty $50.00. October 22, 1862 discharged. October 1862 roll shows his discharge.

SMITH, W. F.: Company E, private. He enlisted as a private in Co. E, 54th Regiment, Georgia Infantry. October 1862 roll shows him detailed to the company commissary.

SMITH, WARREN: Company B, sergeant. He enlisted as a sergeant in Co. B, 54th Regiment, Georgia Infantry.

SMITH, WILLIAM C.: Company F, private. He enlisted as a private in Co. F, 54th Regiment, Georgia Infantry.

SNIDER, H.: Company F, private. May 17, 1861 enlisted as a private in Captain Chisholm's Company, Georgia State Troops. May 1862 mustered out. May 17, 1862 enlisted as a private in Co. F, 54th Regiment, Georgia Infantry at Savannah, Georgia and received bounty pay $50.00. November 20, 1862 discharged at Beaulieu near Savannah, Georgia by Civil Authority. November 1862 roll shows his discharge.

SOLOMON, W. G.: Company F (D), corporal. February 20 (11), 1863 enlisted as a private in Co. F, 54th Regiment, Georgia Infantry at Savannah, Georgia and received bounty pay $50.00. January – February 1863 roll shows him present. October 1863 appointed 1st corporal of Co. F, 54th Regiment, Georgia Infantry. November 1, 1863 received pay. November – December 1863 roll shows him present. January 1864 issued clothing. April 26, 1865 surrendered as 3rd corporal in Co. D, 54th Regiment,

Consolidated Georgia Infantry at Greensboro, North Carolina. May 1, 1865 paroled at Greensboro, North Carolina.

SONNEBORN, CHARLES: Company A (F), private. May 10, 1862 enlisted as a private in Co. A, 54th Regiment, Georgia Infantry at Macon, Georgia and received bounty $50.00. August 1862 roll shows his enlistment (June 23, 1862). October 1862 roll shows him detailed as captain's cook. December 31, 1862 received pay. January 1, 1863 transferred from Co. A, 54th Regiment, Georgia Infantry to Co. F, 54th Regiment, Georgia Infantry. February 8, 1863 he was discharged by Civil Authority. January – February 1863 roll of Company F, 54th Regiment, Georgia Infantry shows his transfer and that he was discharged by Civil Authority on February 8, 1863.

SOREA, C. A.: Company D, private. October 7, 1861 enlisted as a private in Co. I, 5th Regiment, Georgia State Troops. April 1862 mustered out. April 30, 1862 enlisted as a private in Co. D, 54th Regiment, Georgia Infantry at Savannah, Georgia and received bounty pay $50.00. December 31, 1862 received pay. January – February 1863 roll shows him present. January 1864 and May 8, 1864 issued clothing. January 19, 1865 admitted to Way Hospital at Meridian, Mississippi with Debilatis. April 26, 1865 surrendered in Co. D, 54th Regiment, Consolidated Georgia Infantry at Greensboro, North Carolina. May 1, 1865 paroled at Greensboro, North Carolina.

SOWELL, WILLIAM: Company D, private. April 30, 1862 enlisted as a private in Co. D, 54th Regiment, Georgia Infantry at Savannah, Georgia and received bounty pay $50.00. December 31, 1862 received pay. January – February 1863 roll shows him present (absent without leave for 3 days). January 1864 issued clothing. He was born July 10, 1835. He is buried in Doubleheads Baptist Church at Sylvania, Screven County, Georgia. (find a grave # 38265979)

SPEAR (SPEER), G. W.: Company H, private. November 12, 1862 enlisted as a private in Co. H, 54th Regiment, Georgia Infantry at Columbus, Georgia and received bounty pay $50.00. November 1862 roll shows his enlistment. December 31, 1862 received pay. January – February 1863 roll shows him present. March 18, 1863 deserted. April 18, 1863 admitted to U. S. A. General Hospital, Ladies Home at New York City, New York. April 20, 1863 returned to duty. April 20, 1863 admitted to U. S. A. Convalescent Hospital, Fort Wood, Bedloe's Island, New York Harbor for Convalescent. April 21, 1863 transferred to 51st hospital.

SPEAR (SPEER), JAMES F.: Company F, private. He enlisted as a private in Co. F, 54th Regiment, Georgia Infantry. June 19, 1864 captured near Marietta, Georgia. June 26, 1864 received at Military Prison at Louisville, Kentucky from Nashville, Tennessee. June 27, 1864 sent to Camp Morton, Indianapolis, Indiana from Military Prison at Louisville, Kentucky. June 28, 1864 received at Camp Morton, Indianapolis, Indiana from Military Prison at Louisville, Kentucky.

SPEAR (SPEER), JAMES SAMUEL: Company H (F), private. May

12, 1862 enlisted as a private in Co. H, 54th Regiment, Georgia Infantry at Columbus, Georgia and received bounty pay $50.00. January 1, 1863 transferred from Co. H, 54th Regiment, Georgia Infantry to Co. F, 54th Regiment, Georgia Infantry by order of Colonel Way. January – February 1863 rolls show him present and show his transfer. March 3, 1863 transferred from General Hospital No, 1 at Savannah, Georgia to General Hospital at Macon, Georgia with Tertran Fever. November 1, 1863 received pay. November – December 1863 roll shows him present. January 1864 issued clothing. June 19, 1864 captured near Marietta, Georgia (Kennesaw Mountain). July 1, 1864 received at Camp Morton, Indianapolis, Indiana from Military Prison at Louisville, Kentucky May 22, 1865 released on Oath of Allegiance at Camp Morton, Indianapolis, Indiana. He is described as being; a resident of Columbus, Georgia, dark complexion, black hair, black eyes and 5 feet 10 inches high. He is buried in Macedonia Cemetery at Sasser, Terrell County, Georgia. (find a grave # 17976885)

SPEIR, DAVID: Company I, private. September 18, 1861 enlisted as a private in Co. C, 1st Regiment, 1st Brigade, Georgia State Troops. March 18, 1862 mustered out. May 6, 1862 enlisted as a private in Co. I, 54th Regiment, Georgia Infantry at Guyton, Georgia and received bounty pay $50.00. December 31, 1862 received pay. January – February 1863 roll shows him present. October 31, 1863 received pay. November – December 1863 roll shows him present. January 1864 issued clothing. He transferred from Co. D, 54th Regiment, Georgia Infantry to Co. F, 54th Regiment, Georgia Infantry. April 26, 1865 surrendered at Greensboro, North Carolina. May 1, 1865 paroled at Greensboro, North Carolina. He was born August 13, 1832 and died April 8, 1902. He is buried in Old Providence Cemetery in Guyton, Effingham County, Georgia. (find a grave #16708180)

SPEIR, REDDICK J.: Company I, corporal. September 18, 1861 enlisted as a private and appointed corporal in Co. C, 1st Regiment, 1st Brigade, Georgia State Troops. March 18, 1862 mustered out. May 6, 1862 enlisted as a private in Co. I, 54th Regiment, Georgia Infantry at Guyton, Georgia and received bounty pay $50.00. December 31, 1862 received pay. January – February 1863 roll shows him present. October 31, 1863 received pay. November – December 1863 roll shows him present (fisherman for captain). January 1864 and April 25, 1864 issued clothing. He was appointed corporal of Co. I, 54th Regiment, Georgia Infantry. September 2, 1864 captured at Jonesboro, Georgia. October 28, 1864 received at Military Prison at Louisville, Kentucky from Nashville, Tennessee. October 29, 1864 sent to Camp Douglas, Illinois from Military Prison at Louisville, Kentucky. November 1, 1864 received at Camp Douglas, Illinois from Military Prison at Louisville, Kentucky. December 1864 took the Oath of Allegiance at Camp Douglas, Illinois (claims to have been loyal, said he was conscripted in the rebel army. Deserted to avail himself of the amnesty proclamation). April 1, 1865 enlisted in Co I, 5th U. S. Volunteers at Camp Douglas, Illinois. He was born in Guyton, Effingham County, Georgia July 20, 1839 and died in Savannah, Chatham County, Georgia June 1, 1926. He is buried in Laurel Grove Cemetery (North) at Savannah, Chatham County, Georgia. (find a grave # 56534262)

SPEIR (SPEER), WILLIAM S.: Company I, private. May 6, 1862 enlisted as a private in Co. I, 54th Regiment, Georgia Infantry at Guyton, Georgia and received bounty pay $50.00. July 10, 1862 detailed to medical department at Jo Thompson Artillery Hospital as a steward. August, September, October, November and December 1862 rolls show him detailed as a hospital steward. January 1, 1863 received pay. January – February 1863 roll shows his name. March 17, 1863 received pay $ 42.00. May 1, 1863 received pay. October 31, 1863 roll of Bethesda Hospital, Beaulieu Battery near Savannah, Georgia shows him present as a steward and due extra duty pay (184 days plus 87 days due). October 31, 1863 received pay. November – December roll of Bethesda Hospital, Beaulieu Battery near Savannah, Georgia shows him present. January 1864 issued clothing. January – February 1864 roll shows him absent (ordered to report to Surgeon Godfrey on January 6, 1864. June 2, 1864 issued clothing. He was transferred from Co. I, 54th Regiment, Georgia Infantry to Co. F, 54th Regiment, Georgia Infantry. April 26, 1865 surrendered at Greensboro, North Carolina. May 1, 1865 paroled at Greensboro, North Carolina. He was born January 19, 1828 and died November 16, 1912. He is buried in Old Providence Cemetery in Guyton, Effingham County, Georgia. (find a grave #16711584)

SPELL, BENJAMIN: Company D, corporal. October 7, 1861 enlisted and elected 2nd corporal of Co. I, 5th Regiment, Georgia State Troops. April 1862 mustered out. April 30, 1862 enlisted as 2nd corporal in Co. D, 54th Regiment, Georgia Infantry at Savannah, Georgia and received bounty pay $50.00. December 31, 1862 received pay. January – February 1863 roll shows him present. He died in Charleston, South Carolina in 1863-4. He is buried in the confederate section of Magnolia Cemetery at Charleston, South Carolina.

SPENCE, J. D.: Company C, sergeant. May 6, 1862 enlisted as a private in Co. C, 54th Regiment, Georgia Infantry at Savannah, Georgia and received bounty pay $50.00. December 31, 1862 received pay. January – February 1863 roll shows him present. September 1, 1863 received pay. December 1863 appointed 4th sergeant of Co. C, 54th Regiment, Georgia Infantry. January – February 1864 roll shows him present. He was a resident of Emanuel County, Georgia.

SPENCER, HENRY C.: private. He enlisted as a private in the 54th Regiment, Georgia Infantry. February 24, 1864 he took the Oath of Allegiance and is described as: a resident of Lumpkin County, Georgia, light complexion, light hair, blue eyes and 5 feet 11 inches high.

SPILLERS, THOMAS W.: Company G, private. May 12, 1862 enlisted as a private in Co. G, 54th Regiment, Georgia Infantry at Columbus,

Georgia and received bounty $50.00. September 19, 1862 to October 12, 1862 detailed as a butcher at Savannah, Georgia. December 31, 1862 received pay. January – February 1863 roll shows him present. January 1864, April 25, 1864 and May 8, 1864 issued clothing. November 20, 1864 issued clothing at Convalescent Camp Wright at Macon, Georgia. December 29, 1864 appears on a register of Floyd House and Ocmulgee Hospitals at Macon, Georgia (in Hospital B. G.) with a Double Hernia, Hemorrhoids with Prolapsus "Ani". March 1865 he appears on a register of surgical cases at Polk Hospital at Macon, Georgia as having Hemorrhoid Surgery on March 28, 1865 (Multilocular Hemorrhoids – Ecrasument under chloform) (he is shown as age 38 years and a farmer and was doing well after the surgery).

SPIN, W.: Company I, private. He enlisted as a private in Co. I, 54th Regiment, Georgia Infantry. July 1, 1862 detailed to medical department as a nurse. July 1862 roll shows him detailed as a nurse.

SPINKS, CALVIN T.: Company H, private. He enlisted as a private in Co. H, 54th Regiment, Georgia Infantry in 1864. September 1, 1864 wounded and disabled at Jonesboro, Georgia. He was born April 14, 1829 and died March 11, 1901. He is buried in Union Baptist Church Cemetery at Whitesville, Harris County, Georgia. (find a grave # 101112787)

SPINKS, W. W.: Company H, private. He enlisted as a private in Co. H, 54th Regiment, Georgia Infantry. May 14, 1864 deserted. August 1862 roll shows his desertion.

SPIRES, J. J.: Company K, corporal. He enlisted as a private in Co. K, 54th Regiment, Georgia Infantry. He was elected corporal of Co. K, 54th Regiment, Georgia Infantry.

SPIRES, J. N.: Company K, corporal. He enlisted as a private in Co. K, 54th Regiment, Georgia Infantry. He was elected corporal of Co. K, 54th Regiment, Georgia Infantry.

STAFFORD, ELI: Company B, private. October 10, 1861 enlisted as a private in Co. K, 2nd Regiment, 1st Brigade, Georgia State Troops. April 1862 mustered out. April 21, 1862 enlisted as a private in Co. B, 54th Regiment, Georgia Infantry at Savannah, Georgia and received bounty $50.00. December 31, 1862 received pay. January – February 1863 roll shows him present (present in arrest – absent without leave for 2 days).

STALEY, WILLIAM C.: Company F, private. May 17, 1861 enlisted as a private in Chisholm's Company, Georgia State Troops. May 1862 mustered out. April 13, 1863. He enlisted as a private in Co. F, 54th Regiment, Georgia Infantry.

STANFORD, E. G.: Company E, private. He enlisted as a private in Co. E, 54th Regiment, Georgia Infantry.

STANLEY, C. P.: Company E, private. July 29, 1864 enlisted as a private in Co. B, 37^{h} Regiment, Georgia Infantry at Columbus, Georgia. April 26, 1865 surrendered in Co. E, 54th Regiment, Consolidated Georgia Infantry at Greensboro, North Carolina. May 1, 1865 paroled at Greensboro, North Carolina.

STARNES, RUSSELL: Company G, private. He enlisted as a private in Co. G, 54th Regiment, Georgia Infantry.

STEEDLEY, ZACHARIAH: Company B, private. February 5, 1863 enlisted as a private in Co. B, 54th Regiment, Georgia Infantry at Savannah, Georgia and received bounty $50.00. January – February 1863 roll shows him present. January 1864 issued clothing. He was born in 1824 and died in 1883. He is buried in Devil's Bay Cemetery at Argile, Clinch County, Georgia. (find a grave # 104931064)

STEPHENS, C. M.: Company I, private. He enlisted as a private in Co. I, 54th Regiment, Georgia Infantry.

STEPHENS, H. J.: Company B, private. He enlisted as a private in Co. B, 54th Regiment, Georgia Infantry.

STEPHENS (STEVENS), JAMES H.: Company E, private. May 6, 1862 enlisted as a private in Co. E, 54th Regiment, Georgia Infantry at Savannah, Georgia and received bounty $50.00. December 31, 1862 received pay. January – February 1863 roll shows him present. January 1864, April 25, 1864 and May 8, 1864 issued clothing. (According to pension records - April 26, 1865 surrendered at Greensboro, North Carolina. May 1, 1865 paroled at Greensboro, North Carolina). He was born in Jefferson County, Georgia November 7, 1828 and died in Emanuel County, Georgia in 1913. (Identical information for a James H. Stephens, private, Company C, 54th Regiment, Georgia Infantry).

STEPHENS, JOSEPH HAMILTON: Company E, private. May 6, 1862 enlisted as a private in Co. E, 54th Regiment, Georgia Infantry at Savannah, Georgia and received bounty $50.00. December 31, 1862 received pay. January – February 1863 roll shows him present. January 1864, April 25, 1864 and May 8, 1864 issued clothing. May 8, 1864 he was wounded in the left hand resulting in amputation at Dug Gap near Dalton, Georgia. He was born in South Carolina in 1831 and died in Berrien County, Georgia April 12, 1884. He died in Thomas County, Georgia. He is buried in Laurel Hill Cemetery at Thomasville, Thomas County, Georgia. (find a grave # 27033290)

STEVENS, CALEB: Company A, private. May 7, 1862 enlisted as a private in Co. A, 54th Regiment, Georgia Infantry at Macon, Georgia and received bounty pay $50.00. April 30, 1863 received pay. June 30, 1863 roll shows him present (absent from May 3, 1863 to May 5, 1863). October 31, 1863 received pay. November – December 1863 roll shows him present. January 1, 1864 received pay. January – February 1864 roll shows him present. March 31, 1864 issued clothing. 1864 he died in service leaving effects of $17.75. He is buried in the Stonewall Cemetery at Griffin, Spalding County, Georgia. (find a grave # 91188280)

STEVENS, JAMES S.: Company C, private. August 26, 1862 enlisted as a private in Co. C, 54th Regiment, Georgia Infantry at Savannah, Georgia and received bounty $50.00. November 13, 1862 shown as deserted. December 31, 1862 received pay. January – February 1863 roll shows him present. January 1, 1864 received pay. January – February 1864 roll shows him present. April 25, 1864 issued clothing. May 26, 1865 surrendered and paroled at Augusta, Georgia. He was born in Georgia April 20, 1820 and died in Georgia October 28, 1885. He is buried in Stevens Cemetery in Emanuel County, Georgia. (find a grave #61967531)

STEVENS (STEAVENS), JOE: Company A, private. May 2, 1862 enlisted as a private in Co. A, 54th Regiment, Georgia Infantry at Macon, Georgia and received bounty pay $50.00. April 30, 1863 received pay. June 30, 1863 roll shows him present (sick in company hospital). October 31, 1863 received pay. November – December 1863 roll shows him present. January 1, 1864 received pay. January – February 1864 roll shows him present. March 31, 1864 issued clothing.

STEVENS (STEPHENS), JOSEPH: Company A, private. May 6, 1862 enlisted as a private in Co. A, 54th Regiment, Georgia Infantry at Macon, Georgia and received bounty pay $50.00. January – February 1863 roll shows him present. October 31, 1863 received pay. November – December 1863 roll shows him present. January 1, 1864 received pay. January – February 1864 roll shows him present. March 31, 1864 issued clothing. March – April 1865 pension records show he was home on sick furlough. He was born October 10, 1833 and died March 19, 1918 in Jones County, Georgia. He is buried in Fortville Cemetery at Fortville, Jones County, Georgia. (find a grave # 16160216)

STEVENS (STEPHENS), THOMAS J.: Company C, private. He enlisted as a private in Co. C, 54th Regiment, Georgia Infantry. July 20, 1864 captured at Peachtree Creek near Atlanta, Georgia. July 28, 1864 received at Military Prison at Louisville, Kentucky from Nashville, Tennessee. July 30, 1864 sent to Camp Douglas, Illinois from Military Prison at Louisville, Kentucky. August 1, 1864 received at Camp Douglas, Illinois from Military Prison at Louisville, Kentucky. June 16, 1865 discharged from Camp Douglas, Illinois. He is described as being; a resident of Montgomery County, Virginia, fair complexion, brown hair, grey eyes, 5 feet 6 inches high and from Christiansburg, Virginia.

STEVENSON (STEPHENSON), JOSEPH S.: Company H, private. October 8, 1862 enlisted as a private in Co. H, 54th Regiment, Georgia Infantry at Beaulieu near Savannah, Georgia. October 22, 1862 detailed to the medical department as a ward master. October 1862 roll shows his enlistment and that he was detailed to the hospital as a nurse. November 1, 1862 received pay. November 1862 roll shows him detailed in the hospital as a steward. December 1862 roll shows him detailed to the hospital as a nurse. January – February 1863 hospital muster roll shows him present as a ward master.

STEWART, HENRY: Company G, private. January 22, 1863 enlisted as a private in Co. G, 54th Regiment, Georgia Infantry at Columbus, Georgia and received bounty pay $50.00. January – February 1863 roll shows him present. January 1864 issued clothing. February 10, 1865 admitted to Ocmulgee Hospital at Macon, Georgia with Gelaxio. February 13, 1865 his name appears on a register as being in Ocmulgee Hospital at Macon,

Georgia with Ulcers on foot resulting from Frostbite. February 14, 1864 furloughed. April 11, 1865 admitted to Ocmulgee Hospital at Macon, Georgia with ulcers. April 20-21, 1865 captured at Macon, Georgia. April 28, 1865 paroled and returned to duty at Macon, Georgia. He is shown as being a resident of Seal's Station (Store), Russell County, Alabama.

STEWART, JOHN T.: Company A, private. April 29, 1862 enlisted as a private in Co. A, 54th Regiment, Georgia Infantry at Macon, Georgia and received bounty pay of $50.00. April 30, 1863 received pay. June 30, 1863 roll shows him absent on furlough. August 31, 1863 received pay. November – December 1863 roll shows him present. January 1, 1864 received pay. January – February 1864 roll shows him present (pay for the months of September and October 1863 due). April 29, 1864 issued clothing. March 29, 1865 admitted to Ocmulgee Hospital at Macon, Georgia with Chronic Diarrhoea. April 18, 1865 transferred. April 23, 1865 admitted to Ocmulgee Hospital at Macon, Georgia with Chronic Diarrhoea. April 20-21, 1865 captured at Macon, Georgia. April 29, 1865 paroled and returned to duty. He was a resident of Jones County, Georgia.

STEWART (STEWARD), JOHN: Company B, private. He enlisted as a private in Co. B, 54th Regiment, Georgia Infantry.

STEWART, SILAS: Company A, private. October 7, 1862 enlisted as a private in Co. H, 54th Regiment, Georgia Infantry at Beaulieu near Savannah, Georgia and received bounty pay of $50.00. April 30, 1863 received pay. May 1, 1863 to July 31, 1863 detailed as a carpenter (company mechanic). June 30, 1863 roll shows him present (detailed as a carpenter). July 31, 1863 received pay. October 31, 1863 received pay. November – December 1863 roll shows him present. January 1, 1864 received pay. January – February 1864 roll shows him present. April 29, 1864 issued clothing. September 21, 1864 he appears on a register of Floyd House Hospital at Macon, Georgia (Diarrhoea and Bronchitis causing General Debility and Emaciation). He was a resident of Griswold, Georgia.

STOCKS, J. W.: Company B, private. He enlisted as a private in Co. B, 54th Regiment, Georgia Infantry.

STOCKS, JOHN W.: Company G, private. He enlisted as a private in Co. G, 54th Regiment, Georgia Infantry.

STOCKS, T. M.: Company B, private. He enlisted as a private in Co. B, 54th Regiment, Georgia Infantry.

STOTT, ABDIEL (ABDEL): Company H, private. May 8, 1862 enlisted as a private in Co. E, 15th Battalion, Alabama Partisan Rangers. He mustered out. August 25, 1862 enlisted in Co. H, 54th Regiment, Georgia Infantry at Beaulieu near Savannah, Georgia and received bounty pay of $50.00. August and September 1862 rolls show his enlistment. December 31, 1862 received pay. January – February 1863 roll shows him present. October 31, 1863 received pay. November – December 1863 roll shows him present. January 1864 issued clothing. January 1, 1864 received pay. January – February 1864 roll shows him present (on picket).

July 12, 1864 issued clothing in Marshall Hospital at Columbus, Georgia. He died May 19, 1866. He is buried in Stott Cemetery in Butler County, Alabama. (find a grave # 40999287)

STRAWBRIDGE, W. B.: Company H, private. November 3, 1862 enlisted as a private in Co. H, 54th Regiment, Georgia Infantry at Columbus, Georgia and received bounty $50.00. November 1862 roll shows his enlistment. December 31, 1862 received pay. January – February 1863 roll shows him present. October 31, 1863 received pay. November – December 1863 roll shows him present (detailed as ordinance sergeant). December 31, 1863 received pay. January 1864 issued clothing. January – February 1864 roll shows him present. April 25, 1864 and June 2, 1864 issued clothing.

STREET, RICHARD: Company E, sergeant. He enlisted as a sergeant in Co. E, 54th Regiment, Georgia Infantry.

STRICKLAND, ISHAM: Company B, private. October 16, 1861 enlisted as a private in Co. K, 2nd Regiment, 1st Brigade, Georgia State Troops. April 1862 mustered out. April 21, 1862 enlisted as a private in Co. B, 54th Regiment, Georgia Infantry at Savannah, Georgia and received bounty pay of $50.00. December 31, 1862 received pay. January – February 1863 roll shows him present (absent without leave 1 day). January 1864 issued clothing. January 1, 1865 captured at Itawamba County, Mississippi. January 16, 1865 received at Military Prison at Louisville, Kentucky from Nashville, Tennessee. January 16, 1865 sent to Camp Chase, Ohio from Military Prison at Louisville, Kentucky. January 18, 1865 received at Camp Chase, Ohio from Military Prison at Louisville, Kentucky. February 14, 1865 died of pneumonia at Camp Chase, Ohio. He is buried in the Camp Chase Confederate Cemetery in grave #1228 (1/3 mile south of Camp Chase). (find a grave # 55388048)

STRINGER, HENRY W.: Company A, private. He enlisted as a private in Co. A, 54th Regiment, Georgia Infantry.

STRIPLING, BENJAMIN A.: Company H, private. October 1, 1863 enlisted as a private in Co. H, 54th Regiment, Georgia Infantry at Columbus, Georgia and received bounty $50.00. January 1834 issued clothing. January – February 1864 roll shows him present (on guard). April 25, 1864 and June 2, 1864 issued clothing.

STRIPLING (STRIBLING), BERRY A.: Company H, private. October 1, 1863 enlisted as a private in Co. H, 54th Regiment, Georgia Infantry. Pension records show; August 9, 1864 he was wounded through knee and right eye near Decatur, Georgia (Atlanta, Georgia). October 9, 1864 discharged due to disability. He was born in Harris County, Georgia February 17, 1842 and died in Muscogee County, Georgia in 1902.

STRIPLING (STRIBLING), GEORGE M.: Company H, private. November 7, 1862 enlisted as a private in Co. H, 54th Regiment, Georgia Infantry at Columbus, Georgia and received bounty $50.00. November 1862 roll shows his enlistment. December 31, 1862 received pay. January – February 1863 roll shows him present. October 31, 1863 received pay. November – December 1863 roll shows him present (detailed as ordinance sergeant). December 31, 1863 received pay. January 1864 issued clothing. January – February 1864 roll shows him present. April 26, 1865 surrendered at Greensboro, North Carolina. May 1, 1865 paroled at Greensboro, North Carolina.

STRIPLING (STRIBLING), JOHN A.: Company H, private. May 12, 1862 enlisted as a private in Co. H, 54th Regiment, Georgia Infantry at Columbus, Georgia and received bounty $50.00. December 31, 1862 received pay. January – February 1863 roll shows him present (detailed as a teamster in the quartermaster's department). July 1, 1863 to December 31, 1863 detailed as a teamster at Charleston, South Carolina at a rate of $.25 extra per day. October 31, 1863 received pay. November 16, 1863 received pay. December 31, 1863 received pay. November – December 1863 roll shows him present (detailed as teamster – pay due from May 1 until August 31, 1863). January 1864 issued clothing. January – February 1864 roll shows him present. February 29, 1864 received pay. July 29, 1864 admitted to Marshall Hospital at Columbus, Georgia. August 4, 1864 issued clothing in Marshall Hospital at Columbus, Georgia. November 30, 1864 hospital muster roll from Marshall Hospital at Columbus, Georgia shows him present as a patient.

STRIPLING (STRIBLING), MILTON: Company H, private. November 7, 1862 enlisted as a private in Co. H, 54th Regiment, Georgia Infantry at Columbus, Georgia and received bounty $50.00. December 20, 1862 he died of disease in Savannah, Georgia. December 1862 roll shows his death. He was a resident of Harris County, Georgia. He was born in Harris County, Georgia.

STRIPLING, ROBERT: Company G (F), private. May 12, 1862 enlisted as a private in Co. G, 54th Regiment, Georgia Infantry at Columbus, Georgia and received bounty $50.00. October 1, 1862 to October 31, 1862 detailed for extra duty at Beaulieu near Savannah, Georgia at a rate of $.25 extra per day. October 31, 1862 received pay. December 31, 1862 received pay. January – February 1863 roll shows him present. He transferred from Co. G, 54th Regiment, Georgia Infantry to Co. F, 54th Regiment, Georgia Infantry. April 26, 1865 surrendered at Greensboro, North Carolina. May 1, 1865 paroled at Greensboro, North Carolina.

STRIPLING, THOMAS J.: Company G (F), corporal. May 12, 1862 enlisted as 3rd corporal in Co. G, 54th Regiment, Georgia Infantry at Columbus, Georgia and received bounty $50.00. December 31, 1862 received pay. January – February 1863 roll shows him present. January 1864 issued clothing. He transferred from Co. G, 54th Regiment, Georgia Infantry to Co. F, 54th Regiment, Georgia Infantry. April 26, 1865 surrendered at Greensboro, North Carolina. May 1, 1865 paroled at Greensboro, North Carolina.

STRONS, JACOB: Company B, sergeant. He enlisted as a sergeant in Co. B, 54th Regiment, Georgia Infantry.

SUMMERAL (SUMERAL) (SOMMERAL), DAVID W.: Company

B, private. April 21, 1862 enlisted as a private in Co. B, 54th Regiment, Georgia Infantry at Savannah, Georgia and received bounty pay of $50.00. December 31, 1862 received pay. January – February 1863 roll shows him present (nurse in regimental hospital). January 4, 1863 detailed as a nurse at Bethesda Hospital, Beaulieu Battery near Savannah, Georgia. May 1, 1863 received pay. July 1, 1863 returned to duty with company. October 31, 1863 roll of Bethesda Hospital, Beaulieu Battery near Savannah, Georgia shows him present (as a nurse). November – December 1863 roll of Bethesda Hospital, Beaulieu Battery near Savannah, Georgia shows he returned to duty with company July 1, 1863. January 1864 issued clothing. He was born February 3, 1834 in Georgia and died April 15, 1891 in Appling County, Georgia. He is buried in Ten Mile Creek Baptist Church Cemetery in Appling County, Georgia. (find a grave #20253003)

J. A. SUMNER: Company C, private. He enlisted as a private in Co. C, 54th Regiment, Georgia Infantry. He was born November 2, 1864 and died in Jeff Davis County, Georgia September 30, 1923. He is buried in Oak View Cemetery in Jeff Davis County, Georgia. (find a grave #61786332)

SUMNER, JETHRO: Company C, corporal. May 6, 1862 enlisted as 1st corporal in Co. C, 54th Regiment, Georgia Infantry at Savannah, Georgia and received bounty pay of $50.00. December 31, 1862 received pay. January – February 1863 roll shows him present. January 1, 1864 received pay. January – February 1864 roll shows him present. March 12, 1864 discharged by Special Order No. 60 as he was elected clerk of Inferior Court in Emanuel County, Georgia. He was a resident of Emanuel County, Georgia. He was born in Emanuel County, Georgia July 12, 1847 and died in Georgia October 10, 1903. He is buried in Moxley Cemetery at Swainsboro, Emanuel County, Georgia. (find a grave #27037300)

SUTTON, IRA J.: Company E, private. May 6, 1862 enlisted as a private in Co. E, 54th Regiment, Georgia Infantry at Savannah, Georgia and received bounty pay of $50.00. December 31, 1862 received pay. January – February 1863 roll shows him present. January 1864 and April 25, 1864 issued clothing. October 14, 1864 issued clothing in May Hospital at Augusta, Georgia. May 10, 1865 surrendered at Tallahassee, Florida. May 24, 1865 paroled at Thomasville, Georgia. He was born in Wilkinson County, Georgia march 5, 1841 and died in Sirmans, Madison County, Florida April 5, 1909. He is buried in Friendship Cemetery at Sirmans, Madison County, Florida. (find a grave # 58218559)

SUTTON, J. J.: Company E, private. He enlisted as a private in Co. E, 54th Regiment, Georgia Infantry.

SUTTON, S. J.: Company E, private. May 6, 1862 enlisted as a private in Co. E, 54th Regiment, Georgia Infantry at Savannah, Georgia and received bounty pay of $50.00. December 31, 1862 received pay. January – February 1863 roll shows him present. January 1864 issued clothing. May 10, 1865 surrendered at Tallahassee, Florida. May 24, 1865 paroled at Thomasville, Georgia.

SWAIN, JOEL WOOTEN: Company E, lieutenant. May 6, 1862 enlisted as 1st sergeant and elected 2nd lieutenant in Co. E, 54th Regiment, Georgia Infantry at Savannah, Georgia and received bounty pay of $50.00. July 1862 roll shows his name. August 1862 roll shows him present at Beaulieu near Savannah, Georgia. September and October 1862 rolls show him absent with leave. November 24, 1862 list of officers present at Savannah includes his name. November and December 1862 rolls show him present at Beaulieu near Savannah, Georgia. January – February 1863 roll shows him present. March 9, 1863 received pay $80.00. April 3, 1863 received pay $80.00. October 21, 1863 list of officers present at Legare's Point, South Carolina includes his name. October 24, 1863 letter from Colonel Charlton Way of the 54th Georgia Regiment states that Lieutenant Swain deserted his command on Morris Island on August 2, 1863 and has gone to his residence in Berrien County, Georgia and has offered to resign his commission. October 30, 1863 shown as dropped in disgrace by Special Order No. 258/12. He was born June 6, 1836 and died February 3, 1900. He is buried in Fort Drum Cemetery at Fort Drum, Okeechobee County, Florida. (find a grave # 26165425)

TALLEY, H. M.: Company E (D), captain. May 6, 1862 enlisted and elected 1st lieutenant of Co. E, 54th Regiment, Georgia Infantry at Savannah, Georgia. May 16, 1862 detailed as acting assistant surgeon in medical department. July 1862 roll at Savannah, Georgia shows him as acting assistant surgeon. August 1862 roll at Beaulieu near Savannah, Georgia shows him as acting assistant surgeon. September, October, November and December 1862 rolls at Beaulieu near Savannah, Georgia show him present. November 24, 1862 list of officers at Savannah, Georgia shows his name. January – February 1863 roll shows him present (signed rolls as lieutenant commanding company). October 31, 1863 list of officers at Legare's Point, South Carolina shows his name. October 29, 1863 appointed captain of Co E, 54th Regiment, Georgia Infantry. January 16, 1864 granted leave by Special Order No. 15/2. December 8, 1893 is appointed as president of the Court by Special Order No. 265/1. July 15, 1864 received pay $260.00. April 26, 1865 surrendered as captain of Co. D, 54th Regiment, Consolidated Georgia Infantry at Greensboro, North Carolina. May 1, 1865 paroled at Greensboro, North Carolina. He was born May 13, 1834 and died September 1, 1902. He is buried in Sunset Hill Cemetery at Valdosta, Lowndes County, Georgia. (find a grave # 97663937)

TARVIN, GEORGE J.: Company G (F), private. May 12, 1862 enlisted as a private in Co. G, 54th Regiment, Georgia Infantry at Columbus, Georgia and received bounty $50.00. December 31, 1862 received pay. January – February 1863 roll shows him present. January 1864 issued clothing. He transferred from Co. G, 54th Regiment, Georgia Infantry to Co. F, 54th Regiment, Georgia Infantry
April 26, 1865 surrendered at Greensboro, North Carolina. May 1, 1865 paroled at Greensboro, North Carolina. He was born in Harris County, Georgia in 1834.

TARVIN, SOLOMON T.: Company H, private. November 3, 1862 enlisted as a private in Co. H, 54th Regiment, Georgia Infantry at Columbus, Georgia and received bounty $50.00. November 1862 roll shows his enlistment. December 31, 1862 received pay. January – February 1863 roll shows him present. October 31, 1863 received pay. November – December 1863 roll shows him present. December 31, 1863 received pay. January 1, 1864 received pay. January 1864 issued clothing. January – February 1864 roll shows him present. September – October 1864 hospital muster roll of Lee Hospital at Columbus, Georgia shows him present. He was born February 14, 1823 and died January 19, 1904. He is buried in Ellerslie United Methodist Church Cemetery at Ellerslie, Harris County, Georgia. (find a grave # 50820701)

TARVIN, WILLIAM M.: Company H, private. November 3, 1862 enlisted as a private in Co. H, 54th Regiment, Georgia Infantry at Columbus, Georgia and received bounty $50.00. November 1862 roll shows his enlistment. December 31, 1862 received pay. January – February 1863 roll shows him present. October 31, 1863 received pay. November – December 1863 roll shows him present. January 1864 issued clothing. January – February 1864 roll shows him present. December 31, 1863 received pay. Pension records show: April 26, 1865 surrendered at Greensboro, North Carolina. May 1, 1865 paroled at Greensboro, North Carolina. He was born in Columbia County, Georgia March 3, 1825 and died December 29, 1911. He is buried in Riverdale Cemetery at Columbus, Muscogee County, Georgia. (find a grave # 17021215).

TAYLOR, GEORGE: Company F, private. August 1, 1863 enlisted as a private in Co. F, 54th Regiment, Georgia Infantry at Savannah, Georgia and received bounty $50.00. November 1, 1863 received pay. November – December 1863 roll shows him present. January 1864 issued clothing. June 24, 1864 died of Typhoid Febris in Oliver Hospital at La Grange, Georgia. He is buried in Stonewall Confederate Cemetery at LaGrange, Troup County, Georgia. (His stone is marked Co F, 50th Georgia which I believe is an error) (find a grave # 67507870)

TAYLOR, JERRY: Company A (D), private. April 26, 1862 enlisted as a private in Co. A, 54th Regiment, Georgia Infantry at Macon, Georgia and received bounty $50.00. April 30, 1863 received pay. June 30, 1863 roll shows him present. October 31, 1863 received pay. November – December 1863 roll shows him present. January 1, 1864 received pay. January 1864 issued clothing. January – February 1864 roll shows him present. March 31, 1864 issued clothing. May 18, 1865 surrendered and paroled at Augusta, Georgia. He died in 1883.

TAYLOR, LEWIS R.: Company E, private. January 25, 1863 enlisted as a private in Co. E, 54th Regiment, Georgia Infantry at Coffee Bluff near Savannah, Georgia and received bounty $50.00. January – February 1863 roll shows him present. Pension records show; he was at home on sick furlough October 1864 and was unable to rejoin his command. He died in Nashville, Georgia February 26, 1899. He was born in 1845 and died February 26, 1899. He is buried in Empire Primitive Baptist Church Cemetery at Lakeland, Lanier County, Georgia. (find a grave # 38845671)

TAYLOR, NATHAN: Company D, private. April 30, 1862 enlisted as a private in Co. D, 54th Regiment, Georgia Infantry at Savannah, Georgia and received bounty $50.00. December 31, 1862 received pay. January – February 1863 roll shows him present. May 8, 1864 issued clothing. January 1864 issued clothing. August 22, 1864 wounded near Jonesboro, Georgia. August 24, 1864 admitted to Ocmulgee Hospital at Macon, Georgia with a Gunshot Wound to the left thigh and gangrene set in. September 2, 1864 transferred to hospital at Vineville. He was in the hospital at Columbus, Georgia at the close of the war. He was a resident of Screven County, Georgia.

TAYLOR, P. H.: Company B, private. He enlisted as a private in Co. B, 54th Regiment, Georgia Infantry.

TAYLOR, R. L.: Company A, private. April 26, 1862 enlisted as a private in Co. A, 54th Regiment, Georgia Infantry at Macon, Georgia and received bounty $50.00. April 30, 1863 received pay. May 1, 1862 to July 31, 1863 detailed as a teamster at a rate of $.25 extra per day. June 30, 1863 roll shows him present (detailed as teamster in the company). July 31, 1863 received pay. August 10, 1863 to August 31, 1863 detailed as a blacksmith's helper at a rate of $.25 extra per day. August 31, 1863 received pay. October 1, 1863 to October 31, 1863 detailed as a carpenter at a rate of $.40 extra per day. October 31, 1863 received pay. November 3, 1863 received commutation for rations. November – December 1863 roll shows him present (blacksmith – striker for the company – sick in company hospital). January 1, 1864 received pay. January – February 1864 roll shows him present (sick in the company hospital – blacksmith's helper). March 31, 1864 issued clothing. November 9, 1864 admitted to Madison House Hospital at Montgomery, Alabama. November 15, 1864 roll of Madison House Hospital at Montgomery, Alabama shows him present. May 10, 1865 surrendered at Tallahassee, Florida. May 24, 1865 paroled at Thomasville, Georgia.

TAYLOR, R. L.: Company E, private. January 28, 1863 enlisted as a private in Co. E, 54th Regiment, Georgia Infantry at Rose Dew near Savannah, Georgia and received bounty $50.00. April 30, 1863 received pay. December 31, 1863 roll of General Hospital No. 2 (also called Hospital Encampment) at Summerville, South Carolina shows him present. January 1864 issued clothing.

TAYLOR, RICHARD: Company A, private. April 26, 1862 enlisted as a private in Co. A, 54th Regiment, Georgia Infantry at Macon, Georgia and received bounty $50.00. October 31, 1863 received pay. November – December 1863 roll shows him present. June 19, 1864 he died at Marietta, Georgia. October 28, 1864 death benefit claim was filed by his widow, Hepsabeth Taylor.

TAYLOR, W.: Company D, private. He enlisted as a private in Co. D,

54th Regiment, Georgia Infantry.

TAYLOR, WESLEY E.: Company F, private. February 21, 1863 enlisted as a private in Co. F, 54th Regiment, Georgia Infantry at Savannah, Georgia and received bounty $50.00. January – February 1863 roll shows him present. November 1, 1863 received pay. December 1863 detailed provost guard. November – December 1863 roll shows him present (detailed as post teamster). January 1864 and April 25, 1864 issued clothing. He was admitted to St. Mary's Hospital at La Grange, Georgia with Debility from Remitting Febris (able to bear transportation). July 22, 1864 issued clothing in St. Mary's Hospital at La Grange, Georgia. August 3, 1864 received vaccination in St. Mary's Hospital at La Grange, Georgia. August 17, 1864 returned to duty from St. Mary's Hospital at La Grange, Georgia. He was born in Crawford County, Georgia December 15, 1834 and died in Bibb County, Georgia February 5, 1910. He is buried in Grace and Truth Baptist Church Cemetery in Macon, Bibb County, Georgia. (find a grave # 50647957)

TAYLOR, WILLIAM: Company D, private. April 30, 1862 enlisted as a private in Co. D, 54th Regiment, Georgia Infantry at Savannah, Georgia and received bounty $50.00. December 31, 1862 received pay. January – February 1863 roll shows him present (overpaid on roll to October 31, 1862 – 2 months). January 1864, April 25, 1864 and May 8, 1864 issued clothing. He was born in Crawford County, Georgia in 1834.

TAYLOR, WILLIAM A.: Company D, corporal. October 7, 1861 enlisted and was elected 2nd sergeant of Co. I, 5th Regiment, Georgia State Troops. April 1862 mustered out. April 30, 1862 enlisted as 1st corporal of Co. D, 54th Regiment, Georgia Infantry at Savannah, Georgia and received bounty $50.00. December 31, 1862 received pay. January – February 1863 roll shows him present. January 1864 issued clothing. July 3, 1864 wounded (skull fractured) near Marietta, Georgia. Pension records show he contracted fever and was sent home from Decatur, Alabama hospital. March 12, 1865 died at home of disease contracted in service. He was born in Georgia December 8, 1837 and died in Georgia December 14, 1922. He is buried in McDonald Baptist Church Cemetery. (find a grave # 22608198)

TEEL, ALEXANDER: Company H, sergeant. November 3, 1862 enlisted as 2nd sergeant in Co. H, 54th Regiment, Georgia Infantry at Columbus, Georgia and received bounty $50.00. December 31, 1862 received pay. January – February 1863 roll shows him present. October 31, 1863 received pay. November – December 1863 roll shows him present. December 31, 1863 received pay. January 1864 issued clothing. January – February 1864 roll shows him present. June 2, 1864 issued clothing. He died December 22, 1895.

TEEL (TEELE), JAMES: Company A, private. April 26, 1862 enlisted as a private in Co. A, 54th Regiment, Georgia Infantry at Macon, Georgia and received bounty $50.00. August 28, 1862 appointed teamster. August, September, October, November and December 1862 rolls show him detailed as a teamster. August 28, 1862 to December 31, 1862 detailed as a teamster (ambulance driver) at a rate of $.25 extra per day. September, October, November and December 1862 received pay. April 30, 1863 received pay. June 1, 1863 to December 31, 1863 detailed as an ambulance driver at a rate of $.25 extra per day. June 30, 1863 roll shows him present (detailed as ambulance driver for the regiment). June 30, 1863 received pay. November – December 1863 roll shows him absent (detailed as ambulance driver for the regiment). January 1, 1863 to January 31, 1863 detailed as an ambulance driver at a rate of $.25 extra per day. January 21, 1864 detail as ambulance driver revoked by Special Order No. 16/3. January 21, 1864 received pay $164.75 and issued clothing (clothing paid). January – February 1864 roll shows him present (detailed as ambulance driver for the regiment). February 1, 1864 to April 30, 1864 detailed as an ambulance driver at a rate of $.25 extra per day. June 10, 1864 wounded near Marietta, Georgia. March 8, 1865 admitted to Ocmulgee hospital at Macon, Georgia with a Gunshot Wound to the left hand - flesh (C. L. B. S. D.). March 26, 1865 transferred to Vineville Hospital. April 30, 1865 report shows him captured at Macon, Georgia April 20-21, 1865. He was a resident of Bibb County.

TEMPLETON, SAMUEL: Company F, private. May 18, 1863 enlisted as a private in Co. F, 54th Regiment, Georgia Infantry at Savannah, Georgia and received bounty $50.00. November 1, 1863 received pay. November – December 1863 roll shows him present (in arrest). January 1864, April 25, 1864 and May 8, 1864 issued clothing. June 15, 1864 captured near Golgotha (Marietta), Georgia. June 22, 1864 received at Military Prison at Louisville, Kentucky from Nashville, Tennessee. June 22, 1864 sent to Rock Island, Illinois from Military Prison at Louisville, Kentucky. June 24, 1864 received at Rock Island, Illinois from Military Prison at Louisville, Kentucky. October 6, 1864 joined the U. S. Army (for frontier service) at Rock Island Barracks, Illinois.

THIGPEN, A.: Company C, private. December 4, 1863 enlisted as a private in Co. C, 54th Regiment, Georgia Infantry at James Island, South Carolina and received bounty $50.00. January 1, 1864 received pay. January – February 1864 roll shows him present.

THIGPEN, M. T.: Company B, private. He enlisted as a private in Co. B, 54th Regiment, Georgia Infantry.

THOMAS, BANNER: Company K, corporal. May 5, 1863 enlisted and elected 1st corporal of Co. K, 54th Regiment, Georgia Infantry at Savannah, Georgia and received bounty $50.00. January 1, 1863 received pay. January – February 1863 roll shows him present. March 18, 1864 and April 18, 1864 issued clothing. August 8, 1864 discharged by Civil Authority (elected to civil office – Tax Collector of Pierce County) by Special Order No. 186. He was born in Appling County, Georgia January 16, 1843 and died September 16, 1885. He is buried in Overstreet Cemetery in Appling County, Georgia. (find a grave #35627146)

THOMAS, ELIAS D.: Company K, private. October 3, 1861 enlisted as a private in Co. A, 1st Regiment, 1st Brigade, Georgia State Troops. April 1862 mustered out. April 18, 1862 enlisted and as a private in Co. K, 54th Regiment, Georgia Infantry at Savannah, Georgia and received bounty $50.00. January 1, 1863 received pay. January – February 1863 roll shows him present. March 13, 1864, April 25, 1864 and June 2, 1864 issued clothing. July 29, 1864 appears on a register of Floyd House Hospital at Macon, Georgia with a Gunshot Wound of the left hand causing amputation of thumb. He was furloughed for 60 days. May 10, 1865 surrendered at Tallahassee, Florida. May 19, 1865 paroled at Thomasville, Georgia. He is described as; 5 feet 8 inches high, dark hair, blue eyes and dark complexion. He was a resident of Patterson, Georgia. He was born March 29, 1842 and died September 24, 1912. He is buried in Wayfair Cemetery at Bell, Gilchrist County, Florida. (find a grave # 4201293)

THOMAS, GRIGSBY E., SR.: Company G (F), captain. May 12, 1862 enlisted and elected 2nd lieutenant of Co. G, 54th Regiment, Georgia Infantry at Columbus, Georgia and received bounty $50.00. July 1862 roll shows him present at Savannah, Georgia. August, September and October 1862 rolls show him present at Beaulieu near Savannah, Georgia. November 24, 1862 list of officers at Savannah, Georgia includes him. November 1862 roll shows him absent (Enrolling Officer at Columbus, Georgia). December 1862 roll shows him present at Beaulieu near Savannah, Georgia. January 20, 1863 detailed to enrolling and recruiting service. January – February 1863 roll shows him absent on recruiting service. March 9, 1863 received pay $80.00. April 3, 1863 list of absent officers at Savannah, Georgia shows him detached as Enrolling Officer until April 21, 1863. October 21, 1863 list of officers at Legare's point, South Carolina includes him. June 26, 1863 he was in command of Co. G, 54th Regiment, Georgia Infantry at the time. February 15, 1864 appointed 1st lieutenant Co. G, 54th Regiment, Georgia Infantry by Special Order No. 29/1. May 16, 1864 wounded at Resacca, Georgia. June 7, 1864 received pay $80.00. July 22, 1864 wounded at Atlanta, Georgia. August 25, 1864 report of Mercer's Brigade in the field near Atlanta shows him wounded on July 22, 1864 and in the hospital at Columbus, Georgia. September 14, 1864 report of Mercer's Brigade in camp near Jonesboro, Georgia shows him wounded and in the Medical Board Division Hospital. December 2, 1864 received pay $450.00. March 18, 1865 elected captain of Co. G, 54th Regiment, Georgia Infantry for gallantry. Company G and F of the 54th Regiment, Georgia Infantry were combined. April 26, 1865 surrendered as captain of Co. F, 54th Regiment, Georgia Infantry at Greensboro, North Carolina. May 1, 1865 paroled at Greensboro, North Carolina. He was born December 30, 1832 died February 5, 1914 at Linwood Cemetery, Columbus Muscogee County, Georgia. (find a grave # 26503275)

THOMAS, J. B.: private. He enlisted and as a private in the 54th Regiment, Georgia Infantry. May 10, 1865 surrendered at Tallahassee, Florida. May 18, 1865 paroled at Thomasville, Georgia. He is described as; 5 feet 9 inches, dark hair, blue eyes and fair complexion.

THOMAS, LAFAYETTE: Company H (F), private. October 5, 1861 enlisted as a private in Co B, 31st Regiment, Georgia Infantry. He was discharged due to disability. November 6, 1862 enlisted as a private in Co. H, 54th Regiment, Georgia Infantry at Columbus, Georgia and received bounty $50.00. November 1862 roll shows his enlistment. December 31, 1862 received pay. January 17, 1863 transferred from Co. H, 54th Regiment, Georgia Infantry to Co. F, 54th Regiment, Georgia Infantry by order of Colonel Way. January – February 1863 rolls show his transfer and him present. November 1, 1863 received pay. November – December 1863 roll shows him present (in arrest). January 1864 issued clothing. October 13, 1864 issued clothing in Hospital at Fairground at Vineville, Georgia. October 31, 1864 admitted to Stonewall Hospital at Montgomery, Alabama. November 15, 1864 hospital muster roll of Stonewall Hospital at Montgomery, Alabama shows him present. April 26, 1865 surrendered in Co. D, 54th Regiment, Consolidated Georgia Infantry at Greensboro, North Carolina. May 1, 1865 paroled at Greensboro, North Carolina. (Another record shows he was paroled in Thomasville, Georgia on May 25, 1865).

THOMAS, LEWIS II: Company K, private. May 5, 1862 enlisted as a private in Co. K, 54th Regiment, Georgia Infantry at Savannah, Georgia and received bounty $50.00. January 1, 1863 received pay. January – February 1863 roll shows him present. He was assigned to guard the Gulf and Atlantic Railroad. January 22, 1864 received pay $22.00. March 18, 1864 and April 18, 1864 issued clothing. May 10, 1865 surrendered at Tallahassee, Florida. May 25, 1865 paroled at Thomasville, Georgia. He was born November 9, 1830 and died in Pierce County, Georgia August 28, 1893. He is buried in Spring Hill Cemetery in Brantley County, Georgia. (find a grave # 32994827)

THOMAS (THOMS), M. L.: Company E, lieutenant. He enlisted and was elected 1st lieutenant of Co. E, 54th Regiment, Georgia Infantry.

THOMAS, WILLIAM: Company H, private. November 5, 1862 enlisted as a private in Co. H, 54th Regiment, Georgia Infantry at Columbus, Georgia and received bounty $50.00. April 26, 1865 surrendered at Greensboro, North Carolina. May 1, 1865 paroled at Greensboro, North Carolina.

THOMAS, WILLIAM H. H.: Company H, private. December 8, 1862 enlisted as a private in Co. H, 54th Regiment, Georgia Infantry at Columbus, Georgia and received bounty $50.00. December 1862 roll shows his enlistment. December 31, 1862 received pay. January – February 1863 roll shows him present. October 31, 1863 received pay. November – December 1863 roll shows him present. December 31, 1863 received pay. January 1864 issued clothing. January – February 1864 roll shows him present. June 2, 1864 issued clothing. April 26, 1865 surrendered at Greensboro, North Carolina. May 1, 1865 paroled at Greensboro, North Carolina.

THOMPSON, JOHN B.: Company K, private. He enlisted as a private

in Co. K, 54th Regiment, Georgia Infantry.
THOMPSON, STEPHEN H.: Company D, private. April 30, 1862 enlisted as a private in Co. D, 54th Regiment, Georgia Infantry at Savannah, Georgia and received bounty $50.00. December 31, 1862 received pay. January – February 1863 roll shows him present. January 1864 issued clothing. He was born in Screven County, Georgia in1830 and he died at Macon, Georgia in1868. He is buried at Rose Hill Cemetery in Macon, Georgia. (find a grave #105278511)
THOMPSON, S.: lieutenant. He enlisted and was elected lieutenant in Co. D, 54th Regiment, Georgia Infantry May 10, 1865 surrendered at Tallahassee, Florida. May 19, 1865 paroled at Thomasville, Georgia.
THOMPSON, THOMPSON T.: Company E, private. He enlisted as a private in Co. E, 54th Regiment, Georgia Infantry.
THOMPSON, W. R.: Company B, private. November 19, 1862 enlisted as a private in Co. B, 54th Regiment, Georgia Infantry at Savannah, Georgia and received bounty $50.00. December 31, 1862 received pay. January – February 1863 roll shows him present. January 1864 issued clothing.
THORNTON, JAMES ALEXANDER: Company K, private. October 3, 1861 enlisted in and appointed 2nd corporal Co. A, 1st Regiment, 1st Brigade, Georgia State Troops. April 1862 mustered out. April 18, 1862 enlisted as a private in Co. K, 54th Regiment, Georgia Infantry at Savannah, Georgia and received bounty $50.00. August 17, 1862 transferred to Co. C, 1st Georgia Sharpshooters by Special Order No. 259 and was elected 4th sergeant. September 19, 1863 wounded and disabled at Chickamauga, Georgia. He was born September 5, 1840 and died in Ware County, Georgia June 29, 1900. He is buried in Ben James Primitive Baptist Church Cemetery in Pierce County, Georgia. (find a grave #53416771)
THORNTON, JOHN B.: Company K (F), private. April 18, 1862 enlisted as a private in Co. K, 54th Regiment, Georgia Infantry at Savannah, Georgia and received bounty $50.00.   December 1, 1862 transferred from Co. K, 54th Regiment, Georgia Infantry to Co. F, 54th Regiment, Georgia Infantry. December 1862 roll shows his transfer. December 31, 1862 received pay. January – February 1863 roll shows him present. November 1, 1863 received pay. November – December 1863 roll shows him present. January 1864 and April 25, 1864 issued clothing. October 1964 his pension records show he was at home sick with fever. November 1864 his pension records show he attempted to reach his command but the enemy intervened. He was born in Georgia on September 26, 1843 and died at Baxley, Appling County, Georgia February 7, 1920. He is buried in Big Creek Primitive Baptist Church Cemetery in Appling County, Georgia. (find a grave #25663697)
THORNTON, JOHN S.: Company G, private. February 7, 1863 enlisted as a private in Co. G, 54th Regiment, Georgia Infantry at Columbus, Georgia and received bounty $50.00. January – February 1863 roll shows him present.
THORNTON, JOHN T.: Company G, private. February 7, 1863 enlisted

as a private in Co. G, 54th Regiment, Georgia Infantry at Columbus, Georgia and received bounty $50.00. January – February 1863 roll shows him present.

THORNTON, JONATHAN: Company K, private. October 3, 1861 enlisted in and appointed 1st corporal Co. A, 1st Regiment, 1st Brigade, Georgia State Troops. April 1862 mustered out. April 18, 1862 enlisted as a private in Co. K, 54th Regiment, Georgia Infantry at Savannah, Georgia and received bounty $50.00. July 30, 1862 transferred to Co. C, 1st Georgia Sharpshooters by Special Order No. 259. January – February 1864 roll shows him home sick in Appling County, Georgia.

THORNTON, MATTHEW: Company F, sergeant. April 18, 1862 enlisted as 5th sergeant in Co. F, 54th Regiment, Georgia Infantry at Savannah, Georgia and received bounty $50.00. December 31, 1862 received pay. January – February 1863 roll shows him present. October 1863 appointed 5th sergeant of Co. F, 54th Regiment, Georgia Infantry. November 1, 1863 received pay. November – December 1863 roll shows him present. January 1864 and May 8, 1864 issued clothing. He died in service.

THORNTON, S. T.: Company F, private. April 18, 1862 enlisted as a private in Co. F, 54th Regiment, Georgia Infantry.

THORNTON, SILAS: Company K, lieutenant. October 3, 1861 enlisted in and appointed 5th sergeant Co. A, 1st Regiment, 1st Brigade, Georgia State Troops. April 1862 mustered out. April 18, 1862 enlisted as a private and appointed 2nd sergeant in Co. K, 54th Regiment, Georgia Infantry at Savannah, Georgia and received bounty $50.00. December 20, 1862 elected Jr. 2nd lieutenant of Co. K, 54th Regiment, Georgia Infantry. December 1862 roll shows him present and elected Jr. 2nd lieutenant. January – February 1863 roll shows him present. March 4, 1863 received pay $80.00. April 3, 1863 received pay $ 80.00. April 25, 1863 elected 2nd lieutenant of Co. K, 54th Regiment, Georgia Infantry. June 18, 1863 granted a ten day furlough by General Mercer. October 21, 1863 list of officers present at Legare's Point, South Carolina includes his mane. February 27, 1864 shown as commanding Co. K, 54th Regiment, Georgia Infantry. June 7, 1864 received pay $160.00. June 11, 1864 granted leave by Special Order No. 11/8. June 16, 1864 wounded in the right shoulder near Marietta, Georgia. August 25, 1864 report of Mercer's Brigade in the field near Atlanta, Georgia shows him on wounded furlough (wounded June 16, 1864) by the Medical Examining Board. September 14, 1864 report of Mercer's Brigade in camp near Jonesboro, Georgia shows him wounded in the Medical Board Division Hospital. Pension records show; he was at home wounded at the close of the war. May 10, 1865 surrendered at Tallahassee, Florida. May 19, 1865 paroled at Thomasville, Georgia. He is described as; 5 feet 7 inches high, dark hair, blue eyes and light complexion. He was born in Georgia on September 8, 1843 and died in Wayne County, Georgia in 1931. He is buried in Duck Pond Cemetery in Wayne County, Georgia. (find a grave # 52045110)

THORNTON, TIMOTHY: Company K (B), private. October 3, 1861 enlisted in and appointed 3rd corporal Co. A, 1st Regiment, 1st Brigade, Georgia State Troops. April 1862 mustered out. April 18, 1862 enlisted as a private in Co. K, 54th Regiment, Georgia Infantry at Savannah, Georgia and received bounty $50.00. He transferred from Co. K, 54th Regiment, Georgia Infantry to Co. B, 54th Regiment, Georgia Infantry. July 30, 1862 transferred to Co. C, 1st Georgia Sharpshooters by Special Order No. 259 and appointed 5th sergeant. August 1862 roll shows the transfers. September 1, 1864 captured near Jonesboro, Georgia. September 19-22 exchanged at Rough and Ready, Georgia.

THORNTON, WILLIAM: Company B, private. October 10, 1861 enlisted in Co. K, 2nd Regiment, 1st Brigade, Georgia State Troops. April 1862 mustered out. April 21, 1862 enlisted as a private in Co. B, 54th Regiment, Georgia Infantry at Savannah, Georgia and received bounty $50.00. July 31, 1862 transferred to Co. C, 1st Georgia Sharpshooters by Special Order No. 259. August 1862 roll shows his transfer. September 1, 1864 captured near Jonesboro, Georgia. September 19-22 exchanged at Rough and Ready, Georgia. May 10, 1865 surrendered at Tallahassee, Florida. May 21, 1865 paroled at Thomasville, Georgia.

THURMON, JEREMIAH WASHINGTON: Company A, sergeant. October 17, 1861 enlisted as a private in Co. C, 1st Independent Battalion, Georgia State Troops. April 16, 1862 roll shows him present. April 1862 mustered out. May 3, 1862 enlisted as a private and elected 4th sergeant in Co. A, 54th Regiment, Georgia Infantry at Macon, Georgia and received bounty $50.00. April 30, 1863 received pay. June 30, 1863 roll shows him present (sick in the company hospital). October 31, 1863 received pay. November – December 1863 roll shows him present. January 1, 1864 received pay. January – February 1864 roll shows him present. April 29, 1864 issued clothing. June 19, 1864 captured near Marietta, Georgia. June 26, 1864 received at Military Prison at Louisville, Kentucky from Nashville, Tennessee. June 27, 1864 sent to Camp Morton, Indianapolis, Indiana from Military Prison at Louisville, Kentucky. June 28, 1864 received at Camp Morton, Indianapolis, Indiana from Military Prison at Louisville, Kentucky. February 26, 1862 transferred to City Point, Virginia via Baltimore, Maryland for exchange. He was born in Georgia February 19, 1844 and died in Ruston, Lincoln Parrish, Louisiana September 12, 1899. He is buried in Wesley Chapel Cemetery at Ruston, Lincoln Parrish, Louisiana. (find a grave # 90350991)

THURMON, JOHN MITCHEL: Field and Staff, musician. He enlisted as a private in Co. K, 54th Regiment, Georgia Infantry. He was transferred to Field and Staff as a musician. He was born in Georgia November 30, 1846 and died in Ruston, Lincoln Parrish, Louisiana November 19, 1926. He is buried in Greenwood Cemetery at Ruston, Lincoln Parrish, Louisiana. (find a grave # 124675668)

TIDWELL, GEORGE W.: Company A, private. April 25, 1862 enlisted as a private in Co. A, 54th Regiment, Georgia Infantry. April 1864 discharged account of lung trouble. He was born in Georgia in June 3, 1837 and died January 12, 1914. He is buried in Bethel Baptist Church Cemetery in Macon, Bibb County, Georgia. (find a grave #41062920)

TIDWELL, J. D.: Company A, private. May 3, 1862 enlisted as a private in Co. A, 54th Regiment, Georgia Infantry at Macon, Georgia and received bounty pay $50.00. April 30, 1863 received pay. June 30, 1863 roll shows him present. October 31, 1863 received pay. November – December 1863 roll shows him absent (absent on furlough since December 27, 1863). January – February 1864 roll shows him present. March 31, 1864 issued clothing. April 21-22, 1865 captured at Macon, Georgia.

TIDWELL, JAMES A.: Company A, private. May 3, 1862 enlisted as a private in Co. A, 54th Regiment, Georgia Infantry at Macon, Georgia and received bounty $50.00. December 13, 1862 deserted at Savannah, Georgia. July 1864 wounded in the right hand and wrist near Atlanta, Georgia (Unfit for duty). He was born in Twiggs County, Georgia in 1832 and died in 1898. He is buried in Bethel Baptist Church Cemetery in Macon, Bibb County, Georgia. (find a grave #41062893)

TILLEY, W. J.: Company G, private. May 12, 1862 enlisted as a private in Co. G, 54th Regiment, Georgia Infantry at Columbus, Georgia and received bounty $50.00.

TILLMAN, JOSEPH C. (O.): Company B, private. October 10, 1861 enlisted and appointed 5th sergeant in Co. K, 2nd Regiment, 1st Brigade, Georgia State Troops. April 1862 mustered out. April 28, 1862 enlisted as a private in Co. B, 54th Regiment, Georgia Infantry at Savannah, Georgia and received bounty $50.00. September and October 1862 rolls show him detailed as color corporal (guard). December 31, 1862 received pay. January – February 1863 roll shows him present. May 10, 1865 surrendered at Tallahassee, Florida. May 12, 1865 paroled at Thomasville, Georgia. He was born February 22, 1816 and died March 22, 1902. He is buried in Bethel United Methodist Church Cemetery in Appling County, Georgia. (find a grave #65388339)

TIPPINS (TIPPENS), PHILLIP: Company K (F), private. April 18, 1862 enlisted as a private in Co. K, 54th Regiment, Georgia Infantry at Savannah, Georgia and received bounty $50.00. November 1862 roll shows his enlistment January 1, 1863 transferred from Co. K, 54th Regiment, Georgia Infantry to Co. F, 54th Regiment, Georgia Infantry. January 1, 1863 received pay. January – February 1863 rolls show his transfer and him present. November 1, 1863 received pay. November – December 1863 roll shows him absent detailed as timber cutter for post. November 5, 1863 to December 31, 1863 detailed as a carpenter (wood cutter) at Rose Dew near Savannah, Georgia at a rate of $.25 extra per day. January 1864 issued clothing. January 20, 1864 received pay. He is described as; 5 feet 10 inches high, dark hair, blue eyes and dark complexion. His pension records show he was wounded in battle. He was at home on wounded furlough at the close of the war. He was born in Tattnall County, Georgia on August 30, 1834 (1825) and died February 19, 1897. He is buried in Shiloh Primitive Baptist Church Cemetery at Blackshear, Pierce County, Georgia. (find a grave # 56899194)

TOLBERT, W. A.: Company I, corporal. He enlisted as a corporal in Co. I, 54th Regiment, Georgia Infantry.

TOMPKINS, M. W.: Company B, private. He enlisted as a private in Co. B, 54th Regiment, Georgia Infantry.

TRICE, BENJAMIN A: Company B, corporal. He enlisted as a corporal in Co. B, 54th Regiment, Georgia Infantry. He transferred to Co. B, 4th Georgia Sharpshooters. He was born October 17, 1841 and died May 20, 1927. He is buried in Willis Cemetery at Willis, Montgomery County, Texas. (find a grave # 58012682)

TRICE, C.; Company I, private. October 8, 1861 enlisted as a private and appointed Jr. 2nd lieutenant in Co. K, 1st Regiment, Georgia State Troops. October 10, 1861 appointed 2nd lieutenant in Co. K, 1st Regiment, Georgia State Troops. April 1862 mustered out. May 6, 1862 enlisted as a private in Co. I, 54th Regiment, Georgia Infantry January 31, 1863 discharged, furnished D. M. McRae as a substitute.

TRICE, J. C.: Company I, private. May 6, 1862 enlisted as a private in Co. I, 54th Regiment, Georgia Infantry at Guyton, Georgia and received bounty $50.00. January – February 1863 roll show him discharged for substitute McCray.

TRIPP, JOHN R.: Company C, private. March 19, 1863 enlisted as a private in Co. C, 54th Regiment, Georgia Infantry at Savannah, Georgia and received bounty $50.00. November 15, 1863 detailed as quartermaster's clerk by order of Colonel Way. November 1, 1863 to December 31, 1863 detailed as quartermaster's clerk. January 1, 1864 received pay. January 1, 1864 to January 31, 1864 detailed as forage-master. February 1, 1864 to April 30, 1864 detailed as a clerk in the quartermaster's department. January – February 1864 roll shows him absent (detailed as quartermaster's clerk). April 28, 1864 issued clothing. April 12, 1865 captured at Salisbury, North Carolina. April 29, 1865 sent to Military Prison at Louisville, Kentucky from Nashville, Tennessee. May 1, 1865 received at Military Prison at Louisville, Kentucky from Nashville, Tennessee. May 2, 1865 sent to Camp Chase, Ohio from Military Prison at Louisville, Kentucky. May 4, 1865 received at Camp Chase, Ohio from Military Prison at Louisville, Kentucky. June 13, 1865 took Oath of Allegiance at Camp Chase, Ohio. He is described as; a resident of Baldwin County, Georgia, florid complexion, dark hair, grey eyes, 5 feet 10 inches high and 30 years of age.

TOUCHTONE (TETCHSTONE), G. W.: Company K, private. October 3, 1861 enlisted in and appointed 3rd corporal Co. A, 1st Regiment, 1st Brigade, Georgia State Troops. April 1862 mustered out. April 18, 1862 enlisted as a private in Co. K, 54th Regiment, Georgia Infantry at Savannah, Georgia and received bounty $50.00. January 1, 1863 received pay. January – February 1863 roll shows him present (absent without leave 6 days). August 23-30, 1863 wounded (hand shot off) at Battery Wagner on Morris Island near Charleston, South Carolina. October 5, 1863 received pay $44.00. December 16, 1863 received pay $22.00. March 18, 1864 and April 18, 1864 issued clothing. May 10, 1865 surrendered at Tallahassee, Florida. May 19, 1865 paroled at Thomasville, Georgia. He is described as; 5 feet 7 inches high, light hair, blue eyes and light complexion.

TUCKER, ANDREW JACKSON: Company G, private. May 12, 1862 enlisted as a private in Co. G, 54th Regiment, Georgia Infantry at Columbus, Georgia and received bounty $50.00. January – February 1863 roll shows him present.

TUCKER, HIRAM: Company E, private. May 6, 1862 enlisted in Co. E, 54th Regiment, Georgia Infantry. January 1864 transferred from Co. E, 54th Regiment, Georgia Infantry to Co. A, 1st Georgia Regulars. Pension records show; he was at home on sick furlough at the close of the war. He was born in Irwin County, Georgia in 1838 and died in Berrien County, Georgia May 8, 1908 (May 30, 1905). He is buried in Mount Paron Primitive Baptist Church Cemetery at Alapaha, Berrien County, Georgia. (find a grave # 24222766)

TUCKER, J.H.: Company G, private. He enlisted as a private in Co. G, 54th Regiment, Georgia Infantry. January 1864 and April 25, 1864 issued clothing. July 30, 1863 transferred from Co. G, 54th Regiment Georgia Infantry to Co. H, 64th Regiment, Georgia Infantry for W. W. Culverhouse by Special Order No. 149/5.

TUCKER, JAMES MADISON HILL: Company G, private. January 22, 1863 enlisted as a private in Co. G, 54th Regiment, Georgia Infantry. February 1, 1865 sent to Columbus, Georgia hospital with Fever. May 1, 1865 paroled at Columbus, Georgia. He was born in Russell County, Alabama March 12, 1845 and died in Atlanta Georgia January 25, 1925.

TUCKER, JOHN: Company E, private. May 6, 1862 enlisted in Co. E, 54th Regiment, Georgia Infantry at Savannah, Georgia and received bounty $50.00. December 31, 1862 received pay. January – February 1863 roll shows him present. January 1864 issued clothing. January 17, 1865 admitted to Way Hospital at Meridian, Mississippi with Pneumonia (Dircetion).

TUCKER, MOSES J.: Company E, private. May 6, 1862 enlisted in Co. E, 54th Regiment, Georgia Infantry at Savannah, Georgia and received bounty $50.00. June 30, 1862 received pay. January – February 1863 roll shows him absent (absent without leave since January 27, 1863). January 1864 and April 25, 1864 issued clothing.

TUCKER, MOSES: Company A, private. October 17, 1861 enlisted as a private in Co. C, 1st Independent Battalion, Georgia State Troops. April 16, 1862 roll shows him present. April 1862 mustered out. May 3, 1862 enlisted in Co. A, 54th Regiment, Georgia Infantry at Macon, Georgia and received bounty $50.00. April 30, 1863 received pay. June 30, 1863 roll shows him present.

September 1862 roll shows him detailed as company cook. October 31, 1863 received pay. November – December 1863 roll shows him present. January 1, 1864 received pay. January – February 1864 roll shows him present. April 29, 1864 issued clothing. July 4, 1864 wounded in the left leg near Vining Station, Georgia. March 5, 1865 granted wounded furlough at Macon, Georgia. April 4, 1865 Medical Board approved extending his furlough due to condition (he is unable to comply with General Order no. 83 because of Gunshot Wound of the left thigh with hospital Gangrene and much sloughing. It is the opinion he will not be fit for duty in a period of less than 30 days). April 21-22, 1865 captured at Macon, Georgia. He was born March 1840 and died April 1907. He is buried at Mount Pleasant Baptist Church Cemetery at Macon, Bibb County, Georgia. (find a grave # 61362072)

TUCKER, STEPHEN: Company A, private. March 16, 1862 enlisted in Co. A, 54th Regiment, Georgia Infantry at Savannah, Georgia and received bounty $50.00. April 30, 1863 received pay. June 30, 1863 roll shows him present. April 30, 1863 received pay. June 30, 1863 roll shows him present. April 30, 1863 received pay. June 30, 1863 roll shows him claimed by Co. D, 10th Georgia Battalion. He was born in 1845 and died in 1904. He is buried in Mount Pleasant Baptist Church Cemetery at Macon, Bibb County, Georgia. (find a grave # 61363215)

TULIFORD, ARTHUR THOMAS: Company C, sergeant. He enlisted as a sergeant in Co. C, 54th Regiment, Georgia Infantry.

TULLIS, PAUL ALLEN: Company I, private. September 25, 1863 enlisted in Co. I, 54th Regiment, Georgia Infantry at Rose Dew near Savannah, Georgia and received bounty $50.00. October 31, 1863 received pay. November – December 1863 roll shows him present (detailed to oversee in Engineer Corps). January 1864 issued clothing. He was born August 12, 1821 and died August 6, 1884. He is buried in Little Ogeechee Baptist Church Cemetery at Oliver, Screven County, Georgia. (find a grave #24970148)

TURNER, ARTHUR: Company B, private. He enlisted as a private in Co. B, 54th Regiment, Georgia Infantry. He died in service.

TURNER, JOHN W.: Field and Staff, ordinance sergeant. He enlisted as ordinance sergeant in the 54th Regiment, Georgia. He was born February 9, 1842 and died April 12, 1922. He is buried in Rose Hill Cemetery at Alma, Bacon County, Georgia. (find a grave # 125903690)

TURNER, J. W.: Company C, private. He enlisted as a private in Co. C, 54th Regiment, Georgia Infantry.

TURNER, M. H.: Company K, private. He enlisted as a private in Co. K, 54th Regiment, Georgia Infantry.

TURNER, R. G.: Company E, sergeant. May 6, 1862 enlisted in as 2nd sergeant of Co. E, 54th Regiment, Georgia Infantry at Savannah, Georgia and received bounty $50.00. December 31, 1862 received pay. January – February 1863 roll shows him present. August 26, 1863 - September 3, 1863 killed at Battery Wagner on Morris Island near Charleston, South Carolina.

TURNER, WILLIAM H.: Company C, sergeant. December 11, 1861 enlisted as a private and appointed 3rd sergeant in Co. B, 8th Regiment,

Georgia State Troops. He mustered out in 1862. April 22, 1862 enlisted in as 3rd sergeant of Co. C, 54th Regiment, Georgia Infantry at Savannah, Georgia and received bounty $50.00. December 31, 1862 received pay. January – February 1863 roll shows him present. July 16, 1863 appointed 1st sergeant of Co. C, 54th Regiment, Georgia Infantry. January 1, 1864 received pay. January – February 1864 roll shows him present. April 25, 1864 and May 8, 1864 issued clothing. January 13, 1865 admitted to St. Mary's Hospital at West Point, Mississippi with Diarrhoea. Pension records show he was in the hospital at the close of the war.

TWILLY (TWILLEY) (TWILLIE), HENRY E. B.: Company H, private. January 28, 1863 enlisted as a private in Co. H, 54th Regiment, Georgia Infantry at Columbus, Georgia and received bounty $50.00. January – February 1863 roll shows him present. October 31, 1863 received pay. November – December 1863 roll shows him present. December 31, 1863 received pay. January 1864 issued clothing. January – February 1864 roll shows him present (on picket). June 2, 1864 issued clothing. July 22, 1864 wounded at Atlanta, Georgia in the right arm necessitating amputation. He was born in Georgia October 7, 1845 and died in Columbus, Georgia circa 1900-1901.

TYER, JASON: Company F, private. He enlisted in as a private in Co. F, 54th Regiment, Georgia Infantry at Savannah, Georgia and received bounty $50.00. November – December 1863 roll shows him present. January 1864 and April 25, 1864 issued clothing.

TYLER, A. JACKSON: Company G, private. May 12, 1862 enlisted as a private in Co. G, 54th Regiment, Georgia Infantry at Columbus, Georgia and received bounty $50.00. December 31, 1862 received pay. January – February 1863 roll shows him present. January 1864 issued clothing.

TYRE, ISHAM: Company F, private. April 7, 1863 enlisted as a private in Co. F, 54th Regiment, Georgia Infantry at Savannah, Georgia and received bounty $50.00. May 10, 1865 surrendered at Tallahassee, Florida. May 22, 1865 paroled at Thomasville, Georgia. He was born in 1825 and died in 1905. He is buried in Milikin Church Cemetery in Appling County, Georgia. (find a grave #40833912)

TYSON, S.: private. He enlisted in as a private in the 54th Regiment, Georgia Infantry. May 10, 1865 surrendered at Tallahassee, Florida. May 29, 1865 paroled at Albany, Georgia.

UNDERWOOD, G. A.: Company H, private. May 12, 1862 enlisted as a private in Co. H, 54th Regiment, Georgia Infantry at Columbus, Georgia and received bounty $50.00. July 1862 roll shows his enlistment. He was a resident of Warrenton, Georgia.

UNDERWOOD, JOHN D.: Company C (D), private. May 5, 1862 enlisted in as private in Co. C, 54th Regiment, Georgia Infantry at Savannah, Georgia and received bounty $50.00. June 10, 1862 detailed as a teamster in the quartermaster's department at a rate of $.25 extra per day. August 1, 1862 detached as regimental teamster by order of Colonel Way. December 1862 roll shows him detailed as a teamster at a rate of

$.25 extra per day. December 31, 1862 received pay. January – February 1863 roll shows him present (detailed as a teamster). February 1, 1863 to February 28, 1863 detailed as forage-master at a rate of $.25 extra per day. June 1863 received pay. June 1, 1863 to December 31, 1863 detailed as a teamster at a rate of $.25 extra per day. October 31, 1863 list of men detailed at James Island, South Carolina shows him in the quartermaster's department. November 1, 1863 received pay. January – February 1864 roll shows him absent (detailed as a teamster). January 1, 1864 to January 31, 1864 detailed as a wagon master at a rate of $.25 extra per day. March 1, 1864 to April 30, 1864 detailed as forage-master at a rate of $.25 extra per day. April 28, 1864 and May 8, 1864 issued clothing. April 26, 1865 surrendered in Co. D, 54th Regiment, Consolidated Georgia Infantry at Greensboro, North Carolina. May 1, 1865 paroled at Greensboro, North Carolina. He was a resident of Hancock County, Georgia. He was born May 6, 1835 and died May 14, 1915. He is buried in Underwood-Harrison Family Cemetery at Beulah, Hancock County, Georgia. (find a grave # 95353034)

UPTON, JAMES P.: Company H, private. February 6, 1863 enlisted as a private in Co. H, 54th Regiment, Georgia Infantry at Columbus, Georgia and received bounty $50.00. January – February 1863 roll shows him present. October 31, 1863 received pay. November – December 1863 roll shows him present. December 31, 1863 received pay. January 1864 issued clothing. January – February 1864 roll shows him present (on picket). June 2, 1864 issued clothing. February 5, 1865 admitted to Way Hospital at Meridian, Mississippi (note on card - returned).

VANCE, L. H.: Company E, private. He enlisted as a private in Co. E, 54th Regiment, Georgia Infantry.

VANN, ARCHIBALD: Company A, private. August 8, 1862 enlisted in as private in Co. A, 54th Regiment, Georgia Infantry at Savannah, Georgia and received bounty $50.00. August 1862 roll shows his enlistment. November 15, 1862 he died in Macon, Georgia. November 1862 roll shows his death. He is buried in Rose Hill Cemetery at Macon, Bibb County, Georgia. (find a grave # 115649539)

VANN, WILEY: Company H (A), private. September 1, 1862 transferred from Co. H, 54th Regiment, Georgia Infantry to Co. A, 54th Regiment, Georgia Infantry by Special Order No. 6 at Beaulieu near Savannah, Georgia. September 1862 roll records the transfer. September 16, 1862 discharged. September 1862 roll records the discharge.

VEAL, A. J.: Company C, private. January 1, 1864 enlisted in as private in Co. C, 54th Regiment, Georgia Infantry at Camp Rose, South Carolina. January – February 1864 roll shows him absent (detached on picket at Purrysburg, South Carolina by order of Colonel Way). May 8, 1864 issued clothing.

VEAL, JOHN O.: Company H, private. He enlisted in as private in Co. H, 54th Regiment, Georgia Infantry.

VEATCH (VEAIL), FRANKLIN: Company H, private. March 1, 1863 enlisted as a private in Co. H, 54th Regiment, Georgia Infantry at Columbus, Georgia and received bounty $50.00. October 31, 1863 received pay. November – December 1863 roll shows him present. December 31, 1863 received pay. January 1864 issued clothing. January – February 1864 roll shows him present. June 2, 1864 issued clothing. He was captured in Tennessee in 1864. December 30, 1864 took the Oath of Allegiance at Nashville, Tennessee. He is described as; a resident of Muscogee County, Georgia, dark complexion, grown hair, hazel eyed and was 5 feet 5 inches high (has family).

VICKERY, CUYLER, SR.: Company D, private. October 7, 1861 enlisted as a private in Co. I, 5th Regiment, Georgia State Troops. April 1862 mustered out. April 30, 1862 enlisted as a private in Co. D, 54th Regiment, Georgia Infantry. March 1865 sent to the hospital sick. He was born in South Carolina January 26, 1812.

VICKERY (VICKRY), CUYLER (KYLER) JR.: Company D, private. October 7, 1861 enlisted as a private in Co. I, 5th Regiment, Georgia State Troops. April 1862 mustered out. April 30, 1862 enlisted as a private in Co. D, 54th Regiment, Georgia Infantry. January 1864 and May 8, 1864 issued clothing. August 18, 1864 admitted to Ocmulgee Hospital at Macon, Georgia with Chronic Diarrhoea. August 22, 1864 register of Ocmulgee Hospital at Macon, Georgia shows him with Diarrhoea, Anemia and effects of Fractured Tibia and Debility and furloughed to Screven County, Georgia. February 21, 1865 report of Medical Examining Board at Lauderdale, Mississippi granted him a furlough for 60 days to Sardis, Georgia due to Chronic Diarrhoea with extreme Emaciation and Debility for 3 months. He was a resident of Sardis, Screven County, Georgia. He was born in South Carolina January 26, 1812.

VICKERY, HEZEKIAH N.: Company D, private. April 30, 1862 enlisted as a private in Co. D, 54th Regiment, Georgia Infantry at Savannah, Georgia and received bounty $50.00. December 31, 1862 received pay. January – February 1863 roll shows him present (absent without leave for 9 days). January 1864 issued clothing. June 17, 1864 admitted to Ocmulgee Hospital at Macon, Georgia with a Gunshot Wound through the flesh of the left arm. June 24, 1864 report of Ocmulgee Hospital at Macon, Georgia shows him with a Gunshot Wound of the left arm. July 1, 1864 furloughed for 30 days. February 18, 1865 admitted to Way Hospital at Meridian, Mississippi with Chronic Diarrhoea and was furloughed. He was a resident of Screven County, Georgia. He was born October 15, 1839 and died in Georgia February 25, 1912. He is buried in Bascom Cemetery at Hilltonia, Screven County, Georgia. (find a grave # 24373313)

VICKERY, J. H.: Company D, private. April 30, 1862 enlisted as a private in Co. D, 54th Regiment, Georgia Infantry at Savannah, Georgia and received bounty $50.00. December 31, 1862 received pay. January – February 1863 roll shows him present.

VICKERY, WILLIAM: Company D, private. October 7, 1861 enlisted as a private in Co. I, 5th Regiment, Georgia State Troops. April 1862 mustered out. April 30, 1862 enlisted as a private in Co. D, 54th Regiment, Georgia Infantry at Savannah, Georgia and received bounty $50.00. December 31, 1862 received pay. January – February 1863 roll shows him present. January 1864 issued clothing. May 18, 1865 surrendered and paroled at Augusta, Georgia.

VINSON, B.: Company A, private. September 1, 1863 enlisted as a private in Co. A, 54th Regiment, Georgia Infantry at Macon, Georgia and received bounty $50.00. October 31, 1863 received pay. November – December 1863 roll shows him present. January 1, 1864 received pay. January – February 1864 roll shows him present. March 31, 1864 and May 8, 1864 issued clothing.

VINCENT, DANIEL: Company B, private. He enlisted as a private in Co. B, 54th Regiment, Georgia Infantry.

VINSON, JOHN W.: Company F, private. He enlisted as a private in Co. F, 54th Regiment, Georgia Infantry.

VISAGE (VISSAGE), WILLIAM H.: Company A, private. September 1, 1863 enlisted as a private in Co. A, 54th Regiment, Georgia Infantry at Macon, Georgia and received bounty $50.00. October 31, 1863 received pay. November – December 1863 roll shows him present. January 1, 1864 received pay. January – February 1864 roll shows him present. April 29, 1864 issued clothing. Pension records show he was at home sick at the close of the war. He was born in Georgia March 1, 1832.

WADE, NATHANIEL: Company H, private. September 10, 1862 enlisted as a private in Co. H, 54th Regiment, Georgia Infantry at Columbus, Georgia and received bounty $50.00. August and September 1862 rolls show his enlistment. September and October 1862 rolls show him detailed as a butcher. September 19, 1862 to November 8, 1862 detailed as a butcher. December 31, 1862 received pay. January – February 1863 roll shows him present. October 31, 1863 received pay. November – December 1863 roll shows him present (in arrest). December 31, 1863 received pay. January 1864 issued clothing. January – February 1864 roll shows him present (on picket). January 26, 1865 admitted to Way Hospital at Meridian, Mississippi with Pneumonia.

WADE, WILLIAM SCOTT: Company G, private. February 1, 1863 enlisted as a private in Co. G, 54th Regiment, Georgia Infantry at Columbus, Georgia and received bounty $50.00. January 1, 1864 received pay. January 1864 issued clothing. May 19, 1864 captured at Cassville, Georgia. May 24, 1864 received at Military Prison at Louisville, Kentucky from Nashville Tennessee. May 25, 1864 sent to Rock Island, Illinois from Military Prison at Louisville, Kentucky. May 27, 1864 received at Rock Island, Illinois from Military Prison at Louisville, Kentucky. February 15, 1865 transferred from Rock Island, Illinois to Point Lookout, Maryland for exchange. March 6, 1865 muster roll of 5th Division General Hospital Camp Winder at Richmond, Virginia shows him present.

WADELL, HUGH: Company F, private. September 1, 1863 enlisted as a private in Co. F, 54th Regiment, Georgia Infantry at Savannah, Georgia and received bounty $50.00. September 18, 1863 to December 31, 1863 detailed for extra duty with Signal and Telegraph Service at Savannah, Georgia. November – December 1863 roll shows him absent (detailed in Signal Corps). December 31, 1863 received pay $18.33. January 1864 issued clothing. January 1, 1864 to October 31, 1864 detailed for extra duty with Signal and Telegraph Service at Savannah, Georgia. June 30, 1864 received pay. October 31, 1864 muster roll of a Detachment of Men detailed in Signal Corps, Savannah, Georgia shows him absent on sick leave.

WAGONER, J. W.: Company B, private. He enlisted as a private in Co. B, 54th Regiment, Georgia Infantry.

WALDEN, AMOS: Company C, private. October 29, 1863 enlisted as a private in Co. C, 54th Regiment, Georgia Infantry at James Island, South Carolina and received bounty $50.00. January 1, 1864 received pay. January – February 1864 roll shows him present. May 8, 1864 issued clothing. Pension records show he was at home on sick furlough at the close of the war. He was born in Georgia October 12, 1845 and died July 7, 1917. He is buried in Parker Cemetery in Jefferson County, Georgia. (find a grave # 38123327)

WALDEN, THOMAS H.: Company C, private. May 6, 1862 enlisted as a private in Co. C, 54th Regiment, Georgia Infantry at Savannah, Georgia and received bounty $50.00. December 31, 1862 received pay. January – February 1863 roll shows him present. January 1, 1864 received pay. January – February 1864 roll shows him present. April 28, 1864 issued clothing. Pension records show: April 26, 1865 surrendered at Greensboro, North Carolina. May 1, 1865 paroled at Greensboro, North Carolina. He was a resident of Glascock County, Georgia. He was born in Warren County, Georgia in 1842.

WALERS, S: Company D, private. He enlisted as a private in Co. D, 54th Regiment, Georgia Infantry. September 1862 roll shows him detailed as a carpenter with the quartermaster's department.

WALKER, JOHN J.: Company H, corporal. May 12, 1862 enlisted as 3rd corporal in Co. H, 54th Regiment, Georgia Infantry at Columbus, Georgia and received bounty $50.00. December 31, 1862 received pay. January – February 1863 roll shows him present. Pension records show; He enlisted as a private in Co. F, 5th Regiment, Georgia Reserve Infantry in 1864. April 26, 1865 he surrendered at Smithfield, North Carolina. He was born in Muscogee County, Georgia March 12, 1846 and died there September 1919.

WALLACE, GEORGE MILTON: Company D, private. July 1, 1862 enlisted as a private in Co. D, 54th Regiment, Georgia Infantry at Savannah, Georgia and received bounty $50.00. December 31, 1862 received pay. January – February 1863 roll shows him present. January 1864 issued clothing. He was born March 8, 1834 and died in Volusia County, Florida May 3, 1911. He is buried in Pinewood Cemetery at Daytona Beach, Volusia County, Florida. (find a grave # 17739826)

WALSH, V.: Company F, private. December 27, 1862 enlisted as a private in Co. D, 54th Regiment, Georgia Infantry at Savannah, Georgia and received bounty $50.00. December 1862 roll shows his enlistment. December 31, 1862 received pay. January – February 1863 roll shows him present.

WALTERS, JAMES: Company C, private. He enlisted as a private in Co. C, 54th Regiment, Georgia Infantry at Savannah, Georgia and received bounty $50.00. September 16, 1862 he died at Beaulieu near Savannah, Georgia. September 1862 roll shows his death.

WALTERS, JEPTHA: Company H, corporal. May 12, 1862 enlisted as a corporal in Co. H, 54th Regiment, Georgia Infantry.

WALTERS, S.: Company E, private. May 6, 1862 enlisted in as private in Co. E, 54th Regiment, Georgia Infantry at Savannah, Georgia and received bounty $50.00. December 31, 1862 received pay. January – February 1863 roll shows him present. January 1864 and September 13, 1863 issued clothing. November 4, 1864 appears on a register of Floyd House Hospital at Macon, Georgia with Febris Intermittent and Diarrhoea (Y. D. & E.). He was a resident of Nashville, Berrien County, Georgia.

WALTERS, WILLIAM: Company E, private. May 6, 1862 enlisted in as private in Co. E, 54th Regiment, Georgia Infantry at Savannah, Georgia and received bounty $50.00. September 1, 1862 he died. August 28, 1863 death benefit claim was filed by his father, William Walters. He was a resident of Nashville, Berrien County, Georgia.

WALTKINS, MILES B.: Company C, private. He enlisted as a private in Co. C, 54th Regiment, Georgia Infantry.

WALTHOUR (WALDHOWER), GEORGE W. H.: Company I, private. September 18, 1861 enlisted in Co. C, 1st Regiment, 1st Brigade, Georgia State Troops. March 18, 1862 mustered out May 6, 1862 enlisted in as private in Co. I, 54th Regiment, Georgia Infantry at Guyton, Georgia and received bounty $50.00. December 31, 1862 received pay. January – February 1863 roll shows him present (picket guard). October 31, 1863 received pay. November – December 1863 roll shows him present. December 31, 1863 received pay. January 1864 issued clothing. June 13, 1864 issued clothing at Marshall Hospital at Columbus, Georgia. August 20, 1864 admitted to 1st Mississippi C. S. A. Hospital at Jackson, Mississippi with a Hernia (August 20, 1864 admitted to Hospital at Shelby Springs, Alabama). July – August 1864 roll of Hospital at Shelby Springs, Alabama shows him present. September 18, 1864 returned to duty. September 22, 1864 issued clothing.

WARDLAW, WILLIAM E.: Company G, private. May 12, 1862 enlisted as a private in Co. G, 54th Regiment, Georgia Infantry at Columbus, Georgia and received bounty $50.00. He was born December 26, 1843 and died July 18, 1922. He is buried in Linwood Cemetery at Columbus, Muscogee County, Georgia. (find a grave # 34014036)

WARE, WARREN A.: Company G, private. May 12, 1862 enlisted as a private in Co. G, 54th Regiment, Georgia Infantry at Columbus, Georgia and received bounty $50.00. December 31, 1862 received pay. January – February 1863 roll shows him present. January 1864 and April 25, 1864 issued clothing. He transferred from Co. G, 54th Regiment, Georgia Infantry to Co. F, 54th Regiment, Georgia Infantry. April 26, 1865 surrendered at Greensboro, North Carolina. May 1, 1865 paroled at Greensboro, North Carolina.

WARREN, REUBEN A.: Company K, private. October 3, 1861 enlisted as a private in Co. A, 1st Regiment, 1st Brigade, Georgia State Troops. April 1862 mustered out. April 18, 1862 enlisted in as private in Co. K, 54th Regiment, Georgia Infantry at Savannah, Georgia and received bounty $50.00. August 11, 1862 transferred to Co. C, 1st Georgia Sharpshooters by Special Order No. 259. August 1862 roll shows his transfer. December 16, 1864 captured at Nashville, Tennessee. May 15, 1865 released from Camp Chase, Ohio.

WATERHOUSE, J. W.: Company B, private. He enlisted as a private in Co. B, 54th Regiment, Georgia Infantry.

WATERS, AUGUSTUS: Company I (D), private. He enlisted as a private in Co. I, 54th Regiment, Georgia Infantry. January 18, 1865 admitted to Way Hospital at Meridian, Mississippi with a Gunshot Wound. February 6, 1865 he appears on a register of Floyd House and Ocmulgee Hospitals at Macon, Georgia with Bronchitis, Acute Anemia and General Debility. He was a resident of Millen, Georgia. (He appears on the roll of Co. D but no transfer found.)

WATERS, E.: Company D, private. He enlisted as a private in Co. D, 54th Regiment, Georgia Infantry.
January 1864 and May 8, 1864 issued clothing. May 18, 1865 surrendered and paroled at Augusta, Georgia.

WATERS, GEORGE: Company F, private. February 6, 1863 enlisted as private in Co. F, 54th Regiment, Georgia Infantry at Savannah, Georgia and received bounty $50.00. January – February 1863 roll shows him present. March 3, 1863 transferred from General Hospital No. 1 at Savannah, Georgia to General Hospital at Macon Georgia with Chronic Rheumatism. November 1, 1863 received pay. November – December 1863 roll shows him present. January 1864 issued clothing. July 22, 1864 wounded in Atlanta, Georgia. July 25, 1864 admitted to Ocmulgee Hospital at Macon, Georgia with a Gunshot Wound. August 5, 1864 transferred to hospital at Guyton, Georgia. He was a resident of Dooley County, Georgia.

WATERS, JAMES: Company D, private. April 30, 1862 enlisted as a private in Co. D, 54th Regiment, Georgia Infantry at Savannah, Georgia and received bounty $50.00. December 31, 1862 received pay. January – February 1863 roll shows him present. January 1864 and April 25, 1864 issued clothing. He was wounded and at home on wounded furlough near the close of the war. He died September 21, 1864. He is buried in Laurel Grove Cemetery (North) at Savannah, Chatham County, Georgia. (find a grave # 66956732)

WATERS, JAMES: Company D, private. October 5, 1862 enlisted as a private in Co. D, 54th Regiment, Georgia Infantry at Beaulieu near Savannah, Georgia and received bounty $50.00. October 1862 shows his enlistment. He was born in Screven County, Georgia May 14, 1839 and died in Screven County, Georgia December 26, 1907. He is buried in McDonald Baptist Church Cemetery at Sylvania, Screven County, Georgia. (find a grave #83208764)

WATERS (WALTERS), JAMES: Company E, private. May 6, 1862 enlisted as private in Co. E, 54th Regiment, Georgia Infantry at Savannah, Georgia and received bounty $50.00. December 31, 1862 received pay. January – February 1863 roll shows him present (due 2 month's pay). January 1864 and April 25, 1864 issued clothing. September 1864 he died. September 24, 1864 his coffin was requisitioned. He was a resident of Nashville, Berrien County, Georgia.

WATERS, JOHN: Company D, private. August 26, 1862 enlisted as a private in Co. D, 54th Regiment, Georgia Infantry at Beaulieu near Savannah, Georgia and received bounty $50.00. September 18, 1862 to September 30, 1862 detailed for extra duty as a laborer at Beaulieu near Savannah, Georgia at a rate of $.25 extra per day. September 30, 1862 received pay. December 31, 1862 received pay. January – February 1863 roll shows him present. January 1864 and April 25, 1864 issued clothing. He was born August 30, 1844 and died in Georgia November 30, 1910. He is buried in McDonald Baptist Church at Sylvania, Screven County, Georgia. (find a grave #115496448)

WATERS, MICHAEL (MIKE): Company D, private. April 30, 1862 enlisted as a private in Co. D, 54th Regiment, Georgia Infantry at Savannah, Georgia and received bounty $50.00. December 31, 1862 received pay. January – February 1863 roll shows him present. January 1864 and April 25, 1864 issued clothing. According to pension records he was "at home cut off by Sherman's Army" at the close of the war. He was born in Georgia February 10, 1841 and died near Woodcliff, Georgia March 14, 1910. He is buried in McDonald Baptist Church at Sylvania, Screven County, Georgia. (find a grave # 115302253)

WATERS, WILLIAM J.: Company D, private. October 7, 1861 enlisted as a private in Co. I, 5th Regiment, Georgia State Troops. April 1862 mustered out. April 30, 1862 enlisted as a private in Co. D, 54th Regiment, Georgia Infantry at Savannah, Georgia and received bounty $50.00. December 31, 1862 received pay. January – February 1863 roll shows him present (camp guard). January 1864 and April 25, 1864 issued clothing. April 26, 1865 surrendered in Co. D, 54th Regiment, Consolidated Georgia Infantry at Greensboro, North Carolina. May 1, 1865 paroled at Greensboro, North Carolina. He was born in Georgia March 7, 1843 and died May 5, 1917. He is buried in Green Hill Baptist Church Cemetery at Sylvania, Screven County, Georgia. (find a grave # 31325639)

WATKINS, MILLS BENNETT: Company C, private. October 22, 1861 enlisted as a private in Co. A, 2nd Regiment, 1st Brigade, Georgia State

Troops. April 1862 mustered out. May 6, 1862 enlisted as a private in Co. C, 54th Regiment, Georgia Infantry at Savannah, Georgia and received bounty $50.00. December 31, 1862 received pay. January – February 1863 roll shows him present. January 1, 1864 received pay. January – February 1864 roll shows him present. April 28, 1864 issued clothing. May 18, 1865 surrendered and paroled at Augusta, Georgia. He was a resident of Hancock County, Georgia. He was born in Jefferson County, Georgia in 1844. He is buried in Coleman Chapel Cemetery in Wadley, Jefferson County, Georgia. (find a grave #73566766)

WATSON, GEORGE S.: Company G, private. January 22, 1863 enlisted as a private in Co. G, 54th Regiment, Georgia Infantry at Columbus, Georgia and received bounty $50.00. January – February 1863 roll shows him present. January 1864 and May 8, 1864 issued clothing. He transferred from Co. G, 54th Regiment, Georgia Infantry to Co. F, 54th Regiment, Georgia Infantry. April 26, 1865 surrendered at Greensboro, North Carolina. May 1, 1865 paroled at Greensboro, North Carolina.

WATSON, GILBERT: Company G, private. January 22, 1863 enlisted as a private in Co. G, 54th Regiment, Georgia Infantry at Columbus, Georgia and received bounty $50.00. January – February 1863 roll shows him present. January 1864 and May 8, 1864 issued clothing. March 20, 1865 died of Febris Typhoides in Way Hospital No. 3 at Salisbury, North Carolina.

WATSON, JOSEPH: Company E, private. October 6, 1861 enlisted as a private in Co. K, 5th Regiment, Georgia State Troops. April 1862 mustered out. May 6, 1862 enlisted as private in Co. E, 54th Regiment, Georgia Infantry at Savannah, Georgia and received bounty $50.00. November and December 1862 rolls show him detailed as a boatman. December 31, 1862 received pay. January – February 1863 roll shows him present. January 1864 issued clothing. Pension records show; February 1865 he was home on furlough for 30 days and could not reach his command when furlough expired. He was born in Georgia December 19, 1841 and died December 19, 1919. He is buried in Union Primitive Baptist Church Cemetery at Lakeland, Lanier County, Georgia. (find a grave # 59634452)

WATSON, K.: Company E, private (cook). March 1, 1863 enlisted in as private in Co. F, 54th Regiment, Georgia Infantry at Savannah, Georgia and received bounty $50.00. September 1, 1863 received pay. November – December 1863 roll shows he deserted December 10, 1863.

WAY, CHARLTON H.: Field and Staff, colonel. July 18, 1861 elected captain of Way's Independent Company, Georgia infantry (Forest City Rangers). November 1, 1861 mustered out. May 13, 1862 elected Colonel of the 54th Regiment, Georgia Infantry at Guyton, Georgia. June 30, 1862 received pay $298.97. July 1862 roll shows him absent (on sick furlough since July 1, 1862). August and September 1862 rolls show him present at Beaulieu near Savannah, Georgia. October 1862 roll shows him absent on leave since October 30, 1862. November 24, 1862 his name appears on a list of officers at Savannah, Georgia. November and December 1862 rolls show him present at Beaulieu near Savannah, Georgia. January – February 1863 roll shows him absent (detailed to inspect the 32nd Regiment, Georgia Infantry by Special Order No. 57). March 2, 1863 received pay $195.00. April 9, 1863 received pay $195.00. June 23, 1863 to June 29, 1863 he was on furlough approved by General Mercer. August 3, 1863 granted leave by Special Order No. 151/4. October 21, 1863 his name appears on a list of officers at Legare's Point, South Carolina. December 3, 1863 granted leave by Special Order No. 93. January 4, 1864 assigned to General Walker's Division in North Georgia by Special Order No. 4/1. June 4, 1864 admitted to Ocmulgee Hospital at Macon, Georgia with Chronic Dysentery. July 3, 1864 deserted (left hospital without permission). August 25, 1864 his name appears on a report of officers in Mercer's Brigade in the field near Atlanta, Georgia. September 14, 1864 his name appears on a report of officers in Mercer's Brigade in camp near Jonesboro, Georgia. September 20, 1864 he is shown as in command of the 54th Regiment, Georgia Infantry. He was born in Liberty County, Georgia October 5, 1834 and died in Savannah, Chatham County, Georgia July 1, 1901-1900. He is buried in Lot # 753 in Laurel Grove Cemetery (North) at Savannah, Chatham County, Georgia. (find a grave #95936139)

WAY, HARFORD HENRY: (Company G) Field and Staff, adjutant. May 16, 1862 enlisted as a private in Co. G, 54th Regiment, Georgia Infantry at Columbus, Georgia and received bounty $50.00. November 3, 1862 appointed Sergeant Major of the 54th Regiment, Georgia Infantry. October 1862 roll shows him as sergeant major. November 1862 roll shows him transferred to command staff. December 31, 1862 received pay. January 22, 1862 detailed at Coffee Bluff as Drill Officer. January – February 1863 roll shows him absent (detailed at Coffee Bluff as Drill Officer). May 2, 1863 appointed adjutant of the 54th Regiment, Georgia Infantry. October 21, 1863 his name appears on a list of officers at Legare's Point, South Carolina. December 14, 1863 received pay $100.00. August 27, 1864 his name appears on a list of staff officers serving in General Hardee's Corps at Atlanta, Georgia. September 2, 1864 admitted to Medical Board Division Hospital. September 14, 1864 his name appears on a report of officers in Mercer's Brigade in camp near Jonesboro, Georgia as being in Division Hospital. November 7, 1864 his name appears on a list of staff officers serving in General Cheatham's Corps, Smith's Brigade. May 19, 1865 surrendered and paroled at Augusta, Georgia. He was born in 1843 and died in 1907. He is buried in Fairview Cemetery at Eufaula, Barbour County, Alabama. (find a grave # 27114634)

WAYMER, A.: Company E, private. He enlisted as a private in Co. E, 54th Regiment, Georgia Infantry.

WEATHERLY, J. A.: Company B, private. He enlisted as a private in Co. B, 54th Regiment, Georgia Infantry.

WEATHERLY, J. S.: Company B, private. He enlisted as a private in Co. B, 54th Regiment, Georgia Infantry.

WEAVER, JEREMIAH "JERRY" B.: Company E, private. May 6, 1862 enlisted as a private in Co. E, 54th Regiment, Georgia Infantry at Savannah, Georgia and received bounty $50.00. December 31, 1862 received pay. January – February 1863 roll shows him present. January 1864 issued clothing. December 25, 1864 captured at Pulaski, Tennessee. January 2, 1865 received at Military Prison at Louisville, Kentucky from Nashville, Tennessee. January 4, 1865 sent to Camp Chase, Ohio from Military Prison at Louisville, Kentucky. January 6, 1865 received at Camp Chase, Ohio from Military Prison at Louisville, Kentucky. May 12, 1865 died at Camp Chase, Ohio of Pneumonia. He was born in Wilkinson County, Georgia September 20, 1833 and died at Camp Chase, Ohio at Camp Chase, Ohio. He is buried in the Camp Chase Confederate Cemetery, Ohio in Row 39, No. 10, grave 1958 (1/3 mile south of camp). (find a grave #53900754)

WEAVER, JETHRO JOHN WILKINS: Company E, private. February 11, 1863 enlisted as a private in Co. E, 54th Regiment, Georgia Infantry at Coffee Bluff near Savannah, Georgia and received bounty $50.00. January – February 1863 roll shows him present. July 1863 received pay $50.00. January 1864, April 25, 1864 and May 8, 1864 issued clothes. December 25, 1864 captured at Pulaski, Tennessee. January 2, 1865 received at Military Prison at Louisville, Kentucky from Nashville, Tennessee. January 4, 1865 sent to Camp Chase, Ohio from Military Prison at Louisville, Kentucky. January 6, 1865 received at Camp Chase, Ohio from Military Prison at Louisville, Kentucky. January 5, 1865 he died at Camp Chase, Ohio. He was born in Wilkinson County, Georgia October 30, 1825 and died at Camp Chase, Ohio at Camp Chase, Ohio January 5, 1865. He is buried in the Camp Chase Confederate Cemetery, Ohio in row 22, No 12. grave 755 (1/3 mile south of camp). (find a grave #53900421)

WEAVER, JOHN B.: Company E, private. May 6, 1862 enlisted as a private in Co. E, 54th Regiment, Georgia Infantry at Savannah, Georgia and received bounty $50.00. Pension records show; he was at home on sick furlough at the close of the war. He died in Berrien County, Georgia December 15, 1900.

WEBB, ABNER: Company C, private. He enlisted as a private in Co. C, 54th Regiment, Georgia Infantry.

WEBB, JOSEPH: Company C, private. He enlisted as a private in Co. C, 54th Regiment, Georgia Infantry. January 18, 1865 admitted to Way Hospital at Meridian, Mississippi with a Gunshot Wound.

WEBB, J. L.: Company C, private. May 6, 1862 enlisted as a private in Co. C, 54th Regiment, Georgia Infantry at Savannah, Georgia and received bounty $50.00. November 21, 1862 died at Atlanta, Georgia. He is buried at Oakland Cemetery in Atlanta, Georgia. (find a grave #41664359)

WEBB, JAMES ROSS: Company G, corporal. May 12, 1862 enlisted as a private in Co. G, 54th Regiment, Georgia Infantry at Columbus, Georgia and received bounty $50.00. December 31, 1862 received pay. January

– February 1863 roll shows him present. January 1864 and May 8, 1864 issued clothes. He was elected 1st corporal of Co. G, 54th Regiment, Georgia Infantry. He transferred from Co. G, 54th Regiment, Georgia Infantry to Co. F, 54th Regiment, Georgia Infantry. July 22, 1864 wounded at Atlanta, Georgia. April 26, 1865 surrendered at Greensboro, North Carolina. May 1, 1865 paroled at Greensboro, North Carolina. He died in Phoenix City, Alabama June 5, 1899.

WEBB, JOHN: Company E, private. May 6, 1862 enlisted as a private in Co. E, 54th Regiment, Georgia Infantry at Savannah, Georgia and received bounty $50.00. December 31, 1862 received pay. January – February 1863 roll shows him present. January 1864 issued clothing. Pension records show he was home on furlough at the close of the war. He was born in Wilkinson County, Georgia January 22, 1834 and died in Berrien County, Georgia December 15, 1900. He is buried in Futch Cemetery in Cook County, Georgia. (find a grave # 33292885)

WEBB, JORDAN: Company E, private. May 6, 1862 enlisted as a private in Co. E, 54th Regiment, Georgia Infantry at Savannah, Georgia and received bounty $50.00. December 31, 1862 received pay. January – February 1863 roll shows him present. January 1864 issued clothing. He was born June 3, 1831 and died June 30, 1910. He is buried in Spring Hill Baptist Church Cemetery at Sparks, Cook County, Georgia. (find a grave # 8142597)

WELDON (WELDEN), JAMES T.: Company H (F), private. May 12, 1862 enlisted as a private in Co. H, 54th Regiment, Georgia Infantry at Columbus, Georgia and received bounty $50.00. June 30, 1862 deserted. December 31, 1862 received pay. January 16 (17), 1863 transferred from Co. H, 54th Regiment, Georgia Infantry to Co. F, 54th Regiment, Georgia Infantry by order of Colonel Way. January – February 1863 rolls show him transferred due to desertion. November 1, 1863 received pay. November – December 1863 roll shows him present. January 1864 and May 8, 1864 issued clothing.

WELLS, A. J.: Company E, private. February 12, 1862 enlisted as a private in Co. E, 54th Regiment, Georgia Infantry at Beaulieu near Savannah, Georgia and received bounty $50.00. December 31, 1862 received pay. January – February 1863 roll shows him present. January 1864 issued clothing.

WELLS, JACOB H.: Company K, private. October 3, 1861 enlisted as a private in Co. A, 1st Regiment, 1st Brigade, Georgia State Troops. April 1862 mustered out. April 18, 1862 enlisted as a private in Co. E, 54th Regiment, Georgia Infantry at Savannah, Georgia and received bounty $50.00. May 17, 1862 deserted at Savannah, Georgia. August 1862 roll shows his desertion at Savannah, Georgia.

WELLS, JAMES: Company A, private. September 1, 1862 enlisted as a private in Co. A, 54th Regiment, Georgia Infantry at Macon, Georgia and received bounty $50.00. October 31, 1862 received pay. January – February 1863 roll shows him present. January 1, 1864 received pay.

January – February 1864 roll shows him present. November – December 1864 roll of Co E, 1st Regiment, Troops and Defences stationed at Camp Wright near Macon, Georgia shows him absent (Provost Guard – Macon, Georgia). March 31, 1864 and October 29, 1864 issued clothing at Convalescent Camp Wright at Macon, Georgia.

WELLS, A. JAMES: Company D, private. February 12, 1862 enlisted as a private in Co. D, 54th Regiment, Georgia Infantry at Beaulieu near Savannah, Georgia and received bounty $50.00. December 31, 1862 received pay. January – February 1863 roll shows him present. January 1864 issued clothing.

WELLS, JAMES M.: Company E, private. He enlisted as a private in Co. E, 54th Regiment, Georgia Infantry.

WELLS, WILLIAM E.: Company E, corporal. He enlisted as a corporal in Co. E, 54th Regiment, Georgia Infantry.

WELLS, WILLIAM: Company A, private. April 29, 1862 (May 3, 1862) enlisted as a private in Co. A, 54th Regiment, Georgia Infantry at Macon, Georgia and received bounty $50.00. August 31, 1862 received pay. June 30, 1863 roll shows him present. October 31, 1863 received pay. November – December 1863 roll shows him present (sick in camp). January – February 1864 roll shows him present. April 29, 1864 and May 8, 1864 issued clothing. October 27, 1864 issued clothing in Blackie Hospital at Augusta, Georgia. December 2, 1864 admitted to Ocmulgee Hospital at Macon, Georgia with Ulcus. February 15, 1865 shown as deserted from Ocmulgee Hospital at Macon, Georgia. February 16, 1865 admitted to Ocmulgee Hospital at Macon, Georgia with Ulcus. March 20, 1865 returned to duty. He was a resident of Jones County, Georgia.

WEST, ELI H. (TIP): Company G, private. August 12, 1862 enlisted as a private in Co. G, 54th Regiment, Georgia Infantry at Columbus, Georgia and received bounty $50.00. August 1862 roll shows his enlistment. November 1, 1862 to November 30, 1862 detailed as a teamster (ambulance driver) at a rate of $.25 extra per day. November 1862 roll shows him detailed as a teamster. December 31, 1862 received pay. January – February 1863 roll shows him present. June 2, 1863 to December 31, 1863 detailed as an ambulance driver with the Medical Department on James Island, South Carolina at a rate of $.25 extra per day. September 1863 received pay. October 31, 1863 his name appears on a list of men detailed at James Island, South Carolina. October 1863 received pay. November 30, 1863 received pay. January 1, 1864 to April 30, 1864 detailed as an ambulance driver at Charleston, South Carolina at a rate of $.25 extra per day. January 1864 received pay. January 1864 and February 3, 1864 issued clothing. February 1864 received pay. March 31, 1864 received pay. April 7, 1864 issued clothing. 2nd quarter of 1864 received pay. May 21, 1864 granted a furlough by Special Order No. 119/3. July 7, 1864 received pay $66.00.

WESTBERRY, CHARLES M.: Company K, private. He enlisted in as private in Co. K, 54th Regiment, Georgia Infantry at Savannah, Georgia.

WESTBERRY, JOHN MOSES: Company K, private. October 3, 1861 enlisted as a private in Co. A, 1st Regiment, 1st Brigade, Georgia State Troops. April 1862 mustered out. April 18, 1862 enlisted as private in Co. K, 54th Regiment, Georgia Infantry at Savannah, Georgia and received bounty $50.00. January 1, 1863 received pay. January – February 1863 roll shows him present. March 18, 1864, April 18, 1864 and June 2, 1864 issued clothes. July 20, 1864 he was wounded in the left thigh at Peachtree Creek near Atlanta, Georgia. August 1, 1864 admitted to Ocmulgee Hospital at Macon, Georgia with a Gunshot Wound left thigh through the flesh (in battle L. C. B.). August 4, 1864 furloughed to Appling County, Georgia. May 10, 1865 surrendered at Tallahassee, Florida. May 18, 1865 paroled at Thomasville, Georgia. He is described as: 5 feet 8 inches high, red hair, blue eyes and fair complexion. He was a resident of Appling County, Georgia. (Another record shows; He was born in Liberty County, Georgia January 22, 1843 and died October 5, 1916 in Wayne County, Georgia) He was born in Appling County, Georgia May 13, and died November 19, 1909 in Wayne County, Georgia. He is buried in Flint Branch Church Cemetery in Wayne County, Georgia. (find a grave # 23512742)

WESTBERRY, M.: Company F (K), private. September 8, 1862 enlisted as private in Co. F, 54th Regiment, Georgia Infantry at Savannah, Georgia and received bounty $50.00. November 1862 transferred from Co. F, 54th Regiment, Georgia Infantry to Co. K, 54th Regiment, Georgia Infantry.

WESTBERRY, M. G.: Company K, private. September 8, 1862 enlisted as private in Co. K, 54th Regiment, Georgia Infantry at Savannah, Georgia and received bounty $50.00.

WESTBERRY, MOSES JOSHUA: Company K (F), private. October 3, 1861 enlisted as a private in Co. A, 1st Regiment, 1st Brigade, Georgia State Troops. April 1862 mustered out. April 18, 1862 enlisted in as private in Co. K, 54th Regiment, Georgia Infantry at Savannah, Georgia and received bounty $50.00. January 1, 1863 received pay. January – February 1863 roll shows him present.
March 18, 1864, April 18, 1864 and April 25, 1864 issued clothing. May 10, 1865 surrendered at Tallahassee, Florida. May 23, 1865 paroled at Thomasville, Georgia. He was born in Appling County (Another record: November 17, 1836 and died in Wayne County, Georgia April 19, 1936.) He was born in Appling County, Georgia November 29, 1839 and died in Wayne County, Georgia June 30, 1903. He is buried in Flint Branch Church Cemetery in Wayne County, Georgia. (find a grave #29967902)

WESTBERRY, WILLIAM CHARLTON: Company K, private. April 18, 1862 enlisted as private in Co. K, 54th Regiment, Georgia Infantry at Savannah, Georgia and received bounty $50.00. May 25, 1862 deserted at Savannah, Georgia. August 1862 roll shows his desertion. May 1863 he was killed near Charleston, South Carolina (headstone states). He was born in Appling County, Georgia October 16, 1825 and died near Charleston, South Carolina May 1862. He is buried in Old Bethel Cemetery in Wayne County, Georgia. (find a grave #23538581)

WHEATLEY, JOHN: Company K, private. September 10, 1864 enlisted in Co H, 37th Regiment, Georgia Infantry at Washington, Georgia. He transferred to Co K, 54th Regiment, Georgia Infantry. April 26, 1865 surrendered in Co. K, 54th Regiment, Consolidated Georgia Infantry at Greensboro, North Carolina. May 1, 1865 paroled at Greensboro, North Carolina.

WHEELER, ALLEN ORATIO: Company A, private. May 3, 1862 enlisted as private in Co. A, 54th Regiment, Georgia Infantry at Macon, Georgia and received bounty $50.00. April 30, 1863 received pay. June 30, 1863 roll shows him present. October 31, 1863 received pay. November – December 1863 roll shows him present. January 1, 1864 received pay. January – February 1864 roll shows him present. April 29, 1864 issued clothing. June 15, 1864 captured at Golgotha, Georgia (near Marietta, Georgia). June 22, 1864 received at Military Prison at Louisville, Kentucky from Nashville, Tennessee. June 22, 1864 sent to Rock Island, Illinois from Military Prison at Louisville, Kentucky. June 24, 1864 received at Rock Island, Illinois from Military Prison at Louisville, Kentucky. October 15, 1864 he joined the U. S Army at Rock Island, Illinois. He was born in Georgia November 18, 1839 and died in Jones County, Georgia April 14, 1915. He is buried in Wheeler Slocomb Cemetery at Bradley, Jones County, Georgia. (find a grave # 64728343)

WHEELER, J. M.: Company A, private. May 3, 1862 enlisted as private in Co. A, 54th Regiment, Georgia Infantry at Macon, Georgia and received bounty $50.00. April 30, 1863 received pay. June 30, 1863 roll shows him present. May 1, 1863 to October 31, 1863 detailed as a teamster at a rate of $.25 extra per day. July 1863 received pay. August 1863 received pay. October 31, 1863 received pay. November – December 1863 roll shows him present (teamster for company). January 1, 1864 received pay. January – February 1864 roll shows him present (teamster for company).

WHITE, C. H.: Company B, lieutenant. He enlisted in Co. A, 4th Georgia Sharpshooters. He was transferred into Co. B, 54th Georgia Regiment, Consolidated Georgia Infantry. April 26, 1865 surrendered as 1st lieutenant of Co. B, 54th Regiment, Consolidated Georgia Infantry at Greensboro, North Carolina. May 1, 1865 paroled at Greensboro, North Carolina.

WHITE, ELCANAH: Company G, private. He enlisted as a private in Co. G, 54th Regiment, Georgia Infantry.

WHITE, JOHN D.: Company A, private. May 7, 1863 enlisted in as private in Co. A, 54th Regiment, Georgia Infantry at Macon, Georgia and received bounty $50.00. April 30, 1863 received pay. June 30, 1863 roll shows him present. October 31, 1863 received pay. November 1863 received commutation for rations. November – December 1863 roll shows him present. January 1, 1864 received pay. January – February 1864 roll shows him present. February 29, 1864 received pay. April 29, 1864 issued clothing. October 20, 1864 admitted to Stonewall Hospital at Montgomery, Alabama. November 15, 1864 hospital muster roll for Stonewall Hospital at Montgomery, Alabama shows him present as a patient. February 6, 1865 admitted to Ocmulgee Hospital at Macon, Georgia with Ulcus. April 30, 1865 returned to duty. He was a resident of Bibb County, Georgia.

WHITE, J. R.: Company H, private. He enlisted as a private in Co. H, 54th Regiment, Georgia Infantry.

WHITEHEAD, WILLIAM F.: Company H, private. May 12, 1862 enlisted as a private in Co. H, 54th Regiment, Georgia Infantry at Columbus, Georgia and received bounty $50.00. December 31, 1862 received pay. January – February 1863 roll shows him present. October 31, 1863 received pay. November – December 1863 roll shows him present. January 1, 1864 received pay. January 1864 issued clothing. January – February 1864 roll shows him present (on picket). February 29, 1864 received pay. April 25, 1864 issued clothing. June 16, 1864 issued clothing at Marshall Hospital at Columbus, Georgia. August 8, 1864 issued clothing. September 25, 1864 admitted to Marshall Hospital at Columbus, Georgia. November 30, 1864 hospital muster roll of Marshall Hospital at Columbus, Georgia shows him present as a patient.

WHITEHURST, CHARLES L.: Company F, private. August 1, 1863 enlisted as private in Co. F, 54th Regiment, Georgia Infantry at Savannah, Georgia and received bounty $50.00. November 1, 1863 received pay. November – December 1863 roll shows him present. December 31, 1863 received pay. January 1864 issued clothing. August 23, 1864 admitted to Marshall Hospital at Columbus, Georgia. November 30, 1864 hospital muster roll of Marshall Hospital at Columbus, Georgia shows him present as a patient. Pension records state "he was discharged at Macon, Georgia at the close of the war. He was born in Wilkinson County, Georgia July 8, 1845 and died May 2, 1925. He is buried in the Whitehurst Cemetery in Wilkinson County, Georgia. (find a grave # 115337318)

WHITEHURST, THOMAS C.: Company F (D), private. January 1864 and April 25, 1864 issued clothing. December 14, 1864 issued clothing at Convalescent Camp Wright at Macon, Georgia. April 26, 1865 surrendered in Co. D, 54th Regiment, Consolidated Georgia Infantry at Greensboro, North Carolina. May 1, 1865 paroled at Greensboro, North Carolina. He was born in Wilkinson County, Georgia March 20, 1836 and died March 23, 1890. He is buried in the Whitehurst Cemetery in Wilkinson County, Georgia. (find a grave # 115337031)

WIGGINS, JESSE A.: Company C, private. December 11, 1861 enlisted as a private in Co. B, 8th Regiment, Georgia State Troops. April 1862 mustered out. April 22, 1862 enlisted as a private in Co. C, 54th Regiment, Georgia Infantry at Savannah, Georgia and received bounty $50.00. December 31, 1862 received pay. January – February 1863 roll shows him present (in hospital at Bethesda – absent 10 days). January 1, 1864 received pay. January – February 1864 roll shows him present. April 29, 1864 issued clothing. May 24, 1865 surrendered and paroled at Augusta, Georgia. (Pension records show he surrendered at Greensboro, North Carolina on April 26, 1865He was born in Emanuel County, Georgia April

15, 1842 and died April 28, 1911. He is buried in Lewis Primitive Baptist Church Cemetery in Jenkins County, Georgia. (find a grave #60810457)

WIGGINS, JOHN KENT: Company C, private. May 6, 1862 enlisted as a private in Co. C, 54th Regiment, Georgia Infantry at Savannah, Georgia and received bounty $50.00. December 31, 1862 received pay. January – February 1863 roll shows him present (absent without leave 5 days). January 1, 1864 received pay. January – February 1864 roll shows him present. Pension records show he was home on wounded furlough for 30 days and could not reach command when furlough expired. May 24, 1865 surrendered and paroled at Augusta, Georgia. He was a resident of Emanuel County, Georgia. He was born in 1840 and died near Herndon, Georgia in 1888. He is buried in Lewis Primitive Baptist Church Cemetery Jenkins County, Georgia. (find a grave #60813721)

WIGGINS, JOSEPH: Company C, private. May 6, 1862 enlisted as a private in Co. C, 54th Regiment, Georgia Infantry at Savannah, Georgia and received bounty $50.00. October 31, 1862 received pay. January – February 1863 roll shows him present (absent without leave for 2 months 8 days – one month pay retailed by sentence of court martial). January 1, 1864 received pay. January – February 1864 roll shows him present. May 8, 1864 issued clothing. May – June 1864 wounded near Dallas, Georgia. Pension records show he was furloughed for 5 days in March 1865 and could not reach command when furlough expired. May 24, 1865 surrendered and paroled at Augusta, Georgia. He was a resident of Emanuel County, Georgia. He was born in 1837 and died in Jenkins County, Georgia October 19, 1911. He is buried in Lewis Primitive Baptist Church Cemetery in Jenkins County, Georgia. (find a grave #60815594)

WIGGINS, W. W.: Company A, private. February 10, 1863 enlisted as a private in Co. A, 54th Regiment, Georgia Infantry at Savannah, Georgia and received bounty $50.00. April 30, 1863 received pay. June 30, 1863 roll shows him present.

WILDER, JOHN H.: Company A, private. February 16, 1864 enlisted as a private in Co. A, 54th Regiment, Georgia Infantry at Savannah, Georgia. January – February 1864 roll shows him present (pay due since enlistment. March 31, 1864 and April 29, 1864 issued clothing. December 31, 1864 roll of Co. D, 2nd Battalion, Troops and Defences at Macon, Georgia stationed at Camp Wright shows him absent as provost guard at Macon, Georgia. Pension records show he was at home on furlough at the close of the war. He was born in Georgia June 20, 1846.

WILEY, JOHN: Company F, private. February 1, 1863 enlisted as a private in Co. F, 54th Regiment, Georgia Infantry. January – February 1863 roll shows him present

WILKINS, CHARLES SEWELL: Company I, private. September 18, 1861 enlisted as a private in Co. C, 1st Regiment, 1st Brigade, Georgia State Troops. March 18, 1862 mustered out. May 6, 1862 enlisted as a private in Co. I, 54th Regiment, Georgia Infantry at Guyton, Georgia and received bounty $50.00. December 31, 1862 received pay. January

– February 1863 roll shows him present. July 1, 1863 to December 31, 1863 detailed for extra duty as post courier at a rate of $.25 extra per day. September 8, 1863 received pay. October 31, 1863 received pay. November – December 1863 roll shows him present (courier for post). December 31, 1863 received pay. January 1864 and April 25, 1864 issued clothing. July 24, 1864 admitted to Ocmulgee Hospital at Macon, Georgia with Acute Diarrhoea. July 27, 1864 he was transferred. August 17, 1864 he died. He was a resident of Effingham County, Georgia. He was born October 18, 1840 and died August 17, 1864. He is buried in Old Providence Cemetery at Guyton, Effingham County, Georgia. (find a grave #16711313)

WILKINS, THEODORE JASPER: Company I, sergeant. September 18, 1861 enlisted as a private in Co. C, 1st Regiment, 1st Brigade, Georgia State Troops. March 18, 1862 mustered out. May 6, 1862 enlisted as a private in Co. I, 54th Regiment, Georgia Infantry at Guyton, Georgia and received bounty $50.00. December 31, 1862 received pay. January – February 1863 roll shows him present. October 31, 1863 received pay. November – December 1863 roll shows him present (picket guard). He transferred from Co. I, 54th Regiment, Georgia Infantry to Co. F, 54th Regiment, Georgia Infantry and was appointed 2nd sergeant. April 26, 1865 surrendered at Greensboro, North Carolina. May 1, 1865 paroled at Greensboro, North Carolina. He was born in Georgia February 5, 1843 and died in Georgia May 14, 1918. He is buried in Guyton Cemetery at Guyton, Effingham County, Georgia. (find a grave #88703162)

WILKINSON, JAMES: Company A, private. September 1, 1863 enlisted as private in Co. A, 54th Regiment, Georgia Infantry at Macon, Georgia and received bounty $50.00. October 31, 1863 received pay. November – December 1863 roll shows him absent (detailed in Government work at Gordon, Georgia). January – February 1864 roll shows him absent (detailed in Government work at Gordon, Georgia).

WILKINSON, U. L.: Company A, private. He enlisted in as private Co. A, 54th Regiment, Georgia Infantry.

WILLIAMS, ALLEN: Company G, private. May 12, 1862 enlisted as a private in Co. G, 54th Regiment, Georgia Infantry at Columbus, Georgia and received bounty $50.00. November 1862 roll shows him detailed as company cook. December 31, 1862 received pay. January – February 1863 roll shows him present. June 1863 received pay. June 1, 1863 to December 31, 1863 he was detailed as a teamster with the quartermaster's department at a rate of $.25 extra per day. October 31, 1861 his name appears on a list of men detailed at James Island, South Carolina as a teamster with the quartermaster's department. November 16, 1863 received pay. January 1864 issued clothing. April 19, 1865 records of the 10th Michigan Cavalry indicate he was paroled at Newton, North Carolina.

WILLIAMS, ARCHIBALD J.: Company B, private. August 23, 1862 enlisted as a private in Co. B, 54th Regiment, Georgia Infantry at

Savannah, Georgia and received bounty $50.00. August 1862 roll shows his enlistment. December 10, 1862 deserted at Savannah, Georgia.

WILLIAMS, B. A.: Company I, private. May 6, 1862 enlisted as a private in Co. I, 54th Regiment, Georgia Infantry at Savannah, Georgia and received bounty $50.00. August 1862 roll shows he was transferred at Savannah (command not stated). October 2, 1863 he died in Charleston, South Carolina. He is buried in the confederate section of Magnolia Cemetery at Charleston, South Carolina. (find a grave # 20778111

WILLIAMS, B. W.: Company E, private. May 6, 1862 enlisted as a private in Co. E, 54th Regiment, Georgia Infantry at Savannah, Georgia and received bounty $50.00. December 31, 1862 received pay. January – February 1863 roll shows him present. October 2, 1863 he died in Charleston, South Carolina. He is buried in the Confederate Section of Magnolia Cemetery at Charleston, South Carolina. (find a grave # 20778111)

WILLIAMS, EZEKIEL JAMES: Company E, private. May 6, 1862 enlisted as a private in Co. E, 54th Regiment, Georgia Infantry at Savannah, Georgia and received bounty $50.00. November 14, 1862 granted 60 days furlough due to General Disability and Anemia by the Medical Examining Board at Oglethorpe Barracks in Savannah, Georgia. December 31, 1862 received pay. January – February 1863 roll shows him absent (absent without leave since January 27, 1863). January 1864 issued clothing. (Pension records show he was "pressed into service by Enrolling Officer while home on sick furlough and served to the surrender".) He was born in Berrien County, Georgia October 21, 1864 and died in Cook County, Georgia May 4, 1923. He is buried in Wilkes Cemetery in Cook County, Georgia. (find a grave #49279113)

WILLIAMS, GEORGE W.: Company K, sergeant. October 3, 1861 enlisted as a private in Co. A, 1st Regiment, 1st Brigade, Georgia State Troops. April 1862 mustered out. April 18, 1862 enlisted and appointed 4th sergeant in Co. K, 54th Regiment, Georgia Infantry at Savannah, Georgia and received bounty $50.00. January 1, 1863 received pay. January – February 1863 roll shows him present. March 18, 1864, April 25, 1864 and June 2, 1864 issued clothing. July 1864 wounded in the right side near Atlanta, Georgia. He was on wounded furlough at the close of the war. He was born in Tattnall County May 20, 1842 (March 22, 1842) and died in Florida June 21, 1918. He is buried in Oak Grove Community Cemetery in Hardee County, Florida. (find a grave # 25421803). The Southern Cross of Honor was bestowed on him by the Jesup Chapter United Daughters of the Confederacy in 1903.

WILLIAMS, GEORGE WASHINGTON: Company H, private. October 8, 1861 enlisted as a private in Co. K, 1st Regiment, Georgia State Troops. April 1862 mustered out. November 3, 1862 enlisted as a private in Co. H, 54th Regiment, Georgia Infantry at Columbus, Georgia and received bounty $50.00. November 1862 roll shows his enlistment. December 31, 1862 received pay. January – February 1863 roll shows him present. May 1863 received pay $26.40. October 31, 1863 received pay. November – December 1863 roll shows him present. December 31, 1863 received pay. January 1864 issued clothing. January – February 1864 roll shows him present (detailed as a hewer). May 10, 1865 surrendered at Tallahassee, Florida. May 18, 1865 paroled at Thomasville, Georgia. He is described as; 5 feet 10 inches high, auburn hair, blue eyes and fair complexion. He was born July 30, 1836 and died January 30, 1910. He is buried in Bethany Cemetery at Pine Mountain, Harris County, Georgia. (find a grave # 73099974)

WILLIAMS, HENRY A.: Company B, private. December 10, 1863 enlisted in Co. G, 4th Regiment, Georgia Cavalry (Clinch's). July 23, 1863 transferred as a private to Co. B, 54th Regiment, Georgia Infantry in exchange for David Simmons. January 1864 issued clothing. July 16, 1864 admitted to Ocmulgee Hospital at Macon, Georgia with Febris Remitting. July 23, 1864 he was transferred. He was a resident of Appling County, Georgia. October 24, 1864 he took the Oath of Allegiance at Nashville, Tennessee. He took up residence at Patterson, New Jersey.

WILLIAMS J. A.: Company B, private. April 21, 1862 enlisted as a private to Co. B, 54th Regiment, Georgia Infantry at Savannah, Georgia and received bounty $50.00. January – February 1863 roll shows him present.

WILLIAMS, JAMES A.: Company B, private. April 28, 1862 enlisted as a private to Co. B, 54th Regiment, Georgia Infantry at Savannah, Georgia and received bounty $50.00. December 31, 1862 received pay. January – February 1863 roll shows him present. January 1864 issued clothing.

WILLIAMS, JAMES E.: Company E, corporal. May 6, 1862 enlisted as a private and appointed 4th corporal in Co. E, 54th Regiment, Georgia Infantry at Savannah, Georgia and received bounty $50.00. December 31, 1862 received pay. January – February 1863 roll shows him present. November 10, 1863 elected 2nd lieutenant of Co. E, 54th Regiment, Georgia Infantry. June 7, 1864 received pay $200.00. July 2, 1864 received pay $80.00. Pension records show; March 1, 1865 to the close of the war he was on detached detail. He was born in Georgia October 23, 1836 and died July 31, 1926. He is buried in Sparks City Cemetery at Sparks, Cook County, Georgia. (find a grave # 52531595)

WILLIAMS, JOSEPH: Company B, private. April 28, 1862 enlisted as a private to Co. B, 54th Regiment, Georgia Infantry at Savannah, Georgia and received bounty $50.00. January – February 1863 roll shows him discharged by civil authority.

WILLIAMS, M.: Company I, private. May 6, 1862 enlisted as a private in Co. I, 54th Regiment, Georgia Infantry at Savannah, Georgia and received bounty $50.00. August 1, 1862 he was transferred (command unknown). August 1862 roll shows his transfer. April 25, 1864 issued clothing.

WILLIAMS, ROBERT: Company K, private. September 10, 1862 enlisted as a private in Co. K, 54th Regiment, Georgia Infantry at Savannah, Georgia and received bounty $50.00. January 1, 1863 received pay.

January – February 1863 roll shows him present. March 10, 1864 and April 18, 1864 issued clothing. May 10, 1865 surrendered at Tallahassee, Florida. May 18, 1865 paroled at Thomasville, Georgia. He is described as; 5 feet 6 inches high, red hair, dark eyes and fair complexion.
He was born in Appling County, Georgia July 15, 1844 and died in 1910. He is buried in the Blackshear City Cemetery at Blackshear, Pierce County, Georgia. (find a grave # 15450337)

WILLIAMS, SAMUEL: Company G, private. He enlisted as a private in Co. G, 54th Regiment, Georgia Infantry. May 12, 1862 shown as deserted. August 1862 roll shows his desertion. January 1864 and May 8, 1864 issued clothing. November 6, 1864 detailed by Special Order No. 141/11.

WILLIAMS, THOMAS J.: Company E, private. He enlisted as a private in Co. E, 54th Regiment, Georgia Infantry.

WILLIAMS, TIMOTHY: Company K, corporal. October 3, 1861 enlisted as a private in Co. K, 1st Regiment, Georgia State Troops. April 1862 mustered out. April 18, 1862 enlisted as a private and was elected 4th corporal in Co. K, 54th Regiment, Georgia Infantry at Savannah, Georgia and received bounty $50.00. January 1, 1863 received pay. January – February 1863 roll shows him present. March 18, 1864, April 25, 1864 and June 2, 1864 issued clothing. May 10, 1865 surrendered at Tallahassee, Florida. May 19, 1865 paroled at Thomasville, Georgia. He is described as; 5 feet 10 inches high, auburn hair, hazel eyes and florid complexion. He was born in Wayne County, Georgia in 1839 and died in Wayne County, Georgia May 10, 1902.

WILLIAMS, WILLIAM: Company G, private. March 12, 1862 enlisted as a private in Co. G, 54th Regiment, Georgia Infantry at Columbus, Georgia and received bounty $50.00. December 31, 1862 received pay. January – February 1863 roll shows him present. January 1864 and May 8, 1864 issued clothing. December 8, 1864 received pay and clothing allowance $133.00. May 25, 1864 wounded in the leg necessitating amputation at New Hope Church, Georgia.

WILLIAMS, WILLIAM: Field and Staff, musician. April 18, 1862 he enlisted as a musician in the 54th Regiment, Georgia Infantry.

WILLIAMSON, DANIEL LEON, SR.: Company K, private. October 3, 1861 enlisted as a private in Co. A, 1st Regiment, 1st Brigade, Georgia State Troops. April 1862 mustered out. April 18, 1862 enlisted and was elected 4th corporal in Co. K, 54th Regiment, Georgia Infantry at Savannah, Georgia and received bounty $50.00. January 1, 1863 received pay. January – February 1863 roll shows him present. March 18, 1864, April 25, 1864 and June 2, 1864 issued clothing. August 31, 1864 wounded in the stomach and hip at Jonesboro, Georgia. He was in the hospital at Augusta, Georgia at the close of the war. He was born in Georgia October 16, 1844 and died August 2, 1926. He is buried in Antioch Church Cemetery in Appling County, Georgia. (find a grave #24961341)

WILLIAMSON, H.: Company F, private. May 21, 1861 enlisted as a private in Co. B, 8th Regiment, Georgia Infantry. 1863 transferred and enlisted as a private in Co. F, 54th Regiment, Georgia Infantry. November – December 1863 roll shows him absent (transferred from Co. F, 54th Regiment, Georgia Infantry to Co. B, 8th Regiment, Georgia Infantry – absent without leave.).

WILLIAMSON, JOSEPH POTTER: Company F, sergeant. May 21, 1861 enlisted as a private in Co. B, 8th Regiment, Georgia Infantry. May 1862 was temporarily attached to Co. A, 2nd Battalion, North Carolina Local Defense Troops (Booth's Company Ordinance men). June 15-December 30, 1862 on detached duty in the Ordinance Department at Richmond, Virginia. September 11, 1862 received pay in Richmond, Virginia. April 29, 1863 enlisted as a private in Co. F, 54th Regiment, Georgia Infantry. January 1864 and April 25, 1864 issued clothing. May 11, 1864 regiment ordered to proceed to Dalton, Georgia by Special Order No. 105/2. He was appointed Assistant Ordinance Sergeant. December 22, 1864 captured near Columbia, Tennessee. January 2, 1865 received at Military Prison at Louisville, Kentucky from Nashville, Tennessee. January 4, 1865 sent to Camp Chase, Ohio from Military Prison at Louisville, Kentucky January 6, 1865 received at Camp Chase, Ohio from Military Prison at Louisville, Kentucky. March 11, 1865 took the Oath of Alliegence at Camp Chase, Ohio and was released. He is described as; a resident of Chatham County, Georgia, fair complexion, black hair, hazel eyes and 5 feet 7 inches high.

WILLIAMSON, T. J.: Company B, private. He enlisted as a private in Co. B, 54th Regiment, Georgia Infantry.

WILLIFORD, WILLIAM C.: Company G, private. January 22, 1862 enlisted as a private in Co. G, 54th Regiment, Georgia Infantry at Columbus, Georgia and received bounty $50.00. January – February 1863 roll shows him present. January 1864 and April 25, 1864 issued clothing. July 3, 1864 captured near Marietta, Georgia. July 14, 1864 received at Military Prison at Louisville, Kentucky from Nashville, Tennessee. July 16, 1864 sent to Camp Douglas, Illinois from Military Prison at Louisville, Kentucky. July 18, 1864 received at Camp Douglas, Illinois from Military Prison at Louisville, Kentucky. April 6, 1865 enlisted in 6th Regiment, U. S. Volunteers at Camp Douglas, Illinois.

WILLIS, FRANK M.: Company F, corporal. May 17, 1861 enlisted as a private in Chisholm's Company, Georgia State Troops. May 1862 mustered out. May 13, 1862 enlisted as a private and appointed 3rd corporal in Co. F, 54th Regiment, Georgia Infantry at Savannah, Georgia and received bounty $50.00. December 31, 1862 received pay. January – February 1863 roll shows him present. September 1, 1863 transferred to Co. A, 5th Regiment, Georgia Cavalry. August 7, 1864 to December 31, 1864 detached and detailed on duty with Captain Withberger's Horse Infirmary.

WILLIS, JESSE: Company K, private. He enlisted as a private in Co. K, 54th Regiment, Georgia Infantry.

WILLIS, N. R. L.: Company B, private. He enlisted as a private in Co.

B, 54th Regiment, Georgia Infantry.

WILLOBY, S. J.: Company B, private. He enlisted as a private in Co. B, 54th Regiment, Georgia Infantry.

WILLOBY, W. J.: Company B, private. He enlisted as a private in Co. B, 54th Regiment, Georgia Infantry.

WILSON, SAMUEL F. (W.): Company D, private. August 26, 1861 enlisted as a private in 1st Co. D, 25th Regiment, Georgia Infantry. August 16, 1862 discharged at Fort Brown, Georgia. January 18, 1863 enlisted as a private in Co. D, 54th Regiment, Georgia Infantry at Beaulieu near Savannah, Georgia and received bounty $50.00. December 31, 1862 received pay. January – February 1863 roll shows him present (absent without leave for 3 days). January 1864 issued clothing. May 18, 1865 surrendered and paroled at Augusta, Georgia. He was born in Screven County, Georgia February 17, 1822 and died in Georgia February 18, 1906. He is buried in Big Horse Creek Cemetery in Jenkins County, Georgia. (find a grave #10690733)

WILSON, WILLIAM MANASSAS: Company K, private. September 10, 1864 enlisted as a private in Co. H, 37th Regiment, Georgia Infantry. April 26, 1865 surrendered in Co. K, 54th Regiment, Consolidated Georgia Infantry at Greensboro, North Carolina. May 1, 1865 paroled at Greensboro, North Carolina. He was born in Poland April 16, 1826 and died in Waycross, Ware County, Georgia. He is buried in Lott Cemetery at Waycross, Ware County, Georgia. (find a grave # 74921020)

WINN, JAMES: Company K, private. He enlisted as a private in Co. K, 54th Regiment, Georgia Infantry.

WINN, R. R.: Company H, lieutenant. He enlisted as a private and was elected 2nd lieutenant in Co. H, 54th Regiment, Georgia Infantry.

WIRTMAN (WHITMAN), J. F.: Company I, private. May 6, 1862 enlisted as a private in Co. I, 54th Regiment, Georgia Infantry at Savannah, Georgia and received bounty $50.00. September 11, 1862 received pay September 11, 1862 detailed on detached service by Special Order No. 4/2. January – February 1863 roll shows him absent (absent on detached service by Special Order No. 4/2).

WOLFE, R. T.: Company I, private. May 6, 1862 enlisted as a private in Co. I, 54th Regiment, Georgia Infantry at Savannah, Georgia and received bounty $50.00. December 31, 1862 received pay. January – February 1863 roll shows him present. October 31, 1863 received pay. November – December 1863 roll shows him absent (detailed to guard commissary store at # 3 C. R. R. since December 15, 1863). January 1864 issued clothing.

WOOD, A. J.: Company A, private. He enlisted in as private in Co. A, 54th Regiment, Georgia Infantry.

WOOD, A, M.: Company F, private. February 15, 1863 enlisted as a private in Co. F, 54th Regiment, Georgia Infantry at Savannah, Georgia and received bounty $50.00. January – February 1863 roll shows him present. September 1, 1863 received pay. November – December 1863 roll shows him absent (sick in General Hospital No. 1 at Savannah, Georgia). January 1864 issued clothing. July 22, 1864 wounded in Atlanta, Georgia.

WOOD, ANDREW: Field and Staff, musician. January 27, 1863 enlisted as a musician in the 54th Regiment, Georgia Infantry at Beaulieu near Savannah, Georgia and received bounty $50.00. January – February 1863 roll shows him present.

WOOD, BRYANT: Company A, private. June 17, 1863 enlisted as private in Co. A, 54th Regiment, Georgia Infantry at Macon, Georgia and received bounty $50.00. June 30, 1863 roll shows him present. October 31, 1863 received pay. November – December 1863 roll shows him present. January 1, 1864 received pay. January – February 1864 roll shows him present. April 29, 1864 issued clothing. June 18, 1864 captured near Marietta, Georgia. June 26, 1864 received at Military Prison at Louisville, Kentucky from Nashville, Tennessee. June 27, 1864 sent to Camp Morton, Indianapolis, Indiana from Military Prison at Louisville, Kentucky. June 28, 1864 received at Camp Morton, Indianapolis, Indiana from Military Prison at Louisville, Kentucky. July 26, 1864 died of measles at Camp Morton, Indianapolis, Indiana. He is buried at Crown Hill Cemetery (was Green Lawn Cemetery) at Indianapolis, Indiana in grave #987. (find a grave #14736878)

WOOD, DANIEL: Company A, private. July 28, 1863 enlisted in as private in Co. A, 54th Regiment, Georgia Infantry at Macon, Georgia and received bounty $50.00. October 31, 1863 received pay. November – December 1863 roll shows him present. January 1, 1864 received pay. January – February 1864 roll shows him present. April 29, 1864 and May 8, 1864 issued clothing. June 18, 1864 captured near Marietta, Georgia. June 26, 1864 received at Military Prison at Louisville, Kentucky from Nashville, Tennessee. June 27, 1864 sent to Camp Morton, Indianapolis, Indiana from Military Prison at Louisville, Kentucky. June 28, 1864 received at Camp Morton, Indianapolis, Indiana from Military Prison at Louisville, Kentucky. July 28, 1864 died of measles at Camp Morton, Indianapolis, Indiana. He is buried at Crown Hill Cemetery (was Green Lawn Cemetery) at Indianapolis, Indiana in grave #981. (find a grave #14736879)

WOOD, H.: Company A, private. May 13, 1863 enlisted in as private in Co. A, 54th Regiment, Georgia Infantry at Macon, Georgia and received bounty $50.00. April 30, 1863 received pay. June 30, 1863 roll shows him present. October 31, 1863 received pay. November – December 1863 roll shows him present. January 1, 1864 received pay. January – February 1864 roll shows him present. April 29, 1864 issued clothing.

WOOD, J. C.: Company A, private. January 26, 1864 enlisted as private in Co. A, 54th Regiment, Georgia Infantry at Macon, Georgia and received bounty $50.00. January – February 1864 roll shows him present (pay due from enlistment). March 31, 1864 issued clothing.

WOODALL, JAMES WILSON FRANKLIN: Company A, private. November 20, 1863 enlisted as private in Co. A, 54th Regiment, Georgia

Infantry at Savannah, Georgia and received bounty $50.00. November – December 1863 roll shows him present. January – February 1864 roll shows him present (pay due from enlistment). March 31, 1864 issued clothing. He was born in Georgia October 13, 1844 and died in Liberty County, Georgia August 28, 1919. He is buried in Poplar Head Cemetery in Fort Stewart, Long County, Georgia. (find a grave # 40861193)

WOODARD, ROBERT D.: Company E, private. May 6, 1862 enlisted as a private in Co. E, 54th Regiment, Georgia Infantry at Savannah, Georgia and received bounty $50.00. December 31, 1862 received pay. January – February 1863 roll shows him present. December 1, 1863 to December 31, 1863 detailed as a laborer (for forage train) at a rate of $.25 extra per day. January 1864 issued clothing. February 1, 1864 to February 29, 1864 detailed as a mechanic. April 1, 1864 to April 30, 1864 detailed as a teamster at a rate of $.25 extra per day. April 25, 1864 issued clothing. Pension records show he "drove wagon from Mississippi to Macon, Georgia where he was furloughed for 15 days war was over before furlough expired". He was born in Georgia December 1, 1831 and died January 1914. He is buried in Woodlawn City Cemetery at Adel, Cook County, Georgia. (find a grave # 96690317)

WOODS, THOMAS W.: Company K, private. October 3, 1861 enlisted as a private in Co. A, 1st Regiment, 1st Brigade, Georgia State Troops. April 1862 mustered out. April 18, 1862 enlisted as a private in Co. K, 54th Regiment, Georgia Infantry at Savannah, Georgia and received bounty $50.00. January 1, 1863 received pay. January – February 1863 roll shows him present. March 18, 1864 issued clothing. September 9, 1864 he was severely injured in a collision near Barnesville, Georgia. He was sent to the hospital at Macon, Georgia. May 10, 1865 surrendered at Tallahassee, Florida. May 15, 1865 paroled at Thomasville, Georgia. He is described as; 5 feet 8 inches high, dark hair, grey eyes and light complexion. He was born in Holmesville, Appling County, Georgia October 2, 1841 and died in Blackshear, Pierce County, Georgia March 23, 1915. He is buried in the Blackshear City Cemetery at Blackshear, Pierce County, Georgia. (find a grave #15492959)

WOODS, W. R.: private. He enlisted as a private in the 54th Regiment, Georgia Infantry. May 10, 1865 surrendered at Tallahassee, Florida. May 15, 1865 paroled at Thomasville, Georgia.

WOODSON, J.: Company A, private. He enlisted as private in Co. A, 54th Regiment, Georgia Infantry

WRIGHT, EMANUEL: Company G, private. May 12, 1862 enlisted as a private in Co. E, 54th Regiment, Georgia Infantry at Columbus, Georgia and received bounty $50.00. July 26, 1862 he died of Fever at Savannah, Georgia. July and August 1862 rolls show his death.

WRIGHT, JOHN: Company G, private. May 12, 1862 enlisted as a private in Co. E, 54th Regiment, Georgia Infantry at Columbus, Georgia and received bounty $50.00.

WRYE, WILLIAM W.: Company A, corporal. He enlisted as private in Co. A, 54th Regiment, Georgia Infantry. July 30, 1862 transferred to 1st Georgia Sharpshooters at Savannah, Georgia by Special Order No. 259. August 1862 roll shows his transfer.

WYLLY (WYLEY), J. M.: Company F, private. February 1, 1863 enlisted as a private in Co. F, 54th Regiment, Georgia Infantry at Savannah, Georgia and received bounty $50.00. January – February 1863 roll shows him present. March 6, 1863 admitted to General Hospital No. 1 at Savannah with Carditis and Pneumonia. March 25, 1863 he died in General Hospital No. 1 at Savannah, Georgia of Carditis and Pneumonia.

WYLLY (WYLEY), JOHN: Company F, private. February 1, 1863 enlisted as a private in Co. F, 54th Regiment, Georgia Infantry at Savannah, Georgia and received bounty $50.00. January – February 1863 roll shows him present.

WYNN, D.: Company I, sergeant. He enlisted as a private in Co. I, 54th Regiment, Georgia Infantry.

WYNN, H.: Company I, corporal. He enlisted as a private in Co. I, 54th Regiment, Georgia Infantry.

WYNN, SAMUEL: Company A, private. He enlisted as a private in Co. A, 54th Regiment, Georgia Infantry.

YOKUM, JAMES: Company F, private. May 17, 1861 enlisted in Captain Chisholm's Company, Georgia State Troops. May 1862 mustered out. May 13, 1862 enlisted as a private in Co. F, 54th Regiment, Georgia Infantry at Savannah, Georgia and received bounty $50.00. September 5, 1862 discharged at Beaulieu near Savannah, Georgia. September 1862 roll shows his discharge.

YOUNG, HENRY: Company F, private. February 10, 1863 enlisted as a private in Co. F, 54th Regiment, Georgia Infantry at Savannah, Georgia and received bounty $50.00. January – February 1863 roll shows him present. He was born in 1845 and died in 1909. He is buried in Gen Griffin Cemetery in Irwin County, Georgia. (find a grave #9901479)

YOUNG, JEPTHA N.: Company E, private. May 6, 1862 enlisted as a private in Co. E, 54th Regiment, Georgia Infantry at Savannah, Georgia and received bounty $50.00. December 31, 1862 received pay. January – February 1863 roll shows him present. December 31, 1863 received pay. January 1864 and April 25, 1864 issued clothing. July 8, 1864 issued clothing in Cannon Hospital at Union Springs, Alabama. November 8, 1864 admitted to Madison House Hospital at Montgomery, Alabama. November 15, 1864 hospital muster roll of Madison House Hospital at Montgomery, Alabama shows him present (has descriptive roll). May 10, 1865 surrendered at Tallahassee, Florida and was paroled at Thomasville, Georgia. He was born in Georgia March 28, 1835 and died June 30, 1917. He is buried in Crossroads Primitive Baptist Church Cemetery at Adel, Cook County, Georgia. (find a grave # 43353570)

YOUNG, JOEL GREEN: Company E, private. May 6, 1862 enlisted as a private in Co. E, 54th Regiment, Georgia Infantry at Savannah, Georgia and received bounty $50.00. December 31, 1862 received pay. January

– February 1863 roll shows him present. January 1864 issued clothing. February 1, 1865 granted furlough and as pension records show he was at home on furlough at the close of the war. He was born in Washington County, Georgia January 29, 1831 and died February 12, 1915. He is buried in Salem Memorial Gardens at Tifton, Tift County, Georgia. (find a grave # 87863474).

YOUNG, L. G.: Company E, corporal. He enlisted and was appointed corporal of Co. E, 54th Regiment, Georgia Infantry. May 10, 1865 surrendered at Tallahassee, Florida. May 16, 1865 paroled at Thomasville, Georgia. He is described as; 5 feet 8 inches high, light hair, blue eyes and light complexion.

ZEIGLER, GEORGE W.: Company I, private. September 18, 1861 enlisted as a private in Co. C, 1st Regiment, 1st Brigade, Georgia State Troops. March 18, 1862 mustered out. May 6, 1862 enlisted as a private in Co. I, 54th Regiment, Georgia Infantry at Savannah, Georgia and received bounty $50.00. December 31, 1862 received pay. January – February 1863 roll shows him present. October 31, 1863 received pay. November – December 1863 roll shows him present. January 1864 issued clothing. He transferred from Co. I, 54th Regiment, Georgia Infantry to Co. F, 54th Regiment, Georgia Infantry. April 26, 1865 surrendered at Greensboro, North Carolina. May 1, 1865 paroled at Greensboro, North Carolina. He was born August 26, 1837 and died near Rincon, Effingham County, Georgia December 2, 1915. He is buried in Jerusalem Lutheran Church Cemetery in Rincon, Effingham County, Georgia. (find a grave # 67619985)

ZEIGLER, JOHN A.: Company I, private. September 18, 1861 enlisted as a private in Co. C, 1st Regiment, 1st Brigade, Georgia State Troops. March 18, 1862 mustered out. May 6, 1862 enlisted as a private in Co. I, 54th Regiment, Georgia Infantry at Savannah, Georgia and received bounty $50.00. December 31, 1862 received pay. January – February 1863 roll shows him present. October 31, 1863 received pay. November – December 1863 roll shows him present. January 1864 issued clothing. He was born February 22, 1834 and died June 15, 1910. He is buried in Jerusalem Lutheran Church Cemetery in Rincon, Effingham County, Georgia. (find a grave #67620056)

ZIPPERER, BENJAMIN T.: Company I, private. September 18, 1861 enlisted as a private in Co. C, 1st Regiment, 1st Brigade, Georgia State Troops. March 18, 1862 mustered out. May 6, 1862 enlisted as a private in Co. I, 54th Regiment, Georgia Infantry at Savannah, Georgia and received bounty $50.00. June 30, 1862 received pay. January – February 1863 roll shows him absent (absent sick). October 31, 1863 received pay. November – December 1863 roll shows him present. January 1864 issued clothing. November 17, 1864 he died in Scott Hospital at Marion, Alabama of Chronic Diarrhoea.

ZIPPERER, JOHN THEOPHILUS: Company I, private. July 31, 1863 enlisted as a private in Co. I, 54th Regiment, Georgia Infantry at Rose

Dew near Savannah, Georgia and received bounty $50.00. October 31, 1863 received pay. November – December 1863 roll shows him present. January 1864 issued clothing. He was born February 20, 1820 and died April 29, 1866. He is buried in Zion Lutheran Church Cemetery in Guyton, Effingham County, Georgia. (find a grave #46349950)

ZITTMAN, DAVID: Company A, private. He enlisted as a private in Co. A, 54th Regiment, Georgia Infantry. He was captured (date and place not known). 1865 released at Point Lookout, Maryland.

ZITTRAUER (ZITTROUR) (ZITRO), DAVID: Company F, private. May 6, 1862 enlisted as a private in Co. F, 54th Regiment, Georgia Infantry at Savannah, Georgia and received bounty $50.00. December 31, 1862 received pay. January – February 1863 roll shows him present. October 31, 1863 received pay. November – December 1863 roll shows him present. January 1864 and April 25, 1864 issued clothing. December 8, 1864 he was captured in Effingham County, Georgia and taken to Hilton Head, South Carolina. January 10, 1865 arrived at Hilton Head, South Carolina to Point Lookout, Maryland. February 1, 1865 arrived at Point Lookout, Maryland from Hilton Head, South Carolina. June 22, 1865 he was released from Point Lookout, Maryland. He is described as; a resident of Effingham County, Georgia, light complexion, brown hair, grey eyes and was 5 feet 4 inches high.

ZITTRAUER, EMMETT D.: Company I, private. September 18, 1861 enlisted as a private in Co. C, 1st Regiment, 1st Brigade, Georgia State Troops. March 18, 1862 mustered out. May 6, 1862 enlisted as a private in Co. I, 54th Regiment, Georgia Infantry at Savannah, Georgia and received bounty $50.00. December 31, 1862 received pay. January – February 1863 roll shows him present. October 31, 1863 received pay. November – December 1863 roll shows him present. January 1864 issued clothing. He was born in Georgia August 26, 1834 and died August 4, 1918. He is buried in Zion Lutheran Church Cemetery in Guyton, Effingham County, Georgia. (find a grave #67402795)

ZORN, RUSSELL D.: Company G, corporal. He enlisted as a corporal in Co. G, 54th Regiment, Georgia Infantry.

REFERENCES

Roster of the Confederate Soldiers of Georgia 1861 - 1865, Volume III, by Lillian Henderson

Pioneers of Wiregrass Georgia, Volume 1-7, by Judge Folks Huxford. Volumes 8-9, by the Huxford Geaneological Society.

The War of the Rebellion: A Compilation of the Official Records of the Union and the Confederate Armies.

Historical Times - Illustrated Encyclopedia of the Civil War, Patricia L. Faust, Editor

The Civil War - the American Iliad, by Otto Eisenschiml and Ralph Newman

Our Heritage, Volumes I - IV, by Mary Ketus Holland

Footprints in Appling County, by Ruth T. Barron

Wayne Miscellany by Margaret Coleman Jordon

History of Pierce County Georgia, Volume 1 by Dean Broome

Historical Society Papers, edited by Rev J. William Jones, D. D., Secretary - Southern Historical Society

Confederate Military History, edited by General Clement A. Evans of Georgia

Battles and Leaders of the Civil War, Castle

Units of the Confederate States Army, Joseph H. Crute, Jr.

United Daughters of the Confederacy, bound typescripts

Those Gallant Georgians who Served in The War Between the States, by Jimmy E. Arnsdorff

The Coastal War by Peter M. Chaitin (Time Life Books)

Battery Wagner, Timothy E. Bradshaw, Jr.

Battles for Atlanta by Ronald H. Bailey (Time Life Books)

The Campaign For Atlanta, William R, Scaife

The Battle of Resaca, Phillip L. Secrist

The Battles of New Hope Church, Russell W. Blount, Jr.

The Battle at Picketts Mill Along the Dead Line, Brad Butkovich

Historical Guide to Kennesaw Mountain Battlefield Park and Marietta, Georgia by Bowling C. Yates

Clash at Kennesaw, Russell W. Blount, Jr.

Hell's Broke Loose in Georgia, Scott Walker

Charlotte's Boys, Mauriel Phillips Joslyn

The Campaign for Tennessee, William R, Scaife

Col. Charles H. Olmstead C. S. A. His Life and Times edited by Lilla Mills Hawes

The Confederate Veteran March-April 1989 Bloody Footprints in the Snow: Mercer's Brigade by Robert Brawner

Last Stand in the Carolinas: The Battle of Bentonville by Mark L. Bradley

Historical Sketch and Roster, Ga 54th Infantry Regiment, by John Rigdon

We Fought at Kennesaw, by John C. Rigdon

Charles H. Olmstead Papers, #1856, Southern Historical Collection, The Wilson Library, University of North Carolina at Chapel Hill.

To the Manner Born, the Life of General William H. T. Walker, by Russell K. Brown

The History of Pierce County, Georgia, by Dean Broome

Miscellany of Wayne County, by Margaret C. Jordan

In Gray, Lives of the Confederate Commanders by Ezra J. Warner

Sons of Confederate Veterans Ancestor Album by The Sons of Confederate Veterans

America's Civil War magazine, November 1993 edition

Blue and Gray magazine December 1993 edition

Civil War Times magazine December 1992 and April 1993 editions

The Confederate Veteran magazine May 1903 edition

THANKS TO:

Rev. James Bowen, Glennville, Georgia

Deloris Willis Bowers, Baxley, Georgia

William A. Bowers, III, Baxley, Georgia

Elizabeth Bowers Hall, Marietta, Georgia

Charlotte Ray, Georgia Department of Archives and History - Atlanta, Georgia

Steve Thomas, Rincon, Georgia

David Dickey, Savannah, Georgia

John Kindred, Dallas, Georgia

Judge Ken W. Smith, Hazlehurst, Georgia

THANKS ALSO TO THE STAFF AT THE FOLLOWING STATE AND NATIONAL BATTLEFIELDS:

Kennesaw Mountain Battlefield, Kennesaw, Georgia

Fort Sumter National Monument at Charleston, South Carolina

Pickett's Mill Battlefield State Park, Dallas, Georgia

Bentonville Battlefield at Bentonville, North Carolina

Franklin Tennessee Battlefield, Franklin, Tennessee

Tunnel Hill Battlefield Park, Tunnel Hill, Georgia

About the Author

William A. Bowers, Jr., was born August 5, 1947, in San Augustine, Florida, to William Alfred Bowers, Sr., and Lora Elizabeth Tuten. When he was young, his family returned to Baxley, Appling County, Georgia, where he lived, was raised and educated. He is a 1965 graduate of Appling County High School, an Eagle Scout and is retired from the Georgia Department of Transportation as an Area Engineer in South Georgia. He is married to Anna Deloris Willis of Toombs County. He is a member of the First United Methodist Church in Baxley, Georgia.

For the last 22 years he has been involved in researching Confederate units, battles and genealogy. Bill has been to almost all the places that the 47th fought and has stood where they stood in his research of this unit. He has given speeches across south Georgia concerning those Confederate units and their part in the War for Southern Independence. He resides still in Appling County and has served as a scout leader for 30 years, an officer in the Appling Grays Camp #918 Sons of Confederate Veterans, the Appling County Board of Education, the First United Methodist Church Administrative Board and the Appling County Heritage Center Board of Directors.

This is his third regimental history, with the *History of the 47th Georgia Volunteer Infantry* being published in May 2013, and the *History of the 27th Georgia Volunteer Infantry* being published in February 2014. This completes the trilogy of Confederate Regimental Histories which encompasses the four companies of Confederate Infantry which originated in Appling County, Georgia.